Planning
and Design
of Airports

McGraw-Hill Series in Transportation

Dickey *Metropolitan Transportation Planning, 2/e*
Drew *Traffic Flow Theory and Control*
Hennes and Ekse *Fundamentals of Transportation Engineering, 2/e*
Horonjeff and McKelvey *Planning and Design of Airports, 3/e*
Hutchinson *Principles of Urban Transport Planning*
Kanafani *Transportation Demand Analysis*
Morlok *Introduction to Transportation System Engineering and Planning*
Quinn *Design and Construction of Ports and Marine Structures, 2/e*
Wohl and Martin *Traffic System Analysis for Engineers and Planners*

Planning and Design of Airports

THIRD EDITION

Robert Horonjeff
(deceased)
*Professor of Transportation
Engineering
Institute of Transportation
Studies
University of California,
Berkeley*

and **Francis X. McKelvey**

*Associate Professor of
Civil Engineering
Michigan State University*

McGraw-Hill Book Company

New York · St. Louis · San Francisco · Auckland
Bogotá · Hamburg · Johannesburg · London · Madrid
Mexico · Montreal · New Delhi · Panama · Paris
São Paulo · Singapore · Sydney · Tokyo · Toronto

Library of Congress Cataloging in Publication Data

Horonjeff, Robert.
  Planning and design of airports.

  (McGraw-Hill series in transportation)
  Includes bibliographies and index.
  1. Airports—Planning. 2. Airports—Design and
construction. I. McKelvey, Francis X. II. Title.
III. Series.
TL725.3.P5H6 1983   629.136   82-14859
ISBN 0-07-030367-3

1234567890   KGP/KGP   89876543

ISBN 0-07-030367-3

The editors for this book were Joan Zseleczky and Charles P. Ray;
the designer was Off-Broadway Design & Graphics, Inc., and the
production supervisor was Sara Fliess. It was set in Caledonia
by Santype-Byrd.

Printed and bound by The Kingsport Press.

Contents

Preface
to the Third Edition

The technological and legislative developments related to the air-transportation industry in the 1970s and early 1980s are of such significance as to necessitate an updating of the second edition of *The Planning and Design of Airports*, written by Robert Horonjeff and published in 1975. This edition attempts to follow the framework and philosophy of previous editions and draws substantially from the latest information available from the Federal Aviation Administration, the International Civil Aviation Organization, the Air Transport Association of America, the International Air Transportation Association, and other governmental and trade organizations. The basic principles, techniques, and methodologies appropriate to the planning and design of airports are incorporated in this book, and the reader is encouraged to access the publications referenced herein for further explanations of the use and limitations of their application to airport problems.

This edition has updated and expanded the statistical data and legislation associated with air transport. It contains recent developments in environmental, fiscal, and revenue analysis, aircraft characteristics and performance, and air traffic control and navigation. The chapters on air-side capacity and delay, terminal planning and design, and pavement design have been completely rewritten to reflect the recent and significant developments in these areas. The reference section at the end of each chapter has been updated and expanded to reflect the current literature appropriate to the field.

The author is deeply indebted to Mrs. Marian Horonjeff who provided the opportunity and showed the confidence that this work could be completed. The support of Michigan State University in providing the resources needed to complete the manuscript is gratefully acknowledged. The assistance of Aviation Planning Associates, Inc., Landrum and Brown, Inc., and Reynolds, Smith and Hills, Architects, Engineers, and Planners, in providing original drawings, materials, photographs, reports, and other resources is appreciated. Many other organizations and personnel assisted substantially in this effort and are recognized in the Acknowledgments section. Particular and special credit is given to Gregory A. Casto, a student at Michigan State University, who gave unselfishly of his time and abilities in doing research, writing preliminary draft material, proofreading, critiquing, and providing encouragement throughout this effort. Finally, the support and understanding of my wife, Betty, and our three children, Gene, Michael, and Keri, in providing the impetus and strength to complete this work are immeasurable.

This edition of the text is dedicated to the memory of Bob Horonjeff, a man to whom all of us in this profession are forever indebted.

Frank McKelvey

Preface
to the Second Edition

For some years the author has felt the need for a text which would cover the principles governing the planning and design of airports for the use of students and those engaged in practice. As a result a text titled *Planning and Design of Airports* was published by McGraw-Hill Book Company in 1962. Since that time substantial changes have taken place in air transportation; consequently there was a demand to update the text. As in the previous text, the author has included the essential features of the numerous publications of the Federal Aviation Administration, the International Civil Aviation Organization, the Air Transport Association, the International Air Transport Association, and consultants associated with aviation. In preparing this text the author has drawn freely from information published by these sources, especially the Federal Aviation Administration.

For the student a certain amount of historical background in airport development is included. An attempt is made to stress principles and to include just enough detail to illustrate these principles. Airport requirements do undergo revision; therefore a complete bibliography of the basic and frequently revised publications governing airport planning and design is included at the end of each chapter. The text uses English units of measurement, since a change to the metric system is taking place only gradually in the United States; and for those where the metric system has already been adopted, a table showing a conversion from the English to the metric system has been placed at the end of the text.

The author is indebted to Professor A. Kanafani, University of California, Berkeley, and Mr. Hanan Kivett, Kivett and Meyers, for the preparation of Chapter 9, and to Professor Carl Monismith, University of California, Berkeley, for the preparation of Chapter 12. Finally, thanks are extended to industry organizations, consultants, airlines, and aircraft manufacturers for furnishing much useful information for the text and for their valuable suggestions.

Robert Horonjeff

Acknowledgments

The assistance of the following professionals in preparing the material for the third edition of this book is deeply appreciated and gratefully acknowledged.

Leo F. Duggan	Airport Operators Council International
Philip II. Agee	Air Transport Association of America
L. McCarthy Downs III	Aviation Planning Associates, Inc.
David A. Schlothauer	
Cliff. W. Carpenter	Boeing Commercial Airplane Company
Frank M. Lewis	Civil Aeronautics Board
John Leavens	Douglas Aircraft Company
Brady A. Nelson	
William E. Parsons	
Satish K. Agrawal	Federal Aviation Administration
Pat Beardsley	
Robert David	
Ernest P. Gubry	
Richard J. Marek	
Gene S. Mercer	
Thomas P. Messier	
Thomas J. O'Brien	
Bruce M. Singer	
James E. Benedict	Fort Lauderdale–Hollywood International Airport, Broward
L. E. Wagener	County Aviation Division
Stuart S. Holder	Landrum and Brown, Inc.
Jeffrey N. Thomas	
Walter P. Ericksen	Lockheed-California Company
Gregory A. Casto	Michigan State University
William C. Taylor	
Lawrence W. Von Tersch	
Robert T. Taylor	National Aeronautics and Space Administration
Joseph G. Mason	National Association of State Aviation Officials
John F. Gillolly	Orlando International Jetport, Greater Orlando Airport Authority
Vincent E. Bonaventura	Port Authority of New York and New Jersey
Laurence A. Schaefer	
James A. Meehan	Reynolds, Smith and Hills, Inc.
Byron G. McIntyre	
Howard W. Yaws	
Leon Bitners	San Francisco International Airport, Airports Commission
Mark Gorstein	Transportation Systems Center
Edward M. Whitlock	Wilbur Smith and Associates

Planning
and Design
of Airports

Chapter 1

The Nature of Civil Aviation

THE AIR AGE

On December 17, 1903, near Kitty Hawk, North Carolina, a bicycle repairman by the name of Orville Wright propelled himself through the air a distance of 120 ft. This was the first powered flight in a heavier-than-air aircraft known to man; it was the equivalent of twenty-three-hundredths of a passenger-mile, the first such statistic that could be recorded in aviation history. In contrast to this humble beginning, the commercial airlines in the United States in 1980 carried nearly 297 million passengers over 200 billion passenger-miles, which is six times the number of passenger-miles logged by railroads and buses. In 1980, 734 million passengers were recorded worldwide, and they flew 665 billion passenger-miles. In addition to passenger traffic, there has been a substantial increase in the carriage of mail and freight by air. Cargo traffic has been estimated at about 7 billion ton-miles in the United States and 20 billion ton-miles worldwide in 1980.

The impact the commercial air transportation industry has on the economy of the United States can be appreciated by the fact that consumer personal expenditures on this industry were over $5 billion and the air transportation sector of the economy employed well over 400,000 people in 1978. Nearly 20 percent of the national income from the transportation sector of the economy was contributed by the airline industry, in excess of $12 billion in 1978 [14].

The investment in the civil aviation industry consists of commercial aircraft and their supporting facilities and equipment; general aviation aircraft used for business, agricultural purposes, aerial photography, patrol, advertising, and other purposes; airports; and airways. It is difficult to assess the total investment in monetary terms, but in 1979 the total assets of the U.S. domestic airlines exceeded $25 billion, and the investment in aircraft alone exceeded $15 billion [1]. It is projected that in the period from 1980 to 1990, the U.S. airlines will invest nearly $90 billion in new, more efficient commercial aircraft [2].

The availability of air transport, however, has done more than provide a carrier service. It has affected our economic way of life, it has made changes in our social viewpoints, and it has had a hand in shaping the course of political history.

The sociological changes brought about by air transportation are perhaps as important as the changes in the economy. People have been brought closer together and so have reached a better understanding of interregional problems. Industry has found new ways to do business. The opportunity for more frequent exchanges of information has been facilitated, and air transport is enabling more people to enjoy the cultures and traditions of distant lands.

AIR TRANSPORT AND THE NATIONAL ECONOMY

The growth of the American economy has been closely associated with the development of transportation. The amount of money spent for transportation services by all modes of transportation has correlated closely with the level of economic activity as measured by the gross national product (GNP) or national income. The expenditures for domestic intercity travel have averaged 5 to 6 percent of the GNP. Estimates of the GNP in the future vary, but if the average annual increase in GNP is about 2.7 percent in future years [8], by 1992 the real GNP will reach $1984 billion in terms of 1972 dollars. Civil aviation contributions to the GNP have consistently grown at a faster pace than the economy as a whole.

Total intercity travel consists of two major parts: private automobile travel, which accounts for nearly 85 percent of the total, and common-carrier travel (bus, rail, and air), which accounts for the remaining portion. In the last decade (1970 to 1980) a steady rise has continued in both private automobile and common-carrier travel. However, among the common

TABLE 1-1 **Domestic Intercity Passenger-Miles by Mode of Travel and Class of Service, 1950–1980, Millions**

	1950	1960	1970	1975	1980
Total	458,832	748,121	1,161,335	1,331,093	1,496,787
Total common carriers	55,989	67,521	135,335	167,093	233,387
Airlines	7,954	30,557	104,146	131,728	200,087
Railroads	26,781	17,064	6,179	9,765	6,400
Motor buses	21,254	19,900	25,300	25,600	26,900
Air share, %	14.2	45.3	76.8	78.8	85.7
Private automobile	402,843	680,600	1,026,000	1,164,000	1,263,400
Common-carrier share of total, %	12.2	9.0	11.7	12.6	15.6
Air share of total, %	1.7	4.1	9.0	9.9	13.4

SOURCE: Air Transportation Association of America [3].

carriers a drastic reduction has taken place in rail travel, which has been more than offset by the phenomenal growth in air travel. During the period from 1950 to 1980 the air share of common-carrier travel rose from 14 percent to almost 86 percent. Air travel now accounts for over 13 percent of the total intercity traffic in the United States. These relationships are shown in Table 1-1.

The steady rise in consumer income has had a favorable impact on air travel. As incomes have grown, larger proportions have been spent on transportation and other items related to the enjoyment of life. Consumer expenditures have been substantially greater for air travel than for other travel modes. This trend clearly indicates that expenditures for air travel will continue to rise if disposable income continues to increase and people have more time for leisure.

GROWTH OF AIR TRANSPORT AND FUTURE TRENDS

Although more than three-quarters of a century has elapsed since the first successful flight at Kitty Hawk, air transport is essentially a post–World War II development.

Domestic Passenger Traffic

The stature of the United States in the world market for air transportation is clearly indicated by the fact that the airlines in domestic service accounted for about one-third of the passengers and passenger-miles flown in the entire world in 1980. The average annual growth rate in terms of passengers carried from 1960 to 1980 was about 8 percent. Estimates of future growth rates vary from 4 to 8 percent annually through the year 1990. Thus domestic traffic, in terms of passengers and passenger-miles, is expected to almost double in the 10-year period from 1980 to 1990. This is shown in Table 1-2.

It is interesting to examine the pattern of commercial air travel in terms of trip length. While it is common knowledge that air transportation is the predominant mode for long-distance trips, it is interesting to note that in 1980 more than one-half of all trips by air were not more than 500 mi, and almost 87 percent did not exceed 1000 mi. This is illustrated in Fig. 1-1. The same is true of the distribution of scheduled flights in the United States. Figure 1-2 indicates that 67 percent of the flights scheduled were not more than 500 mi, and 90 percent were not more than 1000 mi. This information indicates that a substantial portion of air travel can be classified as *short-haul*, a term generally used to indicate flights of distances under 500 mi.

While the automobile will undoubtedly remain the principal means of

TABLE 1-2 **U.S. Domestic Scheduled Air Carrier Revenue Passengers Enplaned and Passenger-Miles Flown**

Year	Revenue passengers, thousands	Revenue passenger-miles, millions
1940	2,523	1,052
1950	17,345	8,003
1960	56,296	30,555
1970	153,159	103,809
1971	155,727	106,140
1972	171,345	118,127
1973	183,122	126,302
1974	189,576	129,716
1975	188,169	131,656
1976	205,666	145,197
1977	221,528	156,510
1978	253,675	182,664
1979*	316,863	262,023
1980*	296,749	254,180
1985†	308,800	271,100
1990†	454,000	330,000

* Includes newly certified carriers not included in prior years.

† Projections.

SOURCES: Air Transportation Association of America [3] and Federal Aviation Administration [8, 9].

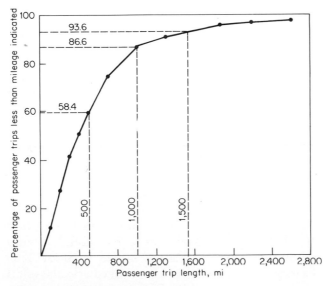

Fig. 1-1 Distribution of passenger trip lengths on scheduled domestic airline flights in the United States, November 1980. (*Civil Aeronautics Board [17].*)

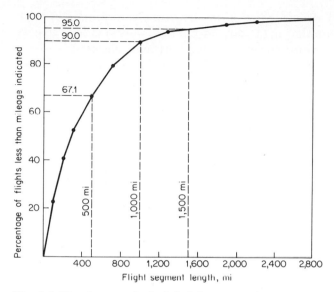

Fig. 1-2 Distribution of scheduled domestic airline flights in the United States, November 1980. (*Civil Aeronautics Board* [17].)

short-haul travel for some time to come, it is useful to compare air transport with the other competing modes of intercity travel. From Table 1-3 it is clear that for household round trips of up to 300 mi travel by bus is predominant, accounting for more than half the trips. However, the majority of round trips in excess of 400 mi are made by air. It is felt that the potential growth of air travel for one-way trips in excess of 100 mi is substantial, provided efficient and economical short-haul aircraft and adequate ground facilities can be developed. This potential, together with

TABLE 1-3 **Household Trips in the United States, 1977**

Round trip length, mi	Percent of trips	Percent by travel mode				
		Auto	Bus	Train	Air	Other
200–299	34	93	4	1	1	1
300–399	17	90	4	1	3	1
400–599	17	82	5	1	9	3
600–799	8	70	4	1	21	4
800–999	5	62	4	1	29	4
1000–1999	10	48	3	1	42	6
2000 and over	9	25	2	1	67	5
Total	100	76	4	1	16	3

SOURCE: Department of Commerce [15].

the severe airspace and airfield congestion occurring at terminals in large metropolitan areas, is stimulating the development of new smaller-capacity aircraft and of satellite airports to service the short-haul markets.

The geographic distribution of domestic passenger traffic is also of interest. Air travel is highly concentrated in relatively few metropolitan areas. In 1980 the 43 airports in the large hub areas generated 72 percent of all air-carrier operations. The large, medium, and small hub airports accounted for 98 percent of all passengers enplaned in the United States. In 1978, 14 airports accounted for one-half of all passengers, while 60 airports accounted for 84 percent of all passenger traffic. The 100 largest airports in the United States enplaned over 92 percent of the passengers (Table 1-4). This situation is expected to continue as the population of the United States continues to concentrate into several distinct regions throughout the country.

Domestic Cargo

The term *air cargo* includes mail, express, and freight. Although quite insignificant in the total intercity domestic cargo market, less than 0.2

TABLE 1-4 **Passenger Enplanements at Major Airports in the United States, 1978**

Cumulative percent of passengers enplaned*	Cumulative number of airports	Airport name
7.78	1	Chicago O'Hare International
14.00	2	Hartsfield-Atlanta International
19.45	3	Los Angeles International
23.71	4	John F. Kennedy International
27.71	5	San Francisco International
31.07	6	Dallas–Fort Worth Regional
34.39	7	Denver Stapleton International
37.37	8	LaGuardia
40.11	9	Miami International
42.51	10	Honolulu International
48.88	13	Detroit Metropolitan
50.53	14	Houston Intercontinental
59.65	20	Newark International
65.60	25	San Diego International
70.21	30	Memphis International
76.28	40	Charlotte Douglas Municipal
80.83	50	Albuquerque International
84.24	60	Rochester-Monroe County
92.07	100	Toledo Express

*Enplaned passengers, total system operations, all services, U.S. certified route carriers (excluding helicopters).

SOURCE: Federal Aviation Administration [20].

TABLE 1-5   **Revenue Ton-Miles of Cargo Flown**
in U.S. Domestic Scheduled Service, Thousands

Year	Mail	Express and freight	Total
1955	61,233	96,134	157,367
1960	240,572	702,937	943,509
1965	482,977	1,820,154	2,303,131
1970	1,470,131	3,514,066	4,984,197
1975	1,097,297	4,495,309	5,892,066
1980	1,312,910	5,676,593	6,989,503

SOURCES: Federal Aviation Administration [9] and Air Transportation Association of America [3].

percent in 1980 [14], air cargo has developed at a very rapid pace, increasing more than seven times during the 20-year period from 1960 to 1980, as shown in Table 1-5. The large increase in the shipment of mail since 1965 is due to the policy of the U.S. Postal Service of sending nonpriority mail by air whenever space is available. In fiscal year 1970 about 40 percent of the air-cargo ton-miles were handled in the bellies of passenger aircraft, the remainder in all-cargo aircraft. Although projections of air-cargo growth vary considerably, annual growth rates averaged 18 percent in the 1960s, but slowed to a little less than 4 percent in the 1970s. The traffic in the period from 1980 to 1990 might be expected to more than double if the average rate of annual growth from the last 20 years continues. Likewise, it has been predicted that the tonnage of air cargo carried in the belly compartments of passenger planes will decrease to somewhere between 10 and 30 percent. Aircraft such as the Lockheed L-500 and the Boeing 747-200F have a lift capacity in excess of 100 tons and provision for end loading rather than side loading. This offers a potential for lowering costs. As air-cargo volumes expand, the continued growth in the use of containerized freight will tend to further reduce costs.

International and Overseas Commerce

Although international air transport was inaugurated in the mid-1930s, rapid growth did not begin until 1950. Since that time the average annual growth rate in the number of passengers was 13 percent from 1960 to 1970 and about 7 percent through the 1970s. International passenger traffic is shown in Table 1-6. Projections of world traffic growth vary considerably, but it has been predicted that an increase to 1.3 billion passengers in 1990 may occur, nearly a doubling of passenger traffic during the period from 1980 to 1990. It has been estimated that the growth rate during this period will average about 6 percent a year.

World air cargo has expanded at a very rapid pace, even more so than

TABLE 1-6 **World Civil Air Transport Revenue Passengers Carried and Passenger-Miles Flown on Domestic and International Routes**

Year	Passengers, thousands	Passenger-miles, millions
1950	31,000	18,000
1960	106,000	68,000
1970	386,000	289,000
1971	411,000	307,000
1972	450,000	348,000
1973	489,000	384,000
1974	515,000	407,000
1975	534,000	433,000
1976	576,000	473,000
1977	610,000	508,000
1978	679,000	582,000
1979	738,000	653,000
1980	734,000	665,000
1985*	974,000	869,000
1990*	1,273,000	1,136,000

* Reflects a projection of an average annual increase of 5.5 percent through 1990.

SOURCES: International Civil Aviation Organization [11] and Boeing Commercial Airplane Company [4].

domestic cargo in the United States. Statistical information on world air cargo is provided in Table 1-7. The average yearly growth rate during the period from 1970 to 1980 was 9 percent, which is considerably higher than the passenger growth of 6 percent during the same period. Domestic cargo in the United States represents about one-third of the total world air cargo. Several aircraft manufacturers and the International Civil Aviation Organization (ICAO) project that the annual growth rate during the period from

TABLE 1-7 **Revenue Ton-Miles of International and Domestic Cargo Flown in the Entire World in Scheduled Service, Millions**

Year	Mail	Express and freight	Total
1955	255	905	1,160
1960	415	1,480	1,815
1965	755	3,400	4,155
1970	1,705	6,895	8,600
1975	1,801	12,033	13,834
1980	2,299	18,047	20,346

SOURCE: International Civil Aviation Organization [11].

TABLE 1-8 **Regional Percentage Distribution of Total Ton-Kilometers Performed on Scheduled Services**

Year	Asia and Pacific	Europe*	North America	Latin America and Caribbean	Africa	Middle East
1968	8.4	19.8	63.8	4.3	2.0	1.5
1972	8.4	35.9	47.6	4.4	2.0	1.7
1976	12.4	36.5	41.0	4.8	2.5	2.8
1980	15.5	35.0	38.6	5.5	2.6	2.8

* Data for 1968 do not include the U.S.S.R. since these data are not available.
SOURCE: International Civil Aviation Organization [11].

1980 to 1990 will be about 17 percent, which will mean that in 1990 the world cargo ton-miles will be five times the amount in 1980.

The geographic distribution of world air transport is also of interest. For statistical purposes ICAO has divided the world into six regions: Asia and Pacific, Europe, North America, Latin America and Caribbean, Africa, and the Middle East. Table 1-8 indicates the regional percentage distributions of total ton-kilometers performed on scheduled services from 1968 to 1980. It will be noted that over 70 percent of all traffic is generated in North America and Europe. The growth of traffic in the Asian and Pacific and the Middle East regions is quite dramatic, paralleling the growth of importance of these areas in the political, social, and economic sectors during the same period.

General Aviation

General aviation is the term used to designate all flying done other than by commercial airlines. For statistical purposes general aviation, in the United States, is usually divided into business flying, that is, transportation not for hire, commercial flying, instructional flying, and personal flying. Some concept of the size of the general aviation activities can be gained from the fact that in 1980 general aviation accounted for about 55 times the number of planes, accumulated nearly twice the mileage, and flew more than four times the number of hours as the scheduled airlines. It also accounted for 75 percent of all civil aircraft operations at airports with FAA control towers. A comparison of the air-carrier fleet with general aviation is presented in Table 1-9.

In 1980 about 67 percent of the air-carrier fleet was turbojets, this percentage being dramatically reduced due to the addition of smaller airlines in certified scheduled service as a direct result of deregulation of the industry. About 80 percent of the general aviation fleet consists of single-engine aircraft. In 1980 the use of general aviation aircraft for business purposes was slightly larger than that for commercial, instruction-

TABLE 1-9 **U.S. Civil Air Fleet**

Calendar year ending	Air carrier			General aviation		
	Jet	Piston, turboprop, rotary wing	Total	Single-engine	Multi-engine	Total*
1960	202	1,933	2,135	69,306	7,243	77,297
1965	725	1,400	2,125	81,134	11,422	95,442
1970	2,136	543	2,679	111,100	16,300	134,000
1975	2,114	381	2,495	136,639	24,106	168,049
1980	2,526	1,279	3,805	168,390	31,313	210,339
1985[†]	2,641	279	2,920	202,100	38,400	254,500
1990[†]	2,869	249	3,118	234,000	46,000	298,100

* Total includes rotorcraft and others not listed in table.
[†] Projections.
SOURCES: Federal Aviation Administration [8, 9].

al, and personal uses in terms of hours flown, as shown in Table 1-10. It is predicted that the use of general aviation aircraft will increase on the average by about 4 percent per year through 1990. Although the aviation fleet has not changed materially in recent years, there has been a marked increase in the number of aircraft equipped for instrument flying. Federal Aviation Administration (FAA) records indicate that in the 4-year period from 1975 to 1979 general aviation instrument operations over the nation's airways have increased by more than 67 percent. At the present time, general aviation represents nearly one-half of all instrument operations monitored by the FAA.

TABLE 1-10 **Hours Flown in General Aviation by Type of Use, Thousands**

Year	Total hours	Business		Commercial		Instructional		Personal		Other	
		Hours	%	Hours	%	Hours	%	Hours	%	Hours	%
1940	3,200	314	10	387	12	1,529	48	970	30	135	1
1951	8,451	2,950	35	1,584	19	1,902	23	1,880	22	57	1
1960	13,121	5,699	44	2,365	18	1,828	14	3,172	24	75	1
1965	16,733	5,857	35	3,348	20	3,346	20	4,016	24	106	1
1970	26,028	7,182	28	4,582	18	6,798	26	6,936	27	530	2
1975	34,165	9,545	28	6,480	19	8,174	24	9,244	27	722	2
1980	43,340	13,980	32	8,064	19	10,668	25	9,471	22	1,052	2
1985*	51,600	15,500	30	9,800	19	12,300	25	11,400	22	1,600	2
1990*	60,900	18,300	30	11,600	19	15,200	25	13,400	22	2,400	2

* Only the total hours flown are projected by the FAA for the years shown. The breakdown by use type is based upon recent trends.
SOURCE: Federal Aviation Administration [9].

Commuter Air Carriers

Commuter air carriers are defined by the Civil Aeronautics Board (CAB) as "those operators which perform, pursuant to published schedules, at least five round trips per week between two or more points, or carry mail." In 1980 there were over 300 operators of over 1300 aircraft, which on the average had about 13 seats. There were over 800 airports served by commuter operators. Of the flights, 51 percent were less than 100 mi and over 89 percent were not more than 200 mi [10]. The distribution of commuter flights by mileage block is shown in Fig. 1-3. It has been estimated that the commuter industry carried 15,600,000 passengers over 2 billion passenger-miles in 1980 [5]. Recent data indicate that the annual growth rate for commuter carriers may average more than 8 percent through 1990. The commuter carrier activity has been concentrated in the large metropolitan regions where commuter airlines have offered an extension of airline service to outlying parts of the region. Recent trend data for the commuter airline industry are shown in Table 1-11.

The passage of the deregulatory legislation in 1978 has had a very favorable impact upon the growth and stability of commuter airline operations. The legislation made these carriers eligible for federal loan guarantees for the purchase of aircraft and extended subsidies to operators of essential air services. Over the last several years the commuter industry has been realigning route structures to increase aircraft utilization and fuel

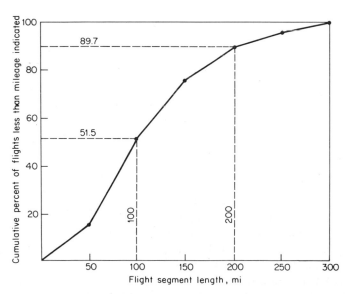

Fig. 1-3 Distribution of commuter airline flights by mileage block, year ended June 30, 1979. (*U.S. Senate [10]*.)

TABLE 1-11 **Commuter Airline Industry Statistics, 1970–1980**

Year	Enplaned passengers, thousands	Passenger-miles, thousands	Average trip length, mi	Number of aircraft	Average number of seats
1970	4,270	399,420	98	741	10.6
1971	4,698	473,243	101	743	11.0
1972	5,262	528,143	100	750	11.1
1973	5,688	575,143	101	855	11.6
1974	6,842	708,709	104	1,041	12.3
1975	6,666	698,473	110	948	13.0
1976	7,305	770,784	106	1,034	12.8
1977	8,505	946,242	111	1,109	13.0
1978	10,074	1,116,931	111	1,187	13.4
1979	11,054	1,324,267	120	1,263	13.0
1980*	15,600	2,060,000	132	1,333	13.1

* Projected preliminary estimates.
SOURCE: Civil Aeronautics Board [6].

efficiency. As a result, the commuters have been able to offer air service in many markets where domestic trunk and local service operations were not viable. Many communities now receive greater schedule frequency than was possible with the high-capacity aircraft used by the larger carriers in these low-density markets. In response to the growth shown in the commuter market in recent years, several aircraft manufacturers are planning the introduction of aircraft designed to meet the particular needs of the commuters. At present commuter carriers are authorized to utilize aircraft with seating capacities of up to 60 passengers on their routes and with payloads of up to 18,000 lb, a significant increase from the restrictions placed upon seating and payload by the CAB in the past.

Continued growth of the commuter industry in the future will depend to a large extent upon a resolution of the problems encountered by the industry in attaining suitable working relationships with the larger carriers, particularly with respect to joint fare agreements and shared reservations systems. With many large airports in this country reaching saturation in terms of airport facility use, provisions for the commuter carriers to gain access to large airports are essential. Advances in the air traffic control system and on-board instrumentation in commuter aircraft would allow these operators to use approach and departure paths and specifically designated runways separate from the larger jet transports. Such developments will significantly improve the ability of commuters to gain access to airports and will increase their performance reliability in the future.

It should be noted that beginning in 1981 the CAB began to classify commercial air-carrier operations based upon the volume of annual operating revenue generated. Therefore, the former classifications based upon

1-15 Annual and Busy-Hour Aircraft Operations at Selected U.S. Air Traffic Hub and General Aviation Airports, Fiscal Year 1980

Airport	Annual		Busy hour	
	Total	Air carrier	Total	Air carrier
Large hub airports:				
Chicago O'Hare International	734,555	577,671	178	141
Hartsfield-Atlanta International	609,466	541,440	145	134
Los Angeles International	534,414	419,506	133	88
Denver Stapleton International	485,695	316,664	169	105
Miami International	376,820	283,457	111	84
Washington National	354,717	204,560	108	56
Boston Logan International	340,896	204,159	112	59
Medium hub airports:				
Memphis International	377,603	143,294	115	48
Salt Lake City International	285,104	83,723	155	27
Milwaukee-Mitchell Field	247,290	85,011	136	35
Portland International	219,404	75,827	107	37
Orlando Jetport	157,535	115,936	67	42
San Diego International	155,914	69,513	54	18
Greater Cincinnati	119,088	59,773	68	25
Small hub airports:				
San Jose Municipal	415,543	47,255	183	19
Daytona Beach Regional	292,534	15,030	164	9
Wichita Mid-Continent	230,128	37,439	169	37
Sacramento Metro	170,733	36,749	106	20
Grand Rapids Kent County	167,922	27,334	126	11
Richmond Byrd International	163,998	33,813	75	17
Knoxville McGhee-Tyson	143,575	19,598	71	7
General aviation:				
Fort Worth Meacham	400,722		284	
Pontiac	274,686		220	
Seattle Boeing Field	408,207		247	
Tamiami	422,867		236	
Teterboro	308,413		231	
Torrance Municipal	370,398		284	
Van Nuys	567,055		310	

SOURCE: Federal Aviation Administration [19].

opened. Some of the early contractors were the Ford Motor Company, Boeing Air Transport (predecessor of United Airlines), and National Air Transport.

Air Commerce Act of 1926

Thus far there was no legislation which fostered and encouraged the orderly development of air transportation. Oddly enough, the first year of

certification have given way to a new classification designating the carriers as majors, nationals, and regionals.

Airports

The number of airports in the United States has grown steadily during the last decade, as shown in Table 1-12. Nearly 68 percent are privately owned. However, it will be noted that of the 15,161 airports on record in 1980 only 38 percent had paved runways, and only 628 were being served by scheduled airline service. There were 574 airports receiving scheduled passenger service from certificated carriers in 1980. There were 43 air-carrier airports in the 26 large hub cities, 36 medium hub airports, 91 small hub airports, and 404 nonhub airports [19]. Only 330 airports had sufficient traffic to justify FAA control towers. Finally, only 3159 airports satisfied the criteria to be included in the National Airport System Plan (NASP). Should commuter travel continue to expand at its present rate, many more airports will undoubtedly be served by scheduled airlines. The distribution of passenger traffic at the 60 largest airports in the United States is shown in Fig. 1-4. One-half of the passengers served were served by 14 airports, and three-quarters by 40 airports. This indicates the high concentration of passenger activity in major metropolitan areas.

In order that the reader may gain an appreciation of the magnitude of traffic at some of the busiest airports in the world, statistical data concerning annual aircraft operations and the annual number of passengers handled are presented in Table 1-13. It is interesting to note the fairly large increase in the number of passengers handled during the period from 1970 to 1980 and the fact that the increase in the number of aircraft operations has been less significant and even decreased in some instances. This latter observation may be attributed to the introduction of wide-body aircraft for passenger travel at the beginning of this period. In Table 1-14 both daily and hourly traffic data are given for those United States airports listed in Table 1-13. It is informative to note the relationships between average and peak traffic on both a daily and an hourly basis. A comparison of the level of total aircraft operations and air-carrier operations on an

TABLE 1-12 Number of Airports in the United States

	1960	1965	1970	1975	1980
Total airports on record with FAA	6,881	9,566	11,340	13,251	15,161
Publicly owned	2,780	3,570	4,260	4,667	4,785
With paved runways	1,893	2,747	3,717	4,865	5,833
With scheduled airline service	575	532	518	653	628
National airport system plan	2,770	3,219	3,236	3,204	3,159

SOURCES: Federal Aviation Administration [9] and Air Transportation Association of America [3].

Fig. 1-4 Distribution of passenger enplanements at U.S. airports, 1978. (*Federal Aviation Administration [20].*)

TABLE 1-13 **Passenger Volumes and Aircraft Operations at Selected Airports in the United States and Europe, 1970 and 1980**

	Total aircraft operations		Total passengers	
Airport	1970	1980	1970	1980
United States:				
Chicago O'Hare International	641,390	724,155	27,918,000	43,653,000
Los Angeles International	544,025	523,961	18,464,000	33,038,000
Hartsfield-Atlanta International	428,392	612,525	16,632,000	40,180,000
John F. Kennedy International	395,938	307,527	19,096,000	26,796,000
San Francisco International	386,674	359,146	12,654,000	22,248,000
Denver Stapleton International	357,849	486,888	7,429,150	20,849,000
LaGuardia	336,449	316,811	11,828,000	17,459,000
Miami International	370,237	369,563	9,584,000	20,505,000
Washington National	319,449	352,166	9,196,000	14,538,000
Boston Logan International	323,425	296,851	8,790,000	14,722,000
Europe:				
London-Heathrow	270,302	294,600	15,607,000	27,472,000
Paris-Orly	191,014	183,850	10,382,000	15,866,557
Frankfurt	195,802	237,765	9,402,000	16,873,000
Rome-Fiumicino	167,981	146,508	7,453,000	11,434,000
Copenhagen	156,757	162,574	6,466,000	8,602,566
Amsterdam	135,520	185,836	5,172,000	9,401,025
Zurich	130,472	161,129	4,530,000	7,255,495

SOURCES: Airport Operators Council International [16, 23] and British Airports Authority [18].

TABLE 1-14 **Profile of Aircraft Operations at Sele Carrier Airports in the United States,**

	Total aircra		
Airport	Annual	Average day	d
Chicago O'Hare International	734,555	2,012	2,6
Los Angeles International	534,414	1,464	1,74
Hartsfield-Atlanta International	609,466	1,670	1,86
John F. Kennedy International	311,777	854	1,167
San Francisco International	371,222	1,017	1,198
Denver Stapleton International	485,695	1,331	1,390
LaGuardia	319,891	876	1,125
Miami International	376,820	1,032	1,340
Washington National	354,717	972	1,289
Boston Logan International	340,896	934	1,219

SOURCE: Federal Aviation Administration [19].

annual and a busy-hour basis for selected air traffic hub aviation airports is shown in Table 1-15. It should be observ carrier traffic is a significant portion of total aircraft operations large hub airports and that the busy-hour operations at other general aviation airports can be quite large.

FEDERAL ROLE IN AVIATION AND AIRPORTS

Commercial air transportation started in the United States with the ca of mail. As early as 1911 the Post Office Department showed an inter the transportation of mail by air, and from then on the department did n to encourage civil aviation. Attempts to obtain federal appropriations airmail began in 1912, but met with little success until 1916, when appropriation for experimental purposes was made. In 1918 the first airma route in the United States was established between Washington, D.C., an New York City. At the start of this service the flying operations were conducted by the War Department, but later that year, the Post Office Department took over the entire operation with its own equipment and pilots. Service was inaugurated between New York City and Chicago in 1919 and was extended to San Francisco in 1920.

The Post Office Department, having demonstrated the practicality of moving mail by air, desired to turn over the operation to private enterprise. By 1925 the development work of the government had reached a stage where private operation seemed feasible. Accordingly, legislation permitting the Post Office Department to contract with private operators for the carriage of mail by air was provided by the Air Mail Act of 1925 (Kelly Act). It was not until 1926, however, that a number of contract routes were the carriage of mail also saw the passage of the first federal law dealing with air commerce, the Air Commerce Act of 1926 (Public Law 64-254). Although this law provided regulatory measures, it did more to aid and encourage civil aviation than to regulate. The principal provisions of this act were:

1. All aircraft owned by U.S. citizens operating in common-carrier service or in connection with any business must be registered.
2. All aircraft must be certificated and operated by certified airmen.
3. Authority was given to the Secretary of Commerce to establish air traffic rules.
4. The Secretary of Commerce was authorized to establish, operate, and maintain lighted civil airways.

In drafting the legislation, Congress relied considerably upon the precedents in maritime law. An analogy was utilized between the role of the government in meeting water navigation needs and the role of the government in air navigation. In water navigation these services included the signing, lighting, and marking of channels, safety inspection of ships and operating personnel, assistance in the development and improvement of ports and waterways, and laws concerning the operations of the industry. The provision of docks and terminal facilities was the responsibility of local government or the private sector of the economy. Therefore, the legislation was adopted in such a framework which held that airports were analogous to the docks of waterborne transportation [22].

Aid for airports was specifically prohibited. This policy remained in effect until the passage of the Civil Aeronautics Act of 1938. The Air Commerce Act had one serious disadvantage, namely, that control of air transportation was divided among several government agencies. The airmail contracts were let by the Post Office Department; airmail rates were subject to regulation by the Interstate Commerce Commission; and matters having to do with registration, certification, and airways were vested in the Bureau of Air Commerce in the Department of Commerce. The result of this divided jurisdiction was a lack of coordination in the efforts of government to develop the air transportation industry.

Civil Aeronautics Act of 1938

The Air Commerce Act of 1926 had been passed before the carriage of mail and passengers had developed into a substantial business enterprise. The failure of this legislation to provide adequate economic control led to wasteful and destructive competitive practices. The carriers had little security in their routes and therefore could not attract private investors and develop traffic volumes sufficient to achieve economic stability. These particular weaknesses in the existing legislation led to the enactment of the

Civil Aeronautics Act of 1938 (Public Law 76-706). This act defined in a precise manner the role of the federal government in respect to the economic phases of air transport. It created one independent agency to foster and regulate air transport in lieu of the three agencies operating under the Air Commerce Act. This new agency was called the Civil Aeronautics Authority (not to be confused with the Civil Aeronautics Administration). It consisted of a five-member Authority, a three-member Air Safety Board, and an Administrator. The five-member Authority was principally concerned with the economic regulation of air carriers; the Air Safety Board was an independent body for the investigation of accidents; and the concerns of the Administrator dealt primarily with the construction, operation, and maintenance of the airways.

During the first year and a half of its existence, a number of organizational difficulties arose within the Civil Aeronautics Authority. As a result, President Franklin D. Roosevelt, acting within the authority granted to him in the Reorganization Act of 1939 (55 Stat. 561), reorganized the Civil Aeronautics Authority and created two separate agencies, the Civil Aeronautics Board and the Civil Aeronautics Administration (CAA). The five-member Authority remained as an independent agency and became known as the CAB; the Air Safety Board was abolished, and its functions were given to the CAB; and the Administrator became the head of an agency within the Department of Commerce, known as the CAA. The duties of the original five-member Authority were unchanged, except that certain responsibilities, such as accident investigation, were added because of the abolition of the Air Safety Board. The Administrator, in addition to retaining the functions of supervising construction, maintenance, and operation of the airways, was required to undertake the administration and enforcement of safety regulations and the administration of the laws with regard to aircraft operation. Subsequently, the Administrator became directly responsible to the Secretary of Commerce (1950).

The Civil Aeronautics Act, like its predecessor, the Air Commerce Act, authorized the federal government to establish, operate, and maintain the airways; but again, authorization for actively aiding airport development was lacking. The act, however, authorized the expenditure of federal funds for the construction of landing areas, provided the Administrator certified "that such landing area was reasonably necessary for use in air commerce or in the interests of national defense." The act also directed the Administrator to make a survey of airport needs in the United States and report to Congress about the desirability of federal participation and the extent to which the federal government should participate.

In accordance with the requirements of the act, the CAA conducted a detailed survey of the airport needs of the nation. An advisory committee was appointed, composed of representatives of interested federal agencies (both military and civil), state aviation officials, airport managers, airline representatives, and others. A report was submitted to Congress on March

23, 1939 (H. Doc. 245, 76th Cong., 1st Sess.). Some of the more important recommendations in this report were:

1. The development and maintenance of an adequate system of airports and seaplane bases should be recognized in principle as a matter of national concern.

2. Such a system should be regarded, under certain conditions, as a proper object of federal expenditure.

3. In passing upon applications for federal expenditure on airport development or improvement, the highest preference should be given to airports which are important to the maintenance of the safe and efficient operation of air transportation along the major trade routes of the nation; and to those rendering special service to the national defense.

4. At such times as the national policy includes the making of grants to local units of government for public-works purposes, or any work-relief activity, a proportion of the funds involved should be allocated to airport purposes. Such purposes should be given preference as rendering an important service to the localities concerned and at the same time being of particular importance to the nation's commerce and defense.

5. Whenever emergency public-works programs may be terminated, or when such programs may be curtailed to a degree not enabling adequate airport development to continue, or when the Congress for other reasons may determine federal assistance for airports should be continued through annual appropriations for that purpose, based upon annual reports which should include a review of the general status of the nation's airport system and of the work recently done or currently in course of being done, and recommendations for future work in the interest of developing and maintaining a system adequate to national needs, expenditures at these periods should be limited to projects of exceptional national interest.

6. In connection with such public-works or work-relief programs as normally involve joint contributions by the federal government and by local government, there should be a provision of supplementary funds to enable the federal government to increase its share of the total expense, in any proportion justified by the importance of the project.

7. All applications for federal airport grants from such a supplementary appropriation should be presented through agencies of state government.

8. In deciding upon the wisdom and propriety of granting any such

applications, and the priority that should be given to them, consideration should be given to the aeronautical policy of the state in question, with reference to such matters as the state's policy in protecting the approaches to airports; the state's policy in respect to the employment of any taxes collected on the fuel used in aircraft; and any measures taken by the state to ensure the proper maintenance of airports and the maintenance of reasonable charges for the services given them.

9. The detailed plans for the location and development of any airport with respect to which there is federal contribution of any kind, should be subject to the approval of the federal agency charged with the establishment of civil airways, landing areas, and necessary air navigation facilities.

10. There should be no direct federal contribution to the cost of maintaining airports, other than federal airports; except that the Administrator of the CAA may, in accordance with the Civil Aeronautics Act and so far as available funds permit, assume the cost of operating any lighting equipment and other air-navigation facility as a part of the cost of operation of the federal airways system.

The airport survey submitted in 1939 was brought up to date with new studies completed in 1940. Continuing studies were made through the war years. While first importance was attached to the military requirements, care was taken whenever possible to anticipate the needs of postwar civil aviation. During the war years the federal government, through the CAA, spent $353 million for the development of military landing areas in the continental United States. This does not include funds spent by the military agencies. During the same period the CAA spent $9.5 million for the development of landing areas in the United States solely for civil purposes.

At the end of World War II, over 500 airports constructed for the military by the CAA were declared surplus and were turned over to cities, counties, and states for airport use. The interest in adequate airport facilities by various political subdivisions of government continued. The needs were made known to Congress by various interests. As a result, the House of Representatives passed a resolution (H. Res. 598, 78th Cong.) directing the CAA to make a survey of "need for a system of airports and landing areas throughout the United States" and report to Congress.

The results of this survey were completed in 1944 (H. Doc. 807, 78th Cong., 2d Sess.) and contained the following principal recommendations:

1. That Congress authorize an appropriation to the Office of the Administrator of Civil Aeronautics not to exceed $100 million annually to be used in a program of Federal aid to public agencies

for the development of a nationwide system of public airports adequate to meet the present and immediate future needs of civil aeronautics. The Administrator be authorized to allocate such funds for any construction work involved in constructing, improving, or repairing an airport, including the construction, alteration, and repair of airport buildings other than hangers, and the removal, lowering, marking, and lighting of airport obstructions; for the acquisition of any lands or property interest necessary either for any such construction or to protect airport approaches; for making field surveys, preparing plans and specifications; for supervising and inspecting construction work; and for any necessary federal expenses in the administration of this program.

2. That such a program be conducted in cooperation with the state and other nonfederal public agencies on a basis to be determined by Congress. That the federal contribution be determined by Congress in passing the necessary enabling legislation. A good precedent for the proportionate sharing of costs exists in the public-roads program which has operated satisfactorily for many years on a 50-50 basis.

3. That any project for which federal aid is requested must meet with the approval of the Administrator of Civil Aeronautics as to the scope of development and cost; must conform to CAA standards for location, layout, grading, drainage, paving, and lighting; and all work thereon must be subject to the inspection and approval of the CAA.

4. In order to participate in the federal-aid program, a state shall:
   a. Establish and empower an official body equipped to conduct its share of the program.
   b. Have legislation adequate for the clearing and protection of airport approaches, and such other legislation as may be necessary to vest in its subdivisions all powers necessary to enable them to participate through the state as sponsors of airport projects.
   c. Have no special tax on aviation facilities, fuel, operations, or businesses, the proceeds of which are not used entirely for aviation purposes.
   d. Ensure the operation of all public airports within its jurisdiction in the public interest, without unjust discrimination or unreasonable charges.
   e. Ensure the proper operation and maintenance of all public airports within its jurisdiction.
   f. Make airports developed with federal aid available for unrestricted use by U.S. government aircraft without charge other than an

amount sufficient to cover the cost of repairing damage done by such aircraft.

    g. Require at all airports for which federal funds have been provided the installation of a standard accounting and fiscal reporting system satisfactory to the Administrator.

5. That sponsors of projects be required to enter into contracts with the CAA ensuring the proper maintenance and protection of airports developed with federal aid and their operation in the public interest.

Federal Airport Act of 1946

In 1944 an airport development bill was introduced into the House of Representatives (H. Res. 5024), but no action was taken on it. After extensive hearings in both houses of Congress, the Senate passed an airport bill (S. 2) in 1945, and later that year the House passed a bill (H. Res. 3615). The language in these two bills differed in several respects. One of the principal differences was the method employed in channeling funds to the municipalities. The Senate bill provided that funds be channeled to the municipalities through appropriate state aviation organizations unless a state did not have an appropriate agency to handle the matter. The House bill permitted channeling of funds either through the state or directly to a municipality or other political subdivision of government. The substitute bill agreed to in conference conformed more nearly to the House language. Another difference had to do with the size of the discretionary fund which, instead of being apportioned among the states by a fixed formula, would be available for use by the Administrator at his sole determination. The House bill provided 25 percent of the total appropriation for airport development as a discretionary fund, the Senate bill 35 percent. The compromise reached in conference retained the House version. Other differences which were worked out in conference concerned whether or not costs of acquisition of land and interest in airspace should be eligible for federal aid, project sponsorship requirements, and the reimbursement for damage to public airports caused by federal agencies.

    The conference report was approved by Congress, and the Federal Airport Act of 1946 was enacted (Public Law 79-377).

Federal Aviation Act of 1958

For a number of years there had been a growing concern about the division of the responsibility in aviation matters among different agencies of the federal government. Unlike highway or other forms of transport, aviation is unique in its relation to the federal government. It is the only mode whose operations are conducted almost wholly within federal jurisdiction, and one subject to little or no regulation by states or local authorities. Thus the federal government bears virtually complete responsibility for the promotion and supervision of the industry in the public interest. The military interest and the entire national defense concept are also intimately related to aviation.

Recognizing that the demands on the federal government in the years ahead would be substantial, the Director of the Bureau of the Budget requested a review of aviation-facilities problems in 1955. A report was issued later that year recommending that a study of "long-range needs for aviation facilities and aids be undertaken" and that such a study be made under the direction of an individual of national reputation.

President Dwight D. Eisenhower accepted these recommendations and appointed Edward P. Curtis as his Special Assistant for Aviation Matters in 1957. Curtis was charged with the responsibility of preparing a comprehensive aviation-facilities plan which would "provide the basis for the timely installation of technically adequate aids, for optimum coordination of the efforts of the civil and military departments, and for effective participation by state and local authorities and the aircraft operators in meeting facilities requirements." Curtis completed his report and submitted it to the President. In this report Curtis stated that "it has become evident that the fundamental reason for our previous failures lies with the inability of our governmental organizations to keep pace with the tremendous growth in private, commercial, and military aviation which has occurred in the last twenty years." Curtis recommended the consolidation of all aviation functions, other than military, into one independent agency responsible only to the President. However, the report recognized that to "develop new management structures and policy, to coordinate proposals within the executive branch and to obtain legislation implementing a new permanent organization might be as long as two or three years." The most urgent matter requiring attention was in the area of air traffic control. The collision of two aircraft over the Grand Canyon in 1956 provided the impetus for rapid legislative action for remedying midair collisions. Curtis recommended that, as an interim measure, there be created an Airways Modernization Board whose function was to "develop, modify, test, and evaluate systems, procedures, facilities, and devices, as well as define the performance characteristics thereof, to meet the needs for safe and efficient navigation and traffic control of all civil and military aviation except for those needs of military agencies which are peculiar to air warfare and primarily of military concern, and select such systems, procedures, facilities, and devices which will best serve such needs and will promote maximum coordination of air traffic control and air defense systems." The Board was to consist of the Secretary of Commerce, the Secretary of Defense, and an independent chairman.

Congress was receptive to this recommendation and passed the Airways Modernization Act of 1957 (Public Law 85-133) establishing the Board for a 3-year term.

In the meantime there were more midair collisions, and reports of near misses were given wide circulation. Costly disagreements between the CAA and the military on the type of navigational aids to be used on the airways no doubt also spurred Congressional action. As a result, instead of taking 2 or 3 years to create a single aviation agency as was predicted, Congress acted favorably on the legislation within a year of the passage of the Airways Modernization Act. This legislation is known as the Federal Aviation Act of 1958 (Public Law 85-726). This law superseded the Civil Aeronautics Act of 1938, but not the Federal Airport Act of 1946.

The principal provision of the law insofar as organizational changes were concerned are as follows:

1. The Federal Aviation Agency was created as an independent agency with an Administrator directly responsible to the President. The agency incorporated the functions of the CAA and the Airways Modernization Board, both of which were abolished.

2. The CAB was retained as an independent agency, including all its functions except its safety-rule-making powers, which were transferred to the Federal Aviation Agency.

Reorganization of Aviation in the Department of Transportation

For many years it had been argued that there had been a proliferation of federal activities with regard to transportation. For example, the Bureau of Public Roads was part of the Department of Commerce, whereas the Federal Aviation Agency was an independent agency. It was felt by different transport interests that there was a lack of coordination and effective administration of the transportation programs of the federal government, resulting in a lack of a sound national transportation policy. It is interesting to note that the first legislative proposal in this direction dates back to 1874. However, in recent years the involvement of the federal government in the development of the transportation systems of the nation has been enormous, requiring much more coordination among federal transport activities than ever before. With this as a background, a cabinet-level Department of Transportation (DOT) was created, headed by the Secretary of Transportation (Public Law 89-670). The department began to function on April 1, 1967.

The agencies and functions transferred to the DOT related to air transportation included the Federal Aviation Agency in its entirety and the safety functions of the CAB, including the responsibility for investigating and determining the probable cause of aircraft accidents, and its appellate safety functions involving the review, on appeal, of the suspension, modification, or denial of certificates or licenses. The name of the Federal Aviation Agency was changed to Federal Aviation Administration. The

Administrator is still appointed by the President, but reports directly to the Secretary of Transportation. A National Transportation Safety Board (NTSB) was established by the same act that created the DOT to determine "the cause or probable cause of transportation accidents and reporting the facts, conditions, and circumstances relating to such accidents" for all modes of transportation. Although created by the act which established the DOT, the NTSB, in carrying out its functions, is "independent of the Secretary and other offices and officers of the Department." The NTSB consists of five members appointed by the President and annually reports directly to Congress.

The creation of the DOT did not alter any legislation in the Federal Aviation Act of 1958, with the exception of the transfer of the safety functions from the CAB to the NTSB. In the act of establishing the new department, however, there was a statutory requirement to establish an Office of Noise Abatement to provide policy guidance with respect to interagency activities related to the reduction of transportation noise. With the introduction of jet aircraft in 1958 the complaints against aircraft noise increased significantly. As a result, in 1968 the Federal Aviation Act was amended by Congress (Public Law 90-411) to require noise abatement regulations. Its principal purpose was to establish noise levels which aircraft manufacturers cannot exceed in the development of new aircraft.

Airport and Airway Development Act of 1970

In the mid-1960s, as air traffic was expanding at a fairly rapid pace, air delays getting into and out of major airports began to increase rapidly. Along with the delays in the air, congestion was taking place in parking areas, access roads, and terminal buildings. It was evident that to reduce congestion, substantial financial resources would be required for investment in airway and airport improvements. It was estimated that $13 billion in new capital improvements would be required for public airports alone in the period from 1970 to 1980. The amount of money authorized by the Federal Airport Act of 1946 was insufficient to assist in financing such a vast program. The normal and anticipated sources of revenue available to public airports were also not sufficient to raise the required funds for capital expenditures. It was argued that much of the congestion in the air at major airports was due to a lack of funds to modernize the airways system. Funds for airport development came from the budget of the FAA authorized by Congress each year and not from the Federal Airport Act. The deficiencies in airport and airway development were documented in several reports. It was the consensus of industry and government that the only way to provide the funds needed for airports and airways was through increased or new taxes imposed upon the users of the air transport system. It was also argued that the revenues from these taxes should be specifically earmarked for aviation and not go to the general fund. The concept of establishing a trust fund similar to that of the national highways program was agreed upon. Finally, after much debate in Congress, the Airport and Airway Development Act of 1970 and the Airport and Airway Revenue Act of 1970 were enacted (Public Law 91-258).

As finally passed, the act was divided into two sections: Title I detailed the airport assistance programs and established a financing program for airport grants, airways hardware acquisition, and research and development; Title II created the Airport and Airway Trust Fund and established a pattern of aviation excise taxes which would provide the resources upon which the Title I capital programs would depend through 1980. The excise taxes adopted were 8 percent on domestic passenger tickets, a flat $3 per passenger on international departures, 7 cents per gallon on all fuel used by general aviation, and 5 percent on all air-cargo waybills. In addition, a $25 per year aircraft registration tax was levied on all aircraft (commercial and general aviation) plus a 2 cents per pound annual surtax (3.5 cents for jet aircraft) for all aircraft weighing in excess of 2500 lb. Finally, revenues from existing taxes on aircraft tires and tubes were transferred from the Highway Trust Fund.

Airline Deregulation Act of 1978

The Airline Deregulation Act (Public Law 95-504) was passed by Congress in October 1978. This legislation will eliminate the statutory authority for the economic regulation of the passenger airline industry in the United States. The CAB will be abolished in 1985 unless legislation is passed in Congress to extend it. The legislation was intended to increase competition in the passenger airline industry by phasing out federal authority to exercise regulatory controls during the period of time from 1978 through 1985.

The principal provisions of this legislation were:

1. Required the CAB to place maximum reliance on competition in its regulation of interstate airline service, while continuing to ensure the safety of air transportation; to maintain service to small communities; and to prevent practices which are deemed anticompetitive in nature.

2. Required CAB approval of airline acquisitions, consolidations, mergers, purchases, and operating contracts; the burden to prove that an action is anticompetitive in nature was placed upon the party challenging that action.

3. Permitted carriers to change rates within a range of reasonableness from the standard industry fare without prior CAB approval; the CAB was authorized to disallow a fare change if it considered the change predatory.

4. Provided interstate carriers an exemption from state regulation of rates and routes.

5. Required the CAB to authorize new routes and services that were consistent with the public convenience and necessity.

6. Allowed carriers to be granted operating rights to any route on which only one other carrier was providing service and on which other airlines were authorized to provide service but were not actually providing a minimum level of service. If more than one airline was providing service on this route, the CAB was required to determine if the granting of additional route authority was consistent with the public convenience and necessity before allowing additional carriers to service the route. An airline not providing the specified minimum level of service on a route (dormant authority) could begin providing such service and retain its authority. Otherwise the CAB was required to revoke the unused authority.

7. Provided for an automatic market entry program, whereby airlines could begin service on one additional route each year during the period from 1979 to 1981 without formal CAB approval. Each carrier was also permitted to protect one of its existing routes each year by declaring it ineligible for automatic market entry by another airline.

8. Authorized the CAB to order an airline to continue to provide "essential air transportation service" and, for a 10-year period, to provide subsidies or seek other willing carriers to assure the continuation of essential service.

9. Required the CAB to determine within 1 year of the enactment of the legislation what it considered to be "essential air transportation service" for each point being serviced at the time of enactment of the legislation.

10. Required the CAB and the DOT to determine the mechanism by which the state and local governments should share the cost of subsidies from the federal government to preserve small community air service and to make policy recommendations to Congress on this matter.

11. Exempted from most CAB regulation commuter aircraft weighing less than 18,000 lb and carrying fewer than 56 passengers.

12. Made commuter and intrastate air carriers eligible for the federal loan guarantee program.

13. Provided that the domestic route authority of the CAB would cease in 1981; its authority over domestic fares, acquisitions, and merg-

ers would cease in 1983; and the CAB would be abolished (sunset) in 1985.

14. Provided that after the CAB was abolished, the local service carrier subsidy program was to be transferred to the DOT; the foreign air transportation authority of the CAB was to be transferred to the Transportation and Justice Departments, in consultation with the State Department; and the mail subsidy program was to be transferred to the U.S. Postal Service.

Some of the more significant developments in the early years of deregulation included the introduction of a great variety of discount fares for the discretionary traveler, the adjustment of fares to more closely reflect the cost of service provided, the realignment of the route systems of airline carriers, the strong growth and apparent acceptance of commuter carriers, and the development and growth of "low-cost airlines" offering basic air transportation service with few of the amenities traditionally associated with air-carrier service [7]. Service patterns to small communities have shifted since deregulation. Less service is being provided between small communities, but more service is being provided between larger communities and small communities. The total number of daily departures has risen since deregulation, the number of competitive markets has increased, and the number of instances of single-plane service between cities has increased [21]. The growth experienced by the local service and commuter carriers has outpaced that of the domestic trunk carriers.

The nature of the airline industry is changing in response to deregulation, but the limited experience reported thus far does not allow for definitive conclusions about the long-term effects on air transportation service in this country.

Airport and Airway Improvement Act of 1982

The Airport and Airway Development Act expired in September 1980 and for nearly 3 years a variety of bills were introduced in Congress to meet future airport development needs. Due to considerable differences about the manner by which the funding of large airports and state airport grants should be implemented, it was not until August 1982 that the Airport and Airway Improvement Act of 1982 was enacted (Public Law 97-248). This act continued the user tax categories outlined in the original airport development legislation with some increases in rates. Expenditures over a 5-year period of nearly $4.8 billion for airport development and $6.3 billion for airway improvement were authorized.

STATE ROLE IN AVIATION AND AIRPORTS

State interest in aviation began as early as 1921, when the state of Oregon established an agency to handle matters concerning aviation. Since that time virtually all states have established aeronautical agencies, as either commissions, departments, bureaus, boards, or divisions. Their responsibilities vary considerably and include channeling federal aid funds, planning state airport systems, providing state aid to local airport authorities, constructing and maintaining navigational equipment, investigating small aircraft accidents, enforcing safety regulations, and licensing airports.

Despite the growing concern of the states in airport development and aviation planning, their participation in the past has had little resemblance to the pattern of highway development. The states have always played a leading role in the development of roads and streets within their boundaries, whereas in airport development this has not been true. The reason for this pattern can be explained best by looking into the background of the entry of the states into aviation.

The majority of airports for civil aviation served by air carriers are municipally owned and operated. In a large number of states these airports were in operation prior to the formation of a state aeronautical agency. From its inception air transportation, because it is inherently of an interstate nature, became a matter of federal concern. The federal government provided much technical and financial assistance to municipalities. During World War II a great number of municipalities were the recipients of federal aid from the CAA through the Defense Landing Area (DLA) Program. Thus in the early stages of airport development in this country, a fairly close relationship was established between the federal government and the municipalities. This relationship was furthered when the Federal Airport Act of 1946 authorized the CAA to issue grants directly to municipalities, as long as such a procedure was not opposed to state policy. In the meantime, the majority of states were doing very little in the way of providing funds to municipalities for airports. While increases in state aid for airport development have occurred in the last several years, the amount of federal aid has been substantially higher.

In those states where monetary aid is made available for airport development, the plans, specifications, and design for airport construction are generally reviewed by the state aeronautical agency.

There is no doubt that participation by the states in airport development is assuming a more significant role with the emergence of recent proposals in Congress to defederalize airport development and to channel funds directly to state aeronautical agencies through block grant programs. The public concern for environmental control has resulted in legislation being passed at the state level, in addition to federal statutes, aimed at the control of aircraft noise and pollution. As general aviation and commuter activities continue to grow, the states will have to share the burden with the federal government in providing facilities for these activities, enforcing safety regulations, and other matters.

AVIATION ORGANIZATIONS AND THEIR FUNCTIONS

The organizations directly involved in U.S. and international air-carrier transportation and general aviation activity have an important influence on airport development as well as on aircraft operations. These organizations can be classified into four groups, namely, international government agencies, federal agencies, state agencies, and industry or trade organizations.

International Government Agencies

International Civil Aviation Organization

Perhaps the most important international agency concerned with airport development is the ICAO, which is now a specialized agency of the United Nations with headquarters in Montreal, Canada. In 1980, 146 nations were members of ICAO.

The ICAO concept was formed during a conference of 52 nations held in Chicago in 1944. This conference was by the invitation of the United States to consider matters of mutual interest in the field of air transportation. The objectives of ICAO as stated in its charter are to develop the principles and techniques of international air transportation so as to:

1. Ensure the safe and orderly growth of international civil aviation throughout the world
2. Encourage the arts of aircraft design and operation for peaceful purposes
3. Encourage the development of airways, airports, and air-navigation facilities for international aviation
4. Meet the needs of the peoples of the world for safe, regular, efficient, and economical air transport
5. Prevent economic waste by unreasonable competition
6. Ensure that the rights of contracting states are fully respected and that every contracting state has a fair opportunity to operate international airlines
7. Avoid discrimination between contracting states
8. Promote safety of flight in international air navigation
9. Promote generally the development of all aspects of international civil aeronautics

The ICAO has two governing bodies, the Assembly and the Council. The Council is a permanent body responsible to the Assembly and is composed of representatives from 30 countries. The Council is the working group for the organization. It carries out the directives of the Assembly and discharges the duties and obligations specified in the ICAO charter.

To the airport planner and designer perhaps the most important document issued by the ICAO is *Aerodromes, Annex 14 to the Convention on International Civil Aviation* [12]. Annex 14 contains the international design standards and recommended practices which are applicable to nearly all airports serving international air commerce. In addition to Annex 14, ICAO publishes a great deal of technical and statistical information relative to international air transport.

Federal Agencies of the U.S. Government

There are three agencies at the federal level which are concerned primarily with air transportation. These are the CAB, the FAA, and the NTSB. The DOT supports the activities of the FAA in many aspects of aviation and develops a national policy with respect to aviation as part of its function of integrating the planning and operations of all modes of transport. The National Aeronautics and Space Administration (NASA) has assumed a basic and applied research role in augmenting the activities of the other agencies concerned with aviation.

Civil Aeronautics Board

The CAB is composed of five members appointed by the President. In general the CAB performs two chief functions:

1. Regulation of the economic aspects of U.S. air-carrier operations, both domestic and international

2. Cooperation and assistance in the establishment and development of international air transportation

As noted earlier, the CAB is to be phased out of existence in 1985, and some of its powers will be transferred to other agencies.

Federal Aviation Administration

The FAA is headed by its chief executive known as the Administrator, who is appointed by the President. The FAA performs the following functions:

1. Encourages the establishment of civil airways, landing areas, and other air facilities

2. Designates federal airways; acquires, establishes, operates, and conducts research and development; and maintains air navigation facilities along such civil airways

3. Makes provision for the control and protection of air traffic moving in air commerce

4. Undertakes or supervises technical development work in the field of aeronautics and the development of aeronautical facilities

5. Prescribes and enforces the civil air regulations for safety standards, including:

   a. Effectuation of safety standards, rules, and regulations

   b. Examination, inspection, or rating of flight personnel, aircraft engines, air navigation facilities, aircraft, and air agencies

   c. Issuance of various types of safety certificates

6. Provides for aircraft registration

7. Requires notice and issues orders with respect to hazards to air commerce

8. Issues airport operating certificates to airports serving air carriers

The FAA develops, directs, and fosters the coordination of a national system of airports, the National Airport System Plan (NASP) [13], and directs the federal aid airport program. In this connection it performs the following functions:

1. Provides consultation and advisory assistance on airport planning, design, construction, management, operation, and maintenance to governmental, professional, industrial, and other individuals and agencies

2. Develops and establishes standards, government planning methods, and procedures; airport and seaplane base design and construction; and airport management, operation, and maintenance

3. Collects and maintains an accurate record of all available airport facilities in the United States

4. Directs, formulates, and keeps current a national plan (NASP) for the development of an adequate system of airports in cooperation with federal, state, and local agencies, and determines and recommends the extent to which portions or units of that system should be developed or improved

5. Develops and recommends principles, for incorporation in state and local legislation, to permit or facilitate airport development, regulation, and protection of approaches through zoning or property acquisition

6. Secures compliance with statutory and contractual requirements relative to airport operation practices, conditions, and arrangements

7. Develops and recommends policies, requirements, and procedures governing the participation of states, municipalities, and other public agencies in federal aid airport projects and secures adherence to such policies, requirements, and procedures

National Transportation Safety Board

The NTSB consists of five members appointed by the President. It performs the following functions:

1. Investigates certain aviation, highway, marine, pipeline, and railroad accidents, and reports publicly on the facts, conditions and circumstances, and the cause or probable cause of such accidents

2. Recommends to Congress and federal, state, and local agencies measures to reduce the incidence of transportation accidents

3. Initiates and conducts transportation safety studies and investigations

4. Establishes procedures for reporting accidents to the CAB

5. Assesses accident investigation techniques and issues recommendations for improving accident investigation procedures

6. Evaluates the adequacy of the procedures and safeguards used for the transportation of hazardous materials

7. Reviews, on appeal, the suspension, amendment, modification, revocation, or denial of certain operating certificates, documents, or licenses issued by the FAA or the U.S. Coast Guard

State Agencies

As mentioned earlier, the states are involved to varying degrees in the many aspects of aviation, including airport financial assistance, flight safety, enforcement, aviation education, airport licensing, accident investigation, zoning, and environmental control. Because of the interstate nature of air transportation, the federal government has preempted the legislative and administative controls since the early days of aviation. However, for those aviation activities that occur wholly within the borders of a state, regulatory agencies have been formed at the state level to see to it that these activities are operated in the best interests of the state.

Industry and Trade Organizations

There are many groups involved in the technical and promotional aspects of aviation. The following is a partial list of those groups that are primarily concerned with the airport aspects of aviation.

1. **Aerospace Industries Association of America (AIA).** The national trade association of companies in the United States engaged in the research, development, and manufacture of aerospace systems. It is located in Washington, D.C.

2. Aircraft Owners and Pilots Association (AOPA). An association of owners and pilots of general aviation aircraft. It is headquartered in Washington, D.C.

3. Air Line Pilots Association (ALPA). An association of airline pilots. It is headquartered in Washington, D.C.

4. Airport Operators Council International (AOCI). An association of large airports located primarily in the United States. It is headquartered in Washington, D.C.

5. Air Transportation Association of America (ATA). An association of scheduled domestic and international airlines in the United States. The headquarters are in Washington, D.C.

6. American Association of Airport Executives (AAAE). An association of the managers of public and private airports. It is in Washington, D.C.

7. General Aviation Manufacturers Association (GAMA). An association promoting the interests of general aviation. It is in Washington, D.C.

8. Industry Working Group (IWG). An informal group of persons from the aircraft manufacturers, airlines, and airports that associate to exchange general technical information and to provide a coordinated industry position on both industrywide problems and governmental activity. This group generally meets in Washington, D.C.

9. International Air Transport Association (IATA). An association of scheduled carriers in international air transportation. It is headquartered in Montreal, Que., Canada.

10. International Civil Airports Association (ICAA). An association of airports located throughout the world. It is headquartered in Paris, France.

11. National Association of State Aviation Officials (NASAO). An association of the representatives of state aviation agencies. Its headquarters are in Washington, D.C.

12. Regional Airline Association of America (RAAA). An association of small regional and commuter aircraft operators, promoting the needs of this segment of the air transportation industry, formerly called the Commuter Airline Association of America (CAAA). It is located in Washington, D.C.

13. Western European Airports Association (WEAA). An association of the principal airports in Western Europe. It is headquartered in Brussels, Belgium.

REFERENCES

1. *Aerospace Facts and Figures,* Aerospace Industries Association of America, Inc., Washington, DC., 1980.

2. *Airline Capital Requirements in the 1980's,* Economics and Finance Department, Air Transportation Association of America, Washington, D.C., September 1979.

3. *Air Transport Facts and Figures,* Air Transportation Association of America, Washington, D.C., annual.

4. *Commercial Air Transportation—1980 and Beyond,* Boeing Commerical Airplane Company, Seattle, Wash., 1981.

5. *Commuter Air, 1981,* yearbook edition, Commuter Airline Association of America, Washington, D.C., April 1981.

6. *Commuter Air Carrier Traffic Statistics,* Civil Aeronautics Board, Washington, D.C., 12 months ended June 30, 1980.

7. *Developments in the Deregulated Airline Industry,* D. R. Graham and D. P. Kaplan, Office of Economic Analysis, Civil Aeronautics Board, Washington, D.C., June 1981.

8. *FAA Aviation Forecasts, Fiscal Years 1981–1992,* Federal Aviation Administration, Washington, D.C.

9. *FAA Statistical Handbook of Civil Aviation,* Federal Aviation Administration, Washington, D.C., annual.

10. *Hearings before Subcommittee on Aviation of the Committee on Commerce, Science, and Transportation,* U.S. Senate, Washington, D.C., August 1980.

11. *ICAO Bulletin,* International Civil Aviation Organization, Montreal, Que., Canada, monthly.

12. *International Standards and Recommended Practices, AERODROMES, Annex 14 to the Convention on International Civil Aviation,* International Civil Aviation Organization, Montreal, Que., Canada, June 1976.

13. *National Airport System Plan, 1978–1987,* Federal Aviation Administration, Department of Transportation, Washington, D.C.

14. *National Transportation Statistics,* annual report, Research and Special Programs Administration, Department of Transportation, Washington, D.C., September 1980.

15. *National Travel Survey, 1977 Census of Transportation,* Department of Commerce, Washington, D.C., October 1979.

16. *Passenger and Cargo Traffic and Aircraft Operations at Major World Airports, Calendar Year 1970,* Airport Operators Council International, Inc., Washington, D.C.

17. *Report on Airline Service, Fares, Traffic, Load Factors, and Market Share,* a staff study, 14th in a series, Civil Aeronautics Board, Washington, D.C., 1981.

18. *Reports and Accounts 1970–1971,* British Airports Authority, London, England.

19. *Terminal Area Air Traffic Relationships, Fiscal Year 1980,* Federal Aviation Administration, Washington, D.C.

20. *Terminal Area Forecasts,* Federal Aviation Administration, Washington, D.C., annual.

21. *The Changing Airline Industry: A Status Report through 1979,* Comptroller General of the United States, General Accounting Office, Washington, D.C., September 1980.

22. *The Federal Turnaround on Aid to Airports 1926–38,* Federal Aviation Administration, Department of Transportation, Washington, D.C., 1973.

23. *Worldwide Airport Traffic Report, Calendar Year 1980,* Airport Operators Council International, Inc., Washington, D.C.

Chapter 2

Airport Financing

INTRODUCTION

Airports are owned and operated by both private interests and public agencies. Over half are privately owned. However, only a small portion of the privately owned fields are paved, as compared to the majority of the publicly owned airports. In the early years of aviation, airport ownership was vested almost entirely in private hands. State and federal financial participation in airport development was virtually nonexistent. The depression period of the twenties witnessed a collapse in private investments in airports and gave rise to public ownership. Today the bulk of this country's aviation activities are carried on at publicly owned airports.

Although public ownership in airports is vested in a number of different types of governmental subdivisions, the majority are owned and operated by municipalities. The next most prevalent ownership is by counties, followed by special districts and authorities. Although both the federal and the state governments may have provisions affecting an airport, it is the decision of the airport owner which ultimately determines the development of the airport.

Airport improvements are financed in a variety of ways. Among these are federal grants, state grants, taxes levied by local governments, general obligation bonds, and revenue bonds. In a few instances, capital improvements of a minor nature have been financed from accumulated surpluses from airport revenues.

The Federal Airport Act made provision for federal grants which were administered by the FAA. The maximum federal grant for an eligible project was for approximately one-half of the total project cost, although this amount has varied over the lives of the various legislations affecting airports, as discussed subsequently.

Virtually all of the states participate financially in airport development, either in conjunction with or independently of the federal aid program. Where state grants are made in conjunction with a federal program, the state usually contributes one-half of the local government share of the project costs.

Local financing has generally been accomplished through the levying of taxes or through the sale of bond issues. For the smaller airports, which have not reached financial maturity, funds for capital improvements have usually been taken from the general tax funds of local governments. This is particularly true if the required amount was small. The bulk of the improvements at the larger airports have been financed by the sale of general obligation or revenue bonds.

FEDERAL PARTICIPATION

Until 1933 airports for civil use were developed mainly through investments by municipalities and private sources. The Depression was largely responsible for the first substantial federal participation in the development of civil airports. The bulk of the funds provided from 1933 until the beginning of World War II were through work-relief programs. The first such program was under the Civil Works Administration (CWA). In the fall of 1933 the CWA provided more than $15 million for airport construction, most of the money going to smaller communities.

In 1934, the CWA was succeeded by the Federal Emergency Relief Administration (FERA). This agency provided over $17 million for the development of 943 airport projects.

The administration of federal aid for airports was taken over in July of 1935 by the Works Progress Administration (WPA). The WPA spent $323 million for airport construction in the United States. It was under this program that contributions by municipalities were encouraged and a pattern of sharing costs emerged. The local contributions amounted to about $110 million.

Another federal program contributing to airport development in the thirties was the Public Works Administration (PWA), which made loans or grants amounting to almost $29 million, primarily to municipalities.

Thus, up to World War II the federal government expended a total of about $384 million for airport development under the four programs of CWA, FERA, WPA, and PWA. It must be recognized that these were primarily work-relief programs and provided no basis for federal support in times of a normal economy.

During World War II the federal government, through the CAA, expended $353 million for the development of landing areas for military use. While first importance in this program was attached to military requirements, the needs of postwar civil aviation were considered in the location and construction of these facilities. During the same period the federal government, through the CAA, spent over $9 million for the development of airports solely for civil use. These two programs are referred to as Defense Landing Areas (DLA) and Development of Civil Landing Areas (DCLA). The DLA and DCLA programs were independent of the airports constructed by the War and Navy departments. After the war some 500 military airports were declared surplus and turned over to cities, counties, and states.

Federal Airport Act

At the end of World War II interest was renewed in establishing a federal program for monetary aid for airport development. A resolution was introduced in Congress (H. Res. 598, 78th Cong.) requiring the CAA to make a survey of airport needs and prepare a report on the subject. These recommendations formed the basis of the Federal Airport Act of 1946 (Public Law 79-377). Appropriations of $500 million over a 7-year period were authorized for projects within the continental United States, plus $20 million for projects in Alaska, Hawaii, Puerto Rico, and the Virgin Islands. In 1950 the 7-year period was extended an additional 5 years (Public Law 81-846). However, annual appropriations approved by Congress were much less than the amounts authorized by the act.

The original act provided that a project shall not be approved for federal aid unless "sufficient funds are available for that portion of the project which is not to be paid by the United States."

Local governments often require 2 to 3 years to make arrangements for raising funds. Most of the larger projects are financed locally through the sale of bonds. This method of financing requires legislation at the local level and, in some cases, also at the state level. General obligation bonds normally require a two-thirds majority of the electorate. Programs to inform the public on the needs for airport improvement must be carefully planned and executed. Thus, after the completion of these events, local governments frequently found that sufficient federal funds were not appropriated to match local funds, and the projects were delayed. Another complaint of local governments had been that Congress failed to fulfill its obligation, since the amount appropriated by Congress fell far short of the amount authorized by the Federal Airport Act. These deficiencies as well as other matters were incorporated in a bill (S. 1855). Hearings on the bill were held before the subcommittee of the Committee on Interstate and Foreign Commerce of the United States Senate in June 1955. Representatives of the Council of State Governments, the American Municipal Association, the National Association of State Aviation Officials, airport and industry associations, and individuals were unanimous in the feeling that air transportation had reached a stage of maturity where many airports were woefully inadequate and greater financial assistance from the federal government would be required to meet the current needs of aviation. After much debate, the bill was approved by the President in August 1955 (Public Law 84-211).

This amending act made no change in the basic policies and purposes expressed in the original act. There were no changes in the requirements with respect to the administration of the grants authorized, such as the distribution and apportionment of funds, the eligibility of the various types of airport constructions, sponsorship requirements, etc. The primary purpose of the act was to substitute for the procedure of authorizing annual appropriations for airport projects, provisions granting substantial annual contract authorization in specific amounts over a period of four fiscal years. Sponsors were thus furnished definite assurance that federal funds would be available at the time projects were to be undertaken.

This law provided $40 million for fiscal year 1956 and $60 million for each of fiscal years 1957, 1958, and 1959 for airport constructon in the continental United States; and $2.5 million in fiscal year 1956 and $3 million for the three succeeding fiscal years for airport construction in Alaska, Hawaii, Puerto Rico, and the Virgin Islands. In addition to the $42.5 million made available in fiscal 1956 by Public Law 84-211, Congress approved an appropriation of $20 million for airport projects.

In 1958 the 85th Congress passed a bill (S. 3502) proposing to extend the Federal Airport Act for 4 years at an annual rate of $100 million. This bill was vetoed by the President in September 1958 with the following statement, in part:

> I am convinced that the time has come for the federal government to begin an orderly withdrawal from the airport grant program. This conclusion is based, first, on the hard fact that the government must now devote the resources it can make available for the promotion of civil aviation programs which cannot be assumed by others, and second, on the conviction that others should begin to assume the full responsibility for the cost of construction and improvement of civil airports.

In the 86th Congress much debate occurred involving a significant increase in the federal airport program. Two bills, one introduced in the House ($297 million over a 4-year period) and the other in the Senate ($465 million for a 4-year period), together with the President's recommended bill for a 4-year program of $200 million, were finally compromised into a 2-year continuation of the existing aid program at $63 million a year (Public Law 86-72).

Significant changes were the removal of the territorial status from Hawaii and Alaska, and the exclusion of automobile parking and certain portions of airport building improvement costs as allowable costs.

A 3-year continuation of the federal aid program providing $75 million annually was enacted by the 87th Congress (Public Law 87-255). The provisions of the bill were very similar to Public Law 86-72. One new feature of the legislation was that it provided the Administrator of the FAA with a discretionary fund of $7 million from the $75 million for developing general aviation airports to relieve congestion at high-density commercial airports.

The Federal Airport Act was again amended on March 11, 1964, authorizing the expenditure of $75 million for fiscal years 1965 to 1967 (Public Law 88-280). The final amendment was accepted on October 13, 1966, authorizing the continuation of the expenditure of $75 million for fiscal years 1968 to 1970 (Public Law 89-647). This marked the end of the

Federal Airport Act, as the Airport and Airway Development Act of 1970 became law in May 1970.

During the life of the Federal Airport Act a total of $1.2 billion was appropriated by the federal government for improvements at 2316 airports.

Airport and Airway Development Act of 1970

Because of the rapidly growing requirements for modernizing the air traffic control system and for airport expansion, neither the federal government nor the local authorities were able to fund the capital improvements badly needed to provide for the growth of aviation. The FAA needed more money in its budget to accelerate the implementation of a program to modernize the air traffic control system. The $75 million authorized annually by the Federal Aviation Act, together with local matching funds, fell far short of the needs of the local airport authorities to meet the current and projected growth of airport traffic. Cities were unable to raise sufficient funds at the local level to meet the rising costs of airport construction. The Federal Aviation Act of 1946 was supported by general rather than user tax revenues; therefore it had to compete annually with other government programs for scarce federal dollars. The increased competition for fewer dollars resulted in delay and postponement of airport construction throughout the nation. As a result of this situation, aviation organizations representing airport owners, airlines, pilots, and general aviation aircraft owners joined in pressing for more funds for airports and airways and the establishment of a trust fund similar to the national highway program. Several bills were introduced in the House and Senate to enact legislation which would remedy the deficiencies in the Federal Airport Act of 1946 (S. 1637, S. 2437, and S. 2651). After much debate, including the question of whether airport terminal buildings should be included in the legislation (initially they were not), Public Law 91-258 was signed into law in May 1970. As stated in Chap. 1, the law consisted of two parts, referred to as Titles I and II. Title I was known as the Airport and Airway Development Act of 1970, which replaced the Federal Airport Act of 1946. Title II was known as the Airport and Airway Revenue Act of 1970, and provided the excise taxes required to furnish the resources necessary to carry out the Title I programs through 1980. The excise taxes were described in Chap. 1.

Title I of the original act provided for $250 million annually for the "acquisition, establishment, and improvement of air navigational facilities," and security equipment required by the sponsor for fiscal years 1971 through 1980. For airport assistance, the Airport Development Aid Program (ADAP) initially authorized a total of $2.5 billion for the 10-year period. The act further specifically authorized $250 million annually through fiscal year 1973 and $275 million for each of fiscal years 1974 and 1975 for airports served by air carriers and for general aviation airports which relieve high-density air-carrier airports. Also authorized was $30 million annually through fiscal year 1973 and $35 million for each of fiscal years 1974 and 1975 for all other general aviation airports (Public Law 93-44). Later amendments (Public Law 94-353) raised the program level to a range from $500 to $610 million annually through 1980. The Aviation Safety and Noise Abatement Act (Public Law 96-193) further raised the final year program to $667 million. These amendments provided $435 to $539 million annually for airports serving all segments of aviation and $65 to $95 million annually for general aviation airports. The act also authorized the issuance of planning grants for the preparation of airport system plans and airport master plans. The Planning Grant Program (PGP) was designed to promote the effective location and development of publicly owned airports and to develop a national airport system plan. System plans were prepared by state and regional agencies to formulate air transportation policy, determine facility requirements needed to meet forecast aviation demand, and establish a framework for detailed airport master planning. Airport master plans, which were developed by the airport owner, focused on the nature and extent of the development required to meet the future aviation demand at specific facilities.

As amended (Public Law 93-44, Public Law 94-353, and Public Law 96-193), the legislation provided over $4 billion for 6152 airport development projects and almost $97 million for 2035 planning grants over the period from 1971 to 1980 [4]. This was about four times greater than the total amount provided by the Federal Airport Act of 1946. A tabulation of the amounts obligated under the Airport and Airway Development Act through fiscal year 1980 is shown in Table 2-1.

TABLE 2-1 **Airport and Airway Development Act Obligations for Airport Development Aid Program (ADAP) and Planning Grant Program (PGP), Fiscal years 1971–1980**

Fiscal year	Airport development		Planning grants	
	Number of projects	Obligations, millions	Number of projects	Obligations, millions
1971	231	$250.0	42	$3.6
1972	464	280.0	180	9.0
1973	450	280.0	275	9.6
1974	646	300.0	277	8.2
1975	643	339.9	286	9.6
1976	525	437.5	122	6.0
1977	757	545.0	205	11.8
1978	761	540.0	242	14.0
1979	858	629.1	241	15.0
1980	817	640.0	165	10.0
Total	6152	$4241.5	2035	$96.8

SOURCE: Federal Aviation Administration [4].

Significant changes from the Federal Airport Act, other than larger amounts of available funds and the establishment of a trust fund, were:

1. The provision of funds to local agencies for airport system planning and master planning

2. The emphasis on airports served by air carriers and on general aviation airports to relieve congested air-carrier airports.

3. The provision of funds for commuter service airports

4. An amendment to the Federal Aviation Act of 1958 to include airport operating certificates to ensure that airports were adequately equipped for safe operations

5. Provision of requirements to ensure that airport projects did not adversely affect the environment and were consistent with long-range development plans of the areas in which the projects were proposed

6. Provision for terminal facility development in non-revenue-producing public areas

Specific Programs Authorized by the Airport and Airway Development Act

The Airport Development Aid Program

To be eligible for the ADAP, airport ownership was required to be vested in a public agency, and the airport had to be included in the NASP. This plan is reviewed and revised as necessary to keep it current. It is prepared by the FAA and submitted to Congress by the Secretary of Transportation. The plan specifies, in terms of general location and type of development, the projects considered necessary to provide a system of public airports adequate to anticipate and meet the needs of civil aeronautics. These projects include all types of airport development eligible for federal aid under the act and are not limited to any classes or categories of public airports. The plan is based on projected needs over 5- and 10-year periods [8].

The funds authorized for airport development for the different classes of airports were apportioned to air-carrier and general aviation airports. In the final amended form of the act, two-thirds of the air-carrier and commuter service funds were made available to air-carrier airports based upon their annual enplaned passengers. The remaining funds were placed in a discretionary fund, of which $15 million was apportioned annually to commuter service airports. Air-carrier airports serving aircraft heavier than 12,500 lb were authorized to receive not less than $150,000 nor more than $10 million annually. Airports serving aircraft weighing less than 12,500 lb were to receive not less than $50,000 annually. Of the funds appropriated for general aviation and general aviation reliever airports, $15 million was apportioned annually to reliever airports. Of the remaining funds 75 percent was allocated to the states on the basis of population and area; 1 percent was allocated to Puerto Rico, Guam, the Virgin Islands, American Samoa, and the Trust Territories of the Pacific Islands and was distributed by the Secretary of Transportation.

The maximum federal grant for any specified project varied from 50 to 90 percent of the total eligible project costs over the life of the act, depending upon the type of project being considered for funding.

A maximum of 75 percent of the allowable project cost was allowed for airports that enplaned 0.25 percent or more of the total number of annual passengers enplaned by air carriers certified by the CAB. A maximum of 90 percent of the allowable project cost was allowed for airports that enplaned less than 0.25 percent of the total number of annual passengers and for general aviation airports.

The original act specifically prohibited the use of federal funds for automobile parking facilities or airport buildings except those parts "intended to house facilities or activities directly related to the safety of persons at the airport." However, the 1976 amendments to the act (Public Law 94-353) provided federal funding for the non-revenue-producing public areas of terminal facilities required for the processing of passengers and baggage. In this case the federal share was limited to 50 percent of the project costs and the airport could not spend more than 60 percent of its enplanement funds on such development.

The Planning Grant Program

There was no state apportionment for planning grant funds. The Secretary prescribed the regulations governing the award and administration of these grants. When the PGP first began, the federal government provided up to two-thirds of the cost of planning grant projects. However, the 1976 amendments to the act increased this share to 75 percent of the cost for airport system plans, 90 percent of the cost for master plans at general aviation airports, and a range from 75 to 90 percent of the cost for master plans at air-carrier airports, depending upon the number of enplaned passengers.

Provisions of the Airport Development Aid Program

Environmental Considerations

Because of the mounting public concern for the enhancement of the environment, the act specifically stated that authorized projects provide for the protection and enhancement of the natural resources and the quality of the environment of the nation. The Secretary of Transportation was required to consult with the Secretary of the Interior and the Secretary of Health, Education and Welfare regarding the effect of certain projects on natural resources and whether "all possible steps have been taken to minimize such adverse effects." The act required that airport sponsors provide the "opportunity for public hearings for the purpose of considering the social, economic, and environmental effect on any project involving the location of an airport, the location of a runway, and a runway extension." In addition, the National Environmental Policy Act of 1969 (Public Law 91-190), supported by a Presidential Executive Order 11514 (March 5, 1970), required the preparation of detailed environmental statements for all major airport development actions significantly affecting the quality of the environment. The environmental statement was required to include the probable impact of the proposed project on both the human and the natural environments, including the impact on ecological systems such as wildlife, fish, and marine life, and any probable adverse environmental effects which could not be avoided if the project was implemented. The act also stipulated that no airport project involving "airport location, a major runway extension, or runway location" could be approved for federal funding unless the Governor of the state in which the project was located certified to the Secretary of Transportation that there was reasonable assurance that the project would comply with applicable air and water quality standards. Finally the project had to be consistent with the plans of other agencies for development of the area, and the airport sponsor had to assure the government that adequate housing was available for any displaced people. The Aviation Safety and Noise Abatement Act of 1979 (Public Law 96-193) amended this legislation to place increased emphasis on reducing the noise impact of airports. Thus one of the principal differences between the Federal Airport Aid Program and the ADAP was the emphasis on environmental protection in the latter.

Selection for the National Airport System Plan

The Airport and Airway Development Act made no mention concerning specific standards for determining airports to be included in the NASP. It did state, however, that:

> The Plan shall set forth, for at least a ten-year period, the type and estimated cost of an airport development considered by the Secretary to be necessary to provide a system of public airports adequate to anticipate and meet the needs of civil aeronautics, to meet the requirements in support of the national defense as determined by the Secretary of Defense, and to meet the special needs of the Postal Service. In formulating and revising the plan, the Secretary shall take into consideration, among other things, the relationship of each airport to the rest of the transportation system in the particular area, to the forecasted technological developments in aeronautics, and to developments forecasted in the other modes of transportation.

With this and other policy guidelines, the FAA developed entry criteria which described a broad and balanced airport system. The 1980 NASP, for example, included about 3600 airport locations, indicating that the federal interest in developing a basic airport system extended well beyond the major airports with scheduled airline service. In an effort to provide a safe and adequate airport for as many communities as possible, NASP criteria were developed to include the general aviation airports which serve smaller cities and towns.

The NASP airport entry criteria evolved from both policy and legislative considerations and focused on two broad categories of airports, those with scheduled service and those without significant scheduled service in the general aviation and reliever categories.

Airports with scheduled service were included in the NASP because of their use by the general public, legislative provisions which specifically designated airports to receive development funds, and their use by CAB certified carriers. Commuter airports were identified in the NASP starting in 1976, when legislation was enacted which designated them as a type of air-carrier airport and provided them with special development funds. About 70 percent of the airports in the NASP are general aviation locations which meet the criteria of viability because of the number of based aircraft or the aircraft activity, and which provide reasonable access for aircraft owners and users to their community. Reliever airports have been included as a separate NASP category since the 1960s when Congress designated special funding for the purpose of relieving congestion in large metropolitan areas by providing additional general aviation capacity.

Eligible Development

In administering the Airport and Airway Development Act, the FAA established, in detail, the types of improvement which were eligible for federal aid under the act. In general, items that were eligible included land acquisition, paving and grading, lighting and electrical work, utilities, roads, removal of obstructions to air navigation, fencing, fire and rescue equipment, snow removal equipment, terminal area development, and physical barriers and landscaping for noise attenuation.

Separate buildings for airport emergency, snow removal, and fire-fighting equipment were eligible. Administration buildings serving air commerce or general aviation were not eligible. Buildings used exclusively for the handling of cargo were also ineligible. The non-revenue-producing public-use areas of terminal facilities became eligible for funding in 1976 (Public Law 94-353) if these areas were "directly related to the movement of passengers and baggage in air commerce within the boundaries of the airport."

Roads and streets were eligible if they were within the boundary of the airport and were needed for the operation and maintenance of the airport, or if they were directly related to the movement of passengers and baggage.

Each eligible project was evaluated separately. It was rated on the basis of the aeronautical necessity of the airport, the volume and character of traffic, and the type of work included in the project. These ratings established a priority score for each increment of work in any one state and were used to program the funds allocated to that state. The ratings were based on such factors as safety, efficiency, and convenience. In the development of priorities, the views of the state aviation agency were solicited. The environmental impact statement included the effect of the project on the ambient noise level, animal and bird life, air or water pollution, recreation areas, areas of unique interest or scenic beauty, and displacement of significant numbers of people.

A community interested in obtaining federal aid contacted the Airport District Office (ADO) of the FAA in the area the airport was located. In states which required that all federal aid be channeled through the state, submission of a request for aid was made through the state aeronautical agency.

If the project qualified for aid, if there were sufficient funds, and if the project was found by the Secretary to be acceptable from the standpoint of its economic, social, and environmental effects on the community, the sponsor was notified that a tentative allocation of the funds had been made for all or part of the items listed in the request. The tentative allocation was an indication that funds had been placed in reserve, pending the completion of arrangements for necessary financing and land acquisition, and the preparation of plans, specifications, and contract documents.

Upon submitting detailed plans and specifications with a project application and upon approval of the FAA, the sponsor secured bids from contractors and made recommendations for the award of the contracts. At this time the sponsor also formally accepted federal aid and the obligations connected therewith by executing what was known as a *grant agreement*.

The execution of the grant agreement legally bound the community to fulfill the obligations (the sponsor's assurances) set forth in the project application. Some of the important obligations on the part of the sponsor were that:

1. It would operate the airport for the use and benefit of the public, on fair and reasonable terms without unjust discrimination.

2. It would keep the airport open to all types, kinds, and classes of aeronautical use without discrimination between such types, kinds, and classes.

3. It would operate and maintain in a safe and serviceable condition the airport and all facilities thereon which are necessary to serve aeronautical uses other than facilities owned or controlled by the United States.

4. It would make every effort to maintain clear approaches to the runways.

5. It would not charge government owned or military aircraft for the use of runways and taxiways unless the use was substantial.

6. These obligations would remain in effect for not more than 20 years.

Airport and Airway Improvement Act of 1982

Although the Airport and Airway Development Act of 1970 significantly expanded the role of the federal government in financing the planning and development of airports in the United States, some of the features of the program have been subject to criticism. Proposals introduced in Congress (S. 1581, S. 1648, and H. Res. 3745, 96th Cong.; S. 508, H. Res. 2643, and H. Res. 2930, 97th Cong.) were directed at alleviating some of the criticism of the previous legislation and refining the nature of federal participation in airport development.

Specific program elements debated included the removal of the largest commercial airports from the federal funding cycle (defederalization), the combination of the planning and development programs into a single grant program, and a lessening of the role of the federal government in the management and decision making associated with airport development through the use of block grants rather than the individual grants of the past [10].

Large commercial airports in the United States are capable of generating the revenues necessary to finance capital development projects without federal funds. These airports appear to have little difficulty financing operating expenses and airport development costs from revenues obtained through airline fees, concessions, rentals, and other charges at the airport. The argument that the loss of ADAP funds would not significantly affect the financial viability of these airports was tempered by concerns about the legality of and ability to renegotiate the leases upon which airport revenues are dependent.

Airports have pressed for provisions to allow for the implementation of passenger facilities charges at the local level to be used for capital development projects for those airports ineligible for ADAP funds. A major question surrounding the defederalization proposals has been the possible loss of continuity in the national airport system where there is little reliance upon federal funds for airport development. The ability for general aviation and new carriers to gain adequate access to major commerical service airports has also been questioned. Such legislation would allow for the direction of airport development funds to those airports least able to support facility improvements without federal aid. It would strengthen the role of local authorities in implementing facility development projects which are most responsive to local needs. In the past, the separation of federal aid into a development program (ADAP) and planning program (PGP) resulted in relatively small grants being available to state and local governments to meet airport needs. Administrative flexibility at all levels of government was lost since the separate programs were restricted in their use. Combination of the two programs into a single grant program may not significantly raise the level of funding available to a state or local entity, but it is likely to provide the flexibility required to respond to local needs and therefore improve investment decision making. Proposals were made to modify the apportionment formula used in the past to reflect the status of an airport as a reliever in addition to the enplanement, area, and population factors. Higher levels of overall funding would allow for long-term funding guarantees to airports, resulting in the implementation of projects which more significantly address long-term local needs. By restructuring the nature of the program away from grants to individual airports and toward the block grant, the role of the states in the administration and management of airport grants at small commercial service and general aviation airports would be enhanced.

Nearly 2 years after the expiration of the ADAP legislation, the Airport and Airway Improvement Act of 1982 was passed as part of the Tax Equity and Fiscal Responsibility Act of 1982 (Public Law 97-248). This law was patterned after the Airport and Airway Development Act and did not allow for the defederalization of airports, eliminated provisions for state block grants, and specifically outlawed passenger facility charges at airports. The program specified the percentages of the total annual authorization which were required to be expended for various types of airport projects rather than continuing the method by which specific sums were spent for each project type. The act designated that 50 percent of the annual authorization was to be spent for primary commerical service airports, those which enplane at least 0.01 percent of the total annual enplanements, 5.5 percent for nonprimary commercial service airports, those which enplane at least 2500 passengers annually and have scheduled passenger service, 12 percent for general aviation airports, 10 percent for general aviation reliever airports, including privately owned public-use airports, 8 percent for airport noise studies, and 1 percent for integrated airport system planning. The remainder of the funds were to be expended at the discretion of the FAA. The enplanement apportionment formula was retained for primary commercial service airports but annual percentage increases in the apportionment were mandated. State funds for general aviation were apportioned by the population-area method used in the past. No apportionment of funds was indicated for the other funding categories. The federal share of eligible projects was set at 75 percent for primary commercial service airports which enplane at least 0.25 percent of the total annual passengers, and 90 percent for all other commercial service airports. A maximum of $200,000 or 60 percent of the entitlement funds may be spent for terminal development in non-revenue-producing public-use areas of the airport with a 75 percent federal share.

The law also required the FAA to conduct studies and report to Congress on the impact of defederalization and airport access. The planning and development programs of the past were combined into a single fund.

STATE PARTICIPATION IN FINANCING AIRPORT IMPROVEMENTS

Airport development and aviation planning is of major concern in many states. Virtually all states provide some financial assistance for airport improvements. Increases in state financial support have been dramatic during the past several years. Census figures show that expenditures by states for airports have risen from $59 million in 1966 to well over $300 million in 1980 [7, 11].

State sharing in airport development varies depending on whether federal aid is involved and whether this aid is channeled through a state aeronautical agency. Most of the states require that federal funds be channeled through the state to local sponsors. In those states where this is a requirement the state normally contributes one-half of the sponsor's share of the project costs, which amounts to approximately one-quarter of the total project cost. If no federal aid is involved, the state often contributes one-half of the project cost. In other states, where revenues are obtained from user taxes, formulas for apportioning the revenues are established.

The several states obtain the revenues to finance aviation and airport improvement projects from a variety of sources including [11]:

1. The general fund
2. Highway or transportation funds or bond issues
3. State-owned airport revenue bonds
4. Fuel taxes on general aviation and air-carrier fuel
5. Sales taxes on the purchase of general aviation or air-carrier fuel
6. Aircraft registration fees
7. Registration fees for flight personnel
8. Airport licensing fees
9. Airline flight property taxes

Some idea of the amounts provided by states for airport improvements in fiscal years 1970 and 1980 can be gained from Table 2-2. It should be emphasized that over half of the funds made available by the states was provided by the states of Alaska and Hawaii. This is because in these states most publicly owned airports are owned and operated by the state.

TABLE 2-2 **State Airport Development and Aviation Funds in Thousands of Dollars, Fiscal Years 1970 and 1980**

	1970	1980		1970	1980
Alabama	350	637	Montana	248	365
Alaska	35,000	71,019	Nebraska	600	1,626
Arizona	200	4,122	Nevada		
Arkansas	125	643	New Hampshire	750	981
California	1,900	4,960	New Jersey		113
Colorado			New Mexico	127	365
Connecticut	7,000	5,970	New York	17,500	4,843
Delaware		67	North Carolina	250	7,000
Florida		4,366	North Dakota	100	2,159
Georgia	250	2,040	Ohio	4,000	2,700
Hawaii	71,952	85,787	Oklahoma	150	828
Idaho	268	624	Oregon	675	662
Illinois	8,458	11,260	Pennsylvania	1,000	15,286
Indiana		2,517	Rhode Island	2,800	6,419
Iowa	200	1,134	South Carolina	907	5,920
Kansas		200	South Dakota	778	417
Kentucky	1,225	2,451	Tennessee	1,350	2,143
Louisiana	500	4,851	Texas	650	2,600
Maine	3,448	3,821	Utah	1,700	304
Maryland	1,300	21,602	Vermont	360	566
Massachusetts	500	323	Virginia	2,500	5,423
Michigan	4,100	2,280	Washington	125	966
Minnesota	4,000	8,895	West Virginia	500	1,303
Mississippi	88	183	Wisconsin	700	922
Missouri	200	231	Wyoming	127	1,570
			Total	178,959	305,464

SOURCES: U.S. Senate [7] and National Association of State Aviation Officals [11].

LOCAL SOURCES OF FUNDS

Municipalities have provided the major portion of the funds for airport improvements. These funds have come from three principal sources, namely, taxes for the support of local governments as a whole, sale of general obligation bonds, and sale of revenue bonds. In the early years of aviation the general tax fund was the principal source of local funds, and it still is for small airports. The taxes levied are not earmarked specifically for airport use, but are the kind that are normally imposed to operate most of the affairs of local government. As long as the amount of funding is relatively small, this method of financing has not met with much opposition from the citizens in whose political jurisdiction the airport is located.

As aviation grew and the amounts of funds required became large in relation to other community expenditures, drawing funds from the general tax fund became no longer practical, and municipalities had to resort to the sale of bonds.

Initially these were mostly of the general obligation type. There were several reasons for resorting to this type of bond financing. First, obligating the entire resources of a local government to back the bonds resulted in much more favorable interest rates than could be obtained by any other form of financing; second, the projected revenues to be derived from the facility to be developed were often insufficient to utilize any other method of financing.

As air transport continued to grow and mature, the requirements for airport capital improvements also grew substantially. At the same time communities were faced with increased demand for schools, streets, sewage disposal, and other public services. In many cases cities either had reached or were reaching the statutory limit on the amount of general obligation bonds which they could issue, and they desired to reserve whatever remaining margin of bonding capacity they had to carry out needed improvements that did not have the revenue potential of airports.

In order to overcome the limitation of financing through the sale of general obligation bonds, many communities are raising funds through the sale of revenue bonds whenever possible. In general only those airports which generate sufficient revenue over the term of the bond issues are candidates for revenue bonds. Agreements between the airlines and the airport are the most common forms of supporting the issuance of revenue bonds. In contrast, most general aviation airports and the smaller air-carrier airports do not generate sufficient revenue to support revenue bonds, and consequently in these cases major capital improvements are usually undertaken with general obligations and combinations of federal and state grants.

Revenue-bond financing is gaining impetus. This is partially due to the fact that the investor has gained confidence in the stability of air transportation and does not consider the investment as much of a risk as it might have been in the earlier years of aviation. While interest rates are generally higher for revenue bonds than they are for general obligation bonds, the differential between the two has decreased considerably since the first issuance of revenue bonds. Revenue-bond financing is most successful for those components of the airport which are good revenue producers, such as terminal buildings and parking garages. Revenues from runways and taxiways, on the other hand, are normally insufficient to finance these specific facilities by the sale of revenue bonds.

Some facilities at an airport, such as hangars, hotels, shopping centers, etc., have been financed through private debt. The tenant constructs the facility on airport property being leased from the airport owner. One advantage of this type of airport financing is that it relieves the community of all capital investment in the facility except for utilities and access roads or taxiways. However, it does require the community to commit the land on the airport for 25 to 30 years, the period normally required in a ground lease if the tenant is to secure private financing.

FINANCIAL PLANNING

The financial plan for the capital improvements at an airport requires a detailed analysis of projected traffic, costs, and revenues. At larger airports significant portions of the capital costs of a project are recovered through revenues from the airlines, concessionaires, and other tenants. The remainder are recovered through capital grants from federal and state sources. Since the airlines become long-term tenants obligated to pay user fees and rents for the facilities utilized in conducting their operations, an evaluation of the conceptual alternatives in the planning phases of a project should only be undertaken with direct input from these users. The financial feasibility of a program is in a large measure determined by the magnitude and reasonableness of the charges and rents paid by airport users and tenants. The financing of general aviation airports continues to be a major problem since the revenue base available is usually insufficient to support significant capital improvements. Therefore, it is imperative that the benefits of such airports to the community at large be carefully analyzed in order that other sources of financing can be demonstrated economically viable.

The determination of the financial feasibility of a project is initiated with an agreement between the airport owners and the airport users, defining the fiscal policies which will govern the setting of rates and charges for the airport users. The basic process consists of a series of steps as defined below [12]:

1. Allocation of the capital costs of the project to the various cost centers established by airport management and airport users. These cost centers are usually categorized as the airfield area, the hangar and other operational support building areas, the terminal area, the concessions area, and other areas of the airport.

2. Projection of the net annual costs of the capital construction program and the assignment of these costs to the various cost centers; these costs are amortized over the period of time specified in the agreement between management and users.

3. Projection and allocation of the net annual administrative, operating, and maintenance costs to each of the cost centers based upon a knowledge of past cost experience and projections of these anticipated costs for the new facility.

4. Conversion of the total annual capital, administrative, operating, and maintenance costs to a schedule of the fees and rents to be paid by the users of the facilities, utilizing available forecasts of aircraft activity, passenger enplanements, parking usage, and other relevant indices of projected airport activity.

Recovery of capital costs requires that the total capital investment in each cost center be determined. Projected costs in the airfield area for runways, taxiways, apron ramps, and land acquisition and improvement, and in the terminal area for terminal building construction, land, and terminal support facilities must be ascertained and assigned to the relevant cost center. It is essential that airport support facilities, such as access roads, service roads, sanitary and storm sewer systems, electrical and mechanical systems, communication and security services, emergency medical services, and crash, fire, and rescue services, be properly apportioned to the appropriate cost centers to eliminate imbalances in the determination of the facility cost center revenue requirements which may result in unreasonable rates and charges. For projects where bond issues are utilized to finance portions of the capital costs, the annual cost of debt service, that is, principal, interest, and the required reserve (coverage) over the recovery period, must be included and assigned to the relevant cost center category.

The anticipated costs of airport administration, operation, and maintenance are assigned to each cost center on an annual basis. These costs generally include all direct costs for salaries, materials, supplies, and outside services, and the related indirect costs.

Terminal costs are divided by terminal area, often considering the location and degree of finishing in ticketing facilities, baggage facilities, office space, and car-rental space, to establish rental rates for the terminal building tenants.

Concession and other airport revenues will normally be applied against the appropriate cost center and the net revenue recovery requirements determined. Forecasts of landing weights are used to determine the landing fees charged to the airlines to recover airfield costs. Often the cost of the apron area is isolated as a separate cost center, and ramp fees are established based upon the frontage required by the airlines.

Concession area costs are derived from rentals paid, and the concessionaire is charged a percentage of the gross receipts. Usually the most significant concession cost center at a large airport is the parking facility. Since the capital costs of a parking structure are considerable, these costs are usually assigned to the terminal area cost center. The administrative, operating, and maintenance costs of these facilities are recovered through a percentage of gross receipts charge.

A breakdown of the items included in the various revenue categories recommended by AOCI is shown in Table 2-3.

The percentage distribution of operating revenue sources for a sampling of air-carrier airports is shown in Table 2-4. This table gives an indication of the percentage of total operating revenue receipts which could be expected from various revenue source items in each cost center category. Based upon data collected from a sample of general aviation

TABLE 2-3   **Airport Report Revenue Classifications**

Landing area:
  Landing fees
  Parking ramp fees
  Fuel flowage fees

Terminal area concessions:
  Advertising
  Bus transportation
  Car rentals
  Coin-operated devices
  Flight insurance
  Hotel
  Limousine and taxi service
  Parking
  Personal services
  Restaurants
  Specialty shops, stores, and facilities
  Miscellaneous

Airline leased areas:
  Ground or land rentals
  Cargo terminals
  Office rentals
  Ticket counters
  Operations and maintenance areas
  Hangars

Other leased areas:
  Fixed-based operators
  Ground or land rentals
  Cargo terminals
  Industrial buildings
  Other buildings
  Fuel and servicing

Other operating areas:
  Sale of insurance
  Other

SOURCE: Airport Operators Council International, Inc. [2].

airports, it was found that such airports needed a strong industrial and commercial base in their service area and total operations in excess of 100,000 annually for the airport to recover operating expenses through operating revenues [3]. A sampling of such general aviation airports demonstrated the operating revenue distributions shown in Table 2-5.

Rate Setting

The airport is designed to service two distinct groups, namely, the airlines and the commercial entities serving them, and the passengers and those retail enterprises which service them [9]. The airport leases its facilities to

TABLE 2-4 **Percent Distribution of Operating Revenue Sources at Air-Carrier Airports by Annual Enplaned Passengers**

Revenue category	Annual enplaned passengers				
	Greater than 2,000,000	500,000 to 2,000,000	250,000 to 500,000	125,000 to 250,000	Less than 125,000
Airfield area	27.6	32.1	31.9	30.2	22.2
Air-carrier landing fees	25.1	22.5	19.0	16.5	8.9
Other landing fees	0.4	0.6	1.0	1.2	2.3
Fuel and oil sales	0.9	4.6	10.0	10.6	8.4
Airline caterings fees	1.1	3.3			
Aircraft parking	0.1	1.1	1.9	1.9	2.6
Hangar and building area	11.4	11.6	13.6	20.2	43.9
Terminal area	12.8	13.3	18.7	14.8	10.5
Systems and services	4.3	3.1	4.0	4.0	4.0
Concessions	43.9	39.9	31.8	30.8	19.4
Airport parking	19.7	15.5	11.5	11.0	2.1
Car rental	8.2	10.3	10.2	8.0	6.8
Restaurants and lounges	4.8	5.5	5.9	3.5	2.5
Advertising	0.6	1.2	0.9	1.5	1.2
Ground transportation	1.9	1.9	0.7	1.9	0.2
Flight insurance	2.3	2.4	0.7	0.7	0.5
Hotel and motel	1.8	1.6	0.1	1.5	0.1
Miscellaneous	4.6	1.5	1.8	2.7	6.0
Total	100.0	100.0	100.0	100.0	100.0

SOURCE: Federal Aviation Administration [3].

the airlines, concessionaires, industries, general aviation, and airport support services. The airlines lease ground for aircraft storage, space for ticket counters, operations, maintenance, and baggage handling, and pay fees for landing and ramp rights. Cargo and hangar facilities are also utilized by the airlines at specific locations. Concessionaires rent space within the terminals and are charged on the basis of the amount and quality of the space rented and a percentage of receipts. Those franchisees outside the terminals, such as taxi cab companies, are charged in various ways. One method is based upon the number of passengers enplaned at the airport and another is a fixed rate based upon the number of times the airport is utilized for the service.

The methods for determining rates varies between airports. The most common method is the residual cost approach. In such an approach the total annualized costs of the airport are reduced by the amount of all nonairline revenues, and the remainder is proportioned out among the airlines based upon level of activity measures. Those costs apportioned to the terminal area are divided by the gross terminal area to determine space rental charges. Those costs apportioned to the airfield are divided by the

TABLE 2-5 **Percent Distribution of Operating Revenue Sources at General Aviation Airports**

Revenue category	
Airfield area	18.7
Hangar and building area	61.6
Terminal area	0.7
Systems and services	8.3
Concessions	10.7
Total	100.0

SOURCE: Federal Aviation Administration [3].

total annual gross landing weight of the carriers at the airport to determine landing fees. This type of cost recovery approach essentially guarantees that the airlines will provide the revenues necessary to cover airport costs. It also places the airlines in a unique position relative to airport management in that the airlines have a vested interest in maximizing nonairline revenues to minimize their costs.

Other approaches to rate setting attempt to classify airport expenses into distinct cost centers and to apportion the cost of each among users through equitable rates, or to assign the expenses associated with certain cost centers to users and group other expenses to be shared by all users.

The test of the validity of any rate setting scheme, however, lies in its ability to reflect rates which are reasonable and justifiable to the airlines, concessionaires, and other tenants.

Evaluation of the Financial Plan

Criteria for measuring the financial effectiveness of an airport plan are usually determined by various evaluative measures, including [12]:

1. The effectiveness of functional areas as measured by the ratios of the amount of public space, revenue space, airline exclusive space, and concession space to the total space within the terminal building

2. The relative effectiveness of areas within the terminal building as indicated by the ratio of airline exclusive space to the number of gates, and the ratio of the ramp area to the total building area

3. An evaluation of annual costs and revenues for various items in each of the cost center categories, as shown by the cost and revenue per enplanement, per operation, per thousand pounds of aircraft landing weight, and per square foot of building space

4. The effectiveness of the schedule plan of the airline as indicated by the number of departures per gate and the number of enplaned passengers per unit of airline exclusive space

The final determination of the most effective plan is made through the process of discussion and negotiation between airport management and users. Various assumptions are made relative to the allocation of costs and revenues between cost centers until a consensus is reached. At this point airline lease agreements and concession policies are developed, which result in long-term commitments by the airlines and tenants to the airport project. In the final analysis, airport expansion plans must not only address the need for changes in physical facilities but must also address the economic, environmental, and financial feasibility associated with such development. In this age of limited financial resources, with energy and aircraft equipment needs foremost in the management of airlines, a clear determination of the feasibility of airport expansion projects will be needed before long-term commitments for support by the airline will be made.

REFERENCES

1. *Airport Revenues and Expenses, Airport Economic Planning,* G. P. Howard, Editor, M.I.T. Press, Cambridge, Mass., 1974.
2. *AOCI Uniform Airport Financial Statement,* Airport Operators Council International, Inc., Washington, D.C.
3. *Economics of Airport Operation, Calendar Year 1972,* J. A. Neiss, Federal Aviation Administration, Washington, D.C., April 1974.
4. *Eleventh Annual Report of Operations under the Airport and Airway Developments Act, Fiscal Year Ended September 30, 1980,* U.S. Department of Transportation, Federal Aviation Administration, Washington, D.C., 1981.
5. *Fort Lauderdale–Hollywood International Airport Economic Feasibility,* Preliminary Report, Aviation Planning Associates, Inc., Cincinnati, Ohio, April 1981.
6. *General Aviation and the Airport and Airway System, An Analysis of Cost Allocation and Recovery,* National Business Aircraft Association, Inc., Washington, D.C., April 1981.
7. *Hearings before the Subcommittee on Aviation of the Committee on Commerce,* U.S. Senate, Washington, D.C., July 1969.
8. *National Airport System Plan, 1978–1987,* Federal Aviation Administration, Department of Transportation, Washington, D.C.
9. *Planning for Airport Access: An Analysis of the San Francisco Bay Area,* Conference Publication 2044, National Aeronautics and Space Administration, Ames Research Center, Moffett Field, Calif., May 1978.
10. *Senate Report No. 97-97, Airport and Airway System Act of 1981,* Committee on Commerce, Science, and Transportation, U.S. Senate, Washington, D.C., May 15, 1981.
11. *State Funding of Airport and Aviation Programs,* National Association of State Aviation Officials, Washington, D.C., 1981.
12. *The Apron-Terminal Complex, Analysis of Concepts for Evaluation of Terminal Buildings,* the Ralph M. Parsons Company, Federal Aviation Administration, Washington, D.C., September 1973.

Chapter 3

Aircraft Characteristics Related to Airport Design

INTRODUCTION

A general knowledge of aircraft is essential in planning facilities for their use. Aircraft used in airline operations have capacities ranging from less than 20 to nearly 500 passengers. General aviation aircraft, on the other hand, have a transportation function similar to that of the private automobile.

A perspective of the variety of aircraft which make up the airline fleet can be gained from Table 3-1, which summarizes the principal characteristics of air-carrier aircraft in terms of size, weight, capacity, and runway length requirements. This list is by no means complete, but it does include the principal aircraft in use or production. In a similar manner, some of the characteristics of typical general aviation and short-haul commuter aircraft, including those used for corporate purposes, are shown in Table 3-2. It is important to recognize that such characteristics as operating empty weight, passenger capacity, and runway length can only be approximated in a very general way in such tabulations because many variables affect these quantities. Main landing gear dimensions and typical tire inflation pressures for some of the more common air-carrier aircraft are shown in Table 3-3. Figure 3-1 illustrates the definition of the principal dimensions shown in Tables 3-1 and 3-2.

The characteristics shown in Tables 3-1 and 3-2 are essential for the planning and design of airports. Aircraft weight is important for determining the thickness of the runway, taxiway, and apron pavements, and it affects the takeoff and landing runway length requirements at an airport. The wingspan and the fuselage length influence the size of parking aprons, which in turn influences the configuration of the terminal buildings. Size

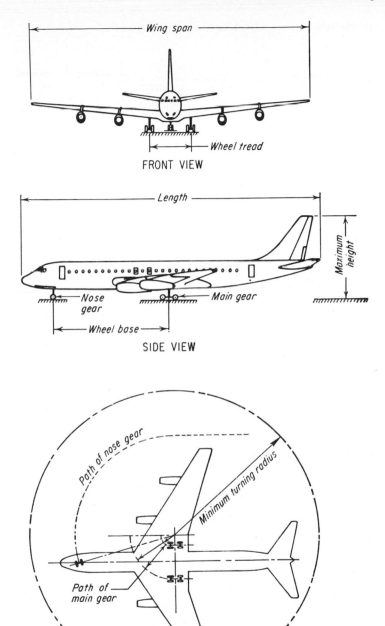

Fig. 3-1 Definition of terms related to aircraft dimensions.

TABLE 3-1 **Characteristics of Principal Transport Aircraft**

Aircraft	Manufacturer	Wingspan	Length	Wheel base	Wheel track
DC-9-32	McDonnell-Douglas	93'04"	119'04"	53'02"	16'05"
DC-9-50	McDonnell-Douglas	93'04"	132'00"	60'11"	16'05"
DC-9-80	McDonnell-Douglas	107'10"	135'06"	72'05"	16'08"
DC-8-61	McDonnell-Douglas	148'05"	187'05"	77'06"	20'10"
DC-8-63	McDonnell-Douglas	148'05"	187'05"	77'06"	20'10"
DC-10-10	McDonnell-Douglas	155'04"	182'03"	72'05"	35'00"
DC-10-30	McDonnell-Douglas	161'04"	181'07"	72'05"	35'00"
B-737-200	Boeing	93'00"	100'00"	37'04"	17'02"
B-727-200	Boeing	108'00"	153'02"	63'03"	18'09"
B-720B	Boeing	130'10"	136'09"	50'08"	21'11"
B-707-120B	Boeing	130'10"	145'01"	52'04"	22'01"
B-707-320B	Boeing	142'05"	152'11"	59'00"	22'01"
B-757-200	Boeing	124'06"	153'10"	60'00"	24'00"
B-767-200	Boeing	156'04"	155'00"	64'07"	30'06"
B-747B	Boeing	195'09"	229'02"	84'00"	36'01"
B-747SP	Boeing	195'09"	176'07"	67'04"	36'01"
L-1011-100	Lockheed	155'04"	177'08"	70'00"	36'00"
L-1011-500	Lockheed	155'04"	164'02"	61'08"	36'00"
Caravelle-B	Aerospatiale	112'06"	108'03"	41'00"	17'00"
Trident 2E	Hawker-Siddeley	98'00"	114'09"	44'00"	19'01"
BAC111-200	British Aircraft	88'06"	92'06"	33'01"	14'03"
Super VC-10	British Aircraft	140'00"	171'08"	72'02"	21'05"
A-300	Airbus Industrie	147'01"	175'11"	61'01"	31'06"
A-310	Airbus Industrie	144'00"	153'01"	40'11"	31'06"
Concorde	British Aircraft-Aerospatial	83'10"	202'03"	59'08"	25'04"
Mercure	Dassault	100'02"	111'06"	39'01"	20'04"
Ilyushine-62	U.S.S.R.	141'09"	174'03"	80'04"	22'03"
Tupolev-154	U.S.S.R.	123'02"	157'02"	62'01"	37'09"
Ilyushine-86	U.S.S.R.	157'08"	197'06"	70'00"	36'07"

* Approximate only; depends upon seating configuration.

† At sea level, standard day, no wind, level runway.

SOURCE: Manufacturers' data.

also dictates the widths of runways and taxiways and the distances between these trafficways, and it affects the required turning radius on pavement curves. The passenger capacity has an important bearing on facilities within and adjacent to the terminal buildings. The runway length influences to a large part the land area required at an airport. The lengths provided in Tables 3-1 and 3-2 are only approximate. For more precise values the appropriate references, such as those listed in this chapter, should be consulted.

An examination of Tables 3-1 and 3-2 reveals some interesting information. The maximum takeoff weight of principal airline aircraft varies from

TABLE 3-1 **Continued**

Maximum structural takeoff weight, lb	Maximum landing weight, lb	Operating empty weight,* lb	Zero fuel weight, lb	Number and Type of engines	Maximum payload, passengers	Runway length† ft
108,000	99,000	56,855	87,000	2 TF	115–127	7,500
120,000	110,000	63,328	98,000	2 TF	130	7,100
140,000	128,000	77,797	118,000	2 TF	155–172	7,190
325,000	240,000	152,101	224,000	4 TF	196–259	11,000
355,000	258,000	158,738	230,000	4 TF	196–259	11,900
430,000	363,500	234,664	335,000	3 TF	270–345	9,000
555,000	403,000	261,094	368,000	3 TF	270–345	11,000
100,500	98,000	59,958	85,000	2 TF	86–125	5,600
169,000	150,000	97,400	138,000	3 TF	134–163	8,600
234,300	175,000	115,000	156,000	4 TF	131–149	6,100
257,340	190,000	127,500	170,000	4 TF	137–174	7,500
333,600	215,000	148,800	195,000	4 TF	141–189	11,500
220,000	198,000	130,700	184,000	2 TF	178–196	6,900
300,000	270,000	178,210	248,000	2 TF	211–230	6,700
775,000	564,000	365,800	526,000	4 TF	362–490	11,000
650,000	450,000	308,400	410,000	4 TF	288–364	8,000
466,000	243,133	243,133	320,000	3 TF	256–400	10,800
496,000	240,139	240,139	338,000	3 TF	246–400	9,300
123,460	190,130	66,260	87,080	2 TF	86–104	6,900
143,500	113,000	73,200	100,000	3 TF	82–115	7,500
79,000	69,000	46,405	64,000	2 TF	65–79	6,900
335,000	237,000	147,000	215,000	4 TF	100–163	8,200
302,000	281,000	186,810	256,830	2 TF	225–345	6,500
291,000	261,250	168,910	239,200	2 TF	205–265	6,100
389,000	240,000	175,000	200,000	4 TJ	108–128	11,300
114,640	108,030	57,022	99,200	2 TF	124–134	6,500
357,000	232,000	153,000	206,000	4 TF	168–186	10,700
198,416	185,188	95,900	139,994	3 TF	128–158	6,900
454,150	385,000			4 TF	350	8,600

79,000 to 775,000 lb. Small general aviation aircraft weights range from 2000 to 8000 lb, while commuter and corporate aircraft vary from 15,000 to 74,600 lb. The maximum number of passengers carried by airline aircraft varies from 65 to nearly 500. On the other hand, small general aviation airplanes seat from 2 to 6 people, and short-haul and corporate aircraft from less than 10 to about 80 persons, depending on the configuration of the interior. Runway lengths for typical airline aircraft vary from 6000 to 12,000 ft, but it is important to note that it is not valid to assume that the larger the weight of an aircraft, the longer the runway length required. For large aircraft especially, the trip length has a profound influence on takeoff weight and, hence, the required runway length. Therefore, in the analysis of runway length requirements, an estimate of trip length is very important.

TABLE 3-2 **Characteristics of General
Aviation and Short-Haul Passenger Aircraft**

Aircraft	Wing span	Fuselage length	Wheel track	Maximum takeoff weight, lb	Maximum number of seats*	Number and type of engines	Runway length, ft
Beech 23 Musketeer	32'09"	25'00"	11'10"	2,200	4	1 P	1,380
Beech V35 Bonanza	33'05"	26'04"	9'07"	3,400	6	1 P	1,320
Beech 58-Baron	37'10"	29'09"	11'00"	6,775	6	2 P	2,380
Beech B80-QueenAir	50'03"	35'06"	12'09"	8,800	11	2 P	1,800
Beech C99	45'10"	44'07"	13'00"	10,900	17	2 TP	2,800
Bellanca 260C	34'02"	22'11"	9'00"	3,000	4	1 P	1,000
Cessna 150	32'08"	23'00"	6'06"	1,600	2	1 P	1,385
Cessna 172 Skyhawk	35'09"	26'11"	7,02"	2,300	4	1 P	1,525
Cessna 182 Skylane	35'10"	28'00"	7'11"	2,950	4	1 P	1,350
Cessna T310	36'11"	29'06"	12'00"	5,500	6	2 P	1,790
Cessna 402	44'01"	36'05"	18'00"	6,850	10	2 P	2,485
Piper PA-23 Aztec	37'02"	30'03"	11'04"	5,200	6	2 P	1,250
Piper PA-28 Cherokee	30'00"	23'06"	10'00"	2,400	4	1 P	
Piper PA-28 Arrow	30'00"	24'02"	10'06"	2,600	4	1 P	
Piper Twin Comanche C	36'00"	25'02"	9'09"	3,600	6	2 P	1,870
Piper PA-31 Navajo	40'08"	32'07"	13'09"	6,500	6	2 P	2,095
Gulfstream II	68'10"	79'11"	13'08"	17,500	22	2 TF	4,070
Metroliner II	46'03"	59'05"	15'00"	12,500	22	2 TF	3,550
Lear Jet 25	35'07"	47'07"	8'03"	15,000	8	2 TJ	5,186
Lockheed Jet Star	54'05"	60'05"	12'03"	42,000	12	4 TJ	4,880
Sabreliner-60	44'05"	48'04"	7'02"	20,000	12	2 TJ	4,875
Jet Falcon 20T	54'03"	60'00"	12'03"	29,100	28	2 TF	4,430
deHavilland TwinOtter	65'00"	51'09"	12'02"	12,500	22	2 TP	1,200
Shorts 330–200	74'08"	58'01"		22,900	32	2 TF	3,880
BAe 146–100	85'05"	78'09"		74,600	84	4 TP	3,530
deHavilland DASH 7	93'00"	80'08"		44,500	52	4 TP	2,260
Fokker F27 Mk500	95'02"	82'03"		45,000	50	2 TP	5,460

* Including pilot.

SOURCE: Manufacturers' data; *Jane's All the World's Aircraft* [27].

Runway lengths for small general aviation aircraft seldom exceed 2000 ft, while for commuter and corporate aircraft this length is on the order of 5000 ft.

In Tables 3-1 and 3-2 aircraft are referred to according to their type of propulsion and thrust-generating medium. The term *piston engine* applies to all propeller-driven aircraft powered by gasoline-fed reciprocating engines. Most small general aviation aircraft are powered by piston engines. The term *turboprop* refers to propeller-driven aircraft powered by turbine engines. A few twin-engine general aviation aircraft and a few of the earlier airline aircraft are powered in this manner. The term *turbojet* makes reference to those aircraft which are not dependent on propellers for thrust, but which obtain the thrust directly from a turbine engine. The early jet airline aircraft, particularly the Comet 707 and the DC-8, were powered by turbojet engines, but these were discarded in favor of turbofan engines principally because the latter are far more economical. When a fan is added in the front or rear of a turbojet engine, it is referred to as a *turbofan*. Most fans are installed in front of the main engine. A fan can be thought of as a

TABLE 3-3 **Main Landing Gear Dimensions for Typical Transport Aircraft**

Main landing gear configuration	Aircraft	Dimensions, in				Typical inflation pressures, psi
		X	Y	Z	U	
	DC-9-80	28.1				170
	B-737	30.5				148
	B-727	34.0				168
	DC-8-61	30.0	55.0			188
	DC-8-62	32.0	55.0			187
	DC-8-63	32.0	55.0			196
	DC-10-10	54.0	64.0			173
	B-720B	32.0	49.0			145
	B-707-120B	34.0	56.0			170
	B-707-320B	34.6	56.0			180
	B-757	34.0	45.0			161
	B-767	45.0	56.0			183
	Concorde	26.4	65.7			184
	L-1011-500	52.0	70.0			184
	A-300B	35.0	55.0			168
	B-747A	44.0	58.0	121.2	142.0	204
	B-747B, C, F	44.0	58.0	121.2	142.0	185
	DC-10-30	54.0	64.0	30.0	216.0	157*
	DC-10-40	54.0	64.0	30.0	216.0	165[†]

* Center gear tire pressure of 134 psi supports 16 percent of total weight.
† Center gear tire pressure of 140 psi supports 16 percent of total weight.
SOURCE: Manufacturers' data.

small-diameter propeller driven by the turbine of the main engine. Nearly all airline transport aircraft are now powered by turbofan engines for the reason just cited.

TRENDS IN SIZE, SPEED, AND PRODUCTIVITY OF TRANSPORT AIRCRAFT

The size, speed, and productivity of aircraft have grown enormously in the last two decades. The introduction of jet transports in the late fifties was a tremendous step forward. Since that time, aircraft grew gradually larger until the introduction of the Boeing 747 in the latter part of 1969, which was a quantum jump in size. On the other hand, there has only been a very nominal increase in speed in subsonic jet aircraft. With the introduction of supersonic transport there was again a quantum jump in speed. In general, the speed of the subsonic jets is about twice that of the piston-engine aircraft of the late fifties, while the speed of the first supersonic transport aircraft is again about twice the speed of the subsonic jets. The trend in the cruising speed of transport aircraft is shown in Fig. 3-2. A perspective of the

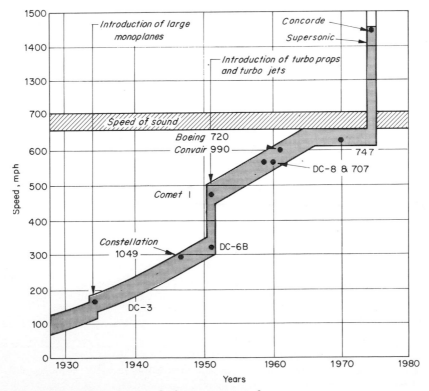

Fig. 3-2 Trends in the speed of transport aircraft.

TABLE 3-4 **Speed of DC-3 Compared to Speed of Other Aircraft**

Aircraft	Cruising speed, mi/h	Ratio of speed to speed of DC-3
DC-3	185	1.0
DC-4	240	1.3
DC-6	305	1.7
DC-9	530	2.9
DC-8	570	3.1
DC-10	600	3.2
B-747	600	3.2
Concorde	1450	6.9

increase in speed in the last 50 years can also be gained by comparing the speeds of various transport aircraft with the speed of the DC-3, as shown in Table 3-4.

During the last three decades we have witnessed an increase not only in the speed of aircraft but also in its size and weight. The trend in maximum weight of transport aircraft is shown in Fig. 3-3. Trends in wingspan and overall length are illustrated in Fig. 3-4.

It will be noted from Fig. 3-3 that in slightly less than 40 years the weight of transport aircraft has increased from slightly over 20,000 lb to nearly 800,000 lb, a fortyfold increase. New technology is not needed to produce aircraft with weights of 1,000,000 lb or more. Demand for travel is the principal factor that should determine the growth in aircraft size.

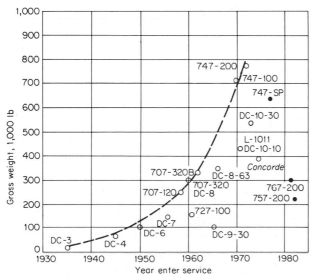

Fig. 3-3 Trends in the gross weight of transport aircraft. (*Aerospace Industries Association of America, Inc. [20].*)

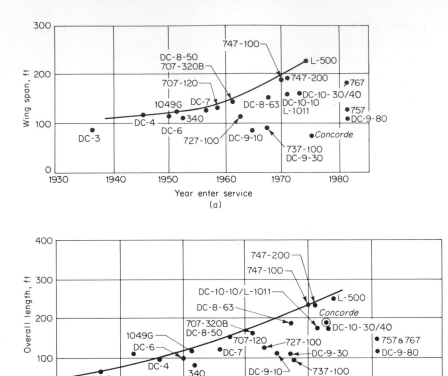

Fig. 3-4 Trends in the wingspan and overall length of transport aircraft. (*Aerospace Industries Association of America, Inc. [20].*)

However, airport facilities may be a limiting factor in growth. The wingspan and overall length of an aircraft are, in general, a function of aircraft weight, that is, the heavier an aircraft, the longer it is and the greater is its wingspan. However, the growth in overall length is dependent upon the extent that multideck aircraft are built. If they become common, the lengths will be shorter than if they are not. For supersonic aircraft the ratio of length to wingspan is larger than for subsonic aircraft of equivalent weight.

The productivity of aircraft in terms of ton-miles per hour has increased enormously since the days of the DC-3. The average productivity is defined as the product of average load and cruising speed. The average productivities of the different aircraft are as follows: for a DC-3, introduced in 1935, 350 ton · mi/h; for a DC-7, introduced in 1953, 2700 ton · mi/h; for a 707-120, introduced in 1959, 8500 ton · mi/h; and for the 747, introduced in 1969, 38,500 ton · mi/h. Thus the increase in productivity in a little less than 40 years has been over 100 times. The supersonic transport, because of its great speed, also has high productivity. However, the first models with their smaller load-carrying capability are not as productive as a 747. The productivity of one large jet transport between New York and London can be equal to or greater than the productivity of a large ocean liner.

The revenue-producing lift capability of transport aircraft, referred to as *payload,* has also grown enormously over two decades, as shown in Table 3-5. The piston-engine transports of the mid and late fifties, DC-7 and Constellation, carried nearly four times more than the DC-3. The first jet transports, 707-120 and DC-8, in the late fifties and early sixties were able to carry about twice the load of piston-engine transports of that time. Through the sixties the growth in payload was gradual until the introduction of the 747, when a very large jump in payload took place.

The distance that aircraft can fly without refueling, *the range,* has also greatly increased since the introduction of the DC-3. The DC-6 could fly about four times farther than the DC-3. The DC-6 was followed by the DC-7, which was able to fly about twice the distance of a DC-6. The DC-7 provided the first regular nonstop coast-to-coast travel in the United States. Then came the jet transports. The early versions were not able to fly as far as the DC-7, but as engine technology improved and turbofan engines were introduced in the sixties, the range of the jet transport exceeded that of the DC-7. This made possible nonstop flights from the West Coast of the United States to Europe. From this point on there was a modest increase in range. Today there are several aircraft that have the capability of flying about 6000 stat mi, making possible nonstop flights from the West Coast of the United States to Europe or the Far East, or from Europe to Africa. The range of these aircraft is so large that it is doubtful any significant increases in range will take place in the next decade.

To the airport designer the matter of runway length is of importance.

TABLE 3-5 **Average Payload
of Transport Aircraft**

Aircraft	Payload, tons
DC-3	2.4
DC-4	7.0
DC-7	9.0
B-707-120	17.9
DC-9-80	20.1
DC-8-61	22.0
B-757-200	26.6
DC-10-10	33.0
B-767-200	34.9
A-310	35.2
B-747	44.0
L1011-500	48.9

Using the DC-3 as a starting point, runway lengths for piston-engine aircraft kept increasing as the DC-4, DC-6, and DC-7 were introduced. A further increase in runway length was required when jet transports were introduced into service. Since that time there has been a leveling off in runway length requirements, as shown in Fig. 3-5. In this figure the lengths are shown relative to the DC-7. One reason for this trend is that many major airports are unable to provide greater lengths because of their inability to obtain additional land. As indicated in Table 3-1, runway lengths for jet transports vary widely, depending on the length of trip. For the longest intercontinental trips a length on the order of 12,000 ft is generally adequate.

CHARACTERISTICS OF TRANSPORT-CATEGORY AIRCRAFT

Engine Types and Thrust

Jet engines can be classified into two general categories, *turbojet* and *turbofan*. A turbojet engine consists of a compressor, a combustion chamber, and a turbine at the rear of the engine. A turbofan is essentially a turbojet engine to which large-diameter blades have been added, usually

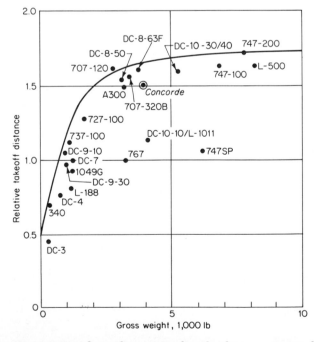

Fig. 3-5 Trends in the runway length of transport aircraft (*Aerospace Industries Association of America, Inc. [20].*)

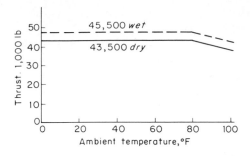

Fig. 3-6 Thrust versus temperature for Pratt and Whitney JT9D-3A engine at sea level.

in front of the compressor. These blades are normally referred to as *the fan*. A single row of blades is referred to as *single-stage*, two rows of blades as *multistage*. The smaller fan engines are all multistage, while the larger engines used to power aircraft like the Boeing 747 and the DC-10 are single-stage. In dealing with turbofan engines reference is made to the *bypass ratio*. This is the ratio of the mass airflow through the fan to the mass airflow through the core of the engine or the turbojet portion. Bypass ratios of engines on aircraft other than the very large ones range from 1.1 to 1.4. For the very large wide-body aircraft the bypass ratio is on the order of 6. In high bypass ratio engines 60 to 70 percent of the thrust is derived from the fan. Engines are usually rated in pounds of thrust in a static position at sea level. If provision is made to use water during takeoff, the engine is referred to as *wet*; if no water is used, it is known as *dry*. Adding water to the engine allows it to operate at higher temperatures than normal, providing slightly more thrust. This larger amount of thrust is available only during takeoff. A typical thrust versus temperature relationship is shown in Fig. 3-6. The engine in this figure would be rated at 43,500 lb dry and 45,500 lb wet. Some dry ratings of typical engines at sea level are given in Table 3-6. When an aircraft is cruising, it is utilizing from one-fifth to one-fourth of the static sea-level thrust rating listed in the table.

TABLE 3-6 **Turbojet Aircraft Engines**

Engine	Manufacturer	Thrust, lb	Aircraft
JT8D-7	Pratt and Whitney	14,000	B-737,B-727,DC-9
JT3D-3B	Pratt and Whitney	18,000	B-707,DC-8-61
JT3D-7	Pratt and Whitney	19,000	DC-8-62,DC-8-63
JT8D-209	Pratt and Whitney	19,250	DC-9-80
PW 2037	Pratt and Whitney	37,000	B-757-200
RB.211-535C	Rolls-Royce	37,400	B-757-200
593Mk.602tj	Olympus	38,000	Concorde
CF-6-60	General Electric	40,000	DC-10-10
JT9D-3A	Pratt and Whitney	43,500	B-747A
JT9D-7R4D	Pratt and Whitney	48,000	B-767-200
CF-6-80A	General Electric	48,000	B-767-200
RB.211-524B	Rolls-Royce	50,000	L-1011-500

TABLE 3-7   **Performance Characteristics of Typical Jet Aircraft Engines**

Aircraft	Weight, kips	Engine	Bypass ratio	Specific fuel consumption*
B-720	180	JT3C-7	0	1.082
DC-8-61	240	JT3D-3B	1.2	0.882
B-747A	520	JT9D-3A	6.0	0.722

* Based on Mach 0.82, 31,000-ft altitude, standard temperature.

Performance

One index of engine performance, insofar as consumption of fuel is concerned, is known as *specific fuel consumption.* It is expressed in terms of pounds of fuel per hour per pound of thrust.

In aviation, fuel consumption is expressed in pounds rather than in gallons. This is because the volumetric expansion and contraction of fuel with changes in temperature can be misleading in the amount of fuel which is available. Each gallon of jet fuel weighs about 6.8 lb.

Specific fuel consumption for a particular type of aircraft is a function of its weight, altitude, and speed. Some approximate values are given in Table 3-7 merely to illustrate the fuel economy of a turbofan engine, particularly at high bypass ratios. The JT3C-7 is a turbojet engine. Note that the JT9D-3A consumes about 30 percent less fuel than the JT3C-7 engine. This of course is the reason why turbojet engines are no longer being installed. Table 3-8 gives the approximate consumption of fuel in cruise for three typical aircraft.

Fuel consumption improvements have been significant in the last decade, and pressures continue to exist for further improvements in this area. New engines, such as the CFM56 and the JT10D, as well as derivatives of current engines, have resulted in significant fuel economy gains. Figure 3-7 illustrates the overall trend in specific fuel consumption improvements. It is likely that advanced turboprop engines will be introduced in the future to take advantage of their fuel economy in applications where speeds below Mach 0.8 are possible [18].

The differences in fuel consumption for the various types of passenger

TABLE 3-8   **Typical Jet Aircraft Fuel Consumption at Cruise**

Aircraft	Engine	Fuel consumption*, lb/h
B-727-200	JT8D-7	7,000
DC-8-61	JT3D-3B	13,000
B-747A	JT9D-3A	21,000

* Based on Mach 0.82, 31,000-ft altitude, standard day.

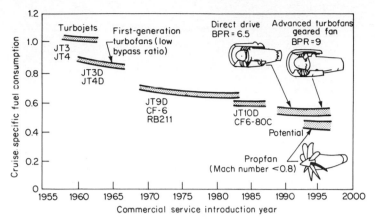

Fig. 3-7 Trends in specific fuel consumption of jet engines. (*Boeing Commercial Airplane Company [18].*)

aircraft in service today and for different trip modes are presented in Table 3-9. It should be pointed out, however, that the data are only indicators of fuel consumption and not of productivity. Those aircraft that burn fuel at higher rates generally are capable of greater speeds and have greater passenger capacity, as indicated in Table 3-10. Finally, Table 3-11 provides an indication of the time spent in the various modes of an aircraft trip and may be combined with Table 3-9 to obtain estimates of fuel consumption for various trip lengths. As may be observed in Fig. 3-8, the fuel consumption in gallons per available seat-mile decreases with increasing route segment length.

Aircraft Operating Costs

Prior to 1973, fuel prices were relatively stable. However, since that time fuel costs have risen very rapidly, resulting in significant changes in the

TABLE 3-9 **Average Fuel Consumption of Passenger Aircraft in Various Trip Modes, gal/h**

Aircraft type	Taxi or idle	Takeoff	Climbout	Cruise	Approach and land
Jumbo jet	1,053	10,335	8,677	3,576	3,154
Long-range jet	528	6,567	5,428	1,879	2,508
Medium-range jet	436	3,980	3,335	1,136	1,550
Turboprop	299	1,450	1,326	582	695
STOL	45	182	152	85	76
General aviation turboprop	44	111	103	61	62

SOURCE: California Department of Transportation [25].

TABLE 3-10 **Average Fuel Consumption**
at Best Cruising Speed for Passenger Aircraft

Aircraft type	Average number of seats	Best cruise speed, mi/h	Fuel consumption Cruise, gal/ seat-mile	Noncruise, gal/seat
Jumbo jet	315	575	0.020	7.2
Long-range jet	140	565	0.024	10.1
Medium-range jet	90	565	0.022	10.1
Turboprop	85	360	0.019	3.0
STOL	19	190	0.028	1.8
General aviation turboprop	10	300	0.020	3.0

SOURCE: California Department of Transportation [25].

operating economics of aircraft. In 1973 fuel costs were less than 30 percent of direct operating costs, while today they are over 50 percent of these costs. An indication of the operating costs for the various types of passenger aircraft is given in Fig. 3-9. In order to counteract the effect of escalating fuel prices, extensive research is being undertaken to investigate the impact of such technological factors as drag reduction, engine efficiency, structural weight changes, and avionics on operating cost [19, 33].

A knowledge of the relative magnitude of the operating expenses of the various aircraft in service today allows one to examine the alternatives available for service by particular aircraft in specific markets. The operating and performance characteristics of an aircraft make it suitable for a particular range of applications, and when the aircraft is utilized in a route context for which it was not designed, considerable diseconomies can result. For example, the Boeing 737 was designed for the short-haul lower-density markets, whereas the Boeing 747 was designed for the long-haul heavily traveled markets. The ability to project the types of aircraft which will be used in the several markets served by an airport is essential to the airport planning and design process.

TABLE 3-11 **Average Time in Operating**
Mode for Passenger Aircraft, h

Aircraft type	Taxi or idle Departure	Arrival	Takeoff	Climbout	Approach and land
Jumbo jet	0.32	0.12	0.012	0.04	0.07
Long-range jet	0.32	0.12	0.012	0.04	0.07
Medium-range jet	0.32	0.12	0.012	0.04	0.07
Turboprop	0.32	0.12	0.010	0.04	0.08
STOL	0.32	0.12	0.010	0.04	0.08
General aviation turboprop	0.32	0.12	0.010	0.04	0.08

SOURCE: California Department of Transportation [25].

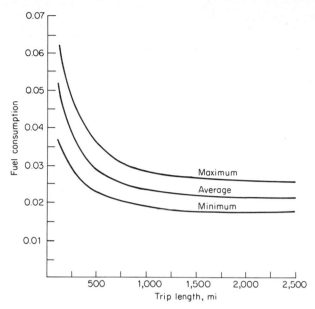

Fig. 3-8 Average passenger aircraft fuel consumption in gallons per seat-mile as a function of route distance. (*California Department of Transportation [25].*)

Noise

The major sources of noise in an engine are the machinery noise and the primary jet. Machinery noise is defined as noise generated primarily by the moving parts of the engine, such as the fan, compressor, and turbine blades. The fan and compressor blade noise is radiated forward of the engine, while the turbine blade noise is radiated aft of the engine. The parts of a jet engine are shown in Fig. 3-10. The primary jet noise is generated by the mixing of the high-velocity exhaust gas from the main body of the engine with the ambient air. The fan exhaust also generates noise, but during high levels of thrust, such as takeoff, the overall noise level from the primary jet is reduced by the presence of the fan exhaust. This is due to the fact that the velocity of the fan exhaust is less than that of the primary jet; therefore it provides for a less abrupt mixing of the primary jet with the ambient air.

The dominant source of noise during takeoff is the primary jet, whereas on approach the dominant source is machinery noise. Acoustical lining of the inlet and ducts for the fan exhaust and removal of the inlet guide vanes have done a great deal to reduce machinery noise. Significant reductions in primary jet noise can be accomplished only by reducing the velocity of the primary jet. Several types of nozzle noise suppressors have been developed to reduce primary jet noise, including corrugated, multitube, and teeth types, but reductions in noise have been marginal.

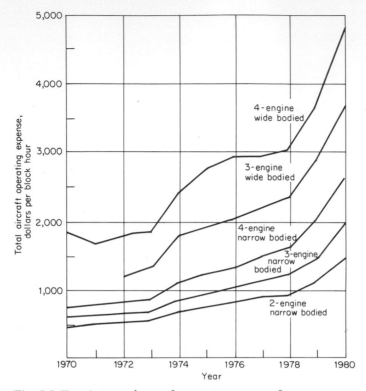

Fig. 3-9 Trends in total aircraft operating expense for average passenger aircraft. (*Civil Aeronautics Board [4].*)

Since the most serious problem facing aviation is noise, a substantial effort is being made by the federal government and engine manufacturers to reduce engine noise [3, 18]. It is interesting to note that since the introduction of commercial jet aircraft in 1958, there has been a reduction of approximately 15 EPDdB (effective perceived noise level in decibels), which is quite significant. An indication of the advancements made in reducing sideline noise levels may be found in Fig. 3-11. Technology has made it possible to substantially reduce noise for a given amount of thrust

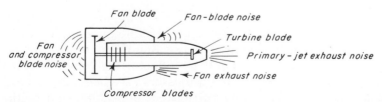

Fig. 3-10 Sources of noise in jet engines.

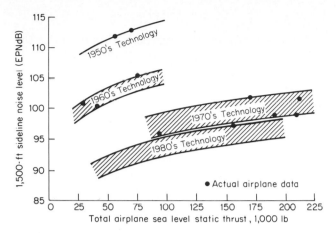

Fig. 3-11 Trends in the relationship between sideline noise and total aircraft thrust. (*Boeing Commercial Airplane Company [18].*)

and to dramatically increase thrust without significantly increasing noise levels. Prospects of producing substantially quieter engines are promising. A more serious problem, however, is to reduce the noise of existing low bypass ratio engines which power most of the earlier jet aircraft, such as the DC-8 and DC-9 and the Boeing 707, 727, and 737.

Components of Aircraft Weight

If the information in Tables 3-1 and 3-2 is to be useful for planning purposes, it is important for the planner to understand the basic components which make up the weight of an aircraft during takeoff and landings, since weight is one of the major factors which govern the length of a runway. A number of different weights which are referenced in airline operations are discussed below.

Operating Empty Weight

The basic weight of the aircraft, including crew and all the necessary gear required for flight, but not including payload and fuel. The operating empty weight is not a constant for passenger aircraft, but varies with the seating configuration.

Zero Fuel Weight

The weight above which all additional weight must be fuel, so that when the aircraft is in flight, the bending moments at the junction of the wing and fuselage do not become excessive.

Payload

A term which refers to the total revenue-producing load. This includes the weight of passengers and their baggage, mail, express, and cargo.

Maximum Structural Payload

The maximum load which the aircraft is certified to carry, whether this load be passengers, cargo, or a combination of both. Theoretically, the maximum structural payload is the difference between the zero fuel weight and the operating empty weight. The maximum payload actually carried is usually less than the maximum structural payload because of space limitations. This is especially true for passenger aircraft, in which seats and other items consume a considerable amount of space.

Maximum Ramp Weight

The maximum weight authorized for ground maneuver, including taxi and run-up fuel. As the aircraft taxis between the apron and the end of the runway, it burns fuel and consequently loses weight. The difference between the maximum structural takeoff weight and the maximum ramp weight is very nominal, only a few thousand pounds.

Maximum Structural Takeoff Weight

The maximum weight authorized at brake release for takeoff. It excludes taxi and run-up fuel and includes the operating empty weight, trip and reserve fuel, and payload.

Maximum Structural Landing Weight

The structural capability of the aircraft in landing. The main gear is structurally designed to absorb the forces encountered during landing; the larger the forces, the heavier must be the gear. Normally the main gears of transport-category aircraft are structurally designed for a weight less than the maximum structural takeoff weight. This is so because an aircraft loses weight en route by burning fuel. This loss in weight is considerable if the journey is long, in excess of 80,000 lb for large jet transports. It is therefore not economical to design the main gear of an aircraft to support the maximum structural takeoff weight during landing since this situation will rarely occur. If it does occur, as in the case of aircraft malfunction just after takeoff, the pilot must jettison fuel prior to returning to the airport so as not to exceed the maximum landing weight. For short-range aircraft, such as the DC-9, the main gear is designed to support, in a landing operation, a weight nearly equal to the maximum structural takeoff weight. This is so because the distances between stops are short, and therefore no large amounts of fuel are consumed between stops.

A portion of the weight of an aircraft before takeoff is composed of fuel. The fuel requirements can be segregated into two components, the amount of fuel needed to make the trip and the reserves required by regulations set forth by the government in the Federal Aviation Regulations, FAR Part 121 [15].

The fuel for the trip depends on the distance to be traveled, the speed, the meteorological conditions, the altitude at which the aircraft is flown, and the payload. The fuel reserve is dependent on the distance to the alternate airport, the amount of specified waiting time to land, and, for international flights, the length of trip.

It can be seen that the aircraft weight is composed of the operating empty weight and the three variables of payload, trip fuel, and fuel reserve.

On landing, the weight of an aircraft is the sum of the operating empty weight, the payload, and the fuel reserve, assuming that the aircraft lands at its destination and is not diverted to an alternate airport. This landing weight cannot exceed the maximum structural landing weight of the aircraft. The takeoff weight is the sum of the landing weight and the trip fuel. This weight cannot exceed the maximum structural takeoff weight of the aircraft.

An approximate estimate of the distribution of the components of aircraft weight is given in Table 3-12. It will be noted that as the range of an aircraft is increased, the proportion of trip fuel to takeoff weight increases, while the percentage of payload decreases.

Payload and Range

A question often asked is, how far can an aircraft fly? The distance it can fly is referred to as *range*. There are a number of factors that influence the range of an aircraft; among the most important is the payload. Normally as the range is increased, the payload is decreased, a weight tradeoff between the fuel to fly to destination and the payload which can be carried. The relationship between payload and range is illustrated in Fig. 3-12. Point A designates the farthest distance that an aircraft can fly with a maximum structural payload. To fly a distance R_a and carry a payload P_a, the aircraft has to take off at its maximum structural takeoff weight; however, its fuel

TABLE 3-12   **Average Distribution of Weight Components for Passenger Turbine-Powered Aircraft, % of Takeoff Weight**

Aircraft type	Operating empty weight	Payload	Trip fuel	Fuel reserve
Short range	66	24	6	4
Medium range	59	16	21	4
Long range	44	10	42	5

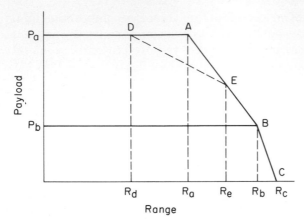

Fig. 3-12 General representation of the relationship between payload and range.

tanks are not completely filled. Point B represents the farthest distance R_b
an aircraft can fly if its fuel tanks are completely filled at the start of the
journey. The corresponding payload that can be carried is P_b. To travel the
distance R_b, the aircraft must take off at its maximum structural takeoff
weight. Therefore to extend the distance of travel from R_a to R_b, the
payload has to be reduced in favor of adding more fuel. Point C represents
the maximum distance an aircraft can fly without any payload. Sometimes
this is referred to as the *ferry range;* it is used if necessary for the delivery
of aircraft. To travel this distance R_c, the maximum amount of fuel is
necessary, but since there is no payload, the takeoff weight is less than
maximum.

In some cases the maximum structural landing weight may dictate how
long an aircraft can fly with a maximum structural payload. If this is the
case, the line DE represents the tradeoff between payload and range, which
must occur since the payload is limited by the maximum structural landing
weight. The shape of the payload versus range curve would then follow the
line $DEBC$ instead of ABC.

The payload versus range depends on a number of factors, such as
meteorological conditions en route, flight altitude, speed, fuel, wind, and
amount of reserve fuel. For an approximate performance comparison of
different aircraft, the payload versus range curves are usually given for
standard day, no wind, and long-range cruise. For this purpose approximate
values of payload versus range for some typical transport aircraft are shown
in Table 3-13 and Fig. 3-13. Note the wide variation in payload and range.

The actual payload, particularly in passenger aircraft, is normally less
than the maximum structural payload, even when the aircraft is completely
full. This is due to the limitation in the use of space when passengers are

TABLE 3-13 **Payload Versus Range Information for Typical Transport Aircraft***

Aircraft	P_A	R_A	P_B	R_B	R_C	R_D	P_E	R_E
DC-9-32	30.1				1600	900	27.5	1230
B-727-200	37.5				2200	950	23.0	1800
B-720B	41.0	2700	13.5	4300	4800			
B-707-320B	46.2				5800	3300	44.0	4300
DC-8-62	51.7	4500	45.0	5100				
DC-8-63	71.2	3300	35.0	4900				
DC-9-80	40.2				2600			
DC-10-10	100.3	2200	46.0	3800				
L-1011	85.0	2200	39.0	4000				
B-747B	160.7	3900	65.0	6100				
Concorde	25.0	3400	15.0	3750				
A-300B	77.6	850	40.0	2000				
B-757-200[†]	53.0	2100	33.0	3300			10.0	3700
B-767-200[†]	42.2	1900	27.0	4100			10.0	4300

* Weights are in 1000 lb, distances in nmi.
[†] Preliminary estimates.
SOURCE: Manufacturers' data.

carried. For computing payload, passengers and their baggage are normally considered as 200-lb units.

Turning Radii

For determining aircraft positions on the apron adjacent to the terminal buildings and establishing the paths of aircraft at other locations on the airport, it is important to understand the geometry of movement of an aircraft. Turning radii are a function of the nose gear steering angle. The larger the angle, the greater are the radii. From the center of rotation the distances to the various parts of the aircraft, such as the wing tips, the nose, or the tail, result in a number of radii. The largest radius is the most critical from the standpoint of clearance to buildings or adjacent aircraft. The minimum turning radius corresponds to the maximum nose gear steering angle specified by the aircraft manufacturer. The maximum angles vary from 60 to 80°. The center of rotation can be determined easily by drawing a line through the axis of the nose gear at whatever steering angle is desired. The intersection of this line with a line drawn through the axes of the two main gears is the center of rotation. For aircraft with more than two main gears, such as the Boeing 747, the axis is drawn midway between the gears. This was illustrated in Fig. 3-1. Some of the newer large aircraft have the capability of swiveling the main gear when making sharp turns. The effect of the swivel is to reduce the turning radius.

Minimum turning radii are not used very often in practice because the maneuver produces excessive tire wear and in some instances results in

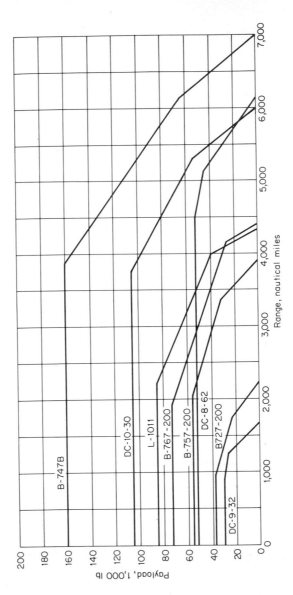

Fig. 3-13 Maximum payload versus range for typical transport aircraft.

scuffing of the pavement surface. Accordingly, lesser angles on the order of 50° are more proper. Maximum turning radii for some typical transport aircraft are given in Table 3-14.

Static Weight on the Main Gears and the Nose Gear

The distribution of the load between the main gears and the nose gear depends on the type of aircraft and the location of the center of gravity of the aircraft. For any gross weight there is a maximum aft and forward center of gravity position to which the aircraft can be loaded for flight in order to maintain stability. Thus the distribution of weight between the nose and main gears is not a constant. An illustration of the variation in main landing gear weight is given in Fig. 3-14. For the design of pavements it is normally assumed that 5 percent of the weight is supported on the nose gear and the remainder on the main gears. Thus if there are two main gears, each gear supports 47.5 percent of the total weight. For example, if the takeoff weight of an aircraft is 300,000 lb, each main gear is assumed to support 142,500 lb. If the main gear has four tires, it is assumed that each tire supports an equal fraction of the weight on the gear, in this example 35,625 lb.

Wing Tip Vortices

Whenever the wings lift an aircraft, vortices form near the ends of the wings. The vortices are made up of two counterrotating cylindrical air masses about a wingspan apart, extending aft along the flight path. The velocity of the wind within these cylinders can be hazardous to other aircraft encountering them in flight. This is particularly true if a light aircraft encounters a vortex generated by a much heavier aircraft. The tangential velocities in a vortex are directly proportional to the weight of the aircraft and inversely proportional to the speed. The more intense vortices are therefore generated when the aircraft is flying slowly near an

TABLE 3-14 **Typical Passenger Aircraft Turning Radii**

Aircraft	Maximum steering angle, °	Radii*, ft		
		Wing tips[†]	Nose	Tail
DC-9-32	82	55.5	61.2	64.0
B-727-200	78	71.0	79.5	80.0
DC-8-63	67	110.4	99.0	109.7
DC-10-10	68	112.4	104.6	101.0
B-747A	70	140.0	109.0	137.0

* From center of rotation.
† Note that the radius of the wing tip is not always the largest of the three radii listed.

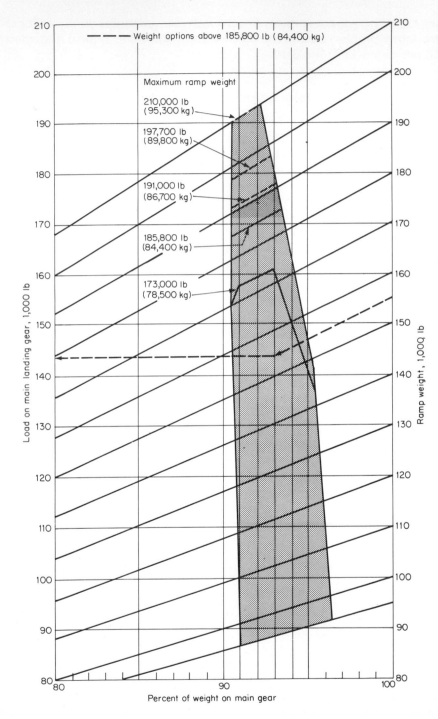

Fig. 3-14 Landing gear pavement loading for the Boeing 727-200 aircraft. Unshaded areas represent operational limits. (*Boeing Commercial Airplane Company [10].*)

airport [39, 43]. The winds created by vortices are often referred to as *wake turbulence* or *wake vortex.*

Once vortices are generated, they move downward and drift laterally in the direction of the wind. The rate at which vortices settle toward the ground is dependent to some extent on the weight of the aircraft; the heavier the vehicle, the faster the vortex will settle. At a height of about one wingspan above the ground the vortices begin to move laterally away from the aircraft, as shown in Fig. 3-15. The duration of a vortex depends to a great extent on the velocity of the wind. When there is very little or no wind, vortices can persist for more than 2 min. It was observed that during flight the vertical displacement of the wake tended to level off about 1000 ft below the flight path of a heavy aircraft [5].

The vortex hazard to small general aviation aircraft has been known for some time. However, when wide-body aircraft were first introduced, it was found that they could create a hazard to smaller-airline aircraft as well. This prompted the federal government through NASA and the FAA to undertake an accelerated flight test program to determine the safe distance that lighter aircraft should keep behind a heavy aircraft. The results of the test program

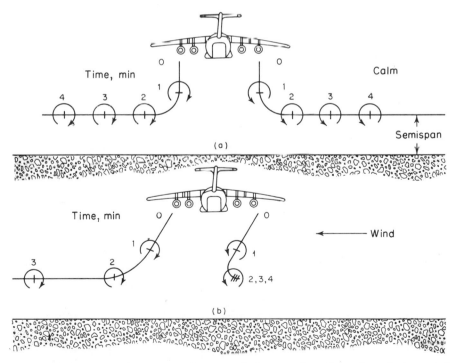

Fig. 3-15 Vortex movement near the ground showing the effect of wind. (*National Aeronautics and Space Administration [5].*)

led the FAA to divide airline jet aircraft into two classes, light and heavy. Light aircraft are defined as those whose maximum takeoff weight is less than 300,000 lb; all other aircraft are classed as heavy. This classification places the DC-9, B-737, B-727, B-720, and B-707-120B in the light category. On the other hand, the 707-320B, DC-8-61, 62, and 63, and all wide-body jets are considered heavy. The minimum headway between a light aircraft and a preceding heavy one was increased as a result of the tests. The spacing between two heavy aircraft following each other was also increased. The headway was not altered for two light aircraft following each other. Likewise the spacing between parallel runways was increased for simultaneous operations in good weather. The specific separation rules are described in the chapter on air traffic control. Since the length of headways has a profound influence on runway capacity, considerable attention is being devoted to the wake vortex problem. NASA has a comprehensive research effort underway to give a better analytical description of vortex behavior and concurrently to develop methods for their detection, early dissipation, or prevention.

Methods of avoiding hazardous wake vortices, particularly for use by operators of small general aviation aircraft, have been published [4]. Among the more important suggestions is to select an approach path which will always be above the path of a heavy aircraft.

THE EFFECT OF AIRCRAFT PERFORMANCE ON RUNWAY LENGTH

The factors which have a bearing on runway length may be grouped into three general categories:

1. Performance requirements imposed by the government on aircraft manufacturers and operators

2. Environment at the airport

3. Those items which establish the operating takeoff and landing gross weights for each aircraft type

Performance Requirements Imposed by the Government

Transport-category aircraft are licensed and operated under a code known as the Federal Aviation Regulations (FAR). This code is promulgated by the federal government in coordination with industry. The regulations govern the aircraft gross weights at takeoff and landing by specifying performance requirements which must be met in terms related to the runway lengths available.

The regulations pertaining to turbine aircraft consider three general cases in establishing the length of a runway necessary for safe operations. These three cases are:

1. A normal takeoff where all engines are available and sufficient runway is required to accommodate variations in liftoff techniques and the distinctive performance characteristics of these aircraft

2. Takeoff involving an engine failure, where sufficient runway is required to allow the aircraft to continue the takeoff despite the loss of power, or else brake to a stop

3. Landing, where sufficient runway is required to allow for normal variation in landing technique, overshoots, poor approaches, and the like

The regulations pertaining to piston-engine aircraft retain in principle the above criteria, but the first criterion is not used. This particular regulation is aimed toward the everyday, normal takeoff maneuver, since engine failure occurs rather infrequently with turbine-powered aircraft.

The runway length needed at an airport by a particular type and weight of turbine-powered aircraft is established by one of the foregoing three cases, whichever yields the longest length.

In the regulations for both piston-engine aircraft and turbine-powered aircraft the word runway refers to *full-strength pavement* (FS). Thus, in the discussion which follows, the terms runway and full-strength pavement are synonymous. In any discussion of the effect of the regulations on the length of the runway, however, it is important to note that the current regulations for turbine-powered aircraft do not require a runway for the entire takeoff distance, while the regulations for piston-engine aircraft normally do.

To indicate why there is a difference in the two regulations with regard to the length of full-strength pavement, it is necessary to examine in more detail the regulations pertaining to turbine-powered transports.

The three cases referred to above, as defined by the current turbine-powered transport regulations, FAR Part 25 [8] and Part 121 [15], are illustrated in Fig. 3-16.

The landing case (Fig. 3-16a) is probably easiest to explain. The regulations state that the *landing distance* (LD) needed for each aircraft using the airport must be sufficient to permit the aircraft to come to a full stop, *stop distance* (SD), within 60 percent of this distance, assuming that the pilot makes an approach at the proper speed and crosses the threshold of the runway at a height of 50 ft. The landing distance must be full-strength pavement. The landing distance for piston-engine aircraft is defined in exactly the same manner.

The normal case, all engine takeoff (Fig. 3-16c), defines a *takeoff distance* (TOD) which, for a specific weight of aircraft, must be 115 percent

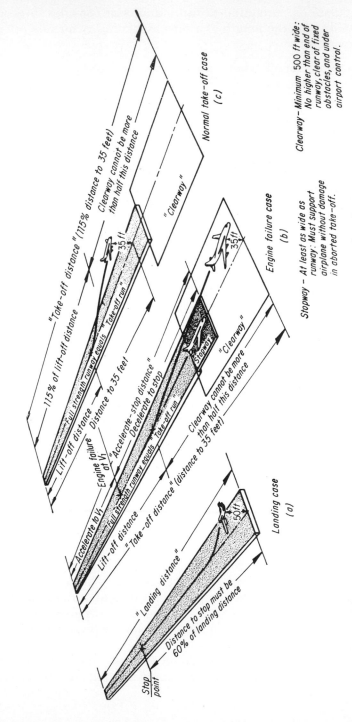

Fig. 3-16 Summary of turbine-powered aircraft performance regulations affecting runway length requirements.

of the actual distance the aircraft uses to reach a height of 35 ft (D35). Not all of this distance has to be of full-strength pavement, however, because pilot techniques would never vary so greatly as to need all of it before lifting off the ground. What is necessary is that all this distance be free from obstructions to protect against an overshooting takeoff. Consequently the regulations permit the use of a *clearway* (CL) for part of this distance. A clearway is defined as an area beyond the runway not less than 500 ft wide, centrally located about the extended centerline of the runway, and under the control of the airport authorities. The clearway is expressed in terms of a clearway plane, extending from the end of the runway with an upward slope not exceeding 1.25 percent above which no object nor any portion of the terrain protrudes, except that threshold lights may protrude above the plane if their height above the end of the runway is not greater than 26 in and if they are located to each side of the runway. Up to one-half the difference between 115 percent of the distance to reach the point of liftoff, the *liftoff distance* (LOD), and the takeoff distance may be clearway. The remainder of the takeoff distance must be full-strength pavement and is identified as the *takeoff run* (TOR).

For the engine-failure case (Fig. 3-16*b*), the regulation specifies that the takeoff distance required is the actual distance to reach a height of 35 ft (D35) with no percentage applied, as in the all-engine takeoff case. This recognizes the infrequency of occurrence of engine failure. The regulations again permit the use of a clearway, in this case up to one-half the difference between the liftoff distance and the takeoff distance, the remainder being full-strength pavement for the entire takeoff distance.

As mentioned previously, the engine-failure case requires that sufficient distance be also available to stop the airplane rather than continue the takeoff. This distance is referred to as the *accelerate-stop distance* (DAS). For piston-engine aircraft only full-strength pavement was normally used for this purpose. The regulations for turbine-powered aircraft, however, recognize that an aborted takeoff is relatively rare and permit use of lesser strength pavement, known as *stopway* (SW), for that part of the accelerate-stop distance beyond the takeoff run. The stopway is defined as an area beyond the runway, not less in width than the width of the runway, centrally located about the extended centerline of the runway, and designated by the airport authorities for use in decelerating the aircraft during an aborted takeoff. To be considered as such, the stopway must be capable of supporting the airplane during an aborted takeoff without inducing structural damage to the aircraft.

The required *field length* FL is generally made up of three components, namely, the full-strength pavement FS, the partial-strength pavement or stopway SW, and the clearway CL.

The above regulations for turbine-powered aircraft may be summarized for each of the cases in equation form to find the required field length.

Normal takeoff case:

$$FL = FS + CL \qquad\qquad (3\text{-}1)$$

where
$$CL = 0.50[TOD - 1.15(LOD)] \qquad\qquad (3\text{-}1a)$$
$$TOD = 1.15(D35) \qquad\qquad (3\text{-}1b)$$
$$FS = TOR \qquad\qquad (3\text{-}1c)$$
$$TOR = TOD - CL \qquad\qquad (3\text{-}1d)$$

Engine-failure takeoff case:

$$FL = FS + CL \qquad\qquad (3\text{-}2)$$

where
$$CL = 0.50(TOD - LOD) \qquad\qquad (3\text{-}2a)$$
$$TOD = D35 \qquad\qquad (3\text{-}2b)$$
$$FS = TOR \qquad\qquad (3\text{-}2c)$$
$$TOR = TOD - CL \qquad\qquad (3\text{-}2d)$$

Engine-failure aborted takeoff:

$$FL = FS + SW \qquad\qquad (3\text{-}3)$$

where
$$FL = DAS \qquad\qquad (3\text{-}3a)$$

Landing case:

$$FS = LD \qquad\qquad (3\text{-}4)$$

where
$$LD = SD/0.60 \qquad\qquad (3\text{-}4a)$$

To determine the required field length and the various components of length which are made up of full-strength pavement, stopway, and clearway, the above equations must each be solved for the critical design aircraft at the airport. This will result in finding each of the following values:

$$FL = \max (TOD, DAS, LD) \qquad\qquad (3\text{-}5)$$
$$FS = \max (TOR, LD) \qquad\qquad (3\text{-}6)$$
$$SW = DAS - \max (TOR, LD) \qquad\qquad (3\text{-}7)$$

and
$$CL = \min (FL - DAS, CL) \qquad\qquad (3\text{-}8)$$

where the minimum allowable value of CL is 0.

If operations are to take place on the runway in both directions, as is the usual case, the field length components must exist in each direction. Example Problem 3-1 illustrates the application of these requirements for a hypothetical aircraft.

Example Problem 3-1

Determine the runway length requirements according to the specifications of FAR 25 and FAR 21 for a turbine-powered aircraft with the following performance characteristics:

Normal takeoff liftoff distance LOD = 7000 ft

Distance to height of 35 ft D35 = 8000 ft

Engine-failure takeoff liftoff distance LOD = 8200 ft

Engine-failure distance to height of 35 ft D35 = 9100 ft

Engine-failure aborted takeoff accelerate-stop distance DAS = 9500 ft

Landing stop distance SD = 5000 ft

Solution

From Eqs. (3-1) for a normal takeoff:

TOD = 1.15 (D35) = 1.15 (8000) = 9200 ft

CL = 0.50 [TOD − 1.15 (LOD)] = 0.50 [9200 − 1.15 (7000)] = 575 ft

TOR = TOD − CL = 9200 − 575 = 8625 ft

From Eqs. (3-2) for an engine-failure takeoff:

TOD = D35 = 9100 ft

CL = 0.50 (TOD − LOD) = 0.50 (9100 − 8200) = 450 ft

TOR = TOD − CL = 9100 − 450 = 8650 ft

From Eq. (3-3) for an engine-failure aborted takeoff:

DAS = 9500 ft

From Eq. (3-4) for a landing:

LD = SD/0.60 = 5000/0.60 = 8333 ft

Using the above quantities in Eqs. (3-5) through (3-8), the runway component requirements become:

FL = max (TOD, DAS, LD) = 9500 ft

FS = max (TOR, LD) = 8650 ft

SW = DAS − max (TOR, LD) = 9500 − 8650 = 850 ft

CL = min [(FL − DAS), CL] = min [(9500 − 9500), 450, 575] = 0 feet

The sketch in Fig. 3-17 shows the required runway field length and the components of this field for operations in both directions. It should be observed that for this case there is a displaced threshold at each end of the runway since the stopway is not available for normal aircraft operations.

It is apparent that both the takeoff distance and the accelerate-stop distance will depend on the speed the aircraft has achieved when an engine fails. The speed at which engine failure is assumed to occur is selected by the aircraft manufacturer and is referred to as the *critical engine-failure speed* V_1. If an engine actually fails prior to this selected speed, the pilot brakes to a stop. If the engine fails at a speed greater than this speed, the pilot has no choice but to continue the takeoff.

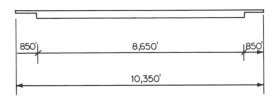

Fig. 3-17 Illustration of runway length components from Example Problem 3-1.

Since for piston engine aircraft, the full-strength pavement was normally used for the entire accelerate-stop distance and the takeoff distance, it was the general practice to select V_1 so that the distance required to stop from the point where V_1 was reached was equal to the distance (from the same point) to reach a specified height above the runway. The runway length established on this basis is referred to as the *balanced-field concept* or *balanced runway* and results in the shortest runway. For turbine-powered aircraft, the selection of V_1 on this basis will not necessarily result in the shortest runway if a clearway or a stopway is provided. For this reason it is necessary to understand the interrelations between V_1 and the various components of the takeoff distance and the accelerate-stop distance. These are illustrated in Fig. 3-18. At increasingly higher V_1 speeds, the takeoff distance becomes shorter and shorter because the aircraft has the benefit of all engine acceleration for greater portions of the takeoff roll, but the accelerate-stop distance is correspondingly increased.

Although Fig. 3-18 is included primarily to illustrate the clearway and stopway concepts, the balanced-field concept is also shown for comparison and corresponds to the crossover of the takeoff and stopping requirements at point D.

When clearways and stopways are utilized, several alternatives are possible:

1. If the same V_1 is selected as in the balanced-field concept, the lengths of the clearway and the stopway are equal. This would mean that the full-strength runway, indicated as L_b in Fig. 3-18, could be shortened a distance equal to the clearway, but a stopway would have to be constructed to the field length L_d.

2. Another alternative is to select V_1 so as to balance the accelerate-stop distance with the takeoff run. In this case the full-strength runway becomes

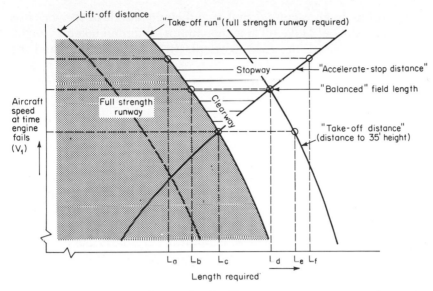

Fig. 3-18 Turbine-powered aircraft takeoff runway requirements in the engine-failure case.

L_c, which is less than L_d, and no stopway is required. Thus the runway has been shortened, but a clearway is required from L_c to L_e.

3. Another alternative is to select a fairly high V_1 in order to reduce the takeoff distance; but when this is done, the accelerate-stop distance is increased greatly. For this case the length of the runway is indicated as L_a, but a stopway must be provided to point L_f because of the greater accelerate-stop distance. This alternative may be advantageous to the operator at airports where there are obstacles near the ends of the runways.

Thus, one can see that the regulations pertaining to turbine-powered aircraft offer a number of alternatives to the aircraft operator. It should be emphasized that the takeoff distance and the takeoff run for the engine-failure case must be compared with the corresponding distance for the normal all-engine takeoff case. The longer distance always governs. A further discussion of these concepts is presented by ICAO [1].

From the presentation thus far, it is apparent that the length of the runway is intimately associated with the heights, speeds, and other requirements specified in the performance regulations.

Both aircraft operators and airport management are interested in clearways, because clearways will, for a fixed available length of runway, allow the operator additional gross takeoff weight with less expense to airport management than the building full-strength pavement would require.

Thus far it has been assumed that if sufficient length of runway was provided, an aircraft could take off at its maximum structural takeoff weight. However, this may not be the case, particularly if it is quite hot and the airport is located at higher elevations. The reason for this is that federal regulations state that the aircraft must be able to climb with one engine inoperative at gradients not less than the minimum specified. This performance must be demonstrated with no obstacles in the flight path. On hot days and at higher elevations an aircraft most likely will be unable to climb at the minimum specified gradients when it is at its maximum structural takeoff weight. Therefore, the weight must be reduced until the climb requirements are met. The resulting weight is referred to as the *climb-limited weight*. It is this weight that the runway must accommodate because an aircraft operator will not be able to take advantage of any longer runway. As an example, at sea level and a temperature of 80°F the maximum allowable takeoff weight of a Boeing 747A is 710,000 lb. This corresponds to its maximum structural takeoff weight. With the same temperature, but an elevation of 2000 ft, the maximum allowable takeoff weight is reduced to 662,000 lb, which corresponds to the climb-limited weight. If at an elevation of 2000 ft there were no climb restriction, the length of runway required for 710,000 lb, the maximum structural takeoff weight, would be 13,400 ft. However, the runway length for the climb-limited weight of 662,000 lb is 11,100 ft. Therefore any length greater than 11,100 ft could not be used by the aircraft operator when the temperature is 80°F.

Thus far no mention has been made of obstacles, sometimes referred to as obstructions, in the flight path. If there are any and they are sufficiently high, the allowable takeoff weight may have to be further reduced to provide adequate clearance of the flight path above these obstacles. The corresponding weight is often referred to as the *obstacle-limited weight*.

Climb and obstacle clearance requirements are too complex to be described in detail in this text, but a summary is shown in Fig. 3-19. The details of these requirements are found in FAR Part 25. The climb regulations pertain to takeoff flight path which extends from a point where the aircraft has reached a height of 35 ft above the pavement surface with one engine inoperative to a point where a height of 1500 ft is reached. The takeoff flight path is divided into several segments, referred to as the first, second, third, and final. Sometimes the third and the final segments are referred to as the *transition segment*. Note that for each segment there are several minimum climb gradients specified, depending on the number of engines on the aircraft. The largest gradients are in the second segment, and therefore this segment is normally the critical one for determining the climb-limited weight. Note that the second segment begins at the point when the landing gear is retracted and ends when the aircraft reaches a

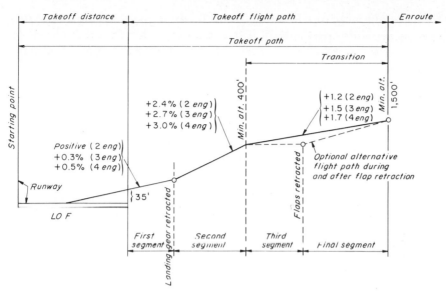

Fig. 3-19 Obstacle-free minimum climb gradients required for turbine-powered aircraft with one engine inoperative.

height of 400 ft above the end of the runway. In the transition segment the aircraft operator has the option of climbing the aircraft in several ways as long as the average gradient is not less than that specified in Fig. 3-19.

If there are obstacles in the flight path and they are high enough, the minimum gradients shown in Fig. 3-19 will no longer be applicable. It is necessary to determine a flight path that will clear the obstacles in a manner specified by the federal regulations. These regulations require that the net takeoff flight path with one engine inoperative clear the obstacle by a distance of not less than 35 ft. The net takeoff flight path is computed by reducing the actual flight path by 0.8 percent for two-engine aircraft, 0.9 percent for three-engine aircraft, and 1.0 percent for four-engine aircraft.

Using the previous example, suppose there was an obstacle 120 ft high, 3400 ft from the takeoff end of the runway. The obstacle-limited weight for this condition is 656,000 lb, slightly less than the climb-limited weight of 662,000 lb. The corresponding runway length to accommodate 656,000 lb is 10,900 ft. However, if it were possible to lower or remove the obstacle, the aircraft would still be limited to its climb-limited weight of 662,000 lb. The removal of the obstacle reduces the weight penalty from 54,000 to 48,000 lb. Beyond this there is nothing that can be done to further reduce the penalty in weight other than to adjust V_1 to the extent that sufficient runway is available. This example points out the importance of selecting airport sites that are relatively free of obstacles in the flight path and are as close to sea level as possible, particularly if it is necessary for aircraft to fly at or near their maximum structural takeoff weights while atmospheric temperatures are high.

The Environs at the Airport

Thus far it has been shown how the requirements imposed by the government can influence runway length. Certain conditions at the airport can also do so. The more important of these conditions are temperature, surface wind, runway gradient, altitude of the airport, and condition of the runway surface. The effect of these conditions on runway length can only be approximated. However, orders of magnitude can be beneficial for planning, and these are therefore presented in this context.

Temperature

The higher the temperature, the longer the runway required because high temperatures reflect lower air densities, resulting in lower output of thrust. The increase in runway length is not linear with temperature. The rate of increase at high temperatures is greater than at lower temperatures. The increase can be specified in terms of the percentage of runway length at 59°F, which is the standard temperature at sea level. For estimating purposes, the approximate variations of runway length with temperature which apply to turbine-powered transport between 59 and 90°F can be used. In this temperature range, the average increase in runway length varies from about 0.42 to 0.65 percent per degree Fahrenheit above the runway requirements at 59°F. Therefore, at 85°F the runway length would be increased by an average range of about 11 to 18 percent over the length required at 59°F.

Surface Wind

The greater the headwind, the shorter the runway length; and also the greater the tailwind, the longer the runway. For computing takeoff weight federal regulations allow operators to use only one-half of the reported headwind. If there is a tailwind, one and one-half times the reported tailwind is used for the computation of takeoff weight, up to a maximum allowable tailwind of 10 kn. The effect of wind varies, depending in part on temperature and aircraft weight. Nevertheless, approximations are useful for planning. A 5-kn headwind reduces takeoff length by about 3 percent, whereas a 5-kn tailwind increases this length by about 7 percent. For airport planning purposes it is desirable to use no wind, particularly if light winds occur at the airport site.

Runway Gradient

An uphill gradient requires more runway length than a level or downhill gradient, the specific amount depending on the elevation of the airport and temperature. Studies indicate that the relationship between uniform gradient and increase or decrease in runway length is nearly linear [41]. For turbine-powered aircraft this amounts to 7 to 10 percent for each percent of uniform gradient. Airport design criteria limit the gradient to a maximum of one and one-half percent. Information provided by aircraft manufacturers in flight manuals is based on uniform gradient, yet most runway profiles are not uniform. In the United States aircraft operators are allowed to substitute an average uniform gradient, which is a straight line joining the ends of the runway, as long as no intervening point along the actual path profile lies more than 5 ft above or below the average line. Fortunately most runways meet this requirement. For airport planning purposes only, the FAA uses an effective gradient. The effective gradient is defined as the difference in elevation between the highest and lowest points on the actual runway profile divided by the length of the runway. Studies indicate that within the degree of accuracy required for airport planning there is not very much difference between the use of the average uniform gradient and the effective gradient.

Altitude

All other things being equal, the higher the altitude of the airport, the longer the runway required. This increase is not linear, but varies with weight and temperature. At higher altitudes the rate of increase is higher than at lower altitudes. For planning purposes an increase from sea level of 7 percent per 1000 ft of altitude will suffice for most airport sites, except those that experience very hot temperatures or are located at high altitudes. Then the rate of increase can be as much as 10 percent. Manufacturer provided performance data are in terms of pressure altitude not geographic altitude. The former is described in a later section. Unless the airport site is very unusual, the two altitudes can be considered equal for the purpose of airport planning.

Condition of Runway Surface

Slush or standing water on the runway has an undesirable effect on aircraft operation. Slush is equivalent to wet snow. It has a slippery texture which makes braking extremely poor. Being a fluid, it is displaced by tires rolling through it, causing a significant retarding force, especially on takeoff. The retarding forces can get so large that the aircraft can no longer accelerate to takeoff speed. In the process slush is sprayed on the aircraft, which further increases the resisting forces on the vehicle and can cause damage to some parts. Considerable experimental work has been conducted by NASA and the FAA on the effect of standing water and slush. As a result of these tests, jet operations are limited to no more than 0.5 in of slush or water. Between 0.25 and 0.5 in depth, the takeoff weight must be reduced substantially to overcome the retarding force of water or slush. It is therefore important to provide adequate drainage on the surface of the runway for the removal of water and a means of rapidly removing slush.

Both water and slush result in a very poor coefficient of braking friction. When tires ride on the surface of the water or slush, the phenomenon is known as hydroplaning. When the tires hydroplane, the coefficient of friction is on the order of wet ice and the steering ability is completely lost. Hydroplaning is primarily a function of tire inflation pressure and to some extent of the condition and type of grooves in the tires. According to tests made by NASA, the approximate speed at which hydroplaning develops may be determined by the formula [2, 34]

$$V_p = 10\sqrt{P} \tag{3-9}$$

where V_p = speed where hydroplaning develops, mi/h
 P = tire inflation pressure, lb/in^2

The range of inflation pressures for commercial jet transports varies from 120 to over 200 lb/in^2. Therefore the hydroplaning speeds would range from 110 to 140 mi/h or more. The landing speeds are in the same range. Therefore hydroplaning can be a hazard to jet operations. Hydroplaning can develop when the depth of water or slush is on the order of 0.2 in or less, the exact depth depending on tire tread design, condition of the tires, and the texture of the pavement surface. Smooth tread operating on a smooth pavement surface requires the least depth of fluid for hydroplaning.

To reduce the hazard of hydroplaning and to improve the coefficient of braking friction, runway pavements have been grooved in a transverse direction. The grooves form reservoirs for the water on the surface. The FAA is conducting extensive research to establish standards for groove dimensions and shape [40]. In the past the grooves were normally 0.25 in deep and spaced 1 in apart [30].

Computation of Runway Length for a Specific Route

The runway length at a particular airport site is based upon the critical aircraft flying the longest nonstop flight segment regularly serviced at the airport. To compute the runway length, the following steps are required:

1. The operating empty weight of the critical aircraft is obtained.
2. The payload for the trip is ascertained.
3. The required fuel reserve is found.
4. The landing weight at the destination is then computed as the sum of

the operating empty weight, the payload, and reserve fuel. This weight should not exceed the maximum structural landing weight of the aircraft.

5. The trip fuel requirements for climb, cruise, and descent are computed.

6. The takeoff weight of the aircraft is obtained by adding the trip fuel requirements to the landing weight. This should not exceed the maximum structural takeoff weight of the aircraft.

7. A determination of the temperature, surface wind, runway gradient, and altitude at origination airport is made.

8. Knowing the takeoff weight of the aircraft with the origination airport temperature, surface wind, runway gradient, and elevation, the approved flight manual for the specific aircraft is used to determine the runway length requirements.

The effect of trip length on the runway length for some typical jet aircraft is shown in Fig. 3-20.

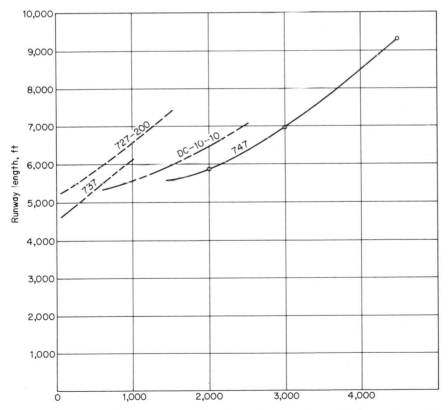

Fig. 3-20 Trip length versus runway length requirements for typical transport aircraft.

Advisory Circular Techniques for Runway Requirements

The FAA has published procedures for determining runway length requirements for airport planning purposes in Advisory Circular 150/5325–4 [36]. In this publication there are two types of procedures available, one based upon aircraft performance curves and the other based upon performance charts. The design runway length is found for the critical aircraft, defined as the aircraft which flies the greatest nonstop route segment from the airport at least 250 times a year and requires the longest runway system. To use these procedures, the following data are necessary:

1. The designation of critical aircraft

2. The longest nonstop route distance flown by the critical aircraft

3. The takeoff and landing weights of the critical aircraft at the airport

4. The airport elevation

5. The mean daily maximum temperature for the hottest month at the airport

6. The effective gradient of the runway, defined as the maximum centerline elevation difference divided by the runway length

The chart procedure, which is discussed here, assumes that the effective runway gradient is zero. To account for actual conditions, the length found from the charts is increased by 10 percent for each percent of effective gradient for turbine-powered aircraft. The charts are based upon wet runway conditions, and no adjustment is made for dry conditions. The utilization of the chart procedure is illustrated in Example Problem 3–2.

Example Problem 3–2

Determine the required runway length at an airport for a Lockheed L–1011–385–1 aircraft equipped with RB211–22B engines. There are to be no weight restrictions in landing or takeoff. The FAA Advisory Circular 150/5325–4 Appendix 6 procedures are to be used under the following conditions:

Flap Settings:
    Takeoff   22°
    Landing   42°

Airport environs:
    Elevation   6300 ft above mean sea level (MSL)
    Temperature   93.5°F
    Runway effective gradient   0.75 percent
    Wet runways

Solution:

Reference to the Advisory Circular yields the takeoff and landing charts for this aircraft shown in Tables 3-15, 3-16.

TABLE 3-15 **Aircraft Landing Performance for Lockheed TriStar L1011-385-1 with Rolls-Royce RB.211-22B Engine at 42° Flap Setting**

	Maximum Allowable Landing Weight, 1000 lb								
Temper-	Airport Elevation, ft								
ature, °F	0	1000	2000	3000	4000	5000	6000	7000	8000
50	358.0	358.0	358.0	358.0	358.0	358.0	358.0	358.0	358.0
55	358.0	358.0	358.0	358.0	358.0	358.0	358.0	358.0	358.0
60	358.0	358.0	358.0	358.0	358.0	358.0	358.0	358.0	358.0
65	358.0	358.0	358.0	358.0	358.0	358.0	358.0	358.0	358.0
70	358.0	358.0	358.0	358.0	358.0	358.0	358.0	358.0	358.0
75	358.0	358.0	358.0	358.0	358.0	358.0	358.0	358.0	357.4
80	358.0	358.0	358.0	358.0	358.0	358.0	358.0	358.0	349.5
85	358.0	358.0	358.0	358.0	358.0	358.0	358.0	355.3	341.6
90	358.0	358.0	358.0	358.0	358.0	358.0	358.0	347.1	333.8
95	358.0	358.0	358.0	358.0	358.0	358.0	352.8	339.0	326.0
100	358.0	358.0	358.0	358.0	358.0	358.0	345.0	331.2	318.4
105	358.0	358.0	358.0	358.0	358.0	351.2	336.8	323.4	310.8
110	358.0	358.0	358.0	358.0	355.6	341.8	328.7	315.9	303.4

	Runway Length, 1000 ft								
Weight,	Airport Elevation, ft								
1000 lb	0	1000	2000	3000	4000	5000	6000	7000	8000
260	5.20	5.31	5.44	5.57	5.70	5.84	5.98	6.12	6.25
270	5.37	5.48	5.60	5.73	5.86	6.00	6.15	6.30	6.44
280	5.52	5.63	5.76	5.89	6.03	6.17	6.32	6.47	6.63
290	5.67	5.79	5.91	6.05	6.19	6.34	6.49	6.65	6.81
300	5.81	5.93	6.07	6.21	6.35	6.50	6.66	6.82	6.99
310	5.94	6.08	6.22	6.36	6.51	6.67	6.83	6.99	7.17
320	6.07	6.22	6.37	6.52	6.67	6.83	6.99	7.16	7.34
330	6.20	6.35	6.51	6.66	6.82	6.98	7.15	7.32	7.50
340	6.33	6.49	6.65	6.81	6.97	7.13	7.30	7.48	7.66
350	6.45	6.62	6.78	6.94	7.10	7.27	7.44	7.62	7.82
360	6.58	6.75	6.90	7.06	7.23	7.40	7.57	7.77	7.97

Airplane Characteristics

Typical operating empty weight plus reserve fuel:	270,300 lb
Average fuel consumption	34 lb/mi
Typical maximum passenger load at 200 lb/passenger:	51,200 lb
Maximum structural payload:	86,183 lb

SOURCE: Federal Aviation Administration [36].

TABLE 3-16   **Aircraft Takeoff Performance for Lockheed TriStar L1011-385-1 with Rolls-Royce RB.211-22B Engines at 22° Flap Setting**

Maximum Allowable Takeoff Weight, 1000 lb									
Temper-	Airport Elevation, ft								
ature, °F	0	1000	2000	3000	4000	5000	6000	7000	8000
50	430.0	428.0	418.0	407.9	397.8	387.7	377.7	367.9	358.3
55	430.0	428.0	418.0	407.9	397.8	387.7	377.7	367.9	358.3
60	430.0	428.0	418.0	407.9	397.8	387.7	377.7	366.7	353.0
65	430.0	428.0	418.0	407.9	397.8	387.7	374.6	360.5	346.8
70	430.0	428.0	418.0	407.9	397.4	382.5	368.0	353.9	340.3
75	430.0	428.0	418.0	405.2	389.9	375.2	360.9	347.0	333.6
80	430.0	428.5	412.5	397.0	382.0	367.5	353.5	339.9	326.7
85	430.0	419.5	403.8	388.5	373.8	359.6	345.8	332.6	319.8
90	426.5	410.4	394.9	379.9	365.4	351.5	338.1	325.2	312.8
95	417.1	401.2	385.9	371.2	357.0	343.4	330.4	317.8	305.7
100	407.7	392.1	377.0	362.6	348.8	335.5	322.8	310.5	298.8
105	398.5	383.1	368.3	354.2	340.7	327.8	315.3	303.4	291.8
110	389.6	374.4	360.0	346.2	333.1	320.4	308.3	296.5	285.1

Reference Factor R									
Temper-	Airport Elevation, ft								
ature, °F	0	1000	2000	3000	4000	5000	6000	7000	8000
50	50.7	53.7	57.0	60.6	64.5	68.8	73.6	78.7	84.4
55	51.0	54.1	57.5	61.2	65.1	69.5	74.2	79.4	85.0
60	51.5	54.6	58.0	61.7	65.7	70.1	74.9	80.2	87.4
65	51.9	55.0	58.4	62.1	66.2	70.7	76.2	82.9	90.4
70	52.2	55.4	58.8	62.6	66.7	72.4	78.8	85.8	93.6
75	52.6	55.8	59.2	63.6	69.0	74.9	81.6	88.9	96.9
80	53.0	56.2	60.8	65.8	71.4	77.6	84.5	92.1	100.5
85	54.1	58.3	62.9	68.2	74.0	80.5	87.7	95.6	104.3
90	56.0	60.3	65.2	70.7	76.8	83.5	91.0	99.2	108.3
95	57.9	62.5	67.7	73.4	79.7	86.8	94.5	103.1	112.5
100	60.0	64.9	70.2	76.2	82.8	90.2	98.2	107.2	117.0
105	62.2	67.3	73.0	79.2	86.1	93.7	102.2	111.5	121.7
110	64.5	69.9	75.9	82.4	89.6	97.5	106.3	116.0	126.7

Runway Length, 1000 ft									
Weight,	Reference Factor R								
1000 lb	50	60	70	80	90	100	110	120	130
260	4.50	4.50	4.50	4.50	4.85	5.31	5.78	6.24	6.71
270	4.50	4.50	4.50	4.70	5.21	5.73	6.24	6.75	7.27
280	4.50	4.50	4.50	5.04	5.60	6.17	6.73	7.30	7.87
290	4.50	4.50	4.78	5.40	6.01	6.63	7.25	7.88	8.50
300	4.50	4.50	5.10	5.78	6.45	7.13	7.81	8.49	9.17
310	4.50	4.71	5.45	6.18	6.92	7.65	8.39	9.13	9.87

TABLE 3-16 **(Continued)**

Weight, 1000 lb	Runway Length, 1000 ft								
	Reference Factor R								
	50	60	70	80	90	100	110	120	130
320	4.50	5.01	5.81	6.60	7.40	8.20	9.00	9.80	10.60
330	4.50	5.32	6.19	7.05	7.91	8.78	9.64	10.51	11.37
340	4.72	5.65	6.59	7.52	8.45	9.38	10.31	11.24	12.17
350	5.00	6.00	7.00	8.01	9.01	10.01	11.01	12.01	13.00
360	5.29	6.36	7.44	8.52	9.59	10.66	11.73	12.80	13.86
370	5.59	6.74	7.89	9.05	10.20	11.34	12.49	13.62	14.75
380	5.90	7.13	8.37	9.60	10.82	12.05	13.27	14.48	
390	6.23	7.55	8.36	10.17	11.48	12.78	14.07		
400	6.57	7.97	9.37	10.76	12.15	13.53	14.90		
410	6.93	8.41	9.89	11.37	12.84	14.31			
420	7.30	8.87	10.44	12.00	13.56				
430	7.68	9.34	11.00	12.66	14.30				

SOURCE: Federal Aviation Administration [36].

For the landing conditions, the top portion of Table 3-15 allows for the interpolation of the maximum allowable landing weight as follows:

Temperature, °F	MALW, 1000 lb		
	Elevation, ft		
	6000	6300	7000
90	358.0		347.1
93.5	354.36	350.48	341.43
95	352.8		339.0

Therefore the maximum allowable landing weight of this aircraft at this airport is found to be 350,480 lb.

The required landing runway length is found by interpolating from the bottom portion of the same exhibit, yielding:

MALW, 1000 lb	Runway length, 1000 ft		
	Elevation, ft		
	6000	6300	7000
350	7.44		7.62
350.5	7.446	7.501	7.628
360	7.57		7.77

Therefore the landing runway length under wet conditions is 7501 ft, which is rounded up to 7525 ft, the next 25 ft. increment.

It should be noted that the chart procedure outlined here yields results for wet and slippery runways and does not contain adjustments for the case where dry runways may be the design condition.

The required takeoff runway length is determined from Table 3-16. From the top table the maximum allowable takeoff weight is found by interpolation as shown:

	MATOW, 1000 lb		
		Elevation, ft	
Temperature, °F	6000	6300	7000
90	338.1		325.2
93.5	332.71	328.90	320.02
95	330.4		317.8

Therefore the maximum allowable takeoff weight at this airport is 328,900 lb. Using the middle table in the exhibit yields the R factor as follows:

	Reference factor R		
		Elevation, ft	
Temperature, °F	6000	6300	7000
90	91.0		99.2
93.5	93.45	95.99	101.93
95	94.5		103.1

This R factor is then used with the maximum allowable takeoff weight in the bottom table of the exhibit to yield the required takeoff runway length:

	Runway length, 1000 ft		
		Reference factor R	
MATOW, 1000 lb	90	95.99	100
320	7.40		8.20
328.9	7.854	8.370	8.716
330	7.91		8.78

The required takeoff runway length is 8370 ft at 0 percent gradient. Correction for gradient of 0.75 percent yields

$$\text{Takeoff runway} = 8370 \, (1 + 0.075) = 8998 \text{ ft}$$

This is rounded to 9000 ft.

In summary, the required landing runway length is 7525 ft and the required takeoff runway length is 9000 ft.

Runway Length Requirements for General Aviation Aircraft

The discussion thus far has been devoted to the primary factors affecting the runway length for transport-category aircraft. The same factors also affect the runway length required for general aviation aircraft. General aviation aircraft are certified under FAR Part 23 [7] in three categories, namely, normal, utility, and acrobatic. The normal category includes aircraft for use in nonacrobatic, nonscheduled passenger and cargo operations. This is the category under which most general aviation aircraft are certified. The utility category involves the same uses as the normal category, but certain acrobatic maneuvers are permitted. Many general aviation aircraft are certified for both normal and utility operations, allowing them to be used for flight instruction. The maximum allowable gross weight, however, is less in the utility than in the normal category. The acrobatic category has no maneuver restrictions. It is a relatively rare category since stunt flying is one of the minor applications of the aircraft. In general, the regulations governing aircraft of less than 6000 lb differ from those for aircraft heavier than 6000 lb. For general aviation aircraft weighing more than 6000 lb the distance to takeoff and climb over a 50-ft obstacle must be determined. From this requirement the takeoff distance can be interpreted as the distance from start of takeoff roll to the attainment of a 50-ft height above the surface of the ground. For landing, the horizontal distance required to bring the aircraft to a stop from a height of 50 ft above the surface must be demonstrated. There is no such requirement for aircraft of less than 6000 lb. Most manufacturers, however, provide the distances for a 50-ft height, and it is these distances that are listed in Table 3-2 as takeoff distance.

AIRCRAFT CERTIFICATION FOR NOISE

The growing concern over jet aircraft noise by the public led to the passage of legislation by Congress which required appropriate federal agencies to take steps "to provide for the control and abatement of aircraft noise" (Public Law 90-411). This resulted in the implementation of FAR Part 36 [31], which prescribes noise standards for subsonic transport-category aircraft and for subsonic jet-powered aircraft regardless of category. The effective date of the regulation was December 1, 1969. Originally the regulation applied only to aircraft with engines having a bypass ratio of 2 or more. This means that all aircraft prior to the introduction of the 747 are exempt from this regulation. Most of these aircraft have noise levels higher than prescribed in Part 36.

In establishing FAR Part 36, the FAA made it clear that the prescribed noise levels would be further reduced as the reductions became technologically practical and economically reasonable. A noise floor of 80 EPNdB was proposed for some future date "as an objective to aim for, and to achieve where economically reasonable."

In 1976, FAR Part 36 was changed to require that all subsonic aircraft with a maximum takeoff weight in excess of 75,000 lb either be retired from the fleet or retrofitted to meet the noise standard levels. A schedule requiring the phasing-in, or staging, of compliance with these standards by January 1, 1985 was adopted.

The measuring points for noise certification are as follows:

1. For takeoff, 3.5 nmi from the start of takeoff roll on the extended centerline of the runway

2. For approach, 1 nmi from the threshold on the extended centerline of the runway

3. For sideline, 0.25 nmi parallel to the runway centerline

The prescribed noise levels to be attained by 1985 are as follows:

1. For approach, a maximum of 105 EPNdB for all aircraft. This value is reduced by 2 EPNdB for each halving of the reference maximum takeoff weight of 850,000 lb down to 98 EPNdB.

2. For sideline, a maximum of 103 EPNdB for all aircraft. This value is reduced for 2- and 3-engine aircraft by 2 EPNdB for each halving of the reference maximum takeoff weight of 882,000 lb down to 96 EPNdB. For 4-engine aircraft a reduction of 2 EPNdB for each halving of the reference maximum takeoff weight of 850,000 lb down to 96 EPNdb.

3. For takeoff, a maximum of 101 EPNdB for 2-engine, 104 EPNdB for 3-engine, and 106 EPNdB for 4-engine aircraft. These values are reduced by 4 EPNdB for each halving of the reference maximum takeoff weight of 850,000 lb down to 89 EPNdB for 2-engine and 90 EPNdB for 3- or 4-engine aircraft.

4. The noise levels prescribed above may be exceeded at one or two of the measuring points if the sum of the excedents is not greater than 3 EPNdB or, at one point, 2 EPNdB. The excedents must be completely offset by reductions at other required measuring points.

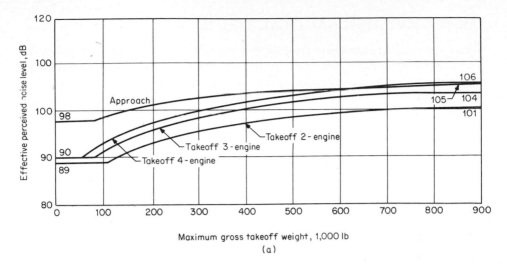

(a)

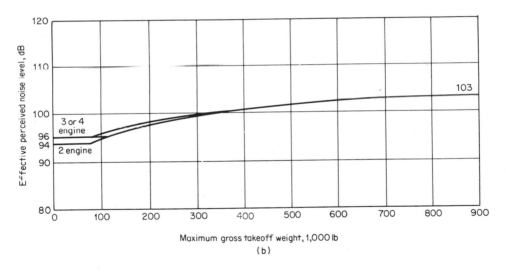

(b)

Fig. 3-21 Aircraft noise certification requirements for takeoff and approach noise level. (*a*) Takeoff and approach noise. (*b*) Sideline noise.

The regulations are illustrated in graphical form in Fig. 3-21. The atmospheric conditions for which the noise levels are prescribed are sea level, 77°F temperature, 70 percent relative humidity, and zero wind on the runway [26].

IMPORTANT AERONAUTICAL TERMS

When dealing with matters concerning aircraft operations as they relate to the design of airports, planners will encounter a number of aeronautical terms with which they should be familiar. These are standard atmosphere, pressure altitude, aircraft speed, and crosswind, track, and heading.

Standard Atmosphere

The actual characteristics of the atmosphere vary from day to day and from place to place, but for the convenience for comparing the performance of aircraft, a standard atmosphere has been adopted by agreement. A *standard atmosphere* represents the average conditions found in the actual atmosphere in a particular geographic region. However, it must be kept in mind that it is a fictitious atmosphere of assumed composition. Several different standard atmospheres are in use, but the one most commonly used is the one proposed by ICAO. In the standard atmosphere it is assumed that from sea level to an altitude of about 36,000 ft the temperature decreases linearly. Above 36,000 to about 65,000 ft, the temperature remains constant; and above 65,000 ft, the temperature rises. Many conventional jet aircraft fly as high as 41,000 ft. The supersonic transports fly at altitudes on the order of 60,000 ft or more. The layer of the earth's atmosphere from sea level to about 36,000 ft is known as the *troposphere.* Immediately above this layer is the *stratosphere.* In the troposphere the standard atmosphere is defined as follows:

1. The temperature at sea level is 59°F.

2. The pressure at sea level is 29.92126 inHg.

3. The temperature gradient from sea level to the altitude at which the temperature becomes −69.7°F is 0.003566°F/ft, and zero above.

The following relation establishes the standard pressure in the troposphere up to a temperature of −69.7°F:

$$\frac{P_0}{P} = \left(\frac{T_0}{T}\right)^{5.2561} \tag{3-10}$$

where P_0 = standard pressure at sea level, 29.92 in
P = standard pressure at a specified altitude
T_0 = standard temperature at sea level, 59°F
T = standard temperature at a specified altitude

In Eq. (3-10) the temperature must be expressed in *absolute* or *Rankine* units (°R). Absolute zero is equal to 459.7°R. Therefore 0°F would be equal to −459.7°R, and 59°F would be equal to 518.7°R.

Using these criteria, the standard temperature at an altitude of 5000 ft is 41.2°F, and the standard pressure is 24.90 inHg. It is common to refer to *standard conditions* or *standard day*. A standard condition is one in which the actual temperature and pressure correspond to the standard tempera- ture and pressure at a particular altitude. When reference is made to the temperature being *above standard*, it means that the temperature is higher than the standard temperature. Table 3-17 contains a partial listing of standard temperatures and pressures.

Pressure Altitude

Aircraft takeoff performance data are related to pressure altitude. The reason for this is that aircraft performance is dependent on the density of the air. When the atmospheric pressure drops, the air becomes less dense, requiring a longer run on the ground to obtain the same amount of lift as on a day when the pressure is high. Thus a reduction in atmospheric pressure at an airport has the same effect on its air density as if the airport had been

TABLE 3-17 **The Standard Atmosphere***

Altitude, ft	Temperature, °F	Pressure, in Hg	Speed of sound, kn
0	59	29.92	661.2
1,000	55.4	28.86	658.9
2,000	51.9	27.82	656.6
3,000	48.3	26.82	654.3
4,000	44.7	25.84	652.0
5,000	41.2	24.90	649.7
6,000	37.6	23.98	647.7
7,000	34.0	23.09	645.1
8,000	30.5	22.23	642.7
9,000	26.9	21.39	640.4
10,000	23.3	20.58	638.0
15,000	5.5	16.89	626.2
20,000	−12.2	13.76	614.1
30,000	−47.8	8.90	589.2
35,000	−65.6	7.06	576.3
37,000	−69.7	6.41	573.3
40,000	−69.7	55.55	573.3
50,000	−69.7	3.44	573.3
60,000	−69.7	2.13	573.3
65,000	−69.7	1.68	573.3
70,000	−67.4	1.32	575.0
80,000	−62.0	0.82	579.0

* Adopted in 1962.

moved to a higher elevation. *Pressure altitude* is defined as the altitude corresponding to the pressure of the standard atmosphere. Thus if the atmospheric pressure is 29.92 inHg, the pressure altitude is zero. If the pressure drops to 28.86 inHg, the pressure altitude is 1000 ft. This can be obtained from the formula relating pressure and temperature. If this lower pressure occurred at a sea-level airport, the geographic altitude would be zero, but the pressure altitude would be 1000 ft. For airport planning purposes, it is satisfactory to assume that the geographic and pressure altitudes are equal, unless the barometric pressures at a particular site are unusually low a great deal of the time.

Aircraft Speed

Reference is made to aircraft speed in several ways. It is important to understand the basic difference between *groundspeed* and *airspeed*. The groundspeed is the speed of the aircraft relative to the ground. True airspeed is the speed of an aircraft relative to the medium in which it is traveling. Thus, if an aircraft is flying at a groundspeed of 500 kn in air where the wind is blowing in the opposite direction at a speed of 100 kn, the true airspeed is 600 kn. Likewise, if the wind were blowing in the same direction and the aircraft maintained a groundspeed of 500 kn, the true airspeed would be 400 kn. Thus, the airspeed is the speed that the aircraft wing (airfoil) encounters.

In examining aircraft performance data, the reader will find that reference is made to two airspeeds, namely, *true airspeed* (TAS) and *indicated airspeed* (IAS). The pilot obtains the speed from an airspeed indicator. This indicator works by comparing the dynamic air pressure due to the forward motion of the aircraft with the static atmospheric pressure. As the forward speed is increased, so is the dynamic pressure. The airspeed indicator works on the principle of the pitot tube. From physics we know that the dynamic pressure is proportional both to the square of the speed and to the density of the air. The variation with the square of the speed is taken care of by the mechanism of the airspeed indicator, but not the variation in density. The indicator is sensitive to the product of the density of the air and the square of the velocity. At high altitudes the density becomes smaller; thus the indicated airspeed is less than the true airspeed.

If the true airspeed is required, it can be found with the aid of tables. As a very rough guide, one can add 2 percent to the indicated speed for each 1000 ft above sea level to obtain true airspeed.

The indicated airspeed is of more importance to the pilot than is the true airspeed. The concern is with the generation of lift, specifically the stall speed, which is dependent on speed and air density. At high altitudes an aircraft will stall at a higher speed than it does at sea level. But at higher altitudes the airspeed indicator is indicating speeds lower than true speeds; consequently this is on the safe side and no corrections are necessary. Thus, an aircraft with a stalling speed of 90 kn will stall at the same indicated airspeed, regardless of altitude. This is why aircraft manufacturers always report stalling speeds in terms of indicated airspeed rather than true airspeed.

With the introduction of jet transports and high-speed military aircraft, the reference datum for speed is often the speed of sound. The speed of sound is defined as *Mach 1* (after Ernst Mach, Austrian scientist). Thus Mach 3 means three times the speed of sound. Most of our current jet transports are *subsonic* (slower than the speed of sound) in the neighborhood of 0.8 to 0.9 Mach. Many military aircraft are *supersonic* (faster than the speed of sound). Again the reader is reminded that when the maximum speed of an aircraft is quoted as 0.9 Mach, this is in terms of true airspeed and not groundspeed. Such an aircraft can conceivably be traveling at a groundspeed higher than the speed of sound, depending on the magnitude of the tail wind.

The speed of sound is not a fixed speed; it depends on temperature and not on atmospheric pressure. As the temperature decreases, so does the speed of sound. The speed of sound at 32°F (0°C) is 1090 ft/s (742 mi/h); at −13°F (−25°C) it is 707 mi/h; and at 86°F (30°C) it is 785 mi/h. In fact, the speed of sound varies 2 ft/s for every change in temperature of 1°C above or below the speed at 0°C. The speed of sound at the altitudes at which jets normally fly is less than 700 mi/h, but at altitudes at which small aircraft normally fly (20,000 ft or less) it is greater than 700 mi/h. The speed of sound may be computed from the formula:

$$V_{sm} = 33.4\sqrt{T} \tag{3-11}$$
$$V_{sf} = 49.04\sqrt{T} \tag{3-12}$$

where V_{sm} = speed of sound at some temperature, in mi/h
   V_{sf} = speed of sound at some temperature, in ft/s
   T = temperature, in °R

For convenience in navigation, aircraft distances and speeds are measured in nautical miles and knots, just like measurements on the high seas. A nautical mile (6080 ft) is practically equal to 1 min of arc of the earth's circumference. A knot is defined as 1 nmi/h. A nautical mile is approximately 1.15 land miles.

Crosswind Track Heading

As an aircraft approaches a runway, its *heading* (direction in which the nose is pointing) is dependent on the strength of the wind blowing across the path of the aircraft (*crosswind*). The approach flight path to the runway is an extension of the centerline of the runway, and it is referred to as the *track*. An aircraft must fly along the track to safely reach the runway. The relation between track, heading, and crosswind is illustrated in Fig. 3-22. In order not to be blown laterally off the track by the wind, the aircraft must fly at an angle x from the track. The magnitude of this angle can be obtained from the following relation:

$$\sin x = \frac{V_c}{V_h} \tag{3-13}$$

where V_h = true airspeed, in mi/h or kn
V_c = crosswind, in mi/h or kn

The crosswind V_c is defined as the component of the wind that is at a right angle to the track. The angle x is referred to as the *crab angle*. It will be noted that the magnitude of the angle is directly proportional to the speed of the wind and indirectly proportional to the speed of the aircraft. This means that when the aircraft is moving slowly, as it does when it approaches a runway, and there is a strong crosswind, the angle x will be large. The term V_t is the true airspeed along the track and is equal to $V_h \cos x$. To obtain the groundspeed along the track, the component of the wind along the track must be subtracted from V_t. In the figure the groundspeed along the track is equal to V_t minus the wind along the track.

Assume that an aircraft was approaching a runway at a speed of 135 kn and the crosswind was 25 kn. The crab angle x would be 10°10′. In order to land properly, the pilot must reduce the crab angle to zero just prior to touchdown. If the crab angle is reduced too early, the aircraft might be blown laterally off the runway. For this reason it is desirable to orient runways so as to minimize crosswinds. Large transport aircraft are capable of landing on a dry runway with crosswinds as high as 30 kn, but this is certainly undesirable from the pilot's standpoint, particularly if the runway is wet. For the orientation of runways, the following criterion is used. Runways should be positioned so that 95 percent of the time the crosswind is not greater than 13 kn (15 mi/h). Even this value is too large for small light aircraft [44].

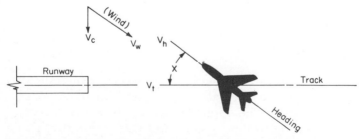

Fig. 3-22 Definition of track, heading, and crab angle for an aircraft.

REFERENCES

1. *Aerodrome Design Manual*, Part 1: *Runways*, International Civil Aviation Organization, Montreal, Que., Canada, Document 9157-AN/901, 1980.

2. *Aircraft Hydroplaning or Aquaplaning on Wet Runways*, Federal Aviation Administration, Washington, D.C., Advisory Circular AC 91-24, September 1969.

3. "Aircraft of the Future," W. E. Parsons and J. A. Stern, International Air Transportation Meeting, Society of Automotive Engineers, Warrendale, Pa., Paper 800743, May 1980.

4. *Aircraft Operating Cost and Performance Report*, Civil Aeronautics Board, Washington, D.C., annual.

5. "Aircraft Wake Turbulence Avoidance," W. A. McGowan, 12th Anglo-American Aeronautical Conference, National Aeronautics and Space Administration, Washington, D.C., Paper 72/6, July 1971.

6. *Air Taxi Operators and Commercial Operators of Small Aircraft*, Federal Aviation Regulations, Federal Aviation Administration, Washington, D.C., FAR Part 135, September 1977.

7. *Airworthiness Standards: Normal, Utility, and Acrobatic Category Airplanes*, Federal Aviation Regulations, Federal Aviation Administration, Washington, D.C., FAR Part 23, June 1974.

8. *Airworthiness Standards: Transport Category Airplanes*, Federal Aviation Regulations, Federal Aviation Administration, Washington, D.C., FAR Part 25, June 1974.

9. *Boeing 707 Airplane Characteristics—Airport Planning*, Boeing Commercial Airplane Company, Seattle, Wash., Document D6-58322, December 1968.

10. *Boeing 727 Airplane Characteristics—Airport Planning*, Boeing Commercial Airplane Company, Seattle, Wash., Document D6-58324-R2, June 1978.

11. *Boeing 737 Airplane Characteristics—Airport Planning*, Boeing Commercial Airplane Company, Seattle, Wash., Document D6-58325, July 1973.

12. *Boeing 747 Airplane Characteristics—Airport Planning*, Boeing Commercial Airplane Company, Seattle, Wash., Document D6-58326, Rev. D., April 1981.

13. *Boeing 757 Airplane Characteristics—Airport Planning*, Boeing Commercial Airplane Company, Seattle, Wash., Preliminary Information, Document D6-58327, Rev. A, March 1981.

14. *Boeing 767 Airplane Characteristics—Airport Planning*, Boeing Commercial Airplane Company, Seattle, Wash., Preliminary Information, Document D6-58328, Rev. B, July 1981.

15. *Certification and Operations—Domestic, Flag, and Supplemental Air Carriers and Commercial Operators of Large Aircraft*, Federal Aviation Regulations, Federal Aviation Administration, Washington, D.C., FAR Part 121, April 1974.

16. *Certification and Operations of Scheduled Air Carriers with Helicopters*, Federal Aviation Regulations, Federal Aviation Administration, Washington, D.C., FAR Part 127, April 1974.

17. *Commercial Air Transportation in the Next Three Decades*, H. W. Withington, Boeing Commercial Airplane Company, Seattle, Wash., 1980.

18. *Commercial Air Transportation, 1980's and Beyond*, H. W. Withington, Boeing Commercial Airplane Company, Seattle, Wash., November 1980.

19. "CTOL Concepts and Technology Development," D. William Conner, *Astronautics and Aeronautics*, American Institute of Aeronautics and Astronautics, July-August 1978.

20. *CTOL Transport Aircraft Characteristics, Trends, and Growth Projections*, Aerospace Industries Association of America, Inc., Washington, D.C., 1979.

21. *DC-8 Airplane Characteristics, Airport Planning*, Douglas Aircraft Company, McDonnell-Douglas Corporation, Long Beach, Calif., Report DAC-67492, March 1969.

22. *DC-9 Airplane Characteristics, Airport Planning*, Douglas Aircraft Company, McDonnell-Douglas Corporation, Long Beach, Calif., Report DAC-67264, September 1978.

23. *DC-10 Airplane Characteristics, Airport Planning*, Douglas Aircraft Company, McDonnell-Douglas Corporation, Long Beach, Calif., Report DAC-67803A, January 1979.

24. *Dimensions of Airline Growth*, Boeing Commercial Airplane Company, Seattle, Wash., March 1980.

25. *Energy and Transportation Systems*, California Department of Transportation, Sacramento, Calif., Final Report, December 1981.

26. *International Standards and Recommended Practices, Aircraft Noise, Annex 16*, International Civil Aviation Organization, Montreal, Que., Canada, 1978.

27. *Jane's All the World's Aircraft*, Franklin Watts, Inc., New York, Annual.

28. "Jet Transport Characteristics Related to Airports," R. Horonjeff and G. Ahlborn, *Journal of the Aero-Space Transport Division*, vol. 91, AT1, American Society of Civil Engineers, New York, April 1965.

29. *L1011 Airplane Characteristics, Airport Planning*, Lockheed California Company, Burbank, Calif., Document CER-12013.

30. *Method for the Design, Construction and Maintenance of Skid Resistant Airport Pavement Surfaces*, Federal Aviation Administration, Washington, D.C., Advisory Circular AC 150/5320-12, June 1975.

31. *Noise Standards: Aircraft Type and Airworthiness Certification*, Federal Aviation Regulations, Federal Aviation Administration, Washington, D.C., FAR Part 36, August 1974.

32. *Outlook for Commercial Aircraft 1980–1994*, Douglas Aircraft Company, McDonnell-Douglas Corporation, Long Beach, Calif., June 1980.

33. *Pavement Grooving and Traction Studies*, Proceedings of Conference at Langley Research Center, National Aeronautics and Space Administration, Langley Field, Va., NASA SP-5073, November 1968.

34. "Pneumatic Tire Hydroplaning and Some Effects on Vehicle Performance," W. B. Horne and U. T. Joyner, Society of Automotive Engineers, New York, Paper 97UC, 1965.

35. "Runway Grooving for Increasing Traction—The Current Program and an Assessment of Available Result," W. B. Horne and G. W. Brooks, Paper at the 20th Annual International Air Safety Seminar, Williamsburg, Va., December 1967.

36. *Runway Length Requirements for Airport Design.*, Federal Aviation Administration, Washington, D.C., Advisory Circular AC 150/5325-4, July 1977.

37. *Short-Haul Transport Aircraft Future Trends*, Aerospace Industries Association of America, Inc., Washington, D.C., January 1978.

38. "Simulated Vortex Encounters by a Twin-Engine Commercial Transport Aircraft During Final Approach," E. C. Hastings, Jr., and G. L. Keyser, Jr., International Air Transportation Meeting, Society of Automotive Engineers, Warrendale, Pa., Paper 800775, May 1980.

39. "Technology Requirements and Readiness for Very Large Vehicles," D. William Conner, Presentation at the AIAA Very Large Vehicle Conference, American Institute of Aeronautics and Astronautics, Arlington, Va., April 1979.

40. *The Braking Performance of an Aircraft Tire on Grooved Portland Cement Concrete Surfaces*, S. K. Agrawal and H. Diautolo, Federal Aviation Administration Technical Center, Federal Aviation Administration, Atlantic City, N.J., Report FAA-RD-80-78, January 1981.

41. *The Effect of Variable Runway Slopes on Takeoff Runway Length for Transport Aeroplanes*, International Civil Aviation Organization, Montreal, Que., Canada, ICAO Circular 91-AN/75, 1970.

42. "Trailing Vortex Hazard," W. A. McGowan, Society of Automotive Engineers, New York, Paper 680220, April 1968.

43. *Water, Slush, and Snow on the Runway*, Federal Aviation Administration, Washington, D.C., Advisory Circular AC 91-6, 1965.

44. "Wind Data Evaluation for Airport Capacity Analysis," Appendix A, *Airport Capacity Criteria Used in Preparing the National Airport Plan*, Federal Aviation Administration, Washington, D.C., Advisory Circular AC 150/5060-1A, July 1968.

Chapter 4

Air Traffic Control

INTRODUCTION

In order that the airport designer may be aware of the importance of air traffic control in airport planning, a very brief summary of what constitutes air traffic control, how it is managed and operated, and of the principal aids to air navigation is presented in this chapter. An appreciation of air traffic control and its problems will focus attention on the fact that any extensive reorientation of runways on existing airports or the construction of entirely new airports requires consultation with the people controlling traffic. This is particularly true in large metropolitan areas where several airports are present. Conflicts in air traffic control procedures can seriously affect the capacity of any single airport. The importance of the segregation of airspace in the vicinity of major airports is illustrated in Fig. 4-1, which shows the location of airports and the low-altitude airways in the Chicago area. In addition, the planning of airports must include provisions for facilities located at airports which support the air traffic control system.

HISTORY OF AIR TRAFFIC CONTROL

The first attempt to set up rules for air traffic control was made by the International Commission for Air Navigation (ICAN), which was under the direction of the League of Nations. The procedures, which the Commission promulgated in July of 1922, were adopted by 14 countries. Although the United States was not a member of the League of Nations and therefore did not officially adopt the rules, many of the procedures established by ICAN were used in the promulgation of air traffic procedures in this country.

The construction and operation of the airways system in this country prior to 1926 were controlled by the military and by the Post Office Department. The formal entry of the federal government into the regulation of air traffic came with the passage of the Air Commerce Act of 1926. This act directed the Bureau of Air Commerce to establish, maintain, and operate lighted civil airways. At the present time the FAA maintains and operates the airways system of the United States, with the exception of a small number of aids provided by private organizations and states at

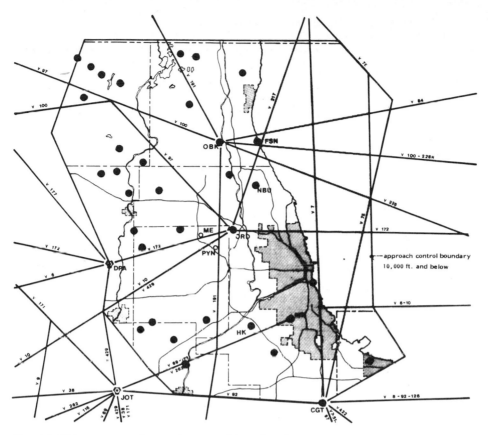

Fig. 4-1 Chicago terminal area airports and low-altitude airways in approach control airspace. (*Landrum and Brown, Inc. [15].*)

locations not involving a substantial volume of interstate commerce, and certain military facilities operated in conjunction with military airfields.

Today the FAA, in providing control and navigational assistance for the movement of air traffic on the airways, has established a pattern of integrated radio signal stations, radar, instrument landing systems, air route traffic control centers, terminal radar approach control facilities, airport traffic control towers, continuous weather reporting, and regulations for the use of these facilities.

AIR TRAFFIC CONTROL DEFINED

The federal government prescribes two basic types of flight rules for air traffic. These are known as *visual flight rules* (VFR) and *instrument flight rules* (IFR). In general, VFR means that the weather conditions are such that aircraft can maintain safe separation by visual means. On the other hand, IFR conditions prevail when the visibility or the ceiling falls below those prescribed under VFR. In IFR conditions safe separation between aircraft is the responsibility of air traffic control personnel, while in VFR conditions it is the responsibility of the pilot. Thus in VFR conditions there is essentially very little air traffic control, and aircraft are allowed to fly on a 'see and be seen' principle. Air traffic control monitors flights under VFR, and intervenes only when apparent conflicts between aircraft develop. This is passive control. Positive traffic control is exercised only when IFR applies. Essentially these rules require the assignment to specific routes and altitudes and the maintenance of minimum separations between aircraft.

As the speed of aircraft and the density of traffic in the airspace increased, there was more concern over the possibility of midair collisions. This concern was substantiated by the occurrence of several such collisions involving many lives. Accordingly, in certain parts of the airspace, IFR has been prescribed regardless of weather conditions. This is referred to as *positive control airspace*. Positive control airspace usually encompasses the airspace where high-speed jet aircraft operate. Therefore it can include the airspace in the vicinity of airports, called the *terminal control area* (TCA), as well as the space in which jets fly en route from one city to another. The limits of positive control airspace can be extended by the FAA as necessary to ensure safe operations. The trend is toward more positive control, especially in those locations where high-speed aircraft operate.

Conformity with IFR requires that, prior to departure, the pilot file with the air route traffic control center a flight plan which indicates the aircraft destination, the desired routes, and the desired altitudes. The flight plan is continuously updated as the flight progresses.

Airways

Aircraft flying from one point to another follow designated routes, which in the United States are referred to as *victor airways* and *jet routes*. These routes have evolved over time, as discussed below.

Colored Airways

The airways were initially given a color designation. The trunk lines east and west were green, the trunk lines north and south were amber, secondary lines east and west were red, and secondary lines north and south were blue. Each of these colored airways was then given a number, such as green 3, red 4, and so on. The numbering for the airways began at the Canadian border and the Pacific Coast and then progressed to the south and east. These airways were then assigned altitude levels, which for green and red were at odd 1000-ft levels eastbound and at even 1000-ft levels westbound. On the amber and blue airways northbound, odd 1000-ft levels were assigned, and southbound even 1000-ft levels. These airways were delineated on the ground by low-frequency/medium-frequency (LF/MF) four-course radio ranges. The colored airways were phased out as aircraft became equipped to use the victor airways, which are described next.

Victor Airways

Following the development of the LF/MF four-course radio ranges, the routes now known as the *victor airways* were established. The victor airways are delineated on the ground by very-high-frequency omnirange equipment (VOR). Each VOR station has a discrete radio frequency, to which a pilot may tune and thus be able to maintain a course from one VOR to the next. The numbering system for these airways is even numbers east and west, odd numbers north and south. The advantages of the victor airways are that the VORs are relatively free of static, and it is thus much easier for a pilot to determine air position relative to a VOR station than with the LF/MF four-course radio range. Victor airways are designated on aeronautical charts as V-1, V-2, and so on. The airway includes the airspace within parallel lines 4 mi each side of the centerline of the airway. If two VORs delineating an airway are more than 120 mi apart, the airspace included in the airway is as described for jet routes.

Jet Routes

With the introduction of commercial jet aircraft in 1958, the altitudes at which aircraft flew increased significantly. At higher altitudes the number of ground stations (VORs) required to delineate a specific route is smaller than at lower altitudes because the signal is transmitted on a line of sight. Therefore there was no need to clutter the high-altitude routes with all the ground stations required for low-altitude flying. All the routes in the continental United States could be placed on one chart. Thus jet routes were established. Although in one sense these routes are airways, they are not referred to as such. Today both victor airways and jet routes exist. Jet routes are delineated by the same aids to navigation on the ground (VORs) as are victor airways, but less stations are used. Victor airways extend from 1200 ft above the terrain to, but not including, 18,000 ft MSL. Jet routes extend from 18,000 to 45,000 ft MSL. Above 45,000 ft there are no designated routes, and aircraft are handled on an individual basis. The numbering system for the jet routes is the same as for the victor airways. Jet routes are designated on aeronautical charts as J-1, J-2, and so on.

Since the VORs delineating a jet route are often more than 120 mi apart, the jet route includes the airspace as indicated in Fig. 4-2 for the case of two VORs 260 nmi apart.

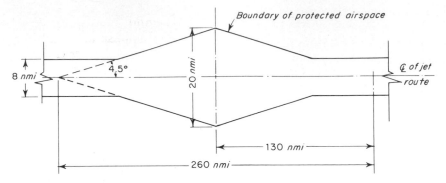

Fig. 4-2 Delineation of a jet route airway.

Area Navigation

For many years all aircraft were required to fly on designated routes, airways, or jet routes. That is, all aircraft had to fly from one VOR to the next, since the VORs delineate the airways and jet routes. This required the funneling of all traffic on designated routes, which resulted in congestion on certain routes. Also the designated routes are often not the shortest distance between two points, resulting in additional fuel consumption, flight time, and cost. Furthermore, if the designated route penetrates into an area of thunderstorms, aircraft have to be vectored around the storm by controllers on the ground. This imposes an extra workload on the controllers.

Area navigation, referred to as RNAV, provides a more flexible routing capability and in so doing allows for better utilization of the airspace. The greater utilization reduces delays in the airspace and results in more economical operation of the aircraft. For example, routes parallel to the designated routes from one VOR to another can be established without requiring additional aids to navigation on the ground. Another example is the establishment of a more direct route from one point to another, resulting in a shorter trip. Routing around a thunderstorm without continuous radar guidance from the ground is another example. RNAV in the terminal areas will provide for more routes to and from airports.

RNAV is accomplished by the installation of special computers in the aircraft. These computers are tuned to VOR stations. Each station provides information on the distance of the aircraft to the station and its azimuth relative to the station. First a route must be established relative to selected VOR stations from which information is fed to the computer. The computer then maintains the selected route by inputs of azimuth and distance from the selected VOR stations. In the aircraft the pilot selects a specified route, in terms of azimuth, and a pictorial display in the cockpit indicates whether the aircraft is following the selected route and any deviation from this route. The route is delineated by intersections, or way points. An intersection is a point in space that is established by providing its latitude and longitude, and by indicating its distance from the nearest VORTAC station. Airborne equipment uses the azimuth and distance from the intersections as inputs for the computers or the latitude and longitude of the way points for inertial navigation systems.

RNAV is not limited to the horizontal plane but can also be utilized in the vertical plane (VNAV). It can also include a time reference capability. A properly equipped aircraft could arrive at a specified point in space, called a fix, with no need for ground vectoring or directions and could additionally be at that point at a specified altitude and time. This is a four-dimensional capability giving latitude, longitude, altitude, and time (4D RNAV). Thus RNAV has the potential of increasing airspace capacity, enhancing safety, and reducing the workload of the pilot and the air traffic controller.

RNAV routes that are frequently used by more than one user appear on published charts, much the same as victor airways and jet routes. The numbering system is as follows. Series 700 is reserved for low altitudes, below 18,000 ft. Each route is labeled V700R, V701R, and so on. The symbol V indicates victor airways as the reference and R indicates area navigation. Above 18,000 ft, series 800 and 900 are used, and the designation is J801R, J802R, and so on. As an additional RNAV route is established, it is given the next available number, irrespective of whether the route is north-south or east-west. Each intersection is given a name similar to VORTAC stations. An RNAV route includes the same airspace as the jet route shown in Fig. 4-2, except that the angle from the VORTAC station may, for example, be 3.25 instead of 4.5. An illustration of a portion of an RNAV chart showing the victor airways is given in Fig. 4-3.

MAJOR COMPONENTS OF THE FEDERAL AIRWAYS SYSTEM AND THEIR FUNCTIONS

The airways system consists of a network of navigational aids and a number of air traffic control facilities, which provide for the safe separation and orderly flow of aircraft within the range of the system. In order to properly manage the traffic in the system, the jurisdiction of control is divided into three parts, namely, en route, terminal, and airport. Each part has a specific function, which in turn is supported by a facility known as the *flight service station* (FSS).

Air Route Traffic Control Centers

Air route traffic control centers (ARTCC) have the responsibility of controlling the movement of en route aircraft along the airways, jet routes, and in other parts of the airspace. Each center has control of a definite geographi-

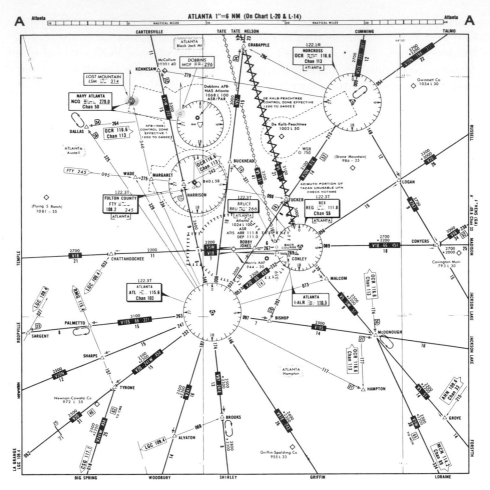

Fig. 4-3 Portion of RNAV chart showing victor airways. (*Federal Aviation Administration* [16].)

cal area which may be greater than 100,000 mi^2 in size. At the boundary points, which mark the limits of the control area of the center, aircraft are released to an adjacent center or to terminal control, an approach control facility. ARTCCs can but need not be located at airports since their functions have nothing to do with airport operations. The ARTCC is concerned primarily with the control of aircraft operating under IFR. In 1981 there were 20 ARTCCs in the continental United States and five more offshore.

Under IFR the pilots are required to file a flight plan indicating the route and altitude they desire to fly. The ARTCC will then check to determine whether the flight plan can be approved so that a safe separation from other aircraft along the same route and altitude is provided. Changes in flight plan en route are permitted if approved by ARTCC.

Each ARTCC geographical area is broken down into sectors. The configuration of each sector is based on equalizing the workload of the controllers. Aircraft are passed from one sector to another. The geographical area is sectored not only in the horizontal but also in the vertical plane. Thus there can be a high-altitude sector above one or more low-altitude sectors. Each sector is manned by one, two, or three controllers, depending on the volume and complexity of traffic. The average number of aircraft that each sector can handle depends on the number of people assigned to the sector, the complexity of traffic, and the degree of automation provided.

Each sector is normally provided with long-range radar, which covers the entire sector and allows for monitoring of the separations between aircraft in the sector. In addition, each sector has information on the identification of the aircraft, destination, flight plan route, estimated speed, and flight altitude, which may be posted on small pieces of paper called *shrimp boats* or may be superimposed on the radarscope adjacent to the blips which identify the position of the aircraft. The strips are continuously updated as the need arises.

At present, communication between pilot and controller is by voice. Therefore each ARTCC is assigned a number of radio communication frequencies. The controller in turn assigns a specific frequency to the pilot.

Terminal Approach Control Facility

The terminal approach control facility has jurisdiction in the control of traffic, arrivals and departures, from the boundary area of the air traffic control tower at an airport to a distance of 25 to 50 mi from the airport. This is commonly referred to as the *terminal area*. Where there are several airports in an urban area, one facility may control traffic to all of these airports. In essence the facility receives aircraft from the ARTCC and guides them to one of several airports. In providing this guidance, it performs the important function of metering and sequencing aircraft to provide uniform and orderly flow to the airports. In 1981 there were about 188 terminal-area control facilities in the United States.

When radar is available, which is in the majority of cases, the approach control facility is referred to as TRACON, an abbreviation for *terminal radar approach control*. There are various degrees of automation in an approach control facility, depending on the volume of traffic it is handling. Various abbreviations are used to designate the type of hardware in an approach control facility. As an example, ARTS III is an abbreviation for automated radar terminal system. The designation III denotes the highest level of automation, while I is the lowest level of automation. Thus one can have ARTS I, II, or III automation capability in a TRACON facility.

The organizational structure of an approach control facility is very similar to the ARTCC. Like the ARTCC, the area of the facility is divided into sectors to equalize the workload of the controllers. The approach control facility hands an arriving aircraft to the airport control tower when it is lined up with the runway about 5 mi from the airport. Likewise departing aircraft are handed to the approach control facility by the airport control tower.

If the flow of aircraft is greater than what the facility can handle, aircraft are delayed by either reducing their speed en route or detaining them at specified radio fixes within the area of the facility. The latter method is referred to as *stacking*. In a stack, aircraft navigate around a fix in a racetrack pattern, a holding pattern, and are separated vertically by 1000-ft intervals. There may be as many as 10 aircraft in a stack, and each one is directed in turn to a landing by the approach control facility.

Airport Traffic Control Tower

The airport traffic control tower (ATCT) is the facility which supervises, directs, and monitors the traffic at the airport and in the immediate airspace, arrivals and departures, up to about 5 mi from the airport. The tower is responsible for issuing clearances to all arriving and departing aircraft, providing pilots with information on wind, temperature, barometric pressure, as well as for operating conditions at the airport and the control of all aircraft on the ground, except in the maneuvering area immediately adjacent to the aircraft parking positions, called the *ramp area*. In 1981 the FAA operated 432 air traffic control towers in the United States.

Flight Service Stations

The FSSs are located along the airways and at airports. Their principal functions are to brief pilots, before flight and in flight, on weather, navigational aids, airports that are out of commission, and changes in procedures and new facilities. A secondary function is to relate traffic control messages between aircraft and the appropriate control facility on the ground. There were more than 1100 FSSs in the United States in 1981.

AIR TRAFFIC SEPARATION RULES

Air traffic rules governing the minimum separation of aircraft in the vertical, horizontal, and lateral directions are established in each country by the appropriate government authority. The current rules described in this text are prescribed by the FAA for use in the United States. These rules apply only when IFR conditions prevail. Minimum separations are a function of aircraft type, aircraft speed, availability of radar facilities, and other factors, such as the severity of wake vortices [3, 17].

Vertical Separation in the Airspace

The minimum vertical separation of aircraft from the ground up to and including 29,000 ft MSL is 1000 ft. Above 29,000 ft MSL the minimum separation is 2000 ft. The first assigned altitude above 29,000 ft is 31,000 ft. Up to and including 29,000 ft, odd altitudes are used for westbound flights (west of north and south). Above 29,000 ft odd altitudes are used for both eastbound and westbound flights in the following manner. For westbound flights altitudes of 31,000, 35,000, 39,000, and 43,000 ft are used; for eastbound flights altitudes of 33,000, 37,000, 41,000, and 45,000 ft are used.

Horizontal Separation in the Airspace

The minimum horizontal separation depends on a number of factors. Among the most important are aircraft size, aircraft speed, and the availability of radar for the control of air traffic. Aircraft size is related to wake turbulence. Heavy aircraft create trailing wake vortices, which are a hazard to light aircraft following them. Heavy aircraft have been classified as those whose maximum certificated takeoff weight is 300,000 lb or more. All other aircraft are considered light.

When the aircraft mix is such that wake turbulence is not a factor and radar coverage is available, the minimum separation for two aircraft traveling in the same direction and at the same altitude is 5 nmi, except that when the aircraft are within 40 nmi of the radar antenna, the separation can be reduced to 3 nmi. For this reason the minimum spacing in the terminal area is 3 nmi because the airport is almost always within 40 nmi of a radar antenna. If wake turbulence is a factor, the minimum separation between a light aircraft and a preceding heavy one is 5 nmi. The spacing between two heavy aircraft following each other is 4 nmi. The spacing between a heavy aircraft and a preceding light aircraft is 3 nmi. The IFR spacings presently used when wake vortices are a factor are shown in Table 4-1. This table also displays the observed actual spacings maintained in VFR at Chicago.

When there is no radar coverage and aircraft are not equipped with distance-measuring equipment (DME), the minimum separations are ex-

TABLE 4-1 **Minimum Horizontal Separation Criteria for Arrival-Arrival Spacing of Aircraft in VFR and IFR Conditions, nmi**

Lead aircraft type	VFR, trail aircraft type			IFR, trail aircraft type		
	Heavy	Light	Small	Heavy	Light	Small
Heavy	2.7	3.6	4.5	4.0	5.0	6.0
Light	1.9	1.9	2.7	3.0	3.0	4.0
Small	1.9	1.9	1.9	3.0	3.0	3.0

SOURCE: Landrum and Brown, Inc. [15].

pressed in terms of time and are as follows:

    1. Three minutes if the lead aircraft is 44 kn faster than the trail aircraft

    2. Five minutes if the lead aircraft is 22 kn faster than the trail aircraft

    3. Ten minutes if both aircraft are at the same speed

    If both aircraft are equipped with DME or RNAV equipment, the corresponding minimum separations are 5, 10, and 20 nmi, respectively. When wake vortices are a factor, the minimum separation is 2 min when a heavy aircraft is following a light aircraft. The controlled separation for the nonradar environment depends on whether the larger separation is dictated by wake vortices or by the normal minimum separations.

    Minimum longitudinal separation over the oceans is normally 20 min, but in some locations it can be slightly more or less than this value.

Lateral Separation in the Airspace

The minimum lateral separation below 18,000 ft MSL is 8 nmi. Above 18,000 ft the lateral separation is 20 nmi. Over the ocean the separation varies from 100 to 200 nmi, depending on location.

Runway Lateral Separation

Lateral separation of runways depends on whether VFR or IFR prevails and whether wake vortices are a factor. If wake vortices are not a factor and VFR prevails, the minimum separation between runways for simultaneous use by arriving or departing aircraft is 700 ft. If IFR prevails, the minimum separation for simultaneous use of one runway by departures and the other runway by arrivals is 3500 ft if the thresholds of the two runways are even with each other. If the two runways are staggered, the separation may be increased or decreased by 100 ft for each 500 ft of stagger, as shown in Fig. 4-4.

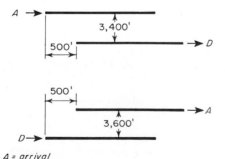

Fig. 4-4 Parallel runway separation criteria.

A = arrival
D = departure

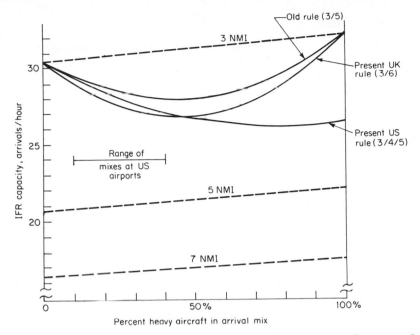

Fig. 4 5 Effect of various wake vortex separation rules on IFR arrival capacity of a typical runway. (*MITRE Corporation [12].*)

The minimum separation for simultaneous use of both runways by arriving aircraft is 4300 ft. There are no adjustments of this distance if the runways are staggered. If wake vortices are a factor, two parallel runways spaced closer than 2500 ft are considered as one runway. The aircraft must be fed to the two runways essentially in a single line, with a light aircraft trailing a heavy one by at least 5 nmi, irrespective of which runway is used.

General Considerations

The horizontal separation standards significantly influence the capacity of the airspace and the airport runways since separations reflect the size of headways between aircraft. The significant influence of radar in reducing headways can be illustrated as follows. With radar the minimum separation is 3 or 5 nmi. If radar is not available, the separation must be increased to 20 mi for aircraft equipped with DME or RNAV equipment and to about 83 mi if none of this equipment is installed in the aircraft. Over the oceans the horizontal separation is close to 170 mi, or about 33 times greater than in a radar environment. These large separations reduce the capacity of the airspace and increase delays, and for this reason efforts are being made to reduce spacing. Figure 4-5 illustrates the impact of a variety of minimum spacing rules on runway capacity.

NAVIGATIONAL AIDS

Aids to aerial navigation can be broadly classified into two groups, external aids, that is, those that are located on the ground, and internal aids, that is, those installed in the cockpit. Some aids are primarily for flying over the oceans, other aids are only applicable to flight over land masses, and finally there are aids that can be used over either land or water. Some aids are used only during the en route portion of the flight, while other aids are necessary in terminal areas or near airports. Aids to navigation can be classified as shown in Fig. 4-6.

External Overland En Route Aids

Very-High-Frequency Omnirange

The advances in radio and electronics during and after World War II led to the installation of the VOR stations. These stations send out radio signals in all directions. Each signal can be considered as a course or a route, referred to as a *radial*, that can be followed by an aircraft. In terms of 1° intervals, there are 360 courses or routes that are radiated from a VOR station, from 0° pointing toward magnetic north, increasing to 360° in a clockwise direction. The VOR transmitter station is a small square building topped with what appears to be a white derby hat. It broadcasts on a frequency just above that of FM radio stations. The very high frequencies it uses are virtually free of static. VOR stations establish the network of airways and jet routes and are also essential to area navigation. The range of a VOR station varies, but is usually less than 200 nmi.

The VOR receiver in the cockpit has a dial for tuning in the desired VOR frequency. Pilots can select the VOR radial or route they wish to follow to the VOR station. In the cockpit there is also a position deviation indicator (PDI), which indicates the heading of the aircraft relative to the direction of the desired radial and whether the aircraft is to the right or left of the radial. Figure 4-7 shows schematically the type of information the PDI provides. At location A the aircraft is on the selected radial and the needle is pointed vertically and passes through the cross, which is a symbol

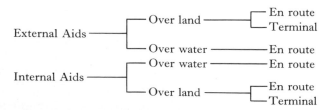

Fig. 4-6 Classification of navigational aids.

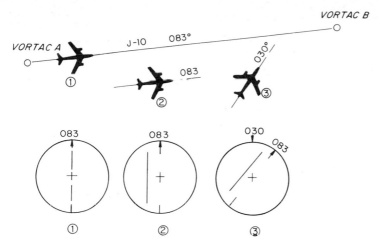

Fig. 4-7 Illustration of pictorial display indicator for aircraft utilizing a VOR radial.

for the aircraft. In other words, the aircraft is heading in the same direction as the desired radial. At location *B* the aircraft is flying parallel, but to the right of the desired radial. At location *C* the aircraft is to the right of the radial and heading across the radial.

Distance-Measuring Equipment

DME has been installed at nearly all VOR stations. It shows the pilot the air distance between the aircraft and a particular VOR station. Since it is the air distance in nautical miles that is measured, the receiving equipment in an aircraft flying at 35,000 ft directly over the DME station would read 5.8 nmi.

An en route air navigation aid which best suited the tactical needs of the military was developed by the Navy in the early 1950s. This aid is known as TACAN, which stands for *tactical air navigation*. This aid combines azimuth and distance measuring into one unit instead of two and is operated in the ultra high-frequency band. As a compromise between civilian and military requirements, the FAA replaced the DME portion of its VOR facilities with the distance-measuring components of TACAN. These stations are known as VOR-DMET. If a station has full TACAN equipment, both azimuth and distance-measuring equipment, and also VOR, it is designated as VORTAC.

Air Route Surveillance Radar

Long-range radar for tracking en route aircraft has been established throughout the continental United States and in other parts of the world.

While in the United States there is complete radar coverage in the 48 contiguous states, this is not the case elsewhere in the world. These radars have a range of about 300 nmi. Strictly speaking, radar is not an aid to navigation. Its principal function is to provide air traffic controllers with a visual display of the position of each aircraft so they can monitor their spacings and intervene when necessary. However, it can be and is used by air traffic controllers to guide aircraft whenever this is necessary. For this reason it has been included as an aid to navigation.

External Overland Terminal Aids

The principal aids in the terminal area are used mainly for landing aircraft, and are described below.

Instrument Landing System

The most widely used method is the instrument landing system (ILS). It consists of two radio transmitters located on the airport. One radio beam is called the *localizer* and the other the *glide slope*. The localizer indicates to pilots whether they are left or right of the correct alignment for approach to the runway. The glide slope indicates the correct angle of descent to the runway. Glide slopes are on the order of 2 to 3°.

In order to further help pilots on their ILS approach, two low-power fan markers, called *ILS markers*, are usually installed so that the pilots may know just how far along the approach to the runway they have progressed. The first is called the *outer marker* (LOM) and is located about 4 to 5 mi from the end of the runway. The other is called the *middle marker* (MM) which is located about 3000 ft from the end of the runway. For category II operations, when visibility is quite poor, an additional marker, called the *inner marker* (IM), is located 1000 ft from the end of the runway. This IM is placed so as to alert pilots that they must have visual reference with the ground at that point, and if not, abandon the approach. When the plane passes over a marker, a light goes on in the cockpit and a high-pitched tone sounds. The ILS system is shown in Fig. 4-8.

The localizer consists of an antenna, which is located on the extension of the runway centerline approximately 1000 ft from the far end of the runway, and a localizer transmitter building located about 300 ft to one side of the runway at the same distance from the end of the runway as the antenna. The glide slope facility is placed 750 to 1250 ft down the runway from the threshold and is located to one side of the runway centerline at a distance which can vary from 400 to 650 ft. The functioning of the localizer and the glide slope facility is affected by the close proximity of moving objects, such as vehicular and aircraft traffic. Stationary objects nearby can also cause a deterioration of signals. Abrupt changes of slope in the

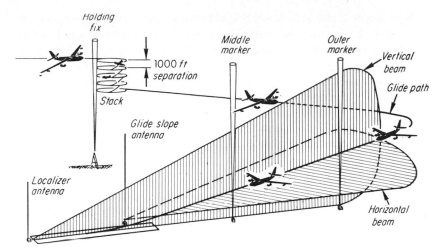

Fig. 4-8 Schematic diagram of an instrument landing system (ILS). (*Scientific American [5].*)

proximity of the antennas are not permitted, or the signal will not be transmitted properly. Another limitation of the ILS is that the glide slope beam is not reliable below a height of about 200 ft above the runway.

Microwave Landing System

The ILS has a number of problems which have made the development of more sophisticated landing systems necessary. The ILS is based on signals reflecting from the surface of the ground. Thus the area adjacent to the antennas must be relatively smooth and kept clear of any obstructions, such as buildings and taxiing aircraft; otherwise the beams are distorted. There have been improvements in the transmission of the localizer beam by the installation of a waveguide antenna which confines the beam spray and reduces the probability of reflections from buildings and other obstructions; but this has not solved all the problems associated with the ILS. The ILS provides only one path in space, which all aircraft must follow if they are using the system. Some aircraft, particularly STOL, can use a steeper approach angle, of about 7°, than conventional aircraft, which use 2.5 to 3° approaches. Other aircraft may wish to make a two-segment approach to reduce noise beneath the flight path. The ILS is unable to provide for these types of operations. Finally, there are only a limited number of frequency channels available for the ILS, and as the number of installations has increased, it is becoming difficult to provide the necessary discrete channels required.

To overcome these limitations, a system has been developed which is referred to as the *microwave landing system* (MLS). Instead of providing only one glide slope as the ILS does, the MLS provides a number of slopes. In the horizontal plane, the MLS provides for any desired routes as long as they are within an area that is from 20 to 60° each side of the runway centerline, whereas the ILS provides for only one route to the runway. Distance-measuring capability can be incorporated into the MLS, providing the pilot with continuous information on the aircraft distance from the end of the runway and removing the need for establishing markers as in the ILS. The MLS is far less susceptible to interference from surrounding objects than the ILS. With the MLS a pilot can choose any desired route to the runway at any glide slope within the vertical coverage of the system. An MLS is shown schematically in Fig. 4-9.

From the standpoint of airport planning, one of the most significant advantages of the MLS is the potential reduction of noise since aircraft can be kept at higher altitudes before making their descent to the airport, or follow curved routes which do not impact as much land as the ILS routes. An illustration of the difference between an ILS and an MLS approach into Kennedy (JFK) and LaGuardia (LGA) airports in the New York area is given in Fig. 4-10. Another advantage is the elimination of the requirement that all aircraft, large or small, follow a common approach route to the runway.

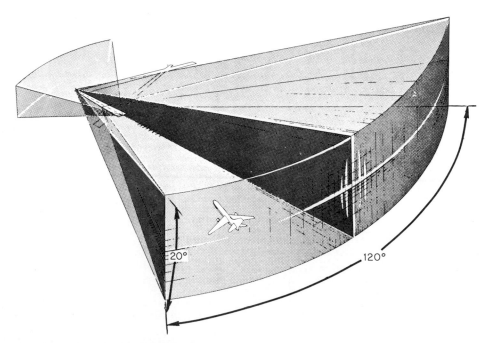

Fig. 4-9 Schematic diagram of a microwave landing system (MLS). The microwave landing system provides volumetric coverage for flexible paths in approach, landing, and departure, and operates at microwave frequencies. (*Federal Aviation Administration [4].*)

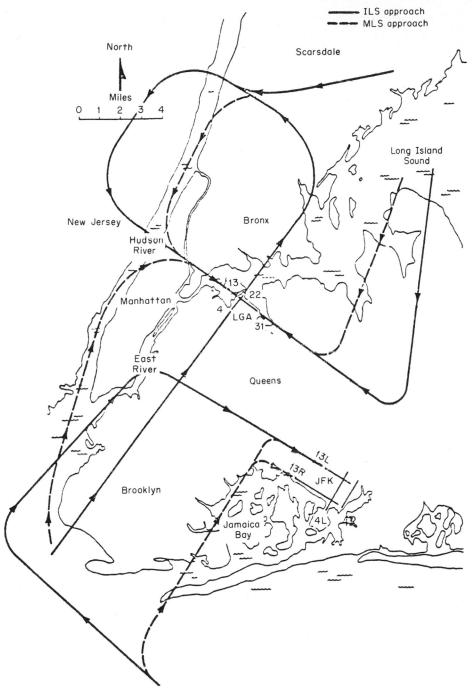

North

Miles

0 1 2 3 4

——— ILS approach
– – – MLS approach

Scarsdale

Long Island
Sound

New Jersey

Bronx

Hudson
River

Manhattan

13
22
4
LGA
31

East
River

Queens

13L
13R
JFK
4L

Brooklyn

Jamaica
Bay

Fig. 4-10 Differences between an ILS and an MLS approach to Kennedy (JFK) and LaGuardia (LGA) airports in the New York metropolitan area. (*Federal Aviation Administration [4].*)

Precision Approach Radar

At a number of airports another landing aid, known as *precision approach radar* (PAR) or *ground control approach* (GCA), has been installed. This equipment was developed by the military during World War II in order to provide a mobile unit which is not dependent on airborne navigation equipment. The PAR radarscope gives controllers a picture of the descending aircraft in both plan and elevation; half the scope is in plan and half in elevation. Thus they can determine whether an aircraft is on glide path and whether it is on the correct alignment. Instructions from controllers to pilots are given by voice communication, and thus no airborne navigation equipment is necessary. This is a very important advantage from a military standpoint, since fighter-type aircraft have very little room for navigation equipment. On the other hand, commercial airline pilots use the ILS almost exclusively, on the grounds that PAR places too much dependence on the controller in the tower and does not provide any direct information to the pilot. At airports where there are both ILS and PAR facilities, commercial airline pilots use ILS, but often request that they be monitored by PAR.

Airport Surveillance Radar

In order to provide the control tower operator with an overall picture of what is going on within the airspace surrounding the terminal, airport surveillance radar (ASR) has been installed at many of the major airports in the country. The ASR rotates through 360°, and the information is received on a scope in the control tower. The range of ASR is from 30 to 60 mi. It shows the aircraft in their relative horizontal position on the scope as blips. The blips of moving aircraft leave a luminous trail, indicate the direction in which they are moving, and may show an indication of their speed. The ASR does not indicate the altitude of aircraft since it simply responds to the reflection of the signal from the skin of the aircraft. This radar is often called *primary radar*.

Approach Lighting Systems

The most critical point of approach to landing comes when the aircraft breaks through the overcast and the pilot must change from instrument to visual conditions. Only a few seconds are available in which to make the transition and complete the landing. To aid in making this transition, lights are installed on the approach to the runway and on the runways themselves. These are generally termed *approach lighting systems* (ALS). There are a number of types and configurations which are used and others which are under experimental testing today. More details concerning these systems are contained in the chapter on signing, marking, and lighting.

Airport Surface Detection Equipment

At large high-density airports, controllers have difficulty in regulating taxiing aircraft because they cannot see the aircraft in poor visibility conditions. A specially designed radar called *airport surface detection equipment* (ASDE) has been developed to aid the controller in regulating traffic on the airport. The radar gives a pictorial display of the runways, taxiways, and terminal area.

Approach Slope Indicators

The visual approach slope indicator (VASI) and the precision approach path indicator (PAPI) provide through a system of lights the proper approach slope to the runway, much the same as the glide slope of an ILS. VASI systems are intended for day or night use during good weather (VFR) conditions. They cannot be used under very poor visibility conditions. A refined version of the visual approach slope indicator, the PAPI system, has undergone recent tests by the FAA and is presently planned for installation at airports in the United States [19]. The PAPI system gives a more definitive indication of approach slope to the pilot and uses only a single set of electronic devices at one point down the runway. More detailed explanations of the VASI and PAPI systems are contained in the chapter on signing, marking, and lighting.

Runway End Identifier Lights

Runway end identifier lights (REIL) are installed to provide the pilot with positive visual identification of the approach end of the runway when there are no approach lights.

The relative location of terminal aids is shown in Fig. 4-11. The siting requirements for visual aids as well as for the ILS antennas can be found [1]. The criteria which are used to establish eligibility for these aids are also found [21].

External Overwater En Route Aids

The principal overwater aid to navigation is LORAN, which consists of stations located on the ground. LORAN is an acronyn for *long-range aerial navigation*. The system was developed during World War II. LORAN stations are located in all parts of the world. The particular system in use is designated LORAN-C. The principle of the LORAN system is as follows. Each element consists of a master station and a slave station located at some distance from the master. The master station sends radio signals into space; at the same time one of the signals goes to the slave station where it is delayed a specified amount of time and then sent into space. At any point in space there is a difference in time between the original signal from the

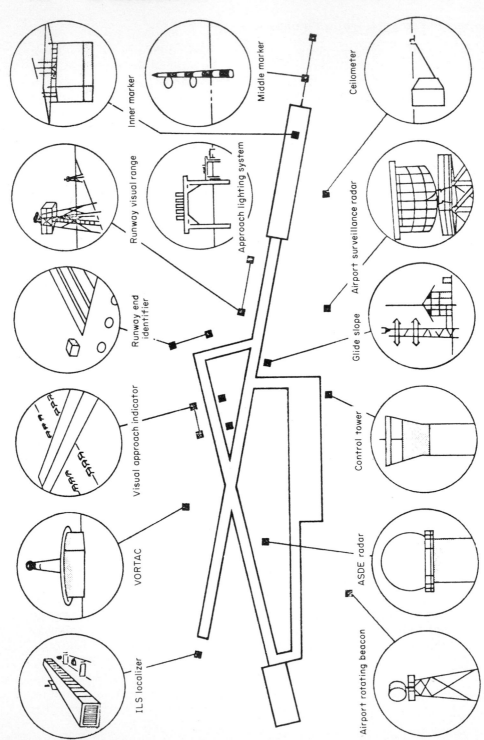

Inner marker

Middle marker

Ceilometer

Runway visual range

Approach lighting system

Airport surveillance radar

Runway end identifier

Glide slope

Visual approach indicator

Control tower

VORTAC

ASDE radar

ILS localizer

Airport rotating beacon

Fig. 4-11 Relative location of terminal aids for an approach to a runway system. *(Federal Aviation Administration [1, 21].)*

master and its intersection with the delayed signal from the slave. Thus a contour of equal time differences can be drawn in space. The same can be done from another master and slave station, resulting in another contour. The intersection of the two contours establishes a position in space. In the aircraft the LORAN receiver tunes in on two master and slave stations, establishing an intersection of two time-difference contours in space. The range of LORAN is affected by the time of day, being greater at night than during daylight hours. LORAN requires the use of a navigator in the cockpit.

Internal Overwater En Route Aids

There are two principal aids used in overwater operation, the doppler navigation system and the inertial navigation system (INS). A third system, which derives its origin from use on ships at sea, is celestial navigation. The latter was quite popular prior to the development of the doppler and inertial systems. The advantages of these later systems are related to the economics of aircraft operation; they do not require the use of a navigator.

Doppler Navigation System

This is a long-range radar-type aid that provides the pilot with the ground speed, the angle of the aircraft axis relative to the desired course (drift angle), the distance of the aircraft right or left of the desired course, and the distance to the destination or way point. Suppose an aircraft is to fly from point A to point B via a great circle route of length L. The length L is usually divided into several shorter lengths or segments. The ends of these segments are established in space by way points. These are imaginary points in space. Inputs into the system are the latitudes and longitudes of points A and B and all way points along the route. The number of way points depends on the length of the trip.

The doppler system is based on the following. The aircraft sends to the ground four beams of continuous-wave energy (8800 MHz), two forward and two toward the rear. The change in frequency of the energy return from the ground is measured. This change is known as doppler shift; it is proportional to the aircraft speed in the directions the beam is pointing. By checking the speed in the four directions in which the beams are pointing, the system derives groundspeed and drift angle. The smoother the surface, the less chance there is for the radiated energy to reflect back to the aircraft antenna. This is a limitation of the system, which is encountered over smooth bodies of water.

Inertial Navigation System

The INS is by far the most popular overwater long-range aid. It will provide all of the information that the doppler system provides, as well as wind speed and direction, the latitude and longitude of the aircraft at any instant in time, and the time to reach the next way point. As for the doppler system, the inputs into the system are the latitudes and longitudes of the origin, destination, and way points. The INS is a development of the space program. It is quite accurate and reliable. Both the inertial and the doppler systems provide azimuth information referenced to true north and not magnetic north.

Internal Overland En Route Aids

Both the doppler systems and the INS can be used over land masses. There are also RNAV systems which can be used only over land. They use as inputs the distance and azimuth information provided by VORTAC stations. The desired course is referenced to way points, as for the other systems. The way points are established by distance and azimuth from the nearest adjacent VORTAC station. Information provided in the cockpit is similar to that of the doppler and inertial systems.

Internal Overland Terminal Aids

RNAV systems used for en route navigation can also be used in the terminal area. In addition to guidance in the horizontal plane, these systems also provide for guidance in the vertical plane. This latter capability is particularly useful for guidance to runways.

AIDS FOR THE CONTROL OF AIR TRAFFIC

The principal aids for the control of air traffic are voice communication and radar. The controller monitors the spacing between aircraft on the radarscope and instructs the pilots by means of voice communication. There are two types of radar, primary and beacon. The primary radar returns appear on the radarscope as small blips. These are reflections from the aircraft body. The primary radar as it appears on a radarscope is shown in Fig. 4-12. Primary radar requires the installation of rotating antennas, the diameter of which depends on the desired range. Beacon radar, sometimes referred to as secondary radar, consists of a radar receiver and transmitter on the ground that transmits a strong coded signal to an aircraft if that aircraft has a transponder. A transponder is an airborne receiver and transmitter which receives the signal from the ground and responds by returning a coded reply to the interrogator on the ground. The coded reply normally contains information on aircraft identity, altitude, and air speed. In essence the interrogator (receiver and transmitter) is the beacon radar antenna. It is usually installed as an integral part of the primary radar antenna. Beacon

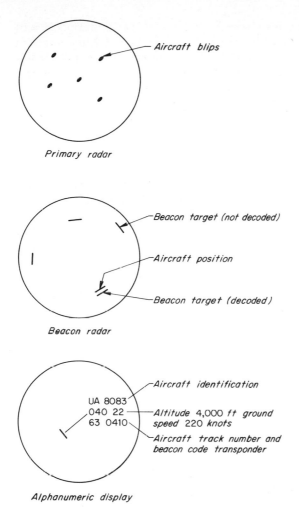

Fig. 4-12 Various displays on radarscope used for air traffic control.

radar returns are presented on the radarscope as two slashes if they are decoded and as a single slash if they are not decoded. Controllers will decode only those aircraft that they are controlling. The slashes will always appear at a right angle to the radial from the location of the antenna to the aircraft, as shown in Fig. 4-12. The center of the slash closest to the antenna is the location of the aircraft. In both the primary and the beacon radar presentations there is no identity of the aircraft or its altitude. This is obtained by voice communication and placed on a small piece of plastic referred to as a *shrimp boat*. The shrimp boat is placed on the aircraft target on the radarscope and is moved as the aircraft moves.

To overcome the deficiencies of the beacon radar presentation and to reduce the amount of communication, a video presentation, which includes identity and altitude, has been developed. This is shown in Fig. 4-12 and is referred to as *alpha-numeric dislay*. The first line shows the identity of the aircraft, the second line its altitude and ground speed, and the third line gives the beacon code transponder number and the aircraft track number. To be able to have this information presented on the radarscope, the aircraft must carry a transponder which has the capability of altitude identity. Most airline aircraft carry a mode C transponder, which satisfies the requirement for reporting altitude. One of the problems with the current beacon radar system is its inability to selectively interrogate aircraft. Proposals have been made to incorporate a modified system to alleviate this difficulty in congested areas through the use of a discrete address beacon system (DABS) [13].

If all aircraft, including general aviation, were equipped with transponders, there would be no need for primary radar except possibly in a backup role.

AUTOMATION IN TERMINAL AND EN ROUTE AIR TRAFFIC CONTROL

Objectives

There are a number of reasons for updating and automating the air traffic control system. The more important are [14]:

1. Having an operational system which is capable of being technically expanded in incremental steps to meet the needs of aviation as time requires

2. Accommodating increasing demand in a manner which permits users to operate in the airspace with a minimum of regulatory constraints and in a fuel-efficient way

3. Reducing the risks of midair and surface traffic collisions, landing and weather related accidents, and collisions with the ground

4. Increasing the productivity of air traffic control personnel in terms of the amount of air traffic monitored

5. Deceasing the technical work force required to maintain and operate the system

6. Maintaining the overall operating costs of the system at reasonable levels

7. Increasing the capacity of the airspace by reducing the spacing between aircraft through improved systems to monitor aircraft and through more accurate airborne systems

Increasing the productivity of a controller is a very important objective for the following reasons. One is simply a matter of economics. In 1981 the number of air traffic personnel employed by the FAA was on the order of 20,000, amounting to an annual payroll cost of nearly three quarters of a billion dollars. It has been estimated that, with the implementation of automation, as indicated in the *National Airspace System Plan* [14], the number of air traffic personnel could be reduced to about one-half of the present level by the year 2000. Without even a modest amount of automation the requirements for controllers would quadruple before the year 2000 [5, 10, 18]. It has been questioned whether it would be possible to maintain such a work force or even manage it. The need for more controllers in the present system stems from the need to increase capacity by establishing more control sectors, but as the number of sectors are increased, more coordination between sectors is required. Coordination therefore imposes a severe constraint on the system.

There have been many discussions relative to the means of increasing controller productivity, but in a broad sense there are two general areas which have been pursued. One is to automate the routine duties of controllers, such as preparing and updating flight strips, or detecting conflicts in flight plans, thus allowing the controller more time to monitor aircraft flow. Another is to reduce communication between pilots and controllers, again allowing the controller more time to monitor aircraft flow.

Some argue that one way to reduce the requirement for additional controllers is to place more responsibility on pilots. These responsibilities would include following a prescribed route and maintaining a time profile over a route. This would leave the controller as a flight monitor, intervening only when necessary.

The FAA has proposed a *National Airspace System Plan* [14] with the expressed purpose of modernizing the air traffic control system of the United States through the year 2000. It is to be a highly automated system, replacing the existing system which has evolved over time. A discussion of the evolution of the existing system follows.

States of Automation

In the United States, the several states of the air traffic control system have been referred to as second-generation, third-generation, and so on. The first-generation system can be considered the state of the system when it first evolved in the early 1940s. The second-generation system which followed was primarily a manual system with regard to control and separation of air traffic, although some functions, such as flight data processing were gradually automated. This was largely the system until the late 1960s, when the transition to the third-generation system began. Both the first- and second-generation systems can be considered largely manual. The third-generation system, which is currently being implemented, provides for limited automation to assist the controller (flight plan processing, updating flight plans, improved video display, reduction in communication) and automated data acquisition and display, including altitude and position provided by the radar beacon system. In this system communication is still by voice, but is reduced by having alpha-numeric displays on the videoscope. Sequencing of aircraft into the final approach to a runway is done manually. It can be considered that computers assist controllers in routine tasks and alert them to potential conflicts, but do not enter into the process of resolving conflicts and recommending solutions.

The beacon radar in the third-generation system lacks measurement accuracy and has limited aircraft capacity and reliability. Furthermore, the system relies heavily on voice communication. There is a limit on the number of voice channels available for air traffic control; consequently the demand could conceivably exceed the capacity of the communication system. Because of these deficiencies, in 1969 the Air Traffic Control Advisory Committee [18] recommended an upgrading of the third-generation system. This upgrading included an improvement in the accuracy and capacity of beacon radars and the incorporation of a ground-to-air and air-to-ground data link. The upgraded third-generation system is fairly automated, providing for flow control [11], sequencing, and spacing in the en route and terminal density airspace. It was estimated that the upgraded third-generation system had the capacity to handle traffic volumes projected into the early 1990s. Sometime thereafter the system would exhibit significant deficiencies. Consequently studies of alternative concepts for a fourth-generation system began in the early 1970s, referred to as advanced air traffic management system study, with a target date of operation around 1990 [13]. The several concepts being studied include the use of satellites for surveillance, navigation, and communication for part or all of these functions. Data processing would be accomplished primarily with a highly integrated network of digital computers. Communication would be largely by data link.

An Automated Air Traffic Control Facility

The automated en route system revises the role of controllers as active participants and allows them to discharge their primary responsibility, that of monitoring and controlling aircraft. Information which was manually acquired and processed is automatically obtained, processed, and presented on the radar display with greater speed and accuracy. Transponder-equipped airplanes provide continuous altitude and identity information, reducing both pilot and communication workload. All information is fed into a computer complex which processes and updates flight data and presents them on a radar display in alpha-numeric form with automatic target tracking. Subsequent stages of development provide for the automatic prediction of potential traffic conflicts, suggestions for resolving conflicts, and preplanning of traffic flow. Another method for reducing the communication workload will be the use of automated ground-to-air and air-to-ground communication (data link). In the terminal area, the ARTS provides for automatic tracking of both primary and beacon radar targets and displays on the radarscope alpha-numeric information for each aircraft being tracked, as in the en route system. VORTAC would continue to be the primary method of en route navigation, although it will be upgraded where required.

The National Airspace System Plan

The FAA proposed a comprehensive 20-year plan for updating and modernizing the air traffic control system of the United States in late 1981. This plan spells out the specific improvements that must be made to the airspace systems and facilities to meet the projected demands of air traffic. The key elements of the plan include the replacement of the current air traffic control computer systems to permit the introduction of higher levels of automation, modernization of the flight service station network to improve the dissemination of flight and weather data to pilots, and the deployment of new radar, communications, and landing systems to enhance safety and provide for more efficient traffic flow.

The projected level and growth of national airspace system activity over the period from 1980 to 2000 is shown in Table 4-2.

In order to meet the aviation demands to be imposed upon the system, the following specific items have been proposed for implementation:

1. The introduction of new high-capacity, high-reliability computer systems to replace the existing computer system

2. The utilization of the same basic computer system in en route and terminal air traffic control facilities and the blending and integration of these facilities from the present level of over 200 to about 60 by the year 2000

3. The implementation of the automated en route air traffic control system (AERA) which would automatically probe aircraft routes, detect and resolve conflicts with other aircraft, weather, and terrain, and issue clearances to ensure the safe, metered, and efficient flow of traffic

4. The consolidation and automation of the present system of FSSs to provide for the rapid retrieval and transmission of flight and weather information to pilots, ultimately through direct pilot access to the computer base

5. The implementation of a new secondary beacon radar system to selectively address aircraft through the mode S transponder

6. The expansion of the new secondary radar system to ultimately include the ability for automatic air-to-ground data link communications

TABLE 4-2 **Total National Airspace System Activity, 1980–2000**

	1980	1985	1990	2000	Percent growth 1980–2000
NASP airports	3163	3637	3631	4000	26.5
Aircraft operations, millions	134.1	179.7	212.7	290.0	116.2
Itinerant operations, millions	74.0	98.8	117.3	159.5	115.5
Instrument operations, millions	38.2	48.1	54.2	65.6	71.7
IFR aircraft handled, millions	30.1	37.2	42.2	53.7	78.7
FSS operations, millions	64.3	83.9	98.6	139.6	117.1
Domestic enplanements, millions:					
Air carrier	278.1	380.8	454.0	589.8	112.1
Commuter	13.1	21.8	30.6	42.0	220.6
Aircraft fleet, thousands:					
Air carrier	2.4	2.7	2.9	3.4	42
Commuter	1.6	2.4	3.2	4.5	175
General aviation	210.3	254.5	298.1	408.5	94
Instrument rated pilots, thousands	247.1	309.5	369.6	481.9	95.0
Total pilots, thousands	814.7	891.0	1050.6	1331.3	63.4

SOURCE: Federal Aviation Administration [14].

7. The phasing out of primary radar for en route air traffic control, but its retention for terminal area air traffic control

8. The development of an enhanced interfacility communications network utilizing state-of-the-art telecommunications technology

9. A modernization of flight inspection and facility maintenance programs

REFERENCES

1. *Airport Design Standards—Site Requirements for Terminal Navigation Facilities*, Federal Aviation Administration, Washington, D.C., Advisory Circular AC 150/5300-2D, 1980.

2. *Air Route Traffic Control*, Federal Aviation Administration, Washington, D.C., Airway Planning Standard 2, Order 7031.3, September 1977.

3. *Air Traffic Control Handbook*, Federal Aviation Administration, Washington, D.C., Order 7110.65B, January 1980.

4. *An Analysis of the Requirements for, and the Benefits and Costs of the National Microwave Landing System (MLS)*, Office of Systems Engineering Management, Federal Aviation Administration, Washington, D.C., Report FAA-EM-80-7, June 1980.

5. *Civil Aviation Research and Development Policy Study*, Department of Transportation and National Aeronautics and Space Administration, Washington, D.C., March 1971.

6. *Designation of Federal Airways, Area Low Routes, Controlled Airspace, and Reporting Points,* Federal Aviation Regulations, Federal Aviation Administration, Washington, D.C., FAA Part 71, 1975.

7. *Enroute Air Traffic Control,* Federal Aviation Administration, Washington, D.C., Handbook 7110.9C, periodically revised.

8. *Enroute High Altitude—U.S.,* Flight Information Publication, National Ocean Survey, National Oceanic and Atmospheric Administration, Department of Commerce, Washington, D.C., December 1975.

9. *Establishment of Jet Routes and Area High Routes,* Federal Aviation Regulations, Federal Aviation Administration, Washington, D.C., FAR Part 75, 1976.

10. *FAA Report on Airport Capacity,* The MITRE Corporation, Federal Aviation Administration, Washington, D.C., Report FAA-EM-74-5, 1974.

11. *Flow Control Procedures,* Federal Aviation Administration, Washington, D.C., Order 7210.76, June 1976.

12. "Future ATC Technology Improvements and the Impact on Airport Capacity," R. M. Harris, The MITRE Corporation, Air Transportation Systems Division, McLean, Va., 1970.

13. "Future System Concepts for Air Traffic Management," W. E. Simpson, Office of Systems Engineering, Department of Transportation, presented at 19th Technical Conference of the International Air Transportation Association, Washington, D.C., October 1972.

14. *National Airspace System Plan,* Facilities, Equipment and Associated Development, Federal Aviation Administration, Washington, D.C., December 1981.

15. *O'Hare Delay Task Force Study,* Vol. 2: *Technical Report, Chicago O'Hare International Airport,* Federal Aviation Administration, Washington, D.C., FAA-AGL-76-1 II, July 1976.

16. *Planning the Metropolitan Airport System,* Federal Aviation Administration, Washington, D.C., Advisory Circular AC 150/5070-5, May 1970.

17. *Procedures for Control of Aircraft Following Heavy Jet Aircraft,* Federal Aviation Administration, Washington, D.C., Order 7110.29.

18. *Report of Department of Transportation Air Traffic Control Advisory Committee,* U.S. Department of Transportation, Washington, D.C., December 1969.

19. "Runway End Safety, PAPI, Among Conference Topics," *Airports International,* London, England, June 1981.

20. *Summary Report 1972,* National Aviation System Planning Review Conference, Federal Aviation Administration, Washington, D.C.

21. *Terminal Air Navigation Facilities and Air Traffic Control Services,* Federal Aviation Administration, Washington, D.C., Airway Planning Standard 1, Order 7031.2B, May 1979.

22. *Terminal Air Traffic Control,* Federal Aviation Administration, Washington, D.C., Handbook 7110.8C, periodically revised.

23. "The Advanced Air Traffic Management System Study," R. L. Maxwell, Office of Systems Engineering, Department of Transportation, presented at the 19th Technical Conference of the International Air Transportation Association, Washington, D.C., October 1972.

24. *United States Aeronautical Information Publication,* 8th ed., Federal Aviation Administration, Washington, D.C., January 1981.

25. *United States Standard for Terminal Instrument Procedures (TERPS),* 3d ed., Federal Aviation Administration, Washington, D.C., July 1976.

Chapter 5

Airport Planning

INTRODUCTION

The planning of an airport is such a complex process that the analysis of one activity without regard to the effect on other activities will not provide acceptable solutions. An airport encompasses a wide range of activities which have different and often conflicting requirements. Yet they are interdependent so that a single activity may limit the capacity of the entire complex. In the past airport master plans were developed on the basis of local aviation needs. In more recent times these plans have been integrated into an airport system plan which assessed not only the needs at a specific airport site, but also the overall needs of the system of airports which service an area, region, state, or country. If future airport planning efforts are to be successful, they must be founded on guidelines established on the basis of comprehensive airport system and master plans.

The elements of a large airport are shown in Fig. 5-1. It is divided into two major components, the airside and the landside. The terminal buildings form the division between the two components. Within the system, the characteristics of the vehicles, both ground and air, have a large influence on planning. The passenger and the shipper of goods are interested primarily in the overall door-to-door travel time and not just in the duration of the air journey. For this reason access to airports is an essential consideration in planning.

The problems resulting from the incorporation of airport operations into the web of metropolitan life are complex. In the early days of air transport, airports were located at a distance from the city, where inexpensive land and a limited number of obstructions permitted a maximum of flexibility in airport operations. Because of the nature of aircraft and the infrequency of flight, noise was not a problem to the community. In many cases this audible evidence of the arrival and departure of passenger and cargo planes was often a source of local pride. In addition, low population density in the vicinity of the airport and light air traffic prevented occasional accidents from alarming the community. In spite of early lawsuits, the relationship between airport and community was relatively free of strife resulting from problems of nuisance or hazard.

Airport operations have been increasingly hampered by obstructions

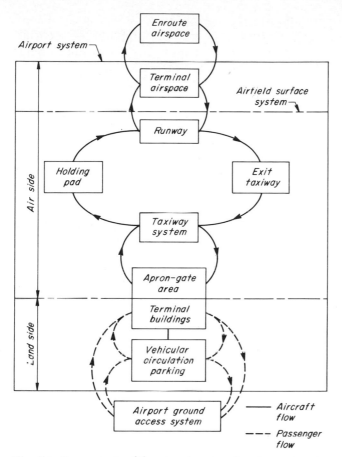

Fig. 5-1 Components of the airport system for a large airport.

resulting from industrial development related to the airport and from industry attracted by adjacent inexpensive land and access to the transportation afforded by the airfield and its associated highways. While increasingly dense residential development has resulted from this economic stimulation, one must not overlook the effects of the unprecedented suburban spread during the postwar era, resulting from the backlog of housing needs and a period of economic prosperity.

Radical developments in the nature of air transport have produced new problems. The phenomenal growth of air traffic has increased the probability of unfavorable community reaction, but developments in the aircraft themselves have had the most profound effect on airport-community relations. The greater size and speed of aircraft have resulted in increases in approach and runway requirements, while increases in the output of power plants have brought almost unavoidable increases in noise. Faced with these problems the airport must cope with the problems of securing sufficient airspace for access to the air, sufficient land for ground operations, and, also, adequate ground access to the metropolitan area.

TYPES OF AIRPORT PLANNING STUDIES

Many different types of studies are performed in aviation and airport planning. These include studies related to facility planning, financial planning, traffic and markets, economics, and the environment. However, each of these studies can usually be classified as being performed at either the system planning or the master planning level.

The Airport System Plan

An airport system plan is a representation of the aviation facilities required to meet the immediate and future needs of a metropolitan area, region, state, or country. It presents the recommendations for the general location and characteristics of new airports and the nature of expansion for existing ones. It includes the timing and estimated costs of development and relates airport system planning to the policy and objectives of the relevant jurisdiction. Its overall purpose is to provide the basis for definitive and detailed airport planning, such as the airport master plan [38, 39].

The airport system plan provides both broad and specific policies, plans, and programs required to establish a viable and integrated system of airports to meet the needs of the region. The objectives of the system plan include:

1. The orderly and timely development of a system of airports adequate to meet present and future aviation needs and to promote the desired pattern of regional growth relative to industrial, employment, social, environmental, and recreational goals

2. The development of aviation to meet its role in a balanced and multimodal transportation system to foster the overall goals of the area as reflected in the transportation system plan and comprehensive development plan

3. The protection and enhancement of the environment through the location and expansion of aviation facilities in a manner which avoids ecological and environmental impairment

4. The provision of the framework within which specific airport programs may be developed consistent with the short- and long-range airport system requirements

5. The implementation of land use and airspace plans which optimize the use of these resources in an often constrained environment

6. The development of long-range fiscal plans and the establishment of priorities for airport financing within the governmental budgeting process

7. The establishment of the mechanism for the implementation of the system plan through the normal political framework, including the necessary coordination between governmental agencies, the involvement of both public and private aviation and nonaviation interests, and compatibility with the content, standards, and criteria of existing legislation

The Airport Master Plan

An airport master plan is a concept of the ultimate development of an airport. The term development includes the entire airport area, both for aviation and nonaviation uses, and use of land adjacent to the airport [13]. The overall objective of the airport master plan is to provide guidelines for future development which will satisfy aviation demand and be compatible with the environment, community development, and other modes of transportation. More specifically it is a guide for:

1. Developing the physical facilities of an airport

2. Developing land in and adjacent to the airport

3. Determining the environmental effects of airport construction and operations

4. Establishing access requirements

5. Establishing the economic and financial feasibility of proposed developments

6. Establishing a schedule of priorities and phasing for the improvements proposed in the plan

Airport planning is based upon a multitude of procedures and criteria for evaluating needs, proposing alternative concepts, ranking, assigning priorities, and justifying the selected alternatives. In the early days of airport planning, the plan evolved primarily as a technically viable solution geared almost entirely to aircraft operational requirements. In today's setting, however, many complex technical, environmental, social, economic, financial, and political considerations influence the airport plan. As a result the plan adopted may not necessarily be the best technical plan, but usually represents a compromise among many diverse physical and non-physical planning requirements.

THE ELEMENTS OF AN AIRPORT PLANNING STUDY

Coordination

Airport planning efforts draw widespread interest from private citizens, community organizations, airport users, areawide planning agencies, and conservation groups. If these groups are not used in a coordinated, consultative, and advisory role at critical stages in the development of the plan, it will likely be unsuccessful when presented to the public. Interested parties should be brought in early in the development of the plan and given access to all relevant information. This process allows vital issues and concerns to be input to and resolved in the planning process and often assists in the ultimate acceptance of the plan.

Content

The content of an airport plan varies in both level of detail and specific requirements depending upon the type of planning effort undertaken. However, the system plan and the master plan should include at least the following elements:

1. An inventory of existing airport facilities and an identification of other planning studies which may impact the airport plan.

2. The demand forecast, including aircraft operations, number of passengers, volume of cargo and mail, and vehicular traffic. The forecast must be made not only on an annual basis, but also for the busiest hours of the day.

3. An analysis of the interaction between the various demand parameters and the capacity of the relevant facilities, including those which affect airfield, terminal, and ground access system operations.

4. The development of alternative solutions to reasonably satisfy forecast demand, taking into account such factors as the functional role of the airport or airports under study and the impacts on the environment, safety, economy, and fiscal resources of the area. An examination of alternative sites, including land use and ground access plans, is essential for the proper consideration and identification of viable alternatives.

5. The determination of the cost-effectiveness of alternative solutions, including not only the tangible but also the more intangible benefits and costs. Tangible benefits include such items as reduction in delays to aircraft. These are the benefits that can readily be quantified in monetary terms. Social costs on the other hand are much more difficult to quantify in monetary terms and are often referred to as intangible. There are many important benefits that are significant in the decision-making process, but which are also difficult to quantify. One of the more important of these is aircraft noise. Therefore one must search for measures of effectiveness in other than monetary terms. For example, in the case of noise, it could be established that one runway layout was more effective than another because the number of people exposed to noise was reduced by one-half. It should be clear that a cost-effectiveness analysis is not an end in itself, but merely an aid to decision making.

6. A financial feasibility analysis, which differs from economic feasibility, for there is no guarantee that if a proposed development is economically feasible, it is also feasible to finance it. Investment priorities must be established among the various individual airport improvements. Frequently airport planning is separated from financial and management planning; the latter being undertaken only after a physical plan is adopted. Because of financial constraints, financial planning should be undertaken concurrently with the planning of the physical facilities.

7. The environmental impact of alternative solutions must be considered and incorporated into the cost-effectiveness analysis. Although aircraft noise is the principal environmental problem faced by airport authorities, there are other factors that must be considered. These are described in the chapter discussing environmental impact.

Inventory

The initial step in the preparation of the plan is the collection of data on existing airport facilities and areawide planning efforts. State and regional transportation authorities should be consulted as they may be sources of valuable data. A key source of data, especially for traffic volumes, is the FAA. The planner should identify all of the physical facilities at the airports, how they are used, and the volumes of traffic in and out of the airport. An identification of the uses of the airspace, the availability of aids to air navigation, and communication facilities which serve the airport should be made. An inventory of land uses adjacent to the airport is also necessary to ascertain the environmental impact of improvements on the airport's neighbors. The collection of socioeconomic and demographic data, such as population, employment, income levels, industrial and commercial activity, and land use, for the service area is of value in demand forecasting. A study of the financing mechanisms available to support airport improvements is necessary for the development of a financial plan.

Forecasts

An airport plan must be developed on the basis of forecasts. From forecasts of demand an evaluation of the performance effectiveness of the various airport facilities can be established. Forecasts are usually needed for the short, intermediate, and long ranges, or approximately 5, 10, and 20 years. As the range of a forecast is increased, it becomes less precise and should be viewed as only an approximation. Earlier it was stated, depending upon the level of detail required in the planning effort, that for some activities, such as aircraft movements and number of passengers, both annual and busy hour forecasts are necessary, while for air cargo and mail an annual forecast may be sufficient. There are a number of ways to forecast future demand. Forecasting methods differ substantially; some are much more sophisticated than others, but all have a certain degree of uncertainty. Some methods are more suited for long-range forecasting. The simplest forecasting techniques simply project into the future past trends of travel volumes. The more complex techniques relate demand to a number of social, economic, and technological factors that affect air travel.

A relationship between social, technological, and economical variables on the one hand and travel demand on the other is called a *demand model*. The development and use of demand models can be outlined by the following steps:

1. Observe past and current trends of air travel demand

2. Inventory the variations in economic, social, and technological factors affecting air travel demand

3. Establish a relationship between travel demand and those factors found to be of significance in altering travel demand

4. Project into the future the values of those factors affecting travel demand

5. Use the model and the forecasts to obtain forecasts of future air travel demand.

A detailed discussion of the techniques available and their applicability to airport planning is contained in the next chapter.

Analysis of Capacity and Delay

The determination of the capacity, delay, and processing times associated with several viable alternative schemes for the improvement of existing airports or the development of a new ones is an essential step in airport planning. The comparison of demand with capacity provides basic information for determining the extent of the required facilities. Delay is an essential input into a benefit-cost analysis. The money saved from reduced delays can be compared with the cost of airfield improvements, thus establishing a relationship between benefits and costs. Table 5-1 presents approximate guidelines for the determination of the levels of annual aircraft demand which cause a need for airside planning efforts.

The capacity analysis of airports includes not only the airfield but also

TABLE 5-1   **Criteria for the Planning of Runway System Changes Based upon Level of Annual Aircraft Operations**

Configuration	% aircraft over 12,500 lb using airport	
	less than 10%	greater than 90%
	Annual operations, [a]	
Single runway	90,000–150,000	80,000–140,000
Two intersecting runways, location of intersection:		
In middle or far end	95,000–160,000	95,000–160,000
At ends, operations away from intersection;		
60% or less of time	95,000–160,000	95,000–160,000
80% of time	120,000–200,000	100,000–170,000
90% of time	135,000–225,000	125,000–210,000
100% of time	160,000–270,000	145,000–230,000
Open V Runways, operations away from intersections:		
60% or less of time	110,000–180,000	100,000–170,000
80% of time	135,000–225,000	120,000–200,000
90% of time	150,000–250,000	135,000–225,000
100% of time	210,000–350,000	160,000–270,000
Three intersecting runways, location of intersections:		
All at middle of runways	100,000–170,000	100,000–170,000
One pair at ends	110,000–180,000	110,000–180,000
Two pairs at ends	125,000–210,000	125,000–210,000
All runways intersecting at ends	160,000–270,000	140,000–230,000
Parallel runways:		
Terminal O < 3500 ft Close parallels No taxiway crossing problem	240,000–400,000	140,000–230,000[b]
Terminal O < 3500 ft Taxiways crossing active runways more than 1/3 from active thresholds	170,000–280,000	140,000–230,000[b]
Terminal O ≥ 5000 ft Open parallels	240,000–400,000	180,000–300,000

[a] Capacity may be less than shown if more than 50% of aircraft cannot use one runway.

[b] Low values were obtained due to IFR limited capacities. For parallel runways spaced greater than 3500 ft the values given may be increased by 20%.

SOURCE: Federal Aviation Administration [7].

the terminal airspace, aircraft gates, passenger terminals, vehicular circulation and parking within the airport boundary, and surface access to the
airport. The proximity of airports to one another, the orientation of
runways, and the type of operations (VFR or IFR) are all factors which can
affect the capacity of an individual airport. As a first approximation, it is
suggested that for instrument operations a rectangular area 10 by 25 mi be
reserved for the airspace for large aircraft with the airport runway approximately centered in the rectangle. For small airplanes, the size of the
rectangle is reduced to 8 by 15 mi [26]. If these requirements cannot be
met, it is suggested that the planner consult with the appropriate governmental authorities.

The capacity of roadways providing access to the airport can be
obtained from references [27] and [28]. For large airports, access can be a
constraint on the development of the entire airport complex [10].

The capacity of the airport system for an area must also be viewed in
light of the functional roles of the airports in the system. A distinction is
required between facilities to accommodate commercial and general aviation operations. Based upon the projected needs ascertained in the demand
forecast, sufficient facilities must be provided for the many diverse aviation
uses consistent with overall policy guidelines.

Facility Requirements

The general location of the various types of airport facilities as well as the
requirements for runways, taxiways, aprons, terminals, cargo and servicing
facilities, roadways, and parking at the various sites are developed from an
analysis of the demand and capacity requirements, and from geometric and
other standards governing the design of airport components. This yields
the number, length, and configuration of runways, the configuration of the
taxiways, the number of gates, and the sizes of passenger terminal buildings, cargo buildings, and facilities for general aviation aircraft. This
information enables the planner to obtain a first approximation of the
overall size and shape for new airports or the expansion of existing sites,
and to analyze the impacts on land use, environment, infrastructure, and
airspace.

Airport Site Selection

The individual who undertakes the selection of a site suitable for new
airports must first establish certain criteria which will serve as a guide in
the determination of its proper location and size. Most of these criteria,
however, are also applicable to the expansion of existing airports. The
location of an airport will be influenced by the following factors:

1. Type of development of the surrounding area
2. Atmospheric and meteorological conditions

3. Accessibility to ground transport

4. Availability of land for expansion

5. Presence of other airports and availability of airspace in the area

6. Surrounding obstructions

7. Economy of construction

8. Availability of utilities

9. Proximity to aeronautical demand

Type of Development of the Surrounding Area

This is an extremely important factor, since airport activities, particularly from the standpoint of noise, are often quite objectionable to the airport's neighbors. Thus a study of current and prospective uses of land adjacent to an airport site is essential. Sites which offer the closest compatibility with airport activities should be given priority [36].

Proximity to residential areas and schools should be avoided whenever possible. If the site is sparsely developed, enactment of zoning ordinances controlling the use of land adjacent to the airport should be considered in order to avoid future conflicts [11]. An airport is essential to a community's transport complex, yet it is an integral part of the community. Hence it is subject to the same principles and policies that govern other elements of a community plan and must be coordinated with existing as well as planned features. It is desirable to provide a buffer zone between the runways, taxiways, aprons, and so on, and the boundaries of the airport property, in order that nuisances created by activities of the airport be at least partially attenuated.

Noise is an extremely important factor where jet aircraft operations are anticipated. Since the introduction of jet aircraft, adverse community reaction to noise has grown rapidly. In several large urban areas the FAA has prescribed specific flight patterns for aircraft to minimize the impact of noise. Regulations on a national scale have also been formulated. Aircraft and engine manufacturers are well aware of this problem, and every effort is being made to reduce noise consistent with the operating economics and safety of aircraft.

Atmospheric and Meteorological Conditions

The presence of fog, haze, and smoke reduces visibility and has the effect of lowering the traffic capacity of an airport, since the capacity when the visibility is poor is less than that when it is good. Fog has a tendency to settle into areas where there is little wind. Lack of wind can be caused by surrounding topography. Likewise, smoke and haze are present in the vicinity of large industrial areas. An examination of specific site conditions as well as a detailed analysis of available weather records should be undertaken for all potential sites. Comparative site evaluations must be made to ensure that the selected site offers characteristics which are commensurate with aviation needs.

Accessibility to Ground Transportation

Transit time from the point of origin to the ultimate destination for passengers and shippers of air freight is a matter of major concern. In many cases the ground time exceeds the air time by a considerable margin. With the introduction of jet transports the margin has increased even more. For a journey of 400 mi between two large metropolitan areas, ground times can be as much as twice the air travel time.

Surveys that have been made of ground transport to the airport indicate that in the United States the majority of passengers, visitors, and airport and airline employees travel by private automobile [42]. Indications are that this trend will continue in the future. Origins and destinations of travelers and shippers relative to airports are widely scattered throughout a metropolitan area. Out-of-town passenger origins and destinations seem to concentrate more in centralized hotel locations near business centers. On the other hand, many of these travelers are using rented automobiles.

Because of the lack of concentration of origins and destinations of air passengers in a metropolitan area and the popularity of the automobile as a personal means of transportation, the use of public transit up to now has not been large [35]. However, as air transport keeps growing, the volume of passengers may be so large as to warrant special means of transportation to the airport. This may be especially true in large urban areas whenever the normal peak traffic periods coincide with the peak traffic periods at the airport. In some cities a train connects the airport with a downtown terminal [43]. Other cities are planning similar installations. While such installations are undoubtedly quite expensive and probably cannot be economically justified on the basis of serving the airport alone, they may become useful in the future as part of a rapid transit facility for an entire metropolitan area. In any event, the private automobile will continue to be an important means of transportation to the airport. Consequently the planning of streets and highways to the airport and parking at the airport are important factors which must be given consideration.

Access to airports is required not only by air passengers but also by other users of the airport, such as employees, visitors, spectators, trucks hauling freight, and businesses dealing with the airport's tenants. All modes of access should be considered. The need for satellite terminals in downtown areas should also be examined.

Statistics have shown that the private automobile is the major form of access to the airport for both passengers and employees. It is expected that this trend will continue in the future despite the greater availability of mass transit. Although air cargo is growing rapidly, truck traffic is not a major contributor to airport traffic. On the other hand, the number of trips by airport employees can be larger than the number generated by airline passengers. This depends on the size of the airport and the presence of commercial enterprises or large maintenance facilities at the airport.

The starting point for estimating the ground traffic generated by air passengers is a forecast of future air travel. It is very desirable to have a forecast of the daily distribution of passenger demand in terms of enplaning and deplaning passengers, at least for the busy hours of the day. The next step is to estimate the modal split of ground transportation among the various available alternatives, including private automobiles, taxis, limousines, and mass transit. After estimating the modal split it is necessary to estimate the occupancy in each mode. Using the modal split of airline passengers and the average occupancy by mode, the number of vehicles generated by airline passengers can be determined. From highway capacity standards the number of lanes required to serve passengers can be established [27, 28]. In addition to an estimate of the number of airline passengers, an estimate must be made of the number of trips generated by spectators and visitors not accompanying passengers. In some cases this may amount to 15 to 25 percent of the air passenger traffic. Another approach is to correlate air passenger activity hour by hour with corresponding ground activity by the use of statistical analysis. Such analyses may include the inherent assumption that the current ground-to-air traffic relationship will be maintained in the future, which may not be true if the modal choice split is altered significantly by providing public transit. For this reason a regression approach is satisfactory for a first approximation, but a more complete knowledge of the various factors generating ground traffic must be known to arrive at more accurate future requirements for ground access. Data have been collected for various trip generators, including the various types of airport facilities, and these may be used as a guide for estimating highway system requirements [44].

As stated earlier, traffic generated by employees during peak periods can exceed that generated by passengers and visitors. This makes it imperative to consider employee access requirements separately. Employees usually have a different origin and destination pattern, which may have some influence on access requirements. Studies have shown that no consistent relationship exists between the number of airport employees and the annual number of air passengers.

Once the total volume of traffic entering the airport is known, an assignment must be made within the airport boundary. It is essential that the circulation of vehicular traffic in the terminal building area be well planned, otherwise congestion and delays are likely to develop.

The circulation of traffic in an airport should generally be one way and counterclockwise. The roads should be wide enough to permit passing.

Direction information to locations of specific airline arrivals and departures and public parking facilities should be adequate in number, size, and legibility [29].

Pedestrian routes should be direct, well marked, and adequately lighted. Covered walkways from public parking lots or to the entrance of the terminal building should be considered if bad weather occurs a substantial amount of the time and walking distances are long.

Provisions for automobile parking must be adequate in order to ensure that the airport functions effectively and efficiently. Despite the use of other means of ground transportation to and from the airport, the use of the private automobile will continue to be substantial. Facilities required to satisfy automobile parking demand for major airports have grown to such magnitude that they have become a dominant consideration in the planning of an airport. A major goal for locating parking facilities for airline passengers is to minimize walking distances and therefore bring the automobile as close as possible to the aircraft. The volume and characteristics of users play a major role in planning parking facilities. Each class of user has a different requirement, depending on the reason for being at the airport. Adequate provisions must also be made for the elderly and handicapped to access airport facilities [2].

Parking at an airport must be provided for airline passengers, visitors accompanying passengers, spectators, people employed at the airport, car rentals and limousines, and people having business with the airport tenants.

Separate parking areas should be provided for employees. These should be located as close as possible to the facilities in which they work. Parking requirements for car rental should be determined by consultation with the rental concessionaires. It is desirable to locate the car rental parking area as close as possible to the terminal building in order to minimize the passengers' walking distance. This close-in parking need not be for the entire car rental fleet but only for cars which have previously been reserved by arriving passengers. Departing passengers can deposit rental cars in an outlying parking area within the airport. This should be conveniently located to the main airport internal access road. From there the car rental firm provides transportation to the passenger terminals. This is a common arrangement at large airports.

Public parking facilities are provided for airline passengers, visitors, and spectators. Surveys at a number of airports in the United States indicate that a large number of airline users, on the order of 80 percent, park 3 hours or less, and a very much smaller group park from 12 hours to several days or longer. The short-term parkers, however, represent only about 15 to 20 percent of the maximum vehicle accumulation in the parking facility. Therefore, many airports designate the most convenient spaces to short-term parkers who represent the highest number of users, and regulate these facilities by charging premium rates for parking. At large airports parking is provided outside the boundary of the airport by private concessionaires who provide transportation to the airport for their patrons.

Projections of future public parking demand at an airport are generally made by some method of correlation with projected growth in air traffic, usually airline passengers. At an existing airport, information on the hourly distribution of automobile traffic entering and leaving the parking facility daily is required. The difference between entering and leaving traffic gives the accumulation of vehicles in the parking facility. A plot of the hourly distribution of accumulated vehicles will yield the peak accumulation and when it occurs. An example of such a plot for determining the parking requirements at O'Hare International Airport is shown in Fig. 5-2 [20]. The peak accumulation represents current needs if the peak demand is to be accommodated.

To project into the future, a relationship between the number of cars entering and leaving a parking facility in a specific period of time, usually 1 hour, and the total number of air passengers arriving and departing during the same period of time is necessary. For example, if there are 2000 arriving and departing passengers per hour and the number of cars entering and leaving the facility in the same time period is 1000, the number of vehicles is one-half the number of passengers. Vehicle occupancy can be affected by the number of visitors accompanying passengers. The number can vary

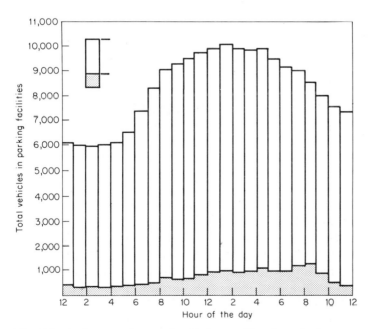

Fig. 5-2 Total accumulation of vehicles in all parking facilities at O'Hare International Airport on a typical day in 1977. (*Landrum and Brown, Inc. [20].*)

considerably, depending on the area in which the airport is located. The forecast of passengers and vehicle occupancy can be used to determine the size of the entrance and exit to the parking facility and the number of spaces required. The busy-hour vehicle flow into and out of the facility can be determined by dividing the forecast of busy-hour passenger demand by vehicle occupancy. The number of spaces in the parking facility can be determined in one of two ways. One way is to obtain a projection of the daily distribution of passengers entering or leaving the airport and converting the number of passengers to vehicles to find the peak accumulation of vehicles. Another way is to correlate the maximum accumulation of vehicles with busy-hour passenger demand during known years, and apply the correlation to projected future busy-hour demand.

It may not be feasible to satisfy demand during the busiest hours of the year. This is a matter of policy which rests with airport management. In part it will be influenced by available space and the costs associated with providing parking. Often remote parking lots are used for overflow.

Methods used for projecting parking requirements range from rules of thumb based on nationwide averages to trend analysis, mathematical models, and simulation. The choice of method depends on the type of planning being undertaken and the accuracy and sensitivity desired. Relatively simple methods based on parking experience at the airport may be sufficient for long-range master planning, but more sophisticated techniques may be required for more precise planning and design, especially when costly parking structures are involved. The planner should always bear in mind that the accuracy of parking projections depends on the accuracy of passenger projections.

The recommended basic parking stall is 8.5 ft wide and 18 ft long. The choice of pattern for parking is dictated by the shape of the area available. For planning purposes about 420 ft^2 is required per parking stall, including circulation. This translates to about 100 vehicles per acre for public and employee parking. Rental car customer parking is provided at the same rate. However, rental car storage is more efficient in space utilization. It is usually recommended that such space be provided at the rate of about 160 vehicles per acre. Estimates of the total number of parking stalls vary, but preliminary estimates may be obtained by allowing about 400 annual originating passengers per public stall and about 750 annual enplaned passengers per rental car stall. Care should be exercised in applying these estimating parameters because of the distinctive nature of travel patterns at different airports.

Availability of Land for Expansion

In a field as dynamic as aviation it is necessary to acquire land in advance or to be able to acquire sufficient real estate in the future for expanding the airport plant. Historically, as the size of aircraft and the volume of traffic increased, runways have had to be lengthened, terminal facilities expanded, and additional support facilities provided. Sufficient real estate must be available to accommodate new facilities. An investigation of policies related to land banking can lead to considerable economies and minimize future environmental impact [11].

Presence of Other Airports and Availability of Airspace

The operations at other airports in the area must be carefully analyzed when a site for a new airport is selected or when additional runways are provided at an existing airport. Airports should be located at a sufficient distance from each other to prevent aircraft which are maneuvering for a landing at one airport from interfering with the movements of aircraft at other airports. The minimum distance between airports depends entirely on the volume and type of traffic and whether the airports are equipped to operate under poor visibility conditions. Many metropolitan areas are experiencing severe air traffic congestion in the limited airspace available to serve the many airports in the region.

Maneuvering in the air is vastly more complicated during periods of poor visibility. Under instrument flying conditions, air traffic control segregates aircraft using the airways and maintains control until each in turn is cleared for an instrument approach to the airport.

The location of several airports in a metropolitan area can greatly influence their respective capacities. If the locations are too near each other, operations can be restricted to the extent that two airports will have no more capacity during IFR weather than a single airport.

Airport location must be consistent with the overhead airway traffic patterns if conflicts in traffic flow are to be avoided. It is imperative that the airport planner consult with the FAA on the adequacy of an airport site insofar as air traffic control is concerned. An illustration of the interaction of airspace for two airports is given in Fig. 5-3.

Surrounding Obstructions

Sites should be selected so that approaches necessary for the ultimate development of the airport are free of obstructions or can be cleared if obstructions exist. The provision and protection of adequate approaches to an airport will necessitate height restrictions in the airport turning zones and in line with the runways. Steps should be taken in the planning stage to preclude the possibility of any future erection of obstructions to aircraft using the airport. The purchase of the real estate necessary to protect approaches may not be economically feasible. Therefore, zoning for height restrictions should be initiated as soon as a site has been selected [19].

The required clearances for the approaches to the runways and in the maneuver area directly above and adjacent to the airport are outlined in

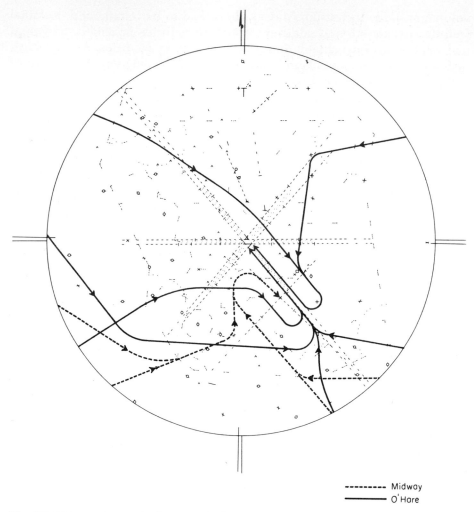

--------- Midway
———— O'Hare

Fig. 5-3 Airspace interaction between Midway and O'Hare International airports. (*Landrum and Brown, Inc. [17].*)

detail by the FAA in FAR Part 77 [34] and by the ICAO in Annex 14 [30]. An object that protrudes above the imaginary surfaces specified in these two references is considered an obstruction to air navigation. If the planner finds that there is an obstruction to air navigation, the appropriate governmental agency must be contacted so that a special aeronautical study may be undertaken to determine the feasibility of a waiver being granted without degrading safety.

In FAR Part 77 airports are classified as shown in Fig. 5-4. Visual runway means a runway intended solely for the operation of aircraft using visual approach procedures. A utility runway means a runway that is constructed for and intended to be used by propeller-driven aircraft weighing 12,500 lb or less. A nonprecision instrument runway means a runway having an instrument approach procedure with only horizontal guidance or RNAV equipment. A precision instrument runway means a runway having an existing instrument approach procedure utilizing ILS or PAR.

In order to determine whether an object is an obstruction to air navigation, several imaginary surfaces are established with relation to the airport and to each runway. The size of the imaginary surfaces depends on the category of each runway, such as utility, and on the type of approach planned for that runway, such as visual, nonprecision instrument, or precision instrument.

If the federal government is to participate in the financing of a new airport or the expansion of an existing one, it will require that clear zones at the ends of runways be provided by the airport operator. Runway clear zones are areas comprising the innermost portions of the runway approach areas as defined in FAR Part 77.

The federal government requires that the airport owner have an adequate property interest in the clear-zone area in order that the require ments of FAR Part 77 can be met and the area protected from future encroachments. Adequate property interest may be in the form of ownership in fee simple, long-term leases or any other demonstration of legal ability to prevent future obstructions in the runway clear zone [19].

The federal government has long recognized that the provision of adequate approaches very near the ends of runways is essential to the interest of safety, yet often quite difficult to maintain, unless positive control of the area can be exercised by the airport owner. Experience has also shown that the exercise of this control by zoning alone has not proved satisfactory, hence the necessity of obtaining some kind of interest in the land itself. Recognizing that such an interest imposes a financial burden on

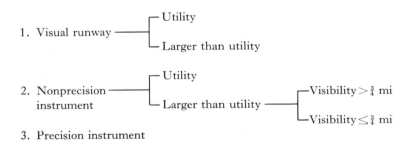

Fig. 5-4 Classification of airport runways by Federal Aviation Regulations Part 77. (*Federal Aviation Administration [34].*)

the airport owner, the federal government has made provision to participate in obtaining adequate property interests in clear-zone areas [31].

The ICAO requirements are similar to FAR Part 77, with several
notable exceptions. ICAO specifies dimensions for each category of runway, coded, 1, 2, 3, and 4, based upon runway length, as shown in Table
5-2. The approach surface defined in Part 77 is for both arriving and
departing aircraft. ICAO separates arrivals and departures and specifies
dimensions for approach surfaces for arrivals and takeoff climb surfaces for
departures. The horizontal surface specified by ICAO is a circle whose
center is at the airport reference point (ARP), whereas in Part 77 it is not a
circle.

A detailed description of these surfaces is presented in the chapter
dealing with airport configuration.

Economy of Construction

It is clear that if alternative sites are available and equally adequate,
the site which is more economical to construct should be given consideration. Sites lying on submerged lands are much more costly to develop than
those on dry land. Rolling terrain requires much more grading than flat
terrain. The availability of local construction materials, including aggre-
gates which can be obtained on site or at nearby locations, can have a
significant impact on construction cost.

Availability of Utilities

An airport, particularly a large one, requires large quantities of water,
natural gas or oil, electric power, and fuel for aircraft and surface vehicles.
In site selection, the provision for these utilities must be given consideration. Most of these utilities will have to be transported to the airport by
either truck, rail, sea, or pipes. On a new site which is not near available
sewers, a disposal plant may have to be constructed. In the case of electric

TABLE 5-2 **Codification of Airports by
the International Civil Aviation
Organization for Obstruction Surfaces**

Runway code	Runway length, meters
1	less than 800
2	800–1200
3	1200–1800
4	1800 and over

SOURCE: International Civil Aviation Organization [30].

power, most large airports must provide generating plants of their own to be used in emergencies in the event that a commercial source fails. In some cases, airports are providing generating facilities which meet a portion of the power needs on a continuing basis due to the efficiency of new technology for energy generation.

Proximity to Aeronautical Demand

In the selection of a new airport site it is quite important that the location be such as to result in the shortest ground access time possible. While much has been said about the establishment of regional airports at considerable distances from the centers of population, the fact remains that about half of the passengers in the United States travel no more than about 500 mi; almost a majority of all scheduled flights are in these short-haul markets. This trend is expected to continue in the future.

It is in the short-haul operations that access time to the airport is quite important. The airline traveler is more interested in overall door-to-door time than just in the portion in the air. Locating an airport a considerable distance from the center of population not only negates the increased speed provided by short-range turbojet transports, but results in loss of patronage as well.

Factors Influencing Airport Size

The necessary size of an airport will depend on such primary factors as:

1. The performance characteristics and size of aircraft expected to use the airport

2. The anticipated volume of traffic

3. Meteorological conditions

4. The elevation of the airport site

The performance characteristics of aircraft will have a direct bearing on the length of runways. Airport designers do not normally have access to information concerning the performance of various types of transport aircraft. This type of information is available from airline engineering departments and aircraft manufacturers. However, most airport planners and designers are not sufficiently familiar with all the technical aspects concerning aircraft performance. In order to provide the airport designer with the information needed on runway length, agencies such as the FAA and ICAO have examined the performance characteristics of many types of aircraft and documented runway length requirements [3, 41]. Whenever possible, the lengths to be provided should be determined by consultation with airlines and other users of the airport.

The volume and character of traffic have an influence on the number of runways required, the configuration of the taxiways, and the size of the ramp area.

Important meteorological conditions which can affect the size of an airport are wind and temperature. Temperature influences runway length, high temperatures requiring longer lengths. The direction of the wind influences the number of runways and their configuration. Techniques for the analysis of the effects of wind are contained in a later chapter.

The elevation of the airport site exerts a significant influence on the runway length requirements of aircraft. As elevation increases runway length requirements increase as discussed in Chap. 3.

Land-Use Planning

A land-use plan for property within the airport boundary and in areas adjacent to the airport is an essential part of an airport master plan. The land-use plan on and off the airport is an integral part of an areawide comprehensive planning program, and therefore it must be coordinated with the objectives, policies, and programs for the area which the airport is to serve. Incompatibility of the airport with its neighbors stems primarily from the objections of people to aircraft noise. A land-use plan must therefore project the extent of aircraft noise that will be generated by airport operations in the future. Contours of equal intensity of noise can be drawn and overlaid on a land-use map, as shown in Fig. 5-5. From these contours an estimate can be made of the compatibility of existing land use with airport operations. If the land outside the airport is underdeveloped, the contours are the basis for establishing comprehensive land-use zoning requirements.

Although zoning is used as a method for controlling land use adjacent to an airport, it is not effective in areas which are already built up because it is not retroactive. Furthermore jurisdictions having zoning powers may not take effective zoning action. Finally the airport operations may be difficult. Despite these shortcomings the planner should utilize zoning as a vehicle to achieve compatibility wherever this approach is feasible.

Airports become involved in two types of zoning. One type is height and hazard zoning, which is mainly to protect the approaches to the airport from obstructions [19]. Both FAR Part 77 [34] and ICAO Annex 14 [30] are the bases for height and hazard zoning. The other type is land-use zoning.

The extent of land use on the airport depends a great deal on the amount of acreage available. Uses can be classified as either closely or remotely related to aviation. Those closely related to aviation use include the runways, taxiways, aprons, terminal buildings, parking, and maintenance facilities. Nonaviation uses include space for recreational, industrial, and commercial activities. When considering commercial or industrial activities, care should be taken to ensure that they will not interfere with aircraft operations, communications equipment, and aids to navigation on

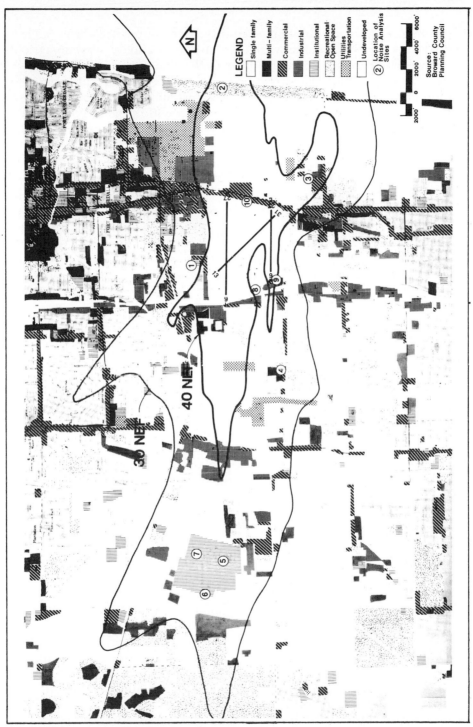

Fig. 5-5 Noise contours superimposed on a land-use plan for Fort Lauderdale–Hollywood International Airport. (*Environmental Sciences and Engineering, Inc. [23].*)

the ground. Smoke can obscure visibility. Recreational facilities such as golf courses may be suitable within the airport boundary. Certain agricultural uses are also appropriate as long as they do not attract birds. When there is acreage within the airport boundary in excess of aviation needs, it is sound fiscal planning to provide the greatest financial return from leases of the excess property. Thus the land-use plan within the airport is a very effective tool in helping airport management make decisions concerning requests for land use by various interests.

The principal objective of the land-use plan for areas outside the airport boundary is to minimize the disturbing effects of noise. As stated earlier, the delineation of noise contours is the most promising approach for establishing noise-sensitive areas. The contours define the areas which are or are not suitable for residential use and, likewise, those which are suitable for light industrial, commercial, or recreational activity. Although the responsibility for developing land uses adjacent to the airport lies with the governing bodies of adjacent communities, the land-use plan provided by the airport authority will greatly influence and assist the governing bodies in their task of establishing comprehensive land-use zoning.

Environmental Impact Assessment

Environmental factors must be considered carefully in the development of a new airport or the expansion of an existing one. This is a requirement of the Airport and Airway Development Act of 1970 (Public Law 91-258) and the Environmental Policy Act of 1969 (Public Law 91—190). Studies of the impact of the construction and operation of a new airport or the expansion of an existing one upon acceptable levels of air and water quality, noise levels, ecological processes, and demographic development of the region must be conducted to determine how the airport requirements can best be accomplished [9].

Aircraft noise is the most severe environmental problem to be considered in the development of airport facilities. Much has been done to quiet engines and modify flight procedures, resulting in substantial reductions in noise. Another effective means for reducing noise is through proper planning of land use for areas adjacent to the airport. For an existing airport this may be difficult as the land may already have been built up. Every effort should be made to orient air traffic away from noise-sensitive land development.

Other important environmental factors include air and water pollution, industrial wastes and domestic sewage originating at the airport, and the disturbance of natural environmental values. With regard to air pollution, the federal government and industry have worked jointly toward alleviating the problem, and there is reason to believe that it will probably be eliminated in the near future as a significant factor. An airport can be a major contributor to water pollution if suitable treatment facilities for airport wastes are not provided. The environmental study must include a statement of how water pollution is to be overcome.

The construction of a new airport or the expansion of an existing one may have major impacts on the natural environment. This is particularly true for large developments where streams and major drainage courses may be changed, the habitats of wildlife may be disrupted, and wilderness and recreational areas may be reshaped. The environmental study should indicate how these disruptions might be alleviated.

In the preparation of an environmental study, or an environmental impact statement, the federal government requires that the findings include the following items [9, 40]:

1. The environmental impact of the proposed development

2. Any adverse environmental effects which cannot be avoided should the development be implemented

3. Alternatives to the proposed development

4. The relationship between local short-term uses of the environment and the maintenance and enhancement of long-term productivity

5. Any irreversible environmental and irretrievable commitments of resources which would be involved in the proposed development should it be implemented

6. Growth-inducing impact

7. Mitigation measures to minimize impact

In the application of these guidelines attention must be directed to the following questions. Will the proposed development

1. Cause controversy

2. Noticeably affect the ambient noise level for a significant number of people

3. Displace a significant number of people

4. Have a significant aesthetic or visual effect

5. Divide or disrupt an established community or divide existing uses

6. Have any effect on areas of unique interest or scenic beauty

7. Destroy or derogate from important recreational areas

8. Substantially alter the pattern of behavior for a species

9. Interfere with important wildlife breeding, nesting, or feeding grounds

10. Significantly increase air or water pollution

11. Adversely affect the water table of an area

12. Cause excessive congestion on existing ground transportation facilities

13. Adversely affect the land-use plan for the region

The preparation of an environmental impact statement is an extremely important part of the airport planning process. The statement should clearly identify the problems that will affect environmental quality and the proposed actions to alleviate them. Unless the statement is sufficiently comprehensive, the entire airport development may be in jeopardy. The details of the preparation of environmental assessments are presented in a later chapter.

Economic and Financial Feasibility

The economic and financial feasibility of alternative plans for a new airport or expansion of an existing site must be clearly demonstrated by the planner. Even if the selected alternative is shown to be economically feasible, it is also necessary to show that the plan will generate sufficient revenues to cover annual costs of capital investment, administration, operation, and maintenance. This must be determined for each stage of development scheduled in the master plan.

An evaluation of economic feasibility requires an analysis of benefits and costs. A comparison of benefits and costs of potential capital investment programs indicates the desirability of a project from an economic point of view. The economic criterion used in evaluating an aviation investment is the total cost of facilities, including quantifiable social costs, compared with the value of increased effectiveness measured in terms of total benefits. The costs include capital investment, administration, operation, maintenance, and any other costs that can be quantified. The benefits include a reduction in aircraft and passenger delays, improved operating efficiency, and other benefits. The costs and benefits are usually determined on an annual basis.

There are a number of techniques for comparing benefits with costs. Most of them consider the time value of money based on an appropriate rate of interest which reflects the opportunity cost of capital. The interest rate is a value by which a unit of money received in the future is multiplied to obtain its present value or present worth. In other words a cost incurred in 1976 has a different economic value from that of the same item incurred in 1980.

If the time value of money is not considered, the ratio of benefits to costs is made for each year by merely dividing the benefits in a particular year by the cost of the project in that year. A project is considered economically feasible when the ratio of the benefits to costs is greater than unity, that is, the benefits exceed the costs. The larger the ratio, the more

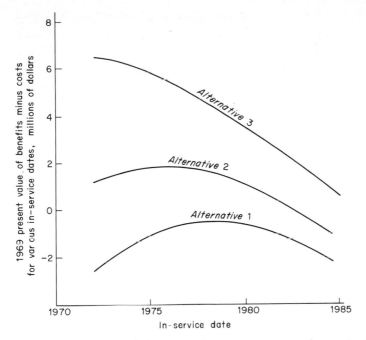

Fig. 5-6 Comparison of alternatives by the net present value method.

attractive is the project from an economic standpoint. A ratio can also be obtained by comparing the present value of benefits with the present value of costs. This approach recognizes the time value of money. Another approach is to plot the *net present value* (NPV) for each year against time. The NPV is defined as the present value of benefits minus the present value of costs. A comparison of three alternatives using the NPV method is shown in Fig. 5-6.

Financing of capital improvements for airports is discussed in an earlier chapter. It was stated that, in the early years of airport development, substantial capital improvement programs were financed at the local level by the sale of general obligation bonds backed by the taxing power of the community. As air transportation became mature and the requirements of the community for capital spending programs increased, airports began to utilize revenue bonds as a source of financing. A financial feasibility study is therefore an analysis to determine if bonds are marketable at reasonable interest rates. It also includes the feasibility of other forms of financing. The analysis requires a thorough evaluation of the revenues to be developed by a proposed improvement and the corresponding costs. Usually this is done in a traffic and earnings study performed over the planning horizon. In such a study, the forecast of demand is utilized, and rates and charges are established for the various revenue categories. This results in annual revenue projections. To make revenue bonds attractive to buyers, a typical airport revenue bond should show an expected coverage by net revenues (gross revenues minus costs) of at least 1.25 times the debt service requirements. If the analysis indicates that the revenues will be insufficient, revisions in the scheduling or scope of the proposed development may have to be made or the rates and charges to the users of the airport may require adjustment.

Continuous Planning Process

A continuous airport system planning process is necessary in order to respond to the needs of air transportation in a changing environment. Changes in aviation demand, community policies, new technology, financial constraints, and other factors can alter the need for and the timing of facility improvements. Current data must be continually collected and assessed relative to airport needs, operations, utilization, environmental impact, and financial capabilities. The staging of airport improvements assists in the reevaluation of continuing needs at the points in time when implementation decisions are required.

REFERENCES

1. "Access to Airports," *Highway Research Record* 274, Transportation Research Board, Washington, D.C., 1969.
2. *Access Travel: Airports, A Guide to Accessibility of Terminals*, Federal Aviation Administration, Washington, D.C., 1979.
3. *Aerodrome Design Manual*, Part 1: *Runways*, International Civil Aviation Organization, Montreal, Que., Canada, 1980.
4. *Aircraft Noise Analyses for the Existing Air Carrier System*, Bolt, Beranek, and Newman, Inc., Aviation Advisory Commission, Federal Aviation Administration, Washington, D.C., Report 2218, September 1972.
5. *Aircraft Sound Description System—Background and Application*, Federal Aviation Administration, Washington, D.C., Report FAA-EQ-73-3, March 1973.
6. "Airport and Air Transport Planning," *Transportation Research Record* 588, Transportation Research Board, Washington, D.C., 1976.
7. *Airport Capacity Criteria Used in the Preparation of the National Airport Plan*, Federal Aviation Administration, Washington, D.C., Advisory Circular AC 150/5060-1A, July 1968.
8. *Airport Curbside Planning Manual*, Wilbur Smith and Associates, Transportation Systems Center, Department of Transportation, Cambridge, Mass., March 1980.
9. *Airport Environmental Handbook*, Federal Aviation Administration, Washington, D.C., Order 5050.4, March 1980.
10. *Airport Ground Access*, Federal Aviation Administration, Washington, D.C., Report FAA-EM-79-4, October 1978.
11. *Airport Land Banking*, Federal Aviation Administration, Washington, D.C., August 1977.

12. *Airport Landside Planning*, Transportation Research Board, Washington, D.C., Special Report 159, 1975.

13. *Airport Master Plans*, Federal Aviation Administration, Washington, D.C., Advisory Circular AC 150/5070-6, February 1971.

14. *Airport Planning Manual*, Part 1: *Master Planning*, International Civil Aviation Organization, Montreal, Que., Canada, 1977.

15. *Airport Planning Manual*, Part 2: *Land Use and Environmental Control*, International Civil Aviation Organization, Montreal, Que., Canada, 1977.

16. *Airport Systems Planning*, R. DeNeufville, M.I.T. Press, Cambridge, Mass., 1976.

17. *Airside Facility Requirements, Chicago Midway Airport Master Plan Study*, Landrum and Brown, Inc., Cincinnati, Ohio, February 1981.

18. "Air Travel and Aviation Facilities Planning," *Transportation Research Record* 529, Transportation Research Board, Washington, D.C., 1975.

19. *A Model Zoning Ordinance to Limit Heights of Objects Around Airports*, Federal Aviation Administration, Washington, D.C., Advisory Circular AC 150/5190-4, August 1977.

20. *Analysis of Vehicular Parking at Chicago O'Hare International Airport*, Landrum and Brown, Inc., Cincinnati, Ohio, February 1978.

21. "An Analysis of Interurban Air Travel," J. B. Lansing, J. C. Lin, and D. B. Suits, *Quarterly Journal of Economics*, February 1961.

22. "Environmental Considerations in Airport Plannings," C. V. Robart, R. Dixon Speas and Associates, Manhasset, NY.

23. *Environmental Impact Assessment for the Expansion of the Existing Terminal Complex at the Fort Lauderdale–Hollywood International Airport*, Environmental Sciences and Engineering, Inc., Tampa, Fla., April 1980.

24. *Fort Lauderdale–Hollywood International Airport, Master Plan Report*, Vol. 1: *Executive Summary*, Landrum and Brown, Inc., Cincinnati, Ohio, August 1977.

25. *Guide for the Planning of Small Airports*, Roads and Transportation Association of Canada, Ottawa, Ont., Canada, 1980.

26. *Guidelines for Airport Spacing and Traffic Pattern Airspace Areas*, Federal Aviation Administration, Washington, D.C., Order 7480.1A, 1971.

27. *Highway Capacity Manual*, Transportation Research Board, Washington, D.C., Special Report 87, 1965.

28. *Interim Materials on Highway Capacity*, Transportation Research Board, Washington, D.C., Circular 212, January 1980.

29. *International Signs to Facilitate Passengers Using Airports*, International Civil Aviation Organization, Montreal, Que., Canada, Document 8881, 1976.

30. *International Standards and Recommended Practices, Aerodromes, Annex 14 to the Convention on International Civil Aviation*, International Civil Aviation Organization, Montreal, Que., Canada, June 1976, as amended November 1982.

31. *Land Acquisition and Relocation Assistance under the Airport Development Aid Program*, Federal Aviation Administration, Washington, D.C., Advisory Circular AC 150/5100-11, February 1975.

32. *Michigan State Airport System Plan*, Michigan Aeronautics Commission, Department of Transportation, Lansing, Mich., Technical Report, May 1972.

33. *Noise Exposure Forecasts—Evolution, Evaluation, Extensions, and Land Use Interpretations*, Federal Aviation Administration, Washington, D.C., Report FAA-NO-70-9, August 1970.

34. *Objects Affecting Navigable Airspace*, Federal Aviation Regulations, Federal Aviation Administration, Washington, D.C., FAR Part 77, January 1975.

35. *Planning for Airport Access: An Analysis of the San Francisco Bay Area*, National Aeronautics and Space Administration, Ames Research Center, Moffett Field, Calif., NASA Conference Publication 2044, May 1978.

36. *Planning the Airport Industrial Park*, Federal Aviation Administration, Washington, D.C., Advisory Circular AC 150/5070-3, September 1965.

37. *Planning for the Airport and Its Environs: The SEA-TAC Success Story*, Federal Aviation Administration, Washington, D.C., April 1978.

38. *Planning the Metropolitan Airport System*, Federal Aviation Administration, Washington, D.C., Advisory Circular AC 150/5070-5, May 1970.

39. *Planning the State Airport System*, Federal Aviation Administration, Washington, D.C., Advisory Circular AC 150/5050-3A, June 1972.

40. *Policies and Procedures for Considering Environmental Impacts*, Federal Aviation Administration, Washington, D.C., Order 1050.1C, January 1980.

41. *Runway Length Requirements for Airport Design*, Federal Aviation Administration, Washington, D.C., Advisory Circular AC 150/5325-4, September 1978.

42. *Survey of Airport Ground Access*, U.S. Aviation Industry Working Group, Washington, D.C., June 1981.

43. *Survey of Fixed Guideway Systems for Access to Airports*, U.S. Aviation Industry Working Group, Washington, D.C., February 1980.

44. *Trip Generation*, Institute of Transportation Engineers, Arlington, Va., Informational Report, 1976.

Chapter **6**

Forecasting in Aviation and Airport Planning

INTRODUCTION

Plans for the development of the various components of the airport system depend to a large extent upon the activity levels which are forecast for the future. Since the purpose of an airport is to process aircraft, passengers, freight, and ground transport vehicles in an efficient and safe manner, airport performance is judged on the basis of how well the demand placed upon the processors within the system is handled. To adequately assess the causes of performance breakdowns in existing airport systems and to plan facilities to meet future needs, it is essential to predict the level and the distribution of the demand on the various components of the airport system. Without a reliable knowledge of the nature and expected variation in the loads placed upon a component, it is impossible to realistically assess the physical and operational requirements of such a component. For example, a forecast to project the mix of aircraft and the types of aviation activity at an airport site is necessary to identify the critical aircraft which dictates the elements of geometric and structural design, the type and extent of physical facilities, the navigational aid requirements, and any special or unique facility needs at the airport [11].

An understanding of future demand patterns allows the planner to assess future airport performance in light of existing and improved facilities, to evaluate the impact of various level of service options on the airlines, travelers, shippers, and community, to recommend development programs consistent with the overall objectives and policies of the airport owner, to estimate the costs associated with these facility plans, and to project the sources and level of revenues to support the capital development program.

It is essential in the planning and design of an airport to have realistic estimates of the future demand to which the airport will be subjected. This is a basic requirement in developing either an airport master plan or an

173

aviation system plan. These estimates determine the future needs for which the physical facilities are designed. A financial plan to achieve the recommended staged development along with required land-use zoning usually accompanies the plan. It should be apparent that an airport is designed for a projected level and pattern of demand, and alterations in the magnitude or configuration of this demand require the implementation of facility modifications to meet changing needs. Facility planning is necessary to provide adequate levels of service to airport users.

The development of accurate forecasts requires a considerable expense of time and monetary resources because of the complex methodologies which must be used and the extensive data acquisition that is often required. The usual justification for a demand forecast in an aviation plan is that the expected level of uncertainty associated with the estimation of essential variables will be reduced, thereby enhancing the decision-making process. The implication, of course, is that the benefits gained due to a better knowledge of the magnitude and fluctuation in demand variables will outweigh the costs incurred in performing the forecast.

To assess the characteristics of future demand, the development of reliable predictions of airport activity is necessary. Pertinent data to be collected to estimate future volumes of aircraft, passenger, freight, mail, and express traffic include information on:

1. The region served by the airport, that is, the airport trade area

2. The origins and destinations of trips by both residents and nonresidents of the area, that is, the air travel market area

3. Demographic and population growth characteristics of the area to be served by the airport

4. The economic character of the area as indicated by such factors as:

a. Per capita disposable income levels

b. The types and levels of business activity, the nature (professional, skilled, unskilled) and size of the labor force employed in industries (agriculture, construction, manufacturing, tourism, mining, finance, insurance, real estate, etc.)

c. Retail and wholesale trade sales, and bank deposits

d. Hotel and motel registrations

5. Trends in the existing transportation activities for passengers, freight, express, and mail by the various modes

6. Trends in national traffic, including estimates of the variables affecting future development

7. Distance, population, and industrial character of nearby areas having air service

8. Geographical factors influencing transportation requirements

9. The existence and degree of competition between airlines and among the several modes of transportation with respect to price, travel time, service frequency, etc.

Forecasts utilizing these types of data give the airport planner a foundation on which to initiate the development of plans to meet the future needs for airport facilities.

Over the years, certain techniques have evolved which enable airport designers to project future aeronautical demand. The principal items for which estimates are usually needed include:

1. The volumes and peaking characteristics of passengers, aircraft, vehicles, freight, express, and mail

2. The number and types of aircraft needed to serve the above traffic

3. The number of based general aviation aircraft and the number of movements generated

4. The performance and operating characteristics of ground access systems

Using forecasting techniques, estimates of these parameters and a determination of the peak-hour volumes of passengers and aircraft movements can be made. From these estimates concepts for the layout and sizing of terminal buildings, runways, taxiways, apron areas, and ground access facilities may be examined.

Forecasting demand in an industry as dynamic as aviation is an extremely difficult matter, and if it could be avoided, it undoubtedly would. Nonetheless estimates of traffic must be made as a prelude to the planning and design of facilities. It is very important to remember that forecasting is not a precise science and that considerable subjective judgment must be applied to any analysis. By anticipating and planning for variations in predicted demand, the airport designer can correct projected service deficiencies before they occur.

LEVELS OF FORECASTING

In aviation demand estimates are prepared for a variety of reasons. Broad large-scale aggregated macroforecasts are made by aircraft and equipment manufacturers, aviation trade organizations, governmental agencies, and others to determine estimates of the market requirements for equipment, trends in travel, personnel needs, air traffic control requirements, and other factors. Similarly, forecasts are made on a smaller scale to examine these needs in particular regions of an area and at specific airports.

In economics, forecasting is done on two levels, and the same holds true in aviation. From the inception of the planning process for an airport consideration is given at both levels. In airport planning, the designer must view the entire airport system as well as the airport under immediate consideration. Macroforecasts are forecasts of the total aviation activity in a large region, such as a country, state, or metropolitan area. Typical macroforecasts are made for such variables as the total revenue passenger-miles, the total enplaned passengers, and the number of aircraft operations, aircraft in the fleet, and licensed airplane pilots and navigators in the country.

Microforecasts deal with the activity at individual airports or on individual routes. Microforecasts for airport planning determine such variables as the number of originations, the passenger origin-destination traffic, the number of enplaned passengers, and the number of aircraft operations by air-carrier and general aviation aircraft at an airport. Separate forecasts are usually made, depending upon the need in a particular study, for cargo movements, commuter service, and ground access vehicular traffic. These forecasts are normally prepared to indicate annual levels of activity and are then disaggregated for airport planning purposes to provide forecasts of the peaking characteristics of traffic during the hours of the day, days of the week, and months of the year. As appropriate to the requirements of an airport planning study, forecasts of such quantities as the number of general aviation aircraft based at an individual airport and the number of general aviation and military operations are also prepared.

In macroforecasting the entire system of airports is examined relative to the geographic, economic, industrial, and growth characteristics of a region to determine the location and nature of airport needs in a region. The microforecast then examines the expected demand at local airports and identifies the necessary development of the airside, landside, and terminal facilities to provide adequate levels of service. Within the two levels of forecasting there are certain techniques which enable the aviation planner to project such parameters as annual, daily, and hourly aircraft operations, passenger enplanements, freight and mail tonnage, and general aviation activity. In microforecasting, there are quite a few variables of significance. The forecast of each variable is quite important because it ultimately determines the size requirements of the facilities which will be necessary to accommodate demand. Often the forecasts of the different variables are linked by a series of steps, that is, originating passengers are forecast first, this then becomes a component in the forecast of enplaned passengers, which leads to a forecast of annual operations, and so on. These techniques are discussed further in the next section.

FORECASTING METHODOLOGIES

There are a considerable variety of forecasting techniques available to airport planners, ranging from subjective judgment to sophisticated mathematical models. The selection of the particular methodology is a function of the use of the forecast, the availability of a data base, the complexity and sophistication of the techniques, the resources available, the time frame in which the forecast is required and is to be used, and the degree of precision desirable. There arc a large number of variables which impact upon a facility plan. It is important that each variable be considered in the context of its use in the plan and that forecasting techniques be utilized which will minimize the uncertainty associated with the range of the forecast variable. For those variables which significantly affect the nature and extent of facilities, more sophisticated techniques are often warranted, and redundancy might be sought through the utilization of several techniques. Such a procedure tends to narrow the expected range of the forecast variable over the planning horizon. Quite often forecasts are prepared under a varying set of assumptions or scenarios to further define the reasonable bounds of the design parameters.

Forecasting by Judgment

An important clement, which should be utilized in any forecasting technique, is the use of professional judgment. A forecast prepared through the use of mathematical relationships must ultimately withstand the test of rationality. In the preparation of the forecast of the annual enplaned passengers at Fort Lauderdale–Hollywood International Airport, the observed trends were modified through the use of judgmental factors. The reason for selecting the projection shown in Fig. 6-1 was a knowledge of the fact that although the enplaned passenger growth rate at this airport was outpacing the national growth rate, this growth rate was also decreasing.

Frequently a group of persons knowledgeable about aviation and the factors influencing aviation trends are assembled to examine forecasts from several different sources, and composite forecasts are prepared in accordance with the information in these sources and the collective judgment of the group. In some cases judgment becomes the principal approach used, with or without an evaluation of economic and other factors that are believed to affect aviation activity.

A common approach being utilized more often today for preparing forecasts by judgment is known as the Delphi method. In this method a panel of experts on a particular subject matter is asked to rate or otherwise arrange in the order of priority a series of questions or projections through a survey technique. The results of the survey are then distributed to the members of the panel, and an opportunity is provided for each member to reevaluate the original rating based upon the collective ratings of the group. The reevaluation phase is often sent through several iterations in order to arrive at a better result. In the Delphi method, the results of the technique do not have to represent a consensus of the panel, and in fact it is

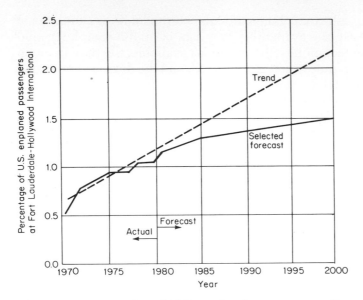

Fig. 6-1 Percentage of total U.S. enplaned passengers at Fort Lauderdale–Hollywood International Airport. (*Aviation Planning Associates, Inc. [22].*)

often quite useful to have a forecast which indicates the spread of the panel in reaching conclusions on a particular issue.

The preparation of judgmental forecasts which reflect the collective wisdom of a broad range of professionals has proven to be very successful in many instances, principally due to the large number of factors which may be considered in such a process. Though there is often a lack of mathematical sophistication in the process, the knowledge and consideration of the many diverse factors influencing aviation forecasts usually improve the results. The disadvantages of this forecasting technique include the absence of statistical measures on which to base the results and the inability, except in the most obvious cases, to gain a significant consensus relative to the expected performance of the explanatory factors in the future.

Trend Projection and Extrapolation

Extrapolation is based upon an examination of the historical pattern of activity and assumes that those factors which determined the variation of traffic in the past will continue to exhibit similar relationships in the future. This procedure utilizes times-series-type data and seeks to analyze the growth and growth rates associated with a particular aviation activity. In practice, trends appear to develop in situations in which the growth rate of a variable is stable in either absolute or percentage terms, there is a gradual increase or decrease in growth rate, or there is a clear indication of a market saturation trend over time [13]. Statistical techniques are used to assist in defining the reliability and the expected range in the extrapolated trend. The analysis of the pattern of demand generally requires that upper and lower bounds be placed upon the forecast and statistics are used to define the confidence levels within which specific projections may be expected to be valid. Quite often smoothing techniques are incorporated into the forecast to eliminate short-run, or seasonal, fluctuations in a pattern of activity which otherwise demonstrates a cyclical pattern in the long run [8]. Several types of extrapolation are commonly used, including linear and curvilinear trend extrapolation. In either case, variables which are suspected to demonstrate relationships to time periods are usually plotted on graph paper, and a determination of the probable functional relationship between the variables is made. In practice it may be necessary to combine several different types of trend extrapolation methods to prepare forecasts, particularly when these forecasts span relatively long time periods. The necessity of such an approach becomes intuitively obvious when one considers the likelihood of variables demonstrating consistent functional relationships throughout the diverse periods of aviation development.

Linear Extrapolation

This technique is used for a pattern of demand which demonstrates an historical linear relationship with a time variable. The underlying relationship may be observed to be constant or to vary in a regular, seasonal, or cyclical pattern. Examples of these types of trends are shown in Fig. 6-2.

Exponential Extrapolation

For a situation in which the dependent variable demonstrates a growth rate which is constant with time, an exponential extrapolation is usually indicated. This phenomenon occurs often in aviation for projections of levels of activity which have shown long-term trends to increase or decrease by an average annual percentage. Population statistics have been shown to demonstrate such a variation in the past. Examples of trends which demonstrate exponential variations are shown in Fig. 6-3. It should be observed that the exponential relationship shows plots as a straight line on logarithmic-linear scale graph paper.

Logistics Curve Extrapolation

In situations where the average annual growth rate begins to diminish gradually with time, it may be appropriate to analyze trends through the use of a logistics curve. As aviation markets evolve, there is often an initial period of gradually increasing annual growth, an intermediate period of fairly constant growth, and a final period in which the growth rate lessens

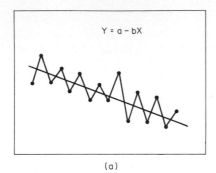

(a)

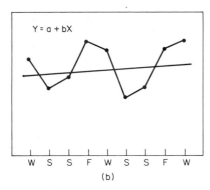

(b)

Fig. 6-2 Typical linear trend data for linear extrapolation of aviation projections. (a) Declining linear trend for annual data; (b) increasing cyclical trend for seasonal data.

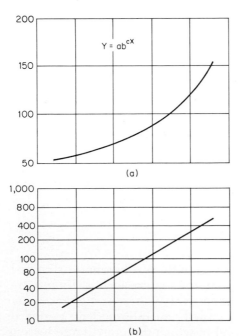

Fig. 6-3 Typical exponential curve trend variation of data. (a) Trend on linear scale graphical plot; (b) trend on log-linear scale graphical plot.

to some point where market saturation has occurred. This type of phenomenon exhibits itself in the fashion of an S-shaped curve, in which the dependent variable asymptotically approaches an upper limit. A curve quite similar to the logistics curve, but of different functional form, is the Gompertz curve. These curves are shown in Figs. 6-4 and 6-5, respectively.

The inability of trend projection techniques to show a causal relationship between the dependent and independent variables is a serious disadvantage. This is particularly true because in the absence of such relationships the degree of uncertainty in such forecasts increases with time. However, trend projections are useful for short-term forecasts in which the response to changes in those factors which stimulate the dependent variables is usually less dynamic. In those cases where cyclic variations may be expected to occur, trend projections may also be quite beneficial.

Market Analysis Methods

Market Share Models

Forecasting techniques which are utilized to proportion a large-scale aviation activity down to a local level are called *market share, ratio,* or *top-*

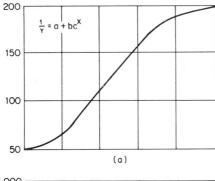

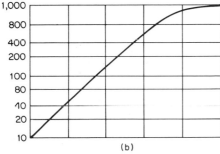

Fig. 6-4 Typical logistics curve trend variation of data. (a) Trend on linear scale graphical plot; (b) trend on log-linear graphical plot.

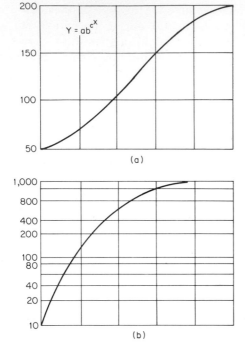

(a)

(b)

Fig. 6-5 Typical Gompertz curve trend variation of data. (a) Trend on linear scale graphical plot; (b) trend on log-linear scale graphical plot.

down models. Inherent to the use of such a method is the demonstration that the proportion of the large-scale activity which can be assigned to the local level is a regular and predictable quantity. This method has been the dominant technique for aviation demand forecasting at the local level, and its most common use is in the determination of the share of total national traffic activity which will be captured by a particular region, traffic hub, or airport. Historical data are examined to determine the ratio of local airport traffic to total national traffic, and the trends are ascertained. From exogenous sources the projected levels of national activity are determined, and these values are then proportioned to the local airport based upon the observed and projected trends. The ratio method is most commonly used in the development of microforecasts for regional airport system plans or for airport master plans.

An example of the data used to prepare a forecast of the number of active aircraft in the State of Florida is given in Table 6-1. These data are plotted in Fig. 6-6 to extrapolate a market share or ratio which can be used to estimate the dependent variable in later years.

These methods are particularly useful in applications in which it can be demonstrated that the market share is a regular, stable, or predictable parameter. For example, the number of annual enplaned passengers at major air traffic hubs has been shown to be a consistent and relatively stable factor, and therefore this method is often used to predict this parameter [6]. An indication of this stability is shown in Table 6-2 for O'Hare International Airport.

Quite often the application of the market share technique is a two-step process in which a ratio is applied to dissaggregate activity forecasts from a national to a regional level, and then another ratio is applied to apportion the regional share among the airports in the region. Table 6-3 illustrates this procedure for the projection of the volume of air cargo at Fort Lauderdale–Hollywood International Airport.

The most compelling advantage of the market share method is its dependence upon existing data sources, which minimizes forecasting cost. However, its principal disadvantages lie in its dependence upon the stability and predictability of the ratios from which the forecasts are made and the uncertainty which may surround market shares in specific applications. An analysis of the factors which determine the scaling of shares may not be explicitly considered, and the introduction of a stimulus or restraint can significantly alter the relationships used to obtain the forecast. There-

TABLE 6-1   **Florida Active General Aviation Aircraft, Historical and Projected Data**

Year	Active aircraft in fleet		Percent of Florida aircraft to U.S. aircraft
	United States	Florida	
Historical			
1960	68,727	2,238	3.26
1961	75,655	2,561	3.39
1962	80,632	2,770	3.44
1963	84,121	2,882	3.43
1964	85,088	3,018	3.55
1965	88,492	3,280	3.71
1966	95,176	3,491	3.67
1967	104,378	4,035	3.87
1968	113,830	4,399	3.86
1969	123,791	4,831	3.90
1970	130,641	5,321	4.07
1971	131,743	5,531	4.20
1972	131,148	5,654	4.31
1973	145,010	6,514	4.49
1974	153,540	7,241	4.72
Forecast			
1980	186,000	9,430	5.07
1985	241,000	13,350	5.54
1990	308,000	18,510	6.01
1995	400,000	25,920	6.48

SOURCE: Landrum and Brown, Inc. [10].

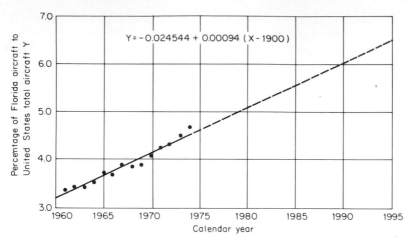

Fig. 6-6 Historical trend and projection of trends for ratio of Florida aircraft to total U.S. aircraft. (*Landrum and Brown, Inc. [10].*)

fore, several forecasts may be required under a differing set of assumptions which are deemed appropriate to the determination of market shares.

Market Definition Models

This type of technique seeks to examine the behavioral characteristics of travelers and to separate travelers into distinct classifications based upon these characteristics. Inherent in the choice of such a method is the belief that certain socioeconomic characteristics influence the propensity for travel, and through the identification and classification of travelers according to such factors it is possible to forecast travel patterns. In general, the population is grouped according to income, occupation, age, type and location of residence, education, and similar factors. From this a study of the travel characteristics of the individual groupings is made. Utilizing the knowledge of these group travel patterns, it is possible to prepare forecasts by simply projecting the size of the group in the future.

This technique does not depend significantly upon the assumed distribution of the underlying data, as is the case in statistically based techniques, such as multiple regression analysis, but only requires sample sizes of significant magnitude to reasonably determine the travel preference of the group. In an early market study performed in New York [3], travel was divided into both personal and business travel. To analyze personal travel, the population was divided into 160 different groups, each characterized by a combination of income, occupation, education, and age. To analyze business travel the labor force was divided into 130 groups, each characterized by a combination of income, occupation, and type of industry [13]. In a more recent study, the travel habits and preferences of firms employing more than 100 persons were determined through surveys to determine air service requirements [12]. The market method does not require complex mathematical relationships and generally uses simple equations to generate a classification table or matrix.

One of the principal advantages of this method is that it allows for a discrimination between discretionary and nondiscretionary travelers and those factors which influence travel behavior in these two distinct groups. The chief disadvantage is that it requires a fairly large sample of the population in order to identify the socioeconomic factors underlying travel choice.

Econometric Modeling Methods

The most sophisticated and complex technique normally found in aviation and airport demand forecasting is the use of econometric models. Trend extrapolation methods do not explicitly examine the underlying relationships between the projected activity descriptor and the many variables which affect its change. There are a wide range of economic, social, and operational factors which affect aviation. Therefore, to properly assess the impact of predicted changes in the other sectors of society upon aviation demand and to investigate the effect of alternative assumptions on aviation, it is often desirable to use mathematical techniques to study the correlations between dependent and independent variables. Econometric models

TABLE 6-2 **Historic Domestic Scheduled Enplaned Passengers on Domestic and Local Service Carriers for the United States and Chicago, 1962–1974**

Year	Domestic scheduled enplanements, thousands		Chicago market share, %
	United States	Chicago	
1962	59,087	5,753	9.74
1963	67,544	6,898	10.21
1964	76,985	7,898	10.26
1965	89,588	9,081	10.14
1966	102,718	10,254	9.98
1967	124,886	11,917	9.54
1968	142,199	13,336	9.38
1969	150,858	13,851	9.18
1970	149,338	13,330	8.91
1971	151,783	13,590	8.95
1972	167,091	14,885	8.91
1973	177,203	15,485	8.74
1974	183,193	16,183	8.83

SOURCE: Landrum and Brown, Inc. [6].

TABLE 6-3 **Domestic Air Cargo Forecast for Fort Lauderdale–Hollywood International Airport (FLL), 1985–2000**

Year	U.S. cargo, million lb	Regional share, %	Regional cargo, thousand lb	FLL share of regional, %	FLL cargo, thousand lb
Historical					
1974	6,854	2.19	149,895	8.06	12,081
1975	6,364	2.05	130,495	6.74	8,794
1976	6,758	2.01	135,869	9.33	12,681
1977	7,174	2.01	144,059	11.64	16,775
1978	7,686	2.09	160,816	15.53	24,967
1979	7,472	2.10	157,123	16.50	25,930
1980*	7,020	2.28	159,842	15.88	25,384
Forecast					
1985	9,494	2.08	197,500	19.00	37,500
1990	12,710	2.08	264,400	21.00	55,500
1995	16,580	2.08	344,900	22.00	75,900
2000	21,720	2.08	451,800	22.50	101,700

* Estimated.

SOURCE: Aviation Planning Associates, Inc. [22].

which relate measures of aviation activity to economic and social factors are extremely valuable techniques in forecasting the future.

There are a great variety of techniques which are used in econometric modeling for airport planning. Classical trip generation and gravity models are quite common in forecasting passenger and aircraft traffic. Simple and multiple regression analysis techniques are often applied to a great variety of forecasting problems to ascertain the relationships between the dependent variables and such explanatory variables as economic and population growth, market factors, travel impedance, and intermodal competition. A compilation of many of the variables used in aviation studies performed by the econometric modeling technique is given in Table 6-4.

The FAA utilized an econometric model to determine through multiple regression techniques projections of the national level of annual air-carrier enplanements over the period from 1976 through 1987 [5]. This macroforecast model is given in Eq. (6-1):

$$ENP = -75.01 + 1.64CMP - 0.04APSU + 1.98PAT - 0.17REL - 5.59STR \tag{6-1}$$

where ENP = level of scheduled domestic revenue enplanements
  CMP = number of civilians employed
  APSU = annual purchase of automobiles
  PAT = private investment in air transportation plants, equipment, etc.

REL = price of air transportation relative to that of other transport modes

STR = a dummy variable to estimate the impact of strikes on the demand for air travel

An econometric model which has been used in several transportation planning studies including the Northeast Corridor Project was adapted for

TABLE 6-4 **Explanatory Variables Used in Air Transportation Studies to Forecast Aviation and Airport Demand**

Factors analyzed	Explanatory variables
Market	
Size and traffic potential	Population
	Industrial production
	Personal income:
	Total per capita
	Disposable
	Discretionary
	Personal expenditures:
	Total
	Travel and recreation
	Propensity for travel
	Leisure time:
	Attractions
	Availability
	Interregional linkages:
	Economic
	Social
Transportation	
Accessibility	Distance to airport
	Travel time to airport
Competition	Alternative airports
	Alternative modes of travel:
	Relative cost
	Relative travel time
	Schedule
	Reliability
Cost of air travel	Average fare
	Fare discounting policies
	Total travel cost
	Value of time
Schedule convenience	Service frequency
	Time of departure
	Necessary connections
Service reliability	On-time performance
	Cancellation history
Transport time	Airport-to-airport time
	Door-to-door time

use in the Michigan State Airport System Plan [14]. In the series of equations which form the model to predict the total intercity passenger demand, projections are required for the population and user cost, travel time, and frequency of service by private automobile, rail, bus, and air transportation between the cities. The principal model equations are given in Eqs. 6-2 and 6-3:

$$V_{ij} = B_i B_j P_i P_j W_{ij}^n \qquad (6\text{-}2)$$

where V_{ij} = total one-way annual passenger flow between city pair ij
B_i, B_j = calibrated constants, indicating measures of economic activity in the cities
P_i, P_j = populations of the cities
W_{ij} = a measure of the total transport impedance between the cities, that is, the sum of the travel impedances by each of the modes
n = a numerical constant

$$w_{ijk} = a_k t_{ijk}^{p_k} c_{ijk}^{q_k} [1 - e^{m f_{ijk}}]^{r_k} \qquad (6\text{-}3)$$

where w_{ijk} = a measure of the travel impedance between cities i and j on mode k

$a_k, p_k, q_k,$
r_k = calibration constants for the various modes of transport k
c_{ijk} = user travel cost on mode k between the two cities i and j
t_{ijk} = travel time on mode k between the two cities i and j
f_{ijk} = frequency of service of mode k between the two cities i and j
m, e = numerical constants

The success in applying mathematical modeling techniques to ascertain the level of future activity depends to a large extent upon the certainty associated with the independent variables and the relative influence of these variables on the dependent variable. Simple and multiple regression analysis methods are often applied to a great variety of forecasting problems to determine the relationships between transport related variables and such explanatory factors as economic and population growth, market factors, travel impedance, and competitive forces. Table 6-5 lists many of the variables required for various purposes in aviation planning studies.

Statistical Testing of Models

There are many statistical tests which can be performed to determine the validity of econometric models in accurately portraying historical phenomena and to reliably project demand. Though the constants may be found to define the general equation of the model, it is possible that the range of error associated with the equation may be large or that the explanatory variables chosen do not directly determine the variation in the dependent variable.

TABLE 6-5 **Typical Air Transportation Forecast Variables and Their Use in Aviation and Airport Studies**

Application in planning studies	Forecast variables required
Macroforecast	
National airport system needs	Revenue passengers
State or regional airport system needs	Revenue passenger-miles
Airlines	Aircraft fleet:
Aircraft and equipment manufacturers	Air carrier
Investment planning	General aviation
Research and development needs	Composition
Route planning	Size
Work force requirements	Capacity
	Enplaned passengers
	Aircraft operations
	Number of airline pilots and navigators
Microforecast	
Airport Facilities:	Aircraft operations:
Airside:	Air carrier:
Runways	Fleet mix
Taxiways	Capacity
Apron area	Peak hour
Navigational aids	General aviation based aircraft
General aviation needs	
Landside:	Passenger traffic:
Gates	Enplaned
Terminal facilities	Origin, destination
Cargo processing	Connections
Ground access:	Freight and cargo tonnage
Curb frontage	Airmail tonnage
Parking	Peaking characteristics
Access highways	Originations
Public transit	Vehicular traffic

There may be a tendency, when performing sophisticated mathematical modeling, to become disassociated from the significance of the results. It is incumbent upon the analyst to consider the reasonableness as well as the statistical significance of the model. Adequate consideration must be given to the rationality of the functional form and the variables chosen for the analysis, and to the logic associated with calibrated constants.

One of the first statistical tests run on a model is the computation of the coefficient of multiple correlation. This coefficient gives an indication of the explanatory power of the equation relative to the dependent variable. A high value indicates that there is a close correlation between the dependent variable and the independent variables, whereas a low value indicates a low correlation between the dependent variable and the independent variables.

The standard error of the estimate is a measure of the dispersion of the data points about the regression line and may be used to establish the confidence limits within which projections made from the equation may be expected to lie. Similarly, tests may be performed to determine the statistical significance of calibrated values. A knowledge of the range in these computed parametric quantities allows the degree of uncertainty in a demand forecast to be ascertained.

In many cases it is essential to determine the sensitivity of forecasts to changes in the explanatory variables. If a particular design parameter being forecast varies considerably with a change in a dependent variable, and there is a significant degree of unreliability in this independent variable, then a great deal of confidence cannot be placed upon the forecast and, more importantly, the design based upon the forecast. Tests are usually performed to determine the explanatory power of the independent variables and their interrelationships. The analyst should carefully investigate the sensitivity of projections within the expected variation of explanatory variables. It is also possible that certain explanatory variables do not significantly affect the modeling equation, and the need for collecting the data associated with these variables required for projections could be eliminated.

One of the more common sensitivity tests conducted in aviation studies is the examination of fare and travel time elasticities of passenger and freight traffic. Elasticity is simply defined as the percentage change in traffic for a 1 percent change in fare or travel time. Though an important factor in projecting demand fluctuations in aviation in the past, it has gained greater significance today due to the vast changes in fares and service offerings in a deregulated industry.

An excellent example of the ability of a mathematical equation to predict aviation traffic trends is shown in Fig. 6-7. In the study from which this figure is extracted, a nonlinear formulation of a regression model was constructed, relating total miles flown per capita on domestic trunk and local service carriers to the per capita gross national product and the fare yield per passenger mile [19]. It is apparent that the equation portrays quite well both the magnitude and the fluctuation of the known trends.

FORECASTING REQUIREMENTS AND APPLICATIONS

The specific forecasting needs depend upon the nature and scope of the study being undertaken. The requirements for a state aviation system plan are very different from those required for an airport master plan. Facility planning requires projections of the parameters which determine physical design, whereas financial planning requires projections of the cost elements and revenue sources associated with physical development. This

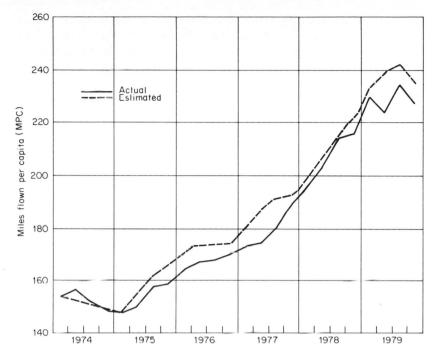

Fig. 6-7 Comparison of actual and estimated total miles flown per capita (MPC) on domestic trunk and local service carriers. (*Port Authority of New York and New Jersey [19].*)

section outlines the general forecasting requirements for various types of aviation and airport studies and discusses the more common methodologies used to arrive at these requirements.

The Aviation System Plan

The purpose of an aviation system plan is to identify the aviation development required to meet the immediate and future aviation needs of a region, state, or metropolitan area [17]. It recommends the general location and characteristics of new and expanded airports, shows the timing, phasing, and estimated cost of development, and identifies revenue sources and legislation for the implementation of the plan. The aviation system plan also provides a basis for the definitive and detailed development of the individual airports in the system.

The primary forecasting requirement for the airport system plan is a projection of the level of aviation activity during the planning period. The forecasts are usually made on an annual basis for the planning entity as a whole and are then proportioned among the various individual airports within this entity. Specific projections are generally made for total aircraft operations, air-carrier and general aviation operations, based aircraft, total air-cargo and airmail tonnage, and passenger enplanements for the short-, medium-, and long-range time frames within the planning period. These demand projections are compared to the inventory of physical facilities to determine development needs. It should be emphasized that these projections are normally made in a very aggregate fashion and tend to examine overall determinates of regional activity rather than the specific factors affecting local activity.

The preparation of a forecast for a systems plan is initiated by the collection of historical data indicative of the various components of aviation activity. These data normally include broad measures of socioeconomic activity as well as aviation activity statistics. Due to the fact that data collection is very expensive, most of the data collection in a system plan depends primarily upon secondary or existing sources and very little survey work is performed. Many of the overall regional projections are made on the basis of trend projections or simple econometric models and these are then apportioned to the individual airports within the region on the basis of ratio methods. In the analysis of observed trends and the preparation of future forecasts, broad indicators are generally used, including an examination of the consistency and realization of past trends and a comparison of growth rates and economic indicators.

The Airport Master Plan

The purpose of the airport master plan is to provide the specific details for the future development of an individual airport to satisfy aviation needs consistent with community objectives. The airport master plan requires detailed projections of the level of demand on the various facilities associated with the airport. Various concepts and alternatives for development are examined and evaluated, and recommendations are made relative to the ordering by priority, scheduling, and financing of the plan [2]. Though the basis for projections in a system plan is the aggregate level of annual demand, this is not sufficient for the master plan. Projections must be made for magnitude, nature, and variation of demand on a monthly, daily, and hourly basis on the many facilities located at the airport.

Annual forecasts of airport traffic during the planning period are the basis for the preparation of the detailed forecasts in the master plan. These forecasts are made for each type of major airport user, including air carrier, commuter, and general aviation aircraft, and are often expressed in terms of upper and lower bounds. The master plan forecasts are usually made under both constrained and unconstrained conditions. An unconstrained forecast is one which is made relative to the potential aviation market in which the basic factors which tend to create aviation demand are utilized, without regard to any constraining factors that could affect aviation growth at the location. A constrained forecast is one which is made in the context of alternative factors which could limit growth at the specific airport. Constraining factors addressed in master plans include limitations on airport capacity due to land availability and noise restrictions, the development of alternative reliever airports to attract general aviation demand, policies which alter access to airports by general aviation and commuter aircraft operations, and the availability and cost of aviation fuel. The determination of the level of general aviation activity at an airport can be significantly changed when land availability is restricted, thereby placing limits on airside capacity. The available capacity may be utilized in the context of policies which favor commercial over general aviation growth [22]. The impacts of such constraints can be quite significant, as shown in Fig. 6-8.

The specific forecasts made for a master plan include the annual, daily, and peak-hour operations by air-carrier, commuter, air-taxi, general aviation, cargo, and military aircraft, passenger originations, enplanements, and connections, annual tonnage and volumes of air freight and airmail, as well as daily and hourly ground access system and parking demand. Projections are also made for the mix or types of aircraft in each of the categories which will utilize the airport during the planning period. In the preparation of these forecasts some variables are projected directly and others are derived from these projections. For example, annual passenger enplanements might be forecast from an econometric model and then, based upon exogenous estimates of average air-carrier fleet passenger capacity and boarding seat load factors, annual air-carrier operations could be derived from these data. An illustration of the derivation of projections of domestic air-carrier operations from domestic passenger enplanements is given in Table 6-6. Similarly, by observing ratios which relate passenger enplane-

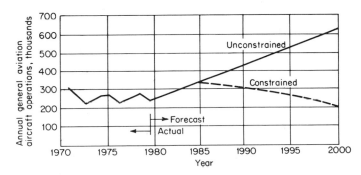

Fig. 6-8 Constrained and unconstrained forecast of general aviation aircraft operations at Fort Lauderdale–Hollywood International Airport. (*Aviation Planning Associates, Inc. [22].*)

TABLE 6-6 **Domestic Major and National Carrier Aircraft Operations at Fort Lauderdale–Hollywood International Airport, 1975–2000**

Year	Domestic passenger enplanements	Average seats per departure	Boarding load factor	Domestic aircraft departures	Domestic aircraft operations
Historical					
1975	1,756,458	123.6	42.8	32,395	64,790
1976	1,944,402	126.4	41.2	36,283	72,566
1977	2,089,373	131.9	41.1	37,703	75,406
1978	2,664,211	142.8	46.8	39,424	78,848
1979	2,881,563	147.6	46.5	42,328	84,656
1980	2,810,525	144.1	46.9	41,612	83,224
Forecast					
1985	4,162,100	170.0	48.0	51,000	102,000
1990	5,436,200	190.0	50.0	57,200	114,400
1995	6,943,200	205.0	52.0	65,100	130,200
2000	8,735,600	210.0	53.0	78,500	157,000

SOURCE: Aviation Planning Associates, Inc. [22].

ments to originating, connecting, and transfer passengers, the forecast of annual enplanements can be used to derive these other quantities.

It is essential for those responsible for preparing aviation forecasts to recognize that patterns of development exist for the various types and sizes of airports, which are useful in the planning function. For example, there is an approximate relationship between the number of peak-hour enplanements on the peak-month average day and the level of annual enplanements for major air-carrier airports serving the large hub areas in the United States. This relationship is shown in Fig. 6-9. Therefore, the analyst might wish to compare forecasts based upon modeling techniques to the relationship observed in this figure.

Similar characteristics have been shown to exist for monthly, daily, and hourly distribution of aircraft operations at air-carrier and general aviation airports of differing levels of activity [15]. An illustration of the variation in peak-hour air-carrier operations with annual enplaned passengers, which is useful for order of magnitude estimates, is given in Fig. 6-10.

Though these factors may not be precisely transferable between airports, they provide a general level of guidance to the airport planner in determining the reasonableness of forecasts in specific applications.

For the most part the methods used in the study of new airports are similar to those used for existing airports. However, the principal difference is the inability of the analyst to obtain a local historical data base to generate extrapolation trends, market shares, or econometric models. To overcome this deficiency, an attempt is usually made to forecast by drawing an analogy between the subject airport and other existing airports which

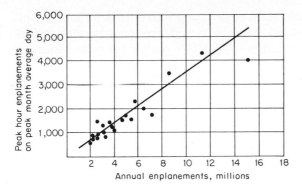

Fig. 6-9 Relationship between peak-hour enplane-ments on the peak-month average day and annual en-planements for large hub major air-carrier airports. (*Landrum and Brown, Inc. [6].*)

demonstrate similar traffic experience, and which are located in areas possessing similar socioeconomic, demographic, and geographic character-istics. Forecasts are then made for the airport under consideration by using these airports as surrogates, and adjustments are performed to accommo-date expected differences between the airports. In the past, the ATA and the FAA have collected and tabulated a significant amount of data for many airports [1, 18]. These data have included the number and distribution of

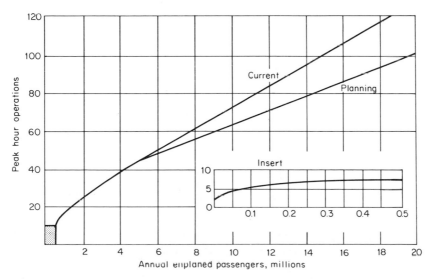

Fig. 6-10 Estimating relation for peak-hour air-carrier operations as a function of annual enplaned passengers. (*Federal Aviation Administration [15].*)

commercial air-carrier operations, fleet mix, and passengers on a peak and average monthly, daily, and hourly basis. It is apparent that one may expect a rather high degree of uncertainty associated with forecasting through such an analogy.

THE FUTURE AVIATION FORECASTING ENVIRONMENT

Many of the forecasts made by the various aviation related organizations become biased by the impact of recent events. Forecasts made in the early 1960s showed rather moderate growth, whereas those made in the late 1960s showed fairly ambitious growth. These forecasts were made in the context of expectations which reflected the behavior of aviation at the time when they were made. In the 1970s the overall economic conditions, the availability and cost of petroleum-based fuels, and airline deregulation considerably affected aviation. Forecasts made in this era attempted to analyze the impact of these factors in projecting the demand for aviation in the future. The effect of existing economic, social, and political factors on forecasts made in the 1960s and 1970s may be inferred from an examination of Fig. 6-11.

In a study of the major factors which would influence aviation over the period from 1980 through 2000, the following conclusions were made [4]:

1. Economic growth in most industrial nations will be moderate compared to historical trends.

2. Inflation rates will remain at or near the double-digit level.

3. Fuel prices will continue to rise at a pace which will exceed the inflation rate.

4. Concerns over jet fuel availability will dominate the demand for aviation services.

5. High to moderate unemployment rates will exist in the aviation industry.

6. The impact of recessions on aviation growth will rise.

7. Difficulties in attracting capital for investment in flight equipment and new markets will continue.

8. There will be continued and rising international tensions in the world.

On the basis of these assumptions, it is expected that over this period competition, high wage scales, and capital requirements will reduce the number of large carriers in long-haul markets and increase the number of specialized carriers providing low fare and cost services in an increasingly competitive environment. Commuter and short-haul service will undergo

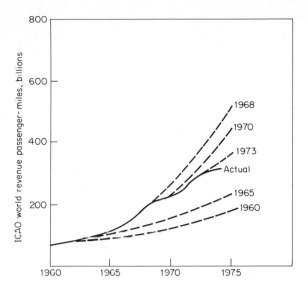

Fig. 6-11 Variation in forecasts made at different points in time for ICAO world revenue passenger-miles. (*Department of Transportation [18].*)

considerable change, which may be constrained by airspace and airside capacity limits, access to large hubs, and the uncertain role of small aircraft in the future. General aviation growth will be stimulated through the evolutionary effect of new technology, particularly avionics. Rising costs, however, will cause a shift away from personal and toward business general aviation flying.

Based upon the error inherent in forecasting and the differences in forecasts made by various organizations at the same point in time, as may be observed in Fig. 6-12, recommendations were made relative to planning needs. These included the presentation of the range in the key assumptions made in the forecast, the use of a variety of techniques to limit uncertainty, the increased use of expert judgment to temper forecasts made using econometric models, and the disaggregation of national forecasts to the regional, local, and market levels.

To adequately cope with the uncertainties associated with the traditional air transportation forecasting process and to react in a timely manner to inaccuracies found in estimates, the planning process is emerging into a phase-oriented, continuing process. For example, the FAA prepares annual forecasts of aviation activity on a national and terminal area basis which extend 10 years into the future [5, 7, 21]. Due to the high costs associated with the traditional planning process and the implementation of physical design changes, and the apparent inability to forecast with any degree of

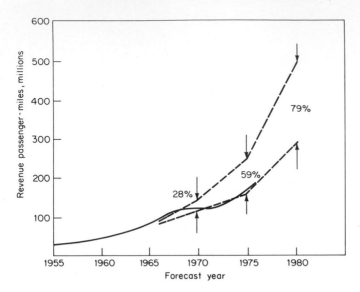

Fig. 6-12 Percentage difference range between the highest and lowest forecasts made by different organizations at the same point in time for revenue passenger-miles in the U.S. domestic markets (*Department of Transportation [18].*)

certainty, it is essential that planning techniques be developed which can respond to changes in the demand parameters prior to the investment decision. Perhaps the key to such a process is the recognition of the interaction of demand and supply parameters. The knowledge of the sensitivity of a physical facility component to a variation in demand can lead to more informed decisions and an understanding of the flexibility in facility design. A continued monitoring of the need for physical facilities in light of changing demand requirements provides a sound basis for the investment decision. Recognition of the uncertainties in the demand forecasting process can prevent a wasteful commitment of valuable resources. Explicit treatment of the variability of demand projections and facility modification recommendations through the use of sensitivity and tradeoff analyses is warranted.

REFERENCES

1. *Aircraft Movement and Passenger Data for 100 U.S. Airports, Average Day in August 1978,* Air Transportation Association of America, Washington, D.C., June 1979.
2. *Airport Master Plans,* Federal Aviation Administration, Washington, D. C., February 1971.

3. "A Market Analysis Approach to Forecasting Domestic Air Travel," J. Legan, Port of New York Authority, New York, 1957.

4. "Assumptions and Issues Influencing the Future Growth of the Aviation Industry," *Transportation Research Circular,* 230, Transportation Research Board, Washington, D.C., August 1981.

5. *Aviation Forecasts, Fiscal Years 1976–1987,* Office of Aviation Policy, Federal Aviation Administration, Washington, D.C., September 1975.

6. *Chicago O'Hare International Airport Master Plan Study,* Vol. III: *Aviation Demand Forecast,* Landrum and Brown, Inc., Cincinnati, Ohio, November 1979.

7. *FAA Aviation Forecasts, Fiscal Years 1981–1992,* Office of Aviation Policy, Federal Aviation Administration, Washington, D.C., September 1980.

8. *Forecasting Methods for Management,* 2d ed., S. C. Wheelwright and S. Makridakis, eds., John Wiley & Sons, Inc., New York, 1977.

9. *Forecasts of Commuter Airlines Activity,* Federal Aviation Administration, Washington, D.C., July 1977.

10. *Fort Lauderdale–Hollywood International Airport Master Plan Report,* Vol. II: *Technical Supplement,* Landrum and Brown, Inc., Cincinnati, Ohio, August 1977.

11. *Guide for the Planning of Small Airports,* Roads and Transportation Association of Canada, Ottawa, Ont., Canada, 1980.

12. *Lambert-St. Louis International Airport, 1980 Air Service Market Study,* Landrum and Brown, Inc., Cincinnati, Ohio, September 1980.

13. *Manual on Air Traffic Forecasting,* International Civil Aviation Organization, Montreal, Que. Canada, Document 8991-AT/722, 1972.

14. *Michigan State Airport System Plan,* Michigan Aeronautics Commission, Department of State Highways and Transportation, Lansing, Mich., Technical Report, May 1975.

15. *Planning and Design Considerations for Airport Terminal Building Development,* Federal Aviation Administration, Washington, D.C., Advisory Circular AC 150/5360-7, 1976.

16. *Planning for Airport Access: An Analysis of the San Francisco Bay Area,* National Aeronautics and Space Administration, Ames Research Center, Moffett Field, Calif., NASA Conference Publication 2044, May 1978.

17. *Planning the Metropolitan Airport System,* Federal Aviation Administration, Washington, D.C., Advisory Circular AC 150/5070-5, May 1970.

18. *Review of Aviation Forecasts and Forecasting Methodology,* Office of Transportation Planning Analysis, U.S. Department of Transportation, Washington, D.C., May 1975.

19. "Some Regression Models, U.S. Domestic Traffic," J. G. Augustinus, Aviation Economics Division, Port Authority of New York and New Jersey, Presentation to the Committee on Aviation Demand Forecasting, Transportation Research Board, Cincinnati, Ohio, May 1980.

20. *Terminal Area Air Traffic Relationships, Peak Day, Busy Hour, Fiscal Year 1980,* Office of Management Systems, Federal Aviation Administration, Washington, D.C., 1981.

21. *Terminal Area Forecasts, Fiscal Years 1981–1992,* Federal Aviation Administration, Washington, D.C., February 1981.

22. *Traffic and Earnings Analysis, Fort Lauderdale–Hollywood International Airport,* Aviation Planning Associates, Inc., Cincinnati, Ohio, January 1982.

Chapter 7

Airport Configuration

INTRODUCTION

Airport configuration is defined as the number and orientation of runways and the location of the terminal area relative to the runways. The number of runways depends on the volume of traffic, and the orientation depends on the direction of the wind and sometimes on the size of the area available for airport development. The terminal buildings serving passengers should be located so as to provide easy and short access to the runways.

RUNWAYS

In general, the runways and the connecting taxiways should be arranged so as to (1) provide adequate separation in the air traffic pattern, (2) cause the least interference and delay in the landing, taxiing, and takeoff operations, (3) provide the shortest taxi distance possible from the terminal area to the ends of runways, and (4) provide adequate taxiways so landing aircraft can leave the runways as quickly as possible and follow routes as short as possible to the terminal area.

At busy airports, holding or run-up aprons should be provided adjacent to the takeoff ends of runways. These aprons should be designed to accommodate three or possibly four aircraft of the maximum size anticipated, with sufficient space for aircraft to bypass one another.

TAXIWAYS

The principal function of taxiways is to provide access from the runways to the terminal area and service hangars. Taxiways should be arranged so that aircraft which have just landed do not interfere with aircraft taxiing to takeoff. At busy airports where taxiing traffic is expected to move simultaneously in both directions, parallel one-way taxiways should be provided. Routes should be selected which will result in the shortest practicable distances from the terminal area to the ends of runways used for takeoff.

Again, at busy airports taxiways should be located at various points along runways, so landing aircraft can leave the runways as quickly as possible to clear them for use by other aircraft; these are commonly referred to as *exit taxiways* or *turnoffs*. Whenever possible, taxiways should be routed so as to avoid crossing of active runways.

During peak traffic periods when a continuous supply of aircraft is available, the capacity of a runway is dependent to a large degree on how quickly landing aircraft can be vacated from the runway. An aircraft which has landed delays succeeding aircraft until it has cleared the runway. At many airports, taxiways are at right angles to the runways, with the result that aircraft must decelerate to very low speeds before they can turn off. A taxiway designed to permit higher turnoff speeds reduces the length of time a landing aircraft occupies the runway. This permits succeeding landing aircraft to be more closely spaced in terms of time, or it might allow a takeoff to be sandwiched in between two successive landings.

RUNWAY CONFIGURATIONS

Many runway configurations exist. Most configurations are combinations of several basic configurations. The basic configurations are (1) single runways, (2) parallel runways, (3) intersecting runways, and (4) open-V runways.

Single Runway

This is the simplest of the runway configurations and is shown in Fig. 7-1*a*. It has been estimated that the hourly capacity of a single runway in VFR conditions is somewhere between 50 and 100 operations per hour, while in IFR conditions the capacity is reduced to 50 or 70 operations, depending on the composition of the aircraft mix and the navigation aids available.

Parallel Runways

The capacities of parallel runway systems depend a great deal on the number of runways and on the spacing between the runways. Two and four parallel runways are common. There are airports with three sets of parallel runways. Airports with more than four parallel runways did not exist at the time this text was written, and it is unlikely that they will exist since few locations can generate the demand to match the capacity of five or more parallel runways. Furthermore, the ability of the air traffic control system to supply five or more runways at the same time becomes progressively more difficult, and the airspace requirement becomes very large. Finally, the availability of land to expand at airports of this size is very restricted.

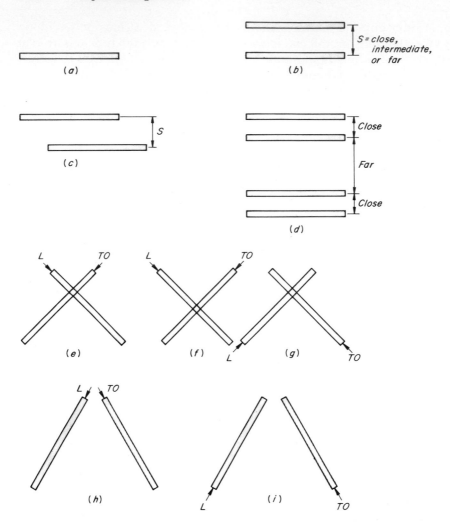

Fig. 7-1 Typical runway configurations. (a) Single runway; (b) two parallel runways—even threshold; (c) two parallel runways—staggered threshold; (d) four parallel runways; (e) intersecting runways; (f) intersecting runways; (g) intersecting runways; (h) open-V runways; (i) open-V runways.

The spacing between parallel runways varies widely. For the purpose of this discussion only, the spacing is classified as *close, intermediate,* and *far,* depending on the degree of independence of the two runways in IFR conditions. Close parallel runways are spaced from a minimum of 700 ft (for air-carrier airports) to less than 2500 ft. In IFR conditions an operation on one runway is dependent on the operation on the other runway. Intermediate parallel runways are spaced from 2500 ft to less than 4300 ft. In IFR conditions an arrival on one runway is independent of a departure on the other runway. Far parallel runways are spaced 4300 ft or more. In IFR conditions the two runways can be operated independently for both arrivals and departures. It is recognized that in the future the spacing for simultaneous operations on parallel runways may be reduced. If this occurs, new spacings can be applied to the same classification.

If the terminal buildings are placed between two parallel runways, runways are always spaced far apart to allow room for the buildings, the adjoining apron, and the appropriate taxiways. When there are four parallel runways, each pair is spaced close, but the pairs are spaced far apart to provide space for the terminal buildings (Fig. 7-1d). The hourly capacities of close-, intermediate-, and far-spaced parallel runways can vary from about 100 to 200 operations in VFR conditions, depending on the composition of the mix of the aircraft; the higher capacity is associated with small general aviation aircraft. Spacing does not affect capacity in VFR conditions, unless large aircraft are present. This is discussed in more detail in Chap. 4. In IFR conditions the hourly capacity of close-spaced parallel runways can vary from 50 to 60 operations, depending on the composition of the aircraft mix, for intermediate-spaced runways the range is 60 to 75 operations per hour, and for far-spaced runways the range is 100 to about 125 operations per hour.

There are times when it may be desirable to stagger the thresholds of parallel runways. The staggering may be necessary because of the shape of the acreage available for runway construction, or it may be desirable for reducing the taxiing distance of takeoff and landing aircraft. The reduction in taxiing distance, however, is based on the premise that one runway is to be used exclusively for takeoff and another for landing. In this case the terminal buildings are located between the runways so that the taxiing distance for each type of operation (takeoff or landing) is minimized (Figs. 7-1c and 7-2c).

Dual-Lane Runway

A dual-lane runway consists of two close-spaced (700 to 2499 ft) parallel runways with appropriate exit taxiways. Although both runways can be used for mixed operations, the desirable mode of operation is to dedicate the runway farthest from the terminal building (outer) for arrivals and the runway closest to the terminal building (inner) for departures. It is estimated that a dual-lane runway can handle at least 70 percent more traffic than a single runway in VFR conditions and about 60 percent more traffic than a single runway in IFR conditions. Capacity was found to be insensitive to centerline spacings between the runways from 1000 to 2499 ft. It is therefore recommended that the two runways be spaced not less than 1000 ft apart where particularly large aircraft are involved. This spacing also provides sufficient runout distance for an arrival to stop between the two runways. A parallel taxiway between the runways will provide for a nominal increase in capacity, but is not essential. The major benefit of a dual-lane runway is to provide an increase in IFR capacity with minimal acquisition of land [5].

Intersecting Runways

Many airports have two or more runways in different directions crossing each other. These are referred to as *intersecting* patterns. Intersecting runways are necessary when relatively strong winds blow from more than one direction, resulting in excessive crosswinds when only one runway is provided. When the winds are strong, only one runway of a pair of intersecting runways can be used, reducing the capacity of the airfield substantially. If the winds are relatively light, both runways can be used simultaneously. The capacity of two intersecting runways depends a great deal on the location of the intersection (e.g., midway or near the ends) and on the way the runways are operated, referred to as *strategy* (takeoff or landing). This is illustrated in Fig. 7-1e to g. The farther the intersection is from the takeoff end of the runway and the landing threshold, the lower is the capacity (Fig. 7-1g). The highest capacity is achieved when the intersection is close to the takeoff end and the landing threshold (Fig. 7-1e). For the strategy shown in Fig. 7-1e, the hourly capacity is from 60 to 70 operations in IFR and from 70 to 175 operations in VFR, depending on mix. For the strategy shown in Fig. 7-1f, the IFR hourly capacity is from 45 to 60, and the VFR capacity is on the order of 60 to 100. For the strategy shown in Fig. 7-1g, the IFR hourly capacity is from 40 to 60, and the VFR capacity is about 50 to 100.

Open-V Runways

Runways in divergent directions which do not intersect are referred to as *open-V runways*. This configuration is shown in Fig. 7-1h and i. Like intersecting runways, open-V runways revert to a single runway when the winds are strong from one direction. When the winds are light, both runways can be used simultaneously.

The strategy which yields the highest capacity is when the operations are away from the V (Fig. 7-1h). In IFR the hourly capacity for this strategy varies from 50 to 80 operations depending on aircraft mix, and in VFR the corresponding numbers are 60 to 180. When the operations are toward the V (Fig. 7-1i), the hourly capacity is reduced to 50 or 60 in IFR, and to between 50 and 100 in VFR.

Comparison of Runway Configurations

From the standpoint of capacity and air traffic control, a single-direction runway configuration is the most desirable. All other things being equal, this configuration will yield the highest capacity compared with other configurations. For air traffic control the routing of aircraft in a single direction is less complex than routing in multiple directions. Comparing the divergent configurations, the open-V runway pattern is more desirable than an intersecting runway configuration. In the open-V configuration an operating strategy that routes aircraft away from the V will yield higher capacities than if the operations were reversed. If intersecting runways cannot be avoided, every effort should be made to place the intersections of both runways as close as possible to their thresholds and to operate the aircraft away from the intersection rather than toward the intersection.

HOLDING APRONS

Holding aprons, often referred to as *run-up* or *warm-up* pads, are necessary at or very near the ends of runways for piston aircraft to make final checks prior to takeoff and for all types of aircraft to wait for takeoff clearance. These aprons are made large enough so that if an aircraft is unable to take off because of some malfunction, another aircraft ready to take off can bypass it. If an aircraft queued up on the taxiway leading to the end of the runway were to have a malfunction, it would have to proceed down the runway and exit at the nearest exit taxiway if there were no holding apron. This would consume more time than if the aircraft were able to be bypassed on the holding apron.

A holding apron should be designed to accommodate two to four aircraft and to allow sufficient space for one aircraft to bypass another. The area allotted for a waiting aircraft will depend on its size and maneuverability. A satisfactory method for establishing size is to use plastic models of aircraft.

Whenever possible, holding aprons should be located as to permit aircraft departing therefrom to enter the runway at an angle of less than 90°. Aircraft should be permitted to enter the runway as close to the end of the runway as possible. Holding aircraft should be placed outside the bypass route so that the blast from the holding aircraft will not be directed toward the bypass route.

Peak traffic volumes at many airports exceed the capacity of a holding apron, resulting in aircraft queues on the taxiway leading to the end of the runway. Despite this situation, holding aprons are useful for allowing one aircraft to bypass another.

HOLDING BAYS

Holding bays are relatively small aprons placed at a convenient location in the airport for the temporary storage of aircraft. At some airports the number of gates may be insufficient to handle the demand during a busy period of the day. If this is the case, aircraft are routed by air traffic control to a holding bay and are held there until a gate becomes available. Holding bays are not required if capacity matches demand. However, fluctuations in future demand are difficult to predict so that a temporary storage facility may be necessary.

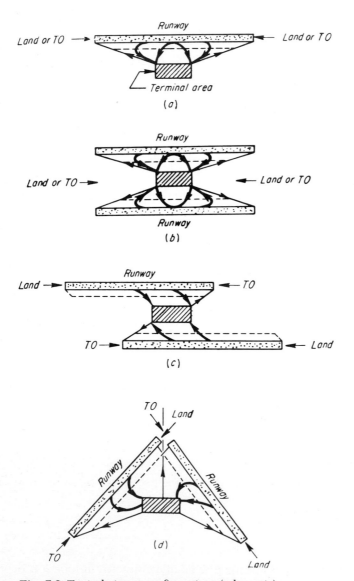

Fig. 7-2 Typical airport configurations (schematic).

RELATION OF TERMINAL AREA TO RUNWAYS

The key to a desirable airport layout is to provide the shortest taxiing distances from the terminal area to the takeoff ends of runways and to shorten the taxiing distances for landing aircraft as much as practicable. This can be illustrated schematically by the sketches shown in Fig. 7-2. The sketches are an attempt to demonstrate principles governing airport configuration and are not to be construed as optimum layouts. The sketches are not complete insofar as taxiways are concerned. For example, two exits for landing aircraft are generally shown, whereas three exits might be more

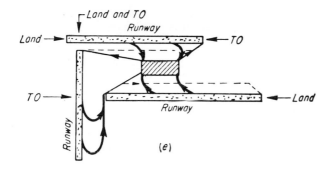

(e)

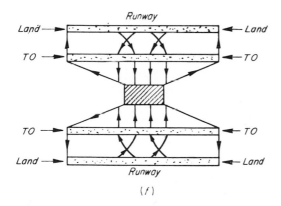

(f)

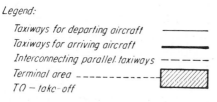

Legend:

Taxiways for departing aircraft
Taxiways for arriving aircraft
Interconnecting parallel taxiways
Terminal area
TO – take-off

Fig. 7-2 (Continued.)

desirable at a specific location, depending on the composition of aircraft and other factors.

Figure 7-2*a* shows a single-runway airport, it being assumed that takeoffs and landings will be about equal in each direction. Note that the taxiing distances are equal, regardless of which end of the runway is used for takeoff, and the terminal is also conveniently located for landing from either direction.

If the volume of traffic justifies a second parallel runway, then the desirable location of the terminal area with respect to the parallel runways is shown in Fig. 7-2*b*. This plan assumes that the wind conditions are such that landings and takeoffs can be made in either direction. At high-traffic-volume airports it is very desirable to have one runway always available for either a landing or a takeoff, should one of the runways be out of service for maintenance or other purposes.

If it is desired to have one runway used exclusively for landing and one for takeoffs, the plan shown in Fig. 7-2*c* should be given consideration. The principal advantage of this layout in comparison with the plan in Fig. 7-2*b* is the reduced taxiing distances for both takeoff and landing. The disadvantages are that the plan is based on the exclusive use of one runway for a specific function (landing or takeoff) and that staggering of the runways may require more land.

Close scrutiny of Fig. 7-2*b* and *c* makes it evident that it is not desirable to place the terminal area to one side of a parallel runway configuration. Taxiing distances are longer, and aircraft traffic on the ground is required to cross active runways.

If the winds at an airport require runways in more than one direction, it is desirable to locate the terminal area centrally, as shown in Fig. 7-2*d*. For this configuration it is assumed that when the winds are light, the traffic controller is able to use both runways for landing or takeoff.

At some airport locations the winds blow fairly regularly in the same general direction throughout the year, except for a small amount of time. If high volumes of traffic are anticipated, three runways may be required, with the terminal area located as shown in Fig. 7-2*e*.

At very-high-density airports serving transport aircraft, four parallel runways, as shown in Fig. 7-2*f*, are necessary. For this type of configuration it is desirable to reserve two runways exclusively for landing and two for takeoffs in order to avoid interference from taxiing aircraft. Note that the runways adjacent to the terminal area, rather than the outer runways, have been designated for takeoff. This was done to prevent takeoff aircraft from crossing active runways for landing. Although landing aircraft must taxi across active takeoff runways, crossings of this kind are preferred by air traffic control rather than crossings by takeoff aircraft.

Wherever possible the terminal area should be so located that aircraft taking off or landing do not pass directly over the area at very low altitudes, creating an aeronautical hazard as well as a nuisance.

The principles in laying out the runways in relation to the terminal can be illustrated by using as actual examples several airports throughout the world. The runway at the Metropolitan Oakland International Airport (Fig. 7-3a) is an example of the single-runway layout shown schematically in Fig. 7-2a. The airport in Hamburg, Germany, (Fig. 7-3b) approximates the schematic arrangement shown in Fig. 7-2b. The Los Angeles International Airport (Fig. 7-3c) illustrates the schematic layout shown in Fig. 7-2c and f. Dulles International Airport in Washington, D.C., (Fig. 7-3d) is an example of the schematic layout shown in Fig. 7-2e. Finally, the Mid-Continent Airport at Wichita, Kan., (Fig. 7-3e) approximates the schematic layout in Fig. 7-2d.

ANALYSIS OF WIND

An analysis of wind is essential for planning runways. As a general rule, the principal traffic runway at an airport should be oriented as closely as practicable in the direction of the prevailing winds. When landing and taking off, aircraft are able to maneuver on a runway as long as the wind component at right angles to the direction of travel (defined as crosswind) is not excessive. The maximum allowable crosswind depends not only on the size of the aircraft, but also on the wing configuration and the condition of the pavement surface. Transport category aircraft can maneuver in crosswinds as high as 30 kn, but it is quite difficult to do so; hence lower values are used for airport planning. For all airports other than "utility" (see Chap. 9 for definition of utility), the FAA requires that "runways should be oriented so planes may be landed at least 95 percent of the time with crosswind components not exceeding 15 mi/h (13 kn)." For utility airports the crosswind component is reduced to 11.5 mi/h (10 kn) [4]. The ICAO also specifies that runways should be oriented so planes may be landed at least 95 percent of the time with crosswind components of 23 mi/h (20 kn) for runways of 1500 meters or more, 15 mi/h (13 kn) for runways between 1200 and 1500 meters, and 11.5 mi/h (10 kn) for runways less than 1200 meters [1].

Once the maximum permissible crosswind component is selected, the most desirable direction of runways for wind coverage can be determined by examination of the wind characteristics for the following conditions:

1. The entire wind coverage regardless of visibility or cloud ceiling

2. Wind conditions when ceiling is between 200 and 1000 ft and/or the visibility is between ½ and 3 mi

The first condition represents the entire range of visibility, from

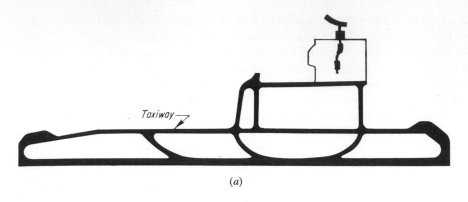

(a)

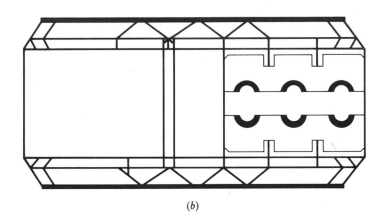

(b)

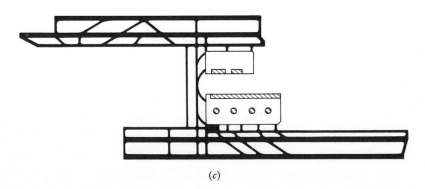

(c)

Fig. 7-3 Typical airports. (a) Metropolitan Oakland International Airport; (b) Hamburg Kaltenkirchen Airport; (c) Los Angeles International Airport; (d) Dulles International Airport, Washington, D.C.; (e) Mid-Continent Airport, Wichita, Kan.

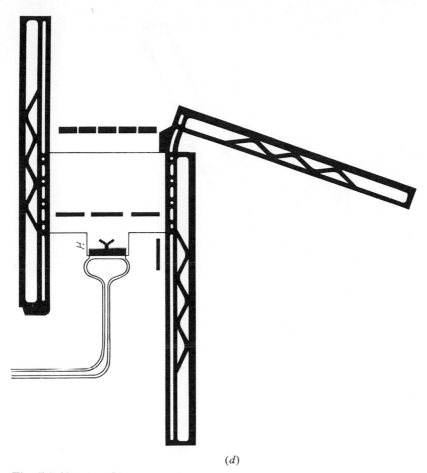

(*d*)

Fig. 7-3 (Continued.)

excellent to very poor. The next condition represents various degrees of poor visibility requiring the use of instruments for landing. It is useful to know the strength of the winds when the visibility is restricted. Normally when the visibility approaches ½ mi and the ceiling is 200 ft, there is very little wind present, the visibility being reduced by fog, haze, smoke, or smog. Sometimes the visibility may be extremely poor, yet there is no distinct cloud ceiling; for that matter, no clouds need be present at all. Examples of this condition are fog, smoke, smog, haze, and so on.

The "95 percent" criterion suggested by the FAA and ICAO is applicable to all conditions of weather; nevertheless it is still useful to examine the data in parts whenever this is possible.

In the United States, weather records can be obtained from the National Weather Records Center in Asheville, N.C. The velocities are

North

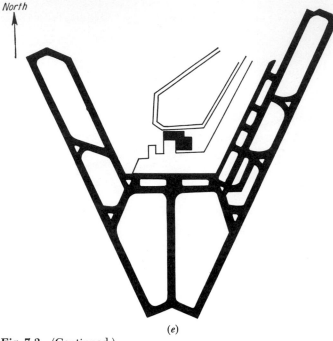

(e)

Fig. 7-3   (Continued.)

generally divided into 22.5° increments* (16 points of the compass). The weather records contain the percentage of time certain combinations of ceiling and visibility occur (e.g., ceiling, 500 to 900 ft; visibility, 3 to 6 mi), and the percentage of time winds of specified velocity occur from different directions (e.g., NNE, 4 to 7 mi/h). The directions are in reference to true north.

The directions of the runways can be determined graphically as follows. Assume that the wind data for all conditions of visibility are those shown in Table 7-1. From these data a wind rose can be plotted, as shown in Fig. 7-4.

The percentage of winds which corresponds to a given direction and velocity range is marked in the proper sector on the wind rose by means of a polar coordinate scale for wind direction and magnitude. Optimum runway directions can be determined from the wind rose by the use of a strip of transparent material on which three parallel and equally spaced lines have been plotted. The middle line represents the runway centerline, and the distance between the outside lines is, to scale, twice the allowable crosswind component (in the example, 15 mi/h). The transparent strip is

_____

* Some wind roses use 10° increments of direction.

placed over the wind rose in such a manner that the centerline on the strip passes through the center of the wind rose. With the center of the wind rose as a pivot point, the transparent overlay is rotated until the sum of the percentages included between the outside lines is a maximum. When one of the outside lines on the transparent strip divides a segment of wind direction, the fractional part is estimated visually to the nearest 0.1 percent. This procedure is consistent with the accuracy of the wind data.

The next step is to read the bearing of the runway on the outer scale of the wind rose where the centerline on the transparent strip crosses the direction scale. Because true north is used for published wind data, this bearing usually will be different from that used in numbering runways which are based on the magnetic bearing. In reference to Fig. 7-4, it will be noted that a runway oriented 150 to 330° (S 30°E true) will permit operations 95 percent of the time with the crosswind components not exceeding 15 mi/h.

Thus far the procedure has been illustrated as it applies to wind records with a velocity break at 15 mi/h. However, it can also be used to obtain estimates of wind coverage for any other velocity break. The concentric circles on the wind rose are drawn to scale and represent breaks in the wind velocity data. Suppose the break was at 12 instead of 15 mi/h. Then the two parallel lines representing the 15-mi/h maximum allowable crosswind component would not be tangent to the 12-mi/h circle, but

TABLE 7-1

Wind direction	Percentage of winds			
	4–15 mi/h	15–31 mi/h	31–47 mi/h	Total
N	4.8	1.3	0.1	6.2
NNE	3.7	0.8	—	4.5
NE	1.5	0.1	—	1.6
ENE	2.3	0.3	—	2.6
E	2.4	0.4	—	2.8
ESE	5.0	1.1	—	6.1
SE	6.4	3.2	0.1	9.7
SSE	7.3	7.7	0.3	15.3
S	4.4	2.2	0.1	6.7
SSW	2.6	0.9	—	3.5
SW	1.6	0.1	—	1.7
WSW	3.1	0.4	—	3.5
W	1.9	0.3	—	2.2
WNW	5.8	2.6	0.2	8.6
NW	4.8	2.4	0.2	7.4
NNW	7.8	4.9	0.3	13.0
Calms	0–4 mi/h			4.6
Total				100.0%

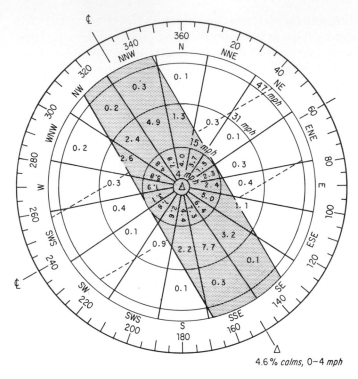

Fig. 7-4 Typical wind rose.

would lie outside of it. An estimate must then be made of the fractional percentage segment between the 12-mi/h circle and the 15-mi/h parallel lines and added to the percentage lying within the 12mi/h circle.

The next step is to examine wind data during restricted visibility conditions cited previously (ceiling between 200 and 1000 ft and visibility between ½ and 3 mi) and plot a wind rose for this condition. From this analysis it can be ascertained whether the runways are capable of accepting aircraft at least 95 percent of the time when restricted visibility conditions prevail. The analysis will also yield information on the percentage of the total time each of the conditions prevails. An example of the form on which restricted visibility data are tabulated is shown in Fig. 7-5. This figure represents observations of winds in one compass direction only, in this instance from the northeast. The total number of observations for all compass directions is 24,081, of which 1106 are for winds from the northeast. To complete the analysis, charts of this type would have to be plotted for other compass directions. On this form, ceilings varying between 0 and 150 ft are considered as a 100-ft ceiling, those between 150 and 250 ft as a 200-ft ceiling, and so on. For the purpose of the example it was assumed that a ceiling of 950 ft was equivalent to 1000 ft. The circled number 7 means that there were seven observations made when the wind was from the northeast with velocities varying from 5 to 9 mi/h, ceiling between 0 and 150 ft, and visibility between 0 and ¼ mi. The crosshatched area conforms to the ceiling and visibility criteria previously cited.

Often wind data for an entirely new location have not been recorded. If that is the case, records of nearby measuring stations should be consulted. If the surrounding area is fairly level, the records of these stations should

NE Wind				Visibility—Miles					Total Obs. 24,081
Ceiling Groups in Feet	Velocity Groups in Miles	0–1/4	1/4–1/2	1/2–3/4	3/4–1	1–1-1/2	1-1/2–3	3+	Total Obs
1000	01–04	4		1	2	4	14	202	227
	05–09	1	5	1	3	6	17	383	416
	10–14	2			1		5	277	285
	15–30							114	114
	30+								
	Total	7	5	2	6	10	36	976	1042
600 thru 900	01–04		1			1		1	3
	05–09			1	1	1	1	8	12
	10–14			1			3	4	8
	15–30								
	30+								
	Total		1	1	2	2	4	13	23
500	01–04			1				1	2
	05–09						2		2
	10–14								
	15–30								
	30+								
	Total			1			2	1	4
400	01–04			1					1
	05–09				1	1	2		4
	10–14						1		1
	15–30								
	30+								
	Total			1	1	1	3		6
300	01–04	1	1		1	1	1		5
	05–09	1			1			1	2
	10–14					1		1	2
	15–30								
	30+								
	Total	2	1		1	1	2	2	9
200	01–04					1			1
	05–09	1	1	1			1	1	5
	10–14						1		1
	15–30				1				1
	30+								
	Total	1	1	1	1	1	2	1	8
100	01–04	3							3
	05–09	⑦	1						8
	10–14		3						3
	15–30								
	30+								
	Total	10	4						14
	% by Velocity Groups		1–4 mi. 10	5–9 19	10–14 12	15–29 5	30 mi.		

▨ Observations to be considered because of ceiling conditions

◥ Observations to be considered because of visibility conditions

▧ Observations to be considered because of ceiling and visibility conditions

Fig. 7-5 Sample of data for analyzing wind coverage in a specific direction during periods of restricted visibility.

indicate the winds at the site of the proposed airport. However, if the terrain is hilly, the wind pattern often is dictated by the topography, and it is dangerous to utilize the records of stations some distance from the site. In that event, a study of the topography of the region and consultation with old-time residents may prove useful.

The wind rose is also a useful device for estimating runway capacity. Suppose it is desired to know what percentage of time during the year two runways can be used simultaneously, with the crosswind component not exceeding 15 mi/h. The answer to this question is illustrated by the following example. Suppose there are two intersecting runways 4 and 33. One runway has a bearing of N 40°E (magnetic), and the bearing of the other runway is N 15°W. The shaded area in Fig. 7-6 indicates the percentage of time both runways (4 and 33) can be used simultaneously; in the case of this example, 29.2 percent. In solving the problem it is assumed that use of the runways is not permitted when tailwinds are present [4].

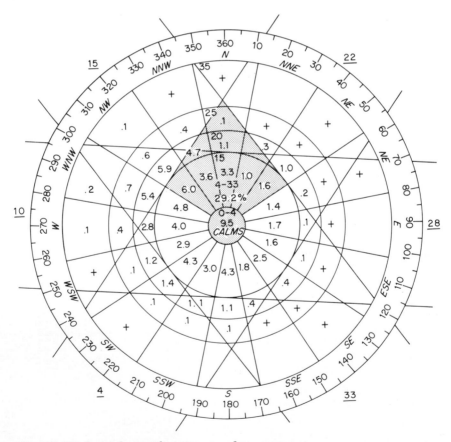

Fig. 7-6 Wind rose for simultaneous use of two runways.

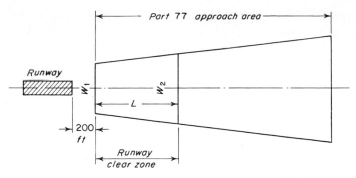

Category	W_1	W_2	L^*
1. Precision instrument	1000	1750	2500
2. Nonprecision instrument for larger than utility with visibility minimum as low as $\frac{3}{4}$ mi	1000	1510	1700
3. Nonprecision instrument for larger than utility with visibility minimum greater than $\frac{3}{4}$ mi	500	1010	1700
4. Visual approach for larger than utility	500	700	1000
5. Nonprecision approach for utility	500	800	1000
6. Visual approach for utility	250	450	1000

* Length of clear zone is determined by the distance required to reach a height of 50 ft for the appropriate approach surface.

SOURCE: Federal Aviation Administration [6].

Fig. 7-7 Runway clear zones. (*Federal Aviation Administration [6].*)

OBSTRUCTION REQUIREMENTS

The federal government requires that clear zones be provided at the ends of runways. *Runway clear zones* are areas comprising the innermost portions of the runway approach areas as defined in FAR Part 77 [6]. The dimensions of the clear zones are shown in Fig. 7-7.

FAR Part 77

In order to determine whether an object is an obstruction to air navigation, several imaginary surfaces are established with relation to the airport and to each runway. The size of the imaginary surfaces depends on the category of each runway (e.g., utility) and on the type of approach planned for that runway (e.g., visual, nonprecision instrument, precision instrument).

The principal imaginary surfaces are shown in Fig. 7-8 and are described as follows:

1. Primary surface. A surface longitudinally centered on a runway is called a *primary surface*. When the runway is paved, the primary surface extends 200 ft beyond each end of the runway.

2. Horizontal surface. A *horizontal surface* is a horizontal plane 150 ft above the established airport elevation, the perimeter of which is constructed by swinging arcs of specified radii from the center of each end of the primary surface of each runway and connecting the adjacent arcs of lines tangent to those arcs.

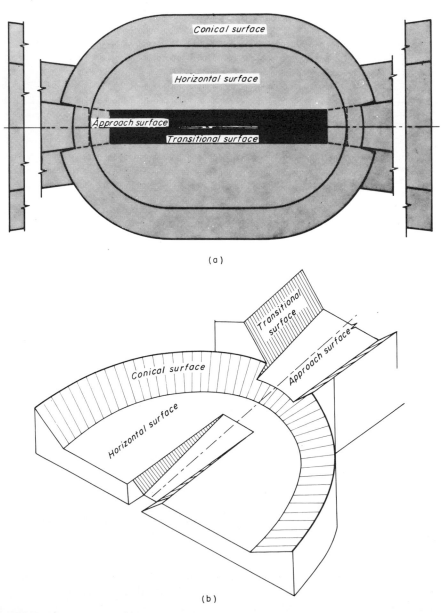

(a)

(b)

Fig. 7-8 Imaginary surfaces (*Federal Aviation Administration [6].*)

TABLE 7-2   **Imaginary Surface Dimensions, FAR Part 77, ft**

Item	Visual runway* A	Visual runway* B	Nonprecision instrument runway[†] A	Nonprecision instrument runway[†] B C	Nonprecision instrument runway[†] B D	Precision instrument runway
Width of primary surface and approach surface at inner end	250	500	500	500	1000	1000
Radius of horizontal surface	5000	5000	5000	10,000	10,000	10,000
Approach surface width at outer end	1250	1500	2000	3500	4000	16000
Approach surface length	5000	5000	5000	10,000	10,000	50,000[‡]
Approach slope	20:1	20:1	20:1	34:1	34:1	50:1[§]

* A = utility runways; B = runways larger than utility.
[†] C = visibility minimum greater than $\frac{3}{4}$ mi; D = visibility minimum as low as $\frac{3}{4}$ mi.
[‡] Inner length 10,000 ft; outer length 40,000 ft.
[§] Inner length 50:1; outer length 40:1.
SOURCE: Federal Aviation Administration [6].

3. **Conical surface.** A surface extending outward and upward from the periphery of the horizontal surface at a slope of 20 to 1 for a horizontal distance of 4000 ft is known as a *conical surface.*

4. **Approach surface.** A surface longitudinally centered on the extended runway centerline and extending outward and upward from each end of the primary surface is called an *approach surface.* It is applied to each end of a runway based on the type of available or planned approach.

5. **Transitional surfaces.** These surfaces extend outward and upward at right angles to the runway centerline plus the runway centerline extended at a slope of 7 to 1 from the sides of the primary surface and from the sides of the approach surfaces.

Dimensions of the several imaginary surfaces are shown in Table 7-2

ICAO Annex 14

The ICAO requirements are similar to FAR Part 77 with the following exceptions. The approach surface defined in FAR Part 77 is for both arriving and departing aircraft. The ICAO separates arrivals and departures and specifies dimensions for approach surfaces for arrivals and *takeoff climb surfaces* for departures. The horizontal surface specified by ICAO is a circle whose center is at the "airport reference point,"* whereas in FAR Part 77 it is not a circle. The height of this surface is 150 ft above the airport

* The center of the circle is the geographic center of the airport.

TABLE 7-3 **ICAO Recommended Dimensions and Slopes of Obstacle Limitation Surface, Meters**

APPROACH RUNWAYS
Runway Classification

	Noninstrument				Nonprecision Approach			Precision Approach Category I		Category II or III
Reference Code Number	1	2	3	4	1,2	3	4	1,2	3,4	3,4
CONICAL										
Slope	20:1	20:1	20:1	20:1	20:1	20:1	20:1	20:1	20:1	20:1
Height	35	55	75	100	60	75	100	60	100	100
INNER HORIZONTAL										
Height	45	45	45	45	45	45	45	45	45	45
Radius	2000	2500	4000	4000	3500	4000	4000	3500	4000	4000
INNER APPROACH										
Width								90	120	120
Distance from threshold								60	60	60
Length								900	900	900
Slope								40:1	50:1	50:1
APPROACH										
Length of inner edge	60	80	150	150	150	300	300	150	300	300
Distance from threshold	30	60	60	60	60	60	60	60	60	60
Divergence (each side)	10:1	10:1	10:1	10:1	6.7:1	6.7:1	6.7:1	6.7:1	6.7:1	6.7:1
First section										
Length	1600	2500	3000	3000	2500	3000	3000	3000	3000	3000
Slope	20:1	25:1	30:1	40:1	30:1	50:1	50:1	40:1	50:1	50:1
Second section										
Length						3600[a]	3600[a]	12000	3600[a]	3600[a]
Slope						40:1	40:1	34:1	40:1	40:1
Horizontal section										
Length						8400[a]	8400[a]		8400[a]	8400[a]
Total length						15,000	15,000	15,000	15,000	15,000
TRANSITIONAL										
Slope	5:1	5:1	7:1	7:1	5:1	7:1	7:1	7:1	7:1	7:1
INNER TRANSITIONAL										
Slope								2.3:1	3:1	3:1

[a] Variable length.

SOURCE: ICAO [1].

elevation, the same as in Part 77. In FAR Part 77 the conical surface extends horizontally 4000 ft at a slope of 20 to 1 irrespective of type of runway and visibility. In ICAO Annex 14 [1] the slope of the conical surface is the same (20 to 1), but the horizontal distance varies depending on the runway reference code; see Table 5-2.

In FAR Part 77 the slope of the transition surface is a constant 7 to 1, whereas in ICAO Annex 14 this slope is specified for runway reference codes 3 and 4. For other runways the slope is 5 to 1.

The dimensions of the imaginary surfaces specified by the ICAO in Annex 14 are summarized in Table 7-3 and Table 7-4.

TABLE 7-4   **ICAO Recommended Dimensions and Slopes of Obstacle Surfaces, Meters**

Takeoff Runways

Surface and Dimensions	Reference Code Number		
	1	2	3 or 4
TAKEOFF CLIMB			
Length of inner edge	60	80	180
Distance from runway end[a]	30	60	60
Divergence (each side)	10:1	10:1	8:1
Final width	380	580	1200
			1800[b]
Length	1600	2500	15,000
Slope	20:1	25:1	50:1

[a] The takeoff climb surface starts at the end of the clearway if the clearway length exceeds the specified distance.

[b] 1800 m when the intended track includes changes of heading greater than 15° for operations conducted at night.

SOURCE: ICAO [1].

REFERENCES

1. *Aerodromes, Annex 14 to the Convention on International Civil Aviation*, International Civil Aviation Organization, Montreal, Que., Canada, June 1976, draft to Amendment 36, August 1982.

2. *Aerodrome Design Manual*, pt. 1: *Runways*, International Civil Aviation Organization, Montreal, Que., Canada, 1980.

3. *Airport Capacity Criteria Used in Long Range Planning*, Federal Aviation Administration, Washington, D.C., Advisory Circular AC 150/5060-3A, 1969.

4. *Airport Capacity Criteria Used in Preparing the National Airport Plan*, Federal Aviation Administration, Washington, D.C., Advisory Circular AC 150/5060-1A, 1968.

5. *Dual Lane Runway Study*, Federal Aviation Administration, Washington, D.C., Rep. FAA-RD-73-60, May 1973.

6. *Objects Affecting Navigable Airspace*, Federal Aviation Administration, Washington, D.C., FAR Part 77, January 1975.

7. *Planning and Design Considerations for Airport Terminal Building Development*, Federal Aviation Administration, Washington, D.C., Advisory Circular AC 150/5360-7, 1976.

8. *Runway Capacity Criteria for Airport Planning Purposes*, 5th ed., Air Transportation Association of America, Washington, D.C.

9. *Techniques for Determining Airport Airside Capacity and Delay*, Federal Aviation Administration, Washington, D.C., Rep. FAA-RD-74-124, June 1976.

10. *The Apron and Terminal Building Planning Report*, Federal Aviation Administration, Washington, D.C., Rep. FAA-RD-75-191, July 1975

11. *The Apron-Terminal Complex*, Ralph M. Parsons Company, Federal Aviation Administration, Washington, D.C., September 1973.

12. *The Dual Lane Runway Concept*, R. M. Harris, MITRE Corporation, McLean, Va., Rep. M72-156, August 1972.

Chapter 8

Airport Airside Capacity and Delay

INTRODUCTION

The effectiveness of a transportation system is commonly measured in terms of its ability to efficiently process the transported unit. Since the performance of the system is dependent upon the individual components which comprise that system, it is usually necessary to evaluate these components to determine system capabilities. In cases where the use of the system requires the sequential utilization of a group of processors, the overall efficiency of the system is usually limited by the characteristics of the least efficient component.

In air transportation particular concern is focused upon the movement of aircraft, passengers, and cargo through both the airport and the aviation system. The experienced air traveler has grown accustomed to delayed flights, overbooking, missed connections, ground congestion, parking shortages, and long lines during peak travel periods. For many air transportation trips, the relative advantage of the speed characteristics of aircraft is considerably diminished by ground access, terminal system, and airborne delays.

In a more general sense, the unprecedented growth in the demand for air transportation services over the past generation has, in many situations, outpaced the ability to provide facilities to adequately accommodate this growth. To a greater and greater extent, elements of the air transport system are being stressed beyond their design capabilities, resulting in significant service deterioration at major airports in this country [6, 20]. It is understandable then that considerable emphasis has been placed upon research to analyze the level and causes of capacity deficiencies. It is now possible to accurately determine the capability of airport and aviation system components to process demand and to pinpoint the causes of deficiencies in these systems. This knowledge allows one to propose solutions to the problems identified.

Information on airport capacity and delay is important to the airport planner. There is a strong belief within the aviation community that significant gains in air transportation efficiency can be realized through an

222

understanding of the factors causing delays and by the application of technological innovation to alleviate delay.

Planners can compare capacity with the existing and forecast demand and ascertain whether improvements to increase capacity will be needed. Comparing the capacity of different configurations at airfields helps determine which are most efficient. Inadequate capacity leads to increasing delays at airports. Delay is an important factor in a benefit-cost analysis. If a monetary value can be placed on delay, the delay reduction savings resulting from an improvement become benefits which can be used to offset the cost of that improvement [14].

CAPACITY AND DELAY

The term *capacity* is used to designate the processing capability of a service facility over some period of time. However, for a service facility to realize its maximum or ultimate capacity there must be a continuous demand for service. In the field of aviation, it is virtually impossible to have a continuous demand throughout the operating period of the system. Even if a continuous demand were artificially created by causing a backlog at the service facilities by limiting its operating periods or providing reduced operating staff, the delays at these facilities would result in such a deterioration in service quality as to make the situation undesirable. Therefore, the facility designer is faced with the problem of providing sufficient capacity to accommodate fluctuating demand with an acceptable level of service. Typically, the design specifications at an airport require that sufficient capacity be provided so that a relatively high percentage of the demand will be subjected to some minimal amount of delay.

This discussion leads to an awareness of the fact that there is a relationship between capacity and delay. To provide sufficient capacity to service a varying demand without delay will normally require facilities which are difficult to justify economically. Therefore, in the design a level of delay acceptable from the perspectives of both the user and the operator is established, and system components of sufficient capacity are chosen to ensure that the delay criteria are met.

The Use of Capacity and Delay in Airfield Planning

Though capacity is an important measure of the effectiveness of an airport, it should not be used as the sole criterion. In preliminary planning, several alternative airfield configurations are usually considered. Capacity is useful for the initial screening of alternatives and for selecting those alternatives which should be subject to further analysis. When demand approaches capacity, delays to aircraft build up very rapidly. Congestion is usually associated with increasing delay, particularly when demand approaches capacity for more than very short periods of time. Because of economic factors, estimating the magnitude of delays often is more important for the justification and establishment of requirements for airfield improvements than the determination of capacity [18].

A primary objective of capacity and delay studies is to determine effective and efficient means to increase capacity and reduce delay at airports. In practice, analyses are conducted to examine the implications of the changes in the nature of the demand and the impact of facility modifications on the service afforded this demand. Some of the typical applications of these analyses might include:

1. The effect of alternative taxiway exit locations and geometry on runway system capacity

2. The impact of airfield restriction due to noise abatement procedures, limited runway capability, or inadequate air traffic control facilities on aircraft processing rates

3. The consequences of introducing heavy aircraft into the aircraft mix at an airport, and an examination of alternative mechanisms for servicing the mix

4. The investigation of alternative runway use configurations on the ability to process aircraft

5. The generation of alternatives for new runway or taxiway construction to facilitate aircraft processing

6. The gains which might be realized in system capacity or delay reduction by the diversion of general aviation aircraft to reliever facilities in large hub areas

The operational and economic implications of delay to aircraft increasingly dictate that delay analyses be included in airfield planning studies being conducted well before demand is expected to reach capacity levels. As an illustration of the magnitude of the impacts of airside delays, reference is made to the delay study conducted at O'Hare International Airport [14]. The computed variation of average daily delay per operation in both VFR and IFR conditions with the variation in average peak-hour demand for this airport is plotted in Fig. 8-1. Based upon these data and the estimated fleet operating cost and fuel consumption shown in Table 8-1, the total annual cost of delay was estimated as over $35 million. In addition, it was estimated that over 53 million gal of aircraft fuel was consumed due to these delays.

Approaches to the Analysis of Capacity and Delay

In this chapter, the analysis of capacity and delay is confined to the airfield which is composed of the runways, taxiways, and apron areas. Capacity and

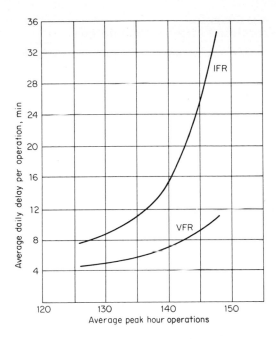

Fig. 8-1 Variation of average daily aircraft delay at O'Hare International Airport. (*Federal Aviation Administration [14].*)

delay have been evaluated by the use of analytical and computer simulation models. The focus here is on analytical models, often referred to as mathematical models.

Mathematical models of airport operations are tools for understanding the important parameters that influence the operation of systems and for investigating specific interactions in systems that are of particular interest. Depending upon the complexity of the system, a large number of conditions may be studied, perhaps more cheaply and quickly than by other methods. To make the mathematics tractable for a complex system, many simplifying assumptions must often be made, which may result in unrealistic answers. In such a case one can resort to a computer simulation model or some other technique. Thus it is necessary, when contemplating the formulation and application of a mathematical model, to examine critically the correspondence between the real world being studied and the abstract world of the model, and to determine the effect of their differences on the decisions to be made.

Computer simulation models are extremely useful for studying complex systems which cannot be represented by equations. These have been used successfully for solving many problems in air transport, including

TABLE 8-1 **Weighted Fleet Operating Costs for
Aircraft at O'Hare International Airport, 1975 dollars**

Representative aircraft type	Percent current mix	Direct operating cost, $/min		Fuel consumption, lb/min	
		Ground	Airborne	Ground	Airborne
B-747	1.9	13.30	25.20	125	345
DC-10	8.5	10.00	17.00	65	205
DC-8, B-707	12.8	8.00	13.20	75	170
B-727	37.1	6.40	10.10	55	125
B-737	18.4	5.10	7.50	35	75
GA jet	2.0	3.00	5.00	15	30
2-engine propeller, >12,500 lb	6.5	3.00	5.00	10	25
2-engine propeller, <12,500 lb	12.8	2.00	2.50	2	3
1-engine propeller	—	—	—	—	—
Weighted fleet average	100.0	5.95	9.48	45.5	108.6

SOURCE: Federal Aviation Administration [14].

airport planning [13]. An important point to remember is that the prime justification for using computer simulation is to reduce the differences between the real world and the abstract world of the model. If the input data required for the model are not very detailed, the results may not be any better than the results obtained from an analytical model of lesser complexity.

Definitions of Capacity

For airport planning, airfield capacity has been defined in two ways. One definition, which has been used extensively in the United States in the past, is that capacity is the number of aircraft operations during a specified interval of time corresponding to a tolerable level of average delay [4]. This is shown in Fig. 8-2 and is referred to as *practical capacity*. Another definition, which is gaining more favor, is that capacity is the maximum number of aircraft operations that an airfield can accommodate during a specified interval of time when there is a continuous demand for service [18]. The continuous demand for service means that there are always aircraft ready to take off or land. This definition has been referred to in several ways, namely, *ultimate capacity, saturation capacity* and *maximum throughput rate*, and is also illustrated in Fig. 8-2.

An important difference in these two measures of capacity is that one is defined in terms of delay and the other is not. There are several reasons for considering two definitions of capacity. There has been a lack of agreement on the specification of acceptable levels of delay applicable to all airports and their airfield components. Because constraints differ from airport to airport, the amount of acceptable delay differs from airport to airport. Ultimate capacity does not include delay and reflects the capability of the airfield to accommodate aircraft during peak periods of activity. However, for this definition one does not have a direct measure of the magnitude of congestion and delay. The magnitude of delay is greatly influenced by the pattern of demand. As an example, when several aircraft wish to use the airfield at the same time, the delay will naturally be larger than if they were spaced an interval of time apart. Since the fluctuation of demand within any hour can vary widely, there may be large variations in average delay for the same level of hourly aircraft demand. The shape of the curve in Fig. 8-2 is therefore influenced by the pattern of demand.

　　Experience has shown that the definition related to ultimate capacity yields values that are slightly larger than the definition which includes delay, but the difference is not considerable. Mathematically, the analysis of ultimate capacity is less complex than that for practical capacity.

The Airfield and Its Components

The airfield is defined as the system of components on which aircraft operate. A simplified diagram of the airfield and its relationship to the adjacent airspace is shown in Fig. 8-3. Air traffic control procedures,

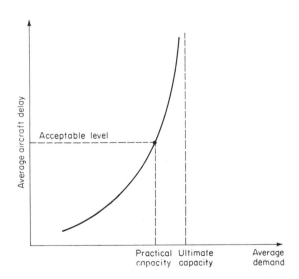

Fig. 8-2 Relationship between delay-related and ultimate capacities.

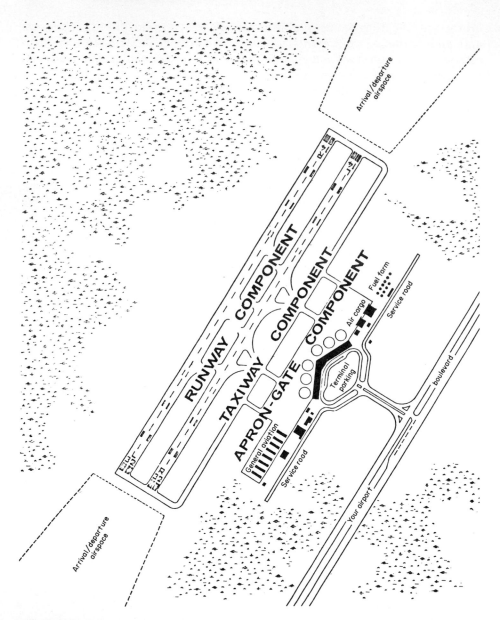

Fig. 8-3 Components of the airfield system. (*Federal Aviation Administration [18].*)

including those reflecting the effects of wake vortices, are major factors that influence runway component capacity and delay. Therefore, the runway component encompasses the common approach and departure paths to and from the runways. The capacity of the taxiway component usually is much greater than are the capacities of the runway or apron-gate components.

The principal exception to this occurs in the situation when a taxiway crosses an active runway. General aviation aircraft do not operate on fixed schedules, and therefore, the time spent by these aircraft in the apron areas fluctuates widely. Techniques generally only consider the capacity and delay on the air-carrier aircraft parking apron. For determining capacity and delay, the operations on the runways, taxiways, and gates at most airports can be considered independent of each other and analyzed separately [17, 18]. For planning purposes it is sufficiently accurate to assume that the capacity of the runways is not affected by operations on either the gates or the taxiways. Because operations on one airfield component generally do not affect the capacity of another component, the capacity of the entire airfield is governed by the capacity of the three components which is most restrictive. In addition, because operations on one component have little influence on the delay to aircraft on another component, the total delay to aircraft on the entire airfield can be estimated by adding the delays to aircraft on each individual airfield component.

Factors that Affect Hourly Capacity

There are many factors that influence the capacity of an airfield, and some are more significant than others. In general, capacity depends on the configuration of the airfield, the environment in which aircraft operate, and the availability of aids to navigation and air traffic control facilities. A listing of the most important factors includes:

1. The configuration, number, spacing, and orientation of the runway system

2. The configuration, number, and location of taxiways and runway exits

3. The arrangement, size, and number of gates in the apron area

4. The runway occupancy time for arriving and departing aircraft

5. The size and mix of aircraft using the facilities

6. Weather, particularly visibility and ceiling, since air traffic rules are different in good weather than in bad weather

7. Wind conditions which may preclude the use of all available runways by all aircraft

8. Noise abatement procedures which may limit the type and timing of operations on the available runways

9. Within the constraints of wind and noise abatement, the strategy which the controllers choose to operate the runway system

10. The number of arrivals relative to the number of departures

11. The number and frequency of touch-and-go operations by general aviation aircraft

12. The existence and frequency of occurrence of wake vortices which require greater separations when a light aircraft follows a heavy aircraft than when a heavy aircraft follows a light one

13. The existence and nature of navigational aids

14. The availability and structure of airspace for establishing arrival and departure routes

15. The nature and extent of the air traffic control facilities

The most significant factor which affects runway capacity is the spacing between successive aircraft. This spacing is dependent upon appropriate air traffic rules, which are functions of weather conditions and aircraft size.

RUNWAY CAPACITY RELATED TO DELAY

In 1960 the FAA contracted with the Airborne Instruments Laboratory to develop mathematical models for estimating the runway capacity [2]. These models rely on steady-state queueing theory. Essentially there are two models, one for runways serving either arrivals or departures and the other for runways serving mixed operations. For runways used exclusively for arrivals or departures the model is that of a simple Poisson-type queue with a first-come, first-served discipline. The demand process for arrivals or departures is characterized as a Poisson distribution with a specified mean arrival or departure rate. For mixed operations, when runways are used for both takeoffs and landings, the process is more complicated, and a preemptive spaced arrivals model was developed. In this model arrivals have priority over departures for the use of the runways. The takeoff demand process is assumed to follow a Poisson distribution; however, the landing process encountered at the end of the runway is not Poisson but more like the output of an airborne queueing system.

It was recognized that steady-state conditions are rarely achieved at airports. However, it was argued that time-dependent solutions, although possible, were quite complex and were out of the question for the large number of situations required for a capacity handbook. Additional support for the use of steady-state solutions came from observations which showed that average delay times yielded by the models were in general agreement with measured delays under a wide variety of operating conditions.

Mathematical Formulation of Delay-Related Capacity

The calculation of delay for runways used exclusively by arrivals may be computed from the following equation:

$$W_a = \frac{\lambda_a(\sigma_a^2 + 1/\mu_a^2)}{2(1 - \lambda_a/\mu_a)} \tag{8-1}$$

where W_a = mean delay to arriving aircraft, time units

λ_a = mean arrival rate, aircraft per unit of time

μ_a = mean service rate for arrivals, aircraft per unit of time, or reciprocal of mean service time

σ_a = standard deviation of mean service time of arriving aircraft

The mean service time may be the runway occupancy time or the time separation in the air immediately adjacent to the runway, whichever value is the largest.

The model for departures is identical to that for arrivals, except for a change in subscripts. The following equation is therefore used for the departure delay:

$$W_d = \frac{\lambda_d(\sigma_d^2 + 1/\mu_d^2)}{2(1 - \lambda_d/\mu_d)} \tag{8-2}$$

where W_d = mean delay to departing aircraft, time units

λ_d = mean departure rate, aircraft per unit of time

μ_d = mean service rate for departures, aircraft per unit of time, or reciprocal of mean service time

σ_d = standard deviation of mean service time of departing aircraft

For mixed operations, arriving aircraft are given priority, and the delay to these aircraft is given by the arrivals equation, Eq. (8-1). However, the average delay to departures can be found from the following equation:

$$W_d = \frac{\lambda_d(\sigma_j^2 + j^2)}{2(1 - \lambda_d j)} + \frac{g(\sigma_f^2 + f^2)}{2(1 - \lambda_a f)} \tag{8-3}$$

where W_d = mean delay to departing aircraft, time units

λ_a = mean arrival rate, aircraft per unit of time

λ_d = mean departure rate, aircraft per unit of time

j = mean interval of time between two successive departures

σ_j = standard deviation of mean interval of time between two successive departures

g = mean rate at which gaps between successive arrivals occur

f = mean interval of time in which no departure can be released

σ_f = standard deviation of mean interval of time in which no departure can be released

During busy periods the second term in Eq. (8-3) would be expected to be zero if it is assumed that aircraft are in a queue at the end of the runway and are always ready to go when permission is granted. It must be emphasized that the above equations are only valid when the mean arrival or departure rate is less than the mean service rate. The use of the model for the arrivals-only case is illustrated in Example Problem 8-1.

Example Problem 8-1

Compute the average delay to arriving aircraft on a runway system which services arrivals only if the mean service time is 60 s per operation with a standard deviation of 12 s, and the average rate of arrivals is 45 aircraft per hour.

Solution

The arrival rate λ_a is equal to 45 aircraft per hour or 0.75 aircraft per minute. The mean service rate μ_a is 1 aircraft per minute with a standard deviation σ_a of 0.2 mins. Therefore substitution into Eq. (8-1) yields

$$W_a = \frac{\lambda_a(\sigma_a^2 + 1/\mu_a^2)}{2(1 - \lambda_a/\mu_a)}$$

or

$$W_a = \frac{0.75 \ (0.2^2 + 1/1^2)}{2 \ (1 - 0.75/1)} = 2.08 \text{ min}$$

Therefore, the average aircraft delay is about 2.08 min per arrival.

The various intervals of time included in the model are shown on the space-time diagram in Fig. 8-4. The space-time diagram is a very useful device for understanding the sequencing of aircraft operations on a runway system and in the airspace adjacent to this system. In the case illustrated in Fig. 8-4, three arrivals and three departures are serviced as indicated. The basic sequencing rules used to service these aircraft are:

1. Two aircraft may not exercise an operation on the runway at the same time.

2. Arriving aircraft have a priority in the use of the runway over departing aircraft.

3. Departures may be released if the runway is clear and the subsequent arrival is at least a certain distance from the runway threshold.

Examination of the space-time diagram shows that the mean departure interval j is the average of the intervals of time between successive departures J_{pq} and J_{qr}. Also, the mean time interval between arrivals, the gap between arrivals I_g during which it may be possible to release departures, is the average of the quantities G_{lm} and G_{mn}. Finally, the mean

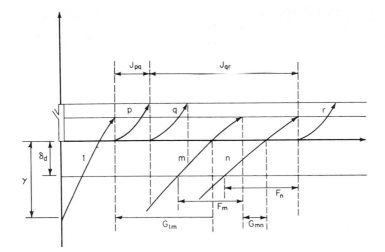

Fig. 8-4 Space-time diagram concepts for mixed operations on runway system.

value of the interval of time in which departures cannot be released f is equal to the average of the quantities F_m and F_n.

Several other observations may be made about the sequence of operations shown on this space-time diagram. The initial departure p could have been released, if it were available, before the first arrival l reached the distance δ_d from the runway threshold, since the runway was clear. The second departure q was released when the previous departure p cleared the runway, since the next arrival m was more than δ_d miles from the threshold at that point in time. However, the third departure r was not released when that departure cleared the runway, because the approaching aircraft m was closer than δ_d miles to the threshold at that point in time. For the same reason, this departure was not released until after the last arrival n cleared the runway. In this exhibit, then, the delays which would occur to aircraft are due to the required separations between different types of operational sequences.

Delay-related capacity can be defined on either an hourly or an annual basis. The former is referred to as the *practical hourly capacity* (PHOCAP) and the latter as the *practical annual capacity* (PANCAP). As indicated in Fig. 8-2, PHOCAP is defined as the number of aircraft movements that the runways can handle corresponding to a tolerable level of delay. There are several levels of tolerable average delay:

1. For departing aircraft, 4 min for mixed runway operations in VFR conditions when more than 10 percent of the aircraft population is large and heavy jet aircraft

2. For departing aircraft, 3 min for mixed runway operations in VFR conditions when 10 percent or less of the aircraft population is large and heavy jet aircraft

3. For departing aircraft, 2 min for mixed runway operations in VFR conditions when there is less than 1 percent large and heavy jet aircraft in the aircraft population

4. For departing aircraft, 4 min for mixed runway operations in IFR conditions, regardless of aircraft class

5. For arriving aircraft, 4 min for mixed operations in IFR conditions, regardless of aircraft class

6. For all arrivals, 1 min in VFR conditions

Since these are averages, some aircraft are delayed more than the specified levels and some less.

Application of Techniques for Practical Hourly Capacity

The mathematical models described were applied to a variety of runway configurations and the results presented in chart form by the FAA [3, 4] and the Airborne Instruments Laboratory [5]. Several of the charts have been included here to illustrate the application of the models. The reader is urged to consult the references for a more detailed explanation of the use of the charts. In applying these models, aircraft are classified as shown in Table 8-2.

The variation of capacity for a single runway in VFR conditions with mixed operations for various aircraft mixes is shown in Fig. 8-5. Similarly, the capacity of a single runway in VFR conditions when the runway is used exclusively for either arrivals or departures is shown in Fig. 8-6. Figure 8-7 shows a single runway for mixed operations, arrivals only, and departures only, as well as open-V and close parallel runways in IFR conditions.

TABLE 8-2   **Aircraft Classification for Practical Capacity Techniques**

Class	Aircraft type
A	Boeing 707, 747, 720 series; Douglas DC-8 and DC-10 series; Lockhead L-1011 series
B	Boeing 727, 737 series; Douglas DC-9 series; BACI-11 series; all large piston and turboprop airliners
C	Small propeller-driven airline aircraft, such as the Fairchild F-27 and business jets
D	Twin-engine propeller-driven general aviation aircraft and some of the larger single-engine models
E	Single-engine propeller-driven general aviation aircraft

SOURCE: Federal Aviation Administration [4].

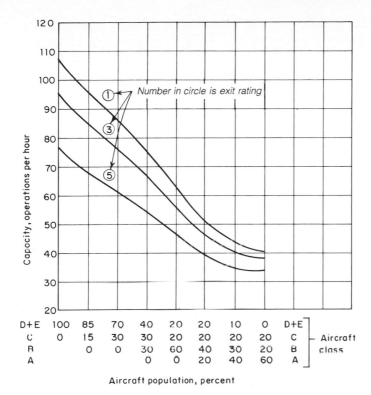

Fig. 8-5 Hourly capacity of a single runway in VFR conditions for mixed operations. (*Federal Aviation Administration [4].*)

The actual aircraft population, or mix, may not correspond to the proportions shown in these figures, and therefore Figs. 8-8 and 8-9 have been provided to interpolate to the mixes given.

It should be noted that in Figs. 8-5 and 8-6 the term *exit rating* appears. Exit rating corresponds to the mean runway occupancy time of an aircraft mix, the higher numbers signifying the larger runway occupancy times. The charts for obtaining exit ratings are shown in Figs. 8-10 and 8-11. When there is a mixture of exit types, a rule of thumb is that three right-angled exits are equivalent to two standard exits or one high-speed exit.

To use the charts to determine the PHOCAP, the following data are required:

1. The aircraft mix using the runway system
2. The length of the runway
3. The number and location of the exits from the runway threshold
4. The types of exits: right-angled, standard, or high-speed

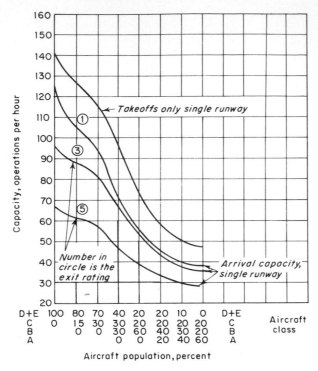

Fig. 8-6 Hourly capacity for single runway in VFR conditions for arrivals only and departures only. (*Federal Aviation Administration [4].*)

5. The flight rules being utilized: VFR or IFR
6. The types of operations taking place on the runway

The charts in this procedure do not reflect the increase in spacing between aircraft due to wake turbulence since they were prepared prior to the establishment of the larger separations required when light aircraft follow heavy aircraft. Heavy aircraft are defined as aircraft whose maximum takeoff weight is 300,000 lb or greater. Therefore, heavy aircraft would fall into the class A group. Whenever there is a mixture of heavy class A aircraft and classes B, C, and D aircraft, the capacity will be smaller than indicated on the charts. This is due to the fact that the separation between heavy aircraft and smaller aircraft is increased to minimize the effect of the wake vortex turbulence generated by the former. The amount of decrease will depend a great deal on the percentage of class A aircraft in the mix. A conservative estimate of the decrease would be about 10 percent.

The use of these charts to obtain the PHOCAP is illustrated in Example Problem 8-2.

Example Problem 8-2

The runway system at an airport consists of a single runway which is 9000 ft long. High-speed exits are located 4000, 5000, and 6000 ft from the runway threshold. The aircraft mix in VFR consists of 30 percent heavy jet aircraft, 50 percent large jet aircraft, and 20 percent small aircraft. The aircraft mix is the same under both VFR and IFR conditions.

The determination of the VFR and IFR PHOCAP of the runway is required.

Solution

Since there is only one runway at the airport, it must be used for both arrivals and departures. Therefore the capacity is found from Fig. 8-5 for VFR and from Fig. 8-7 for IFR conditions. The mix of the aircraft at this airport is determined from Table 8-2 to be 30 percent class A and 50 percent class B. Since this actual mix is different from that given on the capacity charts, Fig. 8-8 must be used to find the interpolated mix.

From Fig. 8-8 it is found that the interpolated mix is about 37 percent class A.

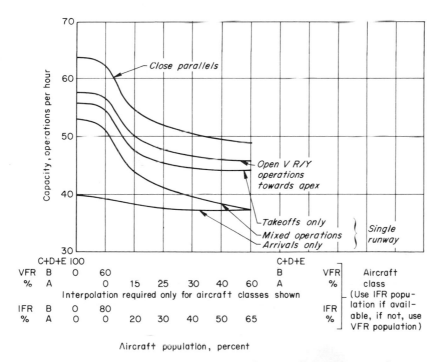

Fig. 8-7 Hourly capacity of single runway, close parallel runways, and open-V runways in IFR conditions. (*Federal Aviation Administration [4].*)

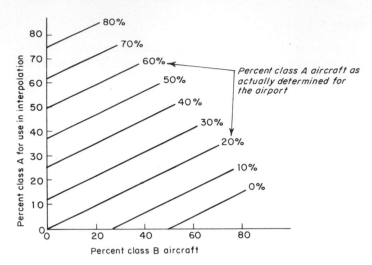

Fig. 8-8 Interpolation of class B aircraft to equivalent class A aircraft. (*Federal Aviation Administration [4]*.)

The exit rating is obtained from Fig. 8-11. In this case there are three high-speed exits for a 9000-ft runway, and these exits are all spaced 1000 ft. Therefore, the exit rating is found to lie between 2 and 3. An exit rating of 3 will be used for illustration.

The VFR capacity is then found from Fig. 8-5 by entering with the percentage of class A equal to 37 to the curve for an exit rating of 3 to give a PHOCAP in VFR of about 43 operations per hour.

Similarly, the IFR capacity is found from Fig. 8-7 by entering with the actual value of the percentage of class A aircraft in the IFR mix, and since interpolation is not necessary here, the PHOCAP in IFR is found to be about 38 operations per hour.

Application of Techniques for Practical Annual Capacity

The PANCAP is an extension of the PHOCAP concept and allows the runway system to be overloaded for short periods of time during the year. An overload is defined as a period of time when demand exceeds the PHOCAP. For commercial airports with a substantial amount of jet traffic an overload is defined as the period of time when the average delay is larger than 4 min. The length of time during which overload is permitted was selected empirically from field observations and can be changed as necessary. At the time the PANCAP was developed it was defined as that level of annual operations in which overload occurs for 10 percent of the aircraft operations or 5 percent of the time, whichever yields the smallest number of annual operations. Average delays during overloaded periods cannot exceed 8 min.

The determination of the PANCAP involves finding the percentage of overloaded hours occurring during the year POH, the percentage of operations during the overloaded hours POM, and the average delay to aircraft during the overloaded hours ADO. Knowing POH, POM, and ADO, the products of POH × ADO and POM × ADO can be found for any assumed level of demand. This process is repeated for a range of airport demand values until two smooth curves corresponding to these products are determined. The smaller of the two levels of demand corresponding to POH × ADO = 40 and POM × ADO = 80 is defined as the PANCAP [8]. This is shown schematically in Fig. 8-12.

Determining a value of PANCAP for an airport is a very time-consuming process which is usually performed by computers. However, an outline of the process is given below:

1. The total daily traffic for each month in a recent year is obtained and divided into three groups of months, namely, three peak months, six average months, and three low months. These months are determined by finding the average daily traffic in each month.

2. For each group of months the traffic on each day of the week is tabulated into two peak days, four average days, and one low day.

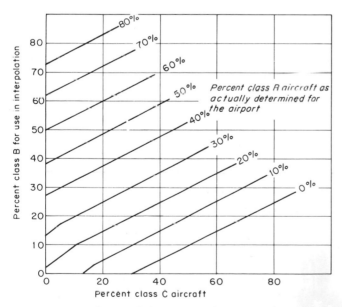

Fig. 8-9 Interpolation of class C aircraft to equivalent class B aircraft. (*Federal Aviation Administration [4].*)

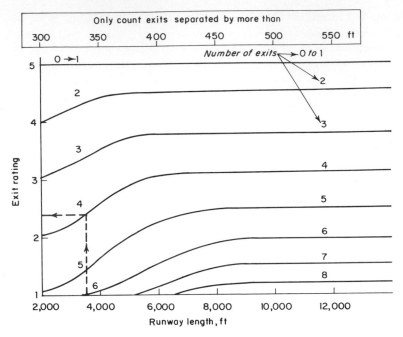

Right angled is considered 60° or sharper

Fig. 8-10 Exit ratings for right-angled exits. For runways serving predominantly small aircraft count only those exits that fall between 800 ft from the landing threshold to 5000 ft, unless four-engine jets are operated on the runway, in which case exits up to 8000 ft should be counted. For runways serving predominantly large aircraft, the exits from 1000 to 6000 ft should be counted (8000 ft if four-engine jets are present). Count only those exits separated by at least the minimum values shown in the rectangular box. *Example:* Exits at 500, 1000, 1500, 1700, 2200, and 3500 ft; runways length 3500 ft. Number of exits = 4 (i.e., those at 500 and 1700 ft are not counted). Exit rating = 2.4. (*Federal Aviation Administration* [4].)

3. The pattern for the variation of traffic at the airport is assumed to be characterized by the traffic on the nine typical days found above. That is, the actual pattern of traffic at the airport is now represented by a hypothetical year, which is made up of nine traffic days, namely, the traffic on the peak, average, and low days in the peak, average, and low months.

4. The hourly variation of traffic on a typical day in both VFR and IFR weather conditions is obtained, and the percentage of the daily traffic which occurs during the two highest consecutive hours on this day is averaged to obtain the peak hour traffic.

5. The variation of hourly traffic on a VFR and an IFR day is then related to the traffic in the peak hour to form a representation of the pattern of hourly traffic demand at the airport.

6. Assumptions of the peak-hour demand at the airport allows the computation of the demand during any hour of the day in any month through these representative patterns of variation.

7. Based upon the hourly capacity of the airport in VFR and IFR conditions, a comparison of the demand in any hour to the capacity is made to find the overloaded hours, the overloaded movements, and the delay. From these data, points on the curve shown in Fig. 8-12 can be found.

8. This process is repeated until two curves are found from which the delay criteria mentioned above can be used to find the PANCAP.

It should be apparent from the above outline that any changes in the assumptions concerning the variation in hourly, daily, or monthly demand will result in a different determination of PANCAP. Therefore, it is incumbent upon the analyst to carefully consider the types of demand variation which are likely to be expected at the subject airport. One of the best sources of these types of data is the historical generation of the variations which may be observed at other similar airports [16].

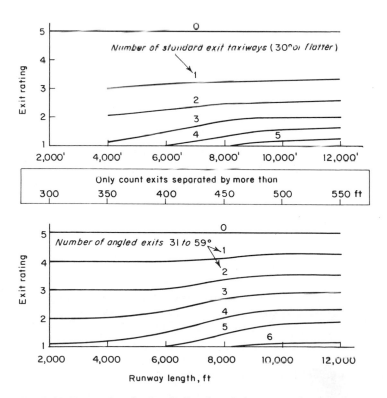

Fig. 8-11 Exit ratings for standard and angled exits. (*Federal Aviation Administration [4].*)

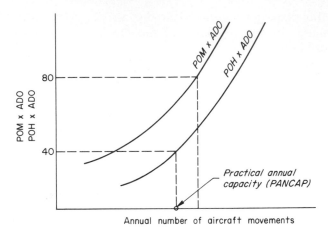

Fig. 8-12 Definition of practical annual capacity.

Estimating Procedures for Practical Capacity and Delay

To facilitate the estimation of capacity and delay, a simplified procedure has been developed [4]. The methodology allows for the approximation of PANCAP and annual delay from the weighted hourly capacity of the runway system. The weighted hourly capacity of a runway system is defined as the hourly capacity averaged over the year and weighted according to the traffic volumes on each runway-use configuration. To find the weighted hourly capacity it is necessary to compute the PHOCAPs of each runway use and weight them according to the factors found in [4]. Once this value is obtained, Fig. 8-13 may be used to estimate the PANCAP. If the projected annual demand is known for the design year, it may be used with the PANCAP to approximate the annual delay which may be expected at the airport. Figure 8-14 is used for this purpose.

The FAA has also estimated the PHOCAP and the PANCAP for several common runway-use configurations under certain assumptions of use [3]. These are shown in Table 8-3. The above figures may also be used with this table for identifying and screening preliminary runway configurations to meet approximate delay criteria for a projected level of annual operations. It should be noted that the values obtained through the use of these procedures are only rough estimates, and any decision related to proposed modifications of the runway system at an airport must rely upon more detailed analyses.

RUNWAY CAPACITY NOT RELATED TO DELAY

Capacity as defined here expresses the maximum physical capability of a runway system to process aircraft. It is the ultimate or maximum aircraft operations rate for a set of specified conditions, and is independent of the level of average aircraft delay. In fact, it has been shown that when traffic volumes reach hourly capacity levels, average aircraft delays may range from 2 to 10 min. Consequently, for the same specific conditions, the capacity values in this technique may tend to be slightly higher than those found by the earlier technique.

Delay is dependent on the capacity as well as on the magnitude, nature, and pattern of demand. Delays can occur even when the demand averaged over 1 h is less than the hourly capacity. Such delays occur because demand fluctuates within an hour so that, during some smaller intervals of time, demand is greater than capacity.

If the magnitude, nature, and pattern of demand are fixed, then delay can be reduced only by increasing capacity. On the other hand, if demand can be manipulated to produce more uniform patterns of demand, then delay can be reduced without increasing capacity. Thus, estimating capacity is an integral step in determining delay to aircraft.

Mathematical Formulation of Ultimate or Saturation Capacity

These types of models determine the maximum number of aircraft operations that a runway system can accommodate in a specified interval of time when there is continuous demand for service [18]. In these models capacity is equal to the inverse of a weighted average service time of all aircraft

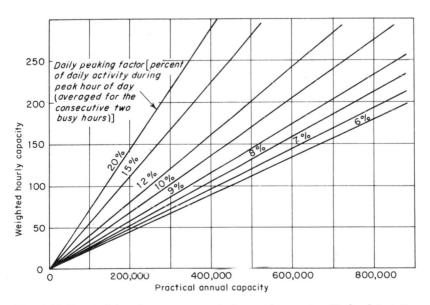

Fig. 8-13 Practical hourly versus practical annual capacity. (*Federal Aviation Administration [4].*)

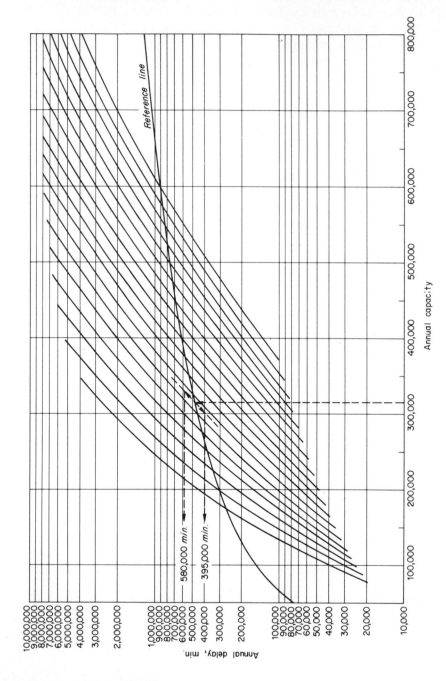

Fig. 8-14 Annual delay versus practical annual capacity. (*Federal Aviation Administration [4].*)

being served. For example, if the weighted average service time is 90 s, the capacity of the runway is 1 operation every 90 s or 40 operations per hour. The models treat the common approach path to the runway together with the runway as the runway system. The runway service time is defined as either the separation in the air in terms of time or the runway occupancy time, whichever is larger. The material presented in this section is taken largely from several references [12, 17, 18].

Development of Models for Arrivals Only

The capacity of a runway system used only for arriving aircraft is influenced by the following factors:

1. The aircraft mix, which is usually characterized by segregating aircraft into several classes according to their approach speeds

2. The approach speeds of the various classes of aircraft

3. The length of the common approach path from the entry or ILS gate to the runway threshold

4. The minimum air traffic separation rules or the practical observed separations if no rules apply

5. The magnitude of errors in arrival time at the gate and of speed error on the common approach path

6. The specified probability of violation of the minimum air traffic separations considered acceptable

7. The mean runway occupancy times of the various classes of aircraft in the mix and the magnitude of dispersion in these mean times

The Error-Free Case

With little loss in accuracy and to make the computations simpler, aircraft are grouped into several discrete speed classes V_i, V_j, etc. To obtain the weighted service time for arrivals, it is necessary to formulate a matrix of the intervals of time between aircraft arrivals at the runway threshold. Having this matrix and the percentages of the various classes in the aircraft mix, the weighted service time can be computed. The inverse of the weighted service time is the capacity of the runway. Let the error-free matrix be designated as $[M_{ij}]$, the minimum time interval at the runway threshold for aircraft of speed class i followed by aircraft of class j, and let the percentage of aircraft of class i in the mix be p_i, and of aircraft of class j be p_j. Then

$$T_j - T_i = [T_{ij}] = [M_{ij}] \tag{8-4}$$

TABLE 8-3 **Practical Annual Capacity of Runways for Long-Range Planning**

| Runway configuration | | | | PHOCAP | |
Layout	Description	Mix	PANCAP	IFR	VFR
Single runway (arrivals = departures)	Single runway (arrivals = departures)	1	215,000	53	99
		2	195,000	52	76
		3	180,000	44	54
		4	170,000	42	45
Less than 3,500 ft	Close parallels (IFR dependent)	1	385,000	64	198
		2	330,000	63	152
		3	295,000	55	108
		4	280,000	54	90
3,500 to 4,999 ft	Independent IFR approach/departure parallels	1	425,000	79	198
		2	390,000	79	152
		3	355,000	79	108
		4	330,000	74	90
5,000 ft or more	Independent IFR arrivals and departures	1	430,000	106	198
		2	390,000	104	152
		3	360,000	88	108
		4	340,000	84	90
5,000 ft or more	Independent parallels plus two close parallels	1	770,000	128	396
		2	660,000	126	304
		3	590,000	110	216
		4	560,000	108	180
	Widely spaced open V with independent operations	1	425,000	79	198
		2	340,000	79	136
		3	310,000	76	94
		4	310,000	74	84
	Open V, dependent, operations away from intersection	1	420,000	71	198
		2	335,000	70	136
		3	300,000	63	94
		4	295,000	60	84
	Open V, dependent, operations toward intersection	1	235,000	57	108
		2	220,000	56	86
		3	215,000	50	66
		4	200,000	50	53

TABLE 8–3 **(Continued)**

| Runway configuration | | | | PHOCAP | |
Layout	Description	Mix	PANCAP	IFR	VFR
Direction of ops	Two intersecting at near threshold	1	375,000	71	175
		2	310,000	70	125
		3	275,000	63	83
		4	255,000	60	69
Direction of ops	Two intersecting in middle	1	220,000	61	99
		2	195,000	60	76
		3	195,000	53	58
		4	190,000	47	52
Direction of ops	Two intersecting at far threshold	1	220,000	55	99
		2	195,000	54	76
		3	180,000	46	54
		4	175,000	42	57

| | | Percent of specified class | | | |
Mix	A	B	C	D + E
1	0	0	10	90
2	0	30	30	40
3	20	40	20	20
4	60	20	20	0

SOURCE: Federal Aviation Administration [3].

where T_i = time that lead aircraft i passes over runway threshold
T_j = time that trail aircraft j passes over runway threshold
$[T_{ij}]$ = matrix of actual time separations at runway threshold for two successive arrivals, an aircraft of speed class i followed by an aircraft of speed class j

$$E[T_{ij}] = \sum p_{ij}M_{ij} = \sum p_{ij}T_{ij} \qquad (8\text{-}5)$$

where $E[T_{ij}]$ = mean service time, or interarrival time at runway threshold for aircraft mix
p_{ij} = probability that lead aircraft i will be followed by trail aircraft j

$$C = \frac{1}{E[T_{ij}]} \tag{8-6}$$

where C = capacity of runway to process this mix of arrivals

To obtain the interarrival time at the runway threshold, it is necessary to know whether the speed of the lead aircraft V_i is greater or less than that of the trailing aircraft V_j, since the separation at the runway threshold will differ in each case. This can be illustrated by drawing space-time diagrams representative of these conditions, as shown in Figs. 8-15, 8-16, and 8-17. In these diagrams the following notation is used:

γ = length of common approach path

δ_{ij} = minimum permissible distance separation between two arriving aircraft, a lead aircraft i and a trail aircraft j, anywhere along this common approach path

V_i = approach speed of leading aircraft of class i

V_j = approach speed of trailing aircraft of class j

R_i = runway occupancy time of lead aircraft of class i

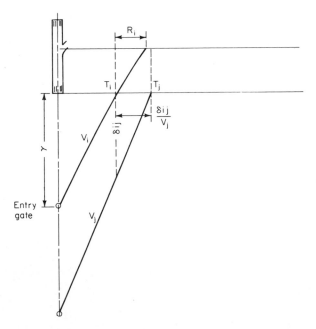

Fig. 8-15 Space-time diagram for interarrival spacing, closing case when $V_i < V_j$.

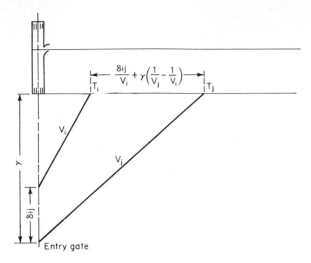

Fig. 8-16 Space-time diagram for interarrival spacing, opening case when $V_i > V_j$, for aircraft control from entry gate to threshold.

The Closing Case ($V_i < V_j$)

Take the case where the lead aircraft approach speed is less than that of the trail aircraft, as shown in Fig. 8-15. The minimum time separation at the threshold may be written in terms of the distance δ_{ij} and the speed of the trail aircraft V_j. However, if the runway occupancy time of the arrival R_i is greater than the airborne separation, then it would be the minimum separation at the threshold. The equation for this case is

$$T_{ij} = T_j - T_i = \frac{\delta_{ij}}{V_j} \qquad (8\text{-}7)$$

The Opening Case ($V_i > V_j$)

For the case where the lead aircraft approach speed is greater than that of the trail aircraft, as shown in Figs. 8-16 and 8-17, the minimum time separation at the threshold is written in terms of the distance δ_{ij}, the length of the common approach path γ, and the approach speeds of the lead and trail aircraft V_i and V_j. This corresponds to the minimum distance separation δ_{ij} along the common approach path, which now occurs at the entry gate instead of the threshold. The equation for the case shown in Fig. 8-16, when control is exercised only from the entry gate to the arrival threshold,

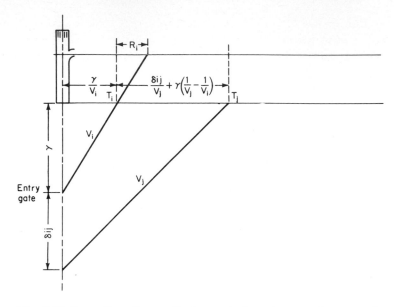

Fig. 8-17 Space-time diagram for interarrival spacing, opening case when $V_i > V_j$, for both aircraft separated in vicinity of entry gate.

is

$$T_{ij} = T_j - T_i = \frac{\delta_{ij}}{V_i} + \gamma \left(\frac{1}{V_j} - \frac{1}{V_i} \right) \qquad (8\text{-}8)$$

When control is exercised to maintain the separations between both aircraft as the lead passes over the entry gate, as shown in Fig. 8-17, the equation is

$$T_{ij} = T_j - T_i = \frac{\delta_{ij}}{V_j} + \gamma \left(\frac{1}{V_j} - \frac{1}{V_i} \right) \qquad (8\text{-}9)$$

It should be carefully noted that the only difference between Eqs. (8-8) and (8-9) is in the first term of the equation, where V_i and V_j are interchanged.

Example Problem 8-3

A mix of aircraft are approaching an airport runway system which services arrivals only. The mix consists of 60 percent aircraft with an approach speed of 150 kn, 20 percent aircraft with an approach speed of 135 kn, and 20 percent aircraft with an approach speed of 120 kn. The minimum separation between these aircraft in the approach airspace is required to be 3 nmi. The length of the common approach path is 6 nmi. Assuming there is no position error, determine the capacity of the runway system to service arrivals if control is exercised only from the entry gate to the runway threshold. Assume also that the time separations in the air are greater than the arrival runway-occupancy times.

Solution

The first step is to determine the error-free matrix $[M_{ij}]$. This is found for the case where the lead aircraft is slower than the trail aircraft, the closing case, in which the minimum separation occurs at the runway threshold, as shown in Fig. 8-15. The equation for the separation at the runway threshold is Eq. (8-7). Since this is the error-free case $[M_{ij}] = [T_{ij}]$, this yields for $V_i = 120$ and $V_j = 135$,

$$T_{ij} = T_j - T_i = \frac{\delta_{ij}}{V_j} = \frac{3(3600)}{135} = 80 \text{ s}$$

and for $V_i = 120$ and $V_j = 150$,

$$T_{ij} = T_j - T_i = \frac{\delta_{ij}}{V_j} = \frac{3(3600)}{150} = 72 \text{ s}$$

and so forth. For the case where the lead aircraft is faster than the trail aircraft, the opening case, the minimum separation occurs at the entry gate, as shown in Fig. 8-16. The equation for the minimum separation at the runway threshold is Eq. (8-8), which yields for $V_i = 150$ and $V_j = 120$,

$$T_{ij} = T_j - T_i = \frac{3(3600)}{150} + 6\left(\frac{1}{120} - \frac{1}{150}\right)3600 = 108 \text{ s}$$

and for $V_i = 150$ and $V_j = 135$,

$$T_{ij} = T_j - T_i = \frac{3(3600)}{150} + 6\left(\frac{1}{135} - \frac{1}{150}\right)3600 = 88 \text{ s}$$

and so forth. For the case where the approach speeds for the lead and trail aircraft are equal, it is apparent that either equation will yield the same results. If the results are tabulated in a matrix, the following gives the minimum time separation at the runway threshold for all cases:

	Trail aircraft speed	Lead aircraft speed		
		150	135	120
$[M_{ij}] = [T_{ij}] =$	150	72	72	72
	135	88	80	80
	120	108	100	90

Therefore, the mean interarrival time $E[T_{ij}]$ is found by using the probability of each combination p_{ij} occurring in the mix. This probability matrix is:

Trail aircraft speed	Lead aircraft speed		
	150	135	120
150	0.36	0.12	0.12
135	0.12	0.04	0.04
120	0.12	0.04	0.04

$[p_{ij}] =$

Substitution into Eq. (8-5) yields

$$E[T_{ij}] = 0.36(72) + 0.12(72) + 0.12(72) + 0.12(88) + 0.04(80) + 0.04(80)$$
$$+ 0.12(108) + 0.04(100) + 0.04(90)$$
$$= 80.72 \text{ s}$$

Finally the capacity of the runway system to service arrivals is found from Eq. 8-6 and yields

$$C = \frac{1(3600)}{80.72} = 44.6 \text{ operations per hour}$$

Consideration of Position Error

The above model represents the situation of a perfect system with no errors. To take care of errors, a buffer time is added to the minimum separation time. The size of the buffer depends upon the probability of violation that is acceptable. Figure 8-18 shows the position of the trail aircraft as it approaches the runway threshold. In the top portion of this illustration, the trail aircraft is sequenced so that its mean position is exactly determined by the minimum separation between the lead and trail aircraft. However, if the aircraft position is a random variable, there is an equal probability that it can be either ahead or behind schedule. Naturally if it is ahead of schedule, the minimum separation criterion will be violated. If the position error is normally distributed, then the shaded area of the bell-shaped curve would correspond to a probability of violation of the minimum separation rule of 50 percent. Therefore, in order to lower this probability of violation, the aircraft may be scheduled to arrive at this position later by building in a buffer to the minimum separation criterion, as shown in the bottom portion of the illustration. In this case, only when the aircraft is so far ahead of schedule as to encroach upon the smaller shaded area of the bell-shaped curve would a separation violation occur. There is of course less of a probability of this occurring. In practice, air

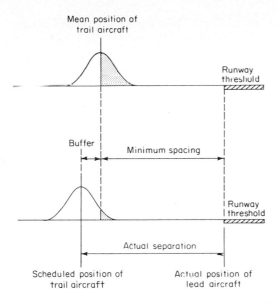

Fig. 8-18 Illustration of buffer spacing on actual separation between aircraft when position error is considered.

traffic controllers schedule aircraft with a buffer so that the probability of violation of the minimum separation rules is at an acceptable level.

As will be shown, in the closing case the buffer is a constant value. However, in the opening case the buffer need not be a constant value and will normally be less than the buffer for the closing case. Having the models for the buffer, a matrix of buffer times $[B_{ij}]$ for aircraft of speed class i followed by aircraft of speed class j is developed. This matrix is added to the error-free matrix to determine the actual interarrival time matrix from which the capacity may be found. The relationship is given by Eq. (8-10)

$$E[T_{ij}] = \sum p_{ij}[M_{ij} + B_{ij}] \qquad (8\text{-}10)$$

The Closing Case

In this case the lead aircraft approach speed is less than that of the trail aircraft, and the separations are as shown in Fig. 8-15. Let us call $[T_{ij}]$ the actual minimum interval of time between aircraft of class i and class j, and assume that runway occupancy is less than $[T_{ij}]$. Designate the mean or expected value of $[T_{ij}]$ as $E[T_{ij}]$ and e_0 as a zero-mean normally distributed random error with a standard deviation of σ_0. Then for each pair of arrivals

$$T_{ij} = E[T_{ij}] + e_0$$

but in order not to violate the minimum separation rule criteria, the value of $E[T_{ij}]$ must be increased by a buffer amount B_{ij}. Therefore, we have

$$E[T_{ij}] = M_{ij} + B_{ij}$$

and also

$$T_{ij} = M_{ij} + B_{ij} + e_0$$

For this case the minimum separation at the runway threshold is given by Eq. (8-7). The objective is to find for a specified probability of violation p_v the required amount of buffer. Thus

$$p_v = P\left(T_{ij} < \frac{\delta_{ij}}{V_j}\right)$$

or

$$p_v = P\left(\frac{\delta_{ij}}{V_j} + B_{ij} + e_0 < \frac{\delta_{ij}}{V_j}\right) \tag{8-11}$$

which simplifies to the relationship

$$p_v = P(B_{ij} < -e_0)$$

Using the assumption that errors are normally distributed with standard deviation σ_0, the value of the buffer can be derived as [12]

$$B_{ij} = \sigma_0 q_v \tag{8-12}$$

where q_v = value for which the cumulative standard normal distribution has the value $(1 - p_v)$

Stated differently, this simply means the number of standard deviations from the mean in which a certain percentage of the area under the normal curve would be found. For example, if $p_v = 0.05$, then q_v is the 95th percentile of the distribution and equals 1.65. In the closing case the buffer time is a constant that depends on the magnitude of the dispersion of the error and the acceptable probability of violation p_v.

The Opening Case

Next consider the case when the lead aircraft is approaching the runway threshold at a speed greater than the trail aircraft. In this case the separation between aircraft increases from the entry gate. The model is premised on the supposition that the trail aircraft should be scheduled not less than δ_{ij} miles behind the lead aircraft when the latter is at the entry gate, but it is assumed that strict separation is enforced by air traffic control only when the trail aircraft reaches the entry gate. This assumption was shown in Fig. 8-16.

For this case the probability of violation is simply the probability that the trail aircraft will arrive at the entry gate before the lead aircraft is a specified distance inside the entry gate. This may be expressed mathematically as follows:

$$p_v = P\left[T_j - \left(\frac{\delta_{ij} + \gamma}{V_j}\right) < T_i - \frac{\gamma}{V_i}\right]$$

or

$$p_v = P\left[T_j - T_i < \frac{\delta_{ij}}{V_j} + \left(\frac{\gamma}{V_j} - \frac{\gamma}{V_i}\right)\right]$$

Using Eq. (8-8) and (8-12) to compute the actual spacing at the arrival threshold and simplifying,

$$B_{ij} = \sigma_0 q_v - \delta_{ij}\left(\frac{1}{V_j} - \frac{1}{V_i}\right) \qquad (8\text{-}13)$$

Therefore, for the opening case the amount of buffer is reduced from that required in the closing case, as shown by Eq. (8-12). Negative values of buffer are not allowed, and therefore, the buffer is some finite positive number with a minimum of zero.

The application of position error to the arrivals-only runway capacity problem is illustrated in Example Problem 8-4.

Example Problem 8-4

Assume that the aircraft approaching the runway in Example Problem 8-3 have a position error of 20 s which is normally distributed. In this environment the probability of violating the minimum separation rule for arrival spacing is allowed to be 5 percent.

Determine the hourly capacity of the runway to service arrivals.

Solution

The error-free interarrival matrix $[M_{ij}]$ was found earlier, and it is now only necessary to find the buffer matrix $[B_{ij}]$ and solve Eq. (8-10), that is,

$$E[T_{ij}] = \sum p_{ij}[M_{ij} + B_{ij}]$$

In the closing case, where the lead aircraft is slower than the trail aircraft,

Eq. (8-12) gives the buffer. For a 5 percent probability of violation, q_v can be found from statistics tables as 1.65.

For all of these cases, the buffer is independent of speed, and therefore

$$B_{ij} = 20(1.65) = 33 \text{ s}$$

In the opening case, where the lead aircraft is faster than the trail aircraft, Eq. (8-13) gives the buffer. Therefore, we have for $V_i = 150$ and $V_j = 135$,

$$B_{ij} = 20(1.65) - 3\left(\frac{1}{135} - \frac{1}{150}\right)3600 = 25 \text{ s}$$

for $V_i = 150$ and $V_j = 120$,

$$B_{ij} = 20(1.65) - 3\left(\frac{1}{120} - \frac{1}{150}\right)3600 = 15 \text{ s}$$

and for $V_i = 135$ and $V_j = 120$,

$$B_{ij} = 20(1.65) - 3\left(\frac{1}{120} - \frac{1}{135}\right)3600 = 23 \text{ s}$$

Summarizing the values found for the buffer in a matrix, we have:

	Trail aircraft speed	Lead aircraft speed		
		150	135	120
	150	33	33	33
$[B_{ij}] =$	135	25	33	33
	120	15	23	33

Combining the error-free matrix $[M_{ij}]$ and the buffer matrix $[B_{ij}]$ yields the actual interarrival time spacing at the runway threshold:

	Trail aircraft speed	Lead aircraft speed		
		150	135	120
	150	105	105	105
$[M_{ij} + B_{ij}]$	135	113	113	113
	120	123	123	123

When this is combined with the mix probability, the mean interarrival time is

$$E[T_{ij}] = 110.2 \text{ s}$$

from which the arrival capacity of the runway in a position error context is

$$C = \frac{1(3600)}{110.2} = 32.7 \text{ operations per hour}$$

which is significantly lower than in the error-free case.

The Development of Models for Mixed Operations

This model is based on the same four operating rules as the model developed by Airborne Instruments Laboratory [2, 5]. These may be listed as follows:

1. Arrivals have priority over departures.

2. Only one aircraft can occupy the runway at any instant of time.

3. A departure may not be released if the subsequent arrival is less than a specified distance from the runway threshold, usually 2 nmi in IFR conditions.

4. Successive departures are spaced at a minimum time separation equal to the departure service time.

A space-time diagram may be drawn to show the sequencing of mixed operations under the rules stated above, and this is done in Fig. 8-19. In this figure T_i and T_j are the times that the lead aircraft i and the trail aircraft j, respectively, pass over the arrival threshold, δ_{ij} is the minimum separation between arrivals, T_1 is the time when the arriving aircraft clears the runway, T_d is the time when the departing aircraft begins its takeoff roll, δ_d is the minimum distance that an arriving aircraft must be from the threshold to release a departure, T_2 is the time which corresponds to the last instant when a departure can be released, R_i is the runway-occupancy time for an arrival, G is the time gap in which a departure may be released, and t_d is the required service time for a departure.

Since arrivals are given priority over departures, the arriving aircraft are sequenced at the minimum separation, and a departure cannot be released unless there is a gap between arrivals G. Therefore, we may write

$$G = T_2 - T_1 > 0$$

but we know that

$$T_1 = T_i + R_i$$

and

$$T_2 = T_j - \frac{\delta_d}{V_j}$$

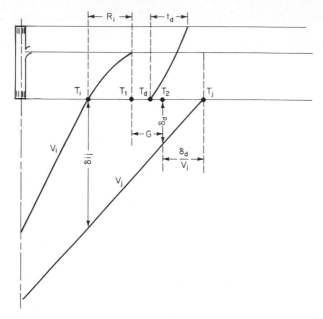

Fig. 8-19 Space-time diagram for interarrival spacing, mixed operations on a runway system.

Therefore, we may write

$$T_2 - T_1 > \left(T_j - \frac{\delta_d}{V_j}\right) - (T_i + R_i) > 0$$

or to release one departure between a pair of arrivals, we have

$$T_j - T_i > R_i + \frac{\delta_d}{V_j}$$

Through a simple extension of this equation it is apparent that the required mean interarrival time $E[T_{ij}]$ to release n departures between a pair of arrivals is given by

$$E\,[T_{ij}] > E[R_i] + E\left[\frac{\delta_d}{V_j}\right] + (n-1)E[t_d] \qquad (8\text{-}14)$$

It should be noted that the last term of this equation is equal to zero when only one departure is to be inserted between a pair of arrivals. An error term $\sigma_G q_v$ may be added to the above equation to account for the violation of the gap spacing. The use of Eq. (8-14) with a gap error is illustrated in Example Problem 8-5.

Example Problem 8-5

Assume that the aircraft mix is the same as for Example Problem 8-4 in which only arrivals were involved and that the standard deviation of the error in the gap is 30 s. The probability of violating the gap in which departures can be released is 10 percent. The runway-occupancy times R_i for the different speed classes are 60, 56, and 52 s for the approach speed classes of 150, 135, and 20 kn, respectively. A departure may be released if the arriving aircraft is at least 2 nmi from the runway threshold.

Determine the minimum separation between arrivals in order to ensure one departure between every two arrivals. Determine if a departure may be released between a pair of arrivals if the actual interarrival spacing is as shown in Example Problem 8-4.

Solution

For a probability of violation of 0.10, q_v is equal to 1.28. Therefore, the error in the gap is

$$\sigma_G q_v = 30(1.28) = 38.4 \text{ s}$$

The mean runway-occupancy time is

$$E[R_i] = 0.6(60) + 0.2(56 + 52) = 57.6 \text{ s}$$

The expected value of the time for an arriving aircraft to travel the final 2 mi to the runway threshold is

$$E\left[\frac{\delta_d}{V_j}\right] = \left[0.6\left(\frac{2}{150}\right) + 0.2\left(\frac{2}{135}\right) + 0.2\left(\frac{2}{120}\right)\right]3600 = 51.5 \text{ s}$$

The last term is, as noted above, equal to zero since only one departure is to be inserted between a pair of arrivals. Therefore, the required interarrival time to release one departure between a pair of arrivals is given by Eq. (8-14), with the error term added on, and this yields

$$E[T_{ij}] > 57.6 + 51.5 + 0 + 38.4 = 147.5 \text{ s}$$

Since the actual interarrival time from Example Problem 8-4 is equal to 110.2 s, a departure cannot be released between a pair of arrivals unless the arrival spacing is increased above the minimum values. In every case the minimum interarrival spacing is less than 147.5 s and therefore a departure can never be released between a pair of arrivals.

Application of Techniques for the Ultimate Hourly Capacity

The hourly capacity of the runway system is defined as the maximum number of aircraft operations that can take place on the runway system in an hour. The maximum number of aircraft operations depends on a number of conditions including, but not limited to, the following:

1. The ceiling and visibility conditions
2. The physical configuration of the runway system
3. The runway-use strategy
4. The mix of aircraft using the runway system
5. The ratio of arrivals to departures
6. The number of touch-and-go operations by general aviation aircraft
7. The number and location of exits from the runway system

It is important to point out that the definition of hourly capacity of runways in this section differs from the earlier discussion since the definition of capacity herein contains no assumptions regarding acceptable levels of delay.

Parameters Required for Runway Capacity

As noted above, to determine the hourly capacity of the runway system it is necessary to ascertain the parameters which will affect capacity. Due to the fact that aircraft separation rules differ in VRF and IFR weather, it is first necessary to determine the ceiling and visibility conditions, or more appropriately, the separation rules applicable to flying conditions when the ceiling is at least 1000 ft and visibility is at least 3 mi. This condition results in VFR. If either or both of these criteria are not met, then IFR is in effect. Of course, all airports have a period of time when conditions are such that IFR applies. Therefore, the hourly capacity of runways is normally specified for each of these conditions.

The physical runway surfaces at an airport can be used in several ways. For example, two parallel runways can be used with arrivals on one runway and departures on the other at some point in time. Also they could be used with arrivals and departures on one surface and arrivals only on the other surface. These runway-use configurations are the runway-use strategies which are dependent upon weather conditions, aircraft types, and the spacing between runways. It is necessary to specify the runway-use strategies and the percentage of time each strategy is used. It is also necessary to specify the types of aircraft which can utilize a given runway, as quite often shorter pavements are constructed for use by general aviation aircraft only. The aircraft which can use a runway surface are defined in terms of a mix index. This index is simply an indication of the level of air-carrier-type operations on the runway. For this procedure aircraft are classified as in Table 8-4. The mix index MI is given by Eq. (8-15)

$$MI = C + 3D \qquad (8\text{-}15)$$

where C = percentage of type C aircraft in mix of aircraft using runway

D = percentage of type D aircraft in mix of aircraft using runway

The percentage of arrival operations which occur on the runway must also be known. This is because the spacing rules for arrivals and departures differ. There are three types of operations which can occur, namely, arrivals, departures, and touch-and-go operations. A touch-and-go operation is most commonly used by general aviation pilots practicing approaches, landings, and takeoffs. These operations are seldom conducted in poor weather. For the purpose of determining capacity, the parameter called *percent arrivals* is used to define the proportion of each type of operation which occurs on the runway. In VFR conditions it is also necessary to find the percentage of touch-and-go operations. At times at small general aviation airports touch-and-go operations can approach 30 percent of all operations.

The location of runway exits for arriving aircraft must also be known since this affects runway-occupancy time. Depending upon the nature of the aircraft using a runway, exits should be located at positions which will allow minimum runway-occupancy times. If this is not the case, the capacity will be reduced because of excessive runway-occupancy times.

As a result of extensive research conducted to determine the capacity of runway systems, the FAA has published a series of charts to determine runway capacity [18]. These charts are used to determine the runway capacity through Eq. (8-16)

$$C = C_b ET \qquad (8\text{-}16)$$

where C = hourly capacity of runway-use configuration in operations per hour

C_b = ideal or base capacity of runway-use configuration

E = exit adjustment factor for number and location of runway exits

T = touch-and-go adjustment factor

The use of this equation and the charts can be illustrated by Example Problem 8-6.

TABLE 8-4 **Aircraft Classification for Ultimate Capacity Techniques**

Aircraft mix class	Aircraft wake turbulence class	Number of engines	Maximum certified takeoff weight, lb
A	Small	Single	12,500 or less
B	Small	Multi	12,500 or less
C	Large	Multi	12,500–300,000
D	Heavy	Multi	300,000 or more

SOURCE: Federal Aviation Administration [18].

Example Problem 8-6

Determine the VFR and IFR hourly capacities of the runway system shown in Fig. 8-20. The runway-use strategy is as shown. In VFR weather, the traffic consists of 13 single-engine, 10 light twin, 25 large transport-type, and 2 wide-body aircraft. Arrivals constitute 40 percent of the operations, and there are approximately 3 touch-and-go operations. In IFR weather, the small aircraft population count drops to 2 single and 5 light twins, the arrival rate increases to 50 percent, and there are no touch-and-go operations.

Solution:

The capacity of intersecting runways is a function of the location of the intersection from both the arrival and the departure thresholds. The closer the intersection to these thresholds, the greater the capacity. The charts used for this configuration in VFR and IFR are given in Fig. 8-21 and 8-22.

Aircraft observed	Classi-fication type	VFR mix		IFR mix	
		Number	%	Number	%
Single engine	A	13	26.0	2	5.9
Twin engine	B	10	20.0	5	14.7
Transport	C	25	50.0	25	73.5
Wide-body	D	2	4.0	2	5.9
Total		50	100.0	34	100.0

From the above data, the mix index can be found for VFR,

$$MI = C + 3D = 50.0 + 3(4.0) = 62.0$$

and for IFR,

$$MI = C + 3D = 73.5 + 3(5.9) = 91.2$$

Using the VFR mix index of 62.0 and the percent arrivals PA equal to 40, the base capacity C_b is found from the left-hand side of Fig. 8-21 as about 95 operations per hour. This base value is then adjusted for touch-and-go operations and the location of exits, using the right-hand side of this figure. From the given data, the touch-and-go operations in VFR are equal to 6 percent. Therefore, the touch-and-go adjustment factor T is equal to 1.03. For the mix index of 62.0, only those exits located between 3500 and 6500 ft from the arrival threshold can be counted. There are two such exits, one at 4500 ft and the other at 6000 ft. The table then gives an exit factor E of 0.97 for 40 percent arrivals.

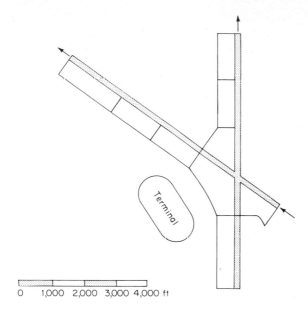

Fig. 8-20 Runway layout for Example Problem 8-6.

Therefore, the hourly capacity of the runway system in VFR is, from Eq. (8-16),

$$C = C_bTE = 95(1.03)(0.97) = 95 \text{ operations per hour}$$

The IFR capacity is determined similarly from Fig. 8-22. This will yield, for an IFR mix index of 91.2 and a percent arrivals PA of 50, the base capacity, touch-and-go factor, and exit factor,

$$C = C_bTE = 58(1.00)(0.97) = 56 \text{ operations per hour}$$

Computation of Delay on Runway Systems

Delay to aircraft is defined as the difference between the actual time it takes an aircraft to maneuver on the runway and the time it would take the aircraft to maneuver without interference from other aircraft. The runway is defined as the entire runway system, including approach and departure airspace [18]. To compute runway system delay it is necessary to analyze each runway-use configuration for the demand placed upon it. To compute annual runway delay, it is necessary to determine the percentage of time each runway-use configuration is used. Normally this will require a knowledge of the following factors:

1. The hourly capacity of the runway-use strategy in VFR and IFR

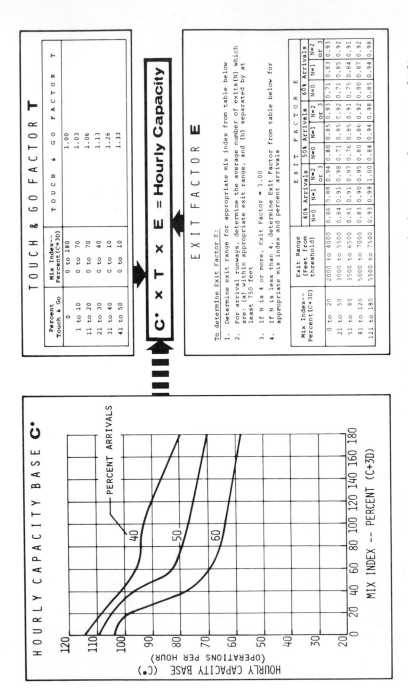

Fig. 8-21 Hourly capacity in VFR for runway operations in Example Problem 8-6. (*Federal Aviation Administration* [18].)

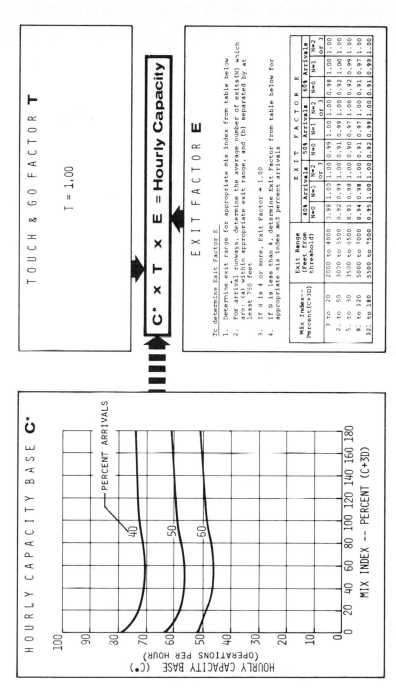

Fig. 8-22 Hourly capacity in IFR for runway operations in Example Problem 8-6. *(Federal Aviation Administration [18].)*

2. The pattern of hourly, daily, and monthly aircraft demand during the design year

3. The peaking of demand during the design hour

4. The frequency of occurrence of runway-use strategies, ceiling, and visibility conditions

The techniques are outlined in detail in [18], but it is sufficient to note that the computation of annual delay is a very tedious and time-consuming process, now generally performed on computers [13]. The elements of the process are exhibited in Example Problem 8-7, which uses charts from [18].

Example Problem 8-7

The hourly delay to aircraft operations on the runway system in Example Problem 8-6 is to be found for both VFR and IFR conditions. It is known that the peak 15-min demand in the peak hour is 20 operations in VFR and 10 operations in IFR.

Solution

The hourly capacity of the runway system was found earlier and yielded 95 operations per hour in VFR and 56 operations per hour in IFR. The hourly demand was 50 operations per hour in VFR and 34 operations per hour in IFR. Therefore, the ratio of hourly demand to hourly capacity is computed for VFR,

$$\frac{D}{C} = \frac{50}{94} = 0.53$$

and for IFR,

$$\frac{D}{C} = \frac{34}{56} = 0.61$$

Figure 8-23 gives the variation of the arrival delay index ADI and the departure delay index DDI for VFR and IFR conditions for this runway use for 40 percent arrivals.

Based upon the respective mix indices for VFR and IFR conditions, this chart gives for VFR,

$$ADI = 0.90$$

$$DDI = 0.88$$

and for IFR,

$$ADI = 1.00$$

$$DDI = 0.84$$

These indices are combined with the respective ratios of demand to capacity to arrive at the arrival delay factor ADF and the departure delay factor DDF as follows:

$$\text{ADF} = (\text{ADI})\frac{D}{C}$$

and

$$\text{DDF} = (\text{DDI})\frac{D}{C}$$

VFR Conditions

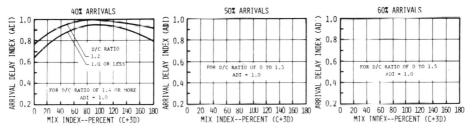

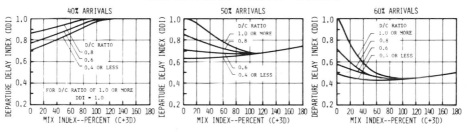

IFR Conditions

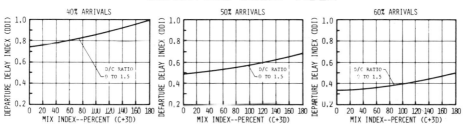

Fig. 8-23 Arrival and departure delay indices for Example Problem 8-7. (*Federal Aviation Administration [18].*)

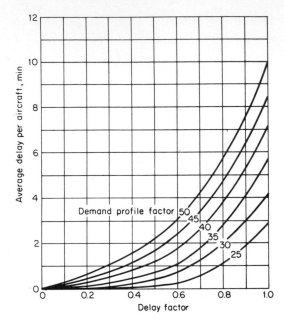

Fig. 8-24 Variation of average aircraft delay with delay factor. (*Federal Aviation Administration [18].*)

Therefore, for arrivals in VFR,

$$\text{ADF} = 0.90(0.53) = 0.48$$

$$\text{DDF} = 0.88(0.53) = 0.47$$

and in IFR,

$$\text{ADF} = 1.00(0.61) = 0.61$$

$$\text{DDF} = 0.84(0.61) = 0.51$$

The average delay for each aircraft is then found from Fig. 8-24 using the above delay factors and the demand profile factor. The demand profile factor is simply a measure of the peaking of demand in the hour and is defined as the peak 15-min demand divided by the hourly demand. Therefore, the demand profile factors DPF are for VFR,

$$\text{DPF} = \frac{20}{50}(100) = 40$$

and for IFR,

$$\text{DPF} = \frac{10}{34}(100) = 34$$

From Fig. 8-24, the average delays are found for VFR,

$$\text{Arrival delay} = 1.6 \text{ min per aircraft}$$

$$\text{Departure delay} = 1.5 \text{ min per aircraft}$$

and for IFR,

$$\text{Arrival delay} = 1.0 \text{ min per aircraft}$$

$$\text{Departure delay} = 0.7 \text{ min per aircraft}$$

Since there are equal arrivals and departures, the total delay to all aircraft in this hour, in both VFR and IFR, can be found:

$$\text{Total delay VFR} = 50[1.6(0.4) + 1.5(0.6)] = 77.0 \text{ min}$$

$$\text{Total delay IFR} = 34[1.0(0.4) + 0.7(0.6)] = 27.9 \text{ min}$$

The computation of annual delay at an airport requires that this procedure be repeated for each runway-use strategy and proportioned throughout the year on the basis of the demand and weather patterns.

Graphic Methods for Approximating Delay

A relatively simple technique for estimating delays when demand exceeds capacity has been used in aviation studies [14]. In this method, a time scale is established on the x axis to represent the time period being analyzed. On the y axis a scale is established for the cumulative number of aircraft which have arrived by some point in time. Therefore, a point on the plot represents the total number of aircraft which have arrived at that point in time. The curve, which results from plotting the succession of points, is actually a representation of the demand $D(t)$. A line of constant or, for that matter, variable slope can be drawn on the same graph to show the service capabilities of a facility. This is the service function $S(t)$. An illustration of such a graph is given in Fig. 8-25.

On this figure, point A represents the time when the demand rate begins to exceed the service rate. Therefore, delays and queues begin to develop. At point B, the delays and queues which have built since time t_1 will have dissipated and the demand rate is now less than the service rate. A review of the results displayed on this figure shows that:

1. Delays occur from time t_1 to time t_4.

2. The total number of aircraft delayed is the difference between P_4 and P_1.

3. From time t_1 to time t_2 the demand rate exceeds the service rate, and delays and queues increase during this time period.

4. The maximum delay and the maximum queue length occur at time t_2 since the demand rate becomes less than the service rate at this time.

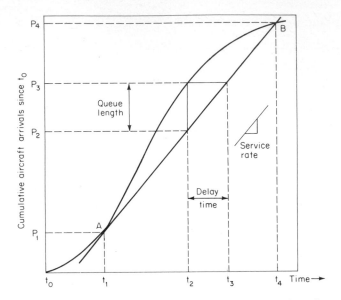

Fig. 8-25 Graphic determination of aircraft delay when demand rate exceeds service rate.

5. The delay to any aircraft is given by the magnitude of a horizontal line drawn between the two curves.

6. The length of a queue at any point in time is given by the magnitude of a vertical line drawn between the two curves at that point in time.

7. The area between the two curves represents the total delay to all aircraft which are delayed from time t_1 to time t_4.

This type of analysis is useful in airport planning to estimate the magnitude of delays, the number of aircraft delayed, and the cost of delay under assumed operating conditions. It does not, however, give an indication of the delays which occur when average demand is less than capacity. These are normally calculated by the equations or methods discussed earlier.

Application of Techniques for Annual Service Volume

Annual service volume is the level of annual aircraft operations that may be used as a reference in preliminary planning. As annual aircraft operations approach annual service volume, the average delay to each aircraft throughout the year may increase rapidly with relatively small increases in aircraft operations, thereby causing levels of service on the airfield to deteriorate.

When annual aircraft operations on the airfield are equal to annual service volume, the average delay to each aircraft throughout the year is on the order of 1 to 4 min. A more precise estimate of the actual average delay to aircraft at a particular airport can be obtained using these procedures if this is required in the planning application.

If the number of annual operations exceeds the annual service volume, moderate or severe congestion may occur, similar to that being at present experienced at several of the major airports in the United States, such as O'Hare International Airport, LaGuardia Airport, and Atlanta International Airport.

For analyses of airfield improvements, aircraft delays can also be important at levels of annual aircraft operations less than the annual service volume. Therefore, delays to aircraft should also be considered in planning and evaluating airfield improvements at levels of annual operations less than the annual service volume. In some instances, when the annual demand is expected to approach one half of the annual service volume within the planning horizon, the normal construction costs of airfield improvements may be balanced by savings in aircraft delay costs.

To determine the annual service volume which can be accommodated at an airport, it is necessary to find the weighted hourly capacity of each of the runway-use configurations at the airport. The weighted hourly capacity is given by the relationship in Eq. (8-17)

$$C_w = \sum \frac{P_n W_n C_n}{P_n W_n} \tag{8-17}$$

where C_w = weighted average hourly capacity of runway system in the year
  C_n = hourly capacity of runway use configuration n
  P_n = percentage of time runway use configuration n is used in the year
  W_n = weight assigned to runway-use configuration n to account for the fact that different delay levels occur on the various runway-use configurations.

Through empirical studies at airports, the weighting factors W_n have been found to equal the values given in Table 8-5 [17].

TABLE 8-5 **Annual Service Volume Weighting Factors for Weighted Hourly Capacity**

Percentage of dominant capacity	Mix index in VFR, 0–180	Mix index in IFR		
		0–20	21–50	51–180
91 or more	1	1	1	1
81–90	5	1	3	5
66–80	15	2	8	15
51–65	20	3	12	20
0–50	25	4	16	25

SOURCE: Federal Aviation Administration [18].

Once the weighted hourly capacity of the runway system has been found, the annual service volume ASV is computed through the relationship given by Eq. (8-18)

$$ASV = C_w HD \qquad (8\text{-}18)$$

where C_w = weighted average hourly capacity of runway system in the year, as found above

H = ratio of average daily operations in peak month to peak-hour operations in peak month

D = ratio of annual operations to average daily operations in peak month

The hourly ratio H and the daily ratio D defined above are used to simulate the fluctuation in the pattern of demand at the airport and can usually be ascertained from existing records or through demand forecasting. However, approximate values of these ratios have been determined for airports in the United States and can be used for estimating purposes [16–18]. These approximate values are given in Table 8-6.

The computation of the annual service volume for an airport is illustrated in Example Problem 8-8.

Example Problem 8-8

The runway system at a large hub commercial airport is shown in Fig. 8-26. The runway-use configuration and the percentage of annual use are given in Table 8-7. The mix index at this airport is 100. The annual demand on this airport is 294,000 operations, the average daily traffic in the peak month is 877 operations, and the peak-hour traffic is 62 operations.

Find the weighted hourly capacity and the annual service volume at this airport if VFR conditions occur 82 percent of the time.

Solution

From the data in Table 8-7, the hourly capacity and percentage use of each configuration can be found. The most frequently used runway configuration has a capacity of 122 operations per hour in VFR weather conditions. This is the predominant capacity. Therefore, the weighting

TABLE 8-6   **Typical Hourly and Daily Ratios for Estimating Annual Service Volume**

Mix index	Hourly ratio H	Daily ratio D
0–20	7–11	280–310
21–50	10–13	300–320
51–180	11–15	310–350

SOURCE: Federal Aviation Administration [18].

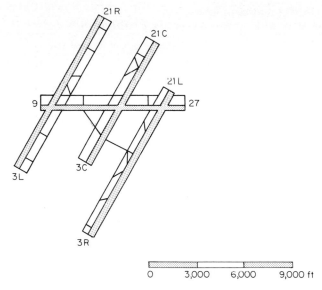

Fig. 8-26 Runway layout for Example Problem 8-8.

factors for each of the runway-use configurations may be found from Table 8-5, and all the required values are tabulated in Table 8-8.

Using the data in Table 8-8, the weighted hourly capacity is found from Eq. (8-17), which yields

$$C_w = \sum \frac{P_n W_n C_n}{P_n W_n}$$

$$= \frac{0.52(1)(122) + 0.17(25)(61) + \cdots + 0.02(25)(48)}{0.52(1) + 0.17(25) + \cdots + 0.02(25)}$$

$$= \frac{720.19}{12.52} = 58 \text{ operations per hour}$$

The annual service volume is computed using the above weighted capacity and the daily and hourly ratios from Eq. (8-18):

$$\text{ASV} = C_w HD$$

$$= 58 \left(\frac{877}{62}\right) \left(\frac{294{,}000}{877}\right) = 275{,}032 \text{ annual operations}$$

TABLE 8–7 **Runway-Use Configurations and Percentage of Annual Use for Example Problem 8-8**

Runway use configuration	Percentage of Annual Use	
	VFR weather	IFR weather
A	63	0
B	21	78
C	9	12
D	7	10

Estimating Procedures for Annual Service Volume and Delay

Simplified estimating procedures are available for airport planning purposes to determine the annual service volume and the average aircraft delay for runway-use configurations existing at airports. These procedures should only be used for preliminary estimating purposes. They allow for approximations of:

1. The hourly capacity of runways in VFR and IFR conditions

2. The annual service volume of runways

3. The average annual delay to aircraft on runways

Hourly capacities and annual service volumes for a number of runway configurations are presented in Table 8-9. An approximate estimate of the average aircraft delay per year for any runway configuration can be obtained from Fig. 8-27. The figures are based on a number of assumptions which include:

1. A representative range of mix indices are sufficient for estimating purposes.

2. The hourly capacities are those that correspond to the runway utilization which produces the largest capacity consistent with current air traffic control procedures and practices, and this configuration is used 80 percent of the time.

3. One half of the demand for the use of the runways is by arriving aircraft, and thus, the number of arriving and the number of departing aircraft in a specified period of time are equal.

4. The percentage of touch-and-go operations is a function of the mix index of the airport.

5. Sufficient taxiways exist to permit the capacity of the runways to be fully realized.

6. The impact on capacity of a taxiway crossing and an active runway is assumed to be negligible.

7. There is sufficient airspace to accommodate all aircraft wishing to use the runways, and aircraft operations are conducted in a radar environment with at least one runway equipped with an ILS.

8. IFR conditions occur 10 percent of the time.

9. Representative hourly and daily ratios are a function of the mix index.

The order of magnitude relationship between the average annual delay per aircraft and the annual service volume depicted in Fig. 8-27 was derived from historical traffic records and a range of assumptions on likely operating conditions, as itemized above. Typically, the upper portion of the shaded band on this figure is representative of airports primarily serving air-carrier operations; airports serving primarily general aviation operations may typically fall anywhere within the entire shaded band. The dotted curve is the average of the upper and lower limits of the band indicated. Example Problem 8-9 shows the use of these approximate procedures.

TABLE 8–8 **Tabulation of Factors for Weighted Hourly Capacity for Example Problem 8-8**

Weather	Runway use	Percentage use	Hourly capacity	Percentage of dominant capacity	Weight
VFR					
	A	52	122	100	1
	B	17	61	50	25
	C	7	52	43	25
	D	6	59	48	25
IFR					
	A	0	—	—	—
	B	14	48	39	25
	C	2	52	43	25
	D	2	48	39	25

TABLE 8-9 **Preliminary Estimates of Hourly and Annual Ultimate Capacities**

Runway configuration	Mix index, % (C + 3D)	Hourly capacity, operations per hour		Annual service volume, operations per year
		VFR	IFR	
A	0–20	98	59	230,000
	21–50	74	57	195,000
	51–80	63	56	205,000
	81–120	55	53	210,000
	121–180	51	50	240,000
B 700' to 2,499'	0–20	197	59	355,000
	21–50	145	57	275,000
	51–80	121	56	260,000
	81–120	105	59	285,000
	121–180	94	60	340,000
C 4,300' or more	0–20	197	119	370,000
	21–50	149	114	320,000
	51–80	126	111	305,000
	81–120	111	105	315,000
	121–180	103	99	370,000
D 700' to 2,499' 2,500' to 3,499'	0–20	295	62	385,000
	21–50	219	63	310,000
	51–80	184	65	290,000
	81–120	161	70	315,000
	121–180	146	75	385,000
E 700' to 2,499' 3,500' or more 700' to 2,499'	0–20	394	119	715,000
	21–50	290	114	550,000
	51–80	242	111	515,000
	81–120	210	117	565,000
	121–180	189	120	675,000
F	0–20	98	59	230,000
	21–50	77	57	200,000
	51–80	77	56	215,000
	81–120	76	59	225,000
	121–180	72	60	265,000
G	0–20	150	59	270,000
	21–50	108	57	225,000
	51–80	85	56	220,000
	81–120	77	59	225,000
	121–180	73	60	265,000

TABLE 8-9 **(Continued)**

Runway configuration	Mix index, % (C + 3D)	Hourly capacity, operations per hour		Annual service volume, operations per year
		VFR	IFR	
H	0–20	132	59	260,000
	21–50	99	57	220,000
	51–80	82	56	215,000
	81–120	77	59	225,000
	121–180	73	60	265,000
I	0–20	150	59	270,000
	21–50	108	57	225,000
	51–80	85	56	220,000
	81–120	77	59	225,000
	121–180	73	60	265,000
J	0–20	132	59	260,000
	21–50	99	57	220,000
	51–80	82	56	215,000
	81–120	77	59	225,000
	121–180	73	60	265,000
K 700' to 2,499'	0–20	197	59	355,000
	21–50	145	57	275,000
	51–80	121	56	260,000
	81–120	105	59	285,000
	121–180	94	60	340,000
L 4,300' or more	0–20	197	119	370,000
	21–50	149	114	320,000
	51–80	126	111	305,000
	81–120	111	105	315,000
	121–180	103	99	370,000
M 700' to 2,499'	0–20	295	59	385,000
	21–50	210	57	305,000
	51–80	164	56	275,000
	81–120	146	59	300,000
	121–180	129	60	355,000

TABLE 8–9   **(Continued)**

Runway configuration	Mix index, % (C + 3D)	Hourly capacity, operations per hour		Annual service volume, operations per year
		VFR	IFR	
N	0–20	295	59	385,000
	21–50	210	57	305,000
	51–80	164	56	275,000
	81–120	146	59	300,000
	121–180	129	60	355,000
O	0–20	197	59	355,000
	21–50	147	57	275,000
	51–80	145	56	270,000
	81–120	138	59	295,000
	121–180	125	60	350,000

SOURCE: Federal Aviation Administration [18].

Example Problem 8-9

An airport has a single runway available to service arrivals and departures. The projected 1990 annual demand is 220,000 operations. The aircraft mix is estimated to consist of 21 percent small single-engine aircraft, 20 percent small multiengine aircraft, 55 percent large commercial aircraft, and 4 percent heavy aircraft. Air-carrier operations predominate at the airport, and very few touch-and-go operations occur.

Determine the annual service volume and the average delay to aircraft for the single runway and for closely spaced parallels which may be constructed.

Solution

The mix index at the airport is computed as

$$MI = 55 + 3(4) = 67$$

From Table 8-9, the annual service volume for each runway is found from runway configuration diagrams A and B, with a mix index range of 51 to 80:

Single runway ASV   205,000 operations

Close parallel runway ASV   260,000 operations

The ratios of annual demand to annual service volume are then computed for both situations as

Single runway $\dfrac{\text{Demand}}{\text{ASV}} = \dfrac{220,000}{205,000} = 1.07$

Close parallel runways $\dfrac{\text{Demand}}{\text{ASV}} = \dfrac{220,000}{260,000} = 0.84$

Using the upper half of the graph in Fig. 8-27, since this is a predominantly air-carrier airport, yields the average annual delay per aircraft. These values are

Single runway   4.0 to 6.0 min per operation

Close parallel runways   1.2 to 1.7 min per operation

It is clear that the construction of close parallel runways will represent a benefit in terms of decreased delays. However, a detailed analysis of this should be performed prior to making a decision on construction modifica-

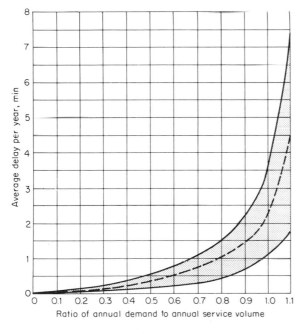

Fig. 8-27 Relationship between average aircraft delay and ratio of annual demand to annual service volume. (*Federal Aviation Administration [18].*)

tions since this procedure is approximate and based upon the assumptions noted above.

APRON-GATE CAPACITY

Gate capacity can be defined as the maximum number of aircraft that a fixed number of gates can accommodate during a specified interval of time when there is a continuous demand for service. Gate capacity can be calculated as the inverse of a weighted average gate-occupancy time of all aircraft being served. For example, if aircraft occupy a gate for an average of 30 min, the capacity of the gate equals 2 aircraft per hour.

The factors that affect gate capacity are as follows:

1. The number and type of gates available to aircraft

2. The mix of aircraft demanding apron gates and the gate-occupancy time for various aircraft

3. The percentage of time gates may be used

4. Restrictions in the use of any or all gates

The type of gate refers to its ability to accommodate a large, medium, or small aircraft. The mix of aircraft refers primarily to size but also to the required gate-occupancy time. Very large aircraft require certain types of gates in order to process passengers. Time is spent maneuvering at a gate, and therefore gate utilization may not be 100 percent of the time. If the gate-occupancy time includes the time to maneuver at gate positions, as well as the normal processing times to board and unboard passengers, fuel and inspect the aircraft, and perform cabin service and other routine service, then the utilization will approach 100 percent. Occupancy times vary depending on the size of the aircraft and whether it is an originating, turnaround, or through flight. Table 8-10 provides typical observed values of occupancy times. These times, however, can be considered as minimal. The gate-occupancy times expected by aircraft manufacturers are usually given in publications. However, this will vary with each airline and their

TABLE 8–10   Typical Observed Values of Aircraft Gate-Occupancy Times

Aircraft	Gate-occupancy time, min
B-747	60
DC-10, L-1011	60
B-727	40
DC-9	40

operating procedures at different stations or airports. Often schedules or lateness of arrivals will result in much greater occupancy times than normally required.

Analytical Models for Gate Capacity

The basis of gate capacity analysis is that the gate time demanded by aircraft should be less than or equal to the gate time available for these aircraft. Two analytical models have been developed for determining the capacity of gates at an airport. One model assumes that all aircraft can use all the gates available at an airport. This is termed an *unrestricted gate-use strategy.* The other model assumes that aircraft of a certain size or airline can only use gates that were specifically designed for these aircraft or airline. This is called a *restricted gate-use strategy.* Both of these models are described, and most situations encountered in practice may be approached through one of the two models.

When there are no restrictions on the use of gates, that is, all aircraft can use all the gates, the capacity of the gates C_g can be derived as follows:

Gate time supplied > gate time demanded

$$u_k N_k = E[T_g]C_g \qquad (8\text{-}19)$$

where u_k = gate utilization factor, or percentage of time in an hour that gates of type k may be used by aircraft of type i

N_k = number of k type gates available to aircraft of type i

$E[T_g]$ = expected value of gate-occupancy time demanded by aircraft which can use gates of type k

C_g = capacity of gates of type k, in aircraft per hour

The expected value of the gate-occupancy time $E[T_g]$ is found from the following expression:

$$E[T_g] = \sum m_i T_{gi} \qquad (8\text{-}20)$$

where m_i = percentage of type i aircraft in fleet mix using airport

T_{gi} = gate-occupancy time required for aircraft of type i at airport

The use of these equations is illustrated for unrestricted gate use in Example Problem 8-10.

Example Problem 8-10

An airport has four gates available to all aircraft. The aircraft mix at the airport during peak hour consists of 30 percent type A, 50 percent type B, and 20 percent type C aircraft. Type A aircraft require a gate-occupancy time of 60 min, type B require 45 min, and type C require 30 min. Normally, due to the distribution of demand, the maximum gate utilization which can be expected is 70 percent.

Find the capacity of the gates at this airport to process aircraft.

Solution

Substitution into Eq. (8-19) yields

$$0.70(4)(60) = [0.3(60) + 0.50(45) + 0.20(30)]C_g$$

which reduces to

$$C_g = 3.61 \text{ aircraft per hour}$$

It should be observed that, since every aircraft at a gate is two operations, an arrival and a departure, the hourly capacity of the gates could also be expressed as $2(3.61) = 7.22$ operations per hour. Also if the gate utilization factor is equal to 1, then the ultimate capacity of the gates becomes equal to 5.16 aircraft per hour.

For restricted gate use, the mix of gates and the mix of aircraft using the airport may not be the same. Therefore, it is necessary to find the gate capacity of each type of gate and then determine the overall capacity of the airport based upon gate capabilities as the minimum gate capacity of any type gate. Mathematically, this becomes

$$C_g = \min[C_{gk}] \qquad\qquad (8\text{-}21)$$

The use of the above analysis for restricted gate use is shown in Example Problem 8-11.

Example Problem 8-11

An airport has 10 gates available for aircraft. These gates are restricted in the types of aircraft which can be accommodated. The 5 type I gates can accommodate any type of aircraft, the 3 type II gates cannot accommodate a type A aircraft, and type III gates can only accommodate a type C aircraft.

The mix and the gate-occupancy times of the aircraft using the airport during peak hour are the same as in Example Problem 8-10. The gate utilization factor is 1.0.

Determine the capacity of the gates to process aircraft at this airport.

Solution

The relationship shown in Eq. 8-19 must be solved for each type of gate. There are 5 gates available for type A, 8 for type B, and 10 for type C aircraft. Solving yields

$$1.0(5)(60) = 0.3(60)C_{gI}$$

$$C_{gI} = 16.67 \text{ aircraft per hour}$$

$$1.0(8)(60) = [0.3(60) + 0.5(45)]C_{gII}$$

$$C_{gII} = 11.85 \text{ aircraft per hour}$$

$$1.0(10)(60) = [0.3(60) + 0.5(45) + 0.2(30)]C_{gIII}$$

$$C_{gIII} = 12.90 \text{ aircraft per hour}$$

Therefore, the type II gates restrict the aircraft capacity of the airport, and

$$C_g = \min[16.67, 11.85, 12.90] = 11.85$$

Therefore, with this mix of aircraft demanding gates at the airport, the gate mix restricts the airport capacity to 11.85 aircraft per hour, or 23.7 operations per hour.

It should be noted that only with this capacity is the gate time supplied greater than or equal to the gate time demanded. This is shown as

$$\text{Gate time supplied} > \text{gate time demanded}$$

$$1.0(10)(60) > [0.3(60) + 0.5(45) + 0.2(30)]11.85$$

$$600 > 551 \quad \text{as required}$$

Graphic Technique for Gate Capacity

A graphic technique to determine gate capacity has also been developed by the FAA [18]. This method assumes a gate utilization factor of 1.0, and the results must be adjusted accordingly if this utilization is not obtainable. The method assumes that all gates which can accommodate a wide-body aircraft can accommodate any other aircraft, but non-wide-body gates will not accommodate the wide-body aircraft. The parameters required to use this technique include the number of gates, the percentage of wide-body and non-wide-body aircraft and gates, and the gate-occupancy times for wide-body and non-wide-body aircraft.

The chart used for gate capacity by this technique is shown in Fig. 8-28, and its use is illustrated in Example Problem 8-12.

Example Problem 8-12

Assume that in Example Problem 8-11 the only wide-body aircraft are the type A. Using the data in this problem, determine the gate capacity of the airport by means of the FAA chart method.

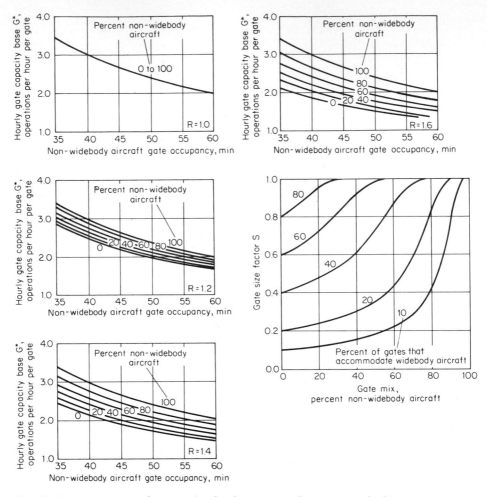

Fig. 8-28 Gate capacity of airports (*Federal Aviation Administration [18].*)

Solution

The percentage of non-wide-body aircraft is equal to 70 percent. The percentage of the gates that accommodate wide-body aircraft is 50 percent. The number of gates equals 10. The ratio of the gate-occupancy time by wide-body aircraft to that by non-wide-body aircraft is

$$R = \frac{60}{(0.5/0.7)(45) + (0.2/0.7)(30)} = \frac{60}{40.7} = 1.47$$

Entering the graph in the upper right-hand corner with a gate mix of 70 and intersecting the interpolated curve for 50 percent wide-body gates, the gate size factor S is 1.0, the chart limit. Using the non-wide-body gate time of 40.7 and interpolating between the results for the values of R of 1.4 and 1.6 on the left-hand curves, the gate capacity hourly base is about 2.57 operations per hour per gate. Therefore,

$$C_g = 2.57\,(1.0)(10) = 25.7 \text{ operations per hour}$$

This agrees well with the previous results.

Delays can be computed for the gate areas by using Fig. 8-24 where the delay factor is now the ratio of demand to capacity for the gates.

TAXIWAY CAPACITY

In connection with the work described on ultimate runway capacity, a model has been developed to determine the capacity of a taxiway crossing an active runway [18]. This capacity is a function of the mix of aircraft using the active runway, the distance of the taxiway from the departure end of the runway, and the nature of operations on the active runway—departures, arrivals, or mixed operations. The capacity of taxiways crossing an active runway for a runway operations rate of 56 to 75 operations per hour is shown in Fig. 8-29.

These models of taxiway capacity are important at airports where the

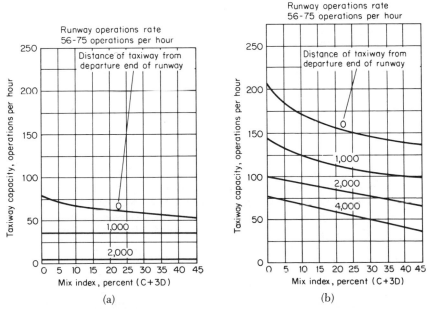

Fig. 8-29 Hourly capacity of taxiway crossing an active runway. (a) Departures only; (b) arrivals only and mixed operations. (*Federal Aviation Administration [18].*)

demand rate is high and the configurations of the taxiways and runways are such that crossings must occur during the peak periods. A complete discussion of the methodology is detailed in [15, 17, 18]. An evaluation of the throughput capacity of a taxiway was omitted, as this capacity is virtually always greater than that of the runway and gate system.

REFERENCES

1. *A Flexible Model for Runway Capacity Analysis*, W.E. Weiss, Master's Thesis, Massachusetts Institute of Technology, Cambridge, Mass., June 1980.
2. *Airport Capacity*, Airborne Instruments Laboratory, Federal Aviation Agency, Office of Technical Services, Department of Commerce, Washington, D.C., Rep. BRD-136, June 1963.
3. *Airport Capacity Criteria Used in Long Range Planning*, Federal Aviation Administration, Washington, D.C., Advisory Circular AC 150/5060-3A, December 1969.
4. *Airport Capacity Criteria Used in Preparing the National Airport Plan*, Federal Aviation Administration, Washington, D.C., Advisory Circular AC 150/5060-1A, July 1968.
5. *Airport Capacity Handbook*, 2nd ed., Airborne Instruments Laboratory, Federal Aviation Administration, Washington, D.C., Rep. SDRS-68-14, June 1969.
6. *Airport Ground Access*, Federal Aviation Administration, Washington, D.C., Rep. FAA-EM-79-4, October 1978.
7. "A Methodology for Airport Capacity Analysis," S.L.M. Hockaday and A. Kanafani, *Transportation Research*, vol. 8, 1974.
8. *Capacity of Airport Systems in Metropolitan Areas—Methodology of Analysis*, Airborne Instruments Laboratory, Federal Aviation Administration, Washington, D.C., Rep. 1400-4, January 1964.
9. *Critique of the Aircraft Delay Curves in Techniques for Determining Airport Airside Capacity and Delay*, C.T. Ball, Institute of Transportation Studies, University of California, Berkeley, Calif., Graduate Rep. UCB-ITS-GR-78-1, August 1978.
10. *FAA Report on Airport Capacity*, Federal Aviation Administration, Washington, D.C., Rep. FAA-EM-74-5, 1974.
11. *Models for Estimating Runway Landing Capacity with Microwave Landing System (MLS)*, V. Tosic and R. Horonjeff, National Aeronautics and Space Administration, Ames Research Center, Moffett Field, Calif., Spec. Rep., September 1975.
12. *Models for Runway Capacity Analysis*, R.M. Harris, MITRE Corporation, Federal Aviation Administration, Washington, D.C., Rep. FAA-EM-73-5, May 1974.
13. *Model Users' Manual for Airfield Capacity and Delay Models*, C.T. Ball, Federal Aviation Administration, Washington, D.C., Rep. FAA-RD-76-128, November 1976.
14. *O'Hare Delay Task Force Study*, Executive Summary and Technical Report, Chicago O'Hare International Airport, Federal Aviation Administration, Washington, D.C., Rep. FAA-AGL-76-1, July 1976.
15. *Procedures for Determination of Airport Capacity*, vols. 1 and 2, Interim Report, Federal Aviation Administration, Washington, D.C., Rep. FAA-RD-73-111, April 1973.
16. *Supporting Documentation for Technical Report on Airport Capacity and Delay Studies*, Federal Aviation Administration, Washington, D.C., Rep. FAA-RD-76-153, June 1976.
17. *Technical Report on Airport Capacity and Delay Studies*, Final Report, Federal Aviation Administration, Washington, D.C., Rep. FAA-RD-76-153, June 1976.

18. *Techniques for Determining Airport Airside Capacity and Delay,* Federal Aviation Administration, Washington, D.C., Rep. FAA-RD-74-124, June 1976.

19. *Terminal Air Traffic Control,* Federal Aviation Administration, Washington, D.C., FAA Handbook 7110.65, Periodically Revised.

20. *Terminal Area Forecasts, Fiscal Years 1980–1991,* Federal Aviation Administration, Washington, D.C., Rep. FAA-AVP-79-12, November 1979.

Chapter 9

Geometric Design of the Landing Area

AIRPORT DESIGN STANDARDS

In order to provide a guide for airport designers and a reasonable amount of uniformity in airport landing facilities, design criteria have been prepared by the ICAO and the FAA. Any criteria involving widths, gradients, separations of runways, taxiways, and other features of the landing area must necessarily incorporate wide variations in aircraft performance, pilot technique, and weather conditions.

The ICAO strives toward uniformity and safety on an international level. Its standards apply to all member nations of the Convention on International Civil Aviation and are published as Annex 14 to that convention [4]. The FAA design standards are very similar to the ICAO requirements, providing for domestic uniformity of airport facilities and serving as a guide to aircraft manufacturers and operators with regard to the facilities which may be expected to be available in the future. The FAA design standards are published in advisory circulars which are revised periodically as the need arises [1]. Requirements for military services are so specialized that they are not included in this chapter.

The design standards prepared by the ICAO and the FAA are presented in the text which follows under the general heading of airport classification, runways, taxiways, and aprons. The material is organized so that the various criteria may be readily compared. It is incumbent upon airport planners to review the latest specifications for airport design at the time studies are undertaken due to the fact that changes are incorporated as conditions dictate.

AIRPORT CLASSIFICATION

For the purpose of stipulating geometric design standards for the various sizes of airports and the functions which they serve, letter and numerical codes or word descriptors have been adopted to classify airports.

The International Civil Aviation Organization

The ICAO now uses a two element reference code to classify the geometric design standards for airports. The code element consists of a numeric and alphabetic designation. The code numbers 1 through 4 classify the length of the runway available and the code letters A through E classify the wingspan and outer main gear wheel span for the aircraft for which the airport has been designed [13]. The aerodrome reference codes are given in Table 9-1.

Federal Aviation Administration

The FAA has recently changed the geometric design specifications for airports to bring them into greater conformity with international standards and to directly reflect the performance and physical characteristics of the critical design aircraft and the types of operations being conducted on the runway system [12, 23]. A description of both classification systems is contained herein. This is useful since the former classification method has been used for many years and will continue to be found in airport plans, reports, and other publications for some time. Therefore, the airport planner will have a source of reference to compare the former and present classification systems and specifications. Figure 9-1 shows the correspondence between the former and present classification systems for airports.

TABLE 9-1 **Aerodrome Reference Codes**

CODE ELEMENT 1		CODE ELEMENT 2		
Code Number	Aeroplane Reference Field Length	Code Letter	Wing Span	Outer Main Gear Wheel Span[a]
1	Less than 800 m	A	Up to but not including 15 m	Up to but not including 4.5 m
2	800 m up to but not including 1200 m	B	15 m up to but not including 24 m	4.5 m up to but not including 6 m
3	1200 m up to but not including 1800 m	C	24 m up to but not including 36 m	6 m up to but not including 9 m
4	1800 m and over	D	36 m up to but not including 52 m	9 m up to but not including 14 m
		E	52 m up to but not including 60 m	9 m up to but not including 14 m

[a] Distance between the outside edges of the main wheel gears.

SOURCE: ICAO [4]

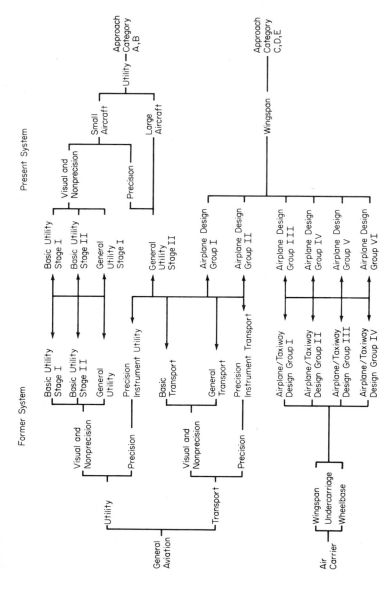

Fig. 9-1 Comparison between former and present FAA airport classification systems. *(Federal Aviation Administration)*

Former Airport Classification System

For the purpose of geometric design standards, the FAA separated airport activity into two general classes, namely, general aviation and air carrier. A further breakdown was made within both of these categories.

Utility airports were defined as those which were used by aircraft weighing not more than 12,500 lb maximum certified takeoff weight, excluding jet aircraft [23]. Transport airports were defined as those which accommodated general aviation aircraft weighing more than 12,500 lb, and jet aircraft [11]. The utility airports were further grouped for visual and nonprecision instrument operations and for precision instrument operations. The visual and nonprecision instrument operation airports were called *basic utility stage* I, *basic utility stage* II, or *general utility*. A basic utility stage I airport had the capability of accommodating about 75 percent of the propeller aircraft not weighing more than 12,500 lb; in general this meant aircraft on the order of 3000 lb or less. A basic utility stage II airport had the capability of accommodating about 95 percent of the propeller aircraft weighing not more than 12,500 lb; in general this meant aircraft weighing on the order of 8000 lb or less. A general utility airport accommodated substantially all propeller aircraft not greater than 12,500 lb. A basic transport airport was one that could accommodate propeller or turbine-powered aircraft up to 60,000 lb maximum certified take off weight. This type of airport was planned for use by business jets, corporate jets, and executive jets. A general transport airport accommodated transport-category aircraft used for general aviation with maximum takeoff weights up to 150,000 lb or more. There were also specifications for a precision instrument transport category airport.

Air-carrier airports had been classified for geometric design purposes according to the wingspan, undercarriage width, and wheel base of the

TABLE 9-2 **Former FAA Taxiway Design Classification System for Air-Carrier Airports**

	Airplane/Taxiway Design Group			
	I	II	III	IV
Aircraft dimension, ft				
Wingspan	Up to 120	Up to 167	Up to 200	Up to 240
Undercarriage width	Up to 30	Up to 41	Up to 41	Up to 50
Wheelbase	Up to 60	Up to 87	Up to 87	Up to 104
Typical aircraft	B-727-100	B-707	B-747	Future
	B-737	B-727-200		
	BAC 1-11	B-757		
	CV 580	B-767		
	DC-9			
		DC-10		
		L-1011		

SOURCE: Federal Aviation Administration [9].

TABLE 9-3 **FAA Aircraft Approach Category Classification**

Approach category	Approach speed, kn
A	Less than 91
B	91–120
C	121–140
D	141–165
E	166 or greater

SOURCE: Federal Aviation Administration [22].

aircraft using the airport [9]. This classification system and the grouping of some common air-carrier aircraft into classifications are shown in Table 9-2.

Present Airport Classification System

The FAA is changing the classification of airports for geometric design purposes so that it is based upon the approach category of aircraft. The approach category, as shown in Table 9-3, is determined by the aircraft approach speed, which is defined as 1.3 times the stall speed in the landing configuration of that aircraft at maximum gross landing weight [23]. Aircraft with maximum certified takeoff weights in excess of 12,500 lb are classified as large aircraft; the rest are small aircraft.

Geometric design specifications for all aircraft in approach categories A and B are governed by utility airport specifications. Utility airports are now classified as basic utility stage I, basic utility stage II, general utility stage I and general utility stage II. A basic utility stage I airport accommodates about 75 percent of most single-engine aircraft and some small twin-engine aircraft for personal and business purposes. This airport is usually designed for aircraft in airplane design group I. A basic utility stage II airport includes a broader spectrum of small business and air taxi type twin-engine aircraft. This airport is normally designed for small aircraft through-

TABLE 9-4 **FAA Airplane Design Group Classification for Geometric Design for Airports**

Airplane design group	Wingspan, ft	Typical aircraft
I	Less than 49	Learjet 24, Rockwell Sabre 75A
II	49 but less than 79	Gulfstream II, Rockwell Sabre 80
III	79 but less than 118	B-727, B-737, BAC1-11, B-757, B-767, Concorde, L-1011, DC-9
IV	118 but less than 171	A-300, A-310, B-707, DC-8
V	171 but less than 197	B-747
VI	197 but less than 262	Future

SOURCE: Federal Aviation Administration [129, 23].

out airplane design group I. A general utility stage I airport accommodates all small aircraft and those up to 25,000 lb maximum certified takeoff weight. This airport is usually designed for all small aircraft throughout airplane design group I. Precision approach operations are not normally anticipated for any of the above type airports. A general utility stage II airport accommodates large aircraft in approach categories A and B. It has the capability for precision approach operations and is usually designed for small and large aircraft in airplane design groups I and II.

A transport airport is defined as an airport which accommodates approach categories C, D, and E aircraft and those with maximum certified takeoff weights above 50,000 lb.

The airplane design groups are defined according to the wingspan of the most demanding aircraft using the airport. These are shown in Table 9-4. The wingspan ranges specified by the ICAO letter codes are similar to those specified by the FAA airplane design groups.

The overall impact of the revised classification is to include the basic and general transport category airports in either general utility stage II specifications for those in approach categories A and B or specifications for transport aircraft for those in approach categories C, D, and E. As an interim measure, however, the specifications for the basic and general transport airports have been retained, which provides an overlap in criteria for general aviation aircraft with maximum certified takeoff weights between 12,500 and 150,000 lb. Ultimately the geometric specifications for airfield design depend upon the functional role of the airport, the approach category, wingspan, and undercarriage width, and the types of approaches being performed on the runway system.

CONTROL TOWER VISIBILITY REQUIREMENTS

At airports with a permanent air traffic control tower, the runways and taxiways must be located and oriented so that all traffic patterns, the final approaches to all runways, all runway structural pavements, and the centerline of taxiways remain continuously visible from the air traffic control tower. At airports without a permanent air traffic control tower, the runways and taxiways should be located and oriented so that a future tower

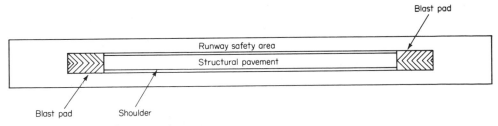

Fig. 9-2 Plan view of runway elements.

TABLE 9-5   **Runway Dimensional Standards**

| | International Civil Aviation Organization | | | |
	1	2	3	4
Width				
Pavement[a]	60–75	75–100	100–150	150
Safety area[b]	200	270	500	500
Shoulder[c]				
Gradient, %				
Pavement, longitudinal				
maximum	2.0	2.0	1.5	1.25
maximum effective	2.0	2.0	1.0	1.0
maximum change	2.0	2.0	1.5	1.5
transition curve rate of				
slope change per 100 ft	0.4	0.4	0.2	0.1
Pavement, transverse				
maximum[d]				
Safety area				
maximum longitudinal	2.0	2.0	1.75	1.5
maximum transverse	3.0	3.0	2.5	2.5

[a] At least 100 ft for precision instrument.

[b] Precision and nonprecision approach requires 500 ft for code 1 and 2, and 1000 ft for codes 3 and 4.

[c] Pavement and shoulders should be at least 200 ft for codes D and E.

[d] 2.0 for codes A and B, 1.5 for codes C, D, and E.

SOURCES: International Civil Aviation Organization [4] and Federal Aviation Administration [12, 23].

may be sited in accordance with the continuous visibility requirements. A clear line of sight to taxi-lane centerlines is also desirable. This requirement may be satisfied where adequate control of aircraft exists by other means [12].

RUNWAYS

The runway system at an airport consists of the structural pavement, the shoulders, the blast pad, and the runway safety area, as shown in Fig. 9-2.

1. The structural pavement supports the aircraft with respect to structural load, maneuverability, control, stability, and other operational and dimensional criteria.

2. The shoulder adjacent to the end of the structural pavement resists jet blast erosion and accommodates maintenance and emergency equipment.

3. The blast pad is an area designed to prevent erosion of the surfaces adjacent to the ends of runways which are subjected to sustained or repeated jet blast. The ICAO requires a 100-ft blast pad, whereas the FAA has determined that the blast pad should be 100 ft in length for airplane design group I, 150 ft for design group II, 200 ft for design groups III and

Federal Aviation Administration									
Approach categories A, B, utility				Approach categories C, D, E, transport					
Visual and Nonprecision		Precision							
I	II	I	II	I	II	III	IV	V	VI
60	75	75	100	100	100	100	150	150	200
120	150	300	300	500	500	500	500	500	500
				10	10	20	25	35	40
2.0	2.0	2.0	2.0	1.5	1.5	1.5	1.5	1.5	1.5
2.0	2.0	2.0	2.0	1.0	1.0	1.0	1.0	1.0	1.0
2.0	2.0	2.0	2.0	1.5	1.5	1.5	1.5	1.5	1.5
0.33	0.33	0.33	0.33	0.1	0.1	0.1	0.1	0.1	0.1
2.0	2.0	2.0	2.0	1.5	1.5	1.5	1.5	1.5	
2.0	2.0	2.0	2.0	1.5	1.5	1.5	1.5	1.5	1.5
5.0	5.0	5.0	5.0	3.0	3.0	3.0	3.0	3.0	3.0

IV, and 400 ft for design groups V and VI. The width of the blast pad should include both the runway and the shoulder width.

4. The runway safety area is an area which is cleared, drained, and graded, and which includes the structural pavement, shoulders, blast pad, and stopway, if provided. This area should be capable of supporting emergency and maintenance equipment as well as providing support for aircraft should they veer off the pavement for one reason or another. The runway safety area required by the ICAO is 275 ft beyond each end of the runway for code elements 3 and 4, and for all runways with instrument operations. The FAA requires that the runway safety area extend 240 ft beyond the end of the runway for small aircraft in airplane design group I, 300 ft for small aircraft in design group II, and 600 ft for precision instrument operations with small aircraft. It also requires 1000 ft for large aircraft in all design groups. The runway safety areas should include the blast pad and its width should be 500 ft for transport category aircraft.

The ICAO and FAA runway standards related to pavement and safety area widths, as well as longitudinal and transverse gradients, are given in Table 9-5.

Sight Distance and Longitudinal Profile

In addition to the information given in Table 9-5, there are other factors that must be considered when establishing the longitudinal profile. One is

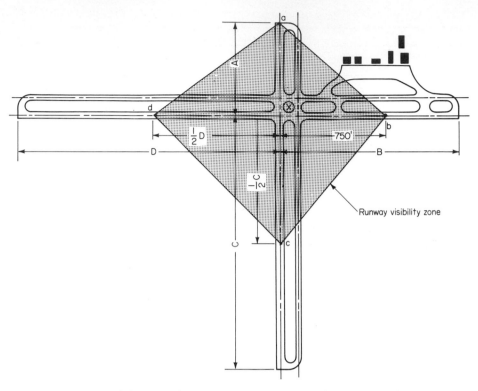

Fig. 9-3 Runway visibility zone for intersecting runways. (*Federal Aviation Administration* [12].)

sight distance and the other is the minimum permissible distance between vertical transition curves. With respect to sight distance, the ICAO requires that there be an unobstructed line of sight from any point 10 ft above the runway within a distance of at least one-half the length of the runway where the runway code is C, D, or E and 7 ft above the runway where the runway code is B, and 5 ft for runway code A [4]. The FAA has no requirement for sight distance on runways at airports with control towers since the standards for longitudinal gradients at these airports provide an adequate line of sight. At other airports the FAA requires that for each runway there be an unobstructed line of sight from any point 5 ft above the runway to all other points 5 ft above the runway for the entire runway length. If a runway has a parallel taxiway for its entire length, the runway grade changes must be such than an unobstructed line of sight will exist from any point 5 ft above the runway centerline to all other points 5 ft above the runway centerline within a distance of one-half the length of the runway. For airports without 24-hour control towers having intersecting runways, the FAA defines a runway visibility zone in which runway grades, terrain, structures, and permanent objects must be such that there will be an unobstructed line of sight from any point 5 ft above one runway centerline to any point 5 ft above an intersecting runway, both points being within this runway visibility zone. The runway visibility zone is an area formed by imaginary lines connecting the visibility points on each runway. The runway visibility zone for intersecting runways is shown in Fig. 9-3. The location of the runway visibility point is on the centerline of the runway at the runway end if the distance from the intersection to the runway end is less than 750 ft, 750 ft from the runway end when the distance from the intersection to the runway end is between 750 and 1500 ft, and equidistant between the runway and the intersection when the distance between the runway end and the intersection is greater than 1500 ft [23]. Airports that do not have control towers are very small in size and traffic activity.

With regard to longitudinal profile, it is desirable to minimize longitudinal grade changes as much as possible. However, it is recognized that this may not be possible for reasons of economy. Therefore both the ICAO and the FAA allow changes in grade, but limit their number and size. The maximum longitudinal slope changes that are permitted are also listed in Table 9-5 and illustrated in Fig. 9-4. Slope changes are accomplished by means of vertical curves. The length of a vertical curve is determined by the magnitude of the change in slope and the maximum allowable change in slope per 100 ft of runway. Both these values are listed in Table 9-5. For example, for an ICAO code 4 airport, if the change in slope was 0.5 percent, the required length of vertical curve would be 500 ft. Vertical curves are normally not necessary if the change in slope is not more than 0.4 percent. The FAA specifies a minimum length of the vertical transition curve of 1000 ft for airports serving approach categories C, D, and E type aircraft.

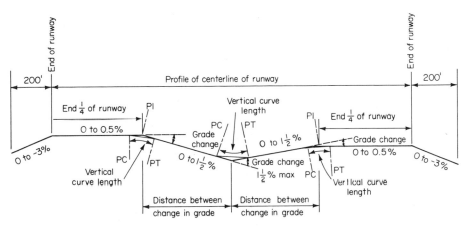

Fig. 9-4 Runway profile.

The number of slope changes is limited by the following rules. The ICAO requires that the distance between the points of intersection of two successive curves be not less than the sum of the absolute percentage values of change in slope multiplied by the appropriate value as follows: 1000 ft for code 4 runways; 500 ft for code 3 runways; and 165 ft for codes 1 and 2 runways; the minimum distance in all cases being 150 ft. The FAA requires 250 ft for utility airports and 1000 ft for transport airports.

The application of this criterion can be illustrated by the following example. Suppose there is a transport-category airport subject to FAA criteria. Further assume that there are two changes in grade, namely, 1.0 and 1.5 percent. What is the minimum permissible distance between the points of intersection (PI) of the two vertical curves? The sum of the grade changes in absolute percentage terms is 1.00 plus 1.50, which is equal to 2.50. Multiply this sum by 1000, which results in 2500 ft.

Table 9-5 lists the maximum longitudinal slope. In addition, for runways that are equipped to be used in bad weather, the slope of the first and last quarters of the runway length must be very flat for reasons of safety. The ICAO requires that this slope not exceed 0.8 percent for runway codes 3 and 4. The FAA limits this slope to 0.5 percent for transport-category runways, but this would also apply to any runway used in bad weather conditions by aircraft equipped with all-weather landing systems.

One more factor concerning longitudinal profile is the maximum effective runway gradient shown in Table 9-5. The effective runway gradient is defined as the slope computed by dividing the difference between the maximum and the minimum elevations along the runway centerline by the entire length of the runway. For air-carrier airports it is normally limited to 1.0 percent.

Transverse Gradient

A typical cross section of a runway is shown in Fig. 9-5. The specifications for transverse slope on the runways are given in Table 9-5. It is recom-

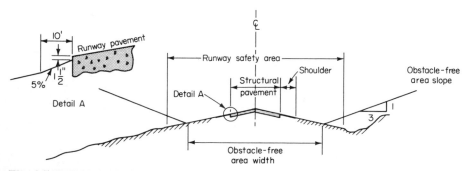

Fig. 9-5 Runway cross section.

mended that a 5 percent transverse slope be provided for the first 10 ft adjacent to a pavement edge to ensure proper drainage.

Another important feature of the runway cross section is the obstacle-free zone. The obstacle-free zone is the volume of space above a surface longitudinally centered on the runway. The elevation of any point on the surface is the same as the elevation of the nearest point on the runway. The runway obstacle-free zone extends 200 ft beyond the ends of the runway, and its width is 250 ft for nonprecision and visual runways, 300 ft for precision instrument runways for aircraft less than 12,500 lb, and 400 ft or greater for runways for larger aircraft. The obstacle-free zone has a transitional slope of 3 horizontal to 1 vertical from the edge of its width up to an elevation of 150 ft. No fixed or movable object may penetrate this zone [23].

Length

It is very difficult to specify runway lengths for different classes of airports because length depends on many factors. These factors are discussed in detail in Chap. 3. Some of the more important are the performance characteristics of a particular type of aircraft, length of trip, and altitude and temperature at the airport. As a guide to airport planners the FAA has published the runway lengths for air-carrier and general aviation aircraft [21]. Additional information on general aviation aircraft is contained in [11, 23]. This information is in the form of performance curves which relate runway length to takeoff or landing weight, temperature, and altitude. The distance that an aircraft can normally travel for a specific takeoff weight is also given. The performance curves are an abstraction of information contained in an aircraft flight operations manual. They are not complete, and thus, if the planner has access to aircraft FAA-approved flight operations manuals, these are the best sources of information for determining runway length. In addition to temperature and altitude contained in the

TABLE 9-6 **Approximate Runway Length Requirements for Various Airport Classifications**

Airport classification	Runway length, ft
Utility airports	
Basic utility stage I	2000
Basic utility stage II	2500
General utility stage I	3000
General utility stage II	3500
Transport airports	
Airplane design groups I and II	5000
Airplane design groups III–VI	7000–12,000

TABLE 9-7   **Taxiway Dimensional Standards**

| | International Civil Aviation Organization | | | | |
	A	B	C	D	E
Width, ft					
Pavement	25	35	50[a]	60[b]	75
Safety	45	65	95	140	155
Shoulder			16	33	38
Gradient, %					
Pavement, longitudinal					
maximum	3.0	3.0	1.5	1.5	1.5
maximum effective					
maximum change					
Transition curve rate of					
[slope change per 100 ft]	1.2	1.2	1.0	1.0	1.0
Pavement transverse					
maximum	2.0	2.0	1.5	1.5	1.5
Safety area					
maximum longitudinal					
maximum transverse	3.0	3.0	2.5	2.5	2.5

[a] Use width of 60 ft if wheelbase is equal to or greater than 60 ft.

[b] 75 ft if outer main gear is greater than 30 ft.

[c] 60 ft if wheelbase is at least 60 ft.

SOURCES: International Civil Aviation Organization [4] and Federal Aviation Administration [12, 23].

advisory circulars, performance curves in the flight operations manuals also include the effects of longitudinal gradient and wind. For the purpose of planning, it is assumed that there is no wind blowing along the runway.

If the planner can determine the runway length required at sea level in standard atmospheric conditions, ICAO Annex 14 provides corrections to this length for altitude at 7 percent for each 1000 ft elevation above mean sea level. This length is further corrected for temperature at the rate of 1 percent for every 1°C that the airport reference temperature exceeds the temperature of the standard atmosphere for that elevation. The airport reference temperature is the monthly mean of the mean daily temperatures for the hottest month of the year, T_1, the hottest month being that which has the highest mean daily temperature, plus one-third of the difference between this monthly mean temperature and the monthly mean of the maximum daily temperature for the same month T_2; in other words, $T_1 + (T_2 - T_1)/3$. Both T_1 and T_2 should be averaged for a period of years. The length corrected for altitude and temperature is further corrected for slope at the rate of 10 percent for each 1 percent of effective runway gradient.

It must be emphasized that these corrections are approximate and that the best source of information is the flight operations manual.

In planning airports, the runways should be long enough to accommodate the aircraft which requires the greatest length. Approximate runway lengths for various categories of airports are given in Table 9-6.

Federal Aviation Administration									
Approach categories A, B, utility				Approach categories C, D, E, transport					
Visual and Non-Precision		Precision		I	II	III	IV	V	VI
I	II	I	II						
25	35	25	35	25	35	50ᶜ	75	75	100
50	80	50	80	49	79	118	171	197	262
				10	10	20	25	35	40
2.0	2.0	2.0	2.0	1.5	1.5	1.5	1.5	1.5	1.5
				3.0	3.0	3.0	3.0	3.0	3.0
				1.0	1.0	1.0	1.0	1.0	1.0
2.0	2.0	2.0	2.0	1.5	1.5	1.5	1.5	1.5	1.5
2.0	2.0	2.0	2.0						
5.0	5.0	5.0	5.0	3.0	3.0	3.0	3.0	3.0	3.0

For transport-category airports serving air-carrier aircraft, runways of 12,000 ft will accommodate long-range flights involving trip lengths on the order of 6000 stat mi. Lengths of 9000 to 10 000 ft can readily serve flights on the order of 3000 stat mi.

TAXIWAYS

Widths and Slopes

Since the speeds of aircraft are considerably less on taxiways than on runways, criteria governing longitudinal slopes, vertical curves, and sight distance are not as stringent as for runways. Also the lower speeds permit the width of the taxiway to be less than that of the runway. The principal geometric design features of interest are listed in Table 9-7.

It will be recalled from Table 9-4 that the FAA now classifies transport aircraft into six groups based upon wingspan. ICAO classifies taxiway geometry based upon the letter codes A through E. Both systems are virtually identical.

Sight Distance and Longitudinal Profile

As in the case of runways, the number of changes in longitudinal profile is limited by sight distance and the minimum distance between vertical curves. With respect to sight distance, the ICAO requires that the surface of the taxiway be seen for a distance of 1000 ft from a point 10 ft above the taxiway for codes C, D, and E runways. For codes A and B runways the comparable dimensions are 650 ft and 7 ft. The FAA does not specify sight distance for taxiways.

With regard to the longitudinal profile of taxiways, the ICAO does not specify the minimum distance between the point of intersection of vertical curves.

The FAA specifies that the minimum distance for transport-category airports should be not less than the product of 1000 ft multiplied by the sum of the absolute percentage values of change in slope.

Exit Taxiway Geometry

The function of exit taxiways, or turnoffs as they are sometimes called, is to minimize runway occupancy by landing aircraft. Exit taxiways can be placed at right angles or at some other angle to the runway. When the angle is on the order of 30°, the term *high-speed exit* is often used to denote that it is designed for higher speeds than other exit taxiway configurations. In this chapter specific dimensions for high-speed and right-angle exit taxiways are presented. The dimensions for high-speed exit taxiways are the result of exhaustive tests conducted for the Airways Modernization Board [17] and subsequent research conducted by the FAA [12].

The earlier tests [17] were conducted on wet and dry concrete and asphalt pavement with various types of civil and military aircraft in order to determine the proper relationship between speed, radius of curvature, and the general configuration of the taxiway. A significant finding of the tests was that at high speeds a compound curve was necessary to minimize tire wear on the nose gear. That is, the central or main curve R_2 should be preceded by a much larger radius curve R_1.

Aircraft paths in the test approximated a spiral. A compound curve is relatively easy to establish in the field and begins to approach the shape of a spiral, thus the reason for suggesting a compound curve. The following pertinent conclusions were reached as a result of the tests [17]:

1. Transport-category and military aircraft can safely and comfortably turn off runways at speeds on the order of 60 to 65 mi/h on wet and dry pavements.

2. The most significant factor affecting the turning radius is speed, not the total angle of turn nor passenger comfort.

3. Passenger comfort was not critical in any of the turning movements.

4. The computed lateral forces developed in the tests were substantially below the maximum lateral forces for which the landing gear was designed.

5. Insofar as the shape of the taxiway is concerned, a slightly widened entrance (100 ft) gradually tapering to the normal width of taxiway is preferred. The widened entrance gives the pilot more latitude in using the exit taxiway.

6. Total angles of turn of 30 to 45° can be negotiated satisfactorily. The smaller angle seems to be preferable because the length of the curved path is reduced, sight distance is improved, and less concentration is required on the part of the pilots.

7. The relation of turning radius versus speed expressed by the formula $R_2 = V^2/15f$, where V is the velocity in miles per hour, will yield a smooth, comfortable turn on a wet or dry pavement when f is made equal to 0.13.

8. The curve expressed by the equation for R_2 should be preceded by a larger-radius curve R_1 at high turn-off speeds of 50 to 60 mi/h. The larger-radius curve is necessary to provide a gradual transition from a straight ahead or tangent direction to a curved path. If the transition curve is not provided, tire wear on large jet transports can be excessive.

9. The length of the transition curve can be roughly approximated by the relation

$$L_1 = \frac{V^3}{CR_2} \tag{9-1}$$

where V is in feet per second and R_2 is in feet. C was found experimentally to be on the order of 1.3.

10. Sufficient distance must be provided to comfortably decelerate an aircraft after it leaves the runway. It is suggested that for the present this distance be based on an average rate of deceleration of 3.3 ft/s². This applies only to transport-category aircraft. Until more experience is gained with this type of operation, the stopping distance should be measured from the edge of the runway.

A chart showing the relationship of exit speed to radii R_1 and R_2 and length of transition curve L_1 is given in Fig. 9-6. The FAA has indicated that the radii of curvature associated with the average speeds of transport-category aircraft when taxiing are as shown in Table 9-8.

A configuration for an exit speed of 60 mi/h and a turnoff angle of 30° is shown in Fig. 9-7. This type of high-speed exit is recommended for airports serving aircraft in approach categories C, D, and E. A high-speed exit with a turnoff angle of 15° is shown in Fig. 9-8. This type of exit is recommended at airports designed for approach category A and B aircraft. ICAO recommends a rapid taxiway exit radius of 1800 ft for runway codes 3 and 4 and 700 ft for codes 1 and 2. These should be capable of exit speeds of about 55

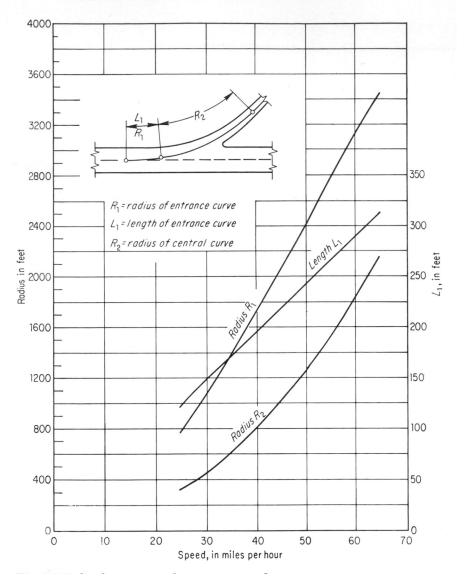

Fig. 9-6 Radii of curvature and entrance curves for taxiways.

and 40 mph, respectively. Intersection angles should be between 25° and 40° with a 30° angle preferable.

Right-angle or 90° exit taxiways, although not desirable from the standpoint of minimizing runway occupancy, are often constructed for other reasons. The configuration for a 90° exit is illustrated in Fig. 9-9. Taxiway intersection details are shown in Figure 9-10.

Location of Exit Taxiways

The location of exit taxiways depends a great deal on the mix of aircraft, the approach and touchdown speeds, the point of touchdown, the exit speed, the rate of deceleration, which in turn depends on the condition of the pavement surface (e.g., dry or wet), and the number of exits.

While the rules for flying transport aircraft are relatively precise, a certain amount of variability among pilots is bound to occur, especially in respect to the braking force applied on the runway and the distance from runway threshold to touchdown. The rapidity and the manner in which air traffic control can process arrivals is an extremely important factor in establishing the location of exit taxiways. The location of exit taxiways is also influenced by the location of the runways relative to the terminal area.

Mathematical analyses or models have been developed for optimizing exit locations. These are described in [13, 19]. While these analyses have been useful in providing an understanding of the significant parameters affecting location, their usefulness to planners has been limited because of the complexity of the analyses and a lack of knowledge of the inputs required for the application of the models. As a result greater use is made of much more simplified methods [9, 12].

The landing process can be described as follows. The aircraft crosses the runway threshold and decelerates in the air until the main landing gear touches the surface of the pavement. At this point the nose gear has not made contact with the runway. It may take as much as 3 s to do so. No form of braking can be applied until the nose gear has made contact with the pavement. When it does, reverse thrust or wheel brakes or a combination of both are used to reduce the forward speed of the aircraft to exit velocity. On the basis of observations [17], the average deceleration of air-carrier aircraft on the runway is about 5 ft/s².

In the simplified procedure [9], an aircraft is assumed to touch down at 1.3 times the stall speed for a landing weight corresponding to 85 percent of

TABLE 9-8   **Radii of Curvature for Transport-Category Aircraft**

Taxiing speed, mi/h	Radius of exit curve, ft
10	50
20	200
30	450
40	800
50	1,250
60	1,800

SOURCE: Federal Aviation Administration [12].

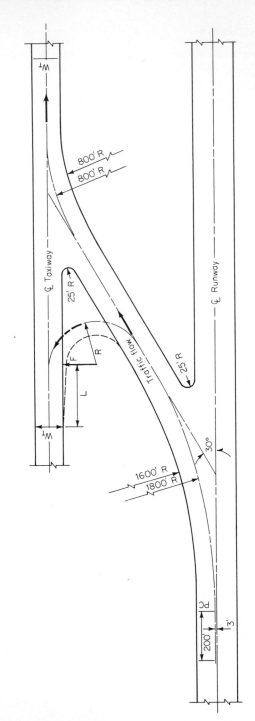

Fig. 9-7 30° high-speed taxiway exit for category C, D, and E aircraft. (See Table 9-10 for dimensions.) *(Federal Aviation Administration [9, 12].)*

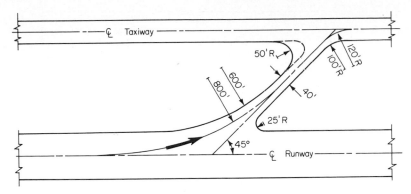

Fig. 9-8 45° high-speed taxiway exit for category A and B aircraft. (See Table 9-10 for dimensions.) (*Federal Aviation Administration [9, 12].*)

the maximum structural landing weight. In lieu of computing the distance from threshold to touchdown, touchdown distances are assumed as fixed values for certain classes of aircraft. To these distances are added the distances to decelerate to exit speed. The simplified procedure is illustrated by the following example.

Suppose the touchdown speed V_{TD} is 140 kn, and the exit speed V_E is 52 kn (60 mi/h). Assume that the touchdown distance is 1500 ft from the threshold and the average deceleration a on the runway is 5 ft/s^2. Then the distance from the threshold to reach exit speed S_E is equal to

$$S_E = \text{touchdown distance} + D$$

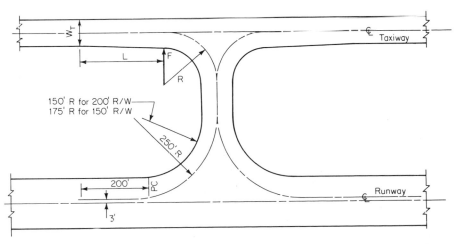

Fig. 9-9 90° taxiway exit. (See Table 9-10 for dimensions.) (*Federal Aviation Administration [9, 12].*)

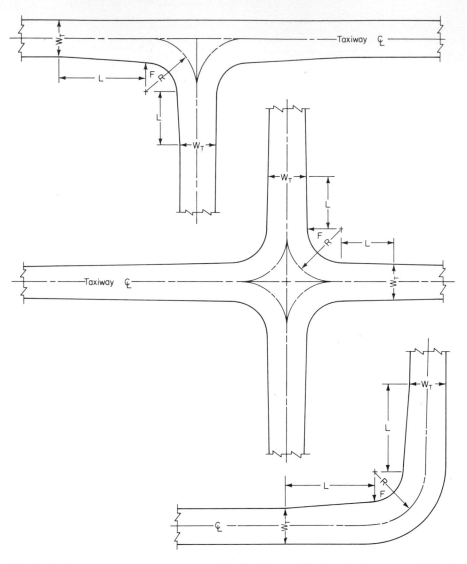

Fig. 9-10 Common taxiway intersection details. (See Table 9-10 for dimensions.) (*Federal Aviation Administration [9, 12].*)

where

$$D = \frac{V_{TD}^2 - V_E^2}{2a} \tag{9-2}$$

The distance for this example becomes 6400 ft.

Although approach and touchdown speeds vary, they can be approximated for locating exit taxiways. At predominantly air-carrier airports air traffic control authorities request general aviation aircraft to increase their speeds above normal to reduce the wide range in speed between air carriers and general aviation. At these airports, therefore, the normal appoach speeds for general aviation are probably not applicable.

The distances to touchdown are assumed to be 1500 ft for air-carrier aircraft and 1000 ft for twin-engine general aviation aircraft. Using these distances, an exit speed to 60 mi/h, and the approximate touchdown speeds, the appropriate exit locations may be found as shown in Table 9-9.

These locations are derived using standard sea-level conditions. Altitude and temperature can affect the location of exit taxiways. Altitude increases distance on the order of 3 percent for each 1000 ft above sea level and temperature 1.5 percent for each 10°F above 59°F.

Planners often find that the runway configuration and the location of the terminal at the airport preclude placing the exits at locations based on the foregoing analysis. This is nothing to be alarmed about since it is far better to achieve good utilization of the exits than to be too concerned about a few seconds lost in occupancy time.

When locating exits it is important to recognize local conditions, such as frequency of wet pavement or gusty winds. It is far better to place the exits several hundred feet farther from the threshold than to have aircraft overshoot the exits a large amount of time. The standard deviation in time required to reach exit speed is on the order of 2 or 3 s; therefore if the exits were placed down the runway as much as two standard deviations from the mean, the loss in occupancy time would only be 4 to 6 s.

The total occupancy time of an aircraft can be roughly estimated using the following procedure. The runway is divided into four components: the flight from the threshold to the touchdown of the main gear, the time required for the nose gear to make contact with the pavement after the main gear has made contact, the time required to reach exit velocity from the time the nose gear has made contact with the pavement and brakes have

TABLE 9-9 **Approximate Taxiway Exit Location from Threshold, ft**

Aircraft type		Touchdown speed, kn	Exit speed, mi/h	
			15	60
Small propeller	GA single-engine	60	1800	2400
	GA twin-engine	95	2800	3500
Light turbojet	2-engine narrow-body	130	4800	5600
	3-engine, narrow-body			
Heavy turbojet	4-engine, narrow-body	140	6400 ·	7100
	3-engine, wide-body			
	4-engine, wide-body			

TABLE 9-10 **Taxiway Exit Geometry Recommended by FAA, ft**

	Airplane design group					
	I	II	III	IV	V	VI
Taxiway width W_T	25	35	50*	75	75	100
Centerline radius R	75	75	100	150	150	170
Length of fillet lead-in L	50	50	150	250	250	250
Fillet radius F	60	55	55*	80	85	85

* If wheelbase is equal to or greater than 60 ft, use a taxiway width of 60 ft and a fillet radius of 50 ft.
SOURCE: Federal Aviation Administration [12].

been applied, and the time required for the aircraft to turn off onto the taxiway and clear the runway. For the first component it can be assumed that the touchdown speed is 5 to 8 kn less than the speed over the threshold. The rate of deceleration in the air is about 2.5 ft/s². The second component is about 3 s, and the third component depends upon exit speed. Time to turnoff from the runway will be on the order of 10 s. Thus the total occupancy time in seconds is

$$R_i = \frac{V_{OT} - V_{TD}}{2a_1} + 3 + \frac{V_{TD} - V_E}{2a_2} + t \qquad (9\text{-}3)$$

where R_i = runway occupancy time, s
V_{OT} = over the threshold speed, ft/s
V_{TD} = touchdown speed, ft/s
V_E = exit speed, ft/s
t = time to turnoff from the runway after exit speed is reached, s
a_1 = average rate of deceleration in the air, ft/s²
a_2 = the average rate of deceleration on the ground, ft/s²

Typical occupancy times for 60-mi/h exits are 40 to 45 s. The corresponding time for a 15-mi/h exit is 60 s or more for air-carrier aircraft.

The FAA recommends that the point of intersection of the centerlines of taxiway exits and runways which are up to 7000 ft in length and accommodate transport-category aircraft, should be located about 3000 ft from the arrival threshold and 2000 ft from the stop end of the runway. To accommodate the average mix of aircraft on runways longer than 7000 ft, intermediate exits should be located at intervals of about 1500 ft. At airports where there are extensive operations with category A and B aircraft, an exit located between 1500 and 2000 ft from the landing threshold is recommended.

Design of Fillets

The basic designs of fillets for three of the most common types of taxiway intersections have been developed by the FAA [12]. These designs are shown in Fig. 9-10. The dimensions recommended by the FAA for the taxiway width, centerline radius, fillet radius, and length of the fillet lead-in are given in Table 9-10. The radii are dependent on the angle of intersection of the taxiways and the wheelbase of the aircraft.

It is not necessary, however, to use the specific dimensions shown in Fig. 9-10 or Table 9-10 since there are methods for determining the path of the main gear when the path of the nose gear is known. The method, which is described in this chapter, had its origin in the United Kingdom [18]. Although this method is approximate, it is sufficiently accurate for the purpose of design. The subject has also been given attention in Australia [15] and in the United States [12, 14, 16].

When a long-wheelbase aircraft negotiates a turn with the nose gear tracking a predetermined curved path, such as a taxiway centerline, the midpoint of the main gear does not follow the same path as the nose gear, as shown in Fig. 9-11. At any point on the curve the distance between the curved path followed by the nose gear and the midpoint of the main landing gear is referred to as the track-in. The track-in varies, increasing progressively during the turning maneuver. It decreases as the nose gear begins to follow the tangent to the curve. Knowing the path of the main gear, the radius of the fillet can be determined by adding an appropriate margin of safety S between the inner tires of the main gear and the edge of the pavement.

The castor angle C is defined as the angle formed by the longitudinal axis of the aircraft and the direction of movement of the nose gear or some other datum point such as the location of the pilot. For design it is sufficiently accurate to assume that the datum point is the nose gear.

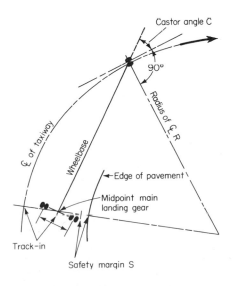

Fig. 9-11 Path of main gear on curve.

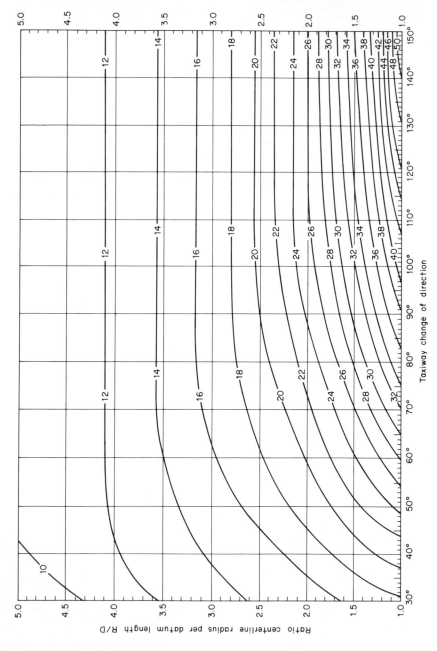

Fig. 9-12 Maximum track-in. (Figures on curves show maximum track-in expressed as percentage of datum length.) (*International Civil Aviation Organization and United Kingdom [18].*)

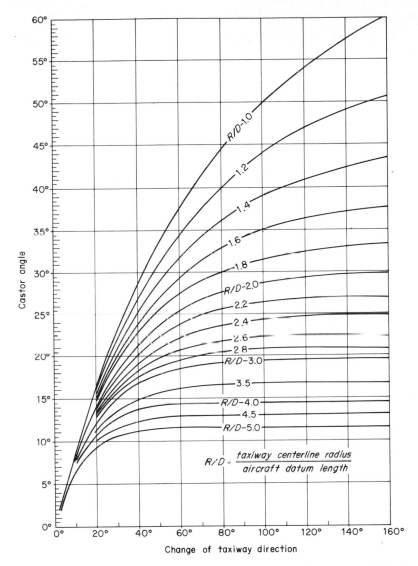

Fig. 9-13 Increase of castor angle during a turn-in. (*International Civil Aviation Organization and United Kingdom [18].*)

The charts presented in this chapter permit designing fillets for any aircraft in a relatively simple manner. They have been taken from [18]. The term *aircraft datum length* on the charts is the distance from the datum point to the midpoint of the main landing gear. For the design of fillets it is sufficiently accurate to assume that the aircraft datum length is equal to the wheelbase, as defined in Chap. 3. The maximum track-in is obtained from

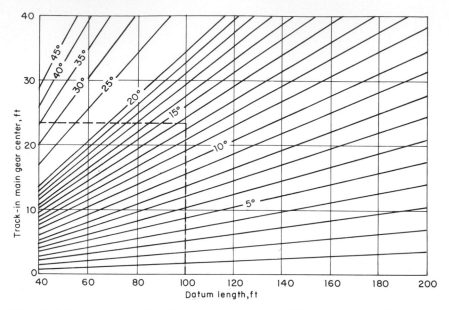

Fig. 9-14 Castor angle and main gear center track-in. (Figures on curve show castor angles.) (*International Civil Aviation Organization and United Kingdom [18].*)

Fig. 9-12. It depends upon the datum length, the radius of curvature of the centerline, and the change in direction. The maximum castor angle of the nose wheel is obtained from Fig. 9-13. Care should be taken to ensure that the castor angle does not exceed the normal operating limits of the aircraft.

The castor angle of the nose wheel at the point where filleting is no longer required is obtained from Fig. 9-14. The distance the nose gear has to travel along the straight centerline to reduce the castor angle at the end of the turn to that at which filleting is no longer required is obtained from Fig. 9-15.

The use of the charts can be illustrated by the following example. Determine the size of the fillet for maneuvering a DC-10 on a 75-ft-wide taxiway which changes direction 90° and has a centerline radius of 250 ft, and a width of 75 ft. The wheelbase for a DC-10 is 72.5 ft. The wheel tread is 35 ft. The desired safety margin between the strut of the inner main landing gear and the edge of the pavement is 15 ft. The ratio of the taxiway centerline radius R to the datum length D is $250/72.5 = 3.45$. Entering Fig. 9-12 with $R/D = 3.45$ and 90° change in direction yields a maximum track-in equal to 14.5 percent of the datum length, or 10.5 ft. Therefore, the radius of the fillet is equal to $R -$ (maximum track-in $+ \frac{1}{2}$ wheel tread $+$ safety margin), which is $250 - (10.5 + 17.5 + 15.0) = 207$ ft. The maximum track-in without filleting is equal to $\frac{1}{2}$ taxiway width $-$ (safety margin $+ \frac{1}{2}$ wheel tread), or $37.5 - (15 + 17.5) = 5$ ft. From Fig. 9-14 this is equivalent to a

Fig. 9-15 Decrease in castor angle during a turn. For datum length in excess of 100 ft, use boxed figures on curves and baseline. For small angles the travel along centerline may be obtained by multiplying the figures in the table by the datum length.

	CASTOR ANGLE REMAINING				
	0°	1°	2°	3°	4°
·0°	∞	4.22	3.53	3.12	2.83
·1°	6.55	4.13	3.48	3.09	2.80
·2°	5.85	4.04	3.43	3.05	2.77
·3°	5.44	3.96	3.39	3.02	2.75
·4°	5.15	3.89	3.34	2.99	2.73
·5°	4.93	3.82	3.30	2.96	2.71
·6°	4.74	3.75	3.26	2.93	2.69
·7°	4.59	3.69	3.23	2.91	2.67
·8°	4.45	3.63	3.19	2.88	2.64
·9°	4.33	3.58	3.15	2.85	2.62

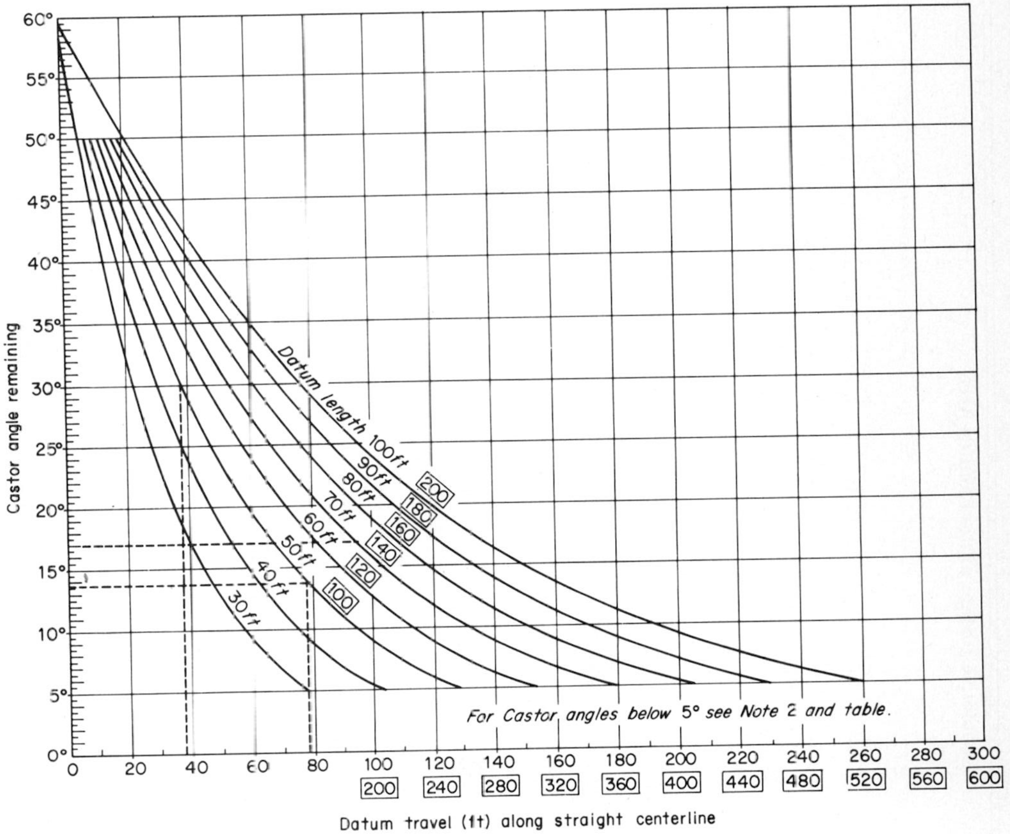

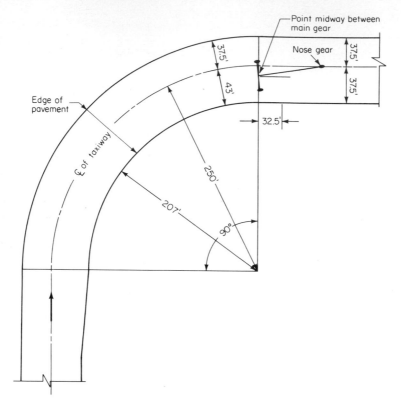

Fig. 9-16 Pictorial solution of turn problem.

castor angle of 4°. Enter Fig. 9-13 to obtain 17° as the castor angle at the end of the turn. These castor angles are converted to travel along the straight centerline by use of Fig. 9-15; 4° yields a distance of 205 ft and 17° yields a distance of 100 ft. The difference, 105 ft, is the travel of the nose gear to reduce the castor angle from 17 to 4°. The distance the main wheels are beyond the end of the curve is obtained by subtracting the aircraft datum length from the difference, that is, 105 − 72.5 = 32.5 ft. The results are shown in Fig. 9-16.

A simple graphic solution of sufficient accuracy is described in [13]. The method consists of the following steps, which are shown in Fig. 9-17:

1. Draw the path followed by the nose wheel to some convenient scale. The scale should be large enough to obtain good accuracy.

2. Set a compass so that it represents the wheelbase of the aircraft at the scale chosen.

3. Mark the initial position of the wheelbase on the guiding line (such as M_1N_1 in the illustration).

4. Place the compass point at M_2, a short distance from M_1, and mark point N_2 on the guiding line. Distance M_1N_2 represents the first increment of the main gear movement at the end of which the nose wheel is at N_2.

5. Place a straightedge in line with points M_2 and N_2. Now move the compass point a short distance along the straightedge to M_3 and mark N_3, the new position of the nose wheel on the path followed by the nose wheel.

6. The straightedge is next lined up with points M_3 and N_3, the compass point is shifted another short distance along the straightedge to N_4, and the corresponding position of the nose wheel is marked on the path followed by the nose wheel.

7. This procedure is repeated until the path of the main gear midpoint, defined by M_1, M_2, M_3, ..., is established for the desired distance. Note that in the initial stage of the turn the increments of main gear movement may be made reasonably large without appreciable loss of accuracy, but that shorter increments are desirable at later stages of the turn to limit the change in the direction of the aircraft axis between successive positions of the nose wheel. After experience with the method the size of the increments to yield reasonable accuracy becomes apparent.

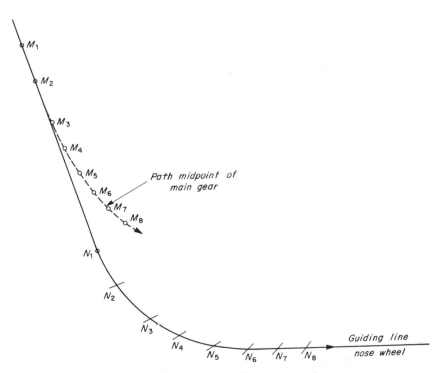

Fig. 9-17 Graphic method of construction of main gear path.

8. A curve drawn through the points $M_1, M_2, M_3, \ldots$, will represent the path of the main gear midpoint. This in turn is superimposed on a taxiway design to establish the desired fillet dimensions.

The size of the fillet depends not only on wheelbase, radius of curve, width of taxiway, and total change in direction, but also on the path that the aircraft follows on the turn. There are two ways in which an aircraft can be maneuvered on a turn. One is to establish the centerline of the taxiway as the path of the nose gear; the other is to assume that the nose gear will follow a path offset outward of the centerline. The latter maneuver will result in the least amount of filleting. While there is no agreement on which procedure is desirable, the authors prefer to assume that the nose gear follows the taxiway centerline.

The FAA has adopted a method for the design of fillets for airport taxiway exits [12]. The method allows one to design for judgmental oversteering, nose-wheel tracking the centerline, or maintaining the cockpit over the centerline. The method presented here will treat only the case of the nose-wheel tracking the centerline.

The maximum angle formed between the tangent to the centerline and the longitudinal axis of the aircraft will occur at the end of the curve when the nose wheel is at the point of tangency. This angle, called A_{max}, may be approximated by

$$A_{max} = \sin\left(\frac{d}{R}\right) \tag{9-4}$$

where d = distance from nose wheel to center of main undercarriage, that is, the wheelbase of the aircraft
   R = radius the nose wheel is tracking on the curve

The required fillet F is given by

$$F = (R^2 + d^2 - 2Rd \sin A_{max})^{0.5} - 0.5u - S \tag{9-5}$$

where u = undercarriage width, that is, the distance between the outside tires on the main gear
   S = minimum distance required between the edge of the outside tire and the edge of the pavement

The length of the lead-in to the fillet is given by

$$L = d \ln\left(\frac{4d \tan 0.5A_{max}}{W_T - u - 2S}\right) - d \tag{9-6}$$

where W_T = taxiway width on tangent
   $\ln$ = natural logarithm

TABLE 9-11   **Minimum Distance from**
Outside of Tire to Pavement Edge, ft

International Civil Aviation Organization		Federal Aviation Administration	
Airport category	Distance	Airplane design group	Distance
A	5.0	I	5.0
B	7.5	II	7.5
C	10.0*	III	10.0
D	15.0	IV	15.0
E	15.0	V	15.0
		VI	20.0

* 15.0 ft if wheelbase greater than or equal to 60 ft.

SOURCES: International Civil Aviation Organization [4] and Federal Aviation Administration [12].

These equations may be solved for a given aircraft tracking a curve of radius R to find the necessary lead-in and fillet radius to maintain a minimum distance between the tire and the pavement edge. The FAA recommends that an entrance spiral be used on taxiway exits to decrease the amount of lead-in to fillets. For a 90° exit it recommends at least a 300-ft entrance spiral from the point of curvature to the 30° deflection point.

The minimum distance between the outside tire of the main landing gear and the edge of the pavement as recommended by the FAA [12] and ICAO [4] is shown in Table 9-11.

SEPARATION CLEARANCES

Taxiways

In order to provide a margin of safety in the airport operating areas, the trafficways must be separated sufficiently from each other and from adjacent obstructions. In Table 9-12 the minimum clearances between a taxiway and a runway, between two parallel taxiways, and between a taxiway and fixed obstructions are summarized. The FAA and ICAO have recently changed these separation criteria [4, 12].

The term *dual parallel taxiways* refers to two taxiways parallel to each other on which airplanes can taxi in opposite directions. A *terminal taxilane* is a taxiway on an apron used for access to gate positions. An *apron taxiway* is a taxiway located usually on the periphery of an apron.

The taxiway to taxiway separations associated with the passage of two aircraft, each being on the centerline of separate parallel taxiways, are predicated on a minimum wing-tip clearance of 0.25 times the wingspan of the most demanding aircraft in the airplane design group plus 7 ft. This

TABLE 9-12   **Separation Criteria on the Airfield, ft**

	International Civil Aviation Organization				
	A	B	C	D	E
Runway centerline to:					
Parallel taxiway centerline	275[a]	285[b]	550[c]	580[d]	600[e]
Aircraft parking area					
Property line					
Building restriction line					
Holding line[f]					
Taxiway centerline to:					
Parallel taxiway centerline	69	103	153	225	251
Fixed or movable objects	44	64	94	139	153
Property line	44	64	94	139	153
Building restriction line	44	64	94	139	153
Taxilane centerline to:					
Fixed or movable objects	39	54	80	118	131

[a] 123 ft for code 1 and 156 ft for code 2 on noninstrument runways.

[b] 138 ft for code 1 and 171 ft for code 2 on noninstrument runways.

[c] 305 ft for noninstrument runways.

[d] 332 ft for noninstrument runways.

[e] 345 ft for noninstrument runways.

[f] See Table 9-13.

[g] 225 ft if large aircraft present.

[h] 250 ft if large aircraft present.

[i] Obstacle-free zone or Part 77 transition surface governs.

[j] Up to 1345-ft elevation; use 450 ft above 1345 up to 6560 ft; use 500 ft above 6560-ft elevation.

SOURCES: International Civil Aviation Organization [4] and Federal Aviation Administration [12, 23].

clearance provides a minimum parallel taxiway centerline to taxiway centerline separation of 1.25 times the wingspan of the most demanding aircraft plus 7 ft. This separation may have to be increased to accommodate pavement fillets. It is recommended that a separation of at least 2.6 times the wheelbase of the most demanding aircraft be provided to accommodate a 180° turn when the pavement fillet is designed for tracking the nose wheel on the centerline. The taxiway to fixed or movable object separation is based upon the same wing-tip clearance between taxiing aircraft. Thus a minimum separation between a taxiway centerline and a fixed or movable object of 0.75 times the wingspan of the most demanding aircraft plus 7 ft is required. This separation is also applicable to aircraft traversing through a

Federal Aviation Administration												
Approach categories A, B, utility				Approach categories C, D, E, transport						Former transport¯c		
Visual and Nonprecision		Precision										
I	II	I	II	I	II	III	IV	V	VI	BT	GT	PT
150	240g	200	300h	400	400	400	400	400j	600	300	300	400
125	200	i	i	500	500	500	500	500	500	375	425	675
200	200	250	500	750	750	750	750	750	750	400	500	750
200	200	250	i	750	750	750	750	750	750	400	500	750
				300	300	300	300	300	300			
69	103	69	103	69	103	153	225	251	340	150	200	200
50	50	50	50	44	64	94	139	153	205	75	100	100
				44	64	94	139	153	205			
				44	64	94	139	153	205			
39	54	39	54	39	54	80	118	131	172			

taxiway on an apron or ramp. The taxi lane to fixed or movable object separation in the terminal area is predicated on a wing-tip clearance of approximately half that required for an apron taxiway. This clearance is based on the consideration that taxiing speed is low in this area, taxiing is precise, and special guidance techniques and devices are provided. This wing-tip clearance establishes a minimum separation between the taxi-lane centerline and an obstacle of 0.63 times the wingspan of the most demanding aircraft plus 7 ft [12]. ICAO Annex 14 does not specify wing-tip clearance.

TABLE 9-13. **ICAO Minimum Recommended Distance from Runway Centerline to Taxiway Holding Line, ft**

	Runway Code Element			
	1	2	3	4
Noninstrument Runway	100	135	250	250
Nonprecision Runway	135	135	250	250
Precision Instrument Category I Runway	200	200	300	300
Precision Instrument Category II or III Runway			300	300

SOURCE: International Civil Aviation Organization [4].

Parallel Runway Spacing

The spacing of parallel runways depends on a number of factors, such as whether the operations are in VFR or IFR and, if in IFR, whether it is desired to have the capability of accommodating simultaneous arrivals or simultaneous arrivals and departures. At those airports serving both heavy and light aircraft simultaneous use of runways even in VFR conditions may be dictated by separation requirements to safeguard against wake vortices.

For VFR operations the ICAO recommends that the minimum separations between parallel runways for simultaneous use, disregarding wake vortices, be 700 ft for codes 3 and 4 airports, 500 ft for code 2 airports, and 400 ft for code 1 airports [4]. The FAA requires 300 ft for single-engine propeller aircraft, 500 ft for twin-engine propeller aircraft, and 700 ft for all other aircraft when the operations are in the same direction. During the daylight hours 1400 ft is required for opposite-direction operations and 2800 ft at all other times [12]. If wake vortices are generated by heavy jets and it is desired to operate on two runways simultaneously in VFR when little or no crosswind is present, the minimum distance specified by the FAA is 2500 ft. However, the designer should contact the nearest governmental aviation body to determine whether for this particular location it is necessary to have such a large separation.

In IFR conditions the FAA specifies 4300 ft as the minimum separation between centerlines of parallel runways for simultaneous instrument approaches. However, there is evidence that this distance is conservative, and steps are being taken to reduce it. The ultimate goal is to reduce this distance by about one half [20].

Two parallel runways may be used simultaneously for departures on each in IFR if the centerlines are separated by at least 3500 ft. If two parallel runways are to be operated independently of each other in IFR, one for arrivals and the other for departures, the minimum separation between the centerlines is 3500 ft when the thresholds are even. If the thresholds are staggered, the runways can be brought closer together or must be separated farther, depending on the amount of the stagger and which runways are used for arrivals and departures. If approaches are to the nearest runway, then the spacing may be reduced by 100 ft for each 500 ft of

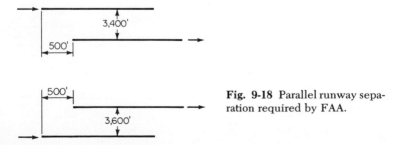

Fig. 9-18 Parallel runway separation required by FAA.

stagger. However, if the approaches are to the farthest runway, then the runway spacing must be increased by 100 ft for each 500 ft of stagger. This is shown in Fig. 9-18.

HOLDING APRONS

Holding aprons, run-up pads, or holding bays, as they are sometimes called, are placed adjacent to the ends of runways. These aprons are used as storage areas for aircraft prior to takeoff. They are designed so that one aircraft can bypass another whenever this is necessary. For piston-engine aircraft the holding apron is an area where the aircraft instrument and engine operation can be checked prior to takeoff. The apron also provides for a trailing aircraft to bypass a leading aircraft in case the takeoff clearance of the latter must be delayed for one reason or another, or if it experiences some malfunction. There are many configurations of holding aprons. The important design criteria are to provide adequate space for aircraft to maneuver easily onto the runway, irrespective of the position of adjacent aircraft on the apron, and to provide sufficient room for an aircraft to bypass parked aircraft on the apron. Space for four average sized aircraft is usually provided. Even when holding aprons are provided, aircraft must often queue on the taxiway leading to the end of the runway since it is not practical to construct aprons large enough to accommodate peak demands.

Apron Surface Gradients

For fueling, ease of towing, and taxiing, apron slopes or grades should be kept to the minimum consistent with good drainage requirements. Slopes should in no case exceed 1.0 percent. At gates where aircraft are being fueled every effort should be made to keep the apron slope within 0.5 percent.

REFERENCES

1. *Advisory Circular Checklist*, Federal Aviation Administration, Washington, D.C., Advisory Circular ACOO-UU, September 1981. Issued three times a year.

2. *Aerodrome Design Manual*, Part 1: *Runways*, International Civil Aviation Organization, Montreal, Que., Canada, 1980.

3. *Aerodrome Design Manual*, Part 2: *Taxiways, Aprons and Holding Bays*, International Civil Aviation Organization, Montreal, Que., Canada, 1977.

4. *Aerodromes, Annex 14 to the Convention on International Civil Aviation*, International Civil Aviation Organization, Montreal, Que., Canada, June 1976 with draft amendment 36, August 1982.

5. *Airport Aprons*, Federal Aviation Administration, Washington, D.C., Advisory Circular AC 150/5335-2, January 1965.

6. *Airport Design Standards—Airports Served by Air Carriers, Bridges and Tunnels on*

Airports, Federal Aviation Administration, Washington, D.C., Advisory Circular AC 150/5335-3, April 1971.

7. *Airport Design Standards—Airports Served by Air Carriers, Runway Geometrics*, Federal Aviation Administration, Washington, D.C., Advisory Circular AC 150/5335-4, July 1975.

8. *Airport Design Standards—Airports Served by Air Carriers, Surface Gradient and Line of Sight*, Federal Aviation Administration, Washington, D.C., Advisory Circular AC 150/5325-2C, February 1975.

9. *Airport Design Standards—Airports Served by Air Carriers, Taxiways*, Federal Aviation Administration, Washington, D.C., Advisory Circular AC 150/5335-1A, May 1980.

10. *Airport Design Standards—Effects and Treatment of Jet Blast*, Federal Aviation Administration, Washington, D.C., Advisory Circular AC 150/5325-6A, July 1972.

11. *Airport Design Standards—General Aviation Airports, Basic and General Transport*, Federal Aviation Administration, Washington, D.C., Advisory Circular AC 150/5300-6A, February 1981.

12. *Airport Design Standards—Transport Airports*, Federal Aviation Administration, Washington, D.C., Draft Advisory Circular AC 150/5300-12, August 1982.

13. "A Mathematical Model for Locating Exit Taxiways," R. Horonjeff, et al., Institute of Transportation and Traffic Engineering, University of California, Berkeley, Calif., 1959.

14. "Calculation of Aircraft Wheel Paths and Taxiway Fillets," J. W. L. van Aswegen, Institute of Transportation and Traffic Engineering, University of California, Berkeley, Calif., Graduate Student Report, July 1973.

15. "Determination of the Path Followed by the Undercarriage of a Taxiing Aircraft," Paper prepared by Department of Civil Aviation, Melbourne, Australia.

16. "Determination of Wheel Trajectories," E. Hauer, *Transportation Engineering Journal*, vol. 96, No. TE4, American Society of Civil Engineers, New York, N.Y., November 1970.

17. *Exit Taxiway Location and Design*, R. Horonjeff et al., Report prepared for the Airways Modernization Board by the Institute of Transportation and Traffic Engineering, University of California, Berkeley, Calif.

18. "Movement of Aircraft and Vehicles on the Ground—Taxiway Fillets," 5th Air Navigation Conference, International Civil Aviation Organization, Montreal, Que., Canada, Working Paper 102 prepared by the United Kingdom, October 1967.

19. "Optimization of Runway Exit Locations," E. S. Joline, R. Dixon Speas and Associates, Manhasset, N.Y.

20. *Report of the Department of Transportation Air Traffic Control Advisory Committee*, vols. 1 and 2, Washington, D.C., December 1969.

21. *Runway Length Requirements for Airport Design*, Federal Aviation Administration, Washington, D.C., Advisory Circular AC 150/5325-4, February 1978.

22. *United States Standard for Terminal Instrument Operations (TERPS)*, 3rd ed., Federal Aviation Administration, Washington, D.C., July 1976.

23. *Utility Airports—Air Access to National Transportation*, Federal Aviation Administration, Washington, D.C., Advisory Circular AC 150/5300-4B, January 1981. Also Draft Change 6, 1982.

Chapter **10**

Planning and Design of the Terminal Area

INTRODUCTION

The terminal area is the major interface between the airfield and the rest of the airport. It includes the facilities for passenger and baggage processing, cargo handling, and airport maintenance, operations, and administrative activities. The passenger-processing system is discussed at length in this chapter. Baggage processing, cargo handling, and apron requirements are also discussed relative to the terminal system.

THE PASSENGER TERMINAL SYSTEM

The passenger terminal system is the major connection between ground access and the aircraft. The purpose of this system is to provide the interface between the passenger and the airport access mode, to process the passenger for the origination or termination of an air transport trip, and to convey the passenger and baggage to and from the aircraft.

Components of the System

The passenger terminal system is composed of three major components. These components and the activities that occur within them are as follows:

1. The access interface where the passenger transfers from the access mode of travel to the passenger-processing component. Circulation, parking, and curbside loading and unloading of passengers are the activities that take place within this component.

2. The processing component where the passenger is processed in preparation for starting or ending an air trip. The primary activities that

take place here are ticketing, baggage check-in, baggage claim, seat assignment, federal inspection services, and security.

3. The flight interface where the passenger transfers from the processing component to the aircraft. The activities that occur here include assembly, conveyance to and from the aircraft, and aircraft loading and unloading.

A number of facilities are provided to perform the functions of the passenger terminal system. These facilities are indicated for each of the components identified above.

The Access Interface

This component consists of the terminal curbs, parking facilities, and connecting roadways that enable originating and terminating passengers, visitors, and baggage to enter and exit the terminal. It includes the following facilities:

1. The enplaning and deplaning curb frontage, which provides the public with loading and unloading positions for vehicular access to and from the terminal building

2. The automobile-parking facilities, which provide short-term and long-term parking spaces for passengers and visitors, and facilities for rental cars, public transit, taxis, and limousine services

3. The vehicular roadways which provide access to the terminal curbs, parking spaces, and the public street and highway system

4. The designated pedestrian walkways for crossing roads, including tunnels, bridges, and automated devices that provide access between the parking facilities and the terminal building

5. The service roads and fire lanes, which provide access to various facilities in the terminal and to other airport facilities such as air freight, fuel truck stands, post office, and so on

The Processing System

The terminal is used to process passengers and baggage for the interface with aircraft and the ground transportation modes. It includes the following facilities:

1. The airline ticket counter and office used for ticket transactions, baggage check-in, flight information, and administrative personnel and facilities

2. The terminal services space, which consists of the public and nonpublic areas such as concessions, amenities for passengers and visitors, truck service docks, food preparation areas, and food and miscellaneous storage

3. The lobby for circulation and passenger and visitor waiting

4. Public circulation space for the general circulation of passengers and visitors, consisting of such areas as stairways, escalators, elevators, and corridors

5. The outbound baggage space, which is a nonpublic area for sorting and processing baggage for departing flights

6. The intraline and interline baggage space used for processing baggage transferred from one flight to another on the same or different airlines

7. The inbound baggage space, which is used for receiving baggage from an arriving flight, and for delivering baggage to be claimed by the arriving passenger

8. Airport administration and service areas used for airport management, operations, and maintenance facilities

9. The federal inspection service facility, which is the area for processing passengers arriving on international flights and which is sometimes incorporated as part of the connector element

The Flight Interface

The connector joins the terminal to parked aircraft and usually includes the following facilities:

1. The concourse, which provides for circulation to the departure lounges and other terminal areas

2. The departure lounge or holdroom, which is used for assembling passengers for a flight departure

3. The passenger boarding device used to transport enplaning and deplaning passengers between the aircraft door and the departure lounge.

4. Airline operations space used for airline personnel, equipment, and activities related to the arrival and departure of aircraft

5. Security facilities used for the inspection of passengers and baggage and the control of public access to passenger boarding areas.

6. The terminal services area, which provides amenities to the public, and those nonpublic areas required for operations, such as building maintenance and utilities

The components of the passenger terminal system together with the specific physical facilities corresponding to them are shown in Fig. 10-1. The relative locations of the various facilities are identified on the plan drawings of the departing and arriving levels of the proposed Fort Lauderdale–Hollywood International Airport given in Fig. 10-2.

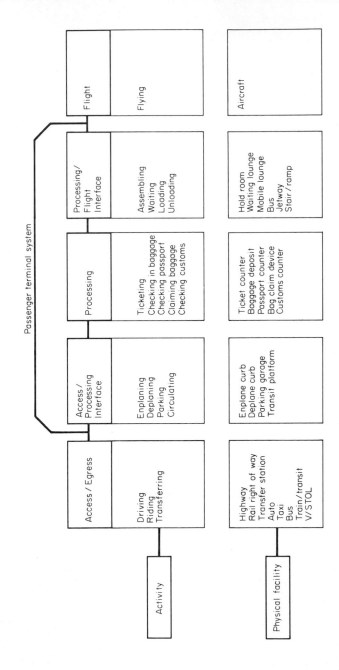

Fig. 10-1 Components of the passenger terminal system.

DESIGN CONSIDERATIONS

In developing criteria for the design of the passenger terminal complex, it is important to realize that there are a number of different factors which enter into the statement of overall design objectives. From these factors, general and specific goals are established which set the framework on which design progresses. For example, in designing modifications to the apron and terminal complex at Geneva Intercontinental Airport, the general design objectives included [19]:

1. Development and sizing to accomplish the stated mission of the airport within the parameters defined in the master plan

2. Capability to meet the demands for the medium- and long-run time frames

3. Functional, practical, and financial feasibility

4. Maximize the use of existing facilities

5. Achievement of a balanced flow between access, terminal, and airfield facilities during the peak hour

6. Consideration of environmental sensitivity

7. Maintenance of flexibility to meet future requirements beyond the current planning horizon

8. Capability to anticipate and implement significant improvements in aviation technology

The following specific design objectives were derived from these overall objectives which included the needs of the various categories of airport users.

Passengers' Objectives

1. Responsiveness to the needs of the people relative to convenience, comfort, and personal requirements

2. Provision of effective passenger and access orientation through concise, comprehensive directional graphics

3. Separation of enplaning and deplaning roadways and curb fronts to ensure maximum operational efficiency

4. Provision of convenient access to public and employee parking facilities, rental car areas, ancillary facilities, and on-site non-aviation facilities

Airline Objectives

1. Accommodation of existing and future aircraft fleets with maximum operational efficiency

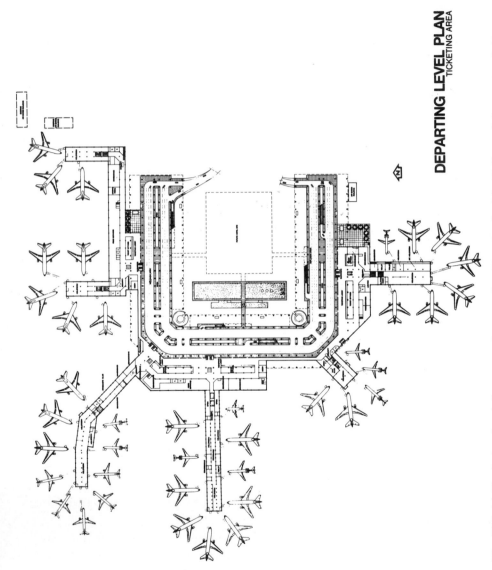

DEPARTING LEVEL PLAN
TICKETING AREA

Fig. 10-2 (a) Enplaning level for proposed terminal at Fort Lauderdale–Hollywood International Airport. *(Reynolds, Smith and Hills [19].)*

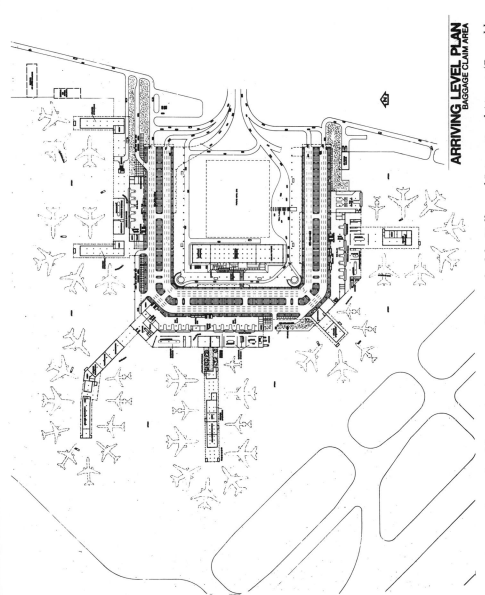

Fig. 10-2 (b) Deplaning level for proposed terminal at Fort Lauderdale–Hollywood International Airport. (*Reynolds, Smith and Hills [19].*)

2. Provision of direct and efficient means of passenger and baggage flow for all passengers, including domestic and international originating, terminating, and transfer passengers

3. Provision for economic, efficient, and effective security

4. Provision of facilities which will embrace the latest energy-conservation measures

Airport Management Objectives

1. Maintenance of the existing terminal operation, access system, runway system, and ancillary facilities during all stages of construction

2. Provision of facilities which generate maximum revenues from concessionaires and other sources

3. Provision of facilities which minimize maintenance and operating expense

Community Objectives

1. Render a unique and appropriate expression and impression of the community

2. Provision of harmony with the existing architectural elements of the total terminal complex

3. Coordination with the existing and planned off-airport highway system

The designer should consider the combination of all these objectives in developing design criteria for a passenger terminal complex. These criteria should be used as performance measures for the evaluation of any particular design alternative. In order to generate their values, a detailed design should be provided. The analyst can then proceed to calculate the various measures using a number of analytical techniques. Some of these techniques are discussed later in this chapter.

Terminal Demand Parameters

The determination of space requirements at passenger terminals is strongly influenced by the level of service desired. A review of passenger terminals in relation to passenger volumes at existing airports shows a wide range in size. However, some guidelines for the determination of space requirements can be defined. The purpose of these guidelines is to give general orders of magnitude for values that are subject to change depending on the requirements of specific designs. The following steps should be followed in determining terminal facility space requirements.

Identify Access Modes and Modal Splits

Vehicle volumes are normally derived from projections of passenger and aircraft forecasts. These volumes critically impact the design of highway access facilities, on-airport roadway and circulation systems, curb frontage requirements for private automobiles, buses, limousines, taxis, and rental cars, and parking. Surveys are normally conducted to determine the access modes of passengers and the vehicle-occupancy rates. In the absence of such surveys, secondary sources may be investigated to ascertain the access characteristics of passengers in similar airport environments [18, 34, 40]. The most important parameters to be obtained include the typical peak-hour volumes of vehicles entering and leaving the airport on the design day, the access facilities used, and the duration of use, including parking and curb front. Care should be exercised to include employees and visitors as well as passengers in these access studies, and to correlate the peaking characteristics and access modes of each group of airport traveler.

Identify Passenger Volumes and Types

Passenger volumes can be obtained from forecasts normally done in conjunction with airport planning studies. Two measures of volume are used. The first is annual passenger volume, which is used for preliminary sizing of the terminal building. The second is a more detailed hourly volume. It is customary to use typical peak-hour passengers as the hourly design volume for passenger terminal design. This figure is a design index and is usually in the range of 0.03 to 0.05 percent of the annual volume.

The identification of passenger types is necessasry because different types of passengers place different demands on the various components. Passenger types are usually broadly classified into domestic and international passengers and then further grouped into originating, terminating, connecting or transfer, through, enplaning, and deplaning passengers. These various passenger groupings are made on the basis of the facilities within the terminal which are normally used by each type of passenger. Historical data and forecasts regarding the proportions of the total volumes that are made up by each of the different types of passengers are useful in obtaining estimates of the parameters needed for the design of the various facilities [3].

Identify Access and Passenger Component Demand

This is done by matching the passenger and vehicle types with facilities in the terminal area. Tabulations such as the one shown in Table 10-1 are quite helpful. This table shows which passengers are using each facility. By indicating the volume of each type of passenger in the rows corresponding to the facilities, it is possible to generate the total load on each facility. This is done by taking the row sums of the volumes entered in the table.

TABLE 10-1 **Determination of Demand for Various Types of Passenger Facilities**

	Passenger type i, arriving			Passenger type i, departing			
Facility j	Domestic, no bags, auto driver*	Domestic, with bags, auto passenger[†]	Inter-national, with bags, auto passenger	Domestic, with bags, auto passenger	Domestic, no bags, auto driver	Inter-national, with bags, auto driver	Total volume V
Curb, arrivals	—	V_{ij}[‡]	V_{ij}	—	—	—	
Curb, departures	—	—	—	V_{ij}	—	V_{ij}	
Domestic lobby	—	V_{ij}	—	V_{ij}	V_{ij}	—	
International lobby	—	—	—	—	—	V_{ij}	
Ticketing counter	—	—	—	V_{ij}	—	V_{ij}	
Assembly	—	—	—	V_{ij}	—	V_{ij}	
Baggage check-in	—	—	—	V_{ij}	V_{ij}	V_{ij}	
Security control	—	—	—	V_{ij}	V_{ij}	V_{ij}	
Customs, health	—	—	V_{ij}				
Immigration	—	—	V_{ij}	—	—	V_{ij}	
Baggage claim	—	V_{ij}	V_{ij}				

* Auto driver = passenger driving a car to and from airport.

† Auto passenger = passenger driven to and from airport.

‡ V_{ij} = Design volume of passengers type i using facility type j.

Facility Classification

The airport terminal facility may be classified by its principal characteristics relative to its functional role. In general, airports are classified as originating-terminating stations, transfer stations, or through stations, and the facilities required are considerably different in magnitude and configuration for each.

An originating-terminating station processes a high level of passengers which are beginning or ending the air transport trip at the airport. At such stations these passengers may be on the order of 70 to 90 percent of the total passengers. Such stations have a relatively long aircraft ground time, and the main flow of passengers is between the aircraft and the ground transportation system. Such stations have relatively high requirements for curb frontage, ticketing and baggage facilities, and parking. Typical data indicate that the hourly movement of aircraft per gate is on the order of 0.9 to 1.1.

A transfer station, on the other hand, has a high percentage of its total passengers connecting between arriving and departing flights. These stations need greater concourse facilities for the processing of connecting passengers and less ground access facility development. Airline ticketing positions and baggage claim facilities are usually less than with originating stations. However, intraline and interline baggage facilities are usually greater. Care must be exercised in the planning of such stations to locate the gate positions of airlines exchanging passengers in close proximity to each other to minimize central terminal flows and connecting times. Data indicate that such airports demonstrate aircraft activity at the rate of 1.3 to 1.5 aircraft per gate per hour in peak periods.

The through station combines a high percentage of originating passengers with a low percentage of originating flights. A high percentage of the passengers remain on the aircraft at such points. Aircraft ground times are minimal, averaging between 1.6 and 2.0 hourly movements per gate in peak periods. Departure lounge space is not as great at such stations, and curb frontage, ticketing, and baggage facilities are less than at originating stations.

Overall Space Approximations

It is possible to estimate order of magnitude ranges for the overall size of a terminal facility prior to performing more detailed calculations for particular space needs. These estimates allow the planner to define broadly the scope of a project based upon information which summarizes the space provided at other existing facilities. The FAA has indicated that gross terminal area space requirements of between 0.08 and 0.12 ft^2 per annual enplaned passenger are reasonable. Another estimate is obtained by applying a ratio of 150 ft^2 per design-hour passenger [30]. Estimates of the level of peak-hour passengers, peak-hour aircraft operations, and gate positions are also obtained based upon the level of annual enplanements by procedures similar to those shown in Figure 10-3. Others have provided

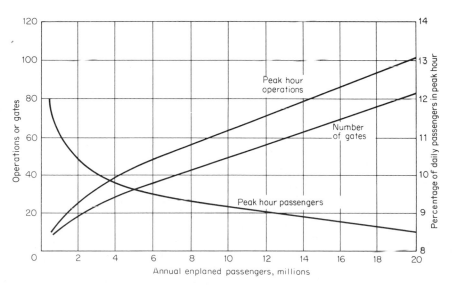

Fig. 10-3 Estimated peak-hour passengers, operations and gate requirements for intermediate-range planning. (*Federal Aviation Administration [30].*)

estimating guidelines for total terminal space as shown in Fig. 10-4 [35]. Approximations of the allocation of space among the various purposes in a terminal building are also useful for preliminary planning. The FAA indicates that approximately 55 percent of terminal space is rentable and 45 percent is not. An approximate breakdown of these space allocations is given as 38 percent for airline operations, 17 percent for concessions and airport administration, 30 percent for public space, and 15 percent for utilities, shops, tunnels, and stairways [35]. A final determination of the actual space allocations is obtained through detailed analyses of the performance of the elements of the system as the design proceeds from space programming through each of the subsequent phases in the process.

THE TERMINAL PLANNING PROCESS

The evolution and development of a terminal design is performed in a series of integrated steps. These may be identified as programming, concept development, schematic design, and design development. The terminal facilities are developed in conformity with the planned development of the airside facilities, considering the most effective use of the airport site, its potential for physical expansion and operational flexibility, its integration with the ground access system, and its compatibility with existing and planned land uses near the airport. The planning process explicitly examines physical and operational aspects of the system.

The programming phase defines the objectives and project scope, including the rationale for the initiation of the study. It includes tentative implementation schedules, estimates of the anticipated level of capital investment, as well as operating, maintenance, and administrative costs,

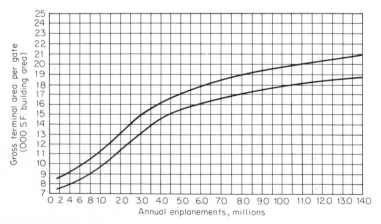

Fig. 10-4 Gross terminal area estimates for intermediate range planning. (*Federal Aviation Administration [35].*)

and the space requirements program. In concept development, studies are undertaken to identify the overall arrangement of building components, functional relationships, and the characteristics of the terminal building. Schematic design translates the concept and functional relationships into plan drawings which identify the overall size, shape, and location of spaces required for each function. Detailed budget estimates are prepared in schematic design so that comparisons may be made between space requirements and costs. In design development the size and character of the entire project is fixed, and detailed plans of the specific design and allocation of space within the complex are prepared. This phase forms the basis for the preparation of construction documents, bidding, construction, and final project implementation [36].

In the programming and concept development phases of a terminal design project, the following evaluative criteria are used to weigh alternatives:

1. Ability to handle expected demand
2. Compatibility with expected aircraft types
3. Flexibility for growth and response to technology changes
4. Compatibility with the total airport master plan
5. Compatibility with on-airport and adjacent land uses
6. Simplicity of passenger orientation and processing
7. Analyses of aircraft maneuvering routes and potential conflicts on the taxiway system and in the apron area
8. Potential for aircraft, passenger, and ground vehicle delay
9. Financial and economic feasibility

In the schematic and design development phases, more specific design criteria are examined such as:

1. The processing cost per passenger
2. Walking distance for various types of passengers
3. Passenger delays in processing
4. Occupancy levels and degree of congestion
5. Aircraft maneuvering delays and costs
6. Aircraft fuel consumption in maneuvering on the airport between runways and terminals
7. Construction costs
8. Administrative, operating, and maintenance costs
9. Potential revenue sources and the expected level of revenues from each source

SPACE PROGRAMMING

General

The space programming phase of terminal planning seeks to establish gross size requirements for the terminal facilities without establishing specific locations for the individual components. The nature of the processing components is such, however, that approximate locations are indicated for new and existing terminal facilities due to the sequential nature of the processing system. This section provides guidance concerning the spatial requirements to accommodate adequately the several functions carried out within the various areas of the airport terminal.

The Access Interface System

The curb element is the interface between the terminal building and the ground transportation system. A survey of the airport users will establish the number of passengers using each of the available ground transportation modes, such as private automobile, taxi, limousine, courtesy car, public bus, rail, or rapid transit. Ratios may be established for both the passenger and the vehicle modal choice for airport access.

Terminal Curb

The length of curb required for the loading and unloading of passengers and baggage is determined by the type and volume of ground vehicle traffic anticipated in the peak period on the design day. Airports with relatively low passenger levels may be able to accommodate both enplaning and deplaning passengers from one curb front. More active airports may find it desirable to physically separate the enplaning from the deplaning passengers, horizontally, if space permits, or vertically if space is limited.

The determination of the amount of curb space which will be required is related to airport policies relative to the assignment of priorities in the use of curb front and the provision of staging areas for taxis, buses, and other public transport vehicles. The parameters required for a preliminary analysis of curb front needs are the number and types of vehicles at the curb, the vehicle length, and the various occupancy times of different types of vehicles at the curb front for arriving and departing passengers. Normally, a slot for a private automobile is considered to be about 25 ft, whereas for taxis 20 ft, for limousines 30 ft, and for transit buses 50 ft are used. Reported dwell times for private automobiles range from 1 to 2 min at the enplaning curb and from 2 to 4 min at the deplaning curb. Taxi dwell times lie closer to the lower range of these values, whereas limousines and buses may be at the curb anywhere from 5 to 15 min. These dwell times are highly influenced by the degree of traffic regulation and enforcement in the vicinity of the curb, and should be verified in specific studies. Normally a wide lane, on the order of 18 to 20 ft, is provided for terminal access to accommodate direct curb access, maneuvering, and standing vehicles. This usually indicates a minimum of one and preferably two additional lanes in the vicinity of terminal entrances and exits to provide adequate capacity for through traffic. Rules of thumb, which may be applied to determine curb front needs, indicate that the full length of the curb adjacent to the terminal plus about 30 percent of the maneuvering lane may be considered as the available curb front. Therefore, a 100-ft curb may be considered to provide 130 ft of curb front in an hour or 7800 ft·min of vehicle occupancy. If 120 automobiles per hour demand curb space for an average dwell time of 2 min, then 6000 ft·min of curb front are required, or the peak hour must provide a curb length of 100 ft. Other methods for approximating curb frontage have been reported in the literature [20, 32]. For example, at Geneva Intercontinental Airport, the preliminary design guidelines have indicated that curb frontage should be made available at the rate of at least 0.5 linear foot per peak-hour enplaning passenger and 0.8 linear foot per peak-hour deplaning passenger [19].

Roadway Elements

The determination of the vehicular demand for the various on and off airport roadways is essential to ensure that adequate service levels are provided to airport users. The main components of the highway system providing for access to airports from population and industrial centers are normally within the jurisdiction of federal, state, and local ground transportation agencies. However, coordination in areawide planning efforts is essential so that the traffic generation potential of airports may be included within the parameters necessary for the proper planning of regional transportation systems. Guidance on the level and peaking characteristics of airport destined traffic may be found in the literature [40].

The provision of adequate feeder facilities from the regional transport network to the airport is largely within the jurisdiction of the airport operator or owner. Vehicle volumes and peaking characteristics are usually determined by correlating modal preference and occupancy rates with flight schedules. Normally roadway facilities are designed for the peak-hour traffic on the design day, with adequate provision for the splitting and recirculation of traffic within the various areas of the airport property. The main roadway elements which must be considered are the feeder roads into the terminal area, the enplaning and deplaning roadways, and recirculation roadways.

The *Highway Capacity Manual* [23, 24] provides criteria for level of service design and quantitative methods for determining the volumes which can be accommodated by various roadway sections. For preliminary planning it is reasonable to assume that feeder roads on the airport property provide acceptable service when they process from 1000 to 1200 vehicles per hour per lane. Enplaning and deplaning roadways, as well as recirculation roadway elements, provide adequate service when they accommodate from 600 to 800 vehicles per hour per lane. It is recommended that for preliminary planning purposes the above ranges of values be used to establish bounds on the sizes of these facilities for a demand-capacity analysis. In schematic design, analysis of the flow characteristics of individual sections of the roadway elements will yield final design parameters.

Parking

Most large airports provide separate parking facilities for passengers and visitors, employees, and rental-car storage. In smaller airports these facilities may be combined in one physical location. Passenger and visitor parking are often segregated into short-term, long-term, and remote parking facilities. Those parking facilities most convenient to the terminal are designated as short-term, and a premium rate is charged for their use. Long-term parking is usually near the main terminal complex, but not as convenient as short-term, and rates are usually discounted for long-term users. Remote parking, on the other hand, is usually quite distant from the terminal complex, and provisions are normally made for courtesy vehicle transportation between these areas and the main terminal complex. The rates in these facilities are usually the most economical.

As noted in Chap. 5, short-term parkers are those which park for 3 h or less, and these account for about 80 percent of the parkers at an airport. However, these short-term parkers account for only 15 to 20 percent of the accumulation of vehicles in the parking facility [30]. Preliminary planning estimates of the number of parking spaces required at an airport may be obtained from Fig. 10-5. In planning for the Geneva airport, preliminary design criteria required two parking spaces per peak-hour passenger on the design day. More refined estimates of the total amount of parking required and the breakdown of short- and long-term space is obtained from analyses performed in the schematic design phase of the terminal planning process.

Entrances to parking facilities through ticket-splitting devices are very common at airports. It has been observed that these devices can process anywhere from 400 to 650 vehicles per hour, depending upon the degree of automation used as well as the continuity of the demand flow. It is recommended that the number of entrances be estimated on the basis of 500 vehicles per hour per device in preliminary planning. Ticket collection points process from 150 to 200 vehicles per hour per position. In parking garages, the capacity of ramps leading from one level to another is

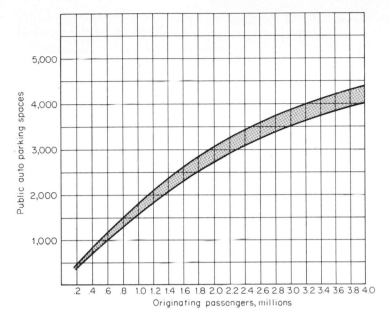

Fig. 10-5 Public automobile-parking space requirements. (*Federal Aviation Administration [35].*)

important during peak periods when considerable searching for an available space may occur, or vehicles may be directed immediately to a particular level. One-way straight ramps can accommodate about 750 vehicles per hour. However, a reduction on the order of 20 percent should be considered when two-way ramps are utilized. Circular or helical ramps, often used for egress from parking facilities, accommodate about 600 vehicles per hour in one direction. The precise volume of vehicles which may be accommodated by a particular design will depend to a large extent on the geometric characteristics of the design, continuity of flow, information systems installed, and characteristics of the vehicles and users of the particular facility. Most often, some type of analytical or simulation model is used in the schematic design phase of the project to test a preliminary design [22].

The Passenger-Processing System

The passenger-processing system consists of those facilities necessary and desirable for the handling of passengers and their baggage prior to and after a flight. It is the element which links the ground access system to the air transportation system. The terminal curb provides the interface on the ground access side of the system, and the aircraft boarding device provides the interface on the air side of the system. In determining the particular needs of a specific component in this system, a knowledge of the types of passengers and the extent of visitors impacting on each component is necesssary.

Entryways and Foyers

Entryways and foyers are located along the curb element and serve as weather buffers for passengers entering and leaving the terminal building. The size of an entryway or foyer depends upon its intended usage. As entrances and exits they may be relatively small; as sheltered public waiting areas they should be sized to meet local needs. Designs must accommodate the physically handicapped. These facilities are sized to process both passengers and visitors during the peak hour. Though the times of the enplaning and deplaning peaks may be different, it is likely that the deplaning peak will occur over a shorter time duration than the enplaning peak. It is often useful to subject a preliminary design proposal not only to an average peak-hour demand, but also to a peak 20- or 30-min demand, particularly for the deplaning elements of the system. Preliminary design processing rates for automated doors in the vicinity of the enplaning and deplaning curb front can be taken as from 20 to 30 persons per minute per unit. These values may be reduced by 50 percent if the doors are not automated.

Terminal Lobby Area

The functions of significance to an air traveler performed in a terminal lobby are passenger ticketing, passenger and visitor waiting, and baggage check-in and claiming. Airports with less than 100,000 annual enplanements frequently carry out these functions in a single lobby. More active airports usually have separate lobbies for each function. The size of the lobby space depends on whether ticketing and baggage claim lobbies are separate, if passenger and visitor waiting areas are to be provided, and the density of congestion acceptable. In general, the lobby area should provide for passenger queueing, circulation, and waiting. Waiting lobby areas are designed to seat from 15 to 25 percent of the design-hour enplaning passengers and visitors if departure lounges are provided for all gates, and from 60 to 70 percent if they are not provided [30, 36]. Usually about 20 ft^2 per person is provided for seating and circulation.

Airline Ticket Counter and Ticket Office Space

The airline ticket counter and office is the area at the airport where airline and passenger make final ticket transactions and check in baggage for a flight. This includes the airline ticket counter, the airline ticket agent service area, the outbound baggage-handling device, and the support office area for the airline ticket agents. There are three types of ticketing and baggage check-in facilities, the linear, pass-through, and island types. Each of these facilities is shown in a typical arrangement in Fig. 10-6.

The ticket transaction takes place at the ticket counter, which is a stand-up desk. To the left and right of the ticket counter position, a low shelf is provided to deposit, check in, tag, and weigh baggage, if necessary, for the flight. Subsequently, the baggage is passed back by the agent to an outbound baggage conveyance device located near the counter. The total number of ticket counter positions required is a function of the level of peak-hour originating passengers, the types of facilities provided, that is,

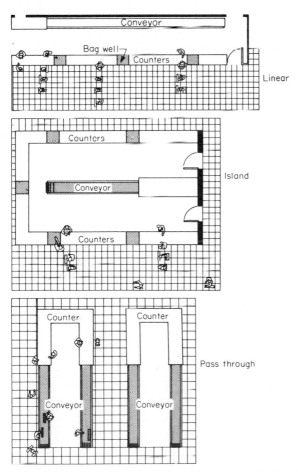

Fig. 10-6 Typical ticket counter configurations. (*Federal Aviation Administration [35].*)

multipurpose, express baggage check-in, and ticketing only, and the queues and delays acceptable to the airlines. In some markets, a considerable number of passengers may be preticketed, and a higher percentage of express check-in positions may be warranted either within the terminal building or at the curb front. This is particularly true at airports serving tourist areas. A reasonable estimate of the number of positions required is gained by assuming the peak loading on the facilities is about 10 percent of the peak-hour originating passengers and that a maximum queue length of 5 passengers per position is a desirable design goal. If this is the case, then 3000 peak-hour originating passengers translates to 300 peak loading passengers, which requires 60 ticketing positions. As indicated in Fig. 10-6, the sizing of the counter length depends upon the mix of position types, but for preliminary estimating purposes a counter length of about 10 ft for two positions is reasonable. Therefore, in this case the total linear footage of counter space would be about 300 ft. If a queueing depth of 3 ft per passenger is provided, then a minimum queueing depth of 15 ft is required. The counter itself requires a 10-ft depth, and a circulation aisle of from 20 to 35 ft is appropriate. Therefore, the area devoted to this function ranges from about 13,500 to 18,000 ft^2. If single-row lobby seating is provided in the area, this increases the area to between 16,500 and 21,000 ft^2. Approximations gained from other techniques yield similar results [36]. In the preliminary design guidelines for Geneva, it was recommended that not less than 40 ft of queueing area be provided in front of the linear ticket counters. The reason for this criterion is to allow for increases in the demand at this airport without requiring major terminal modifications.

The above calculations are useful for linear-type counters where queues form in lines at each position. For corral-type queueing similar results are obtained, the principal advantage of this type of queueing being less restriction to circulation in the ticket lobby area. The pass-through and island-type counters result in a similar number of positions and counter length, but in different geometric arrangements. The circulation and queueing areas may be modified as shown in Fig. 10-6. Normally, in pass-through ticketing and baggage check-in facilities, queueing is along the length of the counter, whereas in island types queueing is in lines at the various ticketing positions.

The final determination of the number and mix of ticketing positions is made through consultation with the various airlines to be served and through the use of analytical or simulation models [12].

The support area may be composed of smaller areas for the operations and functions of accounting and the safekeeping of tickets, receipts, and manifests, communications and information display equipment, and personnel areas for rest, personal grooming, and training. On the wall behind the ticket agents information displays are posted for the latest airline information on arriving and departing flights. Typical estimates of ATO space requirements may be obtained by taking the linear footage of the counters and multiplying this number by a depth of from 20 to 25 ft for this area. This yields a value of about 7500 ft² for 3000 peak-hour originating passengers. As the level of peak-hour passengers increases, various economies of scale may be gained in the use of such facilities. For example, in moving from 3000 to 6000 peak-hour originations, the increase in ATO space may be only about 30 percent. Other estimating procedures yield similar results [30, 36]. Again, the final determination of the space requirements is obtained through consultation with the various airlines using the facility.

Security

Security screening of all airline passengers is an extremely important function to be carried out in an airport terminal. Security screening of passengers and hand-carried articles is required prior to boarding airline aircraft. Depending upon the configuration of the terminal and the policy of the separate airlines, security screening may be conducted at various locations in a terminal within the area lying between the ticketing area and the aircraft boarding position. The area is considered a sterile area. Decisions to bar visitors from sterile areas must consider community reaction. In many cases, signing is used to discourage visitor entrance to sterile areas, but enforcement is purposely lax, except in unusually heavy demand periods.

Security screening is performed in corridors leading to gates, or in some instances at the boarding gate. In most installations the passenger and the visitor must walk through a magnetometer with hand-carried articles subject to manual search or X-ray screening.

A typical manual search station with two tables to accept and two tables to return search articles plus the magnetometer requires approximately 144 ft² of space. A typical X-ray search unit requires approximately 120 ft² of space. These are shown in Fig. 10-7.

The processing rate of screening installations will range from 300 to 600 persons per hour. Care should be exercised to locate the screening positions so that they do not impede the flow of passengers leaving the sterile area and that queues for processing passengers do not restrict other flows within the area. Normally, corridor widths in the vicinity of screening areas should be on the order of 30 to 40 ft to accommodate screening equipment as well as passengers leaving the screening area. Occasionally, screening equipment is placed in tandem along the length of the concourse for use in peak periods without further restricting flow rates or causing long queue lengths.

In many airports, automated facilities are beginning to be used for passengers exiting sterile areas. These may consist of a series of revolving

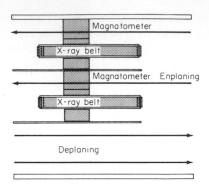

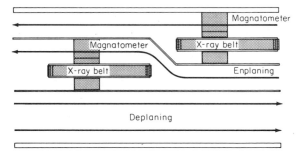

Fig. 10-7 Typical security screening layouts. (*Federal Aviation Administration [35].*)

doors with pressure-sensitive floors to restrict unlawful entrance into the area. For preliminary planning, a revolving door security exit facility will process about 500 to 750 persons per hour per unit.

Departure Lounges

The departure lounge serves as an assembly area for passengers waiting to board a particular flight and as the exit passageway for deplaning passengers. It is generally sized to accommodate the number of boarding passengers expected to be in the lounge 15 min prior to scheduled departure time, assuming this is the point in time when aircraft boarding begins. A conservative estimate of the percentage of passengers in the lounge at this time is 90 percent of the boarding passengers. The space should accommodate seating for these passengers, though not all need be seated, space for airline processing plus passenger queues, and an exitway for deplaning passengers. Design criteria at Geneva airport require that the departure lounge be sized to accommodate an 80-percent load factor for the gate design aircraft, with 80 percent of these passengers seated at 15 ft^2 per passenger and 20 percent standing at 10 ft^2 per passenger. Processing queues should not extend into the corridor to the extent that circulation is impaired. Lounge depths of 25 to 30 ft are considered reasonable for holding boarding passengers. Space for a departure lounge is proportioned on the basis of from 10 to 15 ft² per boarding passenger. Therefore, if a departure lounge is to accommodate 100 boarding passengers for a flight, its area should range from 1000 to 1500 ft². To a greater and greater extent common departure lounge areas are being utilized, and these are sized based upon the total peak-hour boarding passengers for the gates being served by the common lounge. Since it is likely that boarding for these aircraft will occur at different times in the peak hour, the total space required for separate lounges may be reduced by 20 to 30 percent for common lounges.

The corridor provided for deplaning passengers should be about 10 ft in width. The airline-processing area should provide for at least two positions for narrow-body aircraft and up to four positions for wide-body aircraft to minimize queue lengths extending into the corridor. Processing rates range from 1 to 2 passengers a minute at these positions, and peak arrival rates range from 10 to 15 percent of the boarding passengers. Therefore, queue depths of about 10 ft are reasonable values for the preliminary design for individual departure lounges. For common lounges, the position of the processing area should be such as not to interfere with the circulation of passengers in the vicinity of the entrances and exits from the lounge. Typically these positions are located in the center of a satellite facility or at the end of the corridor in a pier facility.

Figure 10-8 shows the layout for a departure lounge seating about 70 passengers.

Corridors

Corridors provide for passenger and visitor circulation between departure lounges and the central terminal areas. These should be designed to accommodate physically handicapped persons during the peak periods of high-density flow. Studies have shown that a typical 20-ft wide corridor will have a capacity ranging from 330 to over 600 persons per minute. For planning purposes, corridor widths should be sized on the basis of about 16.5 passengers per foot of width per minute. The corridor width should be the width required at the most restrictive points, that is, the minimum free-flow width in the vicinity of restaurant entrances, phone booth clusters, or departure lounge check-in points. This standard is based upon a width of 2.5 ft per person and a depth separation of 6.0 ft between people. The corridor width is adversely impacted by the peaking of deplaning passengers in platoons, but the decreased depth separations compensate for the decreased walking rates in these circumstances. At Geneva airport, public circulation corridors are required to be at least 20 ft wide, whereas those in

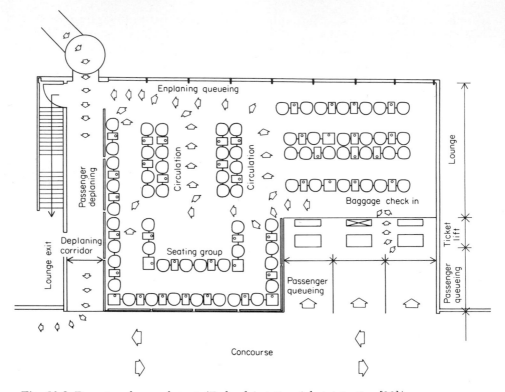

Fig. 10-8 Departure lounge layout. (*Federal Aviation Administration [36].*)

airside connectors are required to be at least 30 ft wide. Further guidance on corridor width design is contained in the literature [11, 30, 36].

Baggage Claim Facilities

The baggage claim lobby should be located so that checked baggage may be returned to terminating passengers in reasonable proximity to the terminal curb. At low-activity airports, checked baggage may be placed on a shelf for passenger claiming. More active airports have installed mechanical delivery and display equipment similar to that depicted in Fig. 10-9. The number of claim devices required is determined by the number and type of aircraft that will arrive during the peak hour, the time distribution of these arrivals, the number of terminating passengers, the amount of baggage checked on these flights, and the mechanism used to transport baggage from the aircraft to the claim area. In the ideal situation, a baggage claim device should not be shared between flight arrivals at the same time, as this leads to considerable congestion in the vicinity of the device and to passenger confusion. Greater utilization of the devices is obtained where airlines time the sharing of claim devices for separate flights.

At the present time, except in the most unusual situations, passenger delays in the baggage claim area are significant due principally to the fact that passengers can travel from aircraft to claim areas much faster than baggage-conveyance systems can transport the baggage from aircraft to claim areas. It is therefore essential that claim lobbies be designed to accommodate waiting passengers adequately and provide for rapid claiming of baggage once the baggage is transferred to the claim device.

Estimating procedures have been provided by the FAA for sizing claiming devices, based upon the equivalent peak 20-min aircraft arrivals. Charts for this purpose are provided in Figs. 10-10 and 10-11. It should be observed that these charts are based upon checked baggage at the rate of 1.3 bags per person, and adjustments may be required as baggage exceeds this rate.

In preliminary planning studies, great care should be exercised in using the above guidelines. Particular attention should be given to the space provided around a claim device, and it is specifically recommended that a clear space of from 13 to 15 ft be provided adjacent to the device for active and waiting claim, as well as for claim area circulation. In some instances baggage lobbies have been designed with adequate waiting areas, and subsequently other facilities have been moved into these areas, considerably diminishing mobility. It is recommended that an additional 15 to 35 ft of circulation space be provided within the deplaning facility to allow for circulation between the claim devices, rental car positions, and deplaning curbs. If ground transportation facilities are located in these areas, they should be physically positioned so as not to restrict passenger flow to and from the claim area.

In many airports, positive claim is now being used to ensure the security of passenger baggage. This system requires that attendants examine baggage claim checks and compare them to baggage tags prior to allowing baggage to leave the facility. Positive claim is provided either by enclosing the claim area with a barrier and restricting exit points or by checking baggage at the exit doors from the baggage claim facility.

International Facilities

Airports with international operations require space for the inspection of passengers, crew, baggage, aircraft, and cargo. The area required for customs, immigration, agriculture, and public health services may be in a separate facility or in the terminal building itself. These facilities should be designed so that passenger flow between the aircraft and the initial processing station is unimpeded and as short as possible, there is no possibility of contact with domestic passengers or any unauthorized personnel until processing is complete, there is no possible way for an international arrival to bypass processing, and there is a segregated area for in-transit international passengers.

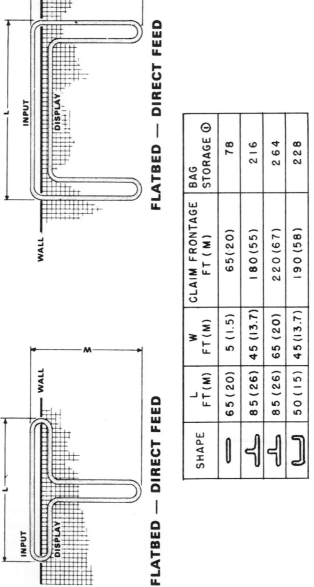

FLATBED — DIRECT FEED

FLATBED — DIRECT FEED

SHAPE	L FT (M)	W FT (M)	CLAIM FRONTAGE FT (M)	BAG STORAGE ①
⎯	65 (20)	5 (1.5)	65 (20)	78
⊥⊤	85 (26)	45 (13.7)	180 (55)	216
⊥⊤	85 (26)	65 (20)	220 (67)	264
⊐	50 (15)	45 (13.7)	190 (58)	228

Fig. 10-9 Mechanized baggage claim devices commonly used at airports. (*Federal Aviation Administration [30].*)

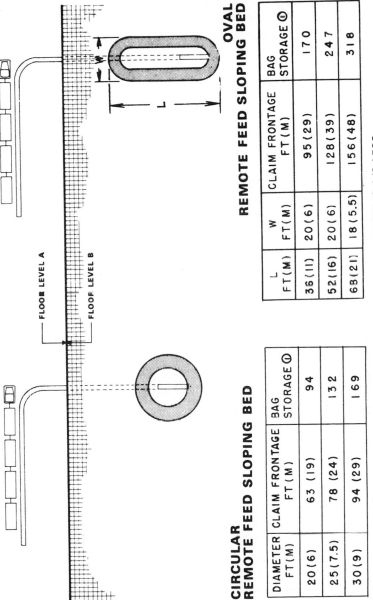

OVAL
REMOTE FEED SLOPING BED

L FT(M)	W FT(M)	CLAIM FRONTAGE FT(M)	BAG STORAGE ⊙
36(11)	20(6)	95(29)	170
52(16)	20(6)	128(39)	247
68(21)	18(5.5)	156(48)	318

CIRCULAR
REMOTE FEED SLOPING BED

DIAMETER FT(M)	CLAIM FRONTAGE FT(M)	BAG STORAGE ⊙
20(6)	63(19)	94
25(7.5)	78(24)	132
30(9)	94(29)	169

⊙ THEORETICAL BAG STORAGE — PRACTICAL BAG STORAGE CAPABILITY IS 1/3 LESS

Fig. 10-9 (Continued).

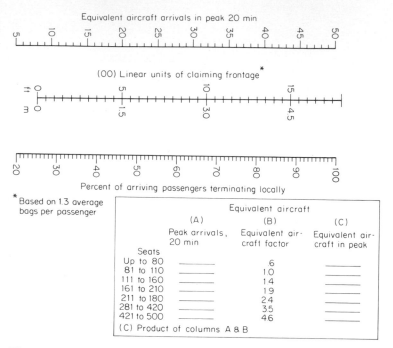

Fig. 10-10 Estimating nomograph for baggage claim linear claim footage requirements. *(Federal Aviation Administration [30].)*

The size of this facility is based on the projection of hourly passengers requiring processing. It is recommended that the appropriate officials and agencies be contacted during the preliminary design phase to determine specific design requirements. Some guidance on the processing rates and sizing of these facilities is found in the literature [30].

Other Areas

Most terminals are developed to accommodate several other activities, and the space needs should be determined for each airport based upon local requirements. These activities are identified below:

Airline Activities—Airline Exclusive Space

The following airline activities may exist at all or some terminal facilities and should be discussed with the airlines which plan on utilizing the facility.

1. Outbound baggage makeup and inbound baggage transfer and conveyance system

2. Cabin services and aircraft maintenance

3. Flight operations and crew ready rooms

4. Storage areas for valuable or outsized baggage

5. Air-freight and mail pickup and delivery

6. Passenger reservations and VIP waiting areas

7. Administrative offices

8. Ramp vehicle and cart parking and maintenance

Passenger Amenities—Revenue-Producing Space

The factors which influence the extent of passenger amenities include passenger volume, community size, the location and extent of off-airport

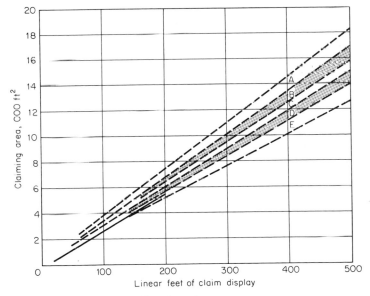

Areas for optimum configurations of:

A Round—sloping bed/remote feed
  Tee—flat bed/direct feed

B Tee and u-shape alternating @ 75'
  (flat bed/direct feed)

C Oval—flat bed/direct feed
  Oval—sloping bed/remote feed

D Tee and u-shape alternating @ 60'
  (flat bed/direct feed)

E ⊥⊥-shape flat bed/direct feed

Fig. 10-11 Estimating chart for total area of baggage claim facilities. (*Federal Aviation Administration [30].*)

services, interests and abilities of potential concessionaires, and rental rates. These generally include:

1. Food and beverage services, news and tobacco stands
2. Drug stores, and gift, clothing, and florist shops
3. Barber shops and shoe-shine stands
4. Counters for car rental and flight insurance companies
5. Public lockers and public and courtesy telephones
6. Manned or automated post offices
7. Amusement arcades and vending machines
8. Public restroom and nursery

Airport Operations and Services—Nonpublic Space

These facilities and services are normal to most public buildings and include the following:

1. Offices for airport management and staff functions, including police, medical and first aid, and building maintenance
2. Building mechanical systems, such as heating, ventilation, and air-conditioning
3. Communication facilities
4. Electrical equipment
5. Government offices for air traffic control, weather reporting, public health and immigration, and customs
6. Conference and press facilities

CONCEPT DEVELOPMENT

In this phase of the process, the block spaces determined in space programming are allocated in a general way to the terminal complex. There are a number of ways in which the facilities of the passenger terminal system are physically arranged, and in which the various passenger-processing activities are performed. Centralized passenger processing means that all the facilities of the system are housed in one building and used for processing all passengers using the building. Centralized processing facilities offer economies of scale in that many of the common facilities may be used to service a large number of aircraft gate positions.

Decentralized processing, on the other hand, means that the passenger facilities are arranged in smaller modular units and repeated in one or more buildings. Each unit is arranged around one or more aircraft gate positions and serves the passengers using those gate positions. There are four basic horizontal distribution concepts, as well as many variations or hybrids which include combinations of these basic concepts. Each can be used with varying degrees of centralization. These concepts are discussed below.

Horizontal Distribution Concepts

The following terminal concepts should be considered in the development of the terminal area plan. Sketches of the various concepts are shown in Fig. 10-12. Many airports have combined one or more terminal types.

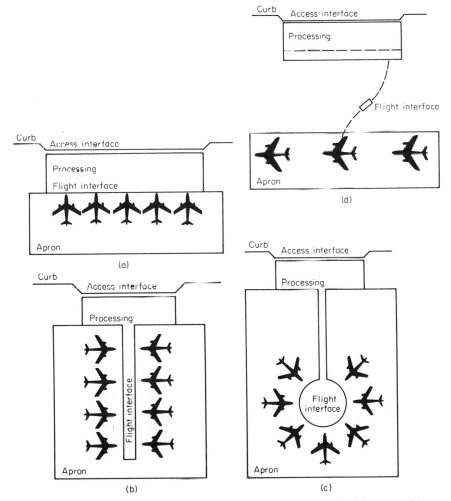

Fig. 10-12 Horizontal distribution concepts for passenger terminals. (*a*) Linear; (*b*) pier; (*c*) satellite; (*d*) transporter.

Pier or Finger Concept

The pier concept has an interface with aircraft along piers extending from the main terminal area. Aircraft are usually arranged around the axis of the pier in a parallel or nose-in parking alignment. Each pier has a row of aircraft gate positions on both sides, with a passenger concourse along the axis which serves as the departure lounge and circulation space for both enplaning and deplaning passengers. This concept usually allows for the expansion of the pier to provide additional aircraft parking positions without the expansion of the central passenger and baggage processing facility. Access to the terminal area is at the base of the connector, or the pier. If two or more piers are employed, the spacing between the two piers must provide for maneuvering of aircraft on one or two apron taxi lanes. When each pier serves a large number of gates, and the probability exists that two or more aircraft may frequently be taxiing between two piers and will be in conflict with one another, then two taxi lanes are advisable. Also, access from this taxiway system by two or more aircraft may require two apron edge taxiways to avoid delays.

The chief advantage of this concept is its ability to be expanded in incremental steps as aircraft or passenger demand warrant. It is also relatively economical in terms of capital and operating cost. Its chief disadvantages are its relatively long walking distance from curb front to aircraft and the lack of a direct curb front relationship to aircraft gate positions.

Satellite Concept

The satellite concept consists of a building surrounded by aircraft, which is separated from the terminal and is usually reached by means of a surface, underground, or above ground connector. The aircraft are normally parked in radial or parallel positions around the satellite. It often affords the opportunity for simple maneuvering and taxiing patterns for aircraft, but requires more apron area than other concepts. It can have common or separate departure lounges. Since enplaning and deplaning from the aircraft is accomplished from a common and often remote area, mechanical systems may be employed to transport passengers and baggage between terminal and satellite.

The main advantages of this concept lie in its adaptability to common departure lounge and check-in functions and the ease of aircraft maneuverability around the satellite structure. However, construction cost is relatively high due to the need to provide connecting concourses to the satellite. It lacks flexibility for expansion, and passenger walking distances are relatively long.

Linear, Frontal, or Gate Arrivals Concept

The simple linear terminal consists of a common waiting and ticketing area with exits leading to the aircraft parking apron. It is adaptable to airports with low airline activity which will usually have an apron providing close-in parking for three to six commercial passenger aircraft. The layout of the simple terminal should take into account the possibility of pier, satellite, or linear additions for terminal expansion. In the gate arrivals or frontal concept, aircraft are parked along the face of the terminal building. Concourses connect the various terminal functions with the aircraft gate positions. This concept offers ease of access and relatively short walking distances if passengers are delivered to a point near gate departure by vehicular circulation systems. Expansion may be accomplished by linear extension of an existing structure or by developing two or more terminal units with connectors.

These concepts provide direct access from curb front to aircraft gate positions and afford a high degree of flexibility for expansion. They do not provide convenient opportunities for the use of common facilities and, as this concept is expanded into separate buildings, may lead to high operating costs.

Transporter, Open-Apron, or Mobile Conveyance Concept

Aircraft and aircraft-servicing functions in the transporter concept are remotely located from the terminal. The connection to the terminal is provided by vehicular transport for enplaning and deplaning passengers. The characteristics of the transporter concept include flexibility in providing additional aircraft parking positions to accommodate increases in schedules or aircraft size, the capability to maneuver an aircraft in and out of a parking position under its own power, the separation of aircraft-servicing activities from the terminal, and reduced walking distances for the passenger.

This concept minimizes the level of capital costs since the building efficiently uses minimal departure lounge space and has gate positions for transporters rather than aircraft. It offers a high degree of flexibility in both operation and expansion. Aircraft maneuverability is very high, and a separation between landside and airside is very obvious. The use of mobile lounges to convey passengers to and from aircraft can increase passenger-processing time, and unless scheduling is carefully coordinated, unnecessary delays may result.

Concept Combinations and Variations

Combinations of concepts and variations are a result of changing conditions experienced from the initial conception of the airport throughout its lifespan. An airport may have many types of passenger activity, varying from originating and terminating passengers using the full range of terminal services to passengers using limited services on commuter or connecting flights.

Each requires a concept that differs considerably from the other. In time, the proportion of traffic handled by flights may change, necessitating modification or expansion of the facilities. Growth of aircraft size or a new combination of aircraft types servicing the airport will affect the type of concept. In the same way, physical limitations of the site may cause a pure conceptual form to be modified by additions or combinations of other concepts.

Combined concepts acquire certain of the advantages and disadvantages of each basic concept. A combination of concept types can be advantageous where more costly modifications would be necessary to maintain the original concept. For example, an airline might be suitably accommodated within an existing transporter concept terminal, while an addition is needed for a commuter operation with rapid turnovers which would be best served by a linear concept extension. In this situation, combined concepts would be desirable. The appearance of concept variations and combinations in a total apron terminal plan may reflect an evolving situation in which altering needs or growth have dictated the use of different concepts. Illustrations of the generation of various horizontal distributions in the concept development phase of Geneva Intercontinental Airport are shown in Fig. 10-13. Applications of several concepts to existing airports are shown in Fig. 10-14.

Vertical Distribution Concepts

The basis for distributing the primary processing activities in a passenger terminal among several levels is mainly to separate the flow of arriving and departing passengers. The decision on the number of levels a terminal facility should have depends primarily on the volume of passengers and the availability of land for expansion in the immediate vicinity. It may also be influenced by the type of traffic, such as domestic, international, or commuter passengers being processed, by the terminal area master plan, and by the horizontal processing concept chosen.

With a single-level system all processing of passengers and baggage occurs at the level of the apron. Separation between arriving and departing passenger flows is achieved horizontally. Amenities and administrative functions may occur on a second level. With this system, stairs are normally used to load passengers onto aircraft. This system is quite economical and is suitable for relatively low passenger volumes. The singe-level terminal is shown in Fig. 10-15a.

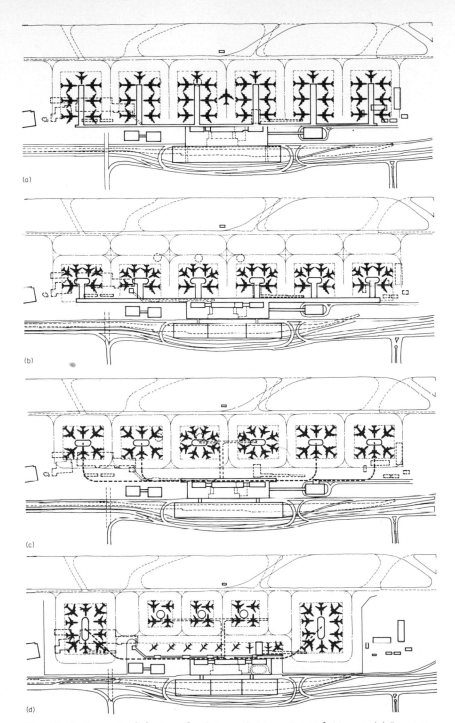

Fig. 10-13 Conceptual designs for Geneva Intercontinental Airport. (*a*) Long pier concept; (*b*) Short pier concept; (*c*) Satellite concept; (*d*) Satellite-linear combination concept.

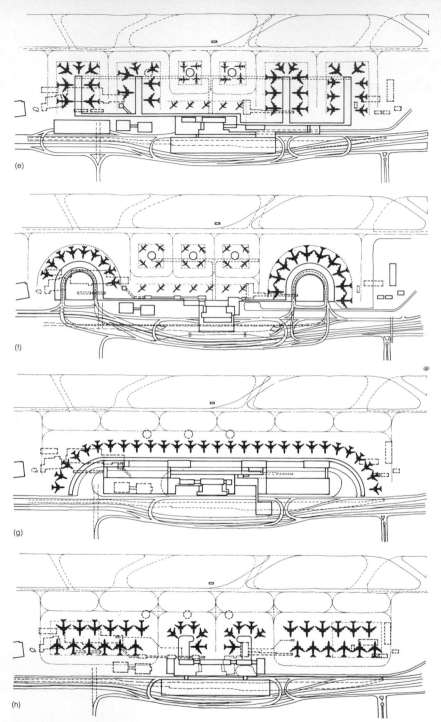

Fig. 10-13 (Continued) (*e*) Satellite-pier combination concept; (*f*) Gate arrivals-pier-satellite combination concept; (*g*) Linear concept; (*h*) Short pier-transport combination concept. (*Reynolds, Smith and Hills [19].*)

Two-level passenger terminal systems may be designed in a number of different ways. In one type, shown in Fig. 10-15*b*, the two levels are used to separate the passenger-processing and the baggage-handling areas. Thus, processing activities including baggage claim occur on the upper level, while airline operations and baggage-handling activities occur at the lower apron level. The advantage of raising the passenger-handling level is that it becomes compatible with aircraft doorsill heights, allowing convenient interface with the aircraft. Vehicular access occurs on the upper level to facilitate the interface with the processing system.

Another articulation of the two-level system separates the arriving and departing passenger streams. In this case departing passenger-processing activities occur on the upper level, and arriving passenger-processing including baggage claim occurs at the apron level. Airline operations and baggage handling also occur at the lower level. Vehicular access and parking occur at both levels, one for arrivals and one for departures, and parking can be surface or structural. An example of this design is shown in Fig. 10-15*c*.

Variations in these basic designs may occur when traffic volumes or the type of traffic so require. For example, for international airport terminals, a third mezzanine level may be needed for international passengers. Also, at large airports where intra-airport transportation systems operate, a special level may be needed to provide for these systems. Figure 10-16*a* shows a multilevel system with structural parking, intra-airport transportation, and underground mass-transit access. Figure 10-16*b* shows another multilevel system with integrated structural parking. In this variation more direct access to the processing component is attained by providing parking above the processing facility.

Based upon an examination of a large number of airports, it is possible to identify those concepts which are candidates for further consideration. Using the level of annual enplanements and the functional nature of the airport, as defined by the relative proportions of originating, terminating, through, and connecting passengers, Fig. 10-17 offers some guidance to the airport planner for the initial identification of appropriate horizontal and vertical distribution concepts. It should be noted, however, that in many instances the constraints of existing terminal facilities, land availability, and the ground access system may restrict the options which are viable alternatives for terminal expansion.

Prior to proceeding with the planning of the airport terminal system, an evaluation of the concepts which have evolved in the conceptual development phase of the project is undertaken to identify those alternatives which should be brought into the schematic design and design development phase of the project. To do this an overall rating of the various concepts relative to the design criteria is performed. The conceptual evaluation factors used for the Geneva airport are given in Table 10-2.

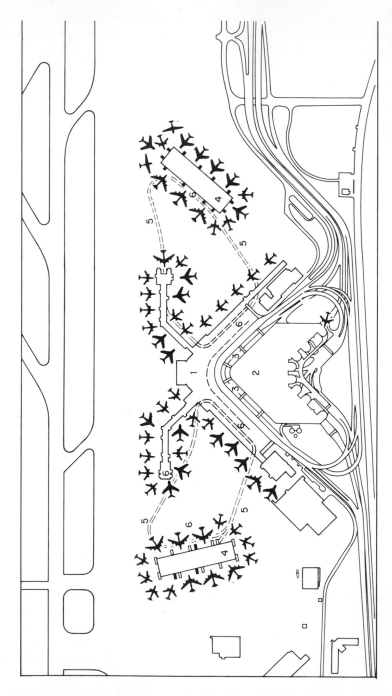

Fig. 10-14 (a) Example of satellite concept, Seattle–Tacoma Airport. (1) Main terminal; (2) parking structure; (3) bridges from parking to terminal; (4) satellites; (5) satellite transit; (6) shuttle station. (*AIA Journal.*)

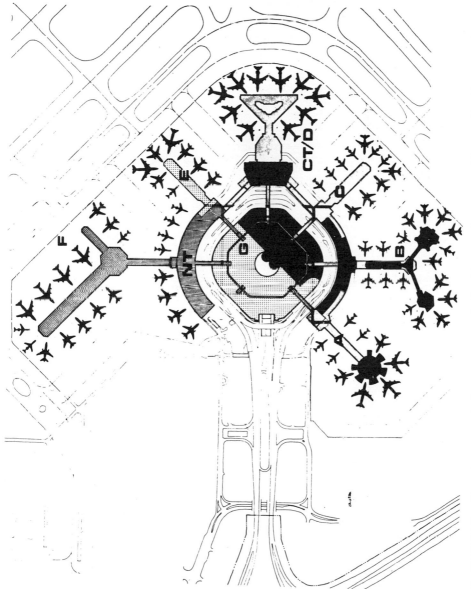

Fig. 10-14 (b) Satellite, pier, gate arrivals concept example, San Francisco International Airport. (*San Francisco Airports Commission.*)

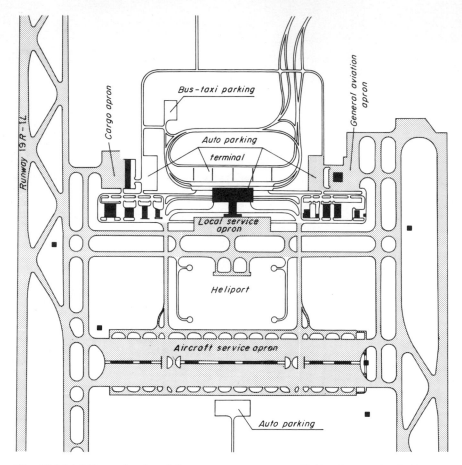

Fig. 10-14 (c) Example of mobile conveyance concept, Dulles International Airport. (*Federal Aviation Administration.*)

SCHEMATIC DESIGN

The schematic design process translates the concept development and overall space requirements into drawings which show the general size, location, and shape of the various elements in the terminal plan. Functional relationships between the components are established and evaluated. The adequacy of the overall space program is evaluated by airport users relative to their specific needs. This phase of the process specifically examines passenger and baggage flow routes through the system and seeks to examine the adequacy of the facility from the point of view of flow levels and flow conflicts.

Modeling techniques are usually employed in this phase of the process to identify passenger-processing, travel, and delay times, and the genera-

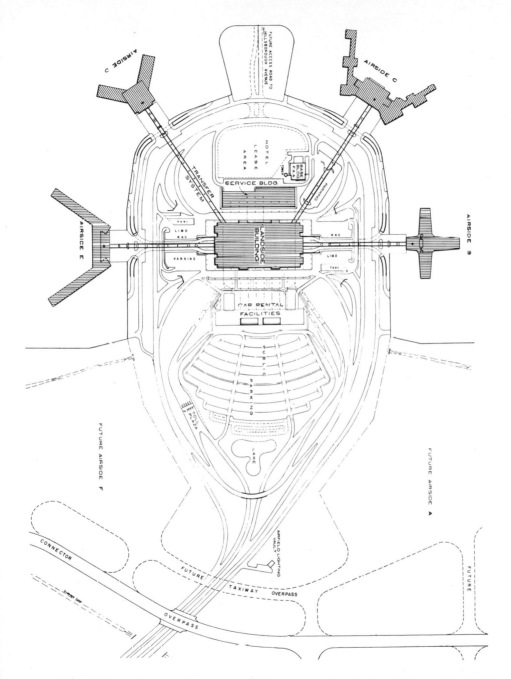

Fig. 10-14 (d) Example of satellite concept, Tampa International Airport. (*Reynolds, Smith and Hills.*)

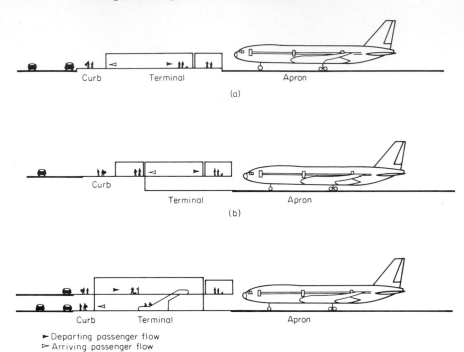

Fig. 10-15 Vertical distribution concepts. (*a*) Single level; (*b*) second-level loading; (*c*) two-level system. (*Federal Aviation Administration [36].*)

tion of lines at processing facilities. The main purpose for analyzing passenger- and baggage-handling systems is the determination of the extent and size of the facilities needed to provide a desired level of convenience to the passenger at reasonable cost. In this analysis alternative layouts can be studied to determine which is the most desirable.

Analysis Methods

A number of system analysis techniques have proved to be useful for the study of facilities for passengers and baggage. These include network models, queueing models, and simulation models.

Network Models

These models are particularly useful for representing and analyzing the interrelationships between the various components of a passenger- or baggage-processing system. For example, passenger processing can be illustrated as a network with the nodes representing service facilities and the links representing the travel paths and passenger splits. This type of

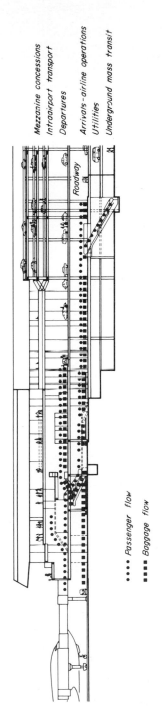

Mezzanine concessions
Intraairport transport
Departures
Arrivals - airline operations
Utilities
Underground mass transit

Roadway

•••• Passenger flow
■■■■ Baggage flow

Fig. 10-16 (a) Multilevel passenger-processing system, structural parking adjacent to terminal. (*Hamburg Airport Authority.*)

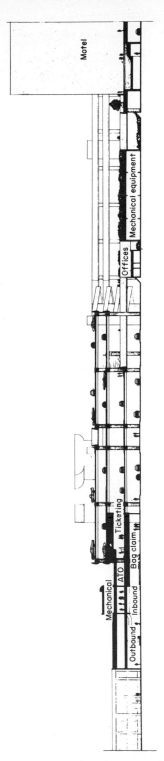

Motel

Offices

Mechanical equipment

Ticketing

Mechanical
ATO
Bag claim
Outbound
Inbound

Fig. 10-16 (b) Multilevel passenger-processing system, structural parking above processing area. (*Reynolds, Smith and Hills.*)

Airport size by enplaned pax/year	Concepts applicable				Physical aspects of concepts							
	Linear	Pier	Satellite	Transporter	Single level curb	Multi level curb	Single level terminal	Multi level terminal	Single level connector	Multi level connector	Apron level boarding	Aircraft level boarding
Feeder under 25,000	X				X		X				X	
Secondary 25,000 to 75,000	X				X		X				X	
75,000 to 200,000	X				X		X		X		X	
200,000 to 500,000	X	X			X		X		X		X	
Primary over 75% pax O/D 500,000 to 1,000,000	X	X	X		X		X		X	X	X	X
Over 25% pax transfer 500,000 to 1,000,000	X	X	X		X		X		X	X	X	X
Over 75% pax O/D 1,000,000 to 3,000,000		X	X	X	X	X			X	X	X	X
Over 25% pax transfer 1,000,000 to 3,000,000		X	X		X	X			X	X	X	X
Over 75% pax O/D over 3,000,000		X	X	X	X	X			X	X	X	X
Over 25% pax transfer over 3,000,000		X	X		X	X			X	X		X

Fig. 10-17 Applicable concepts for airport design. (*Federal Aviation Administration [35].*)

representation allows estimation of delays to the passenger at various locations within the terminal.

An example of a network that has been applied to the evaluation of arriving passenger delay is the critical path model (CPM) [33]. The CPM is used to coordinate the various activities that take place in the system, for handling both passengers and baggage. Nodes that represent critical activities, that is, those that take the greatest amount of time, are easily identified and can be analyzed in more detail to determine their effect on the overall performance of the system. The CPM diagram shown in Fig. 10-18 is a simplified example of the application of a network model. The figure describes the flow of arriving passengers from the aircraft to the baggage claim area and at the same time the flow of baggage between the same points. CPM analysis permits the coordination of these two flows and the determination of the critical links where modifications can lead to the overall improvement in system operations. It also permits scheduling the use of baggage claim areas and devices for a number of flight operations. The CPM analysis can also be applied to identify the critical activities for servicing an aircraft on an apron. Reductions in the time required for these activities may lead to an overall reduction in gate-occupancy time [33].

Another example of a network model which is useful in examining flow paths and overall demand on essential enplaning passenger processing components is shown in Fig. 10-19. In this diagram, the nodes represent service facilities, and the links represent the paths of passengers between these facilities. The diagram shown is generalized so that any level of peak-hour passenger demand can be imposed upon the system to determine overall passenger-processing times as well as delays at the specific service facilities. This is useful for determining critical components that restrict capacity. The numbers above the links represent the percentage of passengers moving from one facility to the other, and the numbers beneath the links represent the travel distance between the specific components. Such a technique may be applied to the entire terminal complex, to separate terminal units within the terminal complex, or to the facilities used by passengers of a particular airline [37]. The link node diagram shown in Fig.

TABLE 10-2 **Conceptual Development Rating Factors for Evaluation of Terminal Planning Concepts**

Passenger convenience:
Walking distance from curb to aircraft
Walking distance for transfer passengers
Walking distance from parking to aircraft
Ease of passenger orientation
Ease of passenger processing
Operational effectiveness:
Efficient taxiing routes
Ground flow coordination of vehicles and aircraft
Apron area maneuverability
Apron adaptation to future aircraft
Vehicular access flows
Direct routes to ancillary facilities
Expansion adaptability:
Ancillary facilities flexible land use
Staging adaptability
Visual character of increments
Gross terminal expandability
Expandability of terminal elements
Economic effectiveness:
Capital cost
Maintenance and operating costs
Ratio of revenue- to nonrevenue-producing areas

SOURCE: Reynolds, Smith and Hills [19].

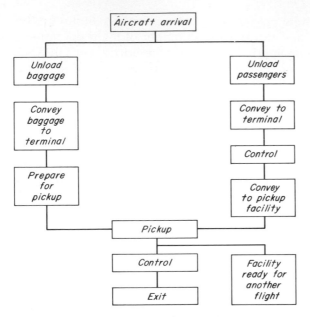

Fig. 10-18 Critical path model (CPM) of arriving passengers and baggage.

10-19 may be readily correlated to the plan of the enplaning level of the proposed North Terminal building at Fort Lauderdale–Hollywood International Airport presented in Fig. 10-20.

The analysis of the service time and waiting time at each facility can be obtained through either analytical queueing models or simulation.

Analytical Queueing Models

Queueing theory permits the estimation of delays and queue lengths for service facilities under specified levels of demand. The application of queueing theory yields useful estimates of processing and delay times from which the required sizes of facilities and operating costs may be derived.

Virtually all of the components of the passenger-handling system can be modeled as service facilities using queueing models. The diagram in Fig. 10-21 shows an example of the application of a deterministic queueing model to the operation of a ticketing counter. Curve $D(t)$ describes the manner by which passengers arrive at the counter for ticketing, the cumulative arrival distribution. Curve $S(t)$ is the cumulative service distribution, which describes the departure of passengers from the ticketing counter. Therefore, the vertical distance between the two curves represents the evolution of the length of the queue in front of the counter. This is useful for sizing the ticket lobby. The horizontal distance between the two curves represents the delays to passengers waiting to be ticketed. Thus the impact of adding ticket agents on delays to passengers and on the size of the queues can be evaluated. With this information it is possible to determine the feasibility of alternative operating strategies for the ticketing facility.

Diagrams similar to this may be constructed for each of the processors for the passenger- and baggage-handling systems and yield satisfactory results when the demand rate exceeds the service rate [13, 28].

For the analysis of component delay and queue length when the average demand rate over some period of time is less than the average service rate, probability theory is used to generate mathematical functions representative of the arrival and service performance of the system. To specify the mathematical formulation of this problem, it is necessary to define the arrival distribution, the service distribution, the number and use of the servers, and the service discipline. Many of the components which service passengers in the airport terminal exhibit a random or Poisson arrival process. The service characteristics are usually exponential or constant. In most cases, there is more than one channel for the performance

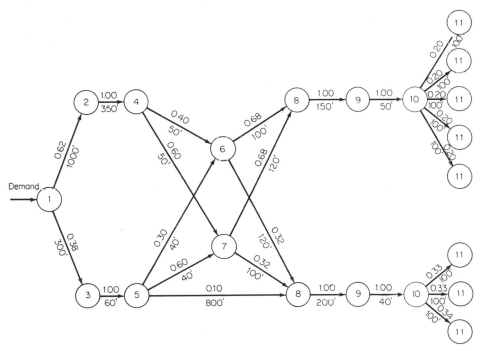

Fig. 10-19 Flow chart for departing passengers at North Terminal building for the proposed Fort Lauderdale–Hollywood International Airport. (1) Ground access system; (2) parking garage; (3) curb front; (4) elevator; (5) terminal entrance doors; (6) regular ticketing; (7) express baggage check-in; (8) security; (9) seat selection; (10) departure lounge; (11) boarding device.

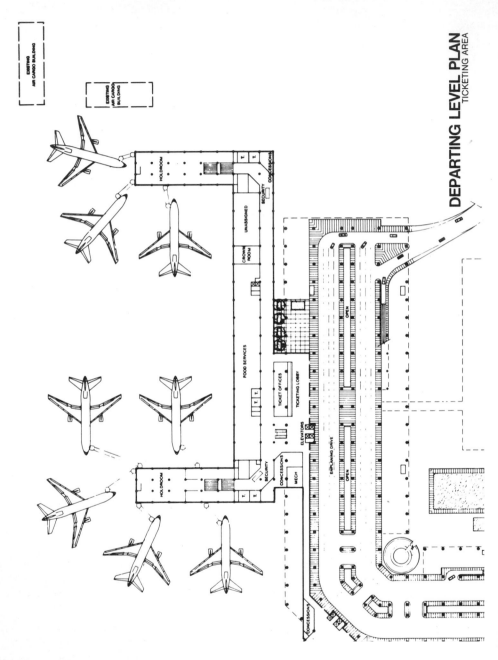

Fig. 10-20 Proposed North Terminal building departing level for Fort Lauderdale–Hollywood International Airport. (*Reynolds, Smith and Hills.*)

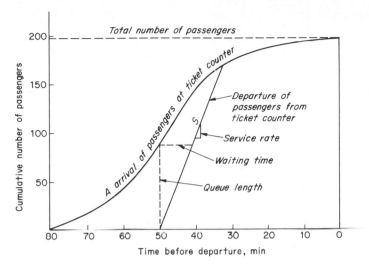

Fig. 10-21 Queueing model of a ticketing counter.

of passenger service, and the queueing mechanism is a first-come, first-served basis. Extensive research has been carried out in recent years to determine mathematical formulations which adequately represent the processing system [1, 9, 15, 37]. Because of the variability associated with passenger behavior at an airport, it is virtually impossible to obtain precise mathematical formulations for delay at processors. However, reasonable estimates of delay and the corresponding queue lengths are possible using simple formulations.

The simplest formulation is that of a single-station queueing system with a Poisson arrival distribution and either exponential or constant service times. For an exponential service time, the following relationships may be derived:

$$L_q = \frac{\lambda^2}{\mu(\mu - \lambda)} \tag{10-1}$$

$$W_t = \frac{\lambda}{\mu(\mu - \lambda)} \tag{10-2}$$

where L_q = average queue length at processor, passengers
$\quad W_t$ = average waiting time or delay time at processor
$\quad \lambda$ = arrival rate, passengers per unit of time
$\quad \mu$ = service rate, passengers per unit of time

If the system exhibits constant service times, then the following relationships are appropriate:

$$L_q = \frac{2\rho - \rho^2}{2(1 - \rho)} \tag{10-3}$$

$$W_t = \frac{\rho}{2\mu(1 - \rho)} \tag{10-4}$$

where ρ = ratio of arrival rate to service rate, which must be less than 1

Estimates of the waiting times and queue lengths for multiple-service channels may be obtained by proportioning the demand equally among processors with the same service characteristics. Better estimates may be obtained though the use of multiple-channel queueing models whose mathematical formulations may be found in the literature [15, 25].

A representation of the passenger delay at baggage claim facilities is given by the relationship [37]

$$W_t = E[t_2] + \frac{nT}{n + 1} - E[t_1] \tag{10-5}$$

where $E[t_2]$ = expected value of time when first piece of baggage arrives at claim area

$E[t_1]$ = expected value of time passengers arrive at claim area

n = number of pieces of baggage to be claimed by each passenger

T = length of time from arrival of first bag until arrival of last bag at claim device

Others have formulated models which show the buildup and the drop-off of passengers and baggage in the claim area, as indicated by Fig. 10-22 [15].

The use of a generalized probability density function, called the *Erlang distribution,* is recommended as a mechanism for evaluating the service characteristics of the various passenger component processors. By collecting a sample of data relative to a specific component, the constant in the Erlang distribution function can be calculated. This constant determines the particular functional relationship for the server. It is possible that this type of distribution may better describe the queueing characteristics of processors. This distribution has been used successfully in passenger terminal modeling [12]. Great care must be exercised in the application of mathematical models and the interpretation of the results. In most cases, the mathematical representation of the terminal system is best suited for the comparison of alternatives and the identification of those components in the system requiring detailed analyses.

Estimates for the observed range of service time for many of the passenger-processing components at an airport are given in Table 10-3.

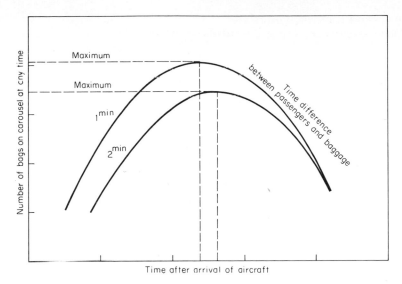

Fig. 10-22 Analytical model of baggage claim facility to determine claim device capacity. (*Pararas [15].*)

Simulation Models

These models become particularly useful when an analysis of the operation of the passenger-handling system is to be performed at a relatively detailed level, or when it is desired to analyze the operation of the system for extended periods of time. They are useful for the analysis of the whole system, as well as of parts of it. When some important inputs to analysis are unobtainable, such as possible future flight schedules, it is possible, with the use of computer simulation, to analyze the operation of the system under randomly generated inputs. Figure 10-23 shows an example of the application of a computer simulation to the analysis of passenger flow along a pier finger. The flow values indicated were generated on the basis of simulated future aircraft flight schedules.

Simulation is also useful when the analysis is to be repeated for varying operating conditions in order to perform sensitivity studies. Computers allow such repeated analyses, which would otherwise be prohibitively expensive and very time-consuming. Most computer systems have standard simulation packages available, which can be adapted to many physical planning problems, including airports.

It is important to note that computer simulation is not a substitute for analysis when information on the system is lacking. In order to construct a simulation model nearly as much detailed information about system operation is necessary as for other analytic techniques. The main feature of simulation is the high speed at which computers can perform lengthy

TABLE 10-3 **Observed Service Times for
Passenger-Processing Facilities at Airports**

Component type	Service rate, seconds per passenger	Standard deviation
Entrance and exit doors		
Automated with baggage	2.0–2.5	0.5
Automated without baggage	1.0–1.5	0.75
Manual with baggage	3.0–5.0	1.0
Manual without baggage	1.5–3.0	0.75
Stairways	3.0–4.0	1.0
Escalators	1.0–3.0	1.0
Moving sidewalks	1.0–3.0	1.0
Apron doors		
With stairs	4.0–8.0	2.0
Without stairs	3.0–7.0	1.5
Jetway	2.0–6.0	1.0
Ticketing and baggage		
Manual with baggage	180–240	60
Manual without baggage	100–200	30
Baggage only	30–50	10
Information	20–40	10
Automated with baggage	160–220	30
Automated without baggage	90–180	40
Security		
Hand check baggage	30–60	15
Automated	30–40	10
Seat selection		
Single flights	25–60	20
Multiple flights	35–60	15
Rental car		
Check-in	120–240	60
Check-out	180–300	90
Automated check-in	60–90	20
Baggage claim		
Manual	10–15	8
Automated carousel	5–10	5
Automated race track	5–10	5
Automated tee	6–12	5

SOURCES: Various airport studies.

calculations. In the analysis of system operations computer simulation should be used with caution, and several runs made so that the statistical reliability of the results may be determined.

Simulation techniques have been studied by the FAA [9, 18] and have been used in many studies to determine facility needs. An outline of the flow of an enplaning passenger through the airport system which can be modeled by the FAA simulation model is given in Fig. 10-24. In the

schematic design phase of the planning project at Fort Lauderdale–
Hollywood International Airport, simulation was used to determine the
parking requirements at the airport and the number of parking toll-
collection facilities needed at the exit [22]. The inputs into the simulation
were the airline flight schedule, the distribution of the total number of
parkers relative to the flight schedule, and the historical distribution of
parking duration as obtained from the analysis of parking ticket stubs.
Alternative flight schedules were used to generate the arrival distribution
at the parking facility, and the parking duration distribution, shown in Fig.
10-25, was used to generate the random service times required by the
arrivals. As a result of the simulation it was possible to determine the
peaking characteristics of arrivals and departures at the parking garage, and
the accumulation of vehicles within the parking facility.

The following steps are recommended in the design of a simulation
model for application to airport terminal projects [36]:

1. Define the scope of the simulation in terms of the questions to be
answered, the components to be included, and the level of detail required.

2. Specify the required output so that an interpretation of the results
will resolve the questions to be addressed.

3. Structure the model so that the abstract representation of the
components in the model and the events and interactions between components are indicative of terminal performance.

4. Define the input data and their variability.

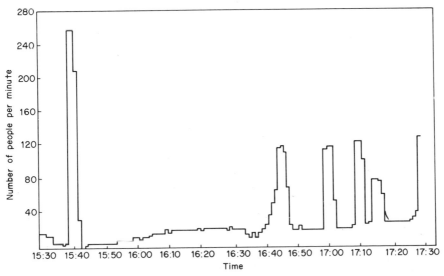

Fig. 10-23 Simulation results of pier finger passenger flows. (*Smith and Murphy [29].*)

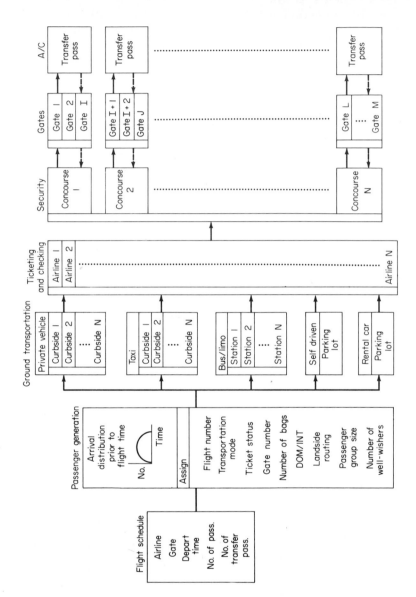

Fig. 10-24 Flow chart for enplaning passenger simulation model. *(Federal Aviation Administration [9].)*

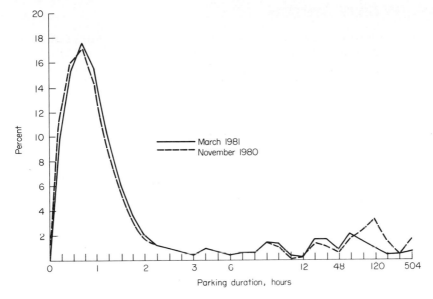

Fig. 10-25 Parking duration at Fort Lauderdale–Hollywood International Airport. (*Aviation Planning Associates, Inc. [22].*)

5. Once the model has been developed, verify through testing on actual systems.

6. Apply the model and modify the facility design in accordance with the model results.

7. Review the findings and design relative to the degree of variability in the output and through reasonableness checks.

DESIGN DEVELOPMENT

The final planning phase in terminal projects is called *design development*. In this phase the size and character of the project are fixed and checked against the findings and recommendations in the prior phases of the project. Acceptance of the project by the airport owner, tenants, and airlines is the final product of this phase. Capital budgeting, operating, maintenance, and administrative costs over the lifetime of the project are determined, and a revenue plan is adopted. Agreements are made on rate and charge structures for the airlines, concessionaires, and other tenants. The project moves on toward implementation through the development of construction documents, bid letting and acceptance, and construction following this phase of planning.

THE APRON-GATE SYSTEM

The apron provides the connection between the terminal buildings and the airfield. It includes aircraft-parking areas, called *ramps*, and aircraft circulation and taxiing areas for access to these ramps. On the ramp, aircraft park in areas designated as gates. The discussion in this section is limited to the apron-gate area.

The size of the apron-gate area depends on three factors, namely, the number of aircraft gates, the size of the gates, and the aircraft parking layout at each gate.

Number of Gates

As in the case with other airport facilities, the number of gates is determined in such a way that a predetermined hourly flow of aircraft can be accommodated. Thus, the number of gates required depends on the number of aircraft to be handled during the design hour, and on the amount of time each aircraft occupies a gate.

The number of aircraft that need to be handled simultaneously is a function of the traffic volume at the airport. As mentioned earlier, it is customary to use the estimated peak-hour volume as the input for estimating the number of gates. However, in order to achieve a balanced airport design, this volume should not exceed the capacity of the runways.

The amount of time an aircraft occupies a gate is referred to as *gate-occupancy time*. It depends on aircraft size and on the type of operation, that is, whether it is a through flight or a turnaround flight. Aircraft parked at a gate are there for passenger and baggage processing and for aircraft servicing and preparation for flight. Larger aircraft normally occupy gates for a longer time than small aircraft. This is because large aircraft require more time for cabin cleaning and refueling. Cabin cleaning and refueling are normally the critical activities that determine gate-occupancy time. The type of operation also affects gate-occupancy time by affecting service requirements. Thus an aircraft on a through flight may require little or no servicing, and consequently, the gate-occupancy time can be as low as 20 to 30 min. On the other hand, an aircraft on a turnaround flight will require complete servicing, resulting in a gate-occupancy time of 40 to 60 min. The table shown in Fig. 10-26 lists the activities that normally take place during a turnaround stop, together with a typical time schedule for these activities.

In calculating the required number of gates, these steps should be followed:

1. Identify the types of aircraft to be accommodated and the percentage of each type in the total mix.

2. Identify the gate-occupancy time for each type.

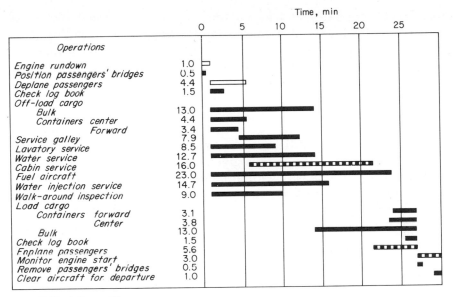

I••• Critical time path

Fig. 10-26 Typical time schedule of aircraft servicing activities at gate. (*Federal Aviation Administration* [36].)

3. Compute the weighted average gate-occupancy time.

4. Determine the total hourly design volume and the percentages of aircraft which are arrivals and departures.

5. Compute the hourly design volume of arrivals and departures by multiplying the percentages of arrivals and departures by the total hourly design volume.

6. Using the larger number of arrivals or departures, the following formula gives the number of gates required:

$$G = \frac{CT}{U} \tag{10-5}$$

where G = number of gates

C = design volume for arrivals or departures, in aircraft per hour

T = weighted average gate-occupancy time, in hours

U = gate utilization factor

The utilization factor used in this formula usually varies between 0.5 and 0.8. This factor must be applied, as it is unlikely that all gates available at a terminal building will be used 100 percent of the time. This is due to the fact that aircraft maneuvering in and out of a gate often block other aircraft attempting to move into or out of their gates. It is also caused by the fact that aircraft schedules often lead to time gaps between the departure of one aircraft and the arrival of another using the same gate. Such time gaps may be too small for the gate to be useful for other flights, thus causing it to be idle. At airports where gates are used mutually by all airlines, the utilization factor should vary between 0.6 and 0.8. At airports where groups of gates are used exclusively by different airlines, the utilization factor drops to about 0.5 or 0.6. The determination of the number of gates needed at an airport should be subjected to the analysis techniques given in Chap. 8 and to the planned gate utilization chart generated by tenant airlines. An example of a gate utilization chart is given in Fig. 10-27.

Gates at most airports vary within the range of 3 to 5 gates per million annual passengers. The total number of gates may have to be modified if not all gates can handle all types of aircraft. This is particularly important at airports where the aircraft mix includes a considerable amount of large jets together with small aircraft. In such situations, and when data are available,

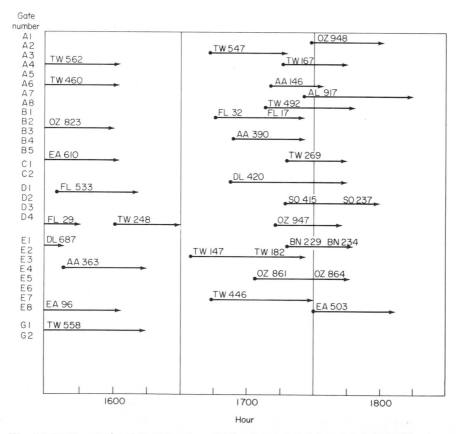

Fig. 10-27 Terminal gate activity chart. (*Federal Aviation Administration [35].*)

it would be preferable to compute gate requirements separately for the different types of aircraft, keeping in mind that the large gates can be used to handle small aircraft, while the reverse is not true. It is also desirable to calculate the gate requirements separately for different types of traffic. For example, at a large international airport separate calculations may be performed for domestic gates, international gates, and charter gates.

Gate Size

The size of a gate depends on the size of aircraft which it is to accommodate and on the type of parking used, that is, nose-in, parallel, or angled parking. The size of the aircraft determines the space required for parking as well as for maneuvering. Furthermore, the aircraft size determines the extent and size of the servicing equipment that needs to be provided to service the aircraft. The type of parking used at the gates affects the gate size since the area required to maneuver into and out of a gate varies depending on the way the aircraft is parked.

In view of the large number of factors that affect the size and exact layout of gates, it is desirable to consult the airlines at an early stage in the design process in order to determine the manner in which they plan to maneuver aircraft and the types of servicing facilities they plan to use.

The design of the gates can be worked out with the aid of procedures and dimensions provided by the FAA [5] and the International Air Transport Association [11]. Included in these references are diagrams which show various dimensions required for different types of aircraft and various parking and maneuvering conditions. An example of such a chart prepared for a Boeing 747-200 aircraft is illustrated in Fig. 10-28.

While a detailed design of aircraft gates requires the aid of charts, such as the one in Fig. 10-27, it is sufficient for preliminary planning to adopt uniform dimensions between centers of gates and to use these for sizing the apron gate area. The dimensions depend on the type of aircraft. The typical dimensions for the case where aircraft enter a gate under their own power and are pushed out by a tractor or taxi out are given in Table 10-4.

A typical preliminary design layout using uniform dimensions is given in Fig. 10-29.

Aircraft-Parking Type

Aircraft-parking type refers to the manner in which the aircraft is positioned with respect to the terminal building and to the manner in which aircraft maneuver in and out of parking positions. It is an important factor, affecting the size of the parking positions and consequently the apron-gate area. Aircraft can be positioned at various angles with respect to the terminal building line and can maneuver in and out of parking positions

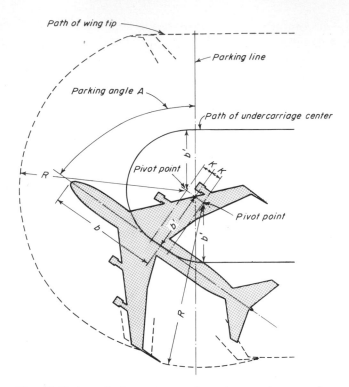

Fig. 10-28 Aircraft dimensions and turning requirements for gate position design, Boeing 747-200. Body length L = 232 ft; wingspan S = 196 ft; nose to centerline of main gear b = 110 ft; forward roll K = 10 ft; turning radius R: minimum 168 ft, maximum 205 ft; pivot point to centerline of airplane b': minimum 60 ft, maximum 100 ft; clearance between aircraft and building C = 35 ft. (*Federal Aviation Administration [5].*)

either under their own power or with the aid of towing equipment. With aircraft towing it is possible to reduce the size of parking positions. It is advisable, in choosing among alternative parking types, to consult with the airline in question, as different airlines have different preferences for the available systems. It is also advisable, in adopting a parking type, to take into consideration the objective of protecting passengers from the adverse elements of noise, jet blast, and weather, and the operating and maintenance costs of needed ground equipment.

The aircraft-parking types which have been successfully used at a variety of airports and should be evaluated in any airport planning study include nose-in, angled nose-in, angled nose-out, and parallel. These parking types are shown in Fig. 10-30 and are discussed separately below.

Nose-in Parking

In this configuration the aircraft is parked perpendicular to the building line, with the nose as close to the building as permissible. The aircraft maneuvers into the parking position under its own power. In order to leave the gate, the aircraft has to be towed out a sufficient distance to allow it to proceed under its own power. The advantages of this configuration are that it requires the smallest gate area for a given aircraft, causes lower noise levels as there is no powered turning movement near the terminal building, sends no jet blast toward the building, and facilitates passenger loading as the nose is near the building. Its disadvantages include the need for towing equipment and the nose is too far from the building to effectively use the rear doors for passenger loading.

Angled Nose-In Parking

This configuration is similar to the nose-in configuration, except that the aircraft is not parked perpendicular to the building. The configuration has the advantage of allowing the aircraft to maneuver in and out of the gate under its own power. However, it requires a larger gate area than the nose-in configuration and causes a higher noise level.

TABLE 10-4 **Comparison of Apron Parking Envelope Dimensions for Aircraft Push-Out and Taxi-Out Gate Use for Nose-In Configuration**

	Push out*			Taxi out*		
Group A/C	L	W	Area, yd²	L	W	Area, yd²
A FH-227	103 ft 1 in	115 ft 2 in	1319	148 ft 10 in	140 ft 2 in	2318
YS-11B	106 ft 3 in	124 ft 11 in	1474	171 ft 0 in	149 ft 11 in	2850
BAC-111	123 ft 6 in	113 ft 6 in	1557	130 ft 0 in	138 ft 6 in	2001
DC-9-10	134 ft 5 in	109 ft 5 in	1634	149 ft 2 in	134 ft 5 in	2228
B DC-9-21, 30	149 ft 4 in	113 ft 4 in	1880	149 ft 0 in	138 ft 4 in	2290
727 (all)	173 ft 2 in	128 ft 0 in	2463	194 ft 0 in	153 ft 0 in	3298
737 (all)	120 ft 0 in	113 ft 0 in	1507	145 ft 4 in	138 ft 0 in	2228
C B-707 (all)	172 ft 11 in	165 ft 9 in	3188	258 ft 0 in	190 ft 9 in	5468
B-720	156 ft 9 in	150 ft 10 in	2627	228 ft 0 in	175 ft 10 in	4454
DC-8-43, 51	170 ft 9 in	162 ft 5 in	3081	211 ft 10 in	187 ft 5 in	4411
D DC-8-61, 63	207 ft 5 in	168 ft 5 in	3882	252 ft 4 in	193 ft 5 in	5423
E L-1011	188 ft 8 in	175 ft 4 in	3676	263 ft 6 in	200 ft 4 in	5865
DC-10	192 ft 3 in	185 ft 4 in	3959	291 ft 0 in	210 ft 4 in	6801
F B 747	241 ft 10 in	215 ft 8 in	5795	328 ft 0 in	240 ft 8 in	8771

* L = perpendicular to face of building; W = parallel to face of building

SOURCE: Federal Aviation Administration [36].

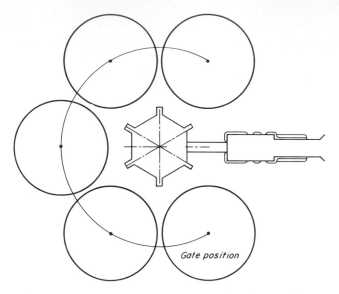

Fig. 10-29 Layout of United Airlines aircraft parking configuration at San Francisco International Airport using uniform gate position dimensions.

Angled Nose-Out Parking

In this configuration the aircraft is parked with its nose pointing away from the terminal building. Like the angled nose-in configuration, it has the advantage of allowing aircraft to maneuver in and out of gate positions without towing. It does require a larger gate area than the nose-in position, but less than the angled nose-in. A disadvantage of this configuration is that the breakaway jet blast and noise are pointed toward the building when the aircraft starts its taxiing maneuver.

Parallel Parking

This configuration is the easiest to achieve from the aircraft maneuvering standpoint. In this case noise and jet blast are minimized, as there are no sharp turning maneuvers required. It does require, however, a larger gate position area, particularly along the terminal building frontage. Another advantage of this configuration is that both forward and aft aircraft doors can be used for loading and unloading passengers, although relatively long loading bridges may be required.

It is evident that no one parking type can be considered ideal. For any planning situation, all the advantages and disadvantages of the different systems have to be evaluated, taking into consideration the preference of the airline that will be using the gates. The trend, however, is toward nose-in parking because of the saving in area and the reduction of noise and blast. Recent experimentation with power-out from the nose-in position is yielding savings in operating and maintenance costs for ground support equipment.

Apron Layout

Another factor that affects apron size and installation requirements is the apron layout. This refers to the manner in which the apron is arranged around the terminal building. The apron layout depends directly on the way the aircraft gate positions are grouped around the building and on the circulation and taxiing patterns dictated by the relative locations of the terminal buildings and the airfield system.

Aircraft are grouped adjacent to the terminal building in a variety of ways, depending on the horizontal terminal concept used. These groupings are referred to as *parking systems* and are classified as the frontal or linear system, the finger or pier system, the satellite system, and the open-apron or transporter system. These were discussed earlier.

The choice of aircraft-parking system is, naturally, strongly influenced by the horizontal passenger-processing concept adopted. For each there are positive and negative attributes that must be weighed against each other. While the open-apron system has the advantage of separating the aircraft and the terminal building from one another, it does require buses or mobile lounges for the conveyance of passengers between them. These vehicles use the apron, and their circulation patterns need careful planning to avoid interference with the flow of aircraft and other service vehicles. While the finger system allows the efficient expansion of gate positions and the efficient use of terminal building space, it may lead to long passenger

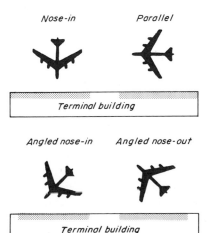

Fig. 10-30 Aircraft parking types. (*International Air Transportation Association [11].*)

walking distances if allowed to become excessively long. The frontal system is suitable for the gate-arrival processing concept. Other features of these systems were discussed earlier in this chapter.

Apron Circulation

In designing the apron layout it is important to take into account aircraft circulation, particularly the movement of aircraft within the apron-gate area and from this area to the taxiways. When the traffic volume is high, it is desirable to provide a taxi lane on the periphery of the apron. It is also important to allow sufficient space to permit easy access of aircraft to gates. This is particularly important when pier fingers are used for aircraft parking and the fingers are parallel to each other. Sufficient space must be provided between the fingers to allow aircraft ready access to the gates. The separation between fingers depends on their length and on the size of the aircraft to be accommodated. The longer the finger, the more aircraft gates can be accommodated. However, the increase in the number of gates may necessitate the provision of two taxi lanes instead of one between the fingers to provide circulation without excessive delay. One taxi lane will probably suffice when there are no more than five or six gates on each side of a finger. A large number of gates may require two taxi lanes.

Passenger Conveyance to Aircraft

Depending on the passenger-processing system used, the type of aircraft parking, and the parking system layout, any of three methods of conveyance can be used between the building and the aircraft. These are walking on the apron, walking through aircraft building connectors such as bridges, and mobile conveyance using any of a variety of apron vehicles.

The first method can be employed with all processing and parking systems. However, as the number of parking positions and the apron size increase, it becomes impractical to use walking for the conveyance of passengers. The economic appeal of this method is overcome by the need to protect the passengers from the elements and from the hazards of walking on the apron.

The second method can be employed for all systems other than where open-apron parking is used. A variety of fixed and movable loading systems have been developed for passenger conveyance. Most common among these are the nose bridges, which are short connectors suitable for use when the aircraft door comes close to the building, such as with nose-in parking. Another common system is the telescoping loading bridge. These have the flexibility of extending from the building to reach the aircraft door and of swinging to accommodate different types of aircraft. A typical boarding bridge is shown in Fig. 10-31.

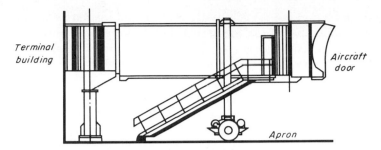

Fig. 10-31 Typical aircraft loading bridge.

The third system is suitable when open-apron parking is used. Here conveyance can be accomplished either with buses or with mobile lounges. With buses, passengers have to walk upstairs to aircraft doors. With the mobile lounges, this need is eliminated, as the lounge is capable of direct interface with aircraft doors through vertical movement. The mobile lounge thus provides for complete passenger protection. There is, of course, a considerable cost difference between the mobile lounge and the conventional bus. A typical mobile lounge is shown in Fig. 10-32.

Apron Utility Requirements

Aircraft need to be serviced at their respective gates. Thus certain fixed installations may be required on the apron. Apron congestion is always a problem, and hence, there is a definite trend at larger airports toward replacing mobile servicing equipment with fixed facilities.

Aircraft Fueling

Aircraft are fueled at the apron by fuel trucks, fueling pits, and hydrant systems. At the smaller and even the larger airports the use of fuel trucks is prevalent, but the pattern is changing in favor of the hydrant system at airports requiring large amounts of fuel.

The principal advantage of fuel trucks is their flexibility. Aircraft can be fueled anywhere on the apron, the units can be added or taken away

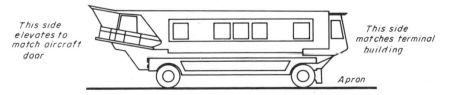

Fig. 10-32 Typical mobile lounge. (*Federal Aviation Administration* [36].)

according to need, and the system is relatively economical insofar as airport management and airline operations are concerned. There are, however, disadvantages associated with the use of fuel trucks. Large jet transports require a considerable amount of fuel, from nearly 8000 U.S. gal for the Boeing 727-100 to almost 50,000 U.S. gal for the Boeing 747-100. Two refueler units are normally required, one under each wing. For the large jets, standby units are sometimes required if the fuel requirements are in excess of two units. This means that there are a large number of vehicles on the apron during peak periods, creating a potential hazard of collision with personnel, other vehicles, and aircraft. Since each truck carries a considerable quantity of fuel, it also constitutes a potential fire hazard when moving around on an apron where a number of other activities are taking place. Trucks are large and awkward and take up valuable space in the operations area. When a truck is empty, it must return to the storage area for refueling before it can be used again. Thus extra trucks must be provided for use during the time when other trucks are being reloaded. When refueling trucks are not in use, parking space must be provided for these vehicles. Modern refuelers are approximately 40 ft in length and weigh as much as 83,000 lb. The capacity of the larger trucks is approximately 8000 gal. For the larger refuelers axle loads are in excess of the legal limits on highways, and consequently, the airport designer must provide adequate pavement strengths to support these vehicles.

Another method of fueling is to install pipelines from a central fuel storage area located adjacent to the landing area to pits located at the gate positions on the apron. Each pit contains a meter, air separator, hose, reel, and filter. Fuel is transferred to the pits by pumps located at the storage tanks. The pits must be located relatively near the fuel intakes in the wings of the aircraft. When an aircraft has been positioned on the apron, the pit cover is opened, the hose reeled out, and fueling begins. The advantages of fuel pits are that a continuous supply of fuel is available at all times, it is safely carried underground, and trucking is eliminated from the apron. The disadvantages are that for each pit a separate meter, filter, and reel are required; thus there is duplication of equipment. Also, a change in future operations at the airport may require a major change in installation. Because a concrete-pad steel pit is required, maintenance costs can be high due to intrusion of moisture. If pits are used, they should be properly ventilated to avoid the accumulation of hazardous fuel vapors.

Pits are considered satisfactory when the rates of fuel are small, but for the high rates required by large turbojet aircraft the equipment is much more bulky. Consequently a much larger pit with a heavy metal cover is required. For this reason, pits are not normally used for fueling large aircraft.

The hydrant system accomplishes the same objectives as the pits, but is simpler insofar as installation is concerned. For this reason, it is far more popular. Essentially, the hydrant system consists of the same elements as the fuel pits, except that the pit is replaced by a special valve mounted in a box in the pavement and flush with the surface, as shown in Fig. 10-33. The hose reel, meter, filter, and air eliminator are contained in a mobile self-propelled or towed hydrant dispenser. One end of the hose has a specially designed valve which is coupled to the valve installed in the pavement. This hose feeds into the meter, filter, and air eliminator, from which another hose, usually on a reel, is led to the fuel intakes on the aircraft.

The principal advantages of the hydrant system are the same as those for the pit system. Additional advantages are eliminating the need for duplicating the hose reel, meter, and filter which are required in each pit, eliminating the need for maintaining pits, and providing a little more flexibility insofar as the positioning of aircraft is concerned. The principal disadvantage is that vehicles are not entirely removed from the apron. However, because of their small size, hydrant dispensers reduce possible collision damage to a minimum.

The amounts of fuel required at many airports are so large that, regardless of the type of fueling system used, a central fuel storage area in the vicinity of the landing area is required. If pits or the hydrant system are used, provision must be made for installing pipes from the storage area to the apron.

The location of the hydrant valves at an individual gate will depend

Fig. 10-33 Typical hydrant valve. (*Standard Oil Company of California.*)

upon the location of the fueling connections in the wings of the aircraft occupying the gate. It is desirable that the hose line from the hydrant dispenser or pit to the intakes in the wings not exceed 20 to 30 ft. If a wide variety of aircraft are to be serviced at a gate position, the precise spacing of the hydrant valves should be established in consultation with the airlines. The number of hydrants required per gate position depends not only on the type of aircraft, but also on the number of grades of fuel required. Each grade of fuel requires a separate layout.

At a number of airports, hydrant systems are installed by oil companies which contract for fuel with a particular airline or airlines. It is not uncommon to have the hydrant system and fuel trucks operate simultaneously at the same airport. The trend at the large airports is definitely toward the hydrant system.

Electric Power

Electric power is required on the apron for the servicing of aircraft prior to engine starting. External electric power is also often required for starting the engines. Power requirements vary widely for different aircraft. Consequently it is necessary to consult with the airlines concerning this matter. Power can be supplied by mobile units or by fixed installations in the pavement. The latter is preferable since it removes the need for a vehicle and to some extent reduces noise which emanates from a motor generator set. For a fixed installation, the most satisfactory technique is to bury conduits under the apron, terminating them at supply points some distance from the hydrant valves, but convenient to the aircraft.

Recently, there has been a trend toward fixed ground power and air-conditioning systems using terminal power sources. The need for these facilities has grown due to the costs of providing power and conditioned air to aircraft during servicing times at the apron gate by using the power generated by the auxiliary power unit on the aircraft. Considerable operating cost economies have been reported in the use of such systems [21].

Aircraft Grounding Facilities

Grounding facilities will be required on the apron to provide protection of parked aircraft and fuel trucks from static discharge, particularly during fueling operations. The location of the grounding facility will be governed by the location of the hydrant valves. With high fueling rates it is essential that grounding facilities be provided.

Apron Lighting and Marking

Adequate lighting and marking are essential on an apron. Wherever possible, each gate should be floodlighted. Floodlighting removes the need for mobile equipment to use headlights, which experience has shown to cause confusion and glare. A system of elevated lights appears to offer the best method of providing apron illumination. Where pier fingers are utilized, the lights can be attached to the fingers. Lighting should be located so as to provide uniform illumination of the apron area, yet not cause glare to the pilot.

When personnel are servicing an aircraft, there is a need for lighting its underside and far side, if the floodlights do not provide the necessary illumination. This can be accomplished by installing flush lights in the pavement. When lights of this type are installed, they should be arranged so as not to confuse the pilot insofar as guidance to the gate position is concerned.

Painted guide lines have proved very desirable as aids to maneuvering aircraft accurately on the apron. The best guide appears to be a single line, usually of yellow color, which is followed by the nose gear of the aircraft. A typical layout is shown in Fig. 10-34. It is recognized that a single line will

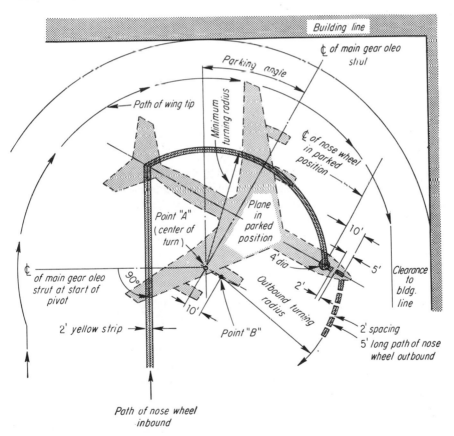

Fig. 10-34 Typical painted guidelines at gate positions.

not provide precise guidance for a variety of different aircraft. Usually the guide line is painted for the most critical aircraft using a particular gate position. Smaller aircraft can use the same lines and maneuver without difficulty, especially if personnel on the ground are available to direct the pilot. Because of possible fuel spillage, it is desirable to paint guide lines with special resistant paint in areas where spillage might occur.

CARGO-HANDLING CONSIDERATIONS

At large airports, where the cargo volume is high, it is usually processed at a cargo terminal that is separate from the passenger terminal. However, the increase in large jet aircraft operations has led to a rise in the occurrence of mixed passenger and cargo operations. This is due to the fact that large jet aircraft have a high cargo-carrying capacity in excess of what is needed to carry passengers and baggage. Therefore, it is essential when planning the apron-gate area to take cargo-handling considerations into account.

Cargo is composed of air freight and airmail. Airmail is usually conveyed by the carrier to a central airport airmail facility. Air freight is conveyed between the aircraft and the cargo terminal either by the carrier or by an air-freight forwarder. Incoming air freight carried on board a passenger-carrying aircraft usually has to be unloaded at the gate and transported to the cargo terminal. Outgoing air freight is conveyed from the cargo terminal before the scheduled departure and has to be stored in designated areas for expedient loading when the aircraft is ready. This operation requires a large area on the apron adjacent to the gate.

Another requirement related to cargo handling is for roadways which facilitate the movement of cargo trucks between the apron-gate area and the cargo terminal. Roadways are sometimes designated for cargo trucks to separate them from the movement of other apron service vehicles [38].

The use of efficient loading equipment is necessary for the loading and unloading of passenger aircraft carrying cargo. This is important in order to avoid delays to passenger operations. Sophisticated aircraft-loading equipment has been developed to cope with the increasing levels of air cargo. Most important are those that are loader-transporter combinations, which have the advantage of reducing the amount of equipment on the apron. Lift-type loaders are used to interface with a variety of aircraft with varying doorsill heights.

Another trend affecting the technology of air-cargo handling is the development of lower deck containers for different types of aircraft. Containers have the advantage that they can be loaded and prepared off the airport, transported directly to the aircraft, and easily loaded on and off the aircraft. As an example, Fig. 10-35 shows an LD-3 container which is designed for wide-body jets. This container has a payload of 2500 lb, with a

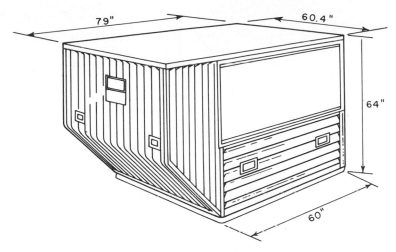

Fig. 10-35 LD-3 cargo container. (*R. J. Roche [38].*)

usable volume of 155 ft³. The lower deck of a DC-10 can be configured to carry a total of 24 such containers, or a total of 60,000 lb. A Boeing 747 can carry up to 30 such containers in the lower deck.

PROTECTION FROM JET BLAST

Inconvenience, discomfort, and even injury may be caused to passengers boarding aircraft on foot and to airline personnel if they are subject to wake velocities greater than 35 mi/h [7]. Likewise wake velocities averaging more than 20 mi/h on a moving vehicle are considered hazardous. Reduction of wake velocities to tolerable limits is accomplished by means of devices commonly referred to as blast fences.

Blast fences are required in areas where engine maintenance checks are made and at the takeoff ends of runways, if the ends are in close proximity to highways, streets, housing, or other developments. Although the primary purpose of blast fences is to reduce wake velocities to tolerable limits, they are also effective in diverting smoke ejected by the engines.

The maximum velocity versus distance for three power settings, takeoff, breakaway, and idle, are shown in [7] for the DC-8, Boeing 727, Boeing 747, and DC-10. These curves are helpful for determining the potential velocities to the rear of the aircraft.

Several types of blast fences are on the market. They can be classified as single-curved vane or multiple-curved vane, and are shown in Fig. 10-36. A comprehensive program for evaluating various types of blast fences was conducted by the Corps of Engineers [26]. The field tests indicated

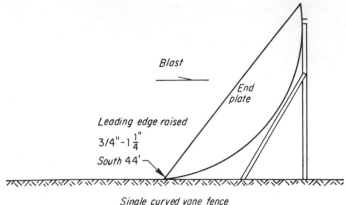

Blast

Leading edge raised

3/4"-1¼"

South 44'

End plate

Single curved vane fence

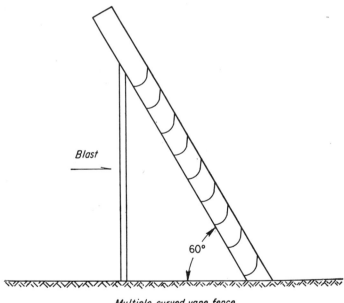

Blast

60°

Multiple curved vane fence

Fig. 10-36 Typical blast fences. (*T. A. Tucker* [26].)

that the performances of single- and multiple-curved vane fences were about equal, although the latter diffused the smoke better.

At runway ends and other areas where takeoff thrust is to be applied, fences of 8 to 10 ft have performed satisfactorily for all types of jet aircraft where the engines are suspended from the wings. Higher fences must be considered for jet aircraft with engines mounted on the fuselage and in the tail of the vehicle. A precise analysis for determining the height of a blast fence is not available, and thus far recommendations are largely based on the results of observations at full-scale installations.

REFERENCES

1. "A Decision Tool for Airport Terminal Building Capacity Analysis," B.F. McCullough and F.L. Roberts, Council for Advanced Transportation Studies, University of Texas at Austin, presented at 58th Annual Meeting of the Transportation Research Board, Washington, D.C., January 1979.

2. "Aircraft Fueling Systems for Jets," J.P. O'Donnell, *Civil Engineering*, American Society of Civil Engineers, New York, N.Y., May 1959.

3. *Aircraft Movement and Passenger Data for 100 U.S. Airports, Average Day in August 1978*, Air Transport Association of America, Washington, D.C., June 1979.

4. *Airline Aircraft Gates and Passenger Terminal Space Approximations*, Air Transport Association of America, Washington, D.C., AD/SC Rep. 4, July 1977.

5. *Airport Design Standards—Airports Served by Air Carriers, Aprons*, Federal Aviation Administration, Washington, D.C., Draft Advisory Circular AC 150/5335-2A.

6. *Airport Design Standards—Airports Served by Air Carriers, Taxiways*, Federal Aviation Administration, Washington, D.C., Advisory Circular AC 150/5335-1A, May 1970.

7. *Airport Design Standards—Effects and Treatment of Jet Blast*, Federal Aviation Administration, Washington, D.C., Advisory Circular AC 150/5325-6A, June 1972.

8. *Airport Landside Capacity*, Transportation Research Board, Washington, D.C., Spec. Rep. 159, 1975.

9. *Airport Landside Planning Through Use of a Computer Simulation Model*, Office of Engineering and Management Systems, Federal Aviation Administration, Washington, D.C., FAA-EM-80-8, June 1982.

10. *Airport Terminal Buildings*, Federal Aviation Agency, September 1960.

11. *Airports Terminal Reference Manual*, 6th ed., International Air Transportation Association, Montreal, Que., Canada, September 1978.

12. "An Airport Passenger Processing Simulation Model," S. Hannig-Smith, Aviation Planning Associates, Inc., Cincinnati, Ohio, January 1981.

13. "Analysis of Passenger and Baggage Flows in Airport Terminal Buildings," R. Horonjeff, *Journal of Aircraft*, vol. 5, no. 5, American Institute of Aeronautics and Astronautics, 1969.

14. "Analysis of Passenger Delays at Airport Terminals," S. Yager, *Transportation Engineering Journal*, vol. 99, no. TE4, American Society of Civil Engineers, New York, N.Y., November 1973.

15. "Analytical Models for the Design of Aircraft Terminal Buildings," J.D. Pararas, Massachusetts Institute of Technology, Cambridge, Mass., Masters Thesis, January 1977.

16. *Baggage Handling*, Report by Ralph M. Parsons Company to the Office of Facilitation, U.S. Department of Transportation, Washington, D.C., April 1971.

17. *Capital City Airport Master Plan, Lansing, Michigan*, vol. II, Landrum and Brown, Cincinnati, Ohio, Tech. Rep., January 1976.

18. *Collection of Calibration and Validation Data for an Airport Landside Dynamic Simulation Model*, Wilbur Smith and Associates, Federal Aviation Administration, Washington, D.C., January 1980.

19. *Conceptual Studies for Geneva Intercontinental Airport*, Reynolds, Smith and Hills, Jacksonville, Fla., March 1981.

20. "Curb Space at Airport Terminals," R. Tolles, *Traffic Quarterly*, October 1973.

21. *Design Guidebook—400 Hz Fixed Power Systems*, Air Transport Association of America, Washington, D.C., January 1980.

22. *Fort Lauderdale–Hollywood International Airport Parking Analysis*, Aviation Planning Associates, Inc., Cincinnati, Ohio, Working Paper, September 1981.

23. *Highway Capacity Manual*, Transportation Research Board, Washington, D.C., Spec. Rep. 87, 1965.

24. *Interim Materials on Highway Capacity*, Transportation Research Board, Washington, D.C., Circular 212, 1980.

25. *Introduction to Transportation Engineering and Planning*, E.K. Morlok, McGraw-Hill, Inc., New York, N.Y., 1978.

26. "Meeting USAF Blast Fence Requirements," T.A. Tucker, *Journal of the Air Transport Division*, vol. 85, no. AT1, American Society of Civil Engineers, New York, N.Y., January 1959.

27. "Moving Sidewalk Systems at Airport Terminals," C.J. Hoch, Institute of Transportation and Traffic Engineering, University of California, Berkeley, Calif., Graduate Report, 1972.

28. "Passenger Flows at Departure Lounges," R.L. Paullin, Institute of Transportation and Traffic Engineering, University of California, Berkeley, Calif., Graduate Report, 1966.

29. "Pier Finger Simulation Model," E.E. Smith and J.T. Murphy, Institute for Transportation and Traffic Engineering, University of California, Berkeley, Calif., Graduate Report, 1968.

30. *Planning and Design Conciderations for Airport Terminal Building Development*, Federal Aviation Administration, Washington, D.C., Advisory Circular AC 150/5360-7, October 1976.

31. *Planning and Design of Airport Terminal Facilities at Nonhub Locations*, Federal Aviation Administration, Washington, D.C., Advisory Circular AC 150/5360-9, April 1980.

32. "Planning Ground Transportation Facilities for Airports," E.M. Whitlock and E. F. Cleary, *Highway Research Record*, no. 274, Washington, D.C., 1969.

33. "Simulating the Turnaround Operation of Passenger Aircraft Using the Critical Path Method," J.B. Braaksma, Waterloo University, Waterloo, Ont., Canada, Doctoral Thesis, 1970.

34. *Survey of Airport Ground Access*, U.S. Aviation Industry Working Group, Washington, D.C., June 1981.

35. *The Apron and Terminal Building Planning Report*, Federal Aviation Administration, Washington, D.C., Rep. FAA-RD-75-191, July 1975.

36. *The Apron Terminal Complex*, Ralph M. Parsons Company, Federal Aviation Administration, Washington, D.C., September 1973.

37. *The FAA's Airport Landside Model, Analytical Approach to Delay Analysis*, Federal Aviation Administration, Washington, D.C., Rep. FAA-AVP-78-2, January 1978.

38. "The Movement of Air Cargo between Cargo Terminals and Passenger Aircraft Gates—Airport Planning Considerations," R.J. Roche, Institute of Transportation and Traffic Engineering, University of California, Berkeley, Calif., Graduate Report, 1972.

39. "The Planning of Passenger Handling Systems," A. Kanafani and H. Kivett, University of California, Berkeley, Calif., Course Notes, 1972.

40. *Trip Generation*, Institute of Transportation Engineers, Arlington, Va., Informational Report, 1976.

Chapter 11

The Design of Heliports and STOL Ports

INTRODUCTION

For a number of years, research and development have been going on in different types of air vehicles which, in effect, "can stand still while flying." The most widely known of this family of vehicles is the helicopter. The helicopter is a vehicle which essentially can lift off the ground in a nearly vertical direction. This is referred as *vertical takeoff and landing* (VTOL). Since the helicopter is by far the most advanced of the vertical takeoff machines, the emphasis in this chapter is on ground facilities for helicopters, referred to as *heliports.*

In recent years considerable research and development effort has been devoted to investigating the potential of *short takeoff and landing* (STOL) vehicles for intercity transportation. These vehicles are unable to rise vertically, but are designed to take off and land on very short runways and to climb and descend at steeper angles than conventional fixed-wing aircraft. The term *short* is undefined. A vehicle requiring 3000 ft or less of runway can be considered as a STOL aircraft. Another way to define a STOL aircraft is that it is a vehicle that requires "powered lift" for its operation rather than relying entirely on "mechanical lift," which conventional aircraft do. Powered lift means that propulsion from the engines is used to blow air over parts of the aircraft body, inproving lift, particularly at low speeds. Mechanical lift relies solely on lift generated by trailing and leading edge flaps and other devices. The argument for the use of STOL aircraft is that they are less noisy and less costly to operate than VTOL, and they require less land for runways than conventional aircraft. Thus the runway lengths at general aviation airports may be adequate for STOL, whereas conventional aircraft could not be accommodated at these airports. No passenger STOL aircraft with a capacity of 50 or more passengers were in service at the time this text was prepared, but many concepts had been studied. The characteristics of these concepts and the corresponding ground requirements are briefly described in this chapter.

NATURE OF HELICOPTER TRANSPORT

Transport by helicopter can be classified into two general categories: private operations and common-carrier operations. Private operations are of the same nature as general aviation flying described in Chap. 1. Common-carrier operations correspond to the scheduled air-carrier activity.

In private operations most of the helicopters are usually of 1- to 3-seat capacity and weigh up to 3000 lb. Helicopters in common-carrier operations are of greater capacity (over 20 passengers) and weigh up to as much as 20,000 lb. Proposed models can accommodate over 50 passengers and weigh as much as 50,000 lb and possibly more. Primarily because of the difference in size, heliport facilities for private operations are normally much smaller than those for common-carrier operations.

Private operations include construction, patrol, dusting, advertising, rescue, and so on. Common-carrier operations can be classified into two types:

1. Transportation in large metropolitan regions between several airports in the region and between the airports and the community center or centers in the region

2. Intercity transportation between cities not necessarily all in one metropolitan region

Experience to date shows that the helicopter has achieved its greatest success in the first type of service, the operating service being within a radius of 50 mi. The development of the second type of service will depend on the ability of helicopters to compete favorably with fixed-wing aircraft or STOL in the matter of speed and economics over stage lengths up to 300 mi.

Despite the growth of transport by helicopter, it represents a small percent of the total number of persons in the United States who travel by air. Operating costs have gradually been reduced, but are still considerably higher than for fixed-wing aircraft.

Characteristics of Helicopters

A helicopter is a powered aircraft which gains its lift from the rotary motion of airfoil surfaces. The distinctive characteristic of a helicopter is its ability to hover through application of power to the rotating airfoils. The practical consequences of this characteristic are a much greater range of flight speeds and flight attitudes than is the case with conventional aircraft and the ability to land on and take off from comparatively small areas. When on the ground, helicopters have the ability of taxiing under their own power. The bulk of the helicopters in private operation cruise at speeds not in excess of 90 kns. Transport-category helicopters now in service cruise at speeds as high as 130 kns.

While helicopters can ascend vertically from the ground, prolonged vertical ascents severely restrict load-carrying capacities. The usual procedure is to employ vertical ascent only to initiate the takeoff. As with other aircraft, takeoffs are usually made into the wind. The initial vertical rise for takeoff is aided by a ground cushion built up by the pressure of the air directed against the ground by the revolving rotors. After a few feet (5 to 10 ft) of vertical ascent, horizontal acceleration is begun until climb-out speed (from 30 to 50 kns) is reached. Prior to reaching climb-out speed, the helicopter can be flown in a horizontal path or in a slightly ascending path. Climb-out and descent speeds vary from 30 to 60 kns. Just before touchdown, the helicopter hovers momentarily 5 to 10 ft above the landing pad.

From a safety standpoint, the operation of single-engine helicopters requires that emergency landing areas be available from any point in the flight path. In case of engine failure, safe landings utilizing autorotation* can be made if space is available. Twin-engine helicopters (S-61 and Vertol 107), on the other hand, are designed to permit continuation of flight and even a moderate rate of climb in the event one engine fails. For these types of helicopters (Figs. 11-1 and 11-2) it is unnecessary from a safety standpoint to have space available for emergency landing along the entire route. All small helicopters in private operation are single-engine. Most of the helicopters, with the exception of a few models (S-61, Vertol 107), are single-engine. Twin-engine helicopters are not, however, designed to hover with only one engine in operation. On takeoff, therefore, in the event an engine fails before the helicopter has reached a one-engine-out flight speed, a landing must be made. To take care of this eventuality, sufficient space must be provided ahead of the landing area for an emergency landing. The single-engine helicopter also needs this area, but in addition requires space for emergency landings all along the flight path. When helicopters are designed to hover with one engine out, space ahead of the landing area is not required.

Because it is not economically practical for a helicopter to ascend and descend vertically, unobstructed approach-departure paths leading to the heliport are required at present. To protect the approach-departure path, obstructions are not permitted to extend above a prescribed inclined plane beginning at the heliport and extending to the en route altitude. The

---

* Continuation of rotor rotation in flight after cessation of power. Sufficient height must be reached by the helicopter in order to utilize the principle of autorotation.

Fig. 11-1 Sikorsky S-61 transport helicopter. (*Sikorsky Aircraft.*)

obstruction clearance requirements specified by the FAA are shown in Fig. 11-3 and tabulated in Table 11-1. ICAO has adopted similar recommendations [6].

Helicopters can be either single-rotor or tandem-rotor and powered by one or two engines. The landing gear can consist of pontoons (for landings and takeoffs on water), skids, or wheels equipped with rubber tires. When wheels are used, the landing gear normally consists of two main wheels and a single nose or tail wheel, or four wheels. The principal dimensions of representative helicopters used for private and common-carrier operations are shown in Fig. 11-4 and tabulated in Table 11-2.

Factors Related to Site Selection

The selection of a heliport site in an urban area requires the consideration of many factors, the most important of which are:

1. Best locations to serve potential traffic

2. Minimum obstructions in the approach and departure areas

3. Minimum disturbance from noise and desirable location with regard to adjacent land use

4. Good access to surface transportation and parking

5. Minimum cost to acquire and develop

6. Two approach paths separated by at least 90° and oriented with respect to prevailing winds

7. Avoidance of traffic conflicts between helicopters and other air traffic

8. Consideration of turbulence and visibility restrictions presented by nearby buildings

9. Provision of emergency landing areas along entire route for single-engine helicopters

Final selection of a heliport site will usually require a compromise

Fig. 11-2 Vertol 107 transport helicopter. (*Vertol Division, Boeing Company.*)

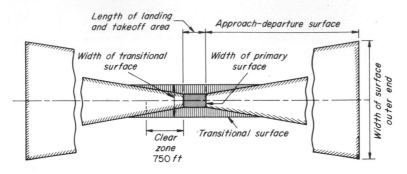

Fig. 11-3 Obstruction clearance requirements for heliports. (*Federal Aviation Administration [5, 18].*)

among these various goals. The most severe problems can be expected in large, highly developed metropolitan areas. In large urban areas heliports should be planned on a regional basis. The first step is to prepare an estimate of the demand for helicopter services and the origins and destinations of this demand. The second step is to select a heliport site or sites which can reasonably satisfy the demand and yet meet the requirements cited in the preceding paragraph.

The principal market for helicopter transportation is in large urban areas between the airport or airports and the central core. Therefore it is essential that the downtown heliport be centrally located near the hotel area and business district. Likewise, adequate provision for helicopters should be made at airports. In extremely large urban complexes (e.g., Los Angeles), where, in addition to a central core, there are outlying smaller

TABLE 11-1 **Obstruction Clearance Requirements**

Item	VFR	IFR
Width of primary surface, ft	1.5L*	300
Width of approach-departure surface, inner end, ft	1.5L	300
Width of approach-departure surface, outer end, ft	500	3,400
Length of approach-departure surface, ft	4000	10,000
Slope of approach-departure surface	8:1	15:1
Slope of transition surface	2:1	4:1
Width of transition surface, ft	500	700
Minimum distance prior to beginning of curved path, ft	300	†
Radius of curved path, ft	700	†

* L overall length of helicopter.
† Not permitted in IFR (see [18]).
SOURCE: Federal Aviation Administration [5, 18].

centers, secondary heliports are needed so that the benefits of air transportation can extend to these centers. A heliport must have good access to streets, highways, and transit facilities so that passengers using buses, personal vehicles, or mass transit can easily reach the facility.

Noise

The noise caused by helicopter operations within or adjacent to built-up urban areas is and will continue to be an extremely important factor in planning for helicopter transport, as it has been with fixed-wing aircraft. Manufacturers are aware of this problem and are studying ways in which noise can be minimized.

A heliport should be located so that the noise generated by helicopters will not cause excessive disturbance to surrounding developments. The noise factor is most critical directly underneath the flight path on takeoff and landing. The amount of sound that can be tolerated by the average person is dependent upon a number of factors, including overall noise level, frequency, duration, the type of development (residential, industrial)

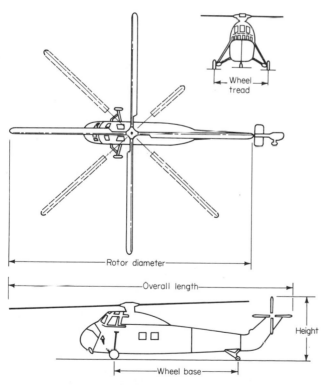

Fig. 11-4 Dimensional definitions for helicopters.

TABLE 11-2 **Dimensions of Typical Helicopters**

Aircraft	Rotor diameter, ft	Overall length, ft	Fuselage length, ft	Height, ft	Wheelbase, ft	Maximum gross weight, lb	Passengers
SA-330J	49.5	59.8	48.6	16.8	13.3	16,300	8–20
Bell-204B	47.9	57.0	42.6	14.5	*	8,500	9
Bell-205A	47.9	57.1	41.9	14.5	*	4,700	14
Bell-222	39.8	47.7	36.0	12.9	11.8	7,650	6–10
B-Vertol 107	48.0	81.7	44.6	16.8	24.8	16,650	25
B-Vertol CH-47C	60.0	98.8	51.0	18.7	22.5	50,000	33–44
Hughes 500D	26.3	30.5	23.1	8.9	7.3	3,000	4–6
Sikorsky S-61	62.0	72.7	59.6	16.8	23.5	19,000	25
Sikorsky S-64E	72.0	88.5	70.1	25.4	24.4	42,000	45

* Uses skids.

SOURCES: International Civil Aviation Organization [6] and Federal Aviation Administration [5].

surrounding the source of noise, and the ambient sound level in the area. A greater amount of noise can be tolerated in industrial areas than in residential areas. Docks and other waterfront sites offer some of the best possibilities for heliport location in large, congested urban centers. Approach and noise problems can usually be overcome by making use of water areas. The downtown heliport in New York City is an example of such a location.

Noise generated by small two- and three-seat helicopters can be tolerated in business and industrial areas, but the noise generated by large multi-engine machines powered by jet engines can exceed tolerable levels even in business and industrial areas. It is well to check with the manufacturers concerning the latest information on the levels of noise generated by the several transport types of helicopters.

To minimize the noise, it is desirable, whenever possible, to orient the landing pad so that landings and takeoffs are made over areas where noise would be least objectionable. Considerably more latitude can be exercised in this respect with helicopters than with fixed-wing aircraft.

Protection of Approach and Departure Paths

Zoning is necessary both to control the location of heliport sites for maximum benefit to the community and to provide safety in helicopter operations by protection of the surrounding airspace. The dimensions of the approach-departure path are shown in Fig. 11-3.

Turbulence and Visibility

Another factor which must be considered in the selecton of a site for a heliport is the effect of turbulence over roof surfaces and downdrafts near buildings. This factor is of particular importance for rooftop heliports. If there is doubt in the planner's mind, the site should be flight-checked with a helicopter.

Poor visibility can be an important factor to consider for sites on tall buildings, 100 ft or more in height. The cloud deck seldom reaches the ground, but at higher levels the heliport might find itself enveloped in fog when the ground is clear.

Physical Characteristics of a Heliport

A heliport is defined as a facility which is intended to be used for the landing and takeoff of helicopters and may include space for helicopter parking, buildings, servicing facilities, and vehicular parking. The takeoff and landing area is where the helicopter actually takes off and lands. The touchdown area is an area within the takeoff and landing area where the helicopter will normally touch down on landing. Functionally, the terminal area requirements for the parking, servicing, and fueling of helicopters and the processing of passengers are no different from the requirements for fixed-wing aircraft.

The FAA [5] classifies heliports according to use as follows:

Military Heliport. Facilities operated by one of the branches of the armed services. The design criteria are specified by the branch of the service and usually prohibit nonmilitary uses.

Federal Heliport. Facilities operated by a nonmilitary agency or department of the federal government. They are used to carry out the functions appropriate to the agency.

Public-Use Heliport. Facilities which are open to the general public and do not require the prior permission of the owner to land. The extent of the facilities available may limit operations to helicopters of specific sizes or weights.

Private-Use Heliport. Facilities which are restricted in use by the owner. These may be publicly owned, but their use is restricted, as in police or fire department use.

Personal-Use Heliport. Facilities which are used exclusively by the owner.

The principal components of a heliport are the landing and takeoff area, the touchdown area, and for large heliports, taxiways and the building area.

Landing and Takeoff Area

The landing and takeoff area is a surface on which the helicopter can land or take off. Its size depends primarily on the overall length of the largest helicopter to be accommodated by the heliport. Because of the dust that can be created by the rotor of a helicopter, it is necessary to prepare the surface of the landing and takeoff area so that it will be free of dust (e.g., turf, pavement). The dimensions of the landing and takeoff area are listed in Table 11-3.

Touchdown Area

Within the landing and takeoff area, an area is designated for the normal everyday landing of helicopters. The touchdown area is usually defined by a solid border painted on the pavement surface (Fig. 11-5). The dimensions of the touchdown area are listed in Table 11-3.

Peripheral Area

A peripheral area surrounding the landing and takeoff area, with a minimum width of one-fourth the overall length of the helicopter but not less than 10 ft, is recommended as an obstruction-free safety zone. The area should be kept free of objects hazardous to the operation of helicopters.

Effect of Wind

Although helicopters can maneuver in much higher crosswinds than fixed-wing aircraft, the takeoff and landing area should preferably be oriented to permit operation into the wind as nearly as possible. At the present time it appears that the crosswind characteristics of the helicopter will be such that for the majority of cases a rectangular takeoff and landing area need be oriented in one direction only.

TABLE 11-3 **Geometric Design Standards for Heliports**

| | | ICAO | |
Item	FAA	Land§	Water§
Length of landing area, ft	1.5A*	50–300	164–330
Width of landing area, ft	1.5A	50–100	100–164
Size of touchdown area	B†	**	**
Taxiway width, ft	20	20–50	66–100
Shoulder width, ft	10	¶	¶
Maximum pavement slope, %	2	2	¶
Shoulder slope, %	3‡	3	¶
Fillet radius, ft	25	¶	¶

  * A = overall length of helicopter; see Fig. 11-4.
  † B = rotor diameter; see Fig. 11-4.
  ‡ For first 10 ft, 5%.
  § See classification by ICAO.
  ¶ Not specified.
  ** See ICAO.
  SOURCES: Federal Aviation Administration [5] and International Civil Aviation Organization [6].

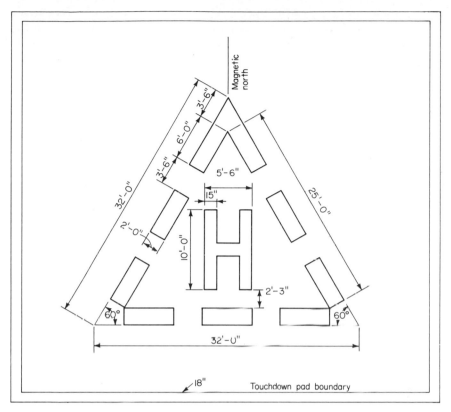

Fig. 11-5 Recommended heliport marking. Dimensions shown are appropriate for touchdown pads 60 ft or larger. Dimensions should be reduced proportionally for smaller touchdown pads. (*Federal Aviation Administration [5].*)

Terminal Area

At heliports where the volume of traffic is relatively small, the loading and unloading of passengers can be accomplished on the takeoff and landing pad. As traffic increases, it will be necessary to provide additional space for the parking of helicopters.

Obstruction Clearance Requirements

Imaginary obstruction clearance surfaces are established for each class of heliport. For heliports the principal surfaces are (1) approach-departure and (2) transitional. The horizontal surface required for airports (Chap. 7) is not necessary for heliports. The requirements for VFR operations are different from IFR. IFR operations by commercial helicopters are very limited, thus VFR requirements will suffice for most heliports. The requirements are shown in Fig. 11-3. It should be noted that curved-path approach and departure are currently not permitted in IFR conditions. However, with the implementation of microwave landing systems, this may change in the future. The specifications for IFR are a function of the nature of the navigational aids, and references [18] should be consulted prior to establishing the landing and takeoff paths.

The relationship between the elements of a typical layout of a heliport is shown in Fig. 11-6.

Marking of Heliports

The primary purpose for marking heliports is to identify the area clearly as a facility for the use of helicopters. The requirements for marking heliports

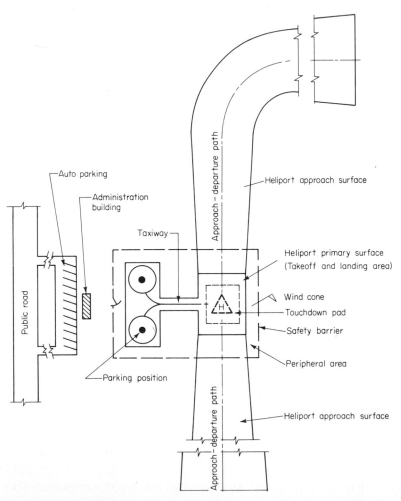

Fig. 11-6 Typical heliport layout. (*Federal Aviation Administration [5].*)

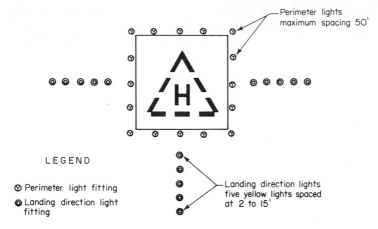

Fig. 11-7 Heliport lighting configuration. (*Federal Aviation Administration [5].*)

are specified by the FAA. Essentially these requirements consist of painting an equilateral triangle with an "H" in the center of the touchdown area, as shown in Fig. 11-5. The marker should be oriented so that the apex is in the direction of magnetic North. Marking on the takeoff and landing area should be white, while on the taxiway and service area markings should be yellow.

Lighting of Heliports

For operation during the hours of darkness various types of lights are suggested [5]. The amount of lighting will depend on the character and volume of operations. Thus more lighting is required for scheduled air-carrier operations than for a private heliport with occasional use. The minimum requirements consist of perimeter lighting and obstruction lighting. Perimeter lighting defines the touchdown area as shown in Fig. 11-7. The lights should have a hemispherical light distribution and a lamp power of at least 30 W. The color is yellow. All objects that penetrate the obstruction clearance surfaces should be lighted (red color).

Other useful lighting aids are the landing direction lights, inset lights, and floodlights. The landing direction lights are miniature approach lights since they extend only 75 ft. The color is yellow. Inset lights are set into the pavement of the touchdown area to provide an aiming point for this area as well as to improve the pilot's depth perception for final approach and landing. White lights of at least 45 W are recommended by the FAA.

Elevated Heliports

When ground-level sites are not available or are unsuitable, an elevated site may be practical. Elevated heliports may be located on piers or other structures over water, as well as on buildings. The dimensions of the touchdown area are the same as for heliports on the ground, but the landing and takeoff area can be smaller and there is no need for a peripheral area. When planning a rooftop heliport, a thorough study should be made of the air currents caused by the presence of adjacent buildings. Roof areas make it possible to locate the heliport closer to the center of business activities in a city, provided the facility is environmentally acceptable. Another advantage is that the land cost is partially absorbed by the tenancy of the lower floors of the building. However, it should be realized that if the operations are of any size, space on the floors below the landing and takeoff area may have to be devoted to uses such as lobby, freight, and baggage handling. The possible disadvantage of height with respect to visibility was mentioned in the section "Factors Related to Site Selection." A heliport 100 ft or more above the ground would require a higher cloud base than a ground heliport to provide the same operating safety. A downtown commercial heliport would require, in addition to lobby space, car parking facilities relatively close by.

Where heliports are built on elevated structures, the strength of the floor should be greater than the strength of the landing gear of the helicopter. The loads imposed by helicopters and recommendations concerning the structural design of elevated structures are discussed in the next section.

Structural Design of Heliports

Helicopters using facilities on land are usually supported on skids or wheels equipped with rubber tires. Helicopters equipped with conventional landing-gear wheels are normally supported by two main wheels and one tail or nose wheel. For the larger helicopters each main landing gear consists of two wheels (such as the DC-9). Each main gear supports 40 to 45 percent of the weight of the helicopter, and the tail or nose wheel the remainder, approximately 10 to 20 percent. If the helicopter is supported by skids, 50 percent of the weight is supported by each skid.

The strength requirements for the landing and takeoff area are determined by considering the helicopter's dynamic and static wheel loads and the landing-gear configuration. For pavements, only the static load is considered. On rooftops, dynamic or impact loads must be considered to ensure that the structure will not fail if a helicopter makes a hard landing. The landing surface should be designed to support a concentrated load equal to 75 percent of the gross weight of the helicopter at each main landing gear. It is assumed that each main landing gear will strike the surface simultaneously. The forces are applied over the footprint area corresponding to the tire inflation pressure or over the area of the landing skid.

Heliports at Airports

A large number of helicopters will operate into airports to serve traffic from the downtown area and surrounding communities. Accordingly, provisions should be made at an airport for the landing and takeoff of helicopters. The takeoff and landing area should be located so as to (1) provide maximum separation from fixed-wing traffic patterns to avoid creating a conflict in takeoff and landing operations, (2) be as close as possible to passenger check-in areas for fixed-wing aircraft to avoid long walking distances, and (3) avoid as much as possible the mixing of taxiing fixed-wing aircraft and helicopters, since helicopters can taxi at relatively low speeds. It is recommended that heliport to runway separations be 300 ft for runways servicing single-engine propeller aircraft, 500 ft for twin-engine propeller aircraft, and 700 ft for all other aircraft [5].

Alternative locations for heliports at an airport are (1) the roof of the terminal building, (2) the apron adjacent to the terminal building used by fixed-wing aircraft, and (3) on ground level, the area adjacent to the terminal building separate from the fixed-wing aircraft apron. There are advantages and disadvantages for all three locations. Normally, a ground-level site is preferred. The most convenient and least expensive method for accomplishing this is to reserve a part of the fixed-wing terminal apron for the takeoff and landing of helicopters. If this is not convenient, a special pad for helicopter operations on the aircraft side of the terminal building should be provided.

STATUS OF STOL TRANSPORT

Continued growth in domestic air travel has placed a strain on the capacity of air-carrier airports serving the larger cities in the United States. The short-haul traveler in particular is quite sensitive to congestion and delay. Although the development of VTOL aircraft offered a possible solution, it was found that their economics and noise generation made them less attractive than STOL aircraft. The use of STOL has therefore been proposed for short-haul intercity transportation to provide better service to the passenger and to relieve airspace and ground congestion at the busy airports. STOL aircraft, because of their high lift capability, can operate off much shorter runways than conventional aircraft. In large metropolitan areas this feature provides the potential of using existing general aviation airports located within the region. The use of these airports can relieve the strain on the major airports and at the same time provide facilities closer to the traveler's origin and destination. Another argument for STOL aircraft is their capability for reducing noise on the ground because of higher approach and departure angles (7° compared with 3° for conventional aircraft approaches). Finally STOL aircraft, because of their substantially lower speeds in the terminal area, have greater maneuverability and hence can make more efficient use of already congested airspace.

Extensive research and development efforts are continuing in the United States, Canada, and elsewhere for the evaluation of STOL as a means of transport. These efforts not only include aircraft technology, but also the potential market, environmental acceptance, ground facilities, aids to navigation, and economic incentives for the manufacturers and operators [10,16]. From these analyses it is quite clear that the operating costs of STOL aircraft depend a great deal on the length of runway available. There is a consensus that downtown STOL ports either on the ground or on a roof will be extremely difficult to develop because of noise and other environmental considerations. Therefore the need for very short runways (such as 2000 ft or less) is questioned. Consequently, lengths of 3000 and even 4000 ft are being considered. It is expected that the first generation of STOL will primarily serve the short-haul intercity market for trips not exceeding 500 nmi.

At the time this text was prepared there was no scheduled STOL airline service of consequence. Further, a consensus had not been reached regarding the size and configuration of passenger aircraft. Alternatives are discussed later in this chapter. It was therefore not possible to provide geometric design standards for STOL ports and obstruction clearance criteria with the same certainty as for helicopters and conventional (CTOL)* aircraft.

Characteristics of STOL Aircraft

Current Aircraft

At the time this text was prepared there were few STOL aircraft in commercial service. These few were relatively small and powered by propellers driven by a jet engine (turboprop). All are able to operate on runways not more than 2000 ft in length. Among those identified with the transport of passengers are the Twin Otter (DHC-6), DHC-7, and the Buffalo (DHC-5). The principal characteristics of these and other current or proposed aircraft are listed in Table 11-4.

The Twin Otter has been successfully used by commuter airlines for relatively short trips connecting a main airport with outlying areas. The DHC-7 "Quiet STOL" airliner was developed by the de Havilland Company of Canada. It is designed for service between downtown STOL ports having 2000-ft runways. Passenger service between Ottawa and Montreal (the distance between the two cities is 110 mi) was approved, on an

---

* CTOL is an acronym for *conventional takeoff and landing*.

TABLE 11-4   **STOL Aircraft Characteristics, Current and Future**

Aircraft	Takeoff weight, lb	Overall length, ft	Wing-span, ft	Height, ft	Passengers	Ramp area, ft²	Wheel-base, ft	Gear tread, ft
BN-2	6,300	35.7	49.0	13.7	10	3,560	12.9	11.3
DHC-5	17,200	77.3	96.0	28.7	50	10,250	27.9	30.5
DHC-6	12,500	51.7	65.0	18.6	20	5,340	14.8	12.5
DHC-7	38,500	80.3	93.0	26.2	48	10,290	28.7	23.5
MDC 188	54,700	80.7	78.5	33.2	67	8,940	23.7	20.0
LG-100-107D	113,900	106.8	136.6	39.5	80	17,970	40.0	15.8
B-751	141,000	132.0	111.0	40.0	150	18,520	44.8	25.5
NR 260C	140,000	118.0	126.5	44.1	150	18,820	43.3	17.3

SOURCES: International Civil Aviation Organization [12] and Federal Aviation Administration [7].

experimental basis, by the Canadian government to determine the market for STOL and evaluate operational factors [3].

Future STOL Concepts

Under the auspices of NASA several aircraft manufacturers have made exhaustive analyses of STOL transportation with respect to the potential market, aircraft technology, economics, ground facilities, and noise [10,16]. In these analyses the three principal variables are: (1) runway length, (2) number of passengers, and (3) method of providing lift. Runway lengths were varied from 2000 to 4000 ft. Aircraft capacities ranged from 150 to 300 passengers. Noise levels were varied from 95 to 98 EPNdB at a distance of 500 ft from the aircraft. Lift concepts included upper surface blowing, external blowing of flaps, augmentor wing,* and mechanical flap. The upper limit of range was 500 nmi.

The principal characteristics of a 150-passenger capacity STOL aircraft are shown in Table 11-5. The data in this table were taken from one of the contractors for NASA. It is presented to show the influence of runway length and lift technique on the physical dimensions and weight of STOL aircraft.

This comparison clearly indicates that the airfield dimensions (e.g., taxiway and runway widths and pavement strengths) for future STOL aircraft carrying up to 150 passengers will be similar to current short-to-medium-range conventional airline aircraft.

Pertinent conclusions from one study [10] indicate the following:

1. Runway lengths of 2000 ft are not economically viable, while 3000-ft lengths are economically viable.

---

* The augmentor wing employs a blown flap system in which the air from a turbofan engine is directed internally along the aircraft wing and expelled rearward through a slot so that the air flows between the upper and lower segments of the trailing edge flap.

TABLE 11-5 **Characteristics of Alternative Concepts for Future STOL Aircraft**

Item	2000-ft runway, 150 passengers			3000-ft runway, 150 passengers		4000-ft runway, 150 passengers, MF
	EBF*	AW	USB	EBF	MF	
Wingspan‡	149'8"	133'10"	164'8"	108'1"	141'8"	124'0"
Overall length†	153'6"	153'7"	159'10"	139'9"	164'6"	131'8"
Height†	54'0"	54'2"	58'6"	41'4"	45'8"	38'0"
Number and type of engines	4TF‡	4TF	4TF	4TF	2TF	2TF
Maximum takeoff weight, lb	196,000	213,000	227,000	149,000	191,000	158,000
Wheel tread§, ft	20	20	25	25	25	25
Cruise speed, Mach no.	0.74	0.78	0.76	0.69	0.70	0.72

* EBF = externally blown flap; AW = augmentor wing; USB = upper surface blowing; MF = mechanical flap.

† Dimensions in feet and inches.

‡ TF = turbofan.

§ Approximate only.

SOURCE: National Aeronautics and Space Administration [10] and McDonnell-Douglas Corporation [16].

2. Payload of 150 passengers is the preferred size.

3. Mechanical flap aircraft are competitive with propulsion-lift aircraft for runway lengths of 3000 to 4000 ft.

4. The noise criteria have a large effect on the economics of the aircraft.

A goal of 95 EPNdB at 500 ft is difficult to achieve; some relaxation of this goal may be necessary.

Although these conclusions are the result of a "paper analysis," they are indicative of the direction in which STOL development will take place in the future.

Physical Characteristics of a STOL Port

STOL Obstruction Clearance Requirements

Obstruction clearance requirements for STOL ports are specified in [7, 12]. Since the characteristics of future STOL aircraft concepts have not been formed, it is premature to consider these requirements as fixed. They are, however, appropriate for current aircraft such as the DHC-6 and DHC-7. Dimensions specified in [7] are as follows (the various surfaces are shown in Fig. 11-3 and in Chap. 7):

1. Primary surface length: runway length plus 100 ft on each end
2. Primary surface width: 300 ft
3. Approach-departure surface length: 10,000 ft
4. Approach-departure surface width at inner end: 300 ft
5. Approach-departure surface width at outer end: 3400 ft
6. Approach-departure surface slope: 15 to 1
7. Transitional surface slope: 4 to 1
8. Width of transitional surface: 1100 ft
9. Length of clear zone: 750 ft
10. Inner width of clear zone: 300 ft
11. Outer width of clear zone: 532 ft

Design Parameters

STOL ports have the same characteristics as airports, only the runways are shorter. Therefore the planning criteria are the same as for conventional airports. For large STOL transports runway widths will range from 100 to 150 ft, depending on aircraft size and the number of engines finally selected. Likewise taxiway widths will vary from 60 to 75 ft. Pavement slopes will remain the same as for conventional aircraft. Spacing between runways and taxiways will be determined by the dimensions of the aircraft selected by the airlines. For small STOL aircraft (DHC-6), the pavement widths and spacing of pavements for utility airports are adequate [19].

STOL runways are marked as shown in Figure 11-8. White is used on runways and yellow on taxiways. Lighting consists of threshold lighting, runway edge lighting, and approach lights. The lighting requirements specified in Chap. 13 apply to STOL ports.

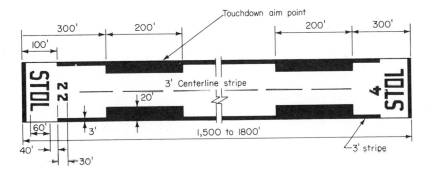

Fig. 11-8 STOL runway marking. (*Federal Aviation Administration [7].*)

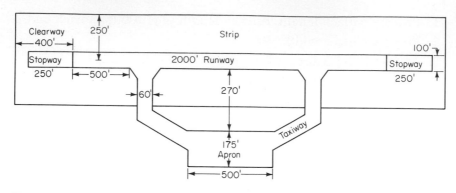

Fig. 11-9 Typical STOL port layout for aircraft similar to DHC-6 Twin Otter. (*International Civil Aviation Organization [12] and Canadian Air Transportation Administration [3, 9].*)

STOL runways should be oriented into the wind as much as possible. A typical STOL port layout to accommodate aircraft such as the DHC-6 Twin Otter is shown in Fig. 11-9.

The design criteria for metropolitan STOL ports recommended by the FAA are given in Table 11-6.

TABLE 11-6   Dimensional Design Criteria for Metropolitan STOL Ports

Item	Recommended Criteria, ft
Runway length	1500–1800*
Runway width	100
Runway safety area length	1700–2000
Runway safety area width	200
Taxiway width	60
Runway centerline to:	
Taxiway centerline	200
Edge of parked aircraft	250
Building line	300
Holding line	150
Separation between parallel runways	700
Taxiway centerline to fixed obstacle	100

* Correction for elevation and temperature required based upon aircraft performance characteristics.
SOURCE: Federal Aviation Administration [7].

REFERENCES

1. *A Canadian STOL Air Transport System—A Major Program*, Canadian Science Council, Ottawa, Ont., Canada, Rep. 11, 1970.

2. *A Guide to STOL Transportation System Planning*, DeHavilland Aircraft of Canada, Limited, Ottawa, Ont., Canada, January 1970.

3. *Canadian STOL Demonstration Service, Montreal STOL Port Master Plan*, Canadian Air Transportation Administration, Ottawa, Ont., ST-71-8, Canada, March 1972.

4. *Guide for the Planning of Small Airports*, Roads and Transportation Association of Canada, Ottawa, Ont., Canada, 1980.

5. *Heliport Design Guide*, Federal Aviation Administration, Advisory Circular AC 150/5390-1B, Washington, D.C., August 1977.

6. *Heliport Manual*, 1st ed., International Civil Aviation Organization, Montreal, Que., Canada, Doc 9261-AN/903, 1979.

7. *Planning and Design Criteria for Metropolitan STOL Ports*, Federal Aviation Administration, Washington, D.C., AC 150/5300-8, April 1975.

8. "Planning STOL Facilities," L. Schaefer, Society of Automotive Engineers, New York, N.Y., Paper 690421, 1969.

9. *Provisional Criteria for STOL Port Zoning*, Canadian Air Transportation Administration, Ottawa, Ont., Canada, August 1973.

10. *Quiet Turbofan STOL Aircraft for Short-Haul Transportation*, National Aeronautics and Space Administration, Washington, D.C., Reps. NASA CR 114612 and CR 114613, June 1973.

11. *STOL Aircraft Future Trends*, Transport Aircraft Council, Aerospace Industries Association of America, Inc., Washington, D.C., May 1971.

12. *STOL Port Manual*, 1st ed., International Civil Aviation Organization, Montreal, Que., Canada, Doc 9150-AN/800, 1976.

13. *STOL-VTOL Air Transportation Systems*, C. Hintz, Jr., Civil Aeronautics Board, Washington, D.C., 1970.

14. *Studies in Short Haul Air Transportation—Effects of Design Runway Length, Community Acceptance, Impact on Return on Investment and Fuel Cost Increases*, R.S. Shevell and D.W. Jones, Jr., Stanford University, National Aeronautics and Space Administration, Ames Research Center, Moffett Field, Calif., July 1973.

15. *Study of Aircraft in Intraurban Transportation Systems, San Francisco Bay Area*, Boeing Company, National Aeronautics and Space Administration, Ames Research Center, Moffett Field, Calif., Rep. NASA CR-114347, 1970.

16. *Study of Quiet Turbofan STOL Aircraft for Short-Haul Transportation*, McDonell-Douglas Corporation, National Aeronautics and Space Administration, Moffett Field, Calif., Rep. MDC-J4371, June 1973.

17. *Study of Short-Haul Aircraft Operating Economies*, National Aeronautics and Space Administration, Ames Research Center, Moffett Field, Calif., Rep. NASA CR-137685, September 1975.

18. *United States Standard for Terminal Instrument Procedures (TERPS)*, Federal Aviation Administration, Washington, D.C., FAA Order 8260.3B, July 1976.

19. *Utility Airports—Air Access to National Transportation*, Federal Aviation Administration, Washington, D.C., Advisory Circular AC 150/5300-4B, October 1981.

20. "V/STOL Aircraft: The Future Role in Urban Transportation as a Pickup and Distribution System," R.H. Miller, *Proceedings of the Symposium on Transportation and the Prospects for Improved Efficiency*, National Academy of Engineering, Washington, D.C., October 12, 1972.

Chapter 12

Structural Design of Airport Pavements

INTRODUCTION

In this chapter various methods for designing pavements are briefly described. The term *structural design of pavements* as used in this text refers to the determination of the thickness of the pavement and its components and not to the design of materials in the pavement (e.g., asphalt concrete or portland cement concrete mixes).

Pavement or *pavement structure* is defined as a structure consisting of one or more layers of processed materials. A pavement consisting of a mixture of bituminous material and aggregate placed on high-quality granular materials is referred to as *flexible*. When the pavement consists of a slab of portland cement concrete, it is referred to as *rigid*.[†]

The pavement is intended to provide a smooth and safe all-weather riding surface, and the thickness of each of the layers must be adequate to ensure that the applied loads will not lead to distress[*] in it or the underlying layers.

Figure 12-1 illustrates the type of structural pavement section suitable for heavy-duty pavements for airports.

A flexible pavement may consist of one or more layers of material classified as *surface course, base course*, and *subbase course*, resting on a *prepared subgrade* layer. This latter material, as seen in Fig. 12-1, is the material on which the pavement structure rests and may be either an embankment or an excavation. The surface course consists of a mixture of bituminous material (generally asphalt) and aggregate ranging in thickness from a minimum of 3 or 4 in (for heavy-duty airfields) to thicknesses of 12 in or more. Its principal functions are to provide for smooth and safe traffic operations, to withstand the effects of applied loads and environmental

---

[†] The terms *flexible* and *rigid* have been retained in the text since this terminology is still used in practice. To consider a thick asphalt concrete layer on subgrade as flexible or a portland cement concrete slab as rigid does not appear "reasonable" at this time. Accordingly the author urges that pavements with a substantial thickness of asphalt concrete in the structural section be referred to as asphalt concrete pavements, while those containing portland cement concrete slabs be referred to as a portland cement concrete pavement.

[*] The term *distress* is preferred to *failure*.

420

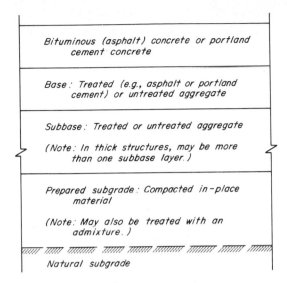

Bituminous (asphalt) concrete or portland
cement concrete

Base: Treated (e.g., asphalt or portland
cement) or untreated aggregate

Subbase: Treated or untreated aggregate

(Note: In thick structures, may be more
than one subbase layer.)

Prepared subgrade: Compacted in-place
material

(Note: May also be treated with an
admixture.)

Natural subgrade

Fig. 12-1 Structural pavement section.

influences for some prescribed period of operation,† and to distribute the applied load to the underlying layers. The base course may consist of treated (e.g., portland cement or asphalt) or untreated granular material. Like the surface course it must be adequate to withstand the effects of load and environment and to distribute the applied loads to the underlying layers. This point is illustrated in Fig. 12-2, which shows the influence of base thickness as well as stiffness (modulus) of the various pavement components on the stress at the surface of the subgrade. The subbase course may be composed of treated or untreated material; quite often unprocessed pit-run material or material selected from a suitable excavation on the site is utilized. Its function is the same as that of the base. It should be noted that not every flexible pavement requires a subbase course. On the other hand, very thick pavements may be composed of several subbase courses.

A rigid pavement consists of a slab of portland cement concrete, 8 to 24 in thick, placed on a prepared layer of imported materials. For heavily trafficked pavements in particular, it would appear desirable that the upper 4 to 6 in of this material be treated with portland cement or asphalt to minimize pumping.* This layer directly under the slab is sometimes referred to as a subbase rather than a base because its quality would not necessarily have to be as high as that of a material directly under a comparatively thin bituminous layer.

† This may be expressed in terms of number of load repetitions or some period of time.
* Pumping is described in this chapter in the section "Design of Rigid Pavements."

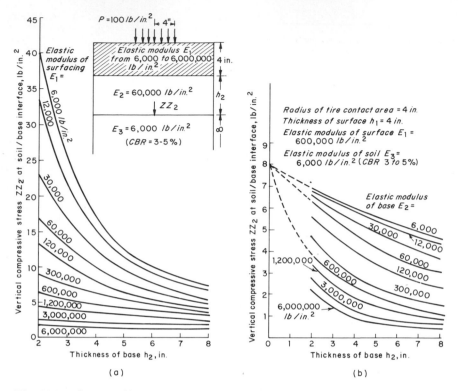

Fig. 12-2 Influence of base thickness and moduli of various layers on vertical stress at surface of subgrade (*Whiffin and Lister [64].*)

Several methods of design for airport pavements are available. Although there is no one method for flexible pavement design accepted by all agencies, a method in widespread use is that developed by the Corps of Engineers and based on the California bearing ratio (CBR) test. Similarly, for rigid pavements, thickness selection based on solutions developed originally by Westergaard are used extensively. These methods are described in this text. Also included are procedures used by the FAA for both flexible and rigid pavements. A method to classify aircraft and airport pavements developed originally by the British Air Ministry, termed the LCN (load classification number) system, is briefly described. A method recently adopted by ICAO, the aircraft classification number–pavement classification number (ACN-PCN), is also discussed. Procedures for the design of asphalt pavements, which treat the structure as a layered elastic solid, developed by Shell Oil Company and by the Asphalt Institute are also briefly summarized.

The design of overlay pavements is treated in some detail since it is considered to be an important aspect of airfield operations in the future. In this regard existing procedures as well as some new developments having the potential to improve overlay design are included.

Details of the aircraft for which the designs have been developed are included in Chap. 3.

THE CBR METHOD OF DESIGN
FOR FLEXIBLE AIRPORT PAVEMENTS

Historical Background

The CBR method of design was developed by the California Division of Highways in 1928.* The method subsequently was adopted for military airport use by the Corps of Engineers, United States Army, shortly after the outbreak of World War II. The outbreak of the war required that a decision be made with little delay concerning a design method. At the time, there were no methods available which were specifically developed for airport pavements. It was apparent that the length of time required to develop a completely new method of design would preclude its use in a war emergency program. Consequently, it was decided to review all available methods for the design of highway pavements and to select one which could readily be adopted for airfield use. The criteria for selecting a method were many. Among the more important were (1) simplicity in procedures for testing the subgrade and the pavement components, (2) a record of satisfactory experience, and (3) adaptation to the airport problem in a reasonable amount of time. After several months of investigating suggested methods, the CBR method was tentatively adopted. Application of the CBR method enables the designer to determine the required thickness of subbase, base, and surface course by entering a set of design curves with the result of a relatively simple soil test.

The CBR Test

The CBR test expresses an index of the shearing strength of soil. Essentially the test consists of compacting about 10 lb of soil into a 6-in-diameter mold, placing a surcharge on the surface of the sample, immersing the sample in water for 4 days, and penetrating the soaked sample with a steel piston approximately 2 in in diameter at a specified rate of loading. The resistance of the soil to penetration, expressed as a percentage of the resistance for a standard crushed stone, is the CBR of the soil. Thus, a CBR of 50 means that the stress necessary for the piston to penetrate the soil sample a specified distance is one-half that required for the piston to

---

* The person most closely associated with its development was O. J. Porter.

penetrate the same distance in the standard crushed stone. The relationship is usually based on a penetration of the piston of 0.1 in, with 1000 lb/in^2 used as the stress required to penetrate the crushed stone at 0.1-in penetration.

The weight placed over the sample prior to immersion in water is commonly referred to as *surcharge*. The unit weight of the surcharge corresponds to an estimate of the unit weight of the pavement structure.

The 4-day soaking period was chosen because a majority of soils approach complete saturation in this time period within the depth affected by the piston. Thus, a soaked sample represents the worst condition of the soil regarding its ability to support a pavement structure. Soaking of the sample is not required where it can be conclusively shown that with the passage of time additional moisture will not be absorbed into the pavement structure.

If the soil in its natural state, for one reason or another, cannot be improved by compaction, the CBR test is performed on an undisturbed sample. On the other hand, if stability can be improved by subsequent compaction, the soil is placed in the CBR mold in five equal layers, and each layer is compacted with a 10-lb weight falling from a height of 18 in. The standard number of blows per layer is 55 (corresponding to the modified AASHO* compactive effort), although a lesser number of blows are also used to establish the CBR for design.

As will be seen subsequently, empirical relationships for various wheel loads have been established between the CBR test value and the thickness of the pavement structure.

Adaptation of the CBR Procedure to Airfield Pavements

Investigations made by the California Highway Department from 1928 to 1942 on both adequate and inadequate pavements furnished data from which the empirical relationship of CBR versus thickness, shown in Fig. 12-3, was developed. Curve B indicates the minimum thickness of the pavement structure for light traffic, and curve A the thickness for average highway traffic conditions. Further analysis of the data from which the two curves were derived indicated that curve A was the more reliable of the two, and that it was reasonable to assume that it represented a 9000-lb truck wheel load. Because aircraft tires are operated at much larger deformations than truck tires, and because highway traffic is much more channelized, it was reasoned that the 9000-lb truck wheel load was equivalent to a 12,000-lb aircraft wheel load. Thus, curve A (Fig. 12-3) was assumed to represent a 12,000-lb aircraft wheel load.

* American Association of State Highway Officials (now the American Association of State Highway and Transportation Officials).

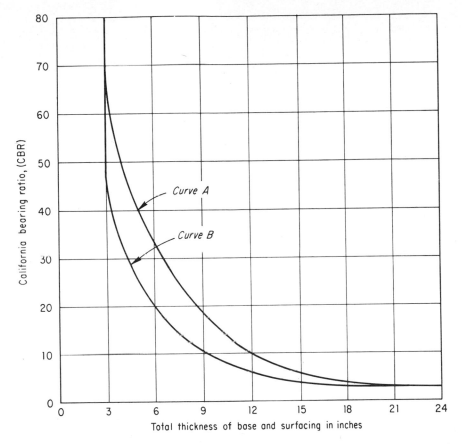

Fig. 12-3 Total thickness of base and surfacing in relation to CBR values. (*Corps of Engineers.*)

At the time the CBR procedure was first adopted by the Corps of Engineers, aircraft tire pressures were on the order of 60 lb/in², and single-wheel loads ranged from 25,000 to 70,000 lb. Because of the war emergency program, an attempt was made to utilize soil mechanics theory to extrapolate from the 12,000-lb wheel load to the larger loads. The following procedure was used.

With a contact pressure of 60 lb/in² contact areas were computed for 12,000-, 25,000-, 40,000-, and 70,000-lb wheel loads. It was assumed that the contact areas were circular. Shear stresses were then computed as shown in Fig. 12-4. The thicknesses of the pavement structure corresponding to CBRs of 3, 5, 7, and 10 on curve A (Fig. 12-3) were plotted on the shear stress curve for the 12,000-lb wheel load, and the corresponding stresses were noted (for example, 5 lb/in² for a CBR of 3). These stress

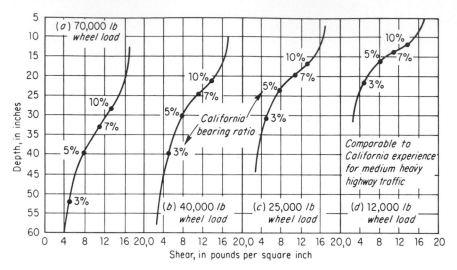

Fig. 12-4 Extrapolation of highway pavement thickness by the elastic theory. (*Corps of Engineers.*)

values were located on the curves for the 25,000-, 40,000-, and 70,000-lb wheel loads, and the corresponding depths noted. The depths, which represent thicknesses, were then plotted on a graph of thickness versus CBR, and a chart similar to the one shown in Fig. 12-5 was developed.

From a strictly theoretical point of view, the conditions assumed in the calculations have several limitations. One such limitation is the assumption of a homogeneous mass for the pavement structure. Nevertheless the analysis was a good beginning and proved to be in substantial agreement with the thicknesses developed later from full-scale test tracks.

Concurrent with the theoretical approach, a comprehensive investigation program involving the construction of a number of full-scale test tracks was initiated. The results of these investigations indicated that the curves established from theoretical considerations appeared to be conservative for the higher CBR values, and for the heavier wheel loads they were not sufficient for the lower CBR values. Accordingly, the basic curves shown in Fig. 12-5 were adjusted to reflect the results of the investigations.

During the greater part of World War II, heavy bombardment aircraft were supported by two main landing gears, each gear consisting of a single wheel. Toward the end of the war, the B-29 entered into service. Its landing gear consisted of dual wheels. An analysis of the effect of this type of gear on pavement thickness and the development of appropriate thickness charts to reflect the new type of landing gear was required.

Subsequent to the introduction of the B-29, as aircraft grew in size it was necessary to spread the load more and more in order to keep the thickness of the pavement structure within tolerable limits, with the result that the number of wheels in each landing gear was increased from two to four (dual-in-tandem arrangement). The analysis developed for the B-29 assembly was extended to develop thickness design relationships for new aircraft with this type of gear. This methodology was used until the middle 1950s, at which time the Corps of Engineers reanalyzed their data and ascertained that the thicknesses were slightly unconservative.

The discussion to follow details the results of a part of this reanalysis, since it is used in the present methodology to develop design thicknesses for new aircraft as they are developed.

One of the principal causes of failure in a pavement is an undesirable amount of movement of material. This movement is manifested as strain or deflection. It was therefore reasoned that an acceptable criterion of failure would be strain or deflection. Since few or no data on strain were available, the curve of the slope or rate of change of deflection versus offset (Fig. 12-6) was considered as a reasonable index of critical strain.

Deflection versus offset curves were computed for single and dual wheels by use of Boussinesq's theory. Some test data on deflection profiles

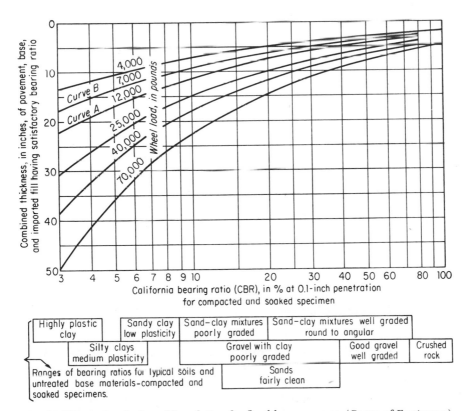

Fig. 12-5 Tentative design of foundation for flexible pavements. (*Corps of Engineers.*)

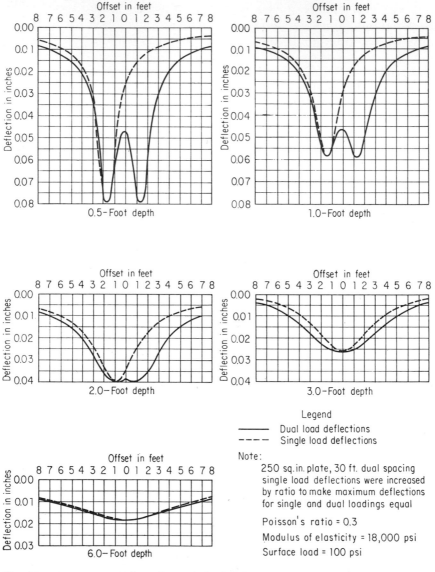

Fig. 12-6 Comparison of single- and dual-deflection profiles theory. (*Waterways Experiment Station, Corps of Engineers.*)

were also available. The test data confirmed the validity of the theoretical computations. It was found, from both the theoretical work and the test data, that without exception the slopes of the deflection versus offset curves for the single loads were equal to or steeper than those for dual wheels at equal depths, as shown in Fig. 12-6. From such an analysis it was demonstrated that a *single-wheel load, which yields the same maximum deflection as a multiple-wheel load, would produce equal or more severe strains in the foundation in comparison with the multiple-wheel load.* For purposes of design, the single-wheel load could be considered equivalent to the multiple-wheel load; thus the concept of the equivalent single-wheel load (ESWL) was introduced. The contact area of this ESWL is equal to the contact area of one of the wheels of the multiple-wheel assembly.

To develop the thickness requirements for a multiple-wheel assembly of known dimensions and total load, ESWLs were computed at various depths by use of the theory of elasticity (Boussinesq's theory as expanded by A.E.H. Love). For each depth there is a different equivalent single-wheel load. The ESWLs are determined for several depths; a curve relating the ESWL to depth is drawn.

To illustrate the procedure, the following example is provided. Assume a dual-in-tandem assembly as shown in Fig. 12-7. Total load on the assembly is 130,000 lb, and the contact pressure is 140 lb/in².

The total contact area is equal to 928 in², and the contact area of each wheel is 232 in². Suppose it is desired to find the maximum ESWL at a depth equal to three times the radius of the contact area of each wheel.

The calculations are as follows:

$$r = \sqrt{\frac{A}{\pi}} = \sqrt{\frac{232}{\pi}} = 8.6 \text{ in}$$

$$3r = 25.8 \text{ in}$$

where r = radius of contact area, in
       A = contact area of wheel, in²

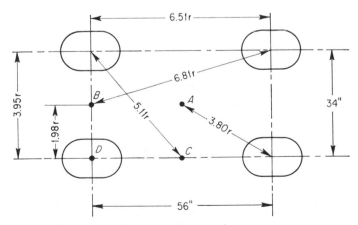

Fig. 12-7 Dual-in-tandem example—reanalysis.

The problem resolves itself to finding the location where the maximum deflection at a depth of 25.8 in will occur. As a trial, four locations were investigated, as shown in Fig. 12.7.* The center of the assembly is designated as location A; midway on the 34-in dimension as location B; midway on the 56-in dimension as location C; and under one wheel of the assembly as location D.

In an elastic medium the deflection W is expressed by Eq. (12-1)

$$W = \frac{prF}{E_m} \tag{12-1}$$

where p = load intensity
$\quad E_m$ = modulus of elasticity
$\quad\ F$ = deflection factor obtained from Fig. 12-8

By using subscripts s and d to denote single and dual wheels, we may write

$$W_s = \frac{r_s}{E_m} p_s F_s \quad \text{and} \quad W_d = \frac{r_d}{E_m} p_d F_d$$

Since $W_s = W_d$ and $r_s = r_d$,

$$\frac{p_s}{p_d} = \frac{F_d}{F_s}$$

The contact area of the single wheel is equal to the contact area of one wheel of the assembly. Thus Eq. (12-2) results:

$$\frac{P_s}{P_d} = \frac{F_d}{F_s} \tag{12-2}$$

or the ratio of the ESWL (P_s) to one wheel of the dual assembly (P_d) is the inverse of the ratio of the maximum deflection factors.

The deflection factors are obtained from Fig. 12-8 and are as follows. For the single wheel the factor at a depth of $3r$ is 0.47 (directly under the axis of load). For the dual-in-tandem assembly the factors must be computed as shown in Table 12-1.

To determine the deflection factors from Fig. 12-8, the distances from each location (A, B, C, and D) to each wheel of the assembly must be expressed in terms of radius r.

In the example, the maximum deflection occurs under the axis of one of the wheels of the assembly (at D). The corresponding deflection factor is 0.89. The various deflection factors are summarized in Table 12-2. The

---

* Tire imprints in Fig. 12-7 are assumed to be circles.

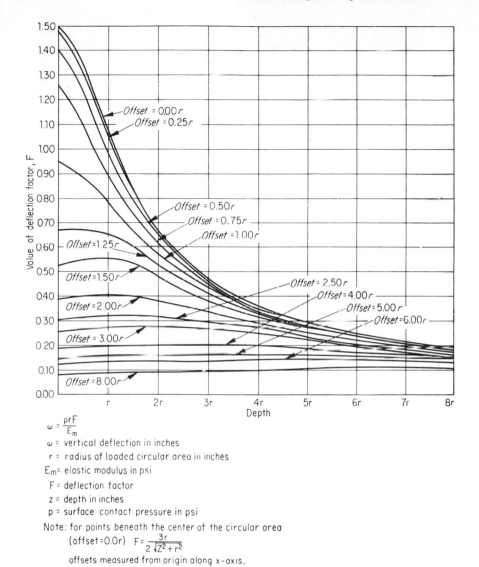

$$\omega = \frac{prF}{E_m}$$

ω = vertical deflection in inches
r = radius of loaded circular area in inches
E_m= elastic modulus in psi
F = deflection factor
z = depth in inches
p = surface contact pressure in psi
Note: for points beneath the center of the circular area
    (offset=0.0r) $F = \dfrac{3r}{2\sqrt{z^2 + r^2}}$
offsets measured from origin along x-axis.

Fig. 12-8 Deflection factor F for uniform load of radius r at points beneath the x axis; Poisson ratio = 0.5. (*Waterways Experiment Station, Corps of Engineers.*)

ESWL at a depth of 25.8 in is then

$$0.475(130,000) = 61,750 \text{ lb}$$

or it may be computed by multiplying the deflection factor of 1.90 by the load on a single wheel of the assembly (32,500 lb).

Analyses of this type, together with the single-wheel load curves

TABLE 12-1

| Depth | Deflection factors for dual-in-tandem assembly | | | |
	At A	At B	At C	At D
$3r$	0.21	0.34	0.25	0.47
$3r$	0.21	0.34	0.25	0.20
$3r$	0.21	0.10	0.16	0.12
$3r$	0.21	0.10	0.16	0.10
Total	0.84	0.88	0.82	0.89

developed over the years (Fig. 12-9 for loads with 100-lb/in^2 tire pressure and Fig. 12-10 for loads with tire pressures of 200 lb/in^2), permit the development of design curves for aircraft with multiple wheels. The method is shown later.

In 1958 an analysis of all available service-behavior data for test sections and prototype airfields indicated that the CBR design criteria for single-wheel loads could be expressed in the parameters: thickness per square root of contact area $(t/\sqrt{A})$ and CBR per tire pressure, which separated failures and nonfailures for near capacity operations (approximately 5000 coverages). The mathematical expression for the relationship was

$$t = \sqrt{\frac{P}{8.1(CBR)} - \frac{A}{\pi}} \qquad (12\text{-}3)$$

where t = design thickness, in
P = single-wheel load, lb
A = tire contact area, in^2

Data from the curves of Figs. 12-9 and 12-10, plotted in this form, are shown in Fig. 12-11. It will be noted that the expression appears valid for CBR values less than about 12. Thicknesses at CBR values greater than 12 are larger because of durability and other requirements.

To account for load repetitions and multiple-wheel gear configurations, the above equation was modified to the following:

$$t = f \sqrt{\frac{ESWL}{8.1(CBR)} - \frac{A}{\pi}} \qquad (12\text{-}4)$$

TABLE 12-2

| Depth, in | Single-wheel deflection factor | Dual-wheel deflection factor | Load ratio | |
			Single to one wheel of assembly	Entire assembly
25.8	0.47	0.89	1.90	0.475

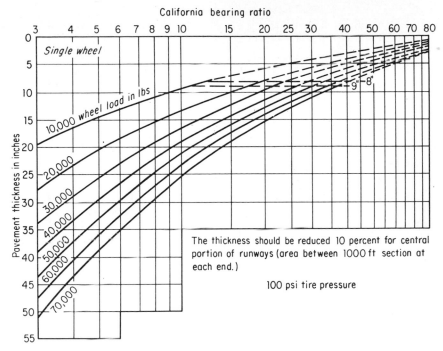

Fig. 12-9 Flexible pavement design curves for taxiways. (*Corps of Engineers.*)

where f = percent of design thickness ($0.23 \log C + 0.15$)
  ESWL = equivalent single-wheel load (determined as described previously)
  C = coverage (sufficient wheel passes to cover every point of traffic lane once)

It is by this procedure that many of the design charts for commercial jet aircraft have been developed. Thickness versus CBR curves for a number of representative jet aircraft are shown in Fig. 12-12. The thicknesses are for taxiways and runway ends (first 1000 ft). Thicknesses for runway interiors are less than those shown by the design relationships [34].*

Recent studies of test pavements subjected to loadings representative of multiple-wheel heavy gear load aircraft (e.g., B-747) have indicated that thicknesses developed at larger repetitions are somewhat conservative if the equation of the preceding paragraph is utilized. Accordingly the present method uses the formula [6]

$$ t = \alpha_i \sqrt{\frac{\text{ESWL}}{8.1(\text{CBR})} - \frac{A}{\pi}} \tag{12-5} $$

* The Corps of Engineers uses a reduced load for a particular aircraft to design the runway interior.

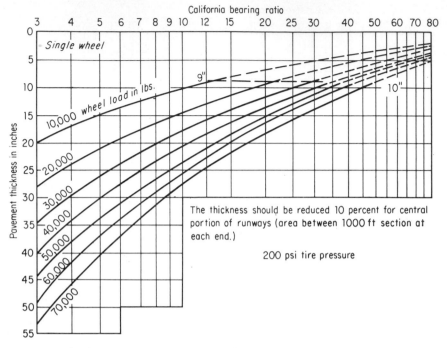

Fig. 12-10 Flexible pavement design curves for taxiways. (*Corps of Engineers.*)

where α_i = load repetition factor, which is dependent on number of wheels for each main landing gear used to compute ESWL; for example, for a B-747, 8 wheels should be used, as shown in Fig. 12-13.

The load repetition factor α_i is based on aircraft passes, whereas the previous relationships were based on coverages.* Relationships between coverages and passes can be found [7, 44]. This equation provides reasonable thicknesses up to CBR values of 15. For CBR values in excess of 15, durability considerations as well as other factors govern pavement thickness.

Thus to develop a CBR versus thickness relationship for any aircraft, the steps may be summarized as follows:

1. For a particular depth t, determine the ESWL according to procedure described previously.

2. For the desired number of aircraft operations (design period), such as 100,000, select α_i from Fig. 12-13.

* A pass is defined as one operation of an aircraft.

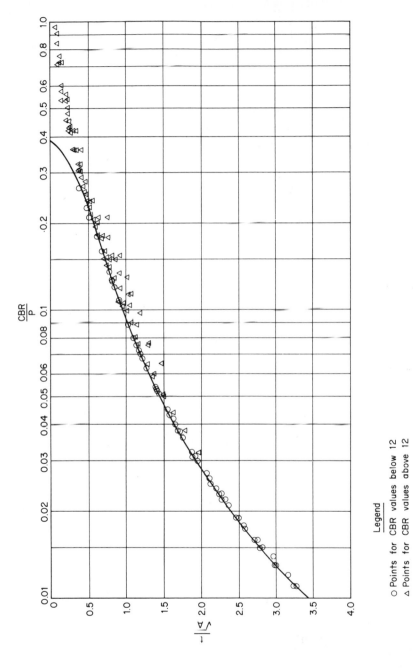

Fig. 12-11 Consolidated CBR design criteria. (*Waterways Experiment Station, Corps of Engineers.*)

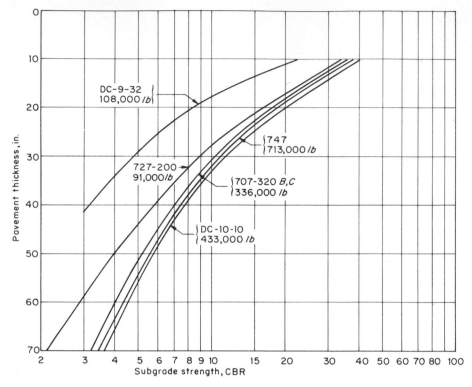

Fig. 12-12 Flexible pavement thickness—Corps of Engineers design method. Weights represent maximum ramp weights with the main landing gears loaded to their maximum.

3. Solve Eq. (12-5) for CBR.

4. Repeat for other depths so that curves of the type shown in Fig. 12-12 can be developed.

Similarly, curves of ESWL versus pavement thickness may be developed for ranges of CBR. The procedure for a particular aircraft is as follows:

1. Determine the ESWL for various depths.

2. Plot the ESWL against the depth.

3. Determine the pavement thickness t required for each ESWL and CBR.

4. Plot the ESWL versus thickness curve on the same graph as in step 2 for each CBR.

5. The point of intersection between the curves determines the required thickness.

This procedure is shown in Fig. 12-14.

Design Example

To illustrate the thickness selection procedure, assume that a pavement is to be designed for a set of conditions where frost and special subgrade treatment are not considerations.

Assume that a taxiway is to be designed for a DC-10-10 using the relationship shown in Fig. 12-12. The design CBR values for the prepared (compacted) subgrade and structural section materials are as follows.

Material	Design CBR
Compacted subgrade soil	5
Select material subbase	25
Crushed rock base	80

The total thickness of pavement is governed by the CBR of the compacted soil. From Fig. 12-12 the required thickness of the pavement structure is 55 in; it is composed of subbase, base, and an asphalt concrete course. Above the subbase a thickness of 17 in is required; thus the subbase thickness is 38 in. If an 8-in asphalt concrete layer is used, the base layer thickness will be 9 in, the difference between 17 and 8 in. For a pavement section of this thickness it is possible that more than one subbase layer might be utilized.

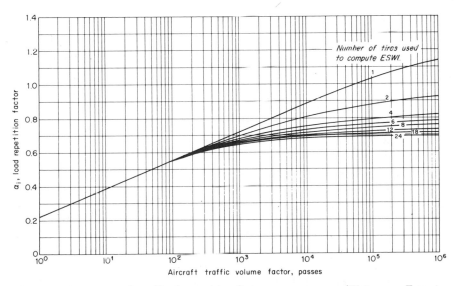

Fig. 12-13 Composite plot of load repetition factors versus passes. (*Waterways Experiment Station, Corps of Engineers.*)

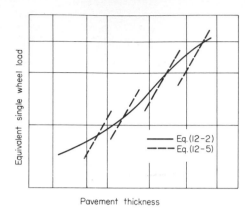

Fig. 12-14 Illustration of the determination of the flexible pavement design curve for an aircraft by equivalent single-wheel load method.

Materials

Bituminous surface courses for airfields should be of sufficient thickness to ensure that excessive stresses will not be transmitted to the underlying layer, and that the stresses in the layer itself will not lead to premature cracking. According to recommendations by the Corps of Engineers, the thickness should be not less than 3 in.*

The base course immediately under the bituminous surface course should be able to withstand the stresses produced in the zone directly under the wheels of an aircraft. The required stability depends on the type and thickness of the surface course and the magnitude of loading. For the surface course noted in the example, the CBR of a crushed stone base course should be in the range of 80 to 100, depending on the load. The minimum thickness of a crushed stone base suggested by the Corps of Engineers is 6 in. A greater thickness is normally preferred.

Recent tests by the Corps of Engineers indicate the advantage of stabilized bases (asphalt or portland cement) in improving the performance of pavements subjected to frequent repetitions of heavy loads. Accordingly it would appear desirable to ensure that the upper 9 to 15 in of the pavement structure be composed of a bituminous surface layer plus a stabilized course. Care should be exercised in the analysis of the benefits of structurally improved layers to consider the economics associated with applications to particular airport projects [16, 19, 28].

Strength characteristics of subbases vary widely, from 20 to 50 CBR. Above 50 CBR materials are generally regarded as base courses.

---

* The authors' experience would suggest larger thicknesses for the bituminous course, particularly for many repetitions of the heavier aircraft.

Compaction Requirements

Field studies by the Corps of Engineers have shown that compaction produced in a given layer by traffic is a function of total load, arrangement of tires, tire pressure, number of repetitions, and depth to a given layer. These parameters can be combined by the use of the design CBR. The term *compaction index* C_i was introduced; this value is the design CBR value for the corresponding depth and load.

Degree of compaction (based on the modified AASHO compaction test) versus compaction index curves for cohesive and cohesionless soils are shown in Fig. 12-15; these curves represent relationships established from field data.

To illustrate the use of the compaction index curves to establish compaction requirements for a specific aircraft, consider the DC-10-10 curve shown in Fig. 12-12. Since the design CBR equals the compaction index, by combining the data of Figs. 12-12 and 12-15 it is possible to develop the density requirements for a specific aircraft, as shown in Fig. 12-16. From this curve it will be noted that any cohesionless material in the upper 3 ft of the pavement section should be compacted to at least 100 percent of the density obtained in the modified AASHO compaction test.

THE DESIGN OF RIGID PAVEMENTS

The design of portland cement concrete pavements for airports is based upon a vast amount of data which have been compiled during many years of research and observation of the behavior of pavements. The Corps of Engineers, the Portland Cement Association (PCA), and the FAA have contributed much to our knowledge of concrete pavements. The material presented herein, much of which has been obtained from publications of

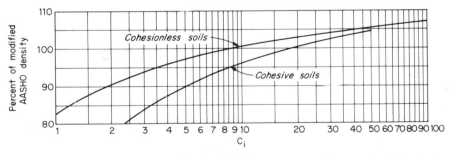

Fig. 12-15 Compaction requirements for flexible pavements. Compaction index is the design CBR value for the corresponding depth and load. (*Waterways Experiment Station, Corps of Engineers.*)

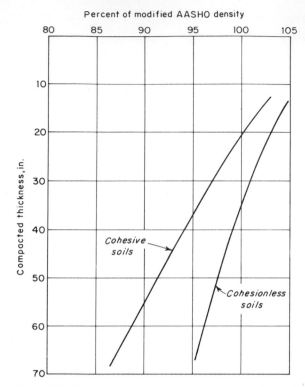

Fig. 12-16 Density requirements for pavement subjected to DC-10-10 loading.

these three agencies, briefly summarizes the design procedures which have been developed from research and practice.

Stress in a concrete pavement is induced in several ways, as follows:

1. Wheel loads

2. Change of shape of slab due to differential in temperature between top and bottom of the slab (commonly referred to as curling)

3. Change of shape of slab due to differential in moisture between top and bottom of the slab

4. Friction developed between slab and foundation when the slab desires to change its volume

The first consideration in the design of any pavement is the load which it is to carry. When the load is known, the next step is to determine the critical stresses which are developed in the slab. Several methods of computing stresses have been proposed, the best known of which is the analysis developed by Westergaard [45]. A number of organizations have conducted comprehensive studies to determine the validity of the analysis.

Approximate solutions for stresses due to curling and friction have also been developed and are summarized in the succeeding paragraphs.

Westergaard's Analysis

Westergaard assumed the pavement slab to be a thin plate resting on a special subgrade which is considered elastic in the vertical direction only. That is, the reaction is proportional to the deflection of the subgrade, $p = kz$, where $z =$ deflection and $k =$ a soil constant, referred to as the *modulus of subgrade reaction*. Other assumptions are that the concrete slab is a homogeneous, isotropic elastic solid and that the wheel load of an aircraft is distributed over an elliptical area. Although these assumptions do not satisfy theory in a strict sense, the results have compared reasonably with observations. The Westergaard analysis can be used to evaluate stress in a pavement slab and the deflection of the slab. The analysis, however, is not applicable for the determination of stresses and deflections in the foundation material.

For airports Westergaard developed formulas for stresses and deflections (1) in the interior of a slab and (2) at an edge of a slab or at a joint that has no capacity for load transfer. These formulas for stress are as follows [45].

Case I

The load is applied in the interior of the area of a panel at a considerable distance from any edge or joint. The total load P is distributed uniformly over an elliptical area defined by the expression

$$\frac{x^2}{a^2} + \frac{y^2}{b^2} = 1$$

The maximum principal tensile stress σ_i at the bottom of the slab under the center of the load may be computed by the following formula:

$$\sigma_i = \frac{P}{d^2}\left\{0.275(1 + \mu)\log_{10}\frac{Ed^3}{k[(a + b)/2]^4} + 0.239(1 - \mu)\frac{a - b}{a + b}\right\} \qquad (12\text{-}6)$$

Case II

The load is applied adjacent to an edge or joint that has no capacity for load transfer. The total load P is distributed uniformly over an elliptical area, the prolate edge of which is tangent to the edge or joint and is defined by the equation

$$\frac{x^2}{a^2} + \frac{(y - b)^2}{b^2} = 1$$

The tensile stress σ_e at the bottom of the slab, along the edge or joint, directly under the point of tangency of the ellipse, may be computed by Eq. (12-7)

$$\sigma_e = \frac{2.2(1 + \mu)P}{(3 + \mu)d^2} \log_{10} \frac{Ed^3}{100k[(a + b)/2]^4}$$

$$+ \frac{3(1 + \mu)P}{\pi(3 + \mu)d^2} \left[1.84 - \frac{4}{3}\mu + (1 + \mu)\frac{a - b}{a + b} \right. \tag{12-7}$$

$$\left. + 2(1 - \mu)\frac{ab}{(a + b)^2} + 1.18(1 + 2\mu)\frac{b}{l} \right]$$

where P = load transmitted through a tire to a panel of the pavement, lb

  a, b = semiaxes of an ellipse which represents the footprint of a tire. If the load is next to an edge or joint, a is the semiaxis parallel to the edge or joint. Either a or b may be the greater semiaxis, depending on whether the joint is longitudinal or transverse.

  x, y = horizontal rectangular coordinates. If the load is next to an edge or joint, the axis of x is along the line of the edge or joint; if the footprint of the tire is represented by an ellipse, the axis of x is in the direction of the semiaxis a.

  d = thickness of slab, in

  E = modulus of elasticity of concrete, lb/in^2

  μ = Poisson's ratio of concrete

  k = modulus of subgrade reaction, lb/in^3

  l = radius of relative stiffness, in

To obtain the allowable stress, it is customary to divide the modulus of rupture of the concrete by a factor of safety, for which the PCA suggests the values tabulated below [24].

Installation	Safety factor
Aprons, taxiways, runway ends	1.7–2.0
Runways (central portion)	1.4–1.7

These safety factors are related to fatigue of concrete. It has been found that if the concrete is stressed repeatedly at a value approximately one-half of the ultimate flexural strength, it can stand an unlimited number of load repetitions. As the stress under repeated loading approaches the ultimate flexural strength, the number of repetitions of load which can be applied without causing failure becomes progressively less. On aprons, taxiways, and runway ends, the traffic is more channelized than in the central portion of runways. Hence, the safety factor is greater for the former group of pavements.

The modulus of rupture used for design is normally the flexural strength at 90 days, although the 28-day value increased by a factor of 1.10 to 1.14 can also be used.

The charts for determining stress which were prepared by the PCA [24] are based on the assumption that the wheel load is in the interior of a panel (case I). This assumption stems from the argument that all interior joints have adequate load transfer devices so that conditions at any point within the pavement panel are nearly the same as though the point under consideration were near the middle of a large slab.

The charts prepared by the Corps of Engineers [58] are derived from Westergaard's edge formula, on the basis that such a loading condition does occur at the edges of joints, and, moreover, it is more critical. However, in order to recognize the action of load transfer devices, it is assumed that when the load is placed at an edge of a slab, one-quarter of the load is transferred to the adjacent slab. The remaining load (0.75P) is increased by 30 percent to take care of curling stresses, load repetitions, and other contingencies. The net load (0.75(1.3) = 0.98P) is used in the Westergaard edge load formula.

Figures 12-17 through 12-20 contain design charts prepared by the PCA for a number of different types of jet aircraft. These design relationships were developed using a computer program based on the Westergaard analysis [14]. This program can be used for a range in gear configurations and loads, making it possible for the designer to develop designs for aircraft to which a specific pavement might be subjected.

In the design charts, gear load rather than gross aircraft weight is used. This information is available from the aircraft manufacturers' data.

An alternative approach to the use of the PCA computer program is to make use of the influence charts developed by Pickett and Ray [38]. Their application is discussed in [24]. A sample chart is shown in Fig. 12-21 with an aircraft gear superimposed. Note that the scale of the chart is expressed in terms of l, the radius of relative stiffness. The scale to which the tire imprint of the multiple-wheel assembly is drawn is based on the ratio of the graphic l on the chart to the actual l. That is, the graphic dimensions are equal to the actual dimensions multiplied by the ratio of the graphic l to the actual l of the pavement. The objective is to place the wheels on the chart so that the maximum number of blocks are incorporated within the tire imprint area. The bending moment M is expressed as:

$$M = \frac{ql^2N}{10,000} \tag{12-8}$$

where q = tire contact pressure, lb/in^2
l = radius of relative stiffness of slab
N = number of blocks enclosed

Application of Fatigue Concept to Traffic Analysis

The fatigue procedure developed by the PCA can be applied to the design and evaluation of pavements at airports serving large volumes of heavy multigeared aircraft of various types as an alternate to the procedure described earlier utilizing the safety factor concept. According to the PCA its applications are:

1. Design for specific volumes of mixed traffic

2. Evaluation of future traffic capacity of existing pavements or of an existing pavement's capacity to carry a limited number of overloads

3. Evaluation of the fatigue effects of future aircraft with complex gear arrangements

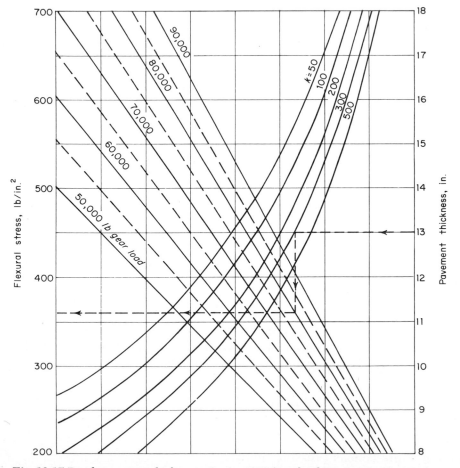

Fig. 12-17 Rigid pavement thickness—Boeing 727. (*Portland Cement Association.*)

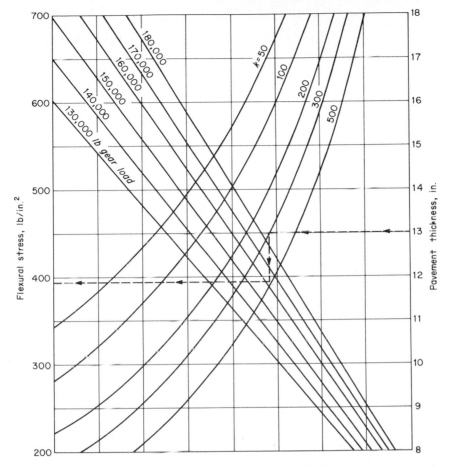

Fig. 12-18 Rigid pavement thickness—DC-8-62, 63. (*Portland Cement Association.*)

4. More precise definition of the comparative thicknesses of runways, taxiways, and other pavement areas depending on operational characteristics

Essentially the procedure involves the analysis of a selected slab thickness* for the expected traffic. For a particular aircraft, the stress corresponding to a specific gear load can be ascertained by means of either the computer program [14] or a chart like Fig. 12-18. To determine the damage produced by the anticipated repetitions of an aircraft, the stress ratio, defined as the ratio of the applied stress to the modulus of rupture, is determined. Fatigue tests on portland cement concrete have indicated that

* This may be either an existing slab thickness or one whose suitability is being ascertained.

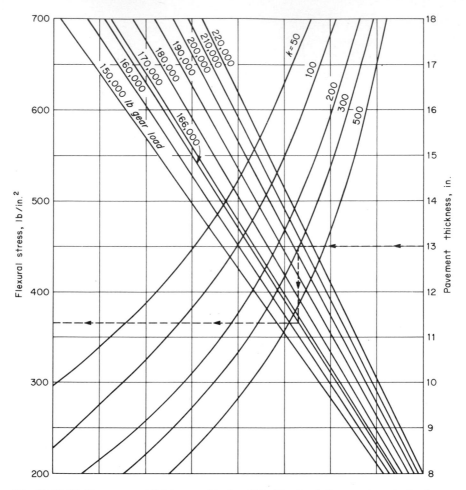

Fig. 12-19 Rigid pavement thickness—Boeing 747. (*Portland Cement Association.*)

test data can be conservatively normalized in terms of this same stress ratio; Table 12-3 contains the basic concrete fatigue data used by the PCA. The structural capacity used up by the anticipated repetitions n_i of an aircraft class i is the ratio of n_i to the allowable number of repetitions to cause failure at the stress ratio N_i, produced by an aircraft of class i. The total structural capacity used is the sum of these cycle ratios for the mix of aircraft structural capacity used, namely,

$$\text{Structural capacity used} = \sum_{i=1}^{n} \frac{n_i}{N_i} \leq 1 \qquad (12\text{-}9)$$

where the term n_i is the actual repetitions of load of a specified aircraft of class i multiplied by a load repetition factor (LRF) which accounts for the lateral wander of the wheels. Typical LRFs are 0.57 for the DC-10, 0.58 for the 747, 0.83 for the 707 and DC-8, and 0.41 for the 727 on taxiways, with a standard deviation of 24 in for the average path tracked. Other values for use on runways are contained in [24]. Values for other aircraft are also listed. Practically this summation should not exceed unity.

Provision is included in the PCA procedure to recognize some lateral distribution of aircraft on both taxiways and runways, variation in concrete strength, and the influence of weak foundation support ($k < 200$ lb/in^3).

Determination of the Modulus of Subgrade Reaction

The modulus of soil reaction k of the subgrade is determined by a field plate bearing test. The test should be made on representative areas of the foundation materials which are to support the pavement. Normally, the procedure consists in applying loads by means of a hydraulic jack through a

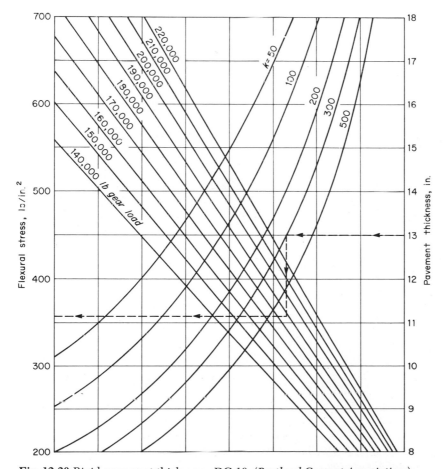

Fig. 12-20 Rigid pavement thickness—DC-10. (*Portland Cement Association.*)

jacking frame onto a steel plate 30 in in diameter. By loading the plate, a load versus deformation curve is obtained. By definition,

$$k = \frac{\text{pressure in lb/in}^2 \text{ to cause a deformation of 0.05 in}}{0.05 \text{ in}}$$

If the tests are made during the dry season, there might be no indication of how much reduction in k would result if the foundation material became saturated. The Corps of Engineers, recognizing that most soils exhibit a

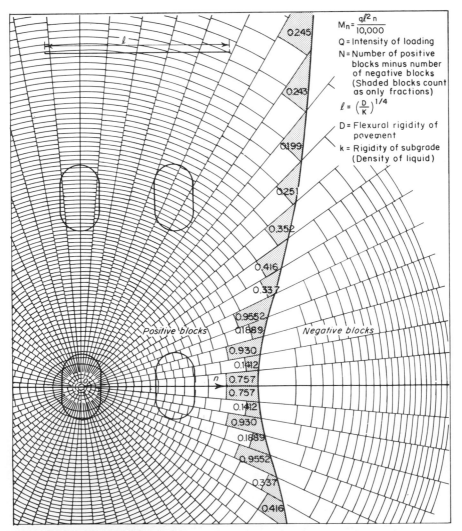

Fig. 12-21 Influence chart for moment M_n due to load at interior of concrete slab. Subgrade assumed to be a dense liquid. Poisson ratio for pavement assumed to be 0.15. (*Portland Cement Association.*)

TABLE 12-3 **Stress Ratios and Allowable Load Repetitions**

Stress* ratio	Allowable repetitions	Stress ratio	Allowable repetitions
0.51[†]	400,000	0.63	14,000
0.52	300,000	0.64	11,000
0.53	240,000	0.65	8,000
0.54	180,000	0.66	6,000
0.55	130,000	0.67	4,500
0.56	100,000	0.68	3,500
0.57	75,000	0.69	2,500
0.58	57,000	0.70	2,000
0.59	42,000	0.71	1,500
0.60	32,000	0.72	1,100
0.61	24,000	0.73	850
0.62	18,000	0.74	650

* Load stress divided by modulus of rupture.

† Unlimited repetitions for stress ratios of 0.50 or less.

SOURCE: Portland Cement Association. [65]

marked reduction in the modulus of soil reaction with increase in moisture content, have developed a more refined procedure for determining k. With a 30-in-diameter plate, the plate is first seated, and then a load of 10 lb/in^2 is applied (7070 lb), and the corresponding deflection is observed. The uncorrected modulus of subgrade reaction is

$$k_\mu = \frac{10 \text{ lb/in}^2}{\text{observed deflection corresponding to 10 lb/in}^2}$$

The value k_μ is further corrected for bending of the plate and for the assumption of full saturation of the foundation material. The correction for saturation is made by use of the consolidation test. The procedure is described in detail in [58].

The choice of a 30-in-diameter plate stems from observations which showed that, for plates less than 26 in in diameter, the size of the plate has a significant influence on k, while for larger plates k is relatively independent of the plate diameter.

Actually, k is not a significant variable in the Westergaard formulas. Fairly large variations in k do not produce large variations in stress. Therefore, for preliminary evaluation k need not be measured, but can be estimated by reference to available correlations with other soil strength indices, such as CBR. The general range of k values is as follows [24]:

Description of foundation material	k
Very poor	Less than 150
Fair to good	200–250
Very good	300 and higher

Foundation for Rigid Pavements

An imported foundation material to support a rigid pavement is often referred to as a subbase, because its quality, in most cases, need not be as high as a base course for flexible pavement. Imported granular and treated material is placed over the native soils to serve one or more of the following functions:

1. To prevent or reduce pumping

2. To prevent damage from frost action

3. To prevent detrimental action due to swell and shrinkage in high-volume soils

4. To improve the supporting capacity of the native soil (very rarely justified)

5. To produce a smooth stable platform during construction

When certain types of fine-grain subgrade soils are saturated, repeated deflection of the pavement causes a mixture of soil and water to be ejected at or near joints and cracks. This is referred to as *pumping.* Three conditions must be present to produce pumping: (1) water, (2) soil that will go into suspension, and (3) traffic. Soils most conducive to pumping are those in which the silt and clay fractions predominate. The best way to minimize pumping is to use a treated subbase using portland cement or asphalt, particularly for heavily trafficked airport pavements.

Stabilized subbases offer a number of benefits in addition to preventing pumping:

1. Provide an impermeable, uniform, and strong support for the pavement

2. Eliminate traffic compaction influences in the material directly under the slab

3. Improve load transfer at joints

4. Expedite construction since stabilized layer will minimize shutdowns due to adverse weather

5. Provide firm support for slip-form paver or side forms, contributing thereby to the construction of smoother pavements

Guidelines for the design of cement-stabilized subbases are contained in [19, 24].

When granular or stabilized layers are used on top of the subgrade, there will be an increase in k value. If it is not feasible to test such a construction, an estimate of the k value can be made from Figs. 12-22 and 12-23.

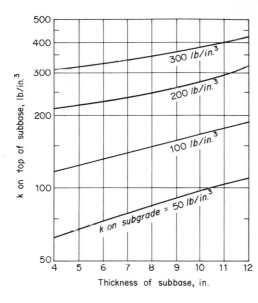

Fig. 12-22 Effect of granular subbase thickness on *k* value. (*Portland Cement Association.*)

Stresses in Rigid Pavements Due to Temperature and Moisture Differentials

Whenever the top and bottom surfaces of a concrete pavement simultaneously have different temperatures, the slab tends to assume a bent or warped shape which induces flexural or so-called *curling* or *warping* stresses. If the slab were weightless and could change shape freely, there would be no warping stress. The stress is caused by the resistance of the slab (due to its weight) to change in shape. Because of the insulating effects of slab thickness, the bottom surface will react to the change more slowly than the top surface.

The subject of warping stresses is complicated and has been treated theoretically by Westergaard [9] and Kelley [10]. Stresses due to temperature warping can, under certain conditions, be equal to and additive to stresses due to load. In the interior the maximum stress due to load causes tension at the bottom of the slab; the same is true of temperature warping.

Warping stresses can also be caused by a differential in moisture content between the top and bottom of the slab. The reason for this is that the slab tends to dry out faster at the top than on the bottom. The greater the moisture content, the more the slab tends to elongate. The following pertinent statement is quoted from a report prepared by the Bureau of Public Roads:

> The annual cyclic variation in moisture conditions within the concrete produces a warping of the slab surface similar to that caused by temperature. The edges of the slab reach their maximum position of upward warping from this cause during the summer and the maximum portion of downward

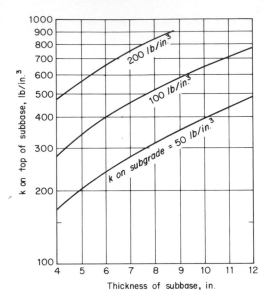

Fig. 12-23 Effect of cement-treated subbase on *k* value. (*Portland Cement Association.*)

warping during the winter, the extent of the upward movement apparently exceeding that of the downward movement appreciably. While sufficient information is not available to permit an estimate to be made of the magnitude of the stresses arising from restrained moisture warping, it appears that at the time of year when the stresses from restrained temperature warping are a maximum (summer months), any stresses caused by restrained moisture warping will be of opposite sense and will thus tend to reduce rather than to increase the state of stress created by restrained temperature warping.

Rarely do the conditions in practice approach those assumed by theory. In a majority of cases, warping stresses are not computed. Warping stresses can be reduced substantially by avoiding long slabs, for example, by introducing joints.

Neither the PCA nor the Corps of Engineers suggests that warping stresses be computed, for it is recognized that only a few times will these stresses be additive. There is usually sufficient margin between the actual stress developed by the wheel load and the ultimate flexural strength of the concrete to take care of warping stresses.

Frictional Stress

Changes in temperature tend to change the length of a slab. Each half of the slab tends to move with reference to the subgrade. If the slab expands, the movement is from the center of the slab toward the free ends. When the slab contracts, the reverse is true. Friction between the foundation and the slab partially resists this movement, and in this way, stress is induced in the slab. The stress is compressive when expansion occurs and tensile when the slab contracts. Referring to Fig. 12-24, horizontal forces are created at the bottom of the slab, inducing stress in the slab (in this case, because of contraction of the slab). If w is the unit weight of the slab in pounds per cubic foot and c is the coefficient of subgrade friction, the force developed per linear foot and width of slab is wc; the total force is $wcL/2$. If the slab is 1 ft wide, the amount of steel required to resist this force per foot of width of slab is

$$A_s f_s = wc \frac{L}{2}$$

or

$$A_s = \frac{wcL}{2f_s} \qquad (12\text{-}10)$$

where L = length of slab between joints
  f_s = allowable tensile stress in reinforcement
  c – coefficient of subgrade (or subbase) resistance to slab movement
  A_s = cross-sectional area of steel

The PCA states [24]:

The resistance coefficient c is sometimes referred to as the coefficient of friction between the slab and subbase (or subgrade). The situation is more complex than pure sliding friction since shearing forces in the subbase or subgrade and warped slabs may be involved in the resistance. For subgrades and granular subbases, coefficients of resistance range from 1 to 2 depending on type of material and moisture conditions. Coefficients for stabilized subbases are likely to be slightly greater. Research indicates that the coefficient also varies with respect to slab length and thickness. While these variations may be taken into account . . ., use of a coefficient other than 1.5 does not seem justified by pavement performance at this time.

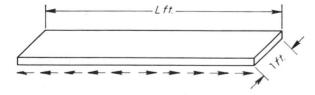

Fig. 12-24 Stress induced by subgrade friction. (*Courtesy of R. D. Bradbury, Wire Reinforcement Institute [54].*)

Amounts and Size of Steel Used in Practice

The advantages claimed for placing steel in portland cement concrete pavements are as follows:

1. Reduces number of joints and, hence, cost of joint maintenance
2. Reduces pumping by keeping cracks tightly closed
3. Prolongs service life when pavement is overloaded
4. Maintains aggregate interlock for load transfer
5. Reduces pavement deflection

The majority of airport pavements constructed in this country are plain slabs without reinforcement. Joints have been spaced no more than 25 ft, obviating the necessity for steel insofar as crack control is concerned. Steel represents an extra expense to the designers, which they must justify. The justification for the use of steel has not been readily apparent for one reason or another. Like all engineering problems, however, the conditions at each airport must be evaluated separately. At one location steel may be justified, while at another it may not. If steel is used, the spacing between contraction joints suggested for plain pavements can be increased. For example, the PCA suggests the distance may be increased up to 50 ft for thick slabs, while the FAA recommends distances between contraction joints in the range 45 to 75 ft for reinforced concrete slabs [7].

Generally pavement thickness for reinforced pavements should be the same as for unreinforced pavements, since distributed steel does not significantly increase flexural strength when used in quantities that are practical from an economic standpoint. This is particularly true for civil airports. For military airfields where traffic delays for routine maintenance may not be as critical, the Corps of Engineers permits a reduction in concrete thickness if steel is used. The procedure is outlined in detail in [58]. Steel placed in concrete pavements is in the form of bar mats or sheets of welded wire. The Corps of Engineers recommends that the steel be placed at a depth of $\frac{1}{4}h + 1$ in from the top of the slab, where h is the thickness of the slab in inches.

One should always keep in mind that the purpose of distributed steel is not to prevent cracking, but to hold the cracks closed after they have formed.

Joints and Joint Spacing

Joints are placed in concrete pavements to permit expansion and contraction of the pavement, thereby relieving flexural stresses due to curling and friction and to facilitate construction. There are three general types of joints: expansion, construction, and contraction. These joints are shown in Fig. 12-25. Their functions are as follows.

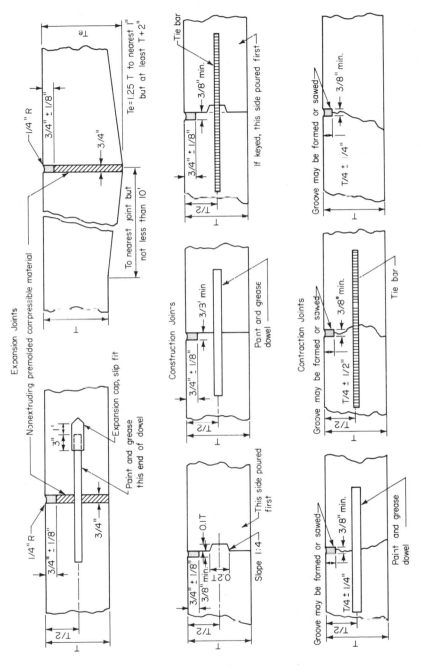

Fig. 12-25 Details of joints in rigid pavements. Shaded area is joint sealer. *(Federal Aviation Administration [7].)*

Expansion Joint

The primary function of an expansion joint is to provide space for the expansion of the pavement, thereby preventing the development of very high compressive stresses, which can cause the pavement to buckle.

Construction Joint

Construction joints are required to facilitate construction. The spacing between longitudinal joints is dictated by the width of the paving machine and by the pavement thickness.

Contraction Joint

Contraction or weakened-plane (dummy) joints are provided to relieve the tensile stresses due to temperature, moisture, and friction, thereby controlling cracking. If contraction joints were not installed, random cracking would occur on the surface of the pavement.

The spacing between contraction joints is dependent on the thickness of the slab, the character of the aggregate, and whether the slab is plain or reinforced. On the basis of experience, it has been found that for plain slabs 8 to 10 in thick, the spacing should be in the range of 15 to 20 ft. For thicker slabs the spacing can be increased to 25 ft. The Corps of Engineers omits placing of contraction joints in a longitudinal direction, provided the thickness of the slab is 8 in or more. If the slab is less than 8 in thick and the spacing between longitudinal construction joints is 20 or 25 ft, a contraction joint is recommended midway between the construction joints. The FAA recommends a longitudinal contraction joint in accordance with the specifications listed in Table 12-4. As a rule of thumb, the joint spacing in feet should not exceed twice the slab thickness in inches to any significant degree.

The spacing between construction joints is primarily dictated by the width of the paving machine. Recent developments in paving equipment permit joint widths up to 50 ft. This allows a selection of joint spacings to satisfy specific design thicknesses.

Generally expansion joints are not used in airfield pavements except

TABLE 12-4 **FAA Recommended Maximum Joint Spacing, ft**

Slab thickness, in	Joint orientation	
	Transverse	Longitudinal
Less than 9	15	12.5
9–12	20	20
Greater than 12	25	25

SOURCE: Federal Aviation Administration [7].

under special conditions. They are necessary where the pavement intersects with other structures or where two pavements intersect each other at an angle. Experience has shown that expansion joints have been a source of trouble; consequently, every effort is made to reduce their number to a minimum. For thick pavements (10 in or more in thickness), the Corps of Engineers suggests that expansion joints can be omitted entirely if the concrete is placed during warm weather. Expansion joints may be necessary, particularly if the thickness of the pavement is less than 10 in and if it is placed during cold weather. Thus, the need for and spacing of expansion joints is primarily a function of factors such as slab thickness, thermal properties of the concrete, seasonal temperature, and temperatures during construction.

Contraction joints are either grooved while the concrete is fresh or sawed after the concrete has hardened. Construction joints are formed by the slab form. In Fig. 12-25 it will be noted that expansion joints can be either thickened at the edge without load-transfer devices or of uniform thickness with a load-transfer device. Although dowels have been shown in the contraction joints, the practice varies. The Corps of Engineers omits dowels from all transverse contraction joints except for the last three joints at the runway and taxiway ends. On the other hand, the FAA recommends doweling of all transverse contraction joints for the entire length of a taxiway and also at the ends of the runways. Doweling of all contraction joints in reinforced concrete pavements is also recommended by the FAA.

Construction joints are either doweled, keyed, or both.

All joints in concrete pavements should be sealed with a sealing compound to prevent infiltration of water or foreign material into the joint spaces.

This joint sealant must be capable of withstanding repeated extension and compression as the pavement changes volume. Moreover, if the sealant is poured, the shape of the reservoir is critical. Guidelines for joint reservoirs are provided in [24].

Dowels are load-transfer devices which permit joints to open but which prevent differential vertical displacement. Usually they are solid round steel bars, although pipe may be used. Tie bars are deformed steel bars which are used to hold certain joints in contact with each other. They are not designed to transfer load from one slab to another.

Tie bars are designed in a manner similar to distributed steel, that is,

$$A_s = \frac{wcb}{f_s} \tag{12-11}$$

where b = distance between joint and the nearest untied joint or free edge, ft

and the other terms have the same meaning as before.

TABLE 12-5 **Dimensions and Spacing of Steel Dowels**

Thickness of slab, in	Diameter, in	Length, in	Spacing, in
	Corps of engineers:		
Less than 8	3/4	16	12
8–11	1	16	12
12–15	1¼	20	15
16–20	1½	20	18
21–25	2	24	18
Over 25	3	30	18
	FAA		
6–7	3/4	18	12
8–12	1	19	12
13–16	1¼	20	15
17–20	1½	20	18
21–24	2	24	18

SOURCES: Federal Aviation Administration [7] and Corps of Engineers [58].

The length of the tie bar may be determined from

$$L_t = \frac{1}{2}\left(\frac{f_s \times d_b}{u}\right) + 3 \tag{12-12}$$

where L_t = length of tiebar, in
  f_s = allowable tensile stress in tie bar, lb/in^2
  d_b = diameter of tie bar, in
  u = allowable bond stress (350 lb/in^2)

The FAA recommends that tiebars be 5/8 in in diameter, 30 in long, and placed 30 in on centers.

Several different analyses have been proposed for the design of dowels. The spacing of dowels depends on the thickness of the pavement, the modulus of subgrade reaction, and the size of the dowel. Table 12-5 contains recommendations for dowel sizes and spacings by the Corps of Engineers and the FAA.

Continuously Reinforced Concrete Pavements

A continuously reinforced concrete pavement (CRCP) is one in which transverse joints have been eliminated* and the longitudinal reinforcing steel is continuous throughout the length of the pavement. Due to the comparatively large amount of steel reinforcement in the longitudinal

* Except where the pavement intersects or abuts existing pavements or structures.

direction, the pavement develops transverse cracks at relatively close intervals, averaging between 3 and 7 ft.

Design for this type of pavement consists of providing sufficient reinforcing steel to keep the cracks tightly closed and adequate pavement thickness for the applied loads. Detailed information on design and construction of this type of pavement is provided in [1, 17].

Thickness selection for CRCP is accomplished in the same way as for plain concrete pavement slabs, that is, with use of charts, such as Figs. 12-17 through 12-20. No reduction in thickness because of the presence of the steel is recommended.

The amount of reinforcing steel required to control volume changes is dependent primarily on slab thickness, concrete tensile strength, and yield strength of the steel. While several procedures have been proposed for estimating the required amount of steel, experience indicates that it should be about 0.6 percent of the gross cross-sectional area and that the yield strength should be at least 60,000 lb/in². The minimum amount may be determined from Eq. (12-13)

$$p_s = \frac{f_t'}{f_s - nf_t'} (1.3 - 0.2c) \, 100 \qquad (12\text{-}13)$$

where p_s = percentage of steel, area of steel/area of concrete
f_t' = tensile strength of concrete, lb/in² (assumed equal to $0.4 \times$ modulus of rupture)
f_s = allowable tensile stress in steel, lb/in²
$n = E_s/E_c$, ratio of elastic modulus of steel to that of concrete
c = coefficient of subgrade friction

The FAA recommends that the cross-sectional area of the reinforcing steel A_s be obtained from Eq. (12-14)

$$A_s = \frac{3.7L \sqrt{Lt}}{f_s} \qquad (12\text{-}14)$$

where A_s = area of steel, in²
L = width of slab, ft
t = slab thickness, in

Recommendations for the size and spacing of this longitudinal steel are summarized in [24]. Steel placement in the slab ranges from middepth (maximum) to one-third depth (minimum) with a minimum cover of $2\frac{1}{2}$ in. Transverse steel is designed in the same way as tie bars.

Terminal provisions are an important part of the design features for CRCP due to large seasonal end movements. End treatments are discussed in [17, 21].

PAVEMENT DESIGN
USING ELASTIC LAYER THEORY

While many of the materials comprising pavement structures exhibit nonlinear and rate-dependent stress-strain characteristics, the response of pavements to moving wheel loads appears "elastic" in nature since the majority of deformation resulting from a single moving wheel load application is recoverable.

Over the years engineers have used elastic theory to assist in the analysis and design of pavement structures. For example, the Corps of Engineers used such theory, as already noted, to extend the design curves established for highway loading conditions to those representative of airfields. Moreover, elastic theory is used in the current CBR procedure to compute the ESWL for any gear arrangement by representing the pavement structure as a semi-infinite elastic solid.

The reader has also observed that design procedures for portland cement concrete pavements utilize elastic theory by considering the concrete slab as an elastic plate resting on a dense liquid subgrade.

Recently design procedures have been developed for asphalt-type pavements in which the structural section is represented as a multilayer elastic solid. Two of these procedures now in use for airfield pavements were developed by the Shell Oil Company [60] and the Asphalt Institute [35].

As will be seen subsequently, multilayer theory also has been used in the overlay design for airfield pavements [49].

Figure 12-26 contains a schematic representation of a pavement structure as a layered elastic solid with the lowest layer semi-infinite in extent. Computer programs are available to permit the calculation of stresses, strains, and displacements at any point in a particular layer for one [46] or a number of loads [31, 37, 39]. Loads are applied to circular areas with uniform contact pressures. The layers are assumed to be infinite in lateral extent, and usually (although not necessarily) full continuity is assumed at each of the interfaces.

In using this approach, engineering judgment is required in the selection of representative material properties: critical stresses, strains, and deformations; limiting values for these quantities, termed distress criteria; and relationships between the distress criteria and performance of the pavement. Both the Shell and the Asphalt Institute procedures are summarized within such a context.

Shell Method

This method of design is applicable for pavement structures consisting of asphalt concrete, untreated granular base, and prepared subgrade or asphalt concrete resting directly on subgrade.

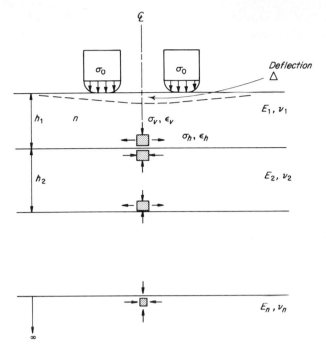

Fig. 12-26 Representation of pavement structure as a multi-layer elastic system.

The structure is represented by a three-layer elastic system (full friction at layer interfaces). Critical conditions for design are:

1. Horizontal tensile strain on the underside of the asphalt-bound layer (ϵ_h, layer 1, Fig. 12-26). If excessive, cracking may occur in the asphalt layer. The value of tensile strain is dependent on the fatigue characteristics of the asphalt mixture with an allowable strain value of 2.30×10^{-4} in/in associated with 10^6 strain repetitions.*

2. Vertical compressive strain in the surface of the subgrade (ϵ_V, layer n, Fig. 12-26). If this value exceeds a specific limit, depending on traffic, permanent deformation may occur at the top of the subgrade, leading, in

---

* The fatigue characteristics of asphalt concrete mixtures can be represented by an equation of the form

$$N_f = k \left(\frac{1}{\epsilon_t} \right)^n$$

where N_f = applications to failure
ϵ_t = tensile strain
k, n = experimentally determined coefficients dependent on mixture characteristics

turn, to permanent deformation (rutting) at the surface of the pavement. The limiting value of vertical compressive strain, which is also dependent on the number of load applications, has been established as 10.3×10^{-4} in/in at 10^6 repetitions.

Materials in each of the layers are assumed to exhibit linear elastic behavior.

For asphalt concrete, time of loading and temperature dependence are recognized. Tensile strains in the asphalt concrete are determined at a stiffness E_1 of 900,000 lb/in² (which corresponds to a temperature of 50°F and a time of loading of 0.02 s). For determining subgrade strain, the air temperature is assumed to be 95°F, and an effective stiffness modulus in the range of 100,000 to 200,000 lb/in² (depending on the thickness of asphalt concrete) is selected.

The modulus of the untreated granular base is a function of the subgrade modulus E_3 and is dependent on the thickness of this layer h_2; it ranges from two to three times E_3.

The modulus of the subgrade soil has been related to the CBR based on dynamic vibratory tests in situ by the relation

$$E_3 = 1500 \text{CBR lb/in}^2$$

The Poisson ratio ν for all layers has been assumed to be 0.35.

Figure 12-27 illustrates the distribution of tensile strain on the underside of an asphalt-bound layer subjected to B-707 aircraft, computed using the BISTRO program [39]. From analyses such as these it is possible to establish thicknesses of the asphalt-bound and granular layers which will ensure that the limiting values for strain are not exceeded. One such design chart is illustrated in Fig. 12-28 for a B-747.

When the subgrade modulus has been established (e.g., by the CBR test), the thickness of granular layer and asphalt concrete, or of asphalt concrete only, can be selected from a chart like that in Fig. 12-28.

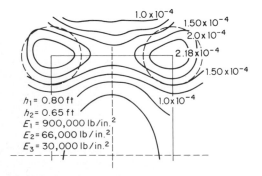

Fig. 12-27 Asphalt strain pattern under B-707. h_1 = asphalt surface course; h_2 = base course. (*Shell Oil Co.*)

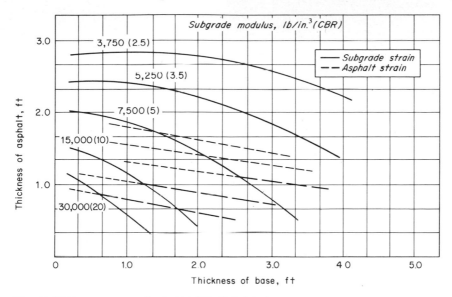

Fig. 12-28 Design curves for B-747. (*Shell Oil Co.*)

Asphalt Institute Method

This procedure is limited to asphalt concrete resting directly on a prepared subgrade (two-layer system). Like the Shell method, thickness design is based on limiting (1) the horizontal tensile strain on the underside of the asphalt layer to minimize fatigue cracking in the asphalt concrete and (2) the vertical compressive strain on the subgrade surface to minimize the potential for surface rutting. A flow diagram detailing the procedure is shown in Fig. 12-29, and the steps used to select the design thickness are shown schematically in Fig. 12-30. Determining the design thickness requires knowing the subgrade modulus, the mean annual air temperature, and the projected forecast of aircraft traffic mix.

Essentially the design procedure then consists of determining:

1. The allowable traffic volume N_a, which is the number of equivalent DC-8-63F strain repetitions that an asphalt concrete layer of specified thickness can withstand for the specific subgrade modulus and environmental condition at the site.

2. The predicted traffic value N_p, which is the number of equivalent DC-8-63F strain repetitions (based on aircraft traffic forecasts) that will actually occur during the design life of the pavement.*

* N_p varies with depth.

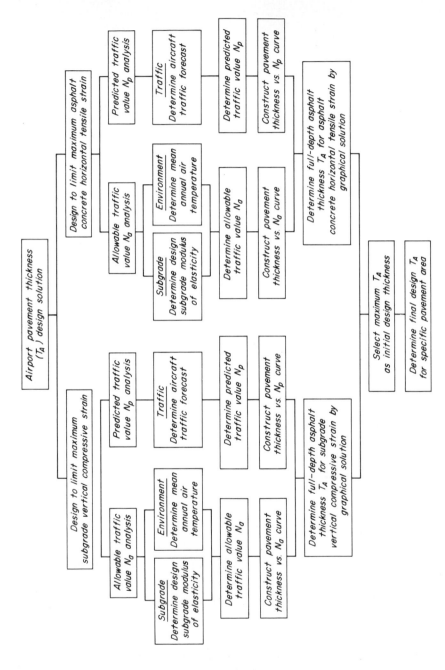

Fig. 12-29 Airport pavement thickness design flow chart. (Asphalt Institute.)

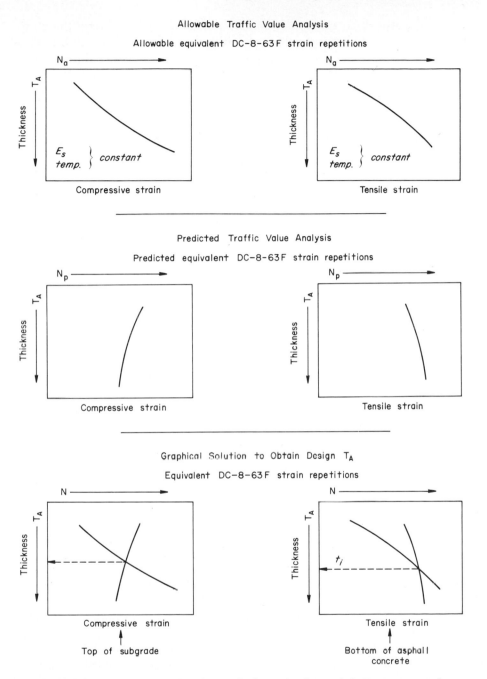

Fig. 12-30 Steps used to determine design thickness by the Asphalt Institute procedure. (*Asphalt Institute.*)

3. The thickness of asphalt concrete T_A required to satisfy the strain criteria for the design input values of subgrade modulus, mean air temperature, and traffic mix. This thickness is determined by a simultaneous graphical solution of N_a and N_p as shown in Fig. 12-30. In the illustration the design thickness is controlled by the asphalt concrete tensile strain since it results in the larger of the two thicknesses.

This method contains a number of innovative concepts for design. For example, like the fatigue procedure, it permits an airfield pavement to be designed for the mixed traffic conditions representative of most large civil airports. In addition, environmental influences are considered in a more realistic fashion for asphalt-bound layers since the influence of temperature on asphalt concrete stiffness is recognized.

EFFECT OF FROST ON PAVEMENT THICKNESS

Frost action, if severe, results in nonuniform heave of pavements during the winter because of ice segregation and in loss of supporting capacity of the subgrade during periods of thaw.

According to the Corps of Engineers, the process of ice segregation can be described as follows [48]:

> The water in void spaces below a critical size can be supercooled and remains liquid below the normal freezing temperature of water. A strong attraction exists between this water and ice crystals which form in the larger voids, and the water flowing to the crystals solidifies on contact. Crystal growth leads to formation of an ice lens. A lens continues to grow in thickness in the direction of heat transfer and at the same time laterally, until ice formation at a lower elevation cuts off the source of water, or until the temperature of the soil just below the surface of ice formation rises above the normal freezing point.

During the spring and early summer, the ice lenses begin to melt, and the water which is released cannot drain through the still-frozen soil at greater depths. Thus, lack of drainage results in loss of strength in the subgrades. It is also possible that a reduction in stiffness will occur in subgrade soils during the thaw period, even though ice lenses may not have formed [12].

The Corps of Engineers has developed a comprehensive design procedure which is briefly summarized herein [48].

Some soils are very susceptible to frost, some are only mildly affected, and others can be considered as non-frost-susceptible. With respect to susceptibility to frost action, the Corps of Engineers has classified soils as shown in Table 12-6.

Depths of frost penetration have been measured in many localities.

TABLE 12-6 **Frost Design Soil Classification**

Frost group	Kind of soil	Percentage finer than 0.02 mm by weight	Typical soil types under unified soil classification system
F1	Gravelly soils	3–10	GW, GP, GW-GM, GP-GM
F2	Gravelly soils	10–20	GM, GW-GM, GP-GM
	Sands	3–15	SW, SP, SM, SW-SM, SP-SM
F3	Gravelly soils	Over 20	GM, GC
	Sands, except very fine silty sands	Over 15	SM, SC
	Clays, PI > 12	—	CL, CH
F4	All silts	—	ML, MH
	Very fine silty sands	Over 15	SM
	Clays, PI < 12	—	CL, CL-ML
	Varved clays and other fine-grained, banded sediments	—	CL and ML; CL, ML, and SM; CL, CH, and ML; CL, CH, ML, and SM

SOURCE: Corps of Engineers.

These depths have been correlated with a number called the *freezing index*,[†] which can be determined from a chart similar to the one shown in Fig. 12-31. The *degree-day* is defined as being the difference between the average daily air temperature and 32°F. The degree-day is minus when the average daily temperature is below 32°F; it is plus when it is above 32°F. The freezing index used in design is the coldest winter in a 10-year period of record, or the average of the three coldest winters in 30 years of record.

Two methods have been developed for designing pavements on frost-susceptible subgrades.[*] One method is to provide a sufficient thickness of pavement to insulate the subgrade, not completely, but substantially so. The other method is to allow freezing of the subgrade and to design the pavement on the basis of reduced supporting capacity during the period of thaw. The choice depends on the type of subgrade material, the economics of construction at a particular site, and the amount of nonuniform heave permitted.

In the first method a correlation between frost penetration and freezing index has been established, as shown in Fig. 12-32. If complete protection of the subgrade is to be provided, the thickness of pavement corresponds to the depth of frost penetration. A normal amount of frost penetration into the

[†] The freezing index is the number of degree-days between the highest and lowest points on a curve of cumulative degree-days versus time for one freezing season.

[*] Complete protection, which is used only in exceptional situations, can be considered as a third method.

subgrade is acceptable; thus, the problem resolves itself into one of determining how much. From its extensive work in the field of frost action, the Corps of Engineers has determined the acceptable amount of penetration of frost into the subgrade, depending on the thickness of the base course. This relationship is shown in Fig. 12-33. The abscissa of the chart represents the thickness of the base for a flexible pavement, assuming no frost penetration into the subgrade, and is obtained by subtracting the thickness of the surface course from the depth of frost penetration, obtained

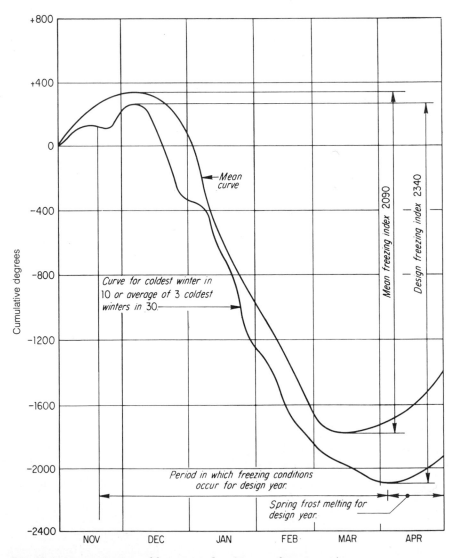

Fig. 12-31 Determination of freezing index. (*Corps of Engineers.*)

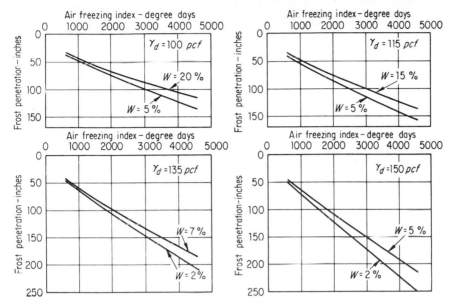

Fig. 12-32 Relationship between air freezing index and frost penetration into granular non-frost-susceptible soil beneath pavements kept free of snow and ice. (*Corps of Engineers.*)

from Fig. 12-32. The ordinate yields the thickness of the base to be used in design and the acceptable amount of frost penetration into the subgrade. If r is greater than 2, use the curve marked 2.0. The pavement thickness obtained in this manner must be compared with the thickness that would be required if frost had not been a consideration. The larger of the two thicknesses should be used for design.

In the second method, charts have been developed for flexible pavements that relate wheel load to thickness of pavement for various classes of subgrade soil. A typical chart for a dual-in-tandem assembly is shown in Fig. 12-34. This procedure is usually not applicable for the F4 type of subgrade soils or for any other soils which will exhibit nonuniform heave.* For such soils, only the first method is applicable.

For rigid pavements the chart shown in Fig. 12-35 has been prepared. The procedure is to compute the thickness of a concrete slab with the appropriate k value, assuming no frost. The next step is to assume that for frost action a thickness of non-frost-susceptible material equal to the thickness of the slab is required (labeled *base* on the chart). By reference to the chart at this thickness of base, the reduced modulus k is obtained, and

* Permissible for F4 subgrades in nonimportant areas where aircraft speeds are very slow and nonuniform heave can be tolerated. In Figs. 12-34 and 12-35 use F3 curve for F4 subgrades.

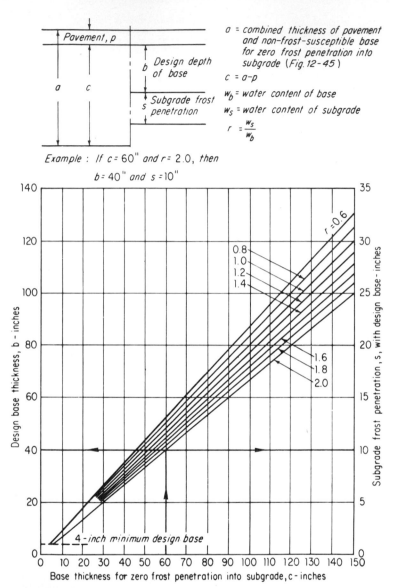

Fig. 12-33 Design depth of non-frost-susceptible base for limited subgrade frost penetration. (*Corps of Engineers.*)

the thickness of the slab is recomputed on the basis of the reduced k. As for flexible pavements, this procedure usually applies only to F1, F2, and F3 soils.

If the thickness of the pavement is less than the depth of frost penetration, it is desirable to have the bottom 4 in of the base consist of non-frost-susceptible gravel, sand, or screenings to act as a soil filter between the subgrade soil and the main body of the base.

THE FAA METHOD OF DESIGN
FOR FLEXIBLE AND RIGID AIRPORT PAVEMENTS

The FAA has recently changed its methods of pavement design to incorporate the unified soil classification system instead of the soil classification system used in the past [7, 57]. To provide continuity in pavement design, the former system may be used to evaluate the characteristics of pavements designed on the basis of the former system. The former system was based upon a gradation analysis of the soil as well as the plastic and liquid limit. It was found that this system was not as reliable or as well known as the unified system, and therefore, the change was made.

Soil Investigations and Evaluation

The accurate identification and evaluation of pavement foundations is essential to the proper design of the pavement structure. The subgrade supports the pavement and the loads placed upon the pavement surface.

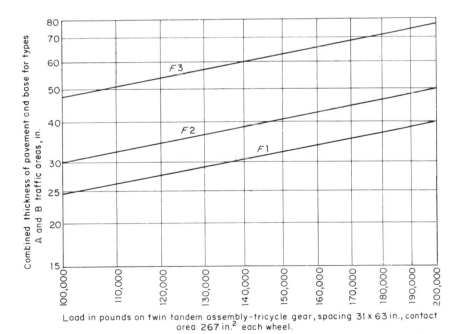

Load in pounds on twin tandem assembly-tricycle gear, spacing 31 x 63 in., contact area 267 in.² each wheel.

Fig. 12-34 Frost condition; reduced subgrade strength design curves for flexible pavements. (*Corps of Engineers.*)

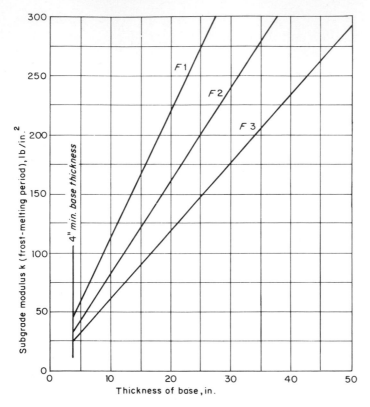

Fig. 12-35 Frost condition; reduced subgrade strength design subgrade modulus curves for rigid pavements. (*Corps of Engineers.*)

The function of the pavement is to distribute the loads to the subgrade, and the greater the capability of the subgrade to support the loads, the less the required thickness of the pavement.

A soil investigation will consist of a soil survey to determine the arrangement of the different layers of soil in relation to the subgrade elevation, a sampling and testing of the various layers of soil to determine the physical properties of the soil with respect to in-place density and subgrade support, and a survey to determine the availability and suitability of local materials for use in the construction of the subgrade and pavement. Surveys and sampling are usually accomplished through soil borings to determine the soil or rock profile and its lateral extent. General criteria for the frequency and depth of soil borings for the different elements of a pavement at an airport are contained in [7]. It should be noted that local site conditions determine the extent of the required boring operations. The sampled materials are then tested to determine soil types, gradation of particle sizes, liquid and plastic limits, plasticity index, moisture-density relationships, shrinkage factors, permeability, organic content, and strength properties including the CBR and the modulus of subgrade reaction.

In the unified system, soils are initially divided by a separation between coarse- and fine-grained soils and highly organic soils. The distinction between coarse- and fine-grained soils is based upon the amount of material retained on the No. 200 sieve. The coarse-grained materials are further subdivided into gravels and sands on the basis of the amounts retained on the No. 4 sieve. Then the gravels and sands are classified according to whether or not fine material is present. Fine-grained soils are subdivided into two groups based upon the liquid limit. A separate division is made for highly organic soils not suitable for construction purposes. A flow chart illustrating the procedure for the classification of soils by the unified system is given in Fig. 12-36. The uses of the various soil materials for pavement foundations are described in Table 12-7.

The strength properties of the soil for use in the FAA design method consist of the CBR value for flexible pavement design and the modulus of subgrade reaction k for rigid pavement design. These two measures of soil strength were described earlier.

Pavement Design Considerations

The design of pavements is a complex engineering problem which involves the consideration of a great number of variables. Flexible pavement design is based upon the CBR method, an essentially empirical method. Rigid pavement design is based upon the Westergaard analysis of edge loading, which has been modified to simulate a jointed edge condition. These methods represent a departure from previous FAA pavement design policy and will result in slightly different thickness determinations. The required parameters for the design of pavements include the gross takeoff weight of the aircraft using the airfield, the landing gear configuration and dimensions, tire contact areas and pressures, and the traffic volume. Separate design curves are presented for single-gear, dual-gear, dual-tandem-gear, and wide-body aircraft.

The first step of the procedure is to determine the forecast of the annual departures by each type of aircraft and to group them into narrow body by gear configuration and wide body by aircraft type. The maximum takeoff weight of each of the aircraft is used, and 95 percent of this weight is assigned to the main landing gear. The design aircraft is then determined as that aircraft which requires the greatest pavement thickness. It is not necessarily the heaviest aircraft which will operate from the airport. Since the aircraft operating from the airport will have different landing gear configurations, it is necessary to determine the equivalent annual depar-

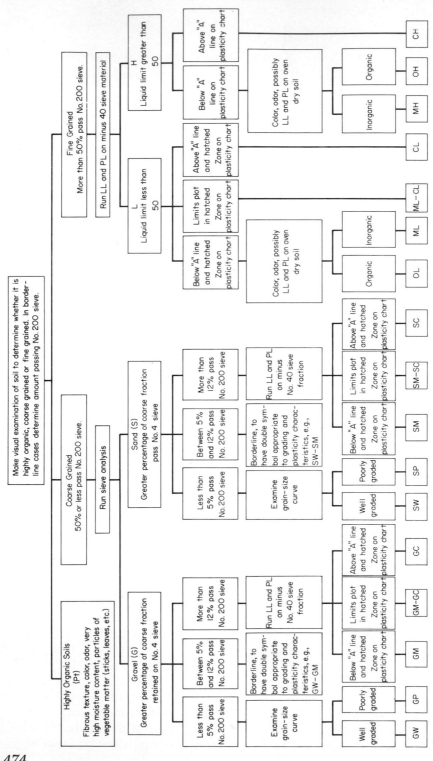

Fig. 12-36 Flow chart of the unified soil classification system. (*Corps of Engineers.*)

tures of each aircraft in terms of the gear configuration of the design aircraft. These equivalencies are given in Table 12-8.

The equivalent annual departures of the design aircraft are determined by summing the equivalent annual departures of each aicraft in the group obtained from Eq. (12-15).

$$\log R_1 = \log R_2 \left(\frac{W_2}{W_1}\right)^{0.5} \qquad (12\text{-}15)$$

where R_1 = equivalent annual departures by design aircraft
R_2 = annual number of departures by an aircraft in terms of the design aircraft landing gear configuration
W_1 = wheel load of design aircraft
W_2 = wheel load of aircraft being converted

Since wide-body aircraft have radically different landing gear configurations than other aircraft, the relative effects on the pavement are considered by assigning a gross takeoff weight of 300,000 lb to any wide-body aircraft and considering it to have a dual-tandem landing gear for the analysis of equivalent departures. The actual curve for the design aircraft is used, however, for the determination of pavement requirements.

Research has shown that aircraft traffic is normally distributed over a lateral range of the pavement surface during operations [33]. Likewise, during a portion of an operation on the runway system, the aerodynamic properties of the aircraft will decrease the actual pavement loading. Therefore, the FAA permits pavement thickness modifications on different surfaces as follows [7]:

1. Full depth thickness T is required where departing aircraft will use the pavement, such as aprons, holding areas, and the center portions of taxiway and runway widths.

2. Pavement thickness of $0.9T$ is required where arriving aircraft will use the surface, such as high-speed runway turnoffs.

3. Pavement thickness of $0.7T$ is required where aircraft traffic is unlikely, such as the outer edges of taxiway and runway pavements.

The FAA also specifies the degree of frost protection required for airport pavements based upon the uniformity of soil conditions, the nature of the airport—large, medium, or small hub—and the particular pavement element—runway, taxiway, or apron. The methods of design to protect from frost effects include [7]:

1. The complete frost protection method which involves the removal of all frost-susceptible material to the depth of frost penetration and replacement with non-frost-susceptible material.

2. The limited subgrade frost penetration method which allows the

TABLE 12-7 Characteristics of Soil Related to Airport Pavements

Major Divisions (1)	(2)	Letter (3)	Name (4)	Value as foundation when not subject to frost action (5)	Value as base directly under wearing surface (6)	Potential frost action (7)	Compressibility and expansion (8)	Drainage characteristics (9)	Compaction equipment (10)	Unit dry weight (pcf) (11)	Field CBR (12)	Subgrade modulus k (pci) (13)
Coarse-grained soils	Gravel and gravelly soils	GW	Gravel or sandy gravel, well graded	Excellent	Good	None to very slight	Almost none	Excellent	Crawler-type tractor, rubber-tired equipment, steel-wheeled roller	125–140	60–80	300 or more
		GP	Gravel or sandy gravel, poorly graded	Good to excellent	Poor to fair	None to very slight	Almost none	Excellent	Crawler-type tractor, rubber-tired equipment, steel-wheeled roller	120–130	35–60	300 or more
		GU	Gravel or sandy gravel, uniformly graded	Good	Poor	None to very slight	Almost none	Excellent	Crawler-type tractor, rubber-tired equipment	115–125	25–50	300 or more
		GM	Silty gravel or silty sandy gravel	Good to excellent	Fair to good	Slight to medium	Very slight	Fair to poor	Rubber-tired equipment, sheepsfoot roller, close control of moisture	130–145	40–80	300 or more
		GC	Clayey gravel or clayey sandy gravel	Good	Poor	Slight to medium	Slight	Poor to practically impervious	Rubber-tired equipment, sheepsfoot roller	120–140	20–40	200–300
	Sand and sandy soils	SW	Sand or gravelly sand, well graded	Good	Poor	None to very slight	Almost none	Excellent	Crawler-type tractor, rubber-tired equipment	110–130	20–40	200–300
		SP	Sand or gravelly sand, poorly graded	Fair to good	Poor to not suitable	None to very slight	Almost none	Excellent	Crawler-type tractor, rubber-tired equipment	105–120	15–25	200–300
		SU	Sand or gravelly sand, uniformly graded	Fair to good	Not suitable	None to very slight	Almost none	Excellent	Crawler-type tractor, rubber-tired equipment	100–115	10–20	200–300

	Symbol	Name						Compaction equipment			
	SM	Silty sand or silty gravelly sand	Good	Poor	Slight to high	Very slight	Fair to poor	Rubber-tired equipment, sheepsfoot roller; close control of moisture	120–135	20–40	200–300
	SC	Clayey sand or clayey gravelly sand	Fair to good	Not suitable	Slight to high	Slight to medium	Poor to practically impervious	Rubber-tired equipment, sheepsfoot roller	105–130	10–20	200–300
Fine grained soils	ML	Silts, sandy silts, gravelly silts, or diatomaceous soils	Fair to poor	Not suitable	Medium to very high	Slight to medium	Fair to poor	Rubber-tired equipment, sheepsfoot roller, close control of moisture	100–125	5–15	100–200
Low compressibility, LL < 50	CL	Lean clays, sandy clays, or gravelly clays	Fair to poor	Not suitable	Medium to high	Medium	Practically impervious	Rubber-tired equipment, sheepsfoot roller	100–125	5–15	100–200
	OL	Organic silts or lean organic clays	Poor	Not suitable	Medium to high	Medium to high	Poor	Rubber-tired equipment, sheepsfoot roller	90–105	4–8	100–200
High compressibility, LL > 50	MH	Micaceous clays or diatomaceous soils	Poor	Not suitable	Medium to very high	High	Fair to poor	Rubber-tired equipment, sheepsfoot roller	80–100	4–8	100–200
	CH	Fat clays	Poor to very poor	Not suitable	Medium	High	Practically impervious	Rubber-tired equipment, sheepsfoot roller	90–110	3–5	50–100
	OH	Fat organic clays	Poor to very poor	Not suitable	Medium	High	Practically impervious	Rubber-tired equipment, sheepsfoot roller	80–100	3–5	50–100
Peat and other fibrous organic soils	Pt	Peat, humus, and other	Not suitable	Not suitable	Slight	Very high	Fair to poor	Compaction not practical			

SOURCE: Corps of Engineers.

TABLE 12-8 **Factors for Converting Annual Departures by Aircraft to Equivalent Annual Departures by Design Aircraft**

Actual aircraft landing gear	Design aircraft landing gear	Multiplier for actual departures to obtain equivalent departures
Single wheel	Dual wheel	0.8
	Dual tandem	0.5
Dual wheel	Single wheel	1.3
	Dual tandem	0.6
Dual tandem	Single wheel	2.0
	Dual wheel	1.7
Double dual tandem	Dual wheel	1.7
	Dual tandem	1.0

SOURCE: Federal Aviation Administration [7].

frost to penetrate a limited depth into the frost-susceptible material, holding deformations to minimal values.

3. The reduced subgrade strength method which provides adequate capacity during the frost melt period and is applicable to situations where aircraft speeds are low and the effects of frost heave are less objectionable.

4. The reduced subgrade frost penetration method which is statistically based and may be used where aircraft speeds are low and some frost heave can be tolerated.

The FAA method also allows for the stabilization and treatment of subgrade, subbase, and base materials to improve pavement performance and economics. Equivalency factors are used to determine the reduction in pavement materials possible under stabilization conditions [7]. Stabilized base and subbase courses are required for new flexible pavements designed to accommodate jet aircraft weighing 100,000 lb or more.

Flexible Pavement Design

Flexible pavements consist of a bituminous wearing surface placed upon a base course and, where required by subgrade conditions, a subbase. The entire flexible pavement structure is ultimately supported by the subgrade. The wearing course prevents the penetration of surface water to the base course, provides a smooth, well-bonded surface free from loose particles, resists the shearing stresses caused by aircraft loading, and furnishes a texture of nonskid qualities not causing undue tire wear. It must also be resistant to fuel spillage and other solvents in areas where maintenance may occur. The base course is the major structural element of the pavement and has the function of distributing the wheel loads to the subbase and subgrade. It must be designed to prevent failure in the subgrade, withstand the stresses produced in the base course, resist vertical pressures tending to produce consolidation and deformation of the wearing course, and resist volume changes caused by fluctuations in its moisture content. The function of the subbase, when required, is similar to that of the base course, but since it is further removed from the area of load application, it is subjected to lower stress intensities. The subgrade soils are subjected to the least loading intensities, and the controlling stresses are usually at the top of the subgrade since stress decreases with depth. However, unusual subgrade conditions, such as layered subgrade materials, can alter the location of controlling stresses. The FAA presents techniques for considering the support strength of layered subgrade materials [7].

Examples of the design charts for flexible pavement design are shown in Figs. 12-37 to 12-40. To determine the thickness of the total pavement thickness (wearing course, base, and subbase), the CBR of the subgrade is used together with the gross takeoff weight and the equivalent annual

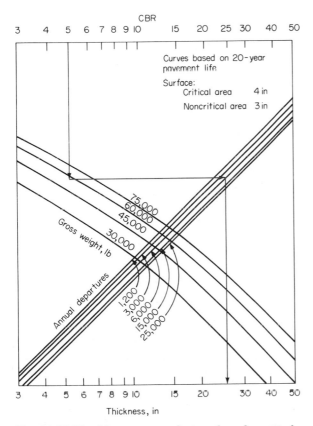

Fig. 12-37 Flexible pavement design chart for critical areas, single-wheel gear. (*Federal Aviation Administration* [7].)

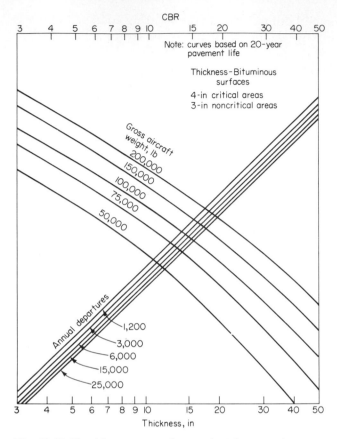

Fig. 12-38 Flexible pavement design chart for critical areas, dual-wheel gear. (*Federal Aviation Administration [7].*)

departures of the design aircraft. To find the required thickness of the wearing course and base, these charts are used with the CBR of the subbase and the gross takeoff weight and the equivalent annual departures of the design aircraft. The minimum base course required, however, is subject to the limitations found from Fig. 12-41. The base must have a minimum thickness of 6 in in critical areas. The thickness of the wearing course is indicated on the design charts for critical, full-depth pavement and for noncritical areas. If the thickness of the wearing and base courses exceeds that determined from the design chart, the subbase may be proportionately decreased.

The design charts are used by entering the chart at the CBR axis, proceeding vertically to the gross takeoff weight curve, then horizontally to the equivalent annual departure curve, and finally vertically to the pavement thickness axis.

Stabilized base and subbase courses may be substituted for granular base and subbase courses in accordance with the equivalency factors given in Table 12-9. Restrictions in the use of these equivalency factors due to construction and other limitations are contained in [7].

Rigid Pavement Design

Rigid pavements for airports consist of a portland cement concrete slab placed upon a granular or treated subbase course resting on a compacted subgrade. A subbase is not required under certain conditions related to the adequacy of drainage and the susceptibility to frost [7]. The concrete slab must provide an acceptable nonskid surface, prevent the infiltration of surface water, and provide the structural support required for aircraft. The subbase provides a uniform stable support for the pavement slab and

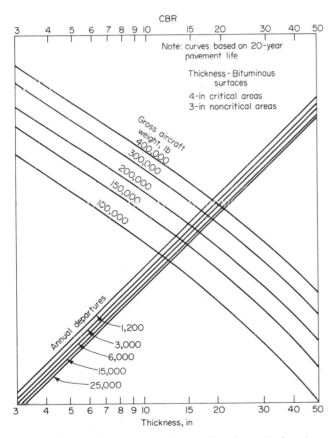

Fig. 12-39 Flexible pavement design chart for critical areas, dual-in-tandem gear. (*Federal Aviation Administration.*)

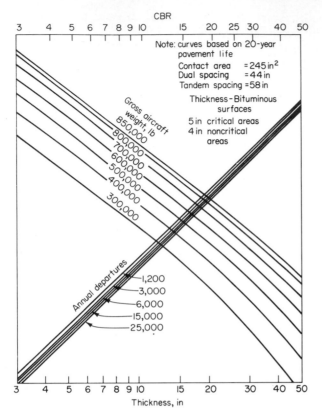

Fig. 12-40 Flexible pavement design chart for critical areas, Boeing 747-100, SR, 200, B, C, F wide-body aircraft only. (*Federal Aviation Administration [7].*)

allows for drainage. It is recommended that the minimum subbase under a concrete slab be at least 4 in, except when not required. The subbase may be increased above this minimum value to increase the modulus of subgrade reaction and, thereby, decrease the thickness of the slab. Stabilized subbases, required in new pavements for aircraft weighing more than 100,000 lb, reflect structural benefits in an increased modulus of subgrade reaction. The effect of a stabilized base on the subgrade modulus is shown in Fig. 12-42. Generally speaking, the most efficient combination of rigid pavement thickness and stabilized subbase thickness for structural capacity is a 1 to 1 ratio [7, 28].

Examples of the design curves for rigid pavements are given in Figs. 12-43 to 12-46. These curves are based upon a jointed edge loading assumption in which the load is tangent to the concrete joint. The use of the design curves is similar to that for flexible pavements in that the gross takeoff weight and the equivalent annual departures of the design aircraft are required in addition to the flexural strength of concrete and the modulus of subgrade reaction for the subgrade. The curves shown give only the thickness of the slab required, and independent methods must be used to obtain the thickness of the subbase. The 90-day flexural strength of concrete is required; however, the 28-day strength may be used and increased by a factor of 1.10 to approximate 90-day strength. Reduction in thickness in noncritical sections to 0.90 of the critical-section thickness is allowed.

The design procedure also allows for modification of the pavement thickness determined from the design charts for high traffic volumes. The increases in thickness are given in Table 12-10.

Pavements for Light Aircraft

Light aircraft pavements are defined as landing areas intended for personal or other small aircraft engaged in nonscheduled flying activities. Pave-

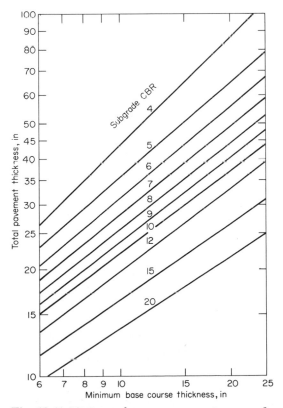

Fig. 12-41 Minimum base course requirements for flexible pavement. (*Federal Aviation Administration* [7].)

TABLE 12-9   **Recommended Equivalency Factors for Stabilized Base and Subbase Materials in Pavements**

Material*	Equivalency factor range†	
	Subbase	Base
Bituminous surface course	1.7–2.3	1.2–1.6
Bituminous base course	1.7–2.3	1.2–1.6
Cold laid bituminous base course	1.5–1.7	1.0–1.2
Mixed in-place base course	1.5–1.7	1.0–1.2
Cement treated base	1.6–2.3	1.2–1.6
Soil cement base course	1.5–2.0	N/A
Crushed aggregate base course	1.4–2.0	1.0‡
Subbase course	1.0§	NA

* See FAA AC 150/5370-10 for specifications.

† Divide granular material thickness by equivalency factor to obtain stabilized material thickness.

‡ A CBR of 20 was used to establish relative factors.

§ A CBR of 80 was used to establish relative factors.

NA = Not applicable.

SOURCE: Federal Aviation Administration [7].

ments are not required to accommodate aircraft which have gross takeoff weights in excess of 30,000 lb, and in many these aircraft will not exceed 12,500 lb. Landing facilities may be turfed, aggregate-turfed, flexible or rigid pavement surfaces. The FAA has established design procedures for flexible and rigid pavements, similar to those for heavier air-carrier type aircraft. No reduction in pavement thickness is allowed for noncritical pavement surfaces.

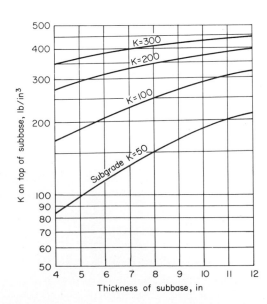

Fig. 12-42 Effect of stabilized subbase on subgrade modulus. (*Federal Aviation Administration [7].*)

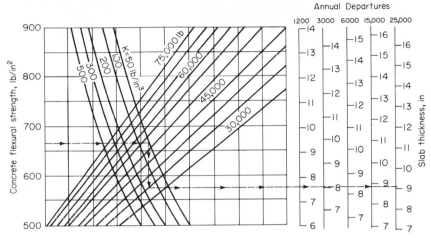

Fig. 12-43 Rigid pavement design chart for critical areas, single-wheel gear. (*Federal Aviation Administration [7].*)

The design of flexible pavements for light aircraft is performed by using Fig. 12-47. The determination of the total flexible structure thickness is found by using the CBR of the subgrade and the gross takeoff weight of the heaviest aircraft using the facility. The thickness of the wearing and base courses is found by using the same chart with a CBR of 20 for the subbase. A minimum thickness of 2 in for the wearing surface and 3 in for the base course is recommended for these facilities [7]. The Asphalt Institute has also prepared design curves and recommendations for light aircraft [36].

Rigid pavement design for light aircraft requires a minimum concrete slab thickness of 5 in for aircraft weighing 12,500 lb or less and 6 in for aircraft weighing between 12,500 and 30,000 lb. Design curves are not presented since these are the only thickness requirements for rigid pavements designed to accommodate light aircraft. For aircraft weighing between 12,500 and 30,000 lb a subbase of 4 in is required under the slab. A subbase of 5 in is required under the slab for aircraft weighing less than 12,500 lb in poor soil conditions [7].

DESIGN OF OVERLAY PAVEMENTS

Overlay pavements are required when existing pavements are no longer serviceable due to either a deterioration in structural capabilities or a loss in riding quality. They are also required when pavements must be strengthened to carry greater loads or increased repetitions of existing aircraft beyond those anticipated in the original design. Overlays also

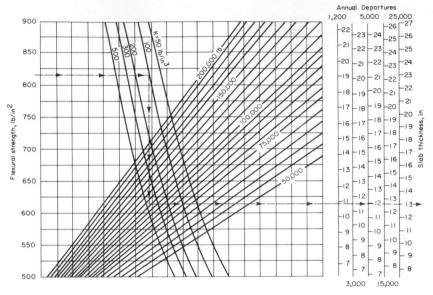

Fig. 12-44 Rigid pavement design chart for critical areas, dual-wheel gear. (*Federal Aviation Administration [7].*)

provide a solution for increased safety (i.e., improved skid resistance and reduced danger of hydroplaning). In this section the discussion will be limited to overlays which are required for structural purposes.

Types of Overlay Pavements

There are several types of overlay pavements. For example, a concrete pavement can be overlaid with additional concrete, a bituminous surfacing, or a combination of aggregate base course and a bituminous surfacing. Likewise, a flexible type of pavement can be overlaid with concrete, a bituminous surfacing, or the combination cited above. The various types of overlay pavements are defined as follows:

1. **Overlay pavement.** The thickness of a rigid or flexible type of pavement placed on an existing pavement

2. **Portland cement concrete overlay.** An overlay pavement constructed of portland cement concrete

3. **Bituminous overlay.** An overlay consisting entirely of a bituminous surfacing

4. **Flexible overlay.** An overlay consisting of a base course and a bituminous surfacing

Overlay design procedures described in this section include those developed by the Corps of Engineers and the FAA. They are based on the results of full-scale test sections together with observations of behavior of overlays in service. Also included are recently developed procedures which make use of layered elastic theory.

Construction details such as treatment of the existing pavement are important, and the reader is referred to references for guidelines for construction of overlays [7, 58].

Bituminous or Flexible Overlays on Flexible Pavements

The same approach is used by the Corps of Engineers and the FAA for determining the thickness of bituminous or flexible overlays. The thickness of pavement for the new wheel load is computed with the assumption that the existing pavement does not exist. The thickness of bituminous or flexible overlay is equal to the difference between the computed thickness and the thickness of the existing pavement. The Corps of Engineers recommends a minimum overlay of 4 in, and the FAA recommends that overlays for increasing strength be a minimum of 3 in. It is recommended that if the base course is less than these minima, the entire overlay should be of the bituminous type.

The FAA permits adjustments to the required thickness of overlay, depending on the condition of the existing pavement and the character of

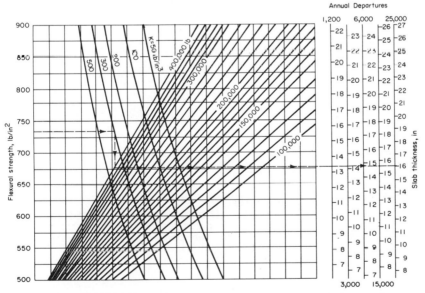

Fig. 12-45 Rigid pavement design chart for critical areas, dual-in-tandem gear. (*Federal Aviation Administration [7].*)

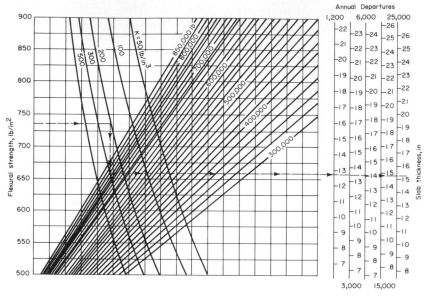

Fig. 12-46 Rigid pavement design chart for critical areas, Boeing 747-100, SR, 200, B, C, F wide-body aircraft only. (*Federal Aviation Administration [7].*)

the materials in the overlay pavement [7]. No adjustments of this kind are permitted by the Corps of Engineers.

The Asphalt Institute procedure [35] is similar in principle to the Corps of Engineers and the FAA methods, except that the difference between the existing and the required pavement thicknesses (overlay) is limited to asphalt concrete, and the components of the existing pavement are expressed in equivalent thicknesses of asphalt concrete.

Portland Cement Concrete Overlays on Flexible Pavements

In the design of portland cement concrete overlays, both the Corps of Engineers and the FAA treat the problem as new construction on a foundation consisting of the existing flexible pavement. The Westergaard

TABLE 12-10 **Rigid Pavement Thickness for High Level of Departures as Percentage of 25,000 Departure Thickness**

Annual departure level	Percentage of 25,000 departure thickness
50,000	104
100,000	108
150,000	110
200,000	112

SOURCE: Federal Aviation Administration [7].

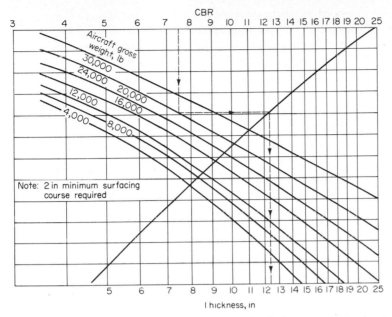

CBR

3 4 5 6 7 8 9 10 11 12 13 14 15 16 17 18 19 20 25

Aircraft gross weight, lb

30,000
24,000
20,000
12,000
16,000
4,000
8,000

Note: 2 in minimum surfacing
course required

5 6 7 8 9 10 11 12 13 14 15 16 17 18 19 20 25

Thickness, in

Fig. 12-17 Flexible pavement design chart for light aircraft. (*Federal Aviation Administration [7].*)

analysis for determining the thickness of the overlay slab is used. Plate bearing tests are made on the existing flexible pavement to establish the value of the subgrade modulus k. The FAA considers the existing flexible pavement as a subbase for the slab. The subgrade on which the existing pavement rests is given a rating, and the thickness of the overlay is determined from the design charts. The minimum thickness of portland cement concrete overlay should not be less than 5 in.

Bituminous or Flexible Overlays on Portland Cement Concrete Pavements

From an analysis of the results of full-scale test sections constructed at several military airfields, the Corps of Engineers developed an empirical relationship which gives the thickness of a bituminous or flexible overlay on an existing rigid pavement. The relationship is as follows:

$$t = 2.5(Fh_d - C_b h) \tag{12-16}$$

where t = thickness of bituminous or flexible overlay, in*

h_d = thickness of portland cement concrete pavement, assuming that the existing pavement did not exist, in

---

* The FAA considers the formula to yield thickness of flexible overlay only.

h = thickness of existing pavement, in

F = a factor which, when multiplied by h_d, is the thickness of a concrete slab that would crack in time, but not so much as to cause undesirable distress in the overlay pavement. The existing slab was assumed to break up into pieces of 5 to 7 ft^2 by the end of the overlay pavement life

C_b = a condition factor for the existing base pavement. This factor ranges from 0.75 to 1.0.

Values of F are given in Fig. 12-48. In determining the thickness h_d, the flexural strength of the existing slab is used.

The Corps of Engineers recommends that the minimum thickness of overlay be 4 in and that for overlays less than 8 in thick a bituminous overlay be used. This implies that the thickness of the base course should not be less than 4 in. The FAA requires that the thickness of bituminous surfacing should not be less than 3 in.

The Asphalt Institute uses the same procedure as for asphalt overlays on flexible pavements, assigning an equivalent thickness of asphalt concrete to the portland cement concrete depending on the condition of the concrete slab.

Portland Cement Concrete Overlays on Portland Cement Concrete Pavements

The thickness of portland cement concrete overlay slabs is determined by both the Corps of Engineers and the FAA by means of the following formulas:

$$h_c = \sqrt[1.4]{h^{1.4} - C h_e^{1.4}} \qquad (12\text{-}17)$$

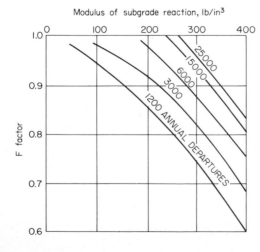

Fig. 12-48 Relationship between overlay factor F and modulus of subgrade reaction for different traffic levels. (*Federal Aviation Administration* [7].)

or

$$h_c = \sqrt{h^2 - Ch_e^2} \qquad\qquad (12\text{-}18)$$

where h_c = thickness of overlay slab, in

h_e = thickness of existing slab, in

h = thickness of equivalent single slab placed directly on subgrade with a working stress equal to that of the overlay slab, in

C = coefficient depending on condition of existing pavement; where C = 1, existing pavement in good condition, 0.75 existing pavement with initial corner cracks due to loading, but no progressive cracks, 0.35 existing pavement badly cracked or crushed (an overlay is not recommended)

These formulas assume that the flexural strength of concrete used for the overlay is approximately equal to that of the existing pavement. Intermediate values of C are not used in design. The change in overlay thickness requirement normally is approximately 1 in for a change of C from 1.0 to 0.75 or from 0.75 to 0.35.

Although the flexural strength of concrete of the overlay does not appear in these formulas, it enters into the computations in the determination of h, the thickness of the equivalent single slab. The flexural strength of the existing slab does not enter into the computations, since it was found that a substantial difference in flexural strength in the two pavements would result in a very small change in thickness.

Overlay Design Using Layered Elastic Theory

A method in which layered elastic theory has been adapted to the evaluation and design of overlays for both rigid and flexible pavements has been described by Vallerga et al. [43, 49]. Figure 12-49 outlines the various steps in this procedure. Briefly they are summarized in the following paragraphs:

Step 1. In the condition survey the condition of the existing pavements, including the nature and extent of distress, is carefully determined and plotted on a large-scale plan of the airfield facilities. This information assists in the sampling and field-test phase as well as in establishing distress related to performance criteria.

Step 2. Deflection measurements* provide a measure of pavement response under known loading conditions and allow differentiation of areas of significant different structural responses.

Step 3. In the drilling and sampling phase pavement cores, layer

---

* Any one of a number of devices, such as the Benkelman beam, can be used.

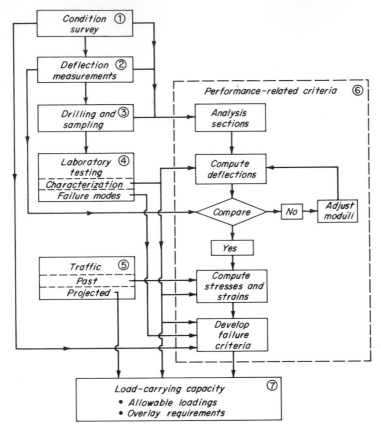

Fig. 12-49 Steps in pavement evaluation method. (*Courtesy of B. A. Valluga.*)

samples, and undisturbed subgrade samples to depths of 10 ft or more are obtained together with information on layer thicknesses, etc.

Step 4. Laboratory testing is primarily concerned with determining representative moduli by a form of dynamic rather than static testing and with establishing failure criteria where appropriate (e.g., fracture strength of cement stabilized base).

Step 5. To determine the traffic, a detailed examination of the past and anticipated future aircraft traffic projections for each specific location (e.g., taxiway) is required. The concept of equating various aircraft into equivalent damage of a standard aircraft can be used effectively in this step [32].

Step 6. From the information established in the previous steps, performance-related criteria are established. Utilizing laboratory properties measured in step 4 as initial input, deflections under the known loadings can be estimated. By comparing these values to those determined in step 2, adjustments in laboratory moduli values are made until predicted (theoretical) deflections agree with the measured deflections. Once this is accomplished, the critical performance parameters for the aircraft in question are determined from layered theory and related to "acceptable" and "not acceptable" performance areas found in step 1, as well as to the laboratory-developed failure criteria of step 4.

Step 7. From the results of step 6 either the load-carrying capacity of the existing pavements or projected overlay requirements for future traffic of a given design life can be readily made.

AIRCRAFT AND AIRPORT PAVEMENT CLASSIFICATION SYSTEMS

The Load Classification Number Method

The LCN (load classification number) method of aircraft evaluation and pavement design was formulated and first published by the Air Ministry Directorate, General of Works, United Kingdom. In this procedure the supporting capacity of a pavement is expressed in terms of a number known as LCN. Likewise, the ESWL of any aircraft can also be expressed in terms of LCN. This latter number is dependent on the gear geometry, tire pressure, and composition and thickness of pavement. Thus, if the LCN of an airfield pavement is larger than the LCN of the aircraft, the aircraft can safely use the pavement.

In order to devise a system whereby the capacity of a pavement could be expressed as a single number, the idea of a standard load classification curve was introduced. This curve, which is shown in Fig. 12-50, is produced by drawing a smooth curve through the arbitrarily chosen points provided by Table 12-11. These values were selected because they were typical of the order of wheel loads and contact areas of aircraft current at the time the LCN system was being developed.

Various types of pavements (both rigid and flexible) were tested with bearing plates having a range of contact areas (200 to 700 in²) representative of a number of aircraft in service at the time. It was found that over this range of contact areas both rigid and flexible pavements showed similar load versus deflection characteristics. The failure load versus contact area relationships for typical flexible and rigid pavements were obtained from a large number of plate tests and are shown in Fig. 12-51. The average curve has the form

$$\frac{W_1}{W_2} = \left(\frac{A_1}{A_2}\right)^{0.44}$$

(12-19)

where W_1, W_2 = respective failure loads, lb
A_1, A_2 = loaded areas, in²

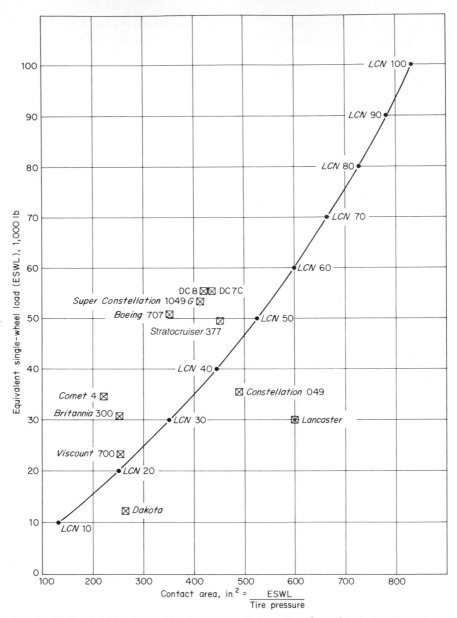

Fig. 12-50 Standard load classification curve. (*International Civil Aviation Organization.*)

It will be noted that the ordinate in Fig. 12-51 is expressed as a percentage of the load required to produce failure when applied through a 26-in-diameter plate (530 in²). This contact area was chosen as a common denominator because it was, at the time of the development of this procedure, representative of heavy aircraft. The failure load for flexible pavements is defined as the load at which the plate deflects progressively without any further load increase. For rigid pavements the failure load is defined as the load which produces an abrupt change in the load deflection curve.

The standard load classification curve and the failure load relationship were combined to produce the chart in Fig. 12-52. This chart was drawn in the following manner:

1. The tire contact area lines were drawn from the relationship

$$\text{Contact area} = \frac{\text{load}}{\text{tire pressure}}$$

2. One point on each LCN line comes directly from the standard load classification curve.

3. Other points on each LCN line have been calculated from Eq. (12-19).

4. The dotted lines are a tentative extension of the LCN system to accommodate contact areas of less than 200 in^2 based on load testing of pavements with small contact areas.

The Aircraft-Pavement Classification Number System

The ICAO has adopted a pavement classification system for reporting airfield strength [3], the ACN-PCN. This system "reports a pavement classification number (PCN) which indicates that an aircraft with an aircraft classification number (ACN) equal to or less than the PCN can operate on the pavement subject to any limitation on the tire pressure."

The bearing strength of the pavement is reported by indicating the ACN-PCN, the pavement type for the ACN-PCN determination, the subgrade category, the maximum allowable tire pressure, and the basis for the evaluation. Different PCNs may be reported if the strength of the

TABLE 12-11

Wheel loading, lb	Tire pressure, lb/in^2	Load classification number
100,000	120	100
90,000	115	90
80,000	110	80
70,000	105	70
60,000	100	60
50,000	95	50
40,000	90	40
30,000	85	30
20,000	80	20
10,000	75	10

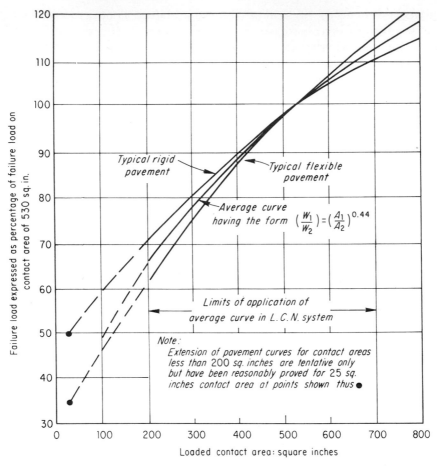

Fig. 12-51 Failure load-contact area relationship curves for typical pavements. (*Courtesy of James A. Skinner and Institution of Civil Engineers, Great Britain.*)

pavement is subject to seasonal variations due to frost or other conditions. A given aircraft will have a different ACN dependent upon the pavement on which it operates, flexible (F) or rigid (R), and the relative strength of the subgrade. The ACN is in subgrade strength units (meganewtons per cubic meter), and can be found by the use of pavement design charts or the analytical equations. One of the primary advantages of this system is that it is independent of the technique used to evaluate pavement strength and relates only to the impact of the aircraft on the supporting subgrade. The PCN is reported for light aircraft, those with a maximum gross takeoff weight less than 5700 kg, in terms of the aircraft weight and the tire pressure. For larger aircraft the system reports the PCN as an ACN, the type of pavement, the subgrade category, the tire pressure category, and the evaluation method used to obtain the PCN.

The concept of the single-wheel load was adopted to determine the ACN so that the interaction between the landing gear and the pavement could be evaluated without reference to pavement thickness. A ratio between the pavement thickness required for the aircraft and that required for the single wheel of a reference aircraft (500-kg weight) at a standard tire pressure defines the ACN. Methods for determining the ACN are presented in [2, 24].

The ACN for any aircraft may be obtained by any established pavement design technique. For example, the ACN for aircraft on rigid pavements was obtained by modifying the PCA computer program for rigid pavement design [14, 24]. The subgrade strength is classified as either high (A), medium (B), low (C), or ultralow (D), based upon whether the CBR is equal to or greater than 13, 8, 4, and 3, respectively, for flexible pavements, or the modulus of subgrade reaction k is equal to or greater than 400, 200, 100, 25 lb/in^3, respectively, for rigid pavements. The maximum allowable tire pressures for aircraft operations are classified as high (W) for no limit, medium (X) for a 217-psi limit, low (Y) for a 145-psi limit, and very low (Z) for a 73-psi limit. If the evaluation is conducted by a specific technical study of the pavement characteristics and behavior, the evaluation method is classed as technical (T). If the evaluation is based upon experience on the type of runway with particular aircraft, it is termed as being performed by aircraft experience (U). The aircraft classification numbers for some

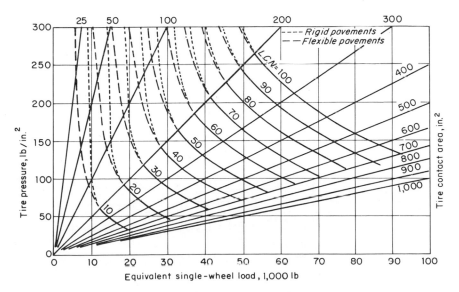

Fig. 12-52 Load classification numbers in terms of load, tire pressure, and contact area for rigid and flexible pavements. The broken lines are tentative extensions of the LCN parameters for contact areas less than 200 in. (*International Civil Aviation Organization.*)

TABLE 12-12 **Aircraft Classification Numbers (ACN) for Selected Aircraft for High Subgrade Strength**

Aircraft	Maximum takeoff weight, lb	Tire pressure, lb/in²	Aircraft classification number	
			Rigid pavement	Flexible pavement
Airbus A-300	313,056	179	37	40
BAC 1-11-400	87,500	135	25	22
Boeing 707-320B	328,000	180	39	42
Boeing 727-200	173,000	167	46	41
Boeing 737-200	111,000	148	27	25
Boeing 747-100	738,000	225	44	46
Concorde	408,000	183	61	65
DC-8-62	353,000	187	47	49
DC-9-32	109,000	152	29	26
DC-10-30	558,000	170	44	53
DCH-7	43,800	107	11	10
L-1011-500	498,000	184	50	60
VC10-1150	335,000	147	38	44

SOURCE: International Civil Aviation Organization [3].

typical aircraft are shown in Table 12-12. A flow chart illustrating the procedure for reporting pavement bearing strength is shown in Fig. 12-53.

To illustrate the PCN reporting system, a PCN of 53/R/B/X/T would indicate that the pavement may be used for unlimited operations by all aircraft with an ACN equal to or less than 46, a Boeing 727-200 with a maximum takeoff weight of 173,000 lb in this case, and that the pavement is a

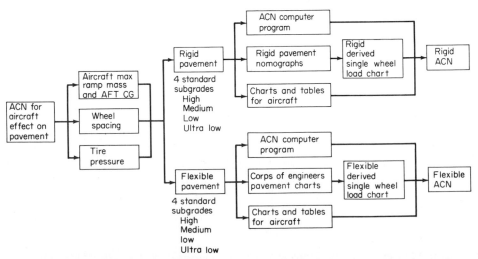

Fig. 12-53 Flow chart indicating the procedure for determining the aircraft classification number (ACN) for pavements. (*Douglas Aircraft Company [63].*)

rigid (R) pavement, which has a modulus of subgrade reaction (B) between 200 and 400 lb/in^3 such that the maximum allowable tire pressure (X) is 217 lb/in^2. This pavement classification number was determined by a technical evaluation (T) of the pavement properties.

ICAO permits some overloading of the pavement by aircraft with ACNs slightly larger than the reported PCN [3]. This allows airport management to assess the optimal operating criteria for airport pavements considering such factors as traffic demand and pavement life. It provides aircraft operators with information essential to the development of effective operating plans related to the aircraft fleet, route network, and strength properties of airports served. Finally, it provides information to aircraft manufacturers relative to the development of aircraft which will operate within the constraints of existing airports.

REFERENCES

1. "A Design Procedure for Continuously Reinforced Concrete Pavements for Highways," ACI Subcommittee VII, Title No. 69-32, *Journal of the American Concrete Institute*, vol. 69, pp. 309–319, Detroit, Mich., June 1972.

2. *Aerodrome Design Manual*, Part 3: *Pavements*, 1st ed., International Civil Aviation Organization, Montreal, Que., Canada, Doc. 9157-AN/901, 1980.

3. *Aerodromes, Annex 14 to the Convention on International Civil Aviation*, 7th ed., International Civil Aviation Organization, Montreal, Que., Canada, June 1976.

4. *Aircraft Data*, Federal Aviation Administration, Washington, D.C., Advisory Circular AC 150/5325-5B, 1975.

5. "Aircraft Pavement Loading: Static and Dynamic," R.C. O'Massey, *Research in Airport Pavements*, Transportation Research Board, Washington, D.C., Spec. Rep. 175, 1978.

6. *Airfield Pavement Requirements for Multi-Wheel Heavy Gear Loads*, Federal Aviation Administration, Washington, D.C., Rep. FAA-RD-70-77, 1971.

7. *Airport Pavement Design and Evaluation*, Federal Aviation Administration, Washington, D.C., Advisory Circular AC 150/5320-6C, 1979.

8. *Air Transportation Bibliography*, Federal Aviation Administration, Washington, D.C., Rep. FAA-EM-78-21, December 1978.

9. "Analysis of Stresses in Concrete Pavements Due to Variations of Temperature," H.M. Westergaard, *Proceedings, 6th Annual Meeting*, Highway Research Board, (Transportation Research Board), Washington, D.C., 1926.

10. "Applications of the Results of Research to the Structural Design of Pavements," E.F. Kelley, *Journal of the American Concrete Institute*, Detroit, Mich., June 1939.

11. *Bibliography: Airports*, Federal Aviation Administration, Washington, D.C., Rep. FAA-EM-77-15, October 1977.

12. "Characterization of Subgrade Soils in Cold Regions for Pavement Design Purposes," A.T. Bergan and C.L. Monismith, *Highway Research Record*, no. 431, Highway Research Board, Washington, D.C., 1973.

13. *Combined CRB Criteria*, U.S. Army Corps of Engineers, Waterways Experiment Station, Vicksburg, Miss., Tech. Rep. 3-495, March 1959.

14. *Computer Program for Airport Pavement Design*, R.G. Packard, Portland Cement Association, Skokie, Ill., 1967.

15. *Computer Program Supplement to Full-Depth Asphalt Pavements for Air Carrier Airports*, Asphalt Institute, College Park, Md., Manual Series 11A (MS-11A), 1973.

16. *Design and Construction and Behavior Under Traffic of Pavement Test Sections*, Federal Aviation Administration, Washington, D.C., Rep. FAA-RD-73-189-I, June 1974.

17. *Design and Construction, Continuously Reinforced Joint and Crack Sealing Materials and Practices*, National Cooperative Highway Research Program, Highway Research Board, Washington, D.C., NCHRP Rep. 38, 1967.

18. *Design and Construction of Airport Pavements on Expansive Soils*, Federal Aviation Administration, Washington, D.C., Rep. FAA-RD-76-66, January 1976.

19. *Design and Construction of MESL*, Federal Aviation Administration, Washington, D.C., Rep. FAA-RD-73-198-III, December 1974.

20. "Design and Evaluation of Aircraft Pavements—1971," F.R. Martin, R.F.A. Judge, and M.B. Chamming, *Transportation Engineering Journal*, vol. 99, no. TE4, American Society of Civil Engineers, New York, N.Y., November 1973.

21. *Design Manual for Continuously Reinforced Concrete Pavement*, P.F. McCullough, United States Steel Corporation, 1968.

22. *Design Manual for Continuously Reinforced Concrete Pavements*, Federal Aviation Administration, Washington, D.C., Rep. FAA-RD-74-33-III, May 1974.

23. *Design of Civil Airfield Pavement for Seasonal Frost and Permafrost Conditions*, Federal Aviation Administration, Washington, D.C., Rep. FAA-RD-74-30, October 1974.

24. *Design of Concrete Airport Pavement*, R.G. Packard, Engineering Bulletin, Portland Cement Association, Skokie, Ill., 1973.

25. "Design of Dowels in Transverse Joints of Concrete Pavements," B.F. Friberg, *Transactions*, vol. 105, American Society of Civil Engineers, New York, N.Y., 1940.

26. *Design of Flexible Airfield Pavements for Multiple-Wheel Landing Gear Assemblies*, Rep. 2: *Analysis of Existing Data*, U.S. Army Corps of Engineers, Waterways Experiment Station, Vicksburg, Miss., Techn. Memo. 3-349, June 1955.

27. *Design of Functional Pavements*, N.C. Yang, McGraw-Hill Book Co., New York, N.Y., 1972.

28. "Design of Pavement with High Quality Structural Layers," G.M. Hammitt, *Research in Airport Pavements*, Transportation Research Board, Washington, D.C., Spec. Rep. 175, 1978.

29. "Development of CBR Flexible Pavement Design Methods for Airfields," A Symposium, *Transactions*, vol. 115, American Society of Civil Engineers, New York, N.Y., 1950.

30. "Effect of Dynamic Loads on Airport Pavements," R.H. Ledbetter, *Research in Airport Pavements*, Transportation Research Board, Washington, D.C., Spec. Rep. 175, 1978.

31. *ELSYM5, Computer Program for Determining Stresses and Deformation in a Five Layer Elastic System*, G. Ahlborn, University of California, Berkeley, Calif., 1972.

32. "Equivalent Passages of Aircraft with Respect to Fatique Distress of Flexible Airfield Pavements," J.A. Deacon, *Proceedings*, Association of Asphalt Paving Technologists, 1971.

33. *Field Survey and Analysis of Aircraft Distribution on Airport Pavements*, Federal Aviation Administration, Washington, D.C., Rep. FAA-RD-74-36, February 1975.

34. *Flexible Airfield Pavements*, U.S. Army Corps of Engineers, A.G. Publication Center, St. Louis, Mo., Tech. Manual TM 5-824-2, February 1969.

35. *Full-Depth Asphalt Pavements for Air Carrier Airports*, Asphalt Institute, College Park, Md., Manual Ser. 11 (MS-11), January 1973.

36. *Full-Depth Asphalt Pavements for General Aviation*, Asphalt Institute, College Park, Md., Information Ser. 154 (IS-154), January 1973.

37. *Geomechanics Computing Programme, N.1, Computer Programmes for Circle and Strip Loads on Layered Anisotropic Media*, W.J. Harrison, C.M. Gerrard, and L.J. Wardel, Division of Applied Geomechanics, SCIRO, Australia, 1972.

38. "Influence Charts for Rigid Pavements," G. Pickett and G.K. Ray, *Transactions*, vol. 116, pp. 49–73, American Society of Civil Engineers, New York, N.Y., 1951.

39. "Layered Systems under Normal Surface Loads," M.G. Peutz, H.P.M. van Kempen, and A. Jones, *Highway Research Record*, no. 228, Highway Research Board, Washington, D.C., 1968.

40. *Mathematical Expressions of the CBR Relations*, U.S. Army Corps of Engineers, Waterways Experiment Station, Vicksburg, Miss., Tech. Rep. 3-441, November 1956.

41. *Methodology for Determining, Isolating and Correcting Runway Roughness*, Federal Aviation Administration, Washington, D.C., Rep. FAA-RD-75-110-II, June 1977.

42. *Methods for the Design, Construction, and Maintenance of Skid Resistant Airport Pavement Surfaces*, Federal Aviation Administration, Washington, D.C., Advisory Circular AC 150/5320-12, 1975.

43. "Modern Pavement Evaluation Techniques," B.A. Vallerga and R.G. Lee, *Airports Challenges of the Future*, American Society of Civil Engineers, New York, N.Y., March 1973.

44. *Multiple-Wheel Heavy Gear Load Pavements Tests*, vol. 1. *Basic Report*, R.G. Ahlvin et al., AFWL, Kirtland Air Force Base, N. Mex., Tech. Rep. AFWL-TR-70 113, November 1971.

45. "New Formulas for Stresses in Concrete Pavements of Airfields," H.M. Westergaard, *Transactions*, vol. 113, American Society of Civil Engineers, New York, N.Y., 1948.

46. "Numerical Computation of Stresses and Strains in a Multiple-Layer Asphalt Pavement System," H. Warren and W.L. Dieckmann, Chevron Research Corporation, Internal Unpublished Report, 1963.

47. *Pavement Classification for Civil and Military Aircraft*, vol. 1, Directorate of Civil Engineering Development, Department of the Environment, Croyden, United Kingdom, 1971.

48. *Pavement Design for Frost Conditions*, U.S. Army Corps of Engineers, A.G. Publication Center, St. Louis, Mo., Tech. Manual TM 5-818-2, July 1965.

49. "Pavement Evaluation and Design for Jumbo Jets," B.A. Vallerga and B.F. McCullough, *Transporation Engineering Journal*, vol. 95, no. TE4, American Society of Civil Engineers, New York, N.Y., November 1969.

50. *Pavement Response to Aircraft Dynamic Loads*, Federal Aviation Administration, Washington, D.C., Rep. FAA-RD-74-39-II, 1974.

51. "Performance of Concrete Pavements Subjected to Wide-Body Jet Aircraft Loading," R.L. Hutchinson, *Proceedings*, Annual Meeting on Roadways and Airport Pavements, Paper SP 51-8, American Concrete Institute, Detroit, Mich., 1975.

52. *Principles of Pavement Design*, 2nd ed., E.J. Yoder and M.W. Witczak, John Wiley & Sons, New York, N.Y., 1975.

53. *Proceedings of the International Air Transportation Conference, 1977 and 1979*, American Society of Civil Engineers, New York, N.Y.

54. *Reinforced Concrete Pavements*, R.D. Bradbury, Wire Reinforcement Institute, Washington, D.C., 1938.

55. "Relative Pavement Bearing Strength Requirements of Aircraft," R.C. O'Massey, Douglas Aircraft Company, McDonnell-Douglas Corporation. Long Beach, Calif., Tech. Paper Ser. 780568, 1978.

56. *Research in Airport Pavements*, Transportation Research Board, Washington, D.C., Spec. Rep. 175, 1978.

57. *Review of Soil Classification Systems Applicable to Airport Pavement Design*, Federal Aviation Administration, Washington, D.C., Rep. FAA-RD-73-169, May 1974.

58. *Rigid Pavements for Airfields Other than Army*, U.S. Army and Air Force, A.G. Publication Center, St. Louis, Mo., Tech. Manual TM 5-824-3, December 1970.

59. *Standards for Specifying Construction of Airports*, Federal Aviation Administration, Washington, D.C., Advisory Circular AC 150/5370-10, August 1981.

60. *Structural Design of Asphalt Pavements for Heavy Aircraft*, J.M. Edwards and C.P. Valkering, Shell International Petroleum Company Limited, London, England, 1970.

61. "Structural Design of Concrete Pavement by Computer," C.E. Warnes, *Transportation Engineering Journal*, vol. 98, no. TE1, American Society of Civil Engineers, New York, N.Y., February 1972.

62. *Structural Design of Pavements for Light Aircraft*, Federal Aviation Administration, Washington, D.C., Rep. FAA-RD-76-179, December 1976.

63. *The ACN/PCN System for Reporting Airfield Bearing Strength*, R.C. O'Massey, Douglas Aircraft Company, McDonnell-Douglas Corporation, Long Beach, Calif., 1980.

64. "The Application of Elastic Theory to Flexible Pavements," A.C. Whiffin and N.W. Lister, *Proceedings*, 1st International Conference on the Structural Design of Asphalt Pavements, University of Michigan, Ann Arbor, Mich., 1963.

65. *Thickness Design for Concrete Pavements*, Portland Cement Association, Skokie, Ill., Cement Information Ser., 1966.

66. *Use of Nondestructive Testing Devices in the Evaluation of Airport Pavements*, Federal Aviation Administration, Washington, D.C., Advisory Circular AC 150/5370-11, 1980.

Chapter 13

Lighting, Marking, and Signing

INTRODUCTION

This chapter is devoted principally to outlining the visual requirements of the pilot and the various lighting systems in use or proposed to meet these requirements. No attempt has been made to describe in detail the hardware or its installation.

The emphasis in this chapter is on the following facilities:

1. Approach lighting
2. Runway threshold lighting
3. Runway edge lighting
4. Runway centerline and touchdown zone lights
5. Taxiway edge and centerline lighting
6. Taxiway guidance sign system

These facilities provide the following functions:

1. The ground-to-air visual information required during landing
2. The visual requirements for takeoff
3. The visual guidance for taxiing

The Pilots' Requirements for Visual Aids

Since the earliest days of flying, pilots have used ground references for navigation when approaching an airport, just as ships' officers at sea have used landmarks on shore when approaching a harbor. Pilots have need for visual aids in good weather as well as in bad weather and in the daytime as well as at night.

In the daytime there is adequate light from the sun and sky, so artificial lighting is not usually required. But it is necessary to have adequate contrast in the field of view and to have a suitable pattern of brightnesses so that the important features of the airport can be identified or oriented with respect to the pilots' positions in space. These requirements are almost automatically met in the daytime when the weather is clear. The runway for conventional aircraft always appears as a long narrow strip with straight sides and is free of obstacles. It can therefore be easily identified from a distance or by flying over the field. Thereafter, the perspective view of the runway and other identifying reference landmarks are used by pilots as visual aids for orientation when they are approaching the airport to land. Experience has demonstrated that the horizon, the runway edges, the runway threshold, and the centerline of the runway are the most important elements for the pilots to see. These features are shown schematically in Figs. 13-1 and 13-2. In order to enhance the daytime visual information, the runway is painted with a standard marking pattern (see Fig. 13-18). The key elements in this pattern are the threshold, the centerline, and the edges, plus multiple parallel lines to increase the perspective and to define the plane of the surface.

In the daytime when the visibility is poor and at night, the visual information is reduced by a very large factor over the clear-weather daytime scene. It is therefore essential to provide visual aids which will be as meaningful to pilots as possible.

The Aircraft Landing Operation

An aircraft landing can be visualized as a sequence of operations involving a transient body suspended in a three-dimensional grid that is approaching

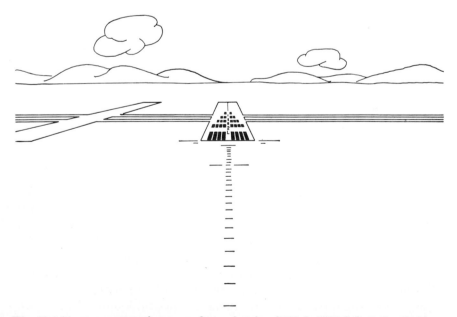

Fig. 13-1 Daytime approach as seen from a height of 200 ft, 3500 ft from threshold.

Fig. 13-2 Daytime approach as seen from a height of 80 ft, 800 ft from threshold.

a fixed two-dimensional grid. While in the air, the aircraft can be considered as a point mass in a three-dimensional orthogonal coordinate system in which it may have translation along three coordinate directions and rotation about three axes. If the three axes are aligned horizontal, vertical, and parallel to the runway, the directions of motion can be described as lateral, vertical, and forward. The rotations are normally called pitch, yaw, and roll for the horizontal, vertical, and parallel axes, respectively. During a landing, pilots must control and coordinate all six degrees of freedom of the aircraft so as to bring it into coincidence with a desired reference path to the touchdown point on the runway. In order to do this, they need translation information regarding the aircraft's alignment, height, and distance; rotation information regarding pitch, yaw, and roll; and information concerning the rate of descent and the rate of closure with the desired path. The glide path, height, time, and distance relationships during a typical landing are shown in Fig. 13-3.

Alignment Guidance

Pilots must know where their aircraft is with respect to lateral displacement from the centerline of the runway. Most runways are from 75 to 200 ft wide and 3000 to 13,000 ft long. Thus any runway is a long narrow ribbon when first seen from several thousand feet away. The predominant alignment guidance comes from the longitudinal lines that constitute the centerline and the edges. All techniques, such as painting, lighting, or surface treatment, that develop contrast and emphasize these linear elements are helpful in providing alignment information.

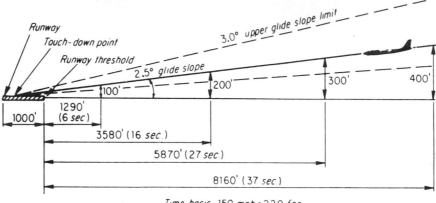

Fig. 13-3 Glide slope, height, time, and distance relationships.

Height Information

The estimation of height above ground from visual cues is one of the most difficult judgments for pilots. It is simply not possible to provide good height information from an approach lighting system; consequently the best source of height information is the instruments in the aircraft. However, use of these instruments requires the availability of an ILS on the ground. Many airports have no ILS at all, and at others only some of the runways have this equipment. Consequently a visual aid defining the desired glide path has been developed, known as the *visual approach slope indicator* (VASI). However, it can be used only when the visibility is reasonably good.

How Much the Pilots See on the Ground

Several parameters influence how much pilots can see on the ground. One of these is the *cockpit cutoff angle*. This is the angle between the longitudinal axis of the fuselage and an inclined plane below which the pilots' views are blocked by some part of the aircraft, indicated as α in Fig. 13-4. Normally the larger the angle α, the more the pilots can see of the ground. Also important is the pitch angle β of the fuselage axis during the approach. Few aircraft approach a runway level with the horizon; they are either pitched up or down. The larger the angle β (in a pitch-up attitude), the larger must be the angle α to have adequate over-the-nose vision. Approach speed has a profound influence on the angle β. As an example, for some aircraft β can be decreased by about 1° with every 5-kn increase in speed above some reference speed.

In Fig. 13-4, VR is the visual range or the maximum distance pilots can see. The horizontal segment on the ground that pilots can see is H.. According to Fig. 13-4,

$$H = VR \cos \theta - h \cot (\alpha - \beta) \quad \text{and} \quad \sin \theta = h/VR$$

Note that for a fixed value of VR the ground segment H increases as the height h of the pilots' eyes above the ground decreases. Some typical values of α and β are provided in Table 13-1.

It has been found through experience that 3 s is approximately the minimum reaction time for pilots to cause the aircraft to react after they see a visual aid [29]. If a minimum of 3 s is necessary for perception, pilot action, airplane response, and checking the response, and if the speed of the aircraft is 150 mi/h (220 ft/s), then the minimum horizontal segment on the ground should be not less than 660 ft. Using the equation for H with a glide slope angle ϕ of 2.5° and $\alpha - \beta = 12°$ results in H being about 200 ft when h is 200 ft. However, when $h = 100$ ft, $H = 687$ ft. Consequently, pilots cannot derive visual guidance from the approach lights until they reach a height of 100 ft above the runway.

APPROACH LIGHTING

Because of the difference in slant range discussed in the preceding paragraph, the approach lights need to meet different photometric requirements than the threshold and runway lights. In general, much higher intensity is required in the approach lighting system, especially in the outermost lighting units. Also, special identification information, such as high-brightness flashing lights, may be warranted where the visibility is extremely bad.

Studies of the visibility in fog [3] have shown that for a visual range of 2000 to 2500 ft it would be desirable to have as much as 200,000

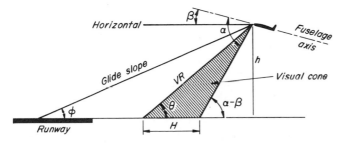

Fig. 13-4 Visual parameters: ϕ = glide slope angle; α = cockpit cutoff angle; β = pitch angle; VR = visual range (maximum distance pilots can see); H = horizontal segment of visual range; h = height of glide slope above runway; θ = angle formed by VR with horizontal.

TABLE 13-1 **Visual Angles for Typical Aircraft**

Aircraft	α	β*	α − β
Boeing 707-320	13°45′	−0°30′	14°15′
Boeing 727	15°24′	−0°30′	15°54′
DC-8	11°30′	+0°30′	11°00′
DC-9	14°00′	+0°31′	13°30′

* Figures are for 100-ft height above the runway, 2.5° glide slope, and approach speed equal to FAR reference speed plus 10 knots; zero wind.

candlepower (cp) available in the outermost approach lights where the slant range is relatively long. Under these same conditions the optimum intensity of the approach lights near the threshold should be on the order of 100 to 500 cp. A transition in the intensity of the light that is directed toward the pilot is highly desirable in order to provide the best visibility at the greatest possible range and to avoid glare and the loss of contrast sensitivity and visual activity at short range.

The configurations which have been accepted are the Calvert system [3] which is widely used in Europe and other parts of the world (Fig. 13-5), and the centerline configuration A system shown in Fig. 13-6, which has been adopted in the United States as a national standard for civil and military use [4]. Both systems are equal in length (3000 ft). The essential difference between them is the number of transverse crossbars. In the Calvert system (developed by E. S. Calvert in Great Britain) there are six transverse rows of lights of variable length spaced on 500-ft centers; in the United States system there is one crossbar 1000 ft from the runway threshold. Roll guidance in the Calvert system is provided principally by the transverse rows of lights; in the United States system roll guidance is provided by bars 14 ft in length, placed at 100-ft centers on the extended centerline of the runway and a single crossbar 1000 ft from the threshold to indicate distance from the threshold. The 14-ft bars consist of five closely

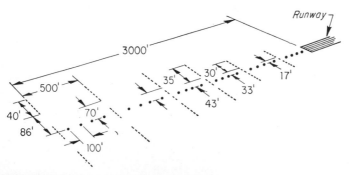

Fig. 13-5 Calvert system of approach lights.

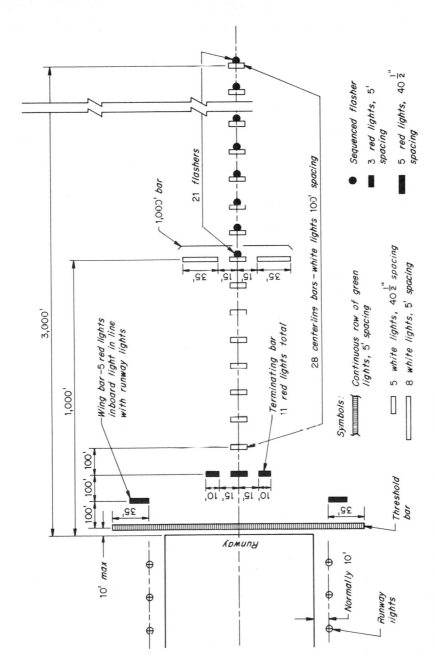

Fig. 13-6 Standard configuration A approach light system.

spaced lights to give the effect of a continuous bar of light. The system is shown in Fig. 13-6.

Approach lights are normally mounted on pedestals of varying height. Details concerning the requirements in the United States are contained in [4].

For operations in very poor visibility, category II or lower, there is a common internationally accepted ICAO system which applies only to the inner 1000 ft of the system closest to the runway threshold. The remaining 2000 ft of the system is unaffected, and consequently it can be either the Calvert, the United States, or another system. The category II system shown in Fig. 13-7 consists of two lines of red barrettes each side of the runway centerline extending 1000 ft from threshold. In addition to the 1000-ft bar, there is an added bar of white light 500 ft from threshold.

At smaller airports where precision approaches are not required, a *medium approach lighting system* (MALS) with or without sequenced flashers is adequate. The system is only 1400 ft long compared with a length of 3000 ft for a precision approach system. It is therefore much more economical, an important factor at smaller airports. The system is illustrated in Fig. 13-8.

Sequenced flashing high-intensity lights are available for airport use and are installed as supplements to the standard approach pattern at those airports where very low visibilities occur frequently. These lights operate from the stored energy in a capacitor which is discharged through the lamp in approximately 5 ms and may develop as much as 30 million cp of light. They are mounted on the same pedestals as the bar lights in configuration A. The lights are sequence-fired, beginning with the unit farthest from the runway. The complete cycle is repeated every 2 s. This results in a brilliant ball of light continuously moving toward the runway. Since the very bright light can interfere with the pilots' eye adaptation, condenser discharge lamps are usually omitted in the 1000 ft of the approach lighting system nearest the runway.

THRESHOLD LIGHTING

During the final approach for landing, pilots must make a decision to complete the landing or to execute a "missed approach." The identification of the threshold is a major factor in pilots' decisions to land or not to land. For this reason, the region near the threshold is given special lighting consideration. The threshold is identified at large airports by a complete line of green lights extending across the entire width of the runway, as shown in Fig. 13-6, and at small airports by four lights on each side of the threshold, as shown in Fig. 13-8. When the lights are extended across the entire width of the runway, they must be of the semiflush types. The lights

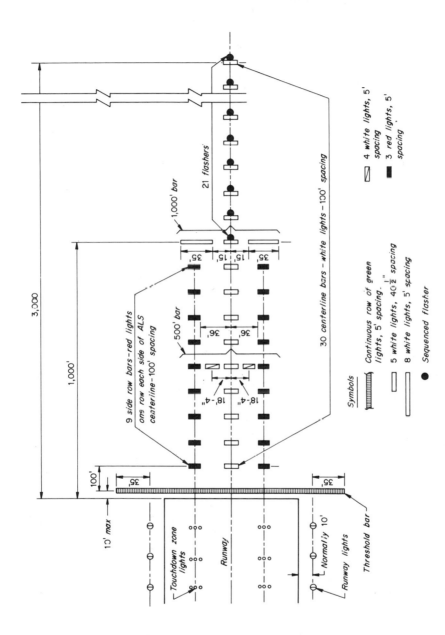

Fig. 13-7 Category II approach light system.

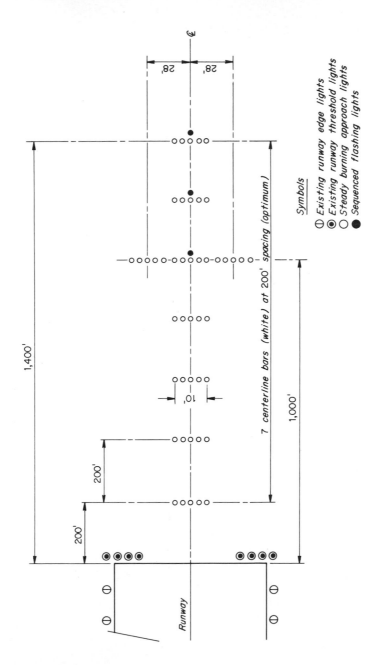

Fig. 13-8 Medium approach light system. Note: This system is a MALS when sequenced flashing lights are omitted. (*Federal Aviation Administration.*)

shown on Fig. 13-8 can be elevated. Threshold lights in the direction of landing are green, as stated previously, but in the opposite direction they are red to indicate the end of the runway.

RUNWAY LIGHTING

After crossing the threshold, pilots must complete a touchdown and roll out on the runway. The runway visual aids for this phase should be designed to give pilots information on alignment, lateral displacement, roll, and distance. The lights should be arranged to form a visual pattern that pilots can easily interpret.

At first, night landings were made by floodlighting a general area. Various types of lighting devices were used, including automobile headlights, arc lights, and search lights. Boundary lights were added to outline the field and to mark hazards such as ditches and fences. Gradually, preferred landing directions were developed, and special lights were used to indicate these directions. Floodlighting was then restricted to the preferred landing directions, and runway edge lights were added along the landing strips. As experience developed, the runway edge lights were adopted as the visual aids on a runway. This was followed by the use of runway centerline and touchdown zone lights for operations in very poor visibility.

Runway Edge Lights

Recommended standards for the design and installation of runway edge lighting systems are described in [20] and in ICAO Annex 14 [1]. The light fixtures are usually elevated units. Semiflush lights, however, are permitted. Each unit has a specially designed lens which projects two main light beams down the runway. Elevated runway lights are mounted on frangible fittings and project no more than 30 in above the surface on which they are installed. They are located along the edge of the runway not more than 10 ft from the edge of the full-strength pavement. The longitudinal spacing is not more than 200 ft. Runway edge lights are white, except that the last 2000 ft of an instrument runway facing the pilot is yellow to indicate a caution zone. A typical layout of high-intensity runway lights is shown in Fig. 13-9. If the runway is displaced, but the area that is displaced is usable for takeoffs and taxiing, the runway edge lights in the displaced area facing the pilot are red, as shown in Fig. 13-10.

Runway Centerline and Touchdown Zone Lights

As an aircraft proceeds over the approach lights, pilots are looking at relatively bright sources on the extended centerline of the runway. Over

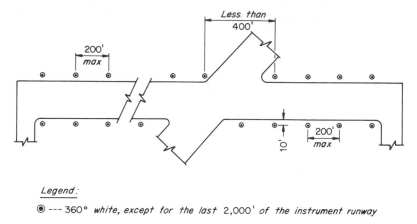

Legend:

◉ --- 360° white, except for the last 2,000' of the instrument runway

Fig. 13-9 High-intensity runway lights.

the runway threshold, they continue to look along the centerline, but the principal source of guidance, namely, the edge lights, has moved far to each side in their peripheral vision. The result is that the central area appears excessively black, and pilots are virtually flying blind, except for the peripheral reference information. Attempts to eliminate the "black hole" by increasing the intensity of the edge lights have proven to be ineffective. In order to reduce the black-hole effect and provide adequate guidance during very poor visibility conditions, runway centerline and touchdown zone lights have been installed in the pavement. These lights are only installed at those airports which are equipped for category II operations. Recommended standards for design are contained in [16].

The touchdown zone lights are white and extend 3000 ft from the threshold of the runway. They are spaced at intervals of 100 ft and are located 60 ft each side of the runway centerline, as shown on Fig. 13-11. The centerline lights are spaced at intervals of 50 ft. They are normally offset 2 ft from the centerline to avoid the paint line and the nose gear of the aircraft from riding over the light fixtures. The lights are white, except for the last 3000 ft of runway facing the pilot, where they are color-coded. The last 1000 ft is red, and the next 2000 ft is alternate red and white, as shown in Fig. 13-12.

When there are displaced thresholds, the centerline and touchdown zone lights are blanked out in the direction of landing.

TAXIWAY LIGHTING

Either after a landing or on the way to takeoff, pilots must maneuver the aircraft on a system of taxiways to and from the terminal and hangar areas.

In a large airport the taxiway system can be very complex; consequently adequate lighting aids should be provided for taxiing at night and also in the daytime when the visibility is very poor. The following design criteria apply to visual aids for taxiways:

1. Taxiways should be clearly identified so that they cannot be confused with runways.

2. Exits from runways should be readily identified. This is especially true for high-speed exits, where the pilots should be able to locate the exit 1200 to 1500 ft ahead of the point of turn.

3. There should be adequate guidance along the taxiway.

4. The specific taxiway should be readily identified to pilots.

5. Intersections of taxiways and runway-taxiway crossings should be clearly marked.

6. The complete route from the runway to the apron should be easily identified.

There are two types of lights. One type delineates the edges of taxiways and is described in detail in [20]. The other type delineates the centerline of the taxiway and is described in detail in [25]. Taxiway edge lights are blue, and taxiway centerline lights are green.

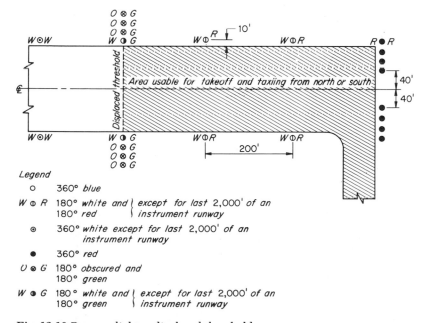

Fig. 13-10 Runway lights—displaced threshold.

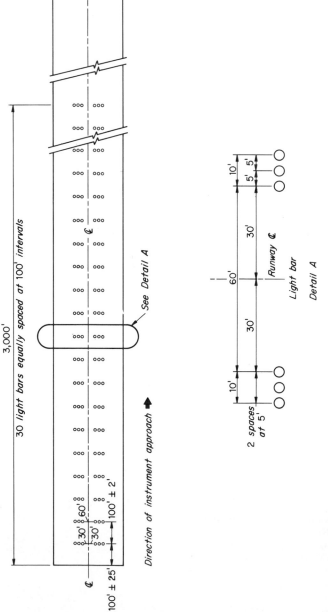

Fig. 13-11 Touchdown zone lights.

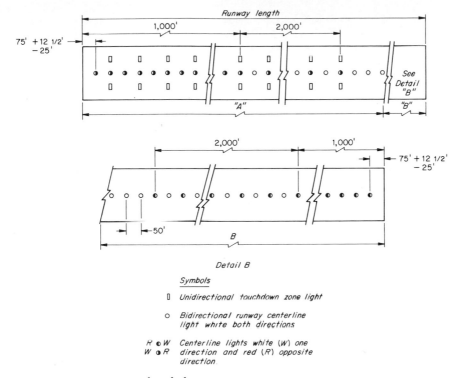

Fig. 13-12 Runway centerline lights.

Taxiway Edge Lights

Elevated bidirectional lights are usually placed at intervals of not more than 200 ft on each side of the taxiway. The exact spacing is influenced by the physical layout of the taxiways. Closer spacing is required on curves. Light fixtures are located not more than 10 ft from the full-strength pavements. The lights cannot extend more than 30 in above the pavement surface. The spacing of lights along a curve is shown in Fig. 13-13. Entrance and exit points to runways are lighted as shown in Fig. 13-14. With the advent of large wide-body jets like the 747 the thrust of the outboard engines tends to impinge on the taxiway lights, causing in some cases damage to the fixtures. Another complaint from pilots is that edge lights do not provide adequate guidance, especially with respect to lateral displacement.

Taxiway Centerline Lighting

Research and experience have demonstrated that guidance from centerline lights is superior to that from edge lights, particularly in low visibility. The spacing of the lights on curves and tangents is given in Table 13-2 [25].

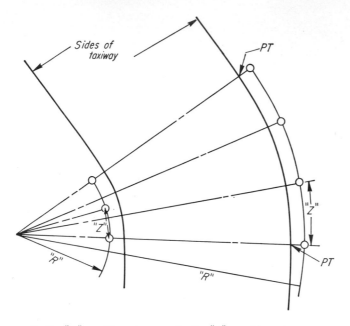

Radius "R" of curve in feet	Dimension "Z" in feet	Radius "R" of curve in feet	Dimension "Z" in feet
15	20	300	80
25	27	400	95
50	35	500	110
75	40	600	130
100	50	700	145
150	55	800	165
200	60	900	185
250	70	1000	200 *max*

Notes:
1. *For radii not listed, "Z" spacing shall be determined by linear interpolation.*
2. *"Z" is the chord length*

Fig. 13-13 Typical taxiway lighting layout on straight and curved sections (*Federal Aviation Administration.*)

For normal exits the centerline lights are terminated at the edge of the runway. At taxiway intersections the lights continue across the intersection. For long-radius high-speed exit taxiways the taxiway lights are extended onto the runway from a point 200 ft back of the point of curve (PC) of the taxiway to the point of tangent of the central curve of the taxiway (see Chap 9). Within these limits the spacing of the lights is 50 ft. They are offset 2 ft from the runway centerline lights and then gradually brought into the centerline of the taxiway.

Where taxiways intersect with runways and aircraft are required to hold short of the runway, several yellow lights spaced at 5-ft intervals are placed transversally across the taxiway.

VISUAL APPROACH SLOPE AIDS

A large percentage of landing accidents have occurred in good visibility weather and have been attributed to poor ground reference data which caused difficulty in judging height.

Visual Approach Slope Indicator

As an aid in defining the desired glide path in relatively good weather conditions, an optical scheme, the VASI, has been developed. The scheme, adopted in the United States, was developed in Great Britain.

There are a number of VASI configurations depending on the desired visual range, the type of aircraft, and whether large wide-body aircraft will be using the runway, as shown in Table 13-3. Each group of lights transverse to the direction of the runway is referred to as a *bar* irrespective of the fact that it may be on one or both sides of the runway. A bar is made up of one, two, or three light units, referred to as *boxes*. Thus the VASI-12 system, shown in Fig. 13-15, is a two-bar system consisting of 12 boxes. The bar that is nearest to the runway threshold is referred to as the *downwind bar*, and the bar that is farthest from the runway threshold is referred to as

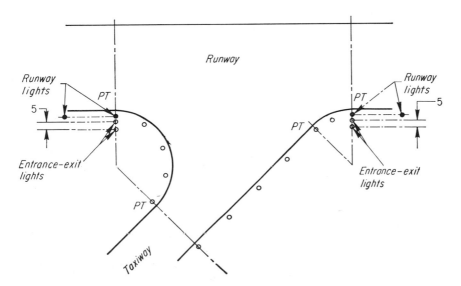

Fig. 13-14 Location of extrance and exit taxiway lights.

TABLE 13-2 **Taxiway Lighting Spacing**

	Maximum longitudinal spacing, ft	
	1000 ft RVR and above	Below 1000 ft RVR*
Curves		
Centerline radius of curve, ft		
125–399	25	12.5
400–1199	50	25
1200 to straight	100	50
Very long radius exits	50	50
Tangents		
Taxiway length, ft		
Up to 350	25	
351–450	50	
451–500	75	
500 or greater	100	

* RVR = "runway visual range."
SOURCE: Federal Aviation Administration.

the *upwind bar*. If pilots are on the proper glide path, the downwind bar appears white and the upwind bar red. If pilots are too low, both bars appear red; and if they are too high, both bars appear white.

In order to accommodate large wide-body jets where the height of the pilots' eyes is much greater than in the smaller jets, a third upwind bar is added, as represented by the VASI-6 and VASI-16 systems in Table 13-3. For wide-body jets the middle bar becomes the downwind bar and the third bar is the upwind bar. In other words, large wide-body aircraft disregard the bar closest to the runway threshold. The location of the lights for VASI-6 systems is shown in Fig. 13-15.

The more common systems in use in the United States are the VASI-2, VASI-4, VASI-12, and VASI-16. VASI systems are particularly useful on runways that do not have an ILS.

Precision Approach Path Indicator

The FAA is at present undertaking operational tests of a new visual approach indicator, called the *precision approach path indicator* (PAPI). This sytem gives more precise indications to the pilots of the approach path of the aircraft and utilizes only one set of lights, as opposed to the minimum of two required by the VASI system. A schematic diagram of the PAPI system is shown in Fig. 13-16. The system consists of a unit with four lights on either side of the approach runway. By utilizing the color scheme indicated in Fig. 13-16, the pilot is able to ascertain five approach angles relative to the proper glide slope, as compared with three with the VASI system. One of the problems with the VASI system has been the lack of an immediate transition from one color indication to another, resulting in shades of colors. The PAPI system resolves this problem by providing an instant transition from one color indication to another as a reaction to the descent path of the aircraft. Another advantage of the system is that it is a one-bar system, as opposed to the two-bar VASI system. This will result in greater operating and maintenance cost economies than the VASI, and eliminates the need for the pilots to look at two bars to obtain glide slope indications.

RUNWAY END IDENTIFIER LIGHTS

Runway end identifier lights (REIL) are installed at airports where there are no approach lights to provide pilots with positive visual identification

TABLE 13-3 **Configuration of Visual Approach Slope Indicators**

Type	Schematic	Day VFR range (nmi)	Comments
VASI-16		5	All aircraft including long large-body turbojet; used at major airports requiring maximum boldness of signal
VASI-12		5	All aircraft except long large-body turbojet; used at major airports requiring maximum boldness of signal
VASI-6		4	For runways with B-747 or C5A operations; two visual glide paths to serve all aircraft types
VASI-4		4	Normally installed on primary runways
VASI-2		3	Normally installed on secondary and utility runways
SAVASI		11/2	Option for VASI-2; for VFR basic utility runways only

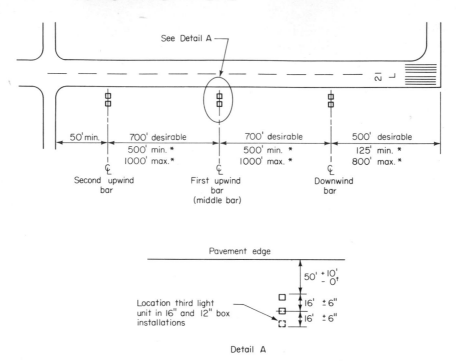

Detail A

Fig. 13-15 Location of visual approach slope indicators. (1) Upwind and downwind light units are located at same distance from runway edge; (2) center of optical aperture of all light units is within ± 1 ft of runway centerline grade. *Longitudinal tolerances to be used only to avoid taxiways, cross runways, etc., or to achieve a desirable height due to terrain. †Lateral tolerances to be used to avoid ditches, catch basins, utility holes, etc. (*Federal Aviation Administration [28].*)

of the approach end of the runway. The system consists of a pair of synchronized white flashing lights located on each side of the runway threshold and is intended for use when there is adequate visibility.

RUNWAY AND TAXIWAY MARKING

In order to aid pilots in guiding the aircraft on the runways and taxiways, pavements are marked with lines and numbers. These markings are of benefit primarily during daylight and dusk; at night, lights are used to guide pilots in landing and maneuvering in the airport. White is used for all markings on runways and yellow on taxiways and aprons. The FAA has developed a comprehensive plan for marking runways and taxiways, which is described in detail in [18]. Similarly the ICAO recommendations for marking are contained in Annex 14 [2]. The FAA and ICAO requirements are quite similar.

Runways

The FAA has grouped runways for marking purposes into three classes: (1) basic runway, (2) nonprecision instrument, and (3) precision instrument. The basic runway is for operations in VFR conditions. The nonprecision instrument runway is one in which straight-in approaches are made with reference to a VOR station. A precision instrument runway is one that is equipped with an ILS.

The end of each runway is marked with a number which indicates the magnetic azimuth (clockwise from north) of the runway in the direction of landing. The marking is given to the nearest 10° with the last digit omitted. Thus an azimuth of 93° would be marked as 9. Likewise the east end of an east-west runway would be marked 27 (for 270°) and the west end 9 (for 90°). When there are more than three parallel runways (e.g., four runways) one pair is marked with the magnetic azimuth to the nearest 10°, while the other pair is marked with the magnetic azimuth to the next nearest 10°.

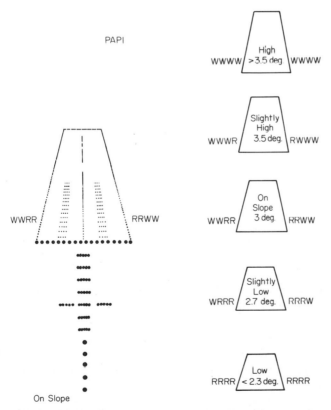

Fig. 13-16 Precision approach path indicator. (*Federal Aviation Administration.*)

Assume there are four runways in an east-west direction. One pair would be marked 9-27, while the other pair would be marked 10-28 or 8-26.

When there is more than one runway in the same direction, the following letters are added to the azimuth numbers:

Two parallel runways	L, R
Three parallel runways	L, C, R
Four parallel runways	L, R, L, R
Five parallel runways	L, C, R, L, R

Figures 13-17 and 13-18 have been taken from [18] to show the essential markings. The amount of marking required on a runway depends on whether the runway is used in VFR or IFR conditions. Markings for the three classes of runways include the following:

1. Basic runway: runway number and centerline

2. Nonprecision runway: runway number, centerline, and threshold

3. Precision runway: runway number, centerline, threshold, touchdown zone, and aiming point.

The aiming point is placed on all runways 4000 ft or longer which are used by turbine-powered aircraft. The marking consists of two bold stripes located 1000 ft from the threshold, as shown in Fig. 13-17.

At some airports it is desirable to "displace" the runway threshold on a permanent basis. A displaced threshold is one which has been moved a certain distance from the end of the runway. Most often this is necessary to clear obstructions in the flight path. The displacement reduces the length of the runway for landings, but takeoffs can use the entire length of the runway. The FAA requires that displaced thresholds be marked as shown in Fig. 13-18.

In order to prevent erosion of the soil, many airports provide a paved *blast pad* 150 to 200 ft in length adjacent to the runway end. This paved area is not designed to support aircraft loads, and yet it may have the appearance of being so designed. Likewise the area adjacent to the edge of a runway may have a paved shoulder not capable of withstanding aircraft loads. These areas are marked with a 3-ft-wide stripe, as shown in Fig. 13-19. Yellow is used for these markings.

Taxiways

Taxiways are marked as shown in Fig. 13-20. The essential features of the taxiway marking system are as follows:

1. A single continuous 6-in yellow stripe is used to mark the centerline of the taxiway.

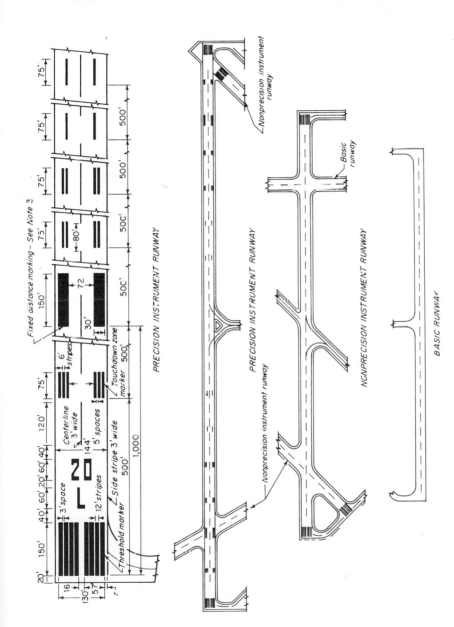

Fig. 13-17 Typical runway marking. *Notes:* (1) Runway numbers are one-tenth of magnetic azimuth measured along runway centerline from approach end; (2) lay out runway centerline spacing from both ends toward center; (3) where fixed distance marker is not used, install three 6 × 75 = ft stripes at that point; (4) all runway markings shall be white, all taxiways yellow. *(Federal Aviation Administration [18].)*

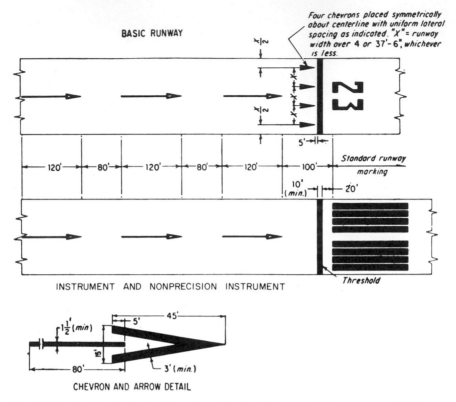

Fig. 13-18 Displaced threshold marking. (*Federal Aviation Administration [18].*)

2. At intersections of taxiways with runway ends the centerline stripe of the taxiway is terminated at the edge of the runway.

3. At all other intersections of taxiways with runways the centerline of the taxiway is extended to the centerline of the runway.

4. Where the edge of the full-strength pavement of a taxiway is not readily apparent, the edge is marked with two continuous 6-in-wide yellow stripes, 6 in apart.

5. For taxiways leading to the end of a runway a *holding line* is placed across the taxiway, as shown in Fig. 13-20. The holding line is located the following minimum distances from the edge of the runway:

　　a. 50 ft at small airports

　　b. 100 ft at airports serving airlines

　　c. 150 ft at airports serving very large airline aircraft

6. If the taxiway shoulder has the same appearance as the load-bearing pavement, it is marked as shown in Fig. 13-19.

Closed Runways and Taxiways

When runways or taxiways are permanently or temporarily closed to aircraft, crosses are placed on these trafficways in accordance with the dimensions shown in [18]. These are painted yellow.

TAXIWAY SIGN SYSTEM

The primary purpose of a taxi sign system is to aid pilots in taxiing aircraft on an airport. At controlled airports, the signs supplement the controller's instructions and aid the pilot in complying with those instructions. The taxi sign system also substantially aids the traffic controller by simplifying instructions for taxiing clearances and routing and holding of aircraft. At locations not served by airport traffic control towers, or for aircraft without radio, the sign system provides guidance to the pilot to major destination areas in the airport.

The system consists of two basic types of signs: *destination*, which indicates the direction to a particular destination, and *intersection*, which identifies intersecting routes [26].

Destination signs show the destination in symbol form and use an arrow to indicate the direction to taxi. The following symbols are used to identify the various inbound destinations:

General parking, servicing, and loading areas	RAMP or RMP
Areas specifically set aside for aircraft parking	PARK
Areas where aircraft are fueled or serviced	FUEL
Gate position at which aircraft are loaded or unloaded	GATE
Areas set aside for itinerant aircraft	VSTR
Areas set aside for military aircraft	MIL
Areas set aside for freight or cargo handling	CRGO
Areas set aside for handling international flights	INTL
Hangar or hangar area	HGR
ILS critical area	ILS

Outbound signs usually designate the direction toward a particular end of a runway.

Intersection signs identify the intersection of runways, taxiways, runways with taxiways, or taxiways with aprons. Taxiways are usually designated by means of capital letters.

The arrangement of destination and intersection signs is illustrated in Fig. 13-21. All signs, including supports, cannot be less than 30 in or more than 42 in in height. They should be located so that the nearest edge of the

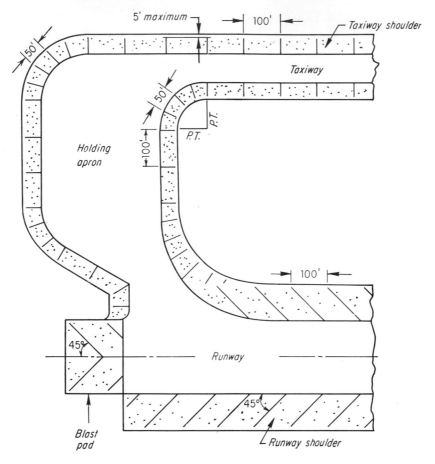

Fig. 13-19 Shoulder marking. (*Federal Aviation Administration [18].*)

sign is not closer than 10 ft from the edge of the pavement. The color of the letters, whether lighted or unlighted, must be yellow, and the color of the background black.

At airports serving large wide-body jets like the B-747 the sign system just described has been subject to damage due to the higher jet-blast velocities and the fact that the engines extend beyond the edge of the pavement farther than for smaller jet aircraft. This demonstrated the need to place the signs further away from the taxiway or runway edge (no closer than 60 ft). A testing program showed that retroreflective highway-type signs could give the guidance needed. The signs are 3 ft high, and the length is determined by the number of letters or numbers that are required. They are supported on frangible fittings, the bottom of the sign being 6 in above the ground. There are three categories of signs: (1) mandatory, (2)

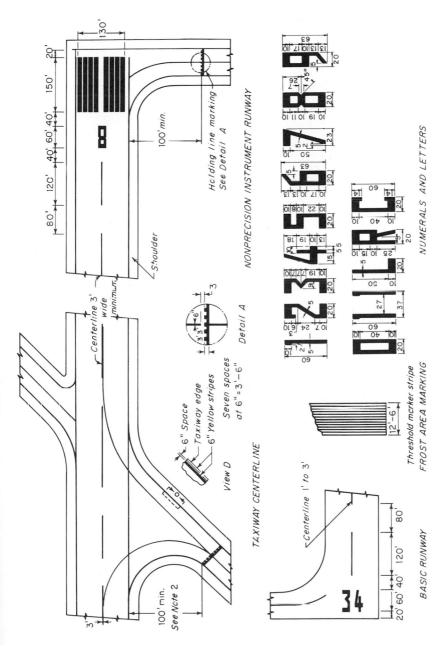

Fig. 13-20 Marking and taxiway typical marking details. *Notes:* (1) Lay out all runway centerline spacing from both ends toward center; (2) locate holding line 100 ft from edge of runway, or 150 ft from edge of runways where heavy jets operate; (3) all stripes and spaces are to be of equal width; (4) maximum width 6 in, minimum width 4 in; (5) all numerals and letters shall by horizontally spaced 15 ft apart, except the numerals in number eleven; (6) work to dimensions, so not scale; (7) all dimensions shown in Numerals and Letters are in feet and inches. (*Federal Aviation Administration [18].*)

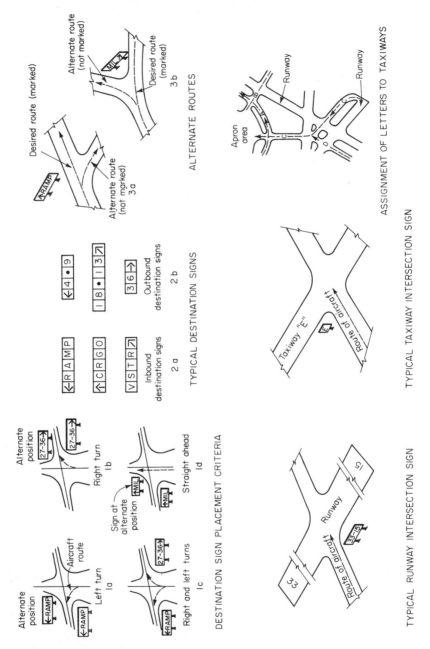

Fig. 13-21 Taxiway signs. (*Federal Aviation Administration [26].*)

informational, and (3) convenience. A mandatory sign is one that, if ignored by a pilot, could cause a hazard involving an aircraft landing or taking off. An example would be a runway intersection sign. An informational sign efficiently determines the route to follow and, if ignored, could cause a hazard to taxiway aircraft. An example would be a taxiway intersection sign. A convenience sign directs pilots to aprons and other specific locations on the airport. Mandatory signs must be lighted; for the other two categories lighting is optional. Mandatory signs have a red retroreflective background with silver-white letters and numerals. For informational signs the background is yellow and the legend is black. Convenience signs have a green background with silver-white legends. The abbreviation system is the same as for the signs previously described. The highway-type signs, which are described in [13], are replacing the signs described elsewhere [26].

RETROREFLECTIVE MARKING OF RUNWAY AND TAXIWAY CENTERLINES

The installation of retroreflective markings is not mandatory; however, it is quite economical, especially at airports where lights cannot be justified because of the volume or the nature of the traffic. The marking is very similar to that used successfully on highways for many years. The system is described in detail in [15].

RELATED VISUAL AIDS

Beacons are lighted to mark an airport. They are designed to produce a narrow horizontal and vertical beam of high intensity which is rotated about a vertical axis so as to produce approximately 12 flashes per minute for civil airports and 18 flashes per minute for military airports [27]. The flashes with a clearly visible duration of at least 0.15 s are arranged in a white-green sequence for land airports and in a white-yellow sequence for landing areas on water. Military airports use a double white flash followed by a longer green or yellow flash to differentiate them from civil airports. The beacons are mounted on the top of the control tower or similar high structure in the immediate vicinity of the airport.

Obstructions are identified by fixed, flashing, or rotating red lights or beacons. All structures that constitute a hazard to aircraft in flight or during landing or takeoff are marked by obstruction lights having a horizontally uniform intensity distribution and a vertical distribution designed to give maximum range at the lower angles (1½ to 8°) from which a colliding approach would most likely come. The criteria for determining which structures need to be lighted are outlined in [5].

VISIBILITY

Throughout this chapter and elsewhere in the text, reference has been made to poor visibility conditions, category II, and runway visual range (RVR). However, these terms were never defined. Various definitions of visibility are used in aviation, and they are briefly described in the following.

Meteorological Visibility and Ceiling

Meteorological visibility is defined differently depending on whether it is night or day. At night it is the distance from which a human can see a 25-candela light. During the day it is the distance that a black circular target subtended by a visual angle of 1° can be seen. Meteorological visibility is also usually associated with the height of the underside of a dense cloud above the airport surface. This height is referred to as *ceiling*. Thus the term *300-¾* means 300-ft ceiling and three quarters of a mile visibility.

Runway Visual Range

While various definitions of visibility have been used by meteorologists, visibility on a runway is being reported more and more in terms of RVR. RVR is the distance that the high-intensity runway edge lights can be seen by pilots. The RVR is determined by transmissometer measurements at the side of the runway near the threshold, and the calibration is correlated with the intensity setting of the edge lights and the time of day or night.

The transmissometer required to measure the RVR consists of a light source with a narrow-beam projector and a receiver having a narrow acceptance angle. The distance between the two units is usually 500 ft. The baseline between the two units should be parallel with the runway, and the light source and the receiver should be about 15 ft above the ground.

For category II and III operations two transmissometer measurements are made, one near the threshold and the other about midway the length of the runway. The latter location provides useful information for aircraft taking off as well as for landing aircraft during the landing roll. The limitation of the transmissometer is that it measures visibility on the ground, whereas pilots approaching a runway like to know the visibility on the approach path.

Visibility Categories

For landing operations primarily, visibilities on the runway have been classified into three categories: I, II, and III. Category III is further subdivided into a, b, and c. The three groups are defined in terms of RVR and *decision height*. Decision height is defined as the lowest height above

TABLE 13-4   **Runway Visual Range Minima and Decision Heights**

ILS category	Lowest minima, ft	
	RVR	Decision height
Non precision	2400	250
Precision, category I	1800	200
Precision, category II	1200	100
Precision, category IIIa	700	0
Precision, category IIIb	150	0
Precision, category IIIc	0	0

SOURCE: Federal Aviation Administration [4].

the runway where pilots make the decision to continue the landing or abort. It is based on the ability of pilots to obtain guidance from visual cues on the ground (i.e., approach lights, runway lights, marking, etc.) rather than on instruments in the cockpit. If pilots are unable to see a sufficient number of visual cues at the decision height, the landing must abort.

The various categories of visibility are defined in Table 13-4. For category IIIa operations, an automatic landing* capability is required rather than manual. The rollout after landing and taxiing to the terminal is manual. For category IIIb operations, an automatic rollout capability in addition to an automatic landing capability is required. For category IIIc operations, the taxiing portion of the landing must also be automatic.

REFERENCES

1. *Aerodrome Design Manual*, Part 4: *Visual Aids*, International Civil Aviation Organization, Montreal, Que., Canada, 1981.
2. *Aerodromes, Annex 14 to the Convention on International Civil Aviation*, 7th ed., International Civil Aviation Organization, Montreal, Que., Canada, June 1976.
3. "Airport Approach, Runway and Taxiway Lighting Systems," E.C. Walter, *Journal of the Air Transport Divison*, vol. 84, no. AT1, American Society of Civil Engineers, New York, N.Y., June 1958.
4. *Airport Design Standards—Site Requirements for Terminal Navigational Facilities*, Federal Aviation Administration, Washington, D.C., Advisory Circular AC 150/5300-2D, 1980.
5. *Airport Miscellaneous Lighting Visual Aids*, Federal Aviation Administration, Washington, D.C., Advisory Circular AC 150/5340-21, 1971.
6. *Airway Planning Standard Number One—Terminal Air Navigation Facilities and Air Traffic Control Services*, Federal Aviation Administration, Washington, D.C., FAA Order 7031.2B, 1976.
7. "Aviation Ground Lighting for All-Weather Operation," M. Latin, *Airport Forum*, vol 7, no. 1, February 1977.
8. *Comparison Between ICAO Annex 14 Standards and Recommended Practices and FAA Advisory Circulars*, Boeing Commercial Airplane Company, Seattle, Wash., Doc. D6-58344, 1979.

* By landing is meant the aircraft touching down on the runway.

9. *Economy Approach Lighting Aids,* Federal Aviation Administration, Washington, D.C., Advisory Circular AC 150/5340-14B, 1970.

10. *Electronic Navigational Aids for Funding Under Airport Development Aid Program (ADAP),* Federal Aviation Administration, Washington, D.C., Advisory Circular AC 150/5100-12, 1976.

11. *Establishment Criteria for Runway End Identification Lights (REIL),* Federal Aviation Administration, Washington, D.C., Rep. FAA-ASP-79-4, 1979.

12. *Establishment Criteria for Visual Approach Slope Indicator (VASI),* Federal Aviation Administration, Washington, D.C., Rep. FAA-ASP-76-2, 1977.

13. *FAA Specification L-853, Runway and Taxiway Retroreflective Markers,* Federal Aviation Administration, Washington, D.C., Advisory Circular AC 150/5345-39A, 1971.

14. *Installation Criteria for the Approach Lighting System Improvement Program (ALSIP),* Federal Aviation Administration, Washington, D.C., Rep. FAA-ASP-78-5, 1978.

15. *Installation Details and Maintenance Standards for Reflective Markers for Airport Runway and Taxiway Centerlines,* Federal Aviation Administration, Washington, D.C., Advisory Circular AC 150/5340-20, 1969.

16. *Installation Details for Runway Centerline and Touchdown Zone Lighting Systems,* Federal Aviation Administration, Washington, D.C., Advisory Circular AC 150/5340-4C, 1978.

17. *Marking and Lighting of Unpaved Runways,* V.F. Dosch, Federal Aviation Administration, Technical Center, Atlantic City, N.J., NAFEC Tech. Letter Rep. NA-78-34-LR, 1978.

18. *Marking of Paved Areas on Airports,* Federal Aviation Administration, Washington, D.C., Advisory Circular AC 150/5340-1E, 1980.

19. *Obstruction Marking and Lighting,* Federal Aviation Administration, Washington, D.C., Advisory Circular AC 70/7460-3, 1978.

20. *Runway and Taxiway Edge Lighting System,* Federal Aviation Administration, Washington, D.C., Advisory Circular AC 150/5340-24, 1977.

21. *Runway Visual Range,* Federal Aviation Administration, Washington, D.C., Advisory Circular AC 97-1A, 1977.

22. *Segmented Circle Airport Marker System,* Federal Aviation Administration, Washington, D.C., Advisory Circular AC 150/5340-5A, September 1971.

23. *Specification for L-858 Taxiway Guidance Signs,* Federal Aviation Administration, Washington, D.C., Advisory Circular AC 150/5345-44B, 1979.

24. *Surface Movement Guidance and Control Systems,* International Civil Aviation Organization, Montreal, Que., Canada, ICAO Circular 148-AN/97, 1979.

25. *Taxiway Centerline Lighting System,* Federal Aviation Administration, Washington, D.C., Advisory Circular AC 150/5340-19, 1968.

26. *Taxiway Guidance Sign System,* Federal Aviation Administration, Washington, D.C., Advisory Circular AC 150/5340-18A, 1980.

27. "The Theory of Visual Judgements in Motion and Its Application to the Design of Landing Aids for Aircraft," E.S. Calvert, *Transactions of the Illuminating Engineering Society,* vol. 22, no. 10, London, England, 1957.

28. *Visual Approach Slope Indicator (VASI) Systems,* Federal Aviation Administration, Washington, D.C., Advisory Circular, AC 150/5340-25, 1977.

29. "Working Papers," A.E. Jenks, International Air Transport Association Special Meeting on Visual Aids to Flare and Landing, Amsterdam, Netherlands, November 14–22, 1955.

Chapter **14**

Airport Drainage

INTRODUCTION

An adequate drainage system for the removal of surface and subsurface water is vital for the safety of aircraft and for the longevity of the pavements. Improper drainage results in the formation of puddles on the pavement surface, which can be hazardous to aircraft taking off and landing. Poor drainage can also result in the early deterioration of pavements. Flat longitudinal and transverse grades and wide pavement surfaces often pose difficulties in making provision for adequate drainage at airports.

The material in this chapter is principally concerned with estimating the amounts of surface and subsurface runoff and not with the hydraulics of pipes or details of installation. These latter items are adequately covered in texts on hydraulics and literature provided by pipe manufacturers.

The FAA and the Corps of Engineers have developed most of the information on airport drainage in the United States. The author has drawn freely from the publications of these two agencies.

PURPOSE OF DRAINAGE

The functions of an airport drainage system are as follows:

1. Interception and diversion of surface and groundwater flow originating from lands adjacent to the airport

2. Removal of surface runoff from the airport

3. Removal of subsurface flow from the airport

In very few cases will the natural drainage on a site be sufficient by itself to satisfy these functions; consequently artificial drainage must be installed.

DESIGN STORM FOR SURFACE RUNOFF

The selection of the severity of the storm which the drainage system should accommodate involves economic consideration. An extremely severe storm

535

occurring very infrequently would undoubtedly cause some damage if the system were designed for a storm of lesser severity. However, if serious interruptions in traffic are not anticipated, a system designed for the larger storm may not be economically justified. Taking these factors into account, the FAA recommends that for civil airports the drainage system be designed for a storm whose probability of occurrence is once in 5 years [1]. The design should, however, be checked with a storm of lesser frequency (10 and 15 years) to ascertain if serious damage or interruption of traffic would result from such a storm. Drainage for military airfields is based on a 2-year storm frequency [5].

Ordinarily no ponding is permitted on paved surfaces, but in the intervening areas ponding is permitted, provided it will not result in undesirable saturation of the subgrades underneath the pavements.

DETERMINING THE INTENSITY-DURATION PATTERN FOR THE DESIGN STORM

The determination of the amount of rainfall which can be expected at the site of the airport is the first step in the design of a drainage system. Rainfall intensity is expressed in inches per hour for various durations of a particular storm. The expected frequency of occurrence is also an important factor to consider. The severity of storms is related to their frequencies; a storm which is expected to occur once in 100 years will be more severe than one having a frequency of occurrence of once in 5 years.

David L. Yarnell of the U.S. Department of Agriculture conducted extensive investigations concerning rainfall intensities, durations, and frequencies throughout the United States [10]. West of the 105th meridian, where the Yarnell information is not as complete, the United States Weather Bureau has compiled rainfall data which appear in [8, 9].

Yarnell developed rainfall intensities for 5-, 10-, 15-, 30-, 60-, and 120-min durations for a storm which can be expected to occur once in 5 years, and the intensities for a 1-h duration for storms whose expected frequencies of occurrence are once in 2, 5, 10, 25, 50, and 100 years. The intensities for a duration of 1 h for frequencies of 2, 5, 10, 25, 50, and 100 years are shown in Fig. 14-1.

The 1-h intensity does not by itself portray the intensity-duration pattern of a storm. The Corps of Engineers made extensive studies of rainfall patterns in the United States and found that irrespective of frequency, the intensity-duration patterns of storms were largely governed by their 1-h intensities. That is to say that two storms of different frequency of occurrence whose 1-h intensities are equal will have similar intensity-duration patterns. This is shown in Fig. 14-2. For example, if the 1-h intensity of storms whose frequencies were 5, 10, or 15 years were all

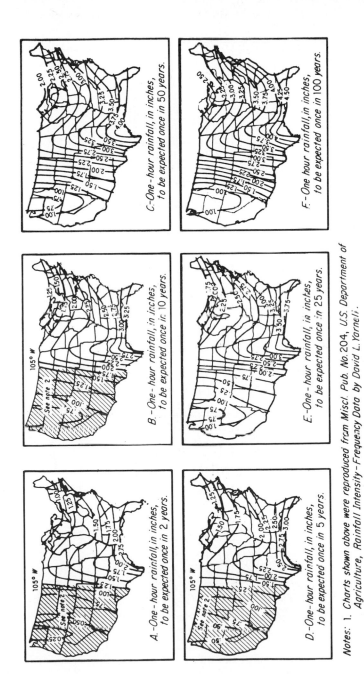

Fig. 14-1 One-hour rainfall intensities for the United States (*Corps of Engineers.*)

Notes: 1. Charts shown above were reproduced from Miscl. Pub. No. 204, U.S. Department of Agriculture, Rainfall Intensity–Frequency Data by David L. Yarnell.

2. For the Western part of the U.S. West of the 105th Meridian, see One Hour Rainfall Data in Weather Bureau Technical Paper No. 24.

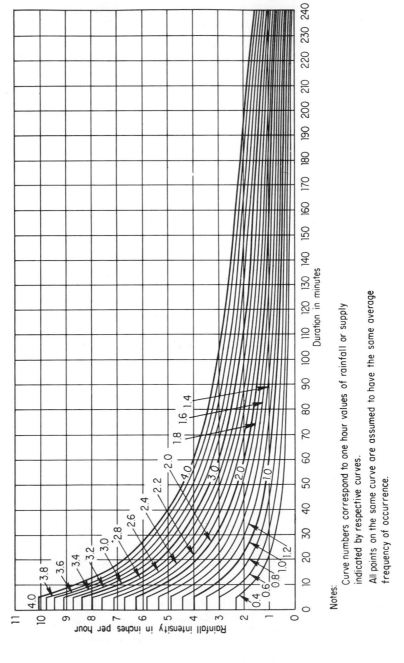

Notes:

Curve numbers correspond to one hour values of rainfall or supply indicated by respective curves.

All points on the same curve are assumed to have the same average frequency of occurrence.

Fig. 14-2 Rainfall intensity-duration curves. (*Corps of Engineers.*)

exactly 2.0 in/h, the intensity-duration patterns would be expected to follow the pattern indicated by the curve labeled 2.0.

If the drainage system is to be designed for a storm whose expected frequency of occurrence is once in 5 years and detailed data concerning the intensity-duration pattern are nonexistent, the pattern can be approximated from Fig. 14-2 provided the 1-h intensity is known. It goes without saying that, if sufficient rainfall data are available at an airport site, the intensity-duration frequency data should be developed from this information rather than from other sources. Rarely, however, does a site have such complete rainfall information.

DETERMINING THE AMOUNT OF RUNOFF BY THE FAA PROCEDURE

The FAA analysis of airport surface drainage revolves about the solution of the rational method expression

$$Q = CIA \qquad (14\text{-}1)$$

where Q = runoff from given drainage basin, ft^3/s
 C = ratio of runoff to rainfall
 I = rainfall intensity for the time of concentration of the runoff, in/h
 A = drainage area, acres

Examples and charts illustrating the FAA procedure for design have been taken largely from [1].

Time of Concentration

The time of concentration is defined as the time taken by water to reach the drain inlet from the most remote point in the tributary area. The most remote point refers to the point from which the time of flow is the greatest. The time of concentration is usually divided into two components, *inlet time* and *time of flow*. The inlet time is the time required for water to flow overland from the most remote point in the drainage area to the inlet. The time of flow is the time taken by the water to flow from the drain inlet through the pipes to the point in the system under consideration. Sometimes the inlet time will be the time of concentration; other times the time of concentration will be the sum of the inlet time and the time of flow.

The time of flow can be computed by the use of well-established hydraulic formulas. The inlet time is obtained largely empirically from the relationship

$$D = kT^2 \qquad (14\text{-}2)$$

where D = distance, ft

T = time, min

k = dimensional empirical factor which is dependent on slope, roughness of terrain, extent of vegetative cover, and distance to drain inlet

Inlet times can be estimated from Fig. 14-3.

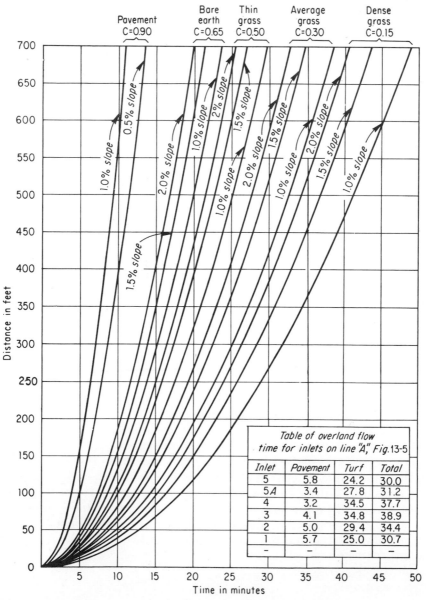

Fig. 14-3 Inlet time curves. (*Federal Aviation Administration [1].*)

Coefficient of Runoff

Application of the rational method requires the exercise of considerable judgment on the part of the engineer. The runoff rate is variable from storm to storm and varies even during a single period of precipitation. The coefficient of runoff depends on antecedent storm conditions, slope and type of surface, and extent of the drainage area. The range of values suggested by the FAA is indicated in Table 14-1.

For drainage basins consisting of several types of surfaces with different infiltration characteristics the weighted runoff coefficient should be computed in accordance with the following expression:

$$C = \frac{A_1 C_1 + A_2 C_2 + A_3 C_3}{A_1 + A_2 + A_3} \tag{14-3}$$

Typical Example—No Ponding

In order that the worst conditions attendant upon the design storm may be used in the design of the pipe system, a separate duration of storm is selected for each subdrainage area tributary to a drain inlet. The duration of the storm is made equal to the sum of the inlet time and the time of flow.

Each reach of pipe must be designed to carry the discharge from the inlet at its upstream end plus the contribution from all preceding inlets. For economy of construction, the grade of each reach is determined largely by topography. A minimum mean velocity on the order of 2.5 ft/s should be maintained to provide scouring action so that reduction of the pipe area due to silting will not be a problem.

To clarify the computation of runoff by the FAA method, the following example is presented.

TABLE 14-1 **Coefficients of Runoff** C

Type of surface	Factor C
For all watertight roof surfaces	0.75–0.95
For asphalt runway pavements	0.80–0.95
For concrete runway pavements	0.70–0.90
For gravel or macadam pavements	0.35–0.70
For impervious soils (heavy)*	0.40–0.65
For impervious soils, with turf*	0.30–0.55
For slightly pervious soils*	0.15–0.40
For slightly pervious soils, with turf*	0.10–0.30
For moderately pervious soils*	0.05–0.20
For moderately pervious soils, with turf*	0.00–0.10

* For slopes from 1 to 2 percent.
SOURCE: FAA [1].

The intensity-duration rainfall pattern for a 5-year-frequency storm at the site of the proposed airport is shown in Fig. 14-4. The layout of the drains on a portion of the airport is shown in Fig. 14-5. Design data for establishing inlet times and coefficients of runoff for drainage areas tributary to drain line A shown in Fig. 14-5 are tabulated in Table 14-2. It is assumed that the coefficients of runoff for pavement and turf are 0.90 and 0.30, respectively.

From these data inlet times have been computed by use of Fig. 14-3 on the basis that the slope of the pavement is 1 percent and the slope of the turfed area is 1.5 percent. The inlet times for this specific problem are shown in Fig. 14-3. The computations for runoff, assuming no ponding, are shown in Table 14-3.

Typical Example—Ponding

In the design of an airfield drainage system, ponding may be used to effect a reduction in the cost of installation. Ponding is simply a means of providing temporary storage of runoff prior to its entry into the underground system. For purposes of design computation the ponded volume may be assumed to be an inverted pyramid or a truncated pyramid, the

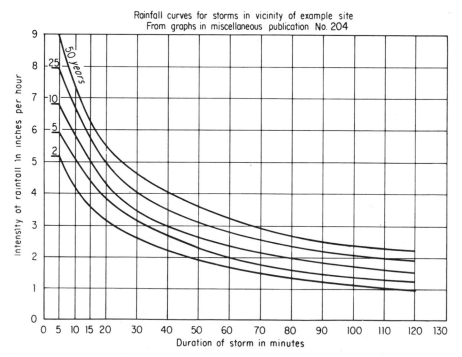

Fig. 14-4 Intensity-duration rainfall pattern for design storm. (*Federal Aviation Administration [1].*)

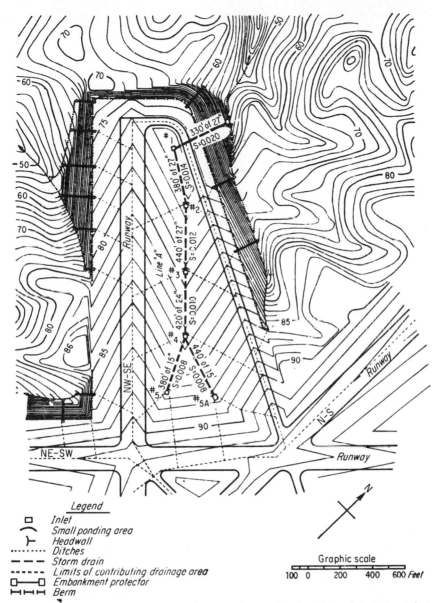

Legend

▫	Inlet
⌒	Small ponding area
⊢	Headwall
··········	Ditches
— — —	Storm drain
-------	Limits of contributing drainage area
▫—▫	Embankment protector
⊢⊢⊢⊢	Berm

Graphic scale

100 0   200   400   600 *Feet*

Fig. 14-5 Portion of airport showing drainage design details. (*Federal Aviation Administration* [1].)

height of which is the depth of water above the inlet at any stage. The area of the base of the pyramid is taken as the surface area of the pond. If ponding were permitted, the layout of the drainage system might be as shown in Fig. 14-6. The most remote point to one of the inlets is 950 ft, comprising 100 ft of pavement and 850 ft of turf. The time of concentration

TABLE 14-2 **Design Data for Line A in Fig. 14-5.**

	Tributary area to inlets, acres				Distance remote point to inlet, ft			Line Segment	Length, ft
	Pave-ment	Turf	Both	Subtotal	Pave-ment	Turf	Total		
Inlets									
5	1.27	1.05	2.32	2.32	200	340	540	5–4	380
5A	1.02	1.86	2.88	2.88	70	450	520	5A–4	440
4	1.40	7.35	8.75	13.95	60	690	750	4–3	420
3	0.78	6.46	7.24	21.19	100	700	800	3–2	440
2	0.83	4.56	5.39	26.58	150	500	650	2–1	380
1	1.14	3.70	4.84	31.42	190	360	550	1–outlet	330
Outlet	—	—	—	—	—	—	330		
Totals	6.44	24.98	31.42						

Weighted average for C

To inlet 5:

$$\frac{1.27}{2.32} (0.90) = 0.49$$

$$\frac{1.05}{2.32} (0.30) = 0.14$$
$$C = 0.63$$

To inlet 5A:

$$\frac{1.02}{2.88} (0.90) = 0.32$$

$$\frac{1.86}{2.88} (0.30) = 0.19$$
$$C = 0.51$$

To inlet 4:

$$\frac{1.40}{8.75} (0.90) = 0.14$$

$$\frac{7.35}{8.75} (0.30) = 0.25$$
$$C = 0.39$$

To inlet 3:

$$\frac{0.78}{7.24} (0.90) = 0.10$$

$$\frac{6.46}{7.24} (0.30) = 0.27$$
$$C = 0.37$$

To inlet 2:

$$\frac{0.83}{5.39} (0.90) = 0.14$$

$$\frac{4.56}{5.39} (0.90) = 0.25$$
$$C = 0.39$$

To inlet 1:

$$\frac{1.14}{4.84} (0.90) = 0.21$$

$$\frac{3.70}{4.84} (0.30) = 0.23$$
$$C = 0.44$$

SOURCE: Federal Aviation Administration [1].

is estimated at 4 + 54 = 58 min. The complete drainage area is 31.42 acres, of which 6.44 acres is paved. Assuming that the coefficients of runoff for pavement and turf are 0.90 and 0.30, respectively, the combined C is 0.423. From Fig. 14-4 the rainfall intensities for durations of 5, 10, 15, 20, 30, 60, 90, 120, and 180 min are obtained and the volumes of runoff computed as shown in Table 14-4.

To visualize the effects of ponding, a comparison is made of the discharge capacity of tentative drainage pipes and the cumulative runoff for the design storm frequency. This comparison is best made as a plot of runoff as ordinates and time as abscissas. An example of such a plot is shown in Fig. 14-7. The discharge capacity for each of four selected pipe sizes is shown as a straight line. These discharge curves were computed for an assigned slope and roughness coefficient n for each pipe by use of the Manning formula. For this example the pipes were assumed to be of concrete with a roughness coefficient n of 0.015 and laid on a 1.0 percent slope. The discharge in cubic feet per second multiplied by 3600 s is the discharge capacity ordinate in cubic feet at the 60-min abscissa in Fig. 14-7. Each discharge capacity curve must pass through the origin of coordinates, and one point as determined above will define the straight-line relationship.

The significance of the cumulative runoff and discharge capacity curves as plotted in Fig. 14-7 is that the difference in ordinates (cumulative runoff minus discharge capacity) represents the amount of ponding at any instant after the beginning of the storm. The maximum amount of ponding is determined by scaling the largest difference between the cumulative runoff curve and the discharge capacity curve.

It is considered essential that all ponding area edges be kept at least 75 ft from the edges of pavements. In this example this would mean that the pond should not reach a level above elevation 88.0. The storage capacity below this elevation is 161,000 ft³. If a 12-in-diameter pipe were used, the maximum ponding would amount to 99,260 ft³, considerably less than the available 161,100 ft³. For practical consideration a pipe of lesser diameter is not recommended.

Although not shown in this text, computations were also made for a 10-year-frequency storm. With a 12-in-diameter pipe such a storm would develop a pond of 123,000 ft³, still less than the available capacity of 161,000 ft³.

DETERMINING THE AMOUNT OF RUNOFF BY THE CORPS OF ENGINEERS PROCEDURE

For determining runoff, the Corps of Engineers makes use of a relationship for overland flow developed by R. E. Horton. This relationship, as modified by the Corps of Engineers, is as follows:

$$q = \sigma \tan h^2 \left[0.922t \left(\frac{\sigma}{nL} \right)^{1/2} S^{1/4} \right] \tag{14-4}$$

where q = rate of overland flow at lower end of an elemental strip of turfed, bare, or paved surface, in/h or ft³/s per acre of drainage area

Q = total discharge from a drainage area, ft³/s; Q is equal to the product of q and the drainage area in acres

S = slope of surface or hydraulic gradient, absolute, i.e., 1 percent = 0.01

TABLE 14-3 **Drainage System Design Data**

Line seg-ment	Length of seg-ment, ft	Inlet time, min	Flow time, min	Time of con-cen-tra-tion, min	Runoff coeffi-cient C	Rainfall intensi-ty I	Tribu-tary area A, acres	Remarks
Inlet								
5A 5A–4	440	31.2	1.8	31.2	0.51	3.10	2.88	$n = 0.015$
5 5–4	380	30.0	1.6	30.0	0.63	3.15	2.32	
4 4–3	420	37.7	1.1	37.7	0.39	2.80	8.75	See accumulated runoff computed below.
3 3–2	440	38.9	1.0	38.9	0.37	2.70	7.24	Accumulated run off adjustment negligible.
2 2–1	380	34.4	0.8	39.9	0.39	2.65	5.39	
1 1-outlet	330	30.7	0.5	40.7	0.44	2.60	4.84	
Outlet								

Calculation of Example

Maximum flow from inlets 5 and 5A will reach inlet 4 in 31.6 and 33.0 min, respectively. All of inlet 4 subarea will be contributing to the system only after 37.7 min. Flow from inlets 5 and 5A must be adjusted for 37.7 min time of concentration. Adjusted time of concentration for inlets 5 and 5A (that is, the inlet time for end-of-line structures) equals the time of concentration to inlet 4 less the flow time through the respective pipe segments.

For inlet 5, adjusted time of concentration = 37.7 − 1.6 = 36.1 min. For inlet 5A, adjusted time of concentration = 37.7 − 1.8 = 35.9 min. Using these adjusted times of concentration, an intensity of rainfall of 2.85 in/h is obtained (slight time difference cannot be read from curves).

Applying these data in the formula $Q = CIA$:

Adjusted flow from inlet 5 = 0.63 × 2.85 × 2.32	= 4.16 ft³/s
Adjusted flow from inlet 5A = 0.51 × 2.85 × 2.88	= 4.18 ft³/s
Flow into inlet 4 from inlets 5 and 5A in 37.7 min =	8.34 ft³/s
Flow from inlet 4 subarea	= 9.56 ft³/s
Accumulated flow entering inlet 4 in 37.7 min	= 17.90 ft³/s

SOURCE: Federal Aviation Administration [1].

t = time or duration, min; time from beginning of supply (storm); total time $t = t_c + t_d$

t_c = duration of supply which produces maximum rate of outflow from a drainage area but not in a pipe

t_d = time water flows in the pipe

σ = rate of supply, or rainfall in excess of the rate of infiltration, in/h

L = effective length of overland or channel flow, ft

n = retardance coefficient

The term t_c is nothing more than the time of concentration for the drainage area under consideration. The term L, the effective length, represents the length of overland sheet flow from the most remote point in

TABLE 14-3 **(Continued)**

	Runoff Q, ft³/s	Accu-mulated runoff, ft³/s	Veloc-ity of drain, ft/s	Size of pipe, in	Slope of pipe, ft/ft	Capacity of pipe, ft³/s	Invert elevation	Remarks
Inlet								
5A	4.55	4.55	4.0	15	0.008	5.0	81.52	$n = 0.015$
5	4.60	4.60	4.0	15	0.008	5.0	81.04	
4	9.56	17.90	6.2	24	0.010	20.0	78.00	See accumulated runoff computed below.
3	7.23	25.13	7.4	27	0.012	30.0	73.80	Accumulated runoff adjustment negligible.
2	5.57	30.70	8.0	27	0.014	33.0	68.52	
1	5.54	36.24	9.5	27	0.020	37.5	63.20	
Outlet							56.60	

the drainage area to the drain inlet measured in a direction parallel to the maximum slope before the runoff has reached a defined channel or ponding basin, plus the length of flow in a channel if one is present. If ponding is permitted, L is measured from the most remote point in the drainage area to the mean edge of the pond.

The term n is referred to as the *retardance coefficient.* Typical coefficients are given in Table 14-5.

When a drainage area is composed of two or three types of surfaces, an average retardance coefficient must be computed. For example, if a drainage area consists of 4 acres of average grass cover and 2 acres of pavement, the average retardance coefficient is equal to

$$\frac{4(0.40) + 2(0.02)}{6} = 0.27$$

Infiltration Rate

Use of the Horton formula requires an estimate of the amount of rainfall which is absorbed in the ground and which therefore does not appear as runoff. This is referred to as *infiltration* and is expressed as a rate in inches per hour. Thus, the intensity of rainfall (in inches per hour) less the infiltration rate is equal to the rate of runoff or the rate of supply σ in the formula for runoff.

The infiltration rate is dependent largely on the structure of the soil

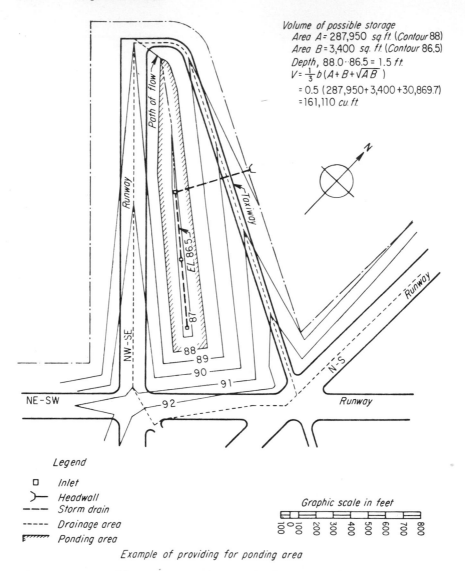

Volume of possible storage
　Area A = 287,950 sq.ft. (Contour 88)
　Area B = 3,400 sq. ft. (Contour 86.5)
　Depth, 88.0·86.5 = 1.5 ft.
　$V = \frac{1}{3}b(A + B + \sqrt{AB}\,)$

　　= 0.5 (287,950 + 3,400 + 30,869.7)
　　= 161,110 cu.ft.

Legend

□	Inlet
⊃—	Headwall
– – –	Storm drain
- - - - -	Drainage area
⌐⁄⁄⁄⁄	Ponding area

Graphic scale in feet

Example of providing for ponding area

Fig. 14-6 Layout of drainage for ponding. (*Federal Aviation Administration [1].*)

cover, the moisture content, and the temperature of the air. The infiltration rate is not constant throughout the duration of the storm, but is assumed so in the computations. It is felt that such an assumption is reasonable, especially when the soil is near saturation.

　The infiltration rate for paved surfaces is usually assumed as zero. Infiltration rates for other types of surfaces and soil cover must be estimated from experience. A value of 0.5 in/h has been suggested for

TABLE 14-4 **Volume of Runoff—Ponding**

Time (min)	Intensity I^*	$Q = CIA$ (ft³/s)	Volume $V = CIAt$ (ft³)
5	5.80	77.1	23,100
10	4.96	65.9	39,600
15	4.33	57.5	51,800
20	3.95	52.5	63,000
30	3.18	42.3	76,100
60	2.00	26.6	95,700
90	1.62	21.5	116,300
120	1.26	16.7	120,600
180	0.87	11.6	125,000

* Hourly intensities from Fig. 14-4.

turfed areas. Thus, if the rainfall intensity on a turfed area was 2.0 in/h, the rate of supply σ would be 1.5 in/h.

Standard Supply Curves

By use of Eq. (14-4) maximum rates of runoff q for rates of supply σ of 0.8, 1.0, 1.6, and 1.8 in/h are shown in Figs. 14-8 and 14 9. Maximum rates of runoff are also shown for rates of supply of 0.4, 0.6, 1.2, 1.4, 2.0, 2.2, 2.4, 2.6, 2.8, 3.0, 3.2, and 3.4 in/h [5].

Maximum rates of runoff for the curve labeled *supply curve no. 1.0* (Fig. 14-8) were obtained in the following manner. From Fig. 14-2 the intensities of runoff for various durations corresponding to the curve labeled 1.0 are obtained. These intensities are entered as σ in Eq. (14-4), and L is varied to produce the family of curves shown in Fig. 14-8. The curve labeled σ is supply curve no. 1.0, obtained from Fig. 14-2. The dotted line labeled t_c represents the maximum rate of runoff q which would occur from an elemental area with various effective lengths L. For example, the maximum rate of runoff from an area whose effective length L is 60 ft is 2.0 ft³/s. Multiplying this rate by the drainage area would yield the maximum total discharge Q.

Figures 14-8 and 14-9 were prepared for $n = 0.40$ and $S = 1$ percent. If these charts are to be used for other cases, the actual effective L for the area under study must be converted in terms of L for $n = 0.40$ and $S = 1$. A conversion chart is shown in Fig. 14-10. For example, if the actual $n = 0.30$ and $S = 2$ percent and the effective length L is 400 ft, the equivalent effective L for $n = 0.40$ and $S = 1$ percent is 140 ft.

Typical Example—No Ponding

In the Corps of Engineers procedure a reach of drain pipe is always designed for a storm whose duration is equal to the time of concentration

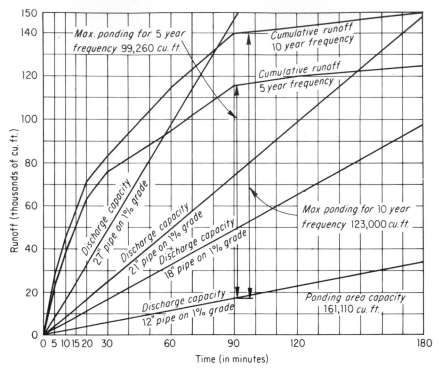

Fig. 14-7 Cumulative runoff for ponding in Fig. 14-6 (*Federal Aviation Administration [1].*)

for the drainage area above the pipe. The time of concentration corresponds to the time necessary to produce maximum flow into a particular inlet (which is the same as the time necessary for water to reach an inlet from the most remote point in the area) plus the flow time in the pipe.

To clarify the computation of runoff by the Corps of Engineers procedure, the following example is presented.

Consider the drainage areas shown in Fig. 14-11. The 1-h intensity of the design storm is assumed as 2.0 in/h. The infiltration rate for the turfed areas is assumed as 0.5 in/h. The retardance coefficient for the pavement is $n = 0.02$, and for the turfed area $n = 0.40$. The drainage areas, retardance

TABLE 14-5 **Retardance Coefficients**

Surface	Value of n
Smooth pavements	0.02
Bare packed soil free of stone	0.10
Sparse grass cover, or moderately rough bare surface	0.30
Average grass cover	0.40
Dense grass cover	0.80

SOURCE: Corps of Engineers, [5].

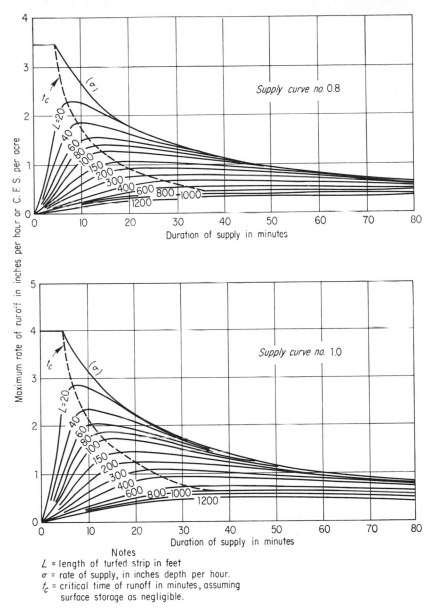

Notes
L = length of turfed strip in feet
σ = rate of supply, in inches depth per hour.
t_c = critical time of runoff in minutes, assuming
        surface storage as negligible.

Fig. 14-8 Standard supply curves, 0.8 and 1.0 in/h. (*Corps of Engineers.*)

coefficients (referred to as roughness factors), and actual effective lengths L
are shown in Table 14-6. Values of L and S were obtained from a grading
plan of the area. The equivalent L's are obtained from Fig. 14-10. Column
14, labeled *adopted for selecting diagrams* designates the nearest whole
number which can be identified on the supply curves (Figs. 14-8 and 14-9).

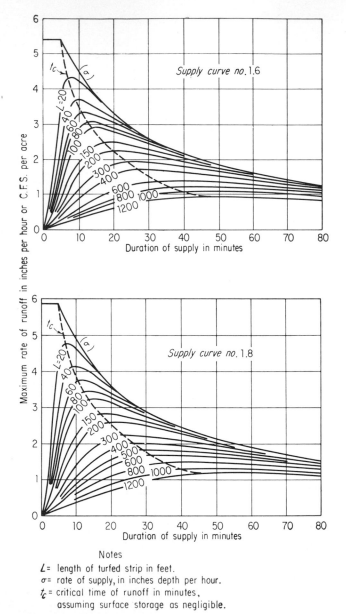

Maximum rate of runoff in inches per hour or C.F.S. per acre

Duration of supply in minutes

Notes
$L=$ length of turfed strip in feet.
$\sigma=$ rate of supply, in inches depth per hour.
$t_c=$ critical time of runoff in minutes,
    assuming surface storage as negligible.

Fig. 14-9 Standard supply curves, 1.6 and 1.8 in/h. (*Corps of Engineers.*)

The standard supply curve to be used for the example is obtained by weighting the supply curves for the paved and turfed areas. For example, for inlet 4, the paved area is 5.97 acres and the supply curve is 2.0 in/h; the turfed area is 26.81 acres and the supply curve is 1.5 in/h. The weighted

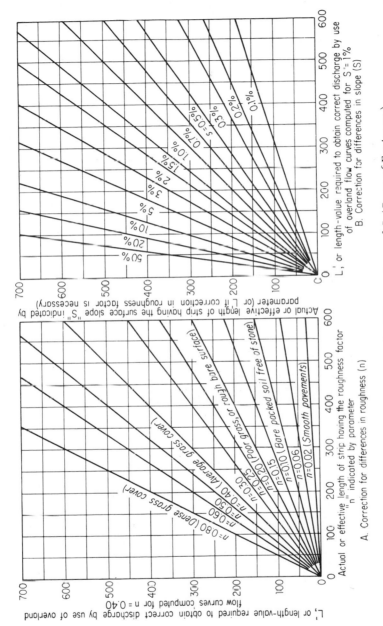

Fig. 14-10 Modification in L required to compensate for difference in n and S. (*Corps of Engineers.*)

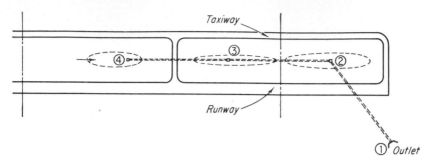

Fig. 14-11 Portion of airport showing drainage layout. (*Corps of Engineers.*)

supply curve is equal to

$$\frac{5.97(2) + 26.81(1.5)}{5.97 + 26.81} = 1.6$$

In columns 20 and 21 the critical inlet time t_c (the time that will produce the maximum discharge) and the corresponding rates of runoff are listed. These values are obtained from Fig. 14-9. In columns 23 and 24 additional rates of runoff for arbitrarily selected times are also listed. This is done to facilitate computation for various times of concentration for the several points along a drainage system.

The next step is to compute the volumes of runoff into inlets 4, 3, and 2. The computations are shown in Table 14-7. Obviously the duration of a

TABLE 14-6   Airfield Drainage—Drain Inlet Capacities

	Supply curve nos.												
For paved areas	2.0												
For bare areas													Drainage
For turfed areas	1.5												

	Drainage area (DA), acres				Permissible ponding				Average roughness factor n	Average slope S, %	Length L, ft		
Inlet no.	Paved, $n =$ 0.02	Bare	Turf $n =$ 0.40	Total	Depth at inlet, ft	Pond area, thousands of ft²	Volume, thousands of ft³	Volume, ft³/acre DA			Actual or effective length, ft	Equivalent L for $n = 0.40$ and $S = 1\%$	L adopted for selecting diagrams
1	*2*	*3*	*4*	*5*	*6*	*7*	*8*	*9*	*10*	*11*	*12*	*13*	*14*
4	5.97		26.81	32.78					0.33	2.0	575	330	330
3	5.69		25.54	31.23					0.33	2.8	575	280	280
2	5.69		25.54	31.23					0.33	2.8	575	280	280

SOURCE: Corps of Engineers, [5].

storm necessary to provide the maximum rate of runoff into inlet 4 is equal to 24 min. The pipe from inlet 4 to inlet 3 is designed for a storm of this duration. At inlet 3 the time of concentration is 24 min plus the flow time in the pipe from inlet 4 to inlet 3 (9.2 min). The pipe from inlet 3 to inlet 2 would be designed for a storm of 33.2-min duration, Enter Fig. 14-9 (supply curves 1.6) with 33 min as the abscissa and read the rates of runoff for effective lengths L of 280 ft (inlet 3) and 330 ft (inlet 4). Multiply these rates by their respective drainage areas. According to the computations at inlet 3, the area directly tributary to it contributes 62.5 ft³/s, and the area tributary to inlet 4 contributes 59.0 ft³/s. Thus the pipe from inlet 3 to inlet 2 should be designed for a capacity of 59.0 + 62.5 = 121.5 ft³/s. The same process would be repeated for the design of the pipe from inlet 2 to the outlet.

It should be emphasized that the duration of the storm for the analysis of a particular point along the drainage system always corresponds to the time of concentration above this point. Had the inlet time t_c for the area directly tributary to inlet 3 been larger than the sum of the inlet time for the area tributary to inlet 4 plus the flow time to inlet 3, the former would have established the duration of the storm for the design of the pipe from inlet 3 to inlet 2.

Typical Example—Ponding

If ponding is permissible, the first step is to establish the limits of the ponding area. From a grading and drainage plan the volumes in the various ponds can be computed. These volumes are then expressed in terms of

section assuming no ponding of runoff

Standard supply curve no. × DA				Weighted supply curve (col. 18 + col. 5)	Drain inlet capacity			Critical contribution to system		
Paved areas	Unpaved areas		Total		t_c, min	q_d, ft³/s. acre DA	Q_d, ft³/s (col. 21 × Col. 5)	t'_c, min	q_d ft³/s. acre DA	Q_d, ft³/s (col. 24 × col. 5)
	Bare	Turf								
15	16	17	18	19	20	21	22	23	24	25
11.94		40.22	52.16	1.6	24	1.8	59.0	30	1.8	59.0
								40	1.7	55.8
11.38		38.31	49.69	1.6	23	2.0	62.5	25	2.0	62.5
								30	2.0	62.5
								40	1.8	56.2
11.38		38.31	49.69	1.6	23	2.0	62.5	25	2.0	62.5
								30	2.0	62.5
								40	1.8	56.2

TABLE 14-7 **Airfield Drainage—Size and Profile of Underground Storm Drains**

	Supply curve nos.												Drainage section
For Paved Areas	2.0												
For Bare Areas													
For Turfed Areas	1.5												

Point of design					Critical runoff time to produce maximum flow in underground drain								Rate of
	Distance, ft						Drain time, min						
Inlet or junction	From main outlet	From preceding inlet	Critical inlet	t_c, min	Assumed velocity in pipe, ft/s	From preceding inlet	Accumulation total	Approximate t'_e (col. 5 + col. 8)	Adopted t'_c, min	4	3	2	
1	2	3	4	5	6	7	8	9	10	11	12	13	14
4	4805	· · · ·	4	24	3.0			24	25	59.0			
3	3155	1650	4	24	3.0	9.2	9.2	33	30	59.0	62.5		
2	1505	1650	4	24	3.0	9.2	18.4	42	40	55.8	56.2	56.2	

SOURCE: Corps of Engineers, [5].

cubic feet per acre of drainage area, as shown in column 9 of Table 14-8. The actual and equivalent L is determined in the same manner as for the case of no ponding, with one exception. The actual L is measured to the mean edge of the pond rather than to the drain inlet. The actual and equivalent effective lengths are listed in columns 12 and 13.

The Corps of Engineers has developed charts which yield drain inlet capacities to prevent ponds from exceeding certain specified volumes. Typical charts are shown in Figs. 14-12 and 14-13. The volumes are computed for various supply curves (Fig. 14-2), assuming the slope of the basins forming the drainage areas is 1 percent. The supply curves represent the intensity-duration pattern for storms whose 1-h intensities correspond

TABLE 14-8 **Airfield Drainage—Drain Inlet Capacities Required to Limit Ponding to Permissible Volumes**

	Supply curve nos.												Drainage
For paved areas	2.0												
For bare areas													
For turfed areas	1.5												

	Drainage area (DA), acres				Permissible ponding				Average roughness factor n	Average slope S, %	Length L, ft		
Inlet	Paved, $n =$ 0.02	Bare	Unpaved Turf $n =$ 0.40	Total	Depth at inlet, ft	Pond area, thousands of ft²	Volume, thousands of ft³	Volume, ft³/acre DA			Actual or effective length, ft	Equivalent L for $n = 0.40$ and $S = 1\%$	L adopted for selecting diagrams
1	2	3	4	5	6	7	8	9	10	11	12	13	14
4	5.97		26.81	32.78	3.0	138	206	6,292	0.33	2.0	525	300	300
3	5.69		25.54	31.23	1.73	145	125	4,016	0.33	2.8	340	200	200
2	5.69		25.54	31.23	2.73	270	368	11,800	0.33	2.8	340	200	200

* Not required when appreciable ponding is permissible
SOURCE: Corps of Engineers, [5].

assuming no ponding of runoff

inflow into underground drains, ft³/s, corresponding to adopted value of t'_c (col 10)

							Inlet								Total
15	16	17	18	19	20	21	22	23	24	25	26	27	28	29	30
															59.0
															121.5
															168.2

to the supply curve numbers. The volumes of runoff for a specific supply curve are computed in a manner similar to the procedure used by the FAA. The cumulative volumes of runoff are compared with the various capacities of drain inlets to arrive at the volumes of storage shown in Figs. 14-12 and 14-13. Since the volumes of runoff depend on L and S, charts must be prepared for a wide range of L values. Figures 14-12 and 14-13 show drain inlet capacities for L equal to 100, 200, 300, and 400 ft. Additional charts have been prepared for $L = 0, 40, 600, 800, 1000,$ and 1200 ft[5].

The physical significance of the charts may be described by reference to the following example. Suppose that L for a large drainage area is 100 ft and the runoff pattern corresponds to supply curve 2. Assume that the maximum permissible ponding is 300 ft³ per acre of drainage area. From Fig. 14-12 a pipe which has a capacity of 1.0 ft³/s per acre of drainage area

section east side of airfield

Standard supply curve no. × DA				Weighted supply curve (col. 18 ÷ col. 5)		Drain inlet capacity			Critical contribution to system	
Paved areas	Unpaved areas		Total		t_c, min	q_d, ft³/ s. acre DA	Q_d, ft³/s (col. 21 × Col. 5)	t'_c, min	q_d, ft³/s. acre DA	Q_d, ft³/s (col. 24 × col. 5)
	Bare	Turf								
15	16	17	18	19	20	21	22	23	24	25
11.94		40.21	52.15	1.6	*	0.52	17.05			
11.38		38.31	49.69	1.6	*	0.52	16.24			
11.38		38.31	49.69	1.6	*	0.52	16.24			

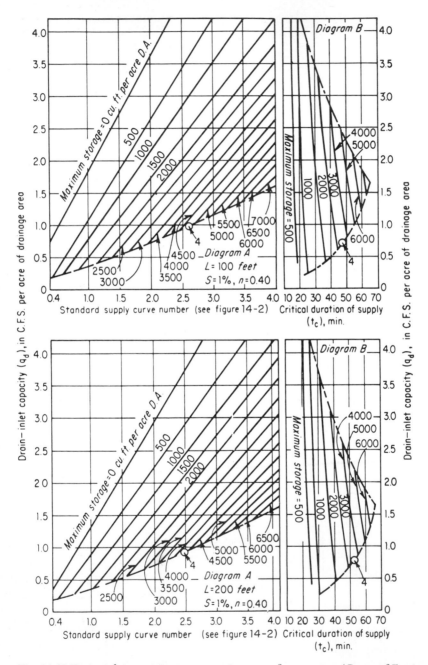

Fig. 14-12 Drain inlet capacity versus maximum surface storage. (*Corps of Engineers.*)

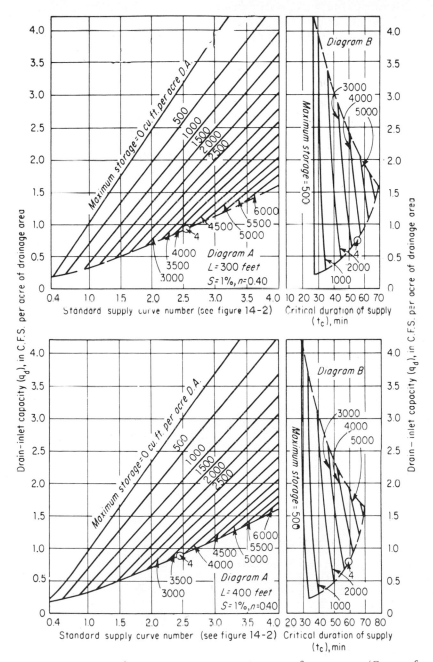

Fig. 14-13 Drain inlet capacity versus maximum surface storage. (*Corps of Engineers.*)

would be adequate to prevent the pond from exceeding a volume of 3000 ft³ during any part of the storm. The dashed lines labeled 4 are equal to rates of supply corresponding to a duration of 4 h. Although smaller drain inlets are possible, it is felt that the sizes corresponding to a duration of 4 h are about the minimum from a practical standpoint.

The required drain inlet capacities required for the drainage layout in Fig. 14-11 were obtained from Figs. 14-12 and 14-13 and are tabulated in Table 14-8. It should be noted that the time of concentration is not a factor in these computations.

LAYOUT OF SURFACE DRAINAGE

A finished grade contour map of the runways, taxiways, and aprons is extremely helpful for the layout of a storm drain system. Several trial drainage layouts may be necessary before the most economical system can be selected. The grades of the storm drain should be such as to maintain a minimum mean velocity on the order of 2.5 ft/s to provide sufficient scouring action so that silting will not become a problem. In order to maintain an adequate cross section for flow at all times, the diameter of the storm drain should not be less than 12 in.

Water from a drainage area is collected into the storm drain by means of inlets. The inlet structure consists of a concrete box, the top of which is covered with a grate made of cast iron, cast steel, or reinforced concrete. The grates must support aircraft wheel loads and should therefore be designed for contact pressures for the aircraft which will be served by the airport.

On long tangents, drain inlets are usually placed at intervals varying from 200 to 400 ft. The location of the inlets depends on the configuration of the airport and on the grading plan. Normally, if there is a taxiway parallel to the runway, the inlets are placed in a valley between runway and taxiways, as indicated in Fig. 14-11. If there is no parallel taxiway, the drains are placed near the edge of the runway pavement or at the toe of the slope of the graded area.*

On aprons, inlets are usually placed in the pavement proper. This is the only way a large apron area can be drained. All grates should be securely fastened to the frames so that they will not be jarred loose with the passage of traffic (see Fig. 14-14).

Adequate depths of cover should be provided over the pipes in order that they can support traffic. The recommended minimum depths of cover are shown in Table 14-9.

---

* The FAA recommends that the inlets should not be closer than 75 ft to the edge of the pavement.

As a guide for the design of storm drains, the coefficient of roughness n for various types of pipes and open channels is listed in Table 14-10.

SUBSURFACE DRAINAGE

The functions of subsurface drainage are to (1) remove water from a base course, (2) remove water from the subgrade beneath a pavement, and (3) intercept, collect, and remove water flowing from springs or pervious strata.

Base drainage is normally required (1) where frost action occurs in the subgrade beneath a pavement, (2) where the ground water is expected to rise to the level of the base course, and (3) where the pavement is subject to frequent inundation and the subgrade is highly impervious.

Subgrade drainage is desirable at locations where the water may rise beneath the pavement to less than 1 ft below the base course.

Intercepting drainage is highly desirable where it is known that subsurface waters from adjacent areas are seeping toward the airport pavements.

Methods for Draining Subsurface Water

Base courses are usually drained by installing subsurface drains adjacent to and parallel to the edges of pavement. The pervious material in the trench should extend to the bottom of the base course, as shown in Fig. 14-15. The center of the drainpipe should be placed a minimum of 1 ft below the bottom of the base course.

Subgrades are drained by pipes installed along the edges of pavement and, in some instances, where the ground water is extremely high, underneath the pavements. The center of the subsurface drain should be placed no less than 1 ft below the level of the ground water. When subgrade drains are installed along the edges of the pavement, they may also serve for draining the base course.

Intercepting drainage can be accomplished by means of open ditches well beyond the pavement areas. If this is not practical, then subdrains can be used.

Types of Pipe

The following types of pipe have been used for subdrainage:

1. Perforated metal, concrete, or vitrified clay pipe. The joints are sealed. The perforations normally extend over about one-third of the circumference of the pipe. The perforated area is usually placed adjacent to the soil.

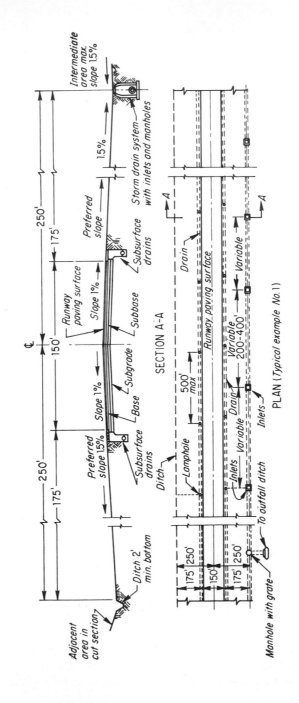

SECTION A-A

PLAN (Typical example No. 1)

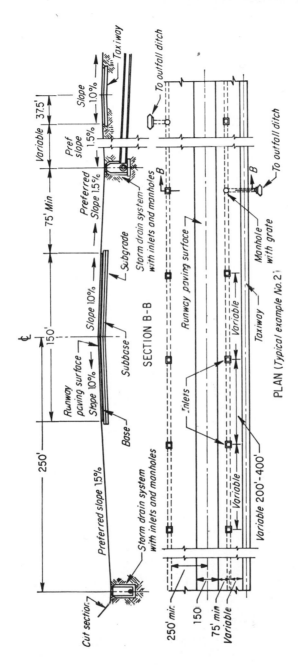

Fig. 14-14 Recommended pavement drainage sections. (*Federal Aviation Administration.*)

TABLE 14-9 **Recommended Minimum Depth of Cover for Pipe, ft**

Kind of pipe	12	18	24	30	36	42	48	60	12	18	24	30	36	42	48	60
Flexible pavement — Pipe cover																
Nominal diameter of pipe, in									Nominal diameter of pipe, in							
Wheel load 15,000 lb									*Wheel load 30,000 lb*							
Clay sewer pipe	2.5	3.0	3.0	3.5	3.5				3.0	3.5	4.0	4.5	4.5			
Clay culvert pipe	1.5	1.5	1.5	2.0	2.0				2.5	3.0	3.0	3.0	3.0			
Concrete sewer pipe	2.5	3.0	3.0						3.0	3.5	4.0					
Concrete sewer pipe (extra strength)	1.5	1.5	2.0						2.5	3.0	3.0					
Reinforced concrete culvert pipe																
Class I						3.0										4.5
Class II	2.5	2.5	2.5	2.5	2.5	2.5	2.5	2.5	3.0	3.0	3.0	3.0	3.0	3.5	3.5	3.5
Class III	2.0	2.0	2.0	2.0	2.0	2.0	2.0	2.0	2.5	2.5	2.5	2.5	2.5	2.5	3.0	3.0
Class IV	1.5	1.5	1.5	1.5	1.5	1.5	1.5	1.5	2.0	2.0	2.0	2.0	2.0	2.0	2.0	2.0
Class V	1.0	1.0	1.0	1.0	1.0	1.0	1.0	1.0	1.5	1.5	1.5	1.5	1.5	1.5	1.5	1.5
Corrugated metal pipe, gauge no.																
16	1.0	1.5	1.5						1.5	2.0	2.0					
14	1.0	1.0	1.0	1.5	2.0				1.0	1.0	1.5	2.0	2.5			
12	1.0	1.0	1.0	1.0	1.5	1.5	2.0		1.0	1.0	1.5	1.5	2.0	2.5	2.5	
10		1.0	1.0	1.0	1.0	1.5	1.5	1.5			1.0	1.5	1.5	2.0	2.0	2.5
8					1.0	1.0	1.0	1.0					1.0	1.5	1.5	2.0
Wheel load 45,000 lb									*Wheel load 60,000 lb*							
Clay culvert pipe	3.0	3.5	3.5	4.0	4.0				3.5	4.0	4.5	4.5	5.0			
Concrete sewer pipe (extra strength)	3.0	3.5	3.5						3.5	4.0	4.5					
Reinforced concrete culvert pipe																
Class I																
Class II	3.0	3.5	3.5	4.0	4.0	4.5	4.5		3.5	4.0	4.5					
Class III	2.5	3.0	3.0	3.5	3.5	3.5	4.0	4.0	3.0	3.5	4.0	4.0	4.5			
Class IV	2.0	2.5	2.5	2.5	2.5	2.5	3.0	3.0	2.5	3.0	3.0	3.0	3.5	3.5	3.5	4.0
Class V	1.5	1.5	2.0	2.0	2.0	2.0	2.5	2.5	2.0	2.0	2.5	2.5	2.5	3.0	3.0	3.0
Corrugated metal pipe, gauge no.																
16	2.0	2.5	3.0						2.5	3.0	3.5					
14	1.5	2.0	2.5	3.0	3.0				2.0	2.5	3.0	3.5	4.0			
12	1.5	2.0	2.0	2.5	2.5	3.0	3.5		1.5	2.0	2.5	3.0	3.5	4.0	4.0	
10			1.5	2.0	2.0	2.5	3.0	3.5			2.0	2.5	3.0	3.5	3.5	4.0
8					1.5	2.0	2.5	3.0					2.5	3.0	3.0	3.5
Wheel load 75,000 lb									*Wheel load 100,000 lb*							
Reinforced concrete culvert pipe																
Class I																
Class II																
Class III	3.0	4.0	4.5	4.5	5.0				3.5	4.5	5.0	5.0	5.5			
Class IV	3.0	3.0	3.5	3.5	4.0	4.0	4.5	5.0	3.5	3.5	4.0	4.0	4.5	5.0	5.0	5.5
Class V	2.5	2.5	3.0	3.0	3.0	3.5	4.0	4.0			3.5	3.5	3.5	4.0	4.5	4.5
Corrugated metal pipe, gauge no.																
16	3.0	3.5	4.0						3.5	4.0	4.5					
14	2.5	3.0	3.5	4.0	4.5				3.0	3.5	4.0	4.5	5.0			
12	2.5	3.0	3.0	3.5	4.0	4.5	5.0		3.0	3.0	3.5	4.0	4.5	5.0	5.5	
10			2.5	3.0	3.5	4.0	4.5	5.0			3.0	3.5	4.0	4.5	5.0	5.5
8					3.0	3.5	4.0	4.5					3.5	4.0	4.5	5.0

Cover depths measured from top of flexible pavement or unsurfaced areas to top of pipe. Cover for pipe in areas not used by aircraft shall be in accordance with cover requirements for 15,000-lb wheel loads.

Rigid pavement

Pipe placed under rigid pavements shall have a minimum cover, measured from the bottom of the slab, of 1.0 ft.

Note: The recommended minimum depth of cover for pipe does not provide protection against freezing conditions in seasonal freezing areas.

SOURCE: Federal Aviation Administration [1].

TABLE 14-10 **Coefficients of Roughness** n

	n
Pipe	
Clay and concrete:	
good alignment, smooth joints, smooth transitions	0.013
less favorable flow conditions	0.015
Corrugated metal	
100% of periphery smoothly lined	0.013
paved invert, 50% of periphery paved	0.018
paved invert, 25% of periphery paved	0.021
unpaved, bituminous-coated or noncoated	0.024
Open channels	
Paved	0.015–0.020
Unpaved:	
bare earth, shallow flow	0.020–0.025
bare earth, depth of flow over 1 ft	0.015–0.020
turf, shallow flow	0.06–0.08
turf, depth of flow over 1 ft	0.04–0.06

SOURCE: Federal Aviation Administration.

2. Bell-and-spigot pipes are laid with the joints open. Vitrified clay, cast iron, and plain concrete are used in the manufacture of bell-and-spigot pipes.

3. Porous concrete pipe collects water by seepage through the concrete wall of the pipe. This type of pipe is laid with the joints sealed.

4. Skip pipe manufactured of both vitrified clay and cast iron is a special type of bell-and-spigot pipe with slots at the bells.

5. Farm tile is made of clay or concrete with the ends separated slightly to permit the entrance of water. This type of pipe is rarely used on airport projects.

Pipe Sizes and Slopes

Experience has shown that a 6-in-diameter drain is adequate, unless extreme groundwater conditions are encountered. If desired, the flow may be estimated by means of the available theories for soil drainage [11]. These theories require a knowledge of the effective porosity and coefficient of permeability of the soil which is being drained, as well as the head on the pipe and the distance which the water must flow to reach the drain. Rarely is reliance made on theory to compute pipe sizes.

The recommended minimum slope for subdrains is 0.15 ft in 100 ft. A minimum thickness of 6 in of filter material should surround the drain. The gradation of the filter material is discussed in the succeeding paragraphs.

Utility Holes and Risers

For cleaning and inspection, utility holes and risers are often installed along the drains. The Corps of Engineers recommends that utility holes be placed at intervals not more than 1000 ft, with one riser approximately midway between the holes [11]. The function of the riser is to be able to insert a hose for flushing the system. The function of a utility hole is to permit inspection of the pipes.

Gradation of Filter Material

The term *filter material* applies to the granular material which is used as backfill in the trenches where subdrains are placed. To permit free water to reach the drain, the filter material must be many times more pervious than the protected soil. Yet if it is too pervious, the particles of soil to be drained will move into the filter material and clog it.

On the basis of some general studies conducted by K. Terzaghi, the Corps of Engineers has developed an empirical design for filter material which has been substantiated by tests [12]. The criteria for selecting the gradation of the filter material are as follows:

1. To prevent clogging of a perforated pipe with filter material, the following requirement must be satisfied:

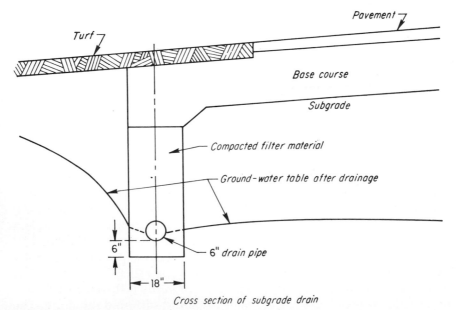

Cross section of subgrade drain

Fig. 14-15 Subgrade subdrainage details. (*Corps of Engineers.*)

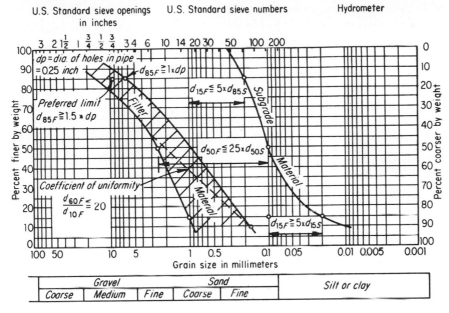

Fig. 14-16 Design example for filter materials. (*Corps of Engineers.*)

$$\frac{85\% \text{ size of filter material*}}{\text{Diameter of perforation}} > 1$$

2. To prevent the movement of particles from the protected soil into the filter material, the following conditions must be satisfied:

$$\frac{15\% \text{ size of filter material}}{85\% \text{ size of protected soil}} \leqq 5$$

and

$$\frac{50\% \text{ size of filter material}}{50\% \text{ size of protected soil}} \leqq 25$$

3. To permit free water to reach the pipe, the following condition must be fulfilled:

$$\frac{15\% \text{ size of filter material}}{15\% \text{ size of protected soil}} \geqq 5$$

A typical example of design is shown in Fig. 14-16. A concrete sand has

* This means that 85 percent (by weight) is finer than the specified size.

proved to be a satisfactory filter material for the majority of fine soils which are drainable. A single gradation of filter material is preferred for simplicity of construction.

Filter materials tend to segregate as they are placed in trenches. In order to minimize this tendency, the material should not have a coefficient of uniformity greater than 20. For the same reason, filter materials should not be skip-graded. Filter material should always be placed in a moist state. The presence of moisture tends to reduce segregation.

Drainability of Soils

Certain types of soils, such as gravelly sands, sand, and sandy loams, are usually self-draining and require very little, if any, subsurface drainage. Subsurface drainage can be effective for draining clay loams, sandy clay loams, and certain silty loams. The amount of sand in these soils largely determines how drainable they are. For soils containing a high percentage of silt and clay, subsurface drainage becomes very problematical.

REFERENCES

1. *Airport Drainage*, Federal Aviation Administration, Washington, D.C., Advisory Circular AC 150/5320-5B, July 1970.

2. *Conduits, Culverts, and Pipes*, Department of the Army, Washington, D.C., Eng. Manual EM 1110-2-2902, March 1969.

3. "Design of Drainage Facilities for Military Airfields," G. A. Hathaway, *Transactions*, Amerian Society of Civil Engineers, New York, N.Y., 1949.

4. *Drainage and Erosion Control Structures for Airfields and Heliports*, Department of the Army, Washington, D.C., Tech. Manual TM 5-820-3, July 1965.

5. *Drainage and Erosion Control—Surface Drainage Facilities for Airfields and Heliports*, Department of the Army, Washington, D.C., Tech. Manual TM 5-820-1, August 1965.

6. *Drainage for Areas Other than Airfields*, Department of the Army, Washington, D.C., Tech. Manual TM 5-820-4, July 1965.

7. *Filter Experiments and Design Criteria*, U.S. Army Corps of Engineers, Waterways Experiment Station, Vicksburg, Miss., Tech. Memo. 3-360, April 1953.

8. "Rainfall Frequency Atlas of the United States," Weather Bureau, Department of Commerce, Washington, D.C., ESSA-Weather Bureau Tech. Paper 40, May 1961.

9. "Rainfall intensities for Local Drainage Design in the U.S.," Weather Bureau, Department of Commerce, Washington, D.C., Tech. Paper 24, pts. I and II, 1953 and 1954.

10. *Rainfall-Intensity Frequency Data*, D. L. Yarnell, Department of Agriculture, Washington, D.C., Miscell. Publ. 204, August 1935.

11. *Subsurface Drainage Facilities for Airfields*, Department of the Army, Washington, D.C., Tech. Manual TM 5-820-2, August 1965.

12. "The Interpretation and Application of Runoff Plat Experiments with Reference to Soil Erosion Problems," R. E. Horton, *Proceedings of the Soil Science Society of America*, vol. 3, 1938.

Chapter 15

Environmental and Economic Assessment of Projects

INTRODUCTION

The current concern for an assessment and understanding of the environmental, ecological, and sociological consequences of development actions has resulted in the emergence of a holistic approach to planning. This approach views all actions as being undertaken in a single system and examines the consequences of these actions in terms of the entire system. Traditionally, proposals for transportation facilities have been evaluated in terms of sound engineering and technological principles, economic criteria, and benefits to the users and community. Policy decisions today, however, are being made with a more complete awareness of the impacts of these decisions on both users and nonusers from economic, social, environmental, and ecological viewpoints.

Airports must be planned in a manner which assures their compatibility with the environs in which they exist. Many serious compatibility problems exist at present in the vicinity of airports which represent a serious confrontation between two important characteristics of urban economics, the need for airports to meet transportation needs and the continuing demand for community expansion [7]. Airport planning must be conducted within the context of a comprehensive regional plan. The location, size, and configuration of an airport must be coordinated with the existing and planned patterns of development in a community, considering the effect of airport operations on people, ecological systems, water resources, air quality, and the other areas of community concern [12].

This chapter presents an overview of the factors which must be considered to assess and evaluate the impact of airport development decisions in the context of a systems approach to planning.

POLICY CONSIDERATIONS

In the United States, the overall basis for policies related to the consideration of the environmental, ecological, and social impacts of airport development is rooted in the National Environmental Policy Act of 1969 (Public Law 91-190). The policy of the FAA is [46] . . . to integrate national environmental objectives into existing agency policies and missions to:

1. Avoid or minimize adverse environmental effects wherever possible by considering project alternatives or measures to mitigate adverse impacts

2. Restore or enhance environmental quality to the fullest extent practicable

3. Make a special effort to preserve the natural beauty of the countryside, public park and recreational lands, wildlife and waterfowl refuges, and historic areas

4. Preserve, restore, and enhance wetlands

5. Preserve an environment free from noise that jeopardizes health and welfare

6. Consult with and inform individuals and groups who are affected by or known to have an interest in an action, or who can speak knowledgeably on the impacts of proposed actions

7. Develop programs and activities in cooperation with state and local governments and Indian tribal governing bodies when appropriate.

To implement this policy it has established an environmental assessment and consultation process which provides the relevant officials, policy makers, and the public with an understanding of the potential environmental consequences of proposed actions and assures that the decision-making process includes environmental assessments as well as economic, technological, and other factors relevant to the decision. It requires that environmental impact statements and negative declarations serve to document and record compliance with this policy and reflect a thorough study of all relevant environmental factors using a systematic, comprehensive, and interdisciplinary approach.

Complementing this overall policy statement, the FAA also established an aviation noise abatement policy [13] to significantly reduce the adverse impacts of aviation noise on existing land uses and to achieve a substantial degree of noise compatibility between airports and their environs. It has endorsed coordinated actions between aircraft operators and owners, the FAA, the airport owners and sponsors, and the community. It proposed several actions to achieve airport noise control and land-use compatibility (ANCLUC), including source noise reductions through aircraft retrofit and replacement, modifications of landing and takeoff procedures, and compatibility plans which have the objective of containing severe noise impacts within airport-controlled areas [7].

Noise is the most apparent impact of the airport upon the community, but due consideration is required for all of those social, economic, environmental, and ecological factors which are influenced by airport activity. These factors may be grouped into four categories which can be identified as pollution factors, social factors, ecological factors, and engineering and economic factors [29]. The pollution factors include air and water quality, noise, and construction impacts. The social factors include land development, the displacement and relocation of businesses and residences, parks and recreational areas, historic places and archeological resources which may be impacted, areas which are unique because of natural or scenic beauty, and the consistency of the proposed development with local planning. The ecological factors include the impact on wildlife and waterfowl, flora and fauna, endangered species, and wetlands or coastal zones. The engineering and economic factors include a consideration of flood hazards, costs of construction and operation, benefits of implementation, and energy and natural resource use.

The FAA has identified the requirements for environmental impact assessment reports (EIAR), environmental impact statements (EIS), and findings of no significant impact (FONSI) for various types of projects, and has also categorically excluded certain types of projects from the requirements of a formal environmental assessment [4]. Table 15-1 lists a breakdown of the type of environmental study required for some common airport planning actions.

The general format for an environmental study consists of a statement of need for the proposal, an inventory of problems and issues, an identification of constraints and opportunities, an identification of the improvement components including physical and nonphysical entities, measures to increase benefits and reduce harm, a discussion of the alternatives and their impacts, and the manner and degree of community and public agency involvement in the process [11].

POLLUTION FACTORS

Air Quality

Many of the larger, more densely populated urban areas are facing serious difficulties associated with the emission of dangerous gaseous and particulate matter into the atmosphere due to industrial processes, combustion, and transportation. Air pollution affects the public welfare, including the personal comfort and health of people, causes damage to soil, water, vegetation, wildlife, and animals, the deterioration of property and the

TABLE 15-1   **Airport Development Project Environmental Study Requirements***

Typical actions normally requiring environmental assessment:
  Airport location
  New runway
  Major runway extension
  Runway strengthening to permit use by noisier aircraft
  Major expansion of terminal or parking facilities
  Establishment or relocation of ILS
  Land acquisition
    Required for facility modifications
    Relocation of business or residences
    Affecting historical, recreational, or archeological resources
    Affecting wetlands, coastal zones, or floodplains
    Affecting endangered or threatened species
Typical actions normally requiring environmental impact statement:
  Adoption of new national airport system plan if criteria are substantially different from former plan
  First-time airport location or airport layout planned
  New runways capable of air-carrier traffic in metropolitan areas

* See Federal Aviation Administration [46].
SOURCE: Federal Aviation Administration [4].

erosion of property values, and a reduction in visibility resulting in losses of aesthetic appeal and increased hazards in transportation. Air pollution is defined as the introduction of foreign substances or compounds into the air or the alteration of the concentrations of naturally occurring elements. Hub airports with a considerable volume of commercial jet aircraft traffic may contribute substantially to this problem.

Air quality is defined by the concentration level of six pollutants for which standards have been adopted, namely, carbon monoxide, hydrocarbons, nitrogen oxides, sulfur dioxide, suspended particulates, and photochemical oxidants. The standards consist of two categories, primary standards related to health and secondary standards related to welfare. These standards, the national ambient air quality standards, adopted by the Clean Air Act, are given in Table 15-2.

The amount of a particular pollutant produced by an aircraft is a function of the type of engines and the mode of operation of the aircraft [19]. An analysis must include a consideration of aircraft idling at the gate and runway threshold, engine power run ups, taxiing, takeoff, climb out, approach, and landing. The dispersion of the pollutants is studied through the use of either emission models or diffusion models. The emission model assumes a uniform dispersion of the pollutants within the atmosphere of concern, whereas the diffusion model uses emissions or emission rates together with physical and meteorological conditions to determine concentrations of pollutants. A study of the air quality impacts for an airport project requires a determination of ambient air quality, local meteorological conditions, the mix, number, and paths of aircraft using the airport, and the emission rate of the aircraft in different operating modes. It also requires a knowledge of the operating characteristics and volume of ground transportation modes providing access to and services at the airport, and the point sources of pollution occasioned by the normal operation of an airport. A flow chart of the interaction of those factors which are normally considered in an air quality study at an airport is given in Fig. 15-1. The results of an air quality study are typically displayed on maps which show the before and after concentration of pollutants in the area of the airport, together with charts indicating the level of compliance with air quality standards.

Water Quality

Water is one of the most valuable resources on earth. Not only is it essential for the maintenance of life itself, but it is also used by people in nearly all daily activities. As the population has grown, so has the demand for water, and today that need is so great that in many areas of the world the need has outpaced the supply. The construction and operation of airport facilities

TABLE 15-2 **National Ambient Air Quality Standards**

Pollutant	Averaging time*	Primary standards	Secondary standards
Particulate matter	Annual[†]	75 μg/m^3	60 μg/m^3
	24 h	260 μg/m^3	150 μg/m^3
Sulfur dioxide	Annual[‡]	80 μg/m^3	—
		(0.03 ppm)	
	24 h	365 μg/m^3	—
		(0.14 ppm)	
	3 h	—	1300 μg/m^3
			(0.5 ppm)
Carbon monoxide	8 h	10 mg/m^3	Same as primary
		(9 ppm)	
	1 h	40 mg/m^3	Same as primary
		(35 ppm)	
Nitrogen dioxide	Annual[‡]	100 μg/m^3	Same as primary
		(0.05 ppm)	
Photochemical oxidants	1 h	160 μg/m^3	Same as primary
		(0.08 ppm)	
Hydrocarbons (nonmethane)	3 h (6–9 a.m.)	160 μg/m^3 (0.24 ppm)	Same as primary

* Except for the annual standards, all standards are specified as not to be exceeded more than once a year.

† Geometric mean.

‡ Arithmetic mean.

SOURCE: Environmental Protection Agency.

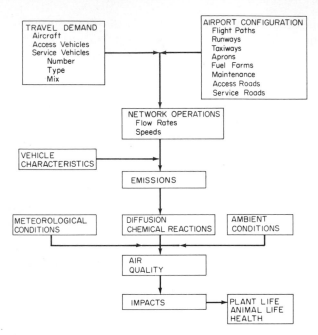

Fig. 15-1 Flow chart illustrating air quality study process for airports.

can contribute to the degradation of the quality and a reduction of the quantity of ground or surface waters. Water quality can be affected by the addition of soluble or insoluble organic or inorganic materials into rivers, streams, and aquifers, resulting in a water source which is inadequate to support aquatic life and other uses such as fishing, swimming, and water supply needs. Changes in the cover, composition, and topography of the ground in the vicinity of airport sites can cause changes in the amount, peaking, routing, and filtration of runoff and the recharge area of aquifers. Construction-related activities may cause the introduction of materials and wastes into streams and water sources, increases in the volumes of sanitary wastes and water supply demand, and increases in storm water management systems.

A water quality study for an airport facility should address both the direct and the indirect effects of the project on water quality [27]. The direct effects include soil erosion, the amount and composition of runoff from the facility, infiltration, spills, turpidity, and the quantities of water supply and sewage disposal needs. Indirect effects include the accelerated weathering of exposed geologic and construction materials, disruption of nutrient cycles for the support of life, and the extraction of construction materials which may alter natural filtering, the degree of imperviousness of soils, and water storage capacity. Typically, a water quality study will

identify the source and receptors of pollutants, and the amount of degradation which the introduction of pollutants will cause. It will also address the
impact on the quantity of water sources through a determination of flow
rates, flow and recharge areas, permeability, infiltration, and flow interruptions. Construction measures utilized to minimize degradation of water
quality and supply include the construction of check dams, sediment traps,
berms, dikes, channels, and slope drains, sodding and seeding, brush
barriers, and paving. Wastewater management plans are usually prepared
integral with a review of this impact area.

Noise

The effect of noise from aircraft operations on land surrounding airports
presents a serious problem to aviation. Since commercial jet transport
operations began in 1958, the reaction to aircraft noise has been vigorous.
Because of this, much has been learned about the generation and propaga-
tion of noise. On the basis of this knowledge, simplified procedures have
been developed which permit the planner to estimate the magnitude and
extent of noise from airport operations and to predict community response.
Several of these procedures are outlined here.

The impact of aircraft noise on a community is dependent upon several
factors, including the magnitude and frequency distribution of the sound,
the duration of noise, the flight paths during takeoff and landing, the
number and types of operations, the operating procedures, the aircraft mix,
the runway system utilization, the time of day and season, and meteorological conditions. The response of communities to exposure to aircraft noise is
a function of the land and building use, the type of building construction,
the distance from the airport, the ambient noise level, sound attentuation
due to physical or meteorological conditions, and sociological considerations [42].

The Physics of Sound

The intensity of sound is usually expressed in decibels (dB). Since the
range of intensities encountered in practice is very great, the intensity level
is expressed as 20 times the logarithm of the ratio of the sound pressure of a
particular sound P to a standard reference pressure P_0. The standard
reference pressure is 20 N/m^2. Thus the level of intensity of sound can be
expressed as

$$\text{dB} = 20 \log \left(\frac{P}{P_0} \right) \tag{15-1}$$

By using decibels as the unit of measure, the large range of sound
intensities can be compressed into a range of from 0 to about 150 dB. On

this scale a doubling of sound intensity is represented by a change in intensity level of about 3 dB, for example, from 60 to 63 dB. Commercial jet operations can generate over 100 dB, while average daytime ambient noise in residential areas varies from 55 to 65 dB.

Frequency is an important factor in the evaluation of sound. Frequency is the rate of vibration of a sound source expressed in hertz. The faster an object vibrates, the greater the number of hertz and the higher the frequency. A source of sound usually generates a range of frequencies. For the purpose of noise analysis, the range of frequencies is divided into smaller ranges known as octave bands. The breakdown of noise into these bands provides a useful and meaningful way of describing the quantity and character of aircraft noise. The human ear can detect sounds over a wide frequency range. For younger people this range usually extends from approximately 16 to 16,000 Hz. A loud roar has a low frequency, while a siren has a high-frequency sound. Some sounds, such as that produced by a simple tuning fork, are usually composed of a single frequency and are known as pure tones.

The final factor which is important for a subjective evaluation of noise is the time variation of the sound level. The fluctuation of sound levels and frequencies over short periods of time tend to be annoying to the listener.

Noise Measures

Noise is usually measured with an instrument called a *sound-level meter* which reads in decibels. One of the readings that can be obtained with the sound-level meter indicates the total amount of sound present at any location and is described as the *overall sound pressure level.* The meter integrates into a single number the intensity levels for the range of frequencies that sound produces without weighting any of the frequencies. For complex noises such as those produced by aircraft, the overall sound pressure level not only provides an inadequate physical description, but it also cannot be related to the subjective reaction to these noises. Two noises can have the same overall sound pressure level and yet, subjectively, be judged very differently. This led to the development of the perceived noise level intensity (PNdB). Perceived noise level is a quantity that is calculated from measured noise levels and adjusted by weighting more heavily those frequencies that are more annoying to the listener. In this way it correlates better with a subjective response of listeners to noises of widely varying character. A further refinement of the PNdB is the effective perceived noise level (EPNdB), which is PNdB corrected for the duration of sound and adjusted for the presence of pure tones. EPNdB is used for the certification of aircraft and for the calculation of noise exposure forecasts (NEF) described later.

It was mentioned earlier that the overall sound pressure level represents an equal weighting of the frequencies generated by a particular sound. Typically the sound-level meter contains three different response weighting networks, A, B, and C. The most commonly used scale on the meter today is the A-weighting since it has been found to account fairly well, although not perfectly, for the response of a listener to sound. It gives greater weight to frequencies which are more objectionable to the listener. Thus the instrument mechanically yields a single number which is reasonably responsive to the listener, whereas PNdB must be derived by calculation. The maximum noise level observed on the A scale is referred to as dBA, or *A-weighted sound level*. Although experts agree that dBA does not correlate quite as well as EPNdB with the subjective response of the listener, it is regarded as sufficiently accurate for the purpose of land-use planning around airports. It has the further advantage of being a simple tool for monitoring aircraft operating at or adjacent to airports. For these reasons the current trend is to use dBA for land-use planning. EPNdB is retained for aircraft certification.

On the basis of extensive measurements made on the ground during aircraft flyovers, one can determine the relationship between the maximum noise level, EPNdB or dBA, observed on the ground and the distance as shown in the upper left-hand corner of Fig. 15-2. From this plot one can determine the maximum noise level at any distance from the aircraft, whether it be passing overhead or passing to one side. Next, the flight profiles for landings and takeoffs must be estimated. As an example, for takeoffs this can best be described by a generalized takeoff profile for a specific type of aircraft, as shown in the upper right-hand corner of Fig. 15-2. Assuming that these two curves are associated with a particular aircraft, one can now construct a set of noise contours representing the maximum noise levels on the ground during takeoff for this aircraft, as shown on the bottom of Fig. 15-2. Noise contours of this type can then be used to describe the noise underneath either a takeoff or a landing path as far as several miles from the runway and several thousand feet to the side. It should be emphasized that these contours represent the sound levels generated by a single flyover of one particular aircraft type. In order to evaluate the response of listeners to aircraft noise, the cumulative effects of many flyovers of several types of aircraft must be considered. The procedures for determining the cumulative effects are described next.

Cumulative Noise Exposure

Every investigation of aircraft noise has shown that the impact of aircraft operations on communities is a function not only of the intensity of a single flyover, but also of the duration and number of operations occurring during

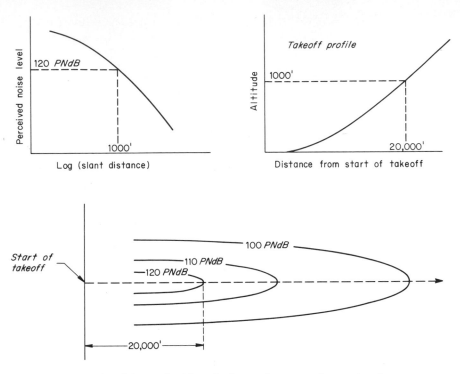

Fig. 15-2 Example of the method by which equal perceived noise level contours are developed.

the day and the night. A number of methods combining the noise from individual aircraft flyovers into measures of cumulative noise exposure have been developed in the United States and other countries. In the United States there is the composite noise rating (CNR) [39], the noise exposure forecast (NEF) [43], the community noise equivalent level (CNEL) [48], the equivalent noise level L_{eq} [37, 38], the day-night average level L_{dn} [15, 35], and the aircraft sound description system (ASDS) [3]. ICAO recommends the use of the total noise exposure level (TNEL), the equivalent continuous perceived noise level (ECPNL), and the weighted equivalent continuous perceived noise level (WECPNL) [2, 12, 42]. In other areas of the world the noise and number index (NNI) [43], the isopsophic index (II) [42], the noise exposure index Q [42], and the total noise load (TNL) [43] are used. These methods, while differing in technical detail, are conceptually very similar and correlate very well with each other. The primary difference is in the unit of measure of sound level.

To be effective, any method for predicting community reaction to noise must have a reasonable correlation between the cumulative noise levels and community annoyance.

Noise Evaluation Systems Used in the United States

Composite Noise Rating

One of the earliest methods for evaluating land use around airports was the CNR [40]. The CNR is equal to the perceived noise level expressed in PNdB adjusted for the number of aircraft operations, whether the operations occurred in the day or the night, and the percentage of time the runway is utilized. The CNR is equal to PNdB plus or minus adjustments. These adjustments are applied in discrete steps of 5 PNdB. Aircraft are segregated into several classes, and air carriers are further grouped according to trip lengths. The CNR contour for each class and trip length is computed and drawn on a land-use map. The contour encompassing the largest area is considered critical. PNdB contours of maximum noise levels for different classes of aircraft and trip lengths are provided in [40], and adjustments can be added or subtracted to result in CNR contours. Although relatively simple, very little use is made of this method today.

Noise Exposure Forecast

The NEF is an extension of the CNR concept. The main differences are that the perceived noise level is expressed in EPNdB instead of PNdB, and adjustments for the number of operations are continuous rather than in discrete steps. Mathematically NEF can be expressed as follows:

$$\text{NEF} = \text{EPNL} + 10 \log \frac{N}{K} - C \qquad (15\text{-}2)$$

where EPNL = effective perceived noise level, EPNdB
N = number of operations during day or night
K = a constant dependent on whether the operations occur at night, $K_n = 1.2$, or in the day, $K_d = 20$
C = a normalization factor to make NEF numbers substantially different from CNR

Daytime operations occur from 0701 to 2200 h, and nighttime operations are considered to occur from 2201 to 0700 h. The day-night average NEF_{ij} of aircraft type i following flight path j is

$$\text{NEF}_{ij} = \text{EPNdB}_i + 10 \log N_j - 88.0 \qquad (15\text{-}3)$$

where N_j = number of daytime operations, N_d plus 16.7 times the number of nighttime operations N_n.

The total day-night average noise exposure for several classes of aircraft i at a point on the ground following the same flight path j is

$$\text{NEF}_j = 10 \log \sum_i \text{antilog} \frac{\text{NEF}_{ij}}{10} \qquad (15\text{-}4)$$

The use of the formulas can be illustrated by the following example. The day-night average NEF is required at a ground position X underneath a flight path j. There are three types of aircraft, A, B, and C, following the same flight path. At point X aircraft type A generates 90 EPNdB, aircraft type B generates 95 EPNdB, and aircraft type C generates 98 EPNdB. The number of aircraft operations and the required computations are tabulated in Table 15-3.

It can readily be seen that manual computation of NEF contours is cumbersome. As a result, a number of computer programs are available for developing NEF contours [9, 37, 38, 50]. NEF contours for O'Hare International Airport in Chicago are shown on Fig. 15-3.

Compatible land uses for various levels of NEF are briefly summarized in Table 15-4. A more detailed description of compatible uses is contained in Table 15-5. This information was excerpted from [7]. Once the contours are plotted, the information in the tables forms the basis for land-use planning or for the determination of community reaction to airport expansion. For illustrative purposes, the variation of EPNdB with the distance from specific types of aircraft is shown in Figs. 15-4 and 15-5.

Community Noise Equivalent Level

The CNEL was developed in the state of California to enforce noise standards enacted by the legislature [48]. It can be used for predicting community reaction as well as for monitoring aircraft operations. The concept is similar to the NEF, except that the dBA is used as the unit of noise measurement. The mathematical expression for day-night average CNEL_{ij} of aircraft of type i following flight path j is

$$\text{CNEL}_{ij} = \text{NEL}_i + 10 \log N_c - 49.4 \qquad (15\text{-}5)$$

TABLE 15-3   **Computation of Noise Exposure Forecast**

Aircraft class	Number of daily operations		$N_f = N_d + 16.7$ N_n	NEF	Antilog $\dfrac{\text{NEF}}{10}$
	Day N_d	Night N_n			
A	20	4	86.8	20.8	120.2
B	2	1	18.7	19.7	93.3
C	5	1	21.7	23.4	218.8
					432.3
			$\text{NEF}_j = 10 \log_{10} 432.3 = 26.4$		

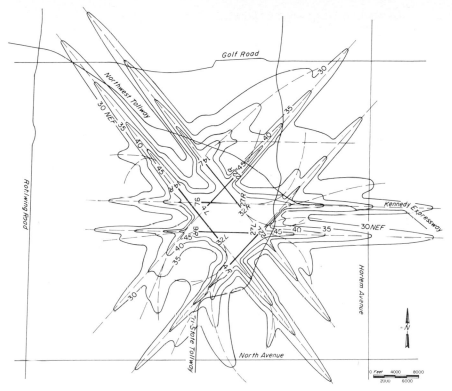

Fig. 15-3 Noise exposure forecast for 1985 civil air carrier operations at Chicago O'Hare International Airport. (*Bolt, Beranek, and Newman [40].*)

where NEL_i = single-flyover noise level of aircraft i on flight path j, dBA, corrected for the duration of sound,

N_c = equivalent number of daily operations, $= N_d + 3N_e + 10N_n$,

N_d = number of daytime operations occurring between 0700 and 1900 h

N_e = number of evening operations occurring between 1900 and 2200 h

N_n = number of nighttime operations occurring between 2200 and 0700 h

The total day-night average exposure for several classes of aircraft i at a point on the ground following the same flight path j is

$$CNEL_j = 10 \log \sum_i antilog \frac{CNEL_{ij}}{10} \tag{15-6}$$

The use of the formulas can be illustrated by the following example. The CNEL is required at a ground position X underneath a flight path j. There are three types of aircraft, A, B, and C, which generate 75, 80, and 85

TABLE 15-4 **Land-Use Guidance Chart for Airport Noise Interpolation**

Land-use guidance zone	Noise exposure class	Inputs: aircraft noise estimating methodologies					
		Day-night average sound level (L_{dn})	NEF	CNR	CNEL	HUD noise assessment guidelines	Suggested noise controls
A	Minimal exposure	0–55	0–20	0–90	0–55	Clearly acceptable	Normally requires no special considerations
B	Moderate exposure	55–65	20–30	90–100	55–65	Normally acceptable	Land-use controls should be considered
C	Significant exposure	65–75	30–40	100–115	65–75	Normally unacceptable	Noise easements, land-use, and other compatibility controls recommended
D	Severe exposure	75 and higher	40 and higher	115 and higher	75 and higher	Clearly unacceptable	Containment within airport boundary or use of positive compatibility controls recommended

SOURCE: Federal Aviation Administration [7].

NEL, respectively. The number of operations and the computations are tabulated in Table 15-6.

CNEL 65 is considered acceptable for residential areas by California standards. CNEL is approximately equal to NEF + 35. Thus CNEL 65 is approximately equivalent to NEF 30. Compatible land uses for various levels of CNEL are also contained in Table 15-4.

Equivalent Noise Level

This measure is used to indicate the average sound energy in dBA received by an observer and is the basis for several noise exposure methods presently in use, including highway systems. The equivalent sound level L_{eq} is expressed by the equation

$$L_{eq} = 10 \log \sum_i p_i \text{ antilog } \frac{L_i}{10} \tag{15-7}$$

where L_i = sound pressure level i, dBA
p_i = percentage of time the sound pressure level is in the interval L_i

TABLE 15-5 **Land-Use Guidance Chart for
Land-Use Noise Sensitivity Interpolation**

Land use		Suggested
SLUCM No.	**Name**	**Land-use guidance zone**
10	Residential:	A–B
11	Household units	
11,11	Single units, detached	A
11,12	Single units, semiattached	A
11,13	Single units, attached row	B
11,21	Two units, side by side	A
11,22	Two units, one above the other	A
11,31	Apartments, walk up	B
11,32	Apartments, elevator	B–C
12	Group quarters	A–B
13	Residential hotels	B
14	Mobile home parks or courts	A
15	Transient lodgings	C
19	Other residential	A–C
20	Manufacturing:*	C–D
21	Food and kindred products, manufacturing	C–D
22	Textile mill products, manufacturing	C–D
23	Apparel and other finished products made from fabrics, leather, and similar materials, manufacturing	C–D
24	Lumber and wood products (except furniture), manufacturing	C–D
25	Furniture and fixtures, manufacturing	C–D
26	Paper and allied products, manufacturing	C–D
27	Printing, publishing, and allied industries	C–D
28	Chemicals and allied products, manufacturing	C–D
29	Petroleum refining and related industries[†]	C–D
30	Manufacturing (continued):*	
31	Rubber and miscellaneous plastic products, manufacturing	C–D
32	Stone, clay, and glass products, manufacturing	C–D
33	Primary metal industries	D
34	Fabricated metal products, manufacturing	D
35	Professional, scientific, and controlling instruments, photographic and optical goods; watches and clocks, manufacturing	B
39	Miscellaneous manufacturing	C–D

TABLE 15-5 **Land-Use Guidance Chart for Land-Use Noise Sensitivity Interpolation (Cont.)**

SLUCM No.	Name	Suggested Land-use guidance zone
40	Transportation, communication, and utilities:	
41	Railroad, rapid rail transit, and street railway transportation	D
42	Motor vehicle transportation	D
43	Aircraft transportation	D
44	Marine craft transportation	D
45	Highway and street right-of-way	D
46	Automobile parking	D
47	Communication	A–D
48	Utilities	D
49	Other transportation, communication, and utilities	A–D
50	Trade:[‡]	
51	Wholesale trade	C–D
52	Retail trade, building materials, hardware, and farm equipment	C
53	Retail trade, general merchandise	C
54	Retail trade, food	C
55	Retail trade, automotive, marine craft, aircraft, and accessories	C
56	Retail trade, apparel and accessories	C
57	Retail trade, furniture, home furnishings, and equipment	C
58	Retail trade, eating and drinking	C–D
59	Other retail trade	
60	Services:[‡]	
61	Finance, insurance, and real estate services	B
62	Personal services	B
63	Business services	B
64	Repair services	C
65	Professional services	B–C
66	Contract construction services	C
67	Governmental services	B
68	Educational services	A–B
69	Miscellaneous services	A–C
70	Cultural, entertainment, and recreational:	
71	Cultural activities and nature exhibitions	A
72	Public assembly	A
73	Amusements	C
74	Recreational activities[§]	B–C
75	Resorts and group camps	A

TABLE 15-5 **Continued**

SLUCM No.	Name	Suggested Land-use guidance zone
76	Parks	A–C
79	Other cultural, entertainment, and recreational[§]	A–B
80	Resource production and extraction:	
81	Agriculture	C–D
82	Agricultural related activities	C–D
83	Forestry activities and related services	D
84	Fishing activities and related services	D
85	Mining activities and related services	D
89	Other resource production and extraction	C–D
90	Undeveloped land and water areas:	
91	Undeveloped and unused land area (excluding noncommercial forest development)	D
92	Noncommercial forest development	D
93	Water areas	A–D
94	Vacant floor area	A–D
95	Under construction	A–D
99	Other undeveloped land and water areas	A–D

* Zone C suggested maximum, except where exceeded by self-generated noise.

† Zone D for noise purposes; observe normal hazard precautions.

‡ If activity is not in substantial, air-conditioned building, go to next higher zone.

§ Requirements likely to vary, individual appraisal recommended.

SOURCE: Federal Aviation Administration [7].

Day-Night Average Level

This is specified by the Environmental Protection Agency for determining community noise [15, 35]. It is nearly the same as CNEL, except that the day is divided into two periods, night and day, instead of three periods. The approximate mathematical expression for L_{dn} is

$$L_{dn_{ij}} = NEL_i + 10 \log N_e - 49.4 \qquad (15\text{-}8)$$

where L_{dn} = day-night average noise level, dBA
NEL_i = same as above
N_e = equivalent number of daily operations, $= N_d + 10N_n$
N_d = total number of operations between 0701 and 2200 h
N_n = total number of operations between 2201 and 0700 h

The total day-night average exposure for several classes of aircraft i at a

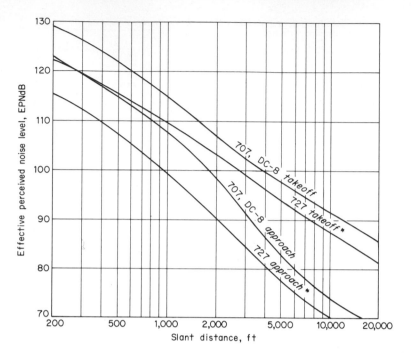

Fig. 15-4 Variation in effective perceived noise levels with distance—Turbofan transport aircraft with untreated nacelles. Subtract 2 dB for two-engine aircraft. (*Bolt, Beranek, and Newman [40].*)

point on the ground following the same flight path j is

$$L_{dn_j} = 10 \log \sum_i \text{antilog} \frac{L_{dn_{ij}}}{10} \tag{15-9}$$

Table 15-4 also shows the relationship between L_{dn} and compatible land uses. The L_{dn} measure is very useful for combining the effects of other airport vehicular traffic since this measure has been adopted by other agencies for this purpose. The FAA recommends that this measure be used for airport land-use compatibility studies [46].

Aircraft Sound Description System

This system was developed by the FAA and is referred to as ASDS [3]. It is straightforward but differs substantially from the preceding methods. At any point near the airport, exposure to aircraft noise is described in terms of the total amount of time (TA) in minutes that sound levels exceed a threshold value of 85 dBA. For example, if a plot of land is exposed to takeoff noise above 85 dBA for a period of 30 min a day, the planner must know if the land is suitable for the construction of a residence. This is needed for land-use planning. Justification for the selection of the 85-dBA threshold is contained in [3]. While durations of sound levels above 85 dBA vary with individual aircraft, average values of 15 s for takeoff and 10 s for landings are considered sufficiently accurate for estimating the duration.

An analysis for a single-runway airport with one aircraft type using three different departure flight paths is shown in Fig. 15-6. The first step is to plot the 85-dBA contour for the aircraft on a land-use map. The next step is to divide the areas into zones and determine the number of operations in each zone. The final step is to multiply the number of operations by the appropriate duration, which results in noise exposure as shown in Fig. 15-6. A typical situation involves a number of aircraft. In this case the 85-dBA contours for each aircraft must be superimposed on each other. From such a plot and with the knowledge of the number of aircraft operations one can determine the areas that will be exposed to more than 85 dBA during fixed intervals of time, for example for 0 to 5, 5 to 10, and 10 to 15 min.

Finally a composite single number, the situation index (SI), is defined as the total integrated value of the product of exposure time in minutes above 85 dBA and the area exposed in acres. The SI, in acre-minutes, is an

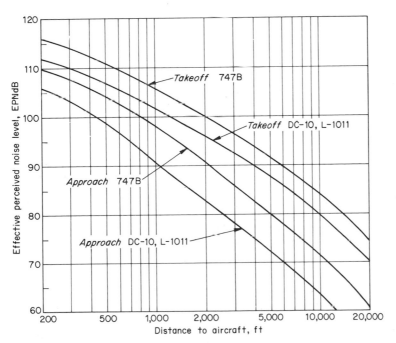

Fig. 15-5 Variation in effective perceived noise levels with distance— Three- and four-engine high-bypass-ratio turbofan transport aircraft. (*Bolt, Beranek, and Newman [40].*)

TABLE 15-6 **Computation of Community Noise Exposure Level**

Aircraft class	Number of operations per time of day			N_c	CNEL	$\dfrac{\text{CNEL}}{10}$ Antilog
	0700–1900 h	1900–2200 h	2200–0700 h			
A	50	10	2	100	45.6	32,310
B	30	5	2	65	48.7	74,140
C	20	5	1	45	52.1	162,200
						268,650

$\text{CNEL}_j = 10 \log 268{,}650 = 10 \times 5.429 = 54.3$

attempt to quantify the overall noise exposure into one number. The mathematical expression is given by

$$SI = \sum_{i=1}^{m} \sum_{j=1}^{n} A_{ij}\, N_{ij}\, TA_i \qquad (15\text{-}10)$$

where A_{ij} = area within the 85-dBA contour for airplane type j for event type i, where events can be differentiated by takeoff or landing flight paths, acres

N_{ij} = total number of events performed by aircraft type j

TA_i = total duration of noise for event i, min

m = total number of airplane types

n = total number of events for aircraft type j

Procedures Recommended by ICAO

The ICAO recommends that noise exposure assessment be conducted by a method which utilizes the physical measurement of sound adjusted for frequency-spectrum irregularities, a tone correction factor, and duration. Therefore, the basic sound measurement unit is the EPNdB or EPNL. Evaluation of the total noise exposure produced by a succession of aircraft during a period of time requires the computation of the TNEL, the ECPNL, and the WECPNL [2, 12, 42]. The primary features of the ICAO method are that it uses the EPNdB as the noise measurement unit rather than the dBA. It permits an adjustment for seasonal factors. The ICAO method contains an approximate procedure to compute the EPNL, intended principally for long-range planning purposes.

The following equations outline the ICAO method. The TNEL produced by a succession of aircraft n is given by

$$TNEL = 10 \log \sum_{n} \text{antilog}\, \frac{EPNL(n)}{10} + 10\left(\frac{T_0}{t_0}\right) \qquad (15\text{-}11)$$

where EPNL(n) = perceived noise level of nth aircraft
$$T_0 = 10 \text{ s}$$
$$t_0 = 1 \text{ s}$$

The ECPNL is equal to

$$ECPNL = TNEL - 10 \log\left(\frac{T}{t_0}\right) \qquad (15\text{-}12)$$

where T = period of time over which the noise level is being computed, s.

The WECPNL weights the sounds at different times during the day and has a seasonal adjustment factor based upon the number of hours in a month that the temperature is in certain specified ranges. This value can be computed using either two time periods, day and night, or three periods, day, evening, and night. The relationship for two time periods is

$$WECPNL = 10 \log\left[\frac{5}{8}\frac{ECPNL_d}{10} + \frac{3}{8}\frac{ECPNL_n}{10} + 10\right] + S \qquad (15\text{-}13)$$

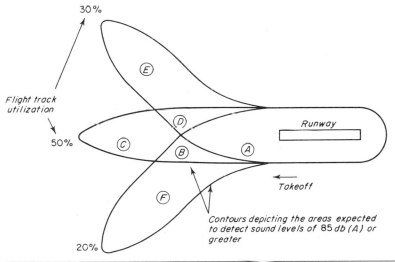

Zone	Exposure
A	(100%) = 180 events = 45 min
B	(70%) = 126 events = 31.5 min
C	(50%) = 90 events = 22.5 min
D	(80%) = 144 events = 36 min
E	(30%) = 54 events = 13.5 min
F	(20%) = 36 events = 9 min

Fig. 15-6 Analysis of takeoff noise exposure for single runway. (*Federal Aviation Administration.*)

where $ECPNL_d$ = equivalent continuous perceived noise level during
0700 to 2200 h

$ECPNL_n$ = equivalent continuous perceived noise level during
2200 to 0700 h

S = seasonal adjustment factor, which adds 5 dB during
warm months or subtracts 5 dB during cold months

The details of the computation of the noise exposure on land uses are contained in [2, 12].

Use of Procedures

The reader should understand that the procedures described herein approximate community response and are used for land-use planning and for assessment of the impact by new airports or the extension of existing ones. The FAA has prepared an extensive computer model for the determination and plotting of noise contours in the vicinity of airports [37, 38]. The noise measures available are the NEF, L_{eq}, L_{dn}, and CNEL. It also allows the computation of the TA. Noise contours may be printed at selected map scales and superimposed on land-use maps. The model includes a data base which contains flight profiles and noise characteristics for common aircraft types. Changes to the data base to alter aircraft noise characteristics and performance data are possible. The use of the model requires the following input data:

1. Airport altitude and temperature
2. Runway configuration
3. Flight track definition
4. Approach and departure profiles
5. Traffic mix
6. Operations by stage length and time of day

Examples of aircraft flight track definition and a typical standard runway approach are given in Figs. 15-7 and 15-8.

The model has many uses to airport owners, consultants, and federal, state, and local governmental entities. It is useful to gain a better understanding of the noise impacts of airport operations, in the preparation of environmental impact assessments and statements, and in reviewing alternative plans for airport expansion or operational changes.

Normally, the results of a noise study at an airport are displayed on land-use maps showing the noise contours for the existing situation and proposed alternatives at different times during the planning horizon. The relative impacts of various project alternatives on population can be expressed in terms of weighting factors and compared by an impact ratio. In this method, the population in a particular noise exposure band is weighted by a factor which is a function of the noise level in the band to determine

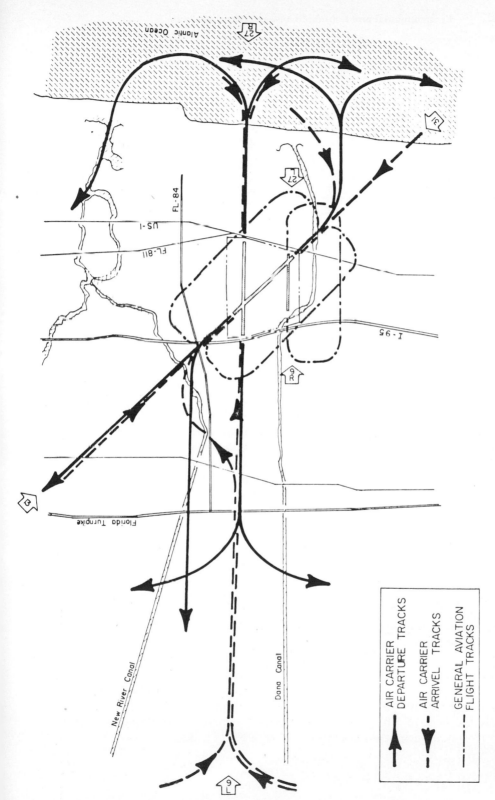

Fig. 15-7 Approach and departure flight tracks for Fort Lauderdale–Hollywood International Airport (*Reynolds, Smith and Hills [32].*)

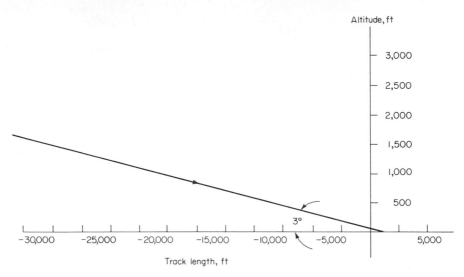

Fig. 15-8 Medium- and long-range approach profile. (*International Civil Aviation Organization [42].*)

the total weighted population exposed to noise by the alternative. The relative impact is gained by taking the weighted ratio of an alternative to that of the base case. Equation (15-14) shows the equation used, and Table 15-7 gives the weighting factors [4]. Mitigation measures to alleviate the adverse consequences of noise exposure on sensitive land uses are identified.

$$P_w = \sum_i P_i W_i \tag{15-14}$$

where P_w = weighted population exposed to noise
   P_i = total population within a noise band of level L_i
   W_i = weight assigned to noise level L_i

Construction Impacts

The construction of facilities at airports can result in temporary and long-term impacts on the community and travelers. Those factors which are of primary concern during the construction process include soil erosion, water and air quality, noise due to construction equipment and methods, the source and quantity of construction materials, disruption and relocation of businesses and residences, the continued operation of existing facilities both on and off the airport during the construction process, and the interference with other construction projects [31, 32].

A review of the environmentally sensitive areas and facilities should be undertaken to identify those which will be subject to impact and the likely duration and consequences of these activities. The location and quantity of cut and fill must be indicated, and methods to minimize the effect of construction activities on soil erosion during construction should be identified. Procedures for the handling of construction materials and wastes to minimize the introduction of particulate matter into the air and water resources are required. Those land uses which will be adversely affected by noise from construction activities should be identified, and the optimal routing of construction vehicles and timing of activities chosen to minimize damage. Obvious positive impacts of a major construction activity are the increases in employment and payroll for personnel associated with the project and the purchase of materials and supplies from local firms which support the local economy. However, certain businesses and residences in the vicinity of the project may be subject to disruption due to the possible rerouting and congestion of vehicular traffic and restrictions on access to land uses.

The study of the direct and indirect socioeconomic impacts on the community should include an identification of the location, timing, and amount of impact throughout the entire construction period.

SOCIAL FACTORS

Land Development

The development of an airport can result in a change in the pattern of land-use activity, both in the vicinity of the airport and in the geographic region. These land-development activities may result in changes in the level of economic activity and population growth and demography. The location of an airport generally results in the inducement of land development in the vicinity of the airport, which may be measured in terms of the density of industrial, commercial, retail, agricultural, and residential use. It usually impacts the nature, magnitude, and operating patterns of other transporta-

TABLE 15-7 **Population Noise Exposure Weighting Factors**

Exposure Range, dB		Weighting factor
NEF	L_{dn}	
35–40	70–75	0.875
30–35	65–70	0.625
25–30	60–65	0.375
20–25	55–60	0.125

SOURCE: Federal Aviation Administration [4].

tion modes providing access to the airport and those land uses associated with its development. The presence of the airport may induce industrial or commercial activities to move into or expand within the region due to increased accessibility to markets and materials.

How an airport will affect land development is a function of its direct economic impact on the region. The following land-development activities should be studied [4, 27]:

1. Plant relocation from outside the region, which will require construction activities

2. Increases in the production or sales of existing business enterprises requiring new or expanded capital facilities

3. Increased expenditures in tourist and recreational facilities resulting in requirements for new or expanded facilities and increases in retail sales

4. Expansion of agricultural markets resulting in increased productivity and resource utilization

5. Increased demand for specialized facilities for such activities as business or convention centers

6. Expansion of commercial and financial markets resulting in a demand for additional facilities

The study of the land-development impacts requires an analysis of those factors which influence industrial, commercial, and residential location decisions, including accessibility to raw materials, labor, and markets, the costs of production and transportation, and those quality-of-life and community factors associated with such decisions. The analysis is usually conducted through an examination of historical trends for the area and similar locations and the use of surveys and economic models to predict land development. The study should identify the nature and extent of existing zoning ordinances in the vicinity of the airport and recommend those changes necessary to accommodate the likely development in a compatible manner. It should also identify those requirements for regional policy decisions needed to stimulate overall land development in accordance with the stated objectives of the communities affected.

Displacement and Relocation

The construction or expansion of an airport often creates a need for additional land, the relocation of residences, businesses, and community facilities, a disruption in business activity and community character and cohesiveness, the impairment of community service functions, and an increased demand for public services. The assessment is directed toward determining the type, extent, characteristics, and effects of displacement and relocation and mitigation measures to minimize adverse consequences.

The boundaries of the areas affected are determined from area maps. The community structure is usually defined in terms of population demography, growth, and density, housing and business characteristics such as the type, distribution, condition, value, occupancy, and vacancy levels, open land, recreational resources, and community services. The availability of relocation resources for those land uses required for airport and ancillary activities are identified. The changes in the demand for public services are quantified. Comparisons of the relative impact of project alternatives are usually made which attempt to address the following items [27]:

1. The nature, location, and extent of the displacement of homes, businesses, and community facilities

2. The creation of physical barriers or divisions

3. The impairment of mobility, accessibility, community services, and community facilities

4. The disruption of homes, businesses, and community facilities during construction

5. The nature, availability, adequacy, and compatibility of relocation resources

6. The nature, location, and extent of land-use changes

7. The aesthetic appeal of the design for the facility and surrounding environment

Parks, Recreational Areas, Historical Places, Archeological Resources, and Natural and Scenic Beauty

Particular attention is required to determine the impact upon parks, recreational areas, open spaces, cultural and historic places, archeological resources, and natural and scenic beauty. The analyst must identify the type of facilities which will be impacted, their size and utilization, and those measures which can be implemented to preserve the nature, character, compatibility, and accessibility of the facilities. It is particularly important to document the relative impact of project alternatives on these types of facilities and to avoid the acquisition of such lands for the implementation of a project alternative.

The assessment can be performed on the basis of a participatory evaluation with those groups which possess expertise or interest in this impact area. Suggested generalized evaluation criteria might include [4, 27]:

1. The existence, nature, and extent of any physical alteration to the facilities

2. The degree of conformity of the planned facilities with the existing environment

3. The disruption of access

4. The disruption of the ambient environment

5. The compatibility of access-induced development with the facilities

Consistency with Local Planning

The planning and design of airports can have significant effects on the economy, land use, infrastructure, and nature of community development. The planning effort must be carried on in an environment which is compatible and coordinated with other local planning efforts and guidelines. Care must be exercised from the inception of planning to assess the impact of project alternatives and operations on the goals and objectives of communities and to identify those facets of the project which may present conflicts with existing plans or community goals. Modifications to airport project proposals which will be in conformity with local policies and plans must be explicitly examined. Policies required to preserve the overall development objectives of the community should be identified and mechanisms to implement such policies proposed.

The assessment of impacts in this area requires an identification of and coordination with those federal, state, and local agencies which have a concern or jurisdiction in matters related to airport and community development actions, the delineation of clear statements of goals and objectives, the integration of airport plans with local comprehensive land-use, economic, and transportation development plans, and the establishment of a continuing dialogue on issues related to these plans. The presentation of the results of planning efforts and development recommendations in public forums, with mechanisms for citizen participation in the planning and review process, together with timely and well-documented responses to community concerns is essential.

ECOLOGICAL FACTORS

Wildlife, Waterfoul, Flora, Fauna, and Endangered Species

The consideration of the impact of airport development on changes in the natural state of land and waterways is essential to protect ecosystems.

Living and nonliving elements, plants, and animals all interact on land and in water to produce a highly interdependent system of aquatic and terrestrial ecosystems. The relationship between species and the ecosystem is essential to maintain the life support system for wildlife, waterfoul, flora, fauna, and endangered species [26, 51, 52]. Of particular importance is plant and animal life. The principal impacts which may occur are the loss of or injury to the organisms or the loss or degradation of the ecosystem.

The use of land for airport development creates disturbances and disruptions to flora and fauna. The specific project elements often include the clearing and grubbing of land areas, changes in the composition and nature of the topography, and interferences with water shed patterns. Thus airports can destroy the natural habitat and feeding grounds of wildlife and eliminate or reduce flora essential to the maintenance of the ecological balance in the area [12]. Particular hazards may be presented to birds and to aircraft due to striking birds, and care must be exercised in choosing airport sites to avoid land which attracts birds and is on natural migration routes. The protection for endangered species in the United States is legislated through the contents of the Endangered Species Act of 1973 (Public Law 93-205). Lists of endangered species are published [26, 51, 52]. Reference should also be made to state and local regulations in this regard.

The assessment techniques used include the identification of the important aquatic and terrestrial organisms present in the area and a determination of the life support systems required for the different species. An analysis is performed to determine the impacts on vegetation requirements, food chains, and habitats of these species, as well as their tolerance to air and water pollution. Care must be taken in the case of aquatic species to examine the effects of soil erosion, flooding, and sedimentation on stream beds where food chains, spawning grounds, and habitats exist [27].

Wetlands and Coastal Zones

Improperly planned or operated drainage systems at airports can cause contaminants to enter streams, lakes, and waterways. The normal operation of an airport results in contamination potential through aircraft and ground vehicle washing, servicing, and fueling, airport and aircraft maintenance, and terminal services. In the construction phase of a project there is a high potential for contamination through clearing, grubbing, pest control, and changes in topography. Changes in the natural drainage patterns of the area are very common due to the nature of airport development projects. Preservation of recharge areas and stream flows, the elimination of flooding and sedimentation problems, and the preservation of the quality and routing of water resources are all vital to the maintenance of water quality and the protection of ecosystems.

ENGINEERING AND ECONOMIC FACTORS

Flood Hazards

The flood hazard potential of any development is a necessary consideration since alterations in the topography, cover, and soil characteristics on the property are inevitable. The storage capacity of local rivers, streams, canals, and groundwater areas can be exceeded due to changes in the magnitude and paths of runoff from storms and high rainfall or thawing events. The analysis of the potential for flooding is conducted by evaluating the characteristics of the ground surface, soil materials, topography, and flood plains, the historical frequency and intensity of storms, and storm water drainage and retention facilities. The methods for conducting such analyses are discussed in an earlier chapter.

If it is found that the project design increases the potential for on- or off-site flooding, those areas subject to these effects are identified, and the mechanisms required to alleviate the hazards are incorporated into the project design. The construction of new or increased-capacity storm sewers and impounding areas, channels, and dikes is most commonly indicated. Changes in the elevation of facilities and the slope and cover of the ground surface at the site can also be of considerable benefit in reducing flood hazards.

Costs of Construction and Operation

All engineering planning studies consider the capital, maintenance, and operating costs of all feasible alternatives as an integral part of the planning process. For airport projects these costs include land acquisition, purchases of land leases and convenants to protect aircraft operations and environmental quality, facility construction, operating, maintenance, and administrative costs. Typically, construction costs are derived from quantity takeoffs of materials which are related to locally appropriate cost indices for the various construction items [23, 24]. The overall cost factor is computed by a concept of benchmark cost indices for various components of the airport [49]. Example indices are tabulated in Table 15-8. The capital costs usually include materials, supplies, labor, and engineering.

The construction costs for the various items are normally made at different points in time and, therefore, for comparative and evaluative purposes these are brought back to some common point in time in order that the values may be properly attributed to the construction needs. The operating, maintenance, and administrative costs are usually annualized. These costs are normally estimated through comparisons with similar installations, historical trends, and economic influences. The costs of capital and the required coverage, as discussed in Chap. 2, are also included to arrive at the total program cost.

TABLE 15-8 **Unit Cost Indices for Space and Special Equipment at Airport Terminal Buildings**

Location	Area category	Area type	Cost unit	Benchmark index per unit		Total cost
				Shell	Tenant	
Terminal	Type A: Passenger-handling facilities	1. Lobbies	ft²	1.00	NA*	
		2. Waiting rooms				
		3. Circulation				
		4. Rest rooms				
		5. Counter areas			2.00	3.00
		6. Baggage claim facilities, including claim device			0.50	1.50
		7. Service and storage areas			NA	
Terminal	Type B: Airline/tenant operations space, partly finished	1. Customer service offices	ft²	0.65	0.40	1.05
		2. Agent supervisor offices, check out, and agent lounge			0.50	1.15
		3. Toilets			1.55	2.20
		4. VIP/PR Rooms			1.10	1.75
		5. Lost and found			0.72	1.37
Terminal or connector	Type C: Airline operations space, lower level unfinished	1. Offices	ft²	0.60.	0.55	1.15
		2. Tire shop (including equipment)			0.62	1.22
		3. Store rooms			0.30	0.90
		4. Ready and lunch rooms			0.43	1.03
		5. Lockers			0.20	0.80
		6. Toilets			1.80	2.40
		7. Planning center and load planning			0.85	1.45
					0.13	0.73
Connector	Type D: Passenger-handling	1. Corridors	ft²	0.80	NA	
		2. Rest rooms				
		3. Service and storage area				
		4. Boarding areas			0.26	1.06

* NA = not applicable.

These cost data have been compiled for new terminal and concourse construction, and may not be applicable for remodeling or small additions to existing facilities. They do not include installed equipment, such as loading bridges, claim devices, ramp utilities, and so on.

SOURCE: Federal Aviation Administration [49].

An overview of the categories and items typically found in airport projects for which capital, operating, maintenance, and administrative cost estimates are required includes:

1. Airfield facilities
   a. Runways, taxiways, and aprons
   b. Fueling and fixed power systems, crash, fire, and rescue units
   c. Air traffic control facilities, lighting, and navigational aids

2. Terminal building facilities
    a. Terminal buildings and connectors
    b. General aviation servicing buildings and hangar areas
    c. Boarding devices, mechanical and electrical systems
    d. Communications and security systems
    e. Air-cargo buildings
    f. Maintenance and administrative buildings
    g. Furnishings

3. Access facilities
    a. Roadways, drives, and curb frontage
    b. Rental car, limousine, and transit areas
    c. Parking lots and garages
    d. Graphics, signage, and lighting

4. Infrastructure facilities
    a. Landscaping and drainage
    b. Utilities including water supply, sewage disposal, power supply systems
    c. Land acquisition

For the purposes of evaluation these costs are usually related to passenger and aircraft traffic characteristics, such as the cost per enplaned passenger or per air-carrier operation. The costs are also allocated among the various users and nonusers of the project, normally tenants, concessionaires, airlines, general aviation, cargo businesses, and federal, state, and local governmental agencies, as appropriate.

Economic Benefits and Fiscal Requirements

The evaluation of the economic and financial feasibility of the project requires an identification of both the level and the allocation of the benefits and costs of the project, as well as a revenue analysis performed for the various cost centers. Both direct and indirect benefits can accrue to the users of the airport and to the community in which the airport is located. Generally user benefits include reductions in delay, fuel consumption, time, and other operating and maintenance costs. These can usually be derived relative to dollar values. Nonuser and community benefits take the form of increased economic activity, rises in employment, and purchases of goods and services. These can also be evaluated through classical economic techniques [4, 27].

Though it may be possible to justify expenditures from an economic standpoint, it may not be possible to generate or capture the value of these benefits from a revenue viewpoint. A revenue analysis seeks to identify the revenue requirements by cost center and the level of revenue required to cover project costs. Normally, the costs are allocated to facility users, and rents, rates, charges, and concession agreements are negotiated on the principle that all users should pay their fair and proportionate share of the costs of providing, maintaining, operating, and administering the facilities they use.

Various indices are used to determine the reasonableness of revenue requirements, including the percentage of revenue generated which is paid for terminal rents or landing fees, and the revenue required per enplaned passenger. A comparison of the bonding capacity of the governmental units concerned with the project is vital in order to determine the influence of the project on other public revenue requirements.

Energy and Natural Resources

The use of new technology in power-generation systems at airports, the efficient layout of apron areas and taxiing routes, improvements in the capacity of runway systems, the installation of navigational aids, and the effective uses of construction materials can substantially reduce the costs and resource use of energy. A detailed examination of the impact of airport design elements on energy consumption should be performed. Typically comparisons between existing and planned systems, and between alternative systems for proposed facility modifications relative to fuel consumption of aircraft and terminal systems may yield essential information concerning their feasibility and merit.

SUMMARY

Though the incentive for the study of environmental, sociological, and ecological factors in the evaluation of engineering projects was initially provided through national, state, and local legislation, the state of the art has evolved to the point that a better and more complete understanding of the short- and long-term implications of these projects is leading to more efficient engineering designs. True, the costs of planning have increased because of the need to study a great number of criteria in the evaluation of planning proposals, but the potential for the overall reduction in the real "costs" of these proposals with regard to the long-term requirements of society through the use of comprehensive planning approaches has also been increased.

REFERENCES

1. *A Guidance Document on Airport Noise Control*, Federal Aviation Administration, Washington, D.C., Rep. FAA-EE-80-37, 1980.

2. *Aircraft Noise—Annex 16 to the Convention on International Civil Aviation*, International Civil Aviation Organization, Montreal, Que., Canada, 1978.

3. *Aircraft Sound Description System—Background and Application*, Federal Aviation Administration, Washington, D.C., Rep. FAA-EQ-73-3, March 1973.

4. *Airport Environmental Handbook*, Federal Aviation Administration, Washington, D.C., Order 5050.4, 1980.

5. *Airport Land Banking*, Federal Aviation Administration, Washington, D.C., Rep. FAA-ASP-77-7, 1977.

6. *Airport Landscaping for Noise Control Purposes*, Federal Aviation Administration, Washington, D.C., Advisory Circular AC 150/5320-14, 1978.

7. *Airport-Land Use Compatibility Planning*, Federal Aviation Administration, Washington, D.C., Advisory Circular AC 150/5050-6, 1977.

8. *Airport Master Plans*, Federal Aviation Administration, Washington, D.C., Advisory Circular AC 150/5070-6, 1971.

9. *Airport Noise Exposure Contour Model, Guide to the Users Manual*, National Transportation Study, Department of Transportation, Washington, D.C., July 1975.

10. *Airport Noise Control and Land Use Compatibility (ANCLUC) Planning under the Planning Grant Program (PGP)*, Federal Aviation Administration, Washington, D.C., Order 5900.4, 1977.

11. *Airport Planning and Environmental Assessment*, Notebook Ser., 4 vol., Department of Transportation, Washington, D.C., DOT P 5600.5, 1978.

12. *Airport Planning Manual*, Part 2: *Land Use and Environmental Control*, 1st ed., International Civil Aviation Organization, Montreal, Que., Canada, Doc. 9184-AN/902, 1977.

13. *Aviation Noise Abatement Policy*, Federal Aviation Administration, Office of the Secretary, Department of Transportation, Washington, D.C., 1976.

14. *Building Construction Cost Data*, R.S. Means Company, Inc., Duxbury, Mass.

15. *Calculation of Day-Night Levels (L_{dn}) Resulting from Civil Aircraft Operations*, Environmental Protection Agency, Washington, D.C., Rep. 550/9-77-450, 1977.

16. *Certified Airplane Noise Levels*, Federal Aviation Administration, Washington, D.C., Advisory Circular AC 36-1B, 1977.

17. *Citizen Participation in Airport Planning*, Federal Aviation Administration, Washington, D.C., Advisory Circular AC 150/5050-4, 1975.

18. *Community Involvement Manual*, Federal Aviation Administration, Washington, D.C., Rep. FAA-EE-79-6, 1979.

19. *Compilation of Air Pollution Emission Factors*, Environmental Protection Agency, Washington, D.C., Rep. AP-42, periodically revised.

20. *Correction Procedures for Aircraft Noise Data*, Federal Aviation Administration, Washington, D.C., Rep. FAA-EE-80-1, 1980.

21. *Developing Noise Exposure Contours for General Aviation Airports*, Federal Aviation Administration, Washington, D.C., Rep. FAA-AS-75-1, 1975.

22. *Development of Regional Impact Application for Development Approval, Fort Lauderdale–Hollywood International Airport*, Aviation Division, Broward County Department of Transportation, Fort Lauderdale, Fla., 1981.

23. *Dodge Guide for Estimating Public Works Construction Costs*, McGraw-Hill Information Systems Company, New York, N.Y.

24. *Dodge Manual for Building Construction Pricing and Scheduling*, McGraw-Hill Information Systems Company, New York, N.Y.

25. *EDB—Environmental Data Bank*, Federal Aviation Administration, Washington, D.C., Rep. FAA-EE-79-1, 1979.

26. *Endangered and Threatened Wildlife and Plants*, Fish and Wildlife Service, Department of the Interior, Washington, D.C.

27. *Environmental Assessment Notebook Series*, 7 vol., Department of Transportation, Washington, D.C., DOT P 5600.4, 1975.

28. *Environmental Assessment of Airport Development Actions*, Federal Aviation Administration, Washington, D.C., Rep. FAA-AP-77-1, March 1977.

29. "Environmental Considerations in Airport Planning," C.V. Robart, PRC Speas, from *Course Notes for Airport Planning and Design Short Course*, University of California, University Extension, Berkeley, Calif., June 1977.

30. *Environmental Enhancement at Airports—Industrial Waste Treatment*, Federal Aviation Administration, Washington, D.C., Advisory Circular AC 150/5320-10, 1973.

31. *Environmental Impact Assessment Report for the Development of a New Terminal Complex, Fort Lauderdale–Hollywood International Airport*, Aviation Division, Broward County Department of Transportation, Fort Lauderdale, Fla., 1979.

32. *Environmental Impact Assessment Report for the Expansion of the Existing Terminal Complex at the Fort Lauderdale–Hollywood International Airport*, Aviation Division, Broward County Department of Transportation, Fort Lauderdale, Fla., 1980.

33. *Estimated Airplane Noise Levels in A-Weighted Decibels*, Federal Aviation Administration, Washington, D.C., Advisory Circular AC 36-3A, 1980.

34. *Evaluation and Sensitivity Analysis of Airport Noise Characterization Methodologies*, MITRE Corporation, McLean, Va., Rep. MTR-6994, 1975.

35. *Impact Characteristics of Noise Including Implementation of Identifying and Achieving Levels of Cumulative Noise Exposure*, Rep. to the Environmental Protection Agency, Washington, D.C., 1973.

36. *Impact of Noise on People*, Federal Aviation Administration, Washington, D.C., May 1977.

37. *INM—Integrated Noise Model Version 2: Programmer's Guide*, Federal Aviation Administration, Washington, D.C., Rep. FAA-EE-79-10, 1979.

38. *INM—Integrated Noise Model Version 2: User's Guide*, Federal Aviation Administration, Washington, D.C., Rep. FAA-EE-79-9, 1979.

39. *Land Acquisition and Relocation Assistance Under the Airport Development Aid Program*, Federal Aviation Administration, Washington, D.C., Advisory Circular AC 150/5100-11, 1975.

40. *Land Use Planning Relating to Airport Noise*, Bolt, Beranek, and Newman, Los Angeles, Calif., 1964.

41. *Measured or Estimated (Uncertified) Airplane Noise Levels*, Federal Aviation Administration, Washington, D.C., Advisory Circular AC 36-2A, 1978.

42. *Noise Assessment for Land-Use Planning*, International Civil Aviation Organization, Montreal, Que., Canada, Circular 116-AN/86, 1974.

43. *Noise Exposure Forecasts: Evolution, Evaluation, Extensions, and Land Use Interpretations*, Federal Aviation Administration, Washington, D.C., Rep. FAA-NO-70-9, 1970.

44. *Noise Standards: Aircraft Type and Airworthiness Certification*, Federal Aviation Administration, Washington, D.C., FAR Part 36, 1974.

45. *Planning for the Airport and Its Environs: The Sea-Tac Success Story*, Federal Aviation Administration, Washington, D.C., April 1978.

46. *Policies and Procedures for Considering Environmental Impacts*, Federal Aviation Administration, Washington, D.C., Order 1050.1C, 1979.

47. *Requirements for Public Hearings in the Airport Development Aid Program*, Federal Aviation Administration, Washington, D.C., Advisory Circular AC 150/5100-7A, 1972.

48. *Supporting Information for the Adopted Noise Regulations for California Airports*, Wyle Laboratories, California Department of Aeronautics, Sacramento, Calif., Rep. WCC 70-3Ce, 1971.

49. *The Apron and Terminal Building Planning Report*, Federal Aviation Administration, Washington, D.C., Rep. FAA-RD-75-191, July 1975.

50. *The Noise Exposure Model MOD-S*, Transportation Systems Center, Department of Transportation, Cambridge, Mass., Rep. DOT-TSC-OST-72-5, 1972.

51. *Threatened Wildlife of the United States*, Fish and Wildlife Service, Department of the Interior, Washington, D.C.

52. *United States List of Endangered Fauna*, Fish and Wildlife Service, Department of the Interior, Washington, D.C.

APPENDIX

Metric Conversion of English Units

English	Metric
1 foot	0.3048 meter
1 inch	0.0254 meter=2.54 centimeters
1 pound	0.4536 kilogram
1 ton (2000 lb)	907.2 kilograms
1 nautical mile	1852 meters=1.852 kilometers
1 statute mile	1609 meters=1.609 kilometers
degrees (°) Fahrenheit	degrees (°) Celsius=(°F−32) 5/9
1 gallon(U.S. liquid)	0.003785 cubic meter
1 acre	4046.8 square meters
1 square mile (statute)	2,589,988 square meters
1 square foot	0.0929 square meter
1 foot per second	0.3048 meter per second

Index

About the Authors

Francis X. McKelvey has over twenty years of experience in teaching and research in engineering and is currently with the Department of Civil Engineering at Michigan State University. He has served as a consultant in transportation and airport planning to federal, state, and local agencies, as well as to private firms here in the United States and abroad. His practical experience in airports includes planning and design work for Fort Lauderdale–Hollywood International Airport and for the Daytona Beach Regional Airport. The author of many technical publications, he is very active in several aviation committees of the Transportation Research Board and is a member of The Advisory Circular Review Committee of the American Society of Civil Engineers. He earned his doctorate from The Pennsylvania State University.

Robert Horonjeff was Professor of Transportation Engineering and Research Engineer at the University of California at Berkeley and an internationally known consultant on airport matters. He was responsible for preparing the plans and specifications for some 14 military and civil airports. The American Society of Civil Engineers awarded him the Arthur Wellington Prize for his work on runway taxiways and the James Laurie Prize for outstanding achievement. He was a Chairman of the Executive Committee of the Air Transport Division of ASCE.